MW00834146

# TEACHING WITH
# *The St. Martin's Handbook*

T HANK YOU FOR CHOOSING *The St. Martin's Handbook,* Eighth Edition, by
Andrea A. Lunsford. This section will offer tips for using the book in the
classroom and also suggest ways to help students get the most from the reference features of the text.

For additional information on resources available for *The St. Martin's
Handbook* and to learn more about Andrea Lunsford and her research,
visit **lunsfordhandbooks.com**.

# A Using the handbook in class and out

*The St. Martin's Handbook,* Eighth Edition, is designed to be both a tool for teachers and students in the classroom and also a handy reference source when no one else is around to answer questions. It's also a book with a clear philosophy of writing: all writers make choices, and students should consider how the choices they make as writers affect the way audiences respond to their writing.

Of course, *The St. Martin's Handbook* offers advice on practical matters—analyzing assignments, planning and drafting a text, revising and editing work, creating multimedia presentations, using a library, documenting sources, and so on—and it's arranged so that students can quickly find the answers they are looking for. But it also asks students to think about their goals for the writing and to reflect on why they made the choices they did.

## ☐ A1. Using the handbook as a teaching tool

Whether or not you're familiar with Andrea Lunsford's work in the field of composition and rhetoric, you'll see that her research findings—from recent and long-range studies—are incorporated throughout this edition of *The St. Martin's Handbook.* Her research on student writing over the past three decades has produced findings with significant implications for professionals, but students may also be interested to learn how much the demands on student writers have changed over the years (and how the mistakes students make most often have correspondingly changed), how much more young people are writing today than previous generations did, and what students can learn from the things they do well as social writers.

### *"The Top Twenty" and your approach to comments on student writing*

As part of a discussion about your own practices for commenting on student work, show students "The Top Twenty" (pp. 1–11), based on the most frequent problems identified in thousands of pieces of student writing from across the United States. Explain when you will and won't pay attention to surface errors, and ask them to consider why such issues "don't always disturb readers."

The current "Top Twenty" reflects a number of changes from the original "Twenty Most Common Errors" study that Andrea Lunsford and Robert Connors conducted in the 1980s. These changes reflect some big changes in technology and in composition teaching: first, spell checkers have become ubiquitous, so spelling mistakes are less frequent while "wrong word" errors happen more often; and second, researched writing has become by far the most common assignment in composition courses, so problems with documentation crop up more often. Your students may be interested to learn that first-year composition students today are required to create much longer texts than were assigned in the past—and that Andrea Lunsford's research shows that writers make about the same number of errors per one hundred words today as they did a century ago. However, as Andrea notes, they're now making *different* errors.

For more content related to "The Top Twenty," see the cross-references accompanying each item on pp. 1–11; these lead to more detailed explanations and examples throughout the book.

### The "literacy revolution" and your expectations about writing assignments

Talk to your students about your expectations for formal writing assignments in your class, and ask them to think about how expectations for informal writing differ from those for formal academic work. Your students are probably very experienced with informal written communication; Andrea's research shows that a "literacy revolution" is underway, that young people today write more than other generations ever have because social writing is now so common, and that many college students have developed skills in informal writing—such as an understanding of audience—that may help them in academic work. Have students read Chapter 1, "Expectations for College Writing," and ask them to reflect on what they do well in social and informal writing and on how those skills might translate to formal projects for their courses.

Another aspect of the "literacy revolution" is that texts are often digital and multimodal, incorporating not just written words but other kinds of media. Tell students what you mean by "writing" and ask them to think about their own definitions, which may not match yours exactly. Talk about the rhetorical aspects of the kinds of texts you will accept in response to assignments. If you accept video texts, for example, what will a revised draft look like? Part 4, "Designing and Performing Writing," includes three chapters of additional advice on presentations, Web texts, and other kinds of multimodal writing.

### The value of reflection

Research demonstrates that learning is more likely to stick when people reflect on what they've learned, how they've learned it, and what they still need to learn. Talk to your students about the need to think critically about their writing and recognize that they are making choices at every step of the way—and that making good choices will result in more effective writing. Of course, college students often have many time-consuming obligations (not least of which is keeping up with coursework), so you may not find it easy to convince them that taking time to reflect carefully after writing is important.

*The St. Martin's Handbook* includes many opportunities for reflection that you might want to point out to students if you need to persuade them of the need to pay attention to this aspect of the writing process.

Many chapters begin with **Connect, Create, Reflect** modules asking students to make connections between material in the chapter and material elsewhere in the book, to create a text, and then to reflect on some aspect of the writing process.

Whether or not you direct students to complete any of these modules, you can use them to point out opportunities for further reflection that arise when writers create any kind of text. (You may also want to use them to point out that the handbook is a reference tool that can help answer student questions—and that to answer some questions, students may want to consult information in more than one chapter.)

> **CONNECT:** How can talking to real people help you with your research project? **11e, 29c–e**
>
> **CREATE:** Draft an email invitation to a person you would like to interview for your project.
>
> **REFLECT:** Record a brief audio or video reflection explaining what you did to find and contact the interview subject, what response (if any) you received, what you learned from the interview (if anything), and what you would do differently the next time.

In addition, most chapters conclude with another opportunity for reflection, a **"Thinking Critically"** exercise that asks students to consider aspects of their own writing and, often, the work of professional writers.

> ▼ ▼ ▼ ▼ ▼ ▼ ▼ ▼ ▼ ▼ ▼ ▼ ▼ ▼ ▼ ▼ ▼ ▼ ▼ ▼ ▼ ▼ ▼ ▼ ▼ ▼
>
> **THINKING CRITICALLY ABOUT YOUR COLLABORATIVE WORK**
>
> Begin by making a list of all the ways in which you collaborate with others. Then reflect on the kinds of collaboration you find most effective. Finally, take an example of a recent collaboration you have been part of, and examine how well it worked by answering the following questions: What did I contribute to the collaboration? What worked well, and what did not work well? What could I have done to improve the collaboration?

### Content for multilingual writers—and their classmates

◆ **MULTI-LINGUAL**  In this edition of *The St. Martin's Handbook*, following the advice of experts on best practices for teaching students from *all* language and educational backgrounds, the information for multilingual writers and U.S. academic writing is integrated into the text. If you teach international students and "Generation 1.5" students whose home language is not English, advise them to look for the **"Multilingual"** icon to find sections and boxed tips that may be of particular interest. Students who have grown up speaking U.S. varieties of English can also benefit from learning that English has particular features not shared by all languages; it's useful for such students to find out more about how much effort is required for non-native English speakers to speak and write effectively in English. And for all students who are new to college writing, *The St. Martin's Handbook* also integrates advice on assessing and creating texts in common U.S. academic genres and on using academic English.

### Examples and models for students

Student writers often find that examples are helpful, and in *The St. Martin's Handbook*, they'll see plentiful models—of effective writing and editing, of annotations for critical reading and peer response, of in-text and bibliographic citations, and of model student writing in various genres. You can ask students to review relevant models in *The St. Martin's Handbook* or in the LaunchPad media at **macmillanhighered.com/smh**, where you'll find twenty-three complete student models in many genres, each of which includes activities and offers more opportunities for reflection.

## ☐ A2. Showing students the print handbook as a reference tool

Whether you've used *The St. Martin's Handbook* in classrooms before or not, take the time to familiarize yourself with the Eighth Edition of the book—and show the quick-access features to your students. Many first-year college students may not have complete confidence in their ability to use a print reference text, so walking students through the book's navigation will help them develop an important skill for academic work—and will ensure that they can easily find information that's more reliable than what turns up in a late-night Google search. You may want to walk students through the print handbook in class, working from the outside in, to point out these reference features. For information on the features of LaunchPad and getting your students enrolled in the online course space and e-book, go to **macmillanhighered.com/smh**, and browse the "Support" links at the bottom of the page.

### Tables of contents

- On the inside front cover, **Brief Contents** pages give an overview of all the chapters in the book.
- On the inside back cover, **Contents** pages list chapter titles and most major headings to make it easy to flip to a particular part of a chapter.

### Page navigation

At the top of each page is a heading that tells readers where they are in the book. Each page has a page number near the outside edge and a chapter number and section letter in a red tab. On left-hand pages, the part title and chapter title appear, and on right-hand pages, readers will find the section heading.

In commenting on student work, some instructors use a chapter number and section letter as shorthand to point students to a particular section for review. (Students using *The St. Martin's Handbook* in LaunchPad will be able to use the same chapter number/section letter navigation to find the information in the e-book.)

## Boxed tips

- Quick Help sections offer quick summaries of important content and appear near the beginnings of chapters. The print book's index also lists each Quick Help section, and users of the LaunchPad e-book can navigate to Quick Help using the search tool.

- Talking the Talk boxes, which are listed in a directory at the back of the print book, answer common student questions about academic writing.

- Considering Disabilities boxes explain ways to make writing accessible to as many readers as possible. A directory to these boxes appears at the back of the book as well.

## Documentation directories

In each documentation section (MLA, APA, *Chicago*, and CSE), students will find quick-access directories to model citations in that documentation style. The APA section, for example, offers a directory for in-text citation models and a directory for models of entries in a list of references. These directories can help

---

### DIRECTORY TO APA STYLE    REFERENCES

**Guidelines for author listings**

**Print books**

students scan all the options available when they are trying to figure out the best model for a source they need to cite. (You may also want to point out the Quick Help boxes called "Citing sources that don't match any model exactly" in the MLA, APA, and *Chicago* sections, since no documentation reference work can include every possible kind of model.)

## Index-glossary

The index at the back of the book doubles as a glossary of terms, with important definitions given alongside cross-references. Designed to be student-friendly, the index also lists both everyday terms and traditional nomenclature for grammatical concepts (students can look up the term *the* as well as the term *articles*, for example).

# B Making *The St. Martin's Handbook* a perfect fit

*The St. Martin's Handbook* is published in both hardcover and paperback print versions—each available packaged free with LaunchPad media that includes an e-book—and in multiple digital formats to accommodate instructor and student needs.

### Print and digital books with LaunchPad

To get the most out of your course, order LaunchPad for *The St. Martin's Handbook* packaged with the print book. (LaunchPad for *The St. Martin's Handbook* can also be purchased on its own.) An activation code is required. LaunchPad for *The St. Martin's Handbook* includes a full e-book you can customize and assign, along with content that goes beyond print: **videos** of student writers, **model student writing** in many genres, and **visual exercises**, all with reflective prompts; **tutorials**; **editing quizzes** with "The Top Twenty" in context; and **LearningCurve adaptive quizzing** that students can do to practice on their own. (For a complete list of the LaunchPad media contents, see the media directory at the back of the book.)

- To order the **hardcover** version of *The St. Martin's Handbook* with LaunchPad, use **ISBN 978-1-319-02136-8**.
- To order the **paperback** version of *The St. Martin's Handbook* with LaunchPad, use **ISBN 978-1-319-02137-5**.

### Other formats

Bedford/St. Martin's offers a range of affordable formats, allowing students to choose the one that works best for them. For details, visit **macmillanhighered.com/smh/formats**.

### Additional resources for instructors and students

For even more advice on planning your composition course, with sample syllabi, teaching tips, and classroom activities, consult *Teaching with Lunsford Handbooks*, **Second Edition**. Request a print copy or download a PDF from the Instructor Resources for *The St. Martin's Handbook* at **macmillanhighered.com/smh/catalog**.

Download the complete answer key for exercises integrated into *The St. Martin's Handbook* from the Instructor Resources for *The St. Martin's Handbook* at **macmillanhighered.com/smh/catalog**.

### Hear more from Andrea Lunsford!

Every week, Andrea's **"Teacher to Teacher" channel** brings you new ideas for the classroom on the award-winning blog **bedfordbits.com**. Andrea always posts on Thursdays, and then during the school year, **"Multimodal Mondays" posts** from Andrea and guest bloggers suggest ways to "go digital" in the composition classroom. (If you're interested in blogging on "Multimodal Mondays," please use the link on the blog to reach Andrea and her editors.)

"Like" Andrea's **author page on Facebook**, where Andrea's updates and links are posted several times each week. And follow **@LunsfordHandbks on Twitter** for even more frequent updates from Andrea.

To read Andrea Lunsford's scholarly work, request or download a copy of *From Theory to Practice: A Selection of Essays* at **macmillanhighered.com**.

# C Integrating *The St. Martin's Handbook* into your course: General strategies

Many students aren't familiar with a handbook or how to use it, so giving students a guided tour of *The St. Martin's Handbook* is essential. This will serve not only to acquaint students with the handbook but also to send the message that this book plays an essential role in the course you are teaching.

## ☐ C1. Introducing the handbook

Ask students to bring the handbook to class. Show them the book's navigation features (see p. IE-5), and explain how these features can be useful in helping them track down important advice. Review the table of contents to give students an overall sense of what the book includes. Finally, lead students through two chapters that will be relevant for your course—perhaps one that gives advice about composing and one that deals with a particular grammatical or mechanical concern—highlighting various types of information and identifying useful features of the text. To check that students understand how to use the handbook, do a scavenger hunt in class using "A Tutorial on Using *The St. Martin's Handbook*" (see pp. xxi–xxvi).

In addition to the contents in the print and e-book versions of *The St. Martin's Handbook*, you can assign video activities, student writing models, quizzes, and more from LaunchPad for *The St. Martin's Handbook*, which can be packaged free with the print book. Go to **macmillanhighered.com/smh** to start setting up your LaunchPad course.

## ☐ C2. Making assignments from *The St. Martin's Handbook*

Even if you expect students to use the book mainly on their own as a reference guide, give at least one substantial reading assignment to the whole class during the first week of the course. A good choice is Chapter 1, "Expectations for College Writing." Take time to talk about the chapter, asking students to discuss what they learned and, in particular, to consider how the book's advice may help them as they draft and revise their papers later in the term. This sort of discussion can help establish a connection between the handbook and the rest of what students will do in the course.

### Integrating the handbook into your assignments

To continue incorporating the handbook into assignments throughout the semester, consider the suggestions below.

#### Discuss purpose and audience

- Determine what objectives you want to accomplish—they should always align with a course outcome—and create writing assignments with a clear purpose (2d). Explain the purpose to students. You may also ask them to reflect afterward on what this piece of writing is for.

- Clearly state the intended audience, or if you want students to choose their audience, say so explicitly (2e).

### Share specific criteria

- Define the terms of the assignment—the range of topics students can choose from, whether research is expected, and so on (Chapter 2).
- Point out the deadline for each part of the assignment that students will submit. Talk about strategies for time management (you may want students to use the calendar in 10b as a model for their own plan).

### Point out the features of the type of writing you expect students to create

- Determine what options are appropriate in student responses to the assignment. Will you require traditional academic formats (such as a researched essay or a review of literature)? Will you accept responses in other media (such as videos or Web essays)? Will students create work for a community or professional audience (Chapters 25 and 26)? Will students be asked to recast a work in another format, such as a presentation (Chapter 17)?
- Take a bit of class time to demonstrate the features of the types of writing you expect students to create, pointing out genre, medium, content, and rhetorical situation. Point out the student writing models available in LaunchPad for *The St. Martin's Handbook* at **macmillanhighered.com /smh** (see the Resources tab for a complete list).
- Consider asking students to do low-stakes, informal assignments as well, such as commenting on a class blog, and to think about how informal writing differs from formal writing (1a).

### Emphasize critical thinking

- Discuss ways to read course materials effectively (Chapter 7) and encourage students to practice critical reading of assigned texts and of possible sources for research (Chapter 12).
- Consider asking students to use a non-print text that makes an argument (such as a public service announcement or political speech) and having them identify the argument and evaluate its effectiveness (Chapter 8).

### Divide the tasks; provide interim deadlines

- Break up the writing assignment into several steps or tasks, each with due dates. This helps students avoid procrastination and plagiarism—and in general produces better writing.
- Offer at least one peer review session for each assignment. Ask students to look over sections 4b and c, and discuss your expectations with them to

help them get the most from the experience. Consider asking students to do a low-stakes practice peer review of Emily Lesk's draft (you can assign this activity at **macmillanhighered.com/smh**).

- Build in time for revising by requiring at least two drafts of each piece of formal writing.

### Expect significant revision and careful editing

- Talk to students about big-picture concerns and sentence-level issues. Explain that you expect them to focus on major issues of planning, drafting, and development (Chapters 3 and 5) before addressing sentence-level issues.

- Point out "The Top Twenty" (on pp. 1–11 of the print book), and discuss the benefits of keeping a personal inventory of writing issues.

- If you point out sentence-level issues in drafts, the revision symbols listed at the back of the book can serve as helpful shorthand. Encourage students to use the handbook to learn more about any distracting issues that you or other reviewers point out.

- Assign students to complete LearningCurve quizzes to give them practice with common editing issues. (To see the full list of LearningCurve topics and assign target scores, go to **macmillanhighered.com/smh**, and click on the Resources tab.)

### Include a rubric for grading

- Be specific about how much each element of an assignment (content, format, etc.) contributes to the final grade.

## ☐ C3. Making the handbook a presence in the classroom

It's important to keep the handbook an active presence in your course throughout the semester. Bring it to class, even when you don't plan to teach from it, and encourage students to do likewise. If you keep the print book in a handy spot on your desk (or use the e-book version in a wired classroom), you can easily consult it when needed during class discussions, demonstrating in a tangible way its value as a writing guide and *showing* students how to use the book to answer questions. If, for example, you tell students that a signal phrase in MLA style should use the present tense and someone asks what "present tense" means, talk the class through ways to find the answer in the handbook. Asking students to look up the information for themselves will help them develop the habit of looking in the book for reference. And the next time a similar question comes up, the student may turn to the handbook before asking you.

You can also utilize the handbook in class to show your students examples of the writing you are asking them to do. You might direct students to examples like these:

- ways to recognize and revise comma splices and fused sentences (Chapter 46)
- how to summarize a text (7d, 13d)
- models of in-text citations and bibliographic entries (Chapters 32–35)
- interim tasks for managing a large research project (Chapter 15)

## ☐ C4. Using the handbook when responding to student work

Responding to student writing is an opportunity to teach a lesson, but trying to teach too much at once can overwhelm students. When considering your purpose in providing feedback, ask yourself: What are the one or two lessons you most want students to take away at this stage of the writing process? What should students do with the information you're providing? How can you clearly convey the most important next steps for revision?

Let students know that your comments on a given draft will focus on certain issues and will necessarily not cover every possible aspect of revision and editing. Explain that comments on early-stage drafts will focus on global issues, not editing concerns, because sentences that need editing may be completely rewritten (or removed) when the student reworks the draft.

If your students will serve as peer reviewers of each other's work as well, ask them to read Chapter 4, "Reviewing, Revising, Editing, and Reflecting," before the first review session.

### Commenting on higher-order concerns in early-stage drafts

Be sure to explain to your students what they should expect from your comments on various stages of their work. If you are responding to work that is in fairly early stages, focus on higher-order issues:

- Is it an appropriate response to the assignment? (Chapter 2)
- Does it have a solid thesis? (3b and c)
- Is it clearly organized? (3e)
- Are main ideas well developed? (Chapter 5)
- Is evidence to support points appropriate? (Chapter 5)
- Are paragraphs unified? (Chapter 5)

Looking at a class's response to an assignment as a group can alert you to significant issues that you may want to address during class time or by assigning handbook content—or both.

If you notice patterns of error in a student's work, make a note of it without correcting every instance. You may want to ask students to keep a writing inventory (see "The Top Twenty" on pp. 1–11) of the errors they make most often so that they can develop the habit of finding and correcting them. You can also ask students to review appropriate chapters in the handbook or to take an adaptive quiz using LearningCurve (see **macmillanhighered.com/smh**).

In later drafts that may not be substantially revised before submission or publication, you may want to pay more attention to lower-order issues—such as grammar, punctuation, spelling, word choice, and proofreading errors—if the situation warrants.

When marking and grading student work in print, use a few key symbols to identify common surface errors (see the list of the most commonly used revision symbols at the back of the book). You can incorporate the handbook by marking the students' work selectively and tying marginal and terminal comments as closely as possible to advice in the book. If, for example, a central weakness of a draft happens to be paragraph coherence, you might describe the problem in a sentence or two. Your comment, like a revision symbol, can send the student to the handbook, but whereas the symbol (*cohere*) gives the student an entire section to read, your advice can be more specific.

Supplying this degree of specificity takes time, but if marking is selective, if you focus on one or two major issues per paper, students are more likely to revise—and to use the book as a reference tool—than they are if you mark every error. Your terminal comment can help focus a student's attention, highlighting strengths to exploit and problems to avoid in the next draft.

## ☐ C5. Encouraging continued use of *The St. Martin's Handbook*

Just as you may start your first-year composition course by orienting students to the book, you may want to end it by explaining how the text can serve them in their other college courses. Reminding your students of the various ways they might use the handbook beyond first-year composition helps place the courses you teach in a larger academic context. Students at the outset of their college years rarely see the "big picture"; they often have little sense of the interconnectedness of the curriculum they are beginning to pursue. You should do what you can to show them the connections—especially the way in which writing, as a way of learning and as a means of communication, cuts across disciplinary boundaries. In a small but significant way, teaching students to make the handbook a trusted guide and reference companion contributes to that effort.

Below are some possible ways in which this handbook may come in handy for students later in their college and life careers. You might mention these in class discussion and encourage students to think of additional possibilities for use of the handbook beyond first-year composition.

- **Editing help.** Checking the Glossary of Usage can help writers be sure that they've used frequently confused or misused words properly (*affect* versus *effect*, for example). Consulting the parts on Grammar, Clarity, Style, Punctuation, and Mechanics makes it easy to correct ineffective grammar—including issues pointed out by tutors, coworkers, and others outside the classroom.

- **Documentation help.**  Documentation guidelines vary from discipline to discipline and class to class. Remind students that Chapter 32 offers comprehensive help with MLA style and that Chapters 33–35 include detailed guidelines for courses requiring APA, *Chicago*, and CSE styles.

- **Help with work-related writing.**  Chapter 23, "Writing for Business," offers important guidelines on writing and formatting effective letters, memos, emails, and résumés. A tutorial on job searching and personal branding appears in the LaunchPad media at **macmillanhighered.com/smh** (click on the Resources tab for a list of tutorials).

- **Help with writing for communities.**  Chapter 26, "Writing to Make Something Happen in the World," can help students accomplish bigger things in the writing they do because they want to achieve a goal outside of school or work.

# D Integrating *The St. Martin's Handbook* into your course: Classroom activities

Following is a sampling of specific teaching ideas and classroom activities that ask students to draw on the handbook for support. For more suggestions, teaching advice, and ready-to-tailor teaching materials, contact your sales representative for a copy of *Teaching with Lunsford Handbooks* or download the PDF from the instructor resources at **macmillanhighered.com/smh/catalog**.

## ☐ D1. Thinking about rhetorical situations

### Activity 1: Thinking about audiences

Have students read Chapter 2, "Rhetorical Situations." Ask students to list all the kinds of writing that they do in a typical day other than writing for school. Then ask them to identify the audience for each kind of writing. How much do they consciously adjust their language, tone, and style for different audiences? Have students respond to the video prompt "Developing a sense of audience" at **macmillanhighered.com/smh** (in the Resources tab under "Videos").

### Activity 2: Audiences for formal and academic writing

Have students read 2e, "Analyzing audiences." Then, have each student find an article, editorial, or column in a newspaper or magazine, print it out, and circle elements in the writing that deliberately exclude or include certain kinds of audiences. Ask students to talk about whether the writer seemed to be aware of doing this and why the writer made the choices he or she made about audience.

### Activity 3: Considering the purpose of your writing

Have students choose a writing assignment they are currently working on and consider the purposes of the assignment (see 2b). What are the instructor's purposes in assigning it? What are their own purposes? How will these purposes affect the way they plan to work on and complete the assignment?

## ☐ D2. Reading critically

### Activity 1: Previewing a text

To have students develop critical reading skills, ask them to compare the same text in two formats: as a written speech and as a short video of the speech. First, choose a speech from the American Rhetoric Web site (at **americanrhetoric .com**), and ask the class to preview it using the questions in 7b. What do students know or find out about the author or creator of the text? Is the author different from the speaker who delivered the speech? What questions do students have about the subject? What was the occasion for the speech? Have them talk about (or write about) their expectations for the speech, and then play the video of the speech for the class. Does anything about the delivery or reception surprise them?

### Activity 2: Reading, annotating, and summarizing a text

Ask students to work in small groups to read and analyze a short review of a product, film, or book from a source such as Amazon.com or the Internet Movie Database (imdb.com). Have the groups work through 7c and d. Ask them to take notes on their first reading of the review and, when they have finished reading and annotating, to agree on a fair one-sentence summary of the review contents. Have each group share their notes and summary, telling the class about the major points of the text and what they learned from a first reading. What, if anything, do they still need to know? What next steps would they take to find additional information?

### Activity 3: Analyzing a text

Ask students to choose a text that they have already previewed and read for analysis. (You might give the option of the review in Activity 2 or the speech in Activity 1.) Have students read 7e and then work collaboratively to create a paragraph of analysis to present to the class.

### Activity 4: Critical reading

Ask students to look at the "Thinking Visually" exercise on critical reading at **macmillanhighered.com/smh** and think about the last film they watched for fun. What did they know about it before watching? What did they feel and learn as they watched? What have they told others about the film, both in terms of summarizing the story and of analyzing what the experience meant to them? Point out that "reading" a film is similar in many ways to "reading" a print text. Ask students to talk about how they might use those same skills—previewing, reading, summarizing, and analyzing—the next time they are asked to read a written-word text.

## ☐ D3. Analyzing arguments

### Activity 1: Identifying elements of an argument

Ask students to analyze Benjy Mercer-Golden's essay (9l and under "Student Writing" in the Resources tab at **macmillanhighered.com/smh**), reading it for its implicit argument. Have them analyze the elements of his argument—its claim, the reasons for the claim, any assumptions it makes, the evidence he presents to support the claim, and any qualifiers that limit the claim. Does the essay succeed as an argument, in their view? Why or why not?

### Activity 2: Analyzing arguments

Have students read Chapter 8, "Analyzing Arguments," and then ask them to work with one or two classmates and choose a brief argumentative text, such as an advertisement or blog post. Have them work together to analyze the text, playing the believing and doubting game; identifying ethical, emotional, and logical appeals; and listing claims, reasons, assumptions, evidence, and qualifiers. Finally, ask each group to collaborate on a critical response and present the results of their analysis to the class.

## ☐ D4. Considering thesis and paragraph development

### Activity 1: Formulating a working thesis

Ask students to read and analyze the "Thinking Visually" panels on developing a working thesis, which can be found under "Exercises" in the Resources tab at **macmillanhighered.com/smh**. How do the steps shown work as a metaphor for the process of planning and drafting a working thesis as described in 3b and c? Have students discuss how well the metaphor in the images describes their own process of creating a working thesis. What changes would they make to the metaphor so that it would fit their personal process? This kind of reflection can prompt students to think (perhaps for the first time) about how they get a writing project started.

### Activity 2: Writing unified paragraphs

One practical way to have students check whether each sentence relates to the main idea of a paragraph is through a collaborative highlighting exercise. Ask students to review 5a and b and then to look at the first draft of Emily Lesk's essay under "Student Writing" in the Resources tab at **macmillanhighered.com /smh**. Print out a page or two of her draft, and ask students to go through it, highlighting the main idea of each paragraph and noting the relevance of each sentence in a given paragraph to the highlighted one. Then ask the class to discuss their highlighting together and see whether they agree about the unity of the paragraphs. Does each paragraph stand on its own as a unified whole? Does any paragraph have too many new ideas? Do the details fit together to support the topic sentence?

## ☐ D5. Thinking about the research process

### Activity 1: Evaluating sources

Have students spend some time thinking about the everyday Internet research they have done recently—typing health symptoms into Google for a diagnosis, examining blogs and forums to determine the best media player to buy, and so on. What kinds of research do they commonly do online? What kinds of sources do they turn to most often? Then ask students to look at the guidelines in 12d for evaluating the usefulness and credibility of a source. Do the sources they use most often meet the criteria for a reliable source? Why or why not?

### Activity 2: Differentiating kinds of sources

Ask students to read Chapter 11, "Conducting Research," and then to consider a research assignment they are currently working on (in your class or in another course). Then, have each student draw up a preliminary list of types of sources that they think would be most relevant for finding information on their particular research topic. Which information will require a trip to the library? Which information might be found on the Internet? How can they determine which Internet sources might be acceptable for their purpose? As a class, draw up a list of guidelines for exploring a topic and finding potentially useful sources.

### Activity 3: Evaluating sources

After students have begun their preliminary research, have them read sections 12a–c and prepare a working bibliography. Ask them to examine either the working bibliography example by Tony Chan or the reflective working bibliography by Nandita Sriram in the media resources at **macmillanhighered.com /smh** (click on "Student Writing" in the Resources tab) and respond to the writing prompt. Ask students to create a sample annotated bibliography entry for one source they are thinking of using in their own project and explain, either in class discussion or in writing, the purpose the source could serve in their own work.

### Activity 4: Synthesizing sources

Ask students to read section 12f and then look closely at each source they are using for a research project they are working on now or have done in the past. How do the sources fit into the overall pattern of the argument? How are the sources brought together and integrated into the writing? Ask students to reflect on how they tried to make the sources support rather than overwhelm their own ideas. You might have them try sketching a picture that captures the role the sources play in their argument.

### Activity 5: Integrating sources

To facilitate students' understanding of source integration, review Chapter 13 with them, and then have them work in pairs to discuss each other's research projects. Ask them to analyze their partner's integration of sources (including visuals and media files), identifying any areas where source integration could be improved. Have students write comments for each other and then discuss the feedback with the class.

## ☐ D6. Considering multimodality

### Activity: *Translating to a new genre*

Ask students to read Chapter 18, "Communicating in Other Media," and bring in an idea for turning a traditional print essay they have completed for your course or another class into a multimodal genre that includes visuals or media (or both) in some way. What genre would be an appropriate way to use the information they have created? What steps would they need to take to "translate" the assignment into a new genre? Would the thesis, purpose, and audience for the content be the same? Ask students to describe or sketch their initial plan.

## ☐ D7. Analyzing visuals

### Activity: *Words and images*

Ask students to analyze the illustration on one or more of the part-opening pages in *The St. Martin's Handbook*. What items appear in the photograph? If the title of the part were removed, what title would they give the collection of objects? How do the words on the page affect the way they understand what the image depicts? Does the photograph clarify the title or contents of the section in any way, or does it seem chiefly decorative? Ask students to work in small groups to discuss whether the image works well, to determine what makes the image work (or not), and to identify other ways the concept might be effectively illustrated.

Illustration for Part 2, "Critical Thinking and Argument"

## ☐ D8. Thinking about language choice

### Activity 1: Avoiding language that stereotypes

Have students read Chapter 28, "Language That Builds Common Ground," in their handbook. Then, ask them to read the comments on a popular online video of their choosing and identify two or three comments that use biased language or hurtful stereotypes. Ask them to submit a sentence or two analyzing why each comment they have chosen might upset some readers. Lead a brainstorming session asking students to think about what prompts hateful comments and what kind of response is appropriate (comments denouncing the hatred? silence? requesting the removal of the comments or the commenter? legal action? something else?). Do they see YouTube and other online spaces as more likely locations for inflammatory remarks than face-to-face public spaces? How can online writers determine what kind of language and behavior is acceptable in a given community?

### Activity 2: Understanding the Glossary of Usage

Ask students to examine the Glossary of Usage in *The St. Martin's Handbook* and choose three entries that they see as stumbling blocks. Have students work in small groups to analyze their selections and explain appropriate usage to each other. Do any nonstandard usage examples seem acceptable under at least some circumstances to members of the group? Ask each group to report to the class as a whole, and keep track of the most commonly identified glossary entries overall and of any nonstandard examples that may be widely accepted by your students. Discuss what your class has reported, pointing out to them that "surface errors . . . don't always disturb readers," as Andrea Lunsford notes in the introduction to "The Top Twenty" in your handbook. In what contexts do they think the class's common stumbling blocks will probably be disturbing (and to whom)? In what contexts do they see these as acceptable usage?

### Activity 3: Learning specialized vocabulary

Ask students to read 19d and to bring to class two copies of a short passage taken from an article, Web site, or textbook in a field with which they are (or want to become) familiar. Have students work in groups of three and give a copy of the passage to their partners, asking them (1) to list terms, phrases, or concepts that involve highly specialized language, and (2) to try to define or explain these terms. After students have worked on each other's passages, have them retrieve their partners' lists and check their efforts. Discuss what, if anything, they found confusing about each other's passages.

This exercise gives students practice explaining terms in fields they are familiar with to a general audience, so it serves two purposes. It helps students develop an awareness of how to adapt their language and explanations to audiences with different degrees of expertise or familiarity with a field, and it also allows students to test their own understanding of terms and concepts—one way we determine how well we understand concepts is to try to explain them to someone else.

# E Aligning WPA outcomes with *The St. Martin's Handbook*

The following chart shows how content in *The St. Martin's Handbook*, Eighth Edition, aligns with the WPA Outcomes Statement ratified in July 2014.

| WPA Outcomes | Relevant Features of *The St. Martin's Handbook* |
|---|---|
| **Rhetorical Knowledge** | |
| **Learn and use key rhetorical concepts through analyzing and composing a variety of texts.** | Chapter 1, "Expectations for College Writing," introduces the idea that social writing and academic writing are different but related skills and spells out the requirements of academic writing. |
| | Chapter 2, "Rhetorical Situations," examines the rhetorical triangle and the aspects of rhetorical situations for all kinds of communication. |
| | Chapter 7, "Reading Critically," walks students through the process of analyzing various kinds of texts, from scholarly articles to images. |
| | Chapter 8, "Analyzing Arguments," looks closely at analyzing explicitly persuasive texts. |
| | Chapter 12, "Evaluating Sources and Taking Notes," offers suggestions for determining how authoritative and useful a text is for a given purpose. |
| | Part 4 (Chapters 16–18), "Designing and Performing Writing," discusses composing texts beyond print. |
| | Part 5 (Chapters 19–26), "Academic, Professional, and Public Writing," examines writing beyond the English classroom and beyond the academy. |
| | Chapter 27, "Writing to the World," asks students to consider the rhetorical implications of texts for global audiences. |

| WPA Outcomes | Relevant Features of *The St. Martin's Handbook* |
| --- | --- |
| **Gain experience reading and composing in several genres to understand how genre conventions shape and are shaped by readers' and writers' practices and purposes.** | 2f, "Thinking about genres and media," asks students to think about genre conventions. |
| | 7a, "Reading print and digital texts," discusses differences in reading practices in various media. |
| | Chapter 8, "Analyzing Arguments," helps students analyze writers' purposes in persuasive texts. |
| | Chapter 9, "Constructing Arguments," asks students to consider their own purposes and practices as writers of persuasive texts. |
| | 12c, "Keeping a working bibliography," asks students to compose in a conventional genre and evaluate how other texts will work with their own writing purpose. |
| | Chapter 17, "Presentations," offers advice on moving between genres. |
| | Chapter 18, "Communicating in Other Media," discusses rhetorical aspects of multimodal genres. |
| | Part 5 (Chapters 19–26), "Academic, Professional, and Public Writing," discusses conventions of genres beyond composition. |
| | 19g, "Using conventional patterns and formats," asks students to consider expectations for particular genres and disciplines. |
| | Chapter 27, "Writing to the World," asks students to consider cultural aspects of genre conventions. |
| | Chapter 29, "Language Variety," discusses the conventions of academic genres and when it's appropriate to depart from those conventions purposefully. |

| WPA Outcomes | Relevant Features of *The St. Martin's Handbook* |
|---|---|
| **Develop facility in responding to a variety of situations and contexts, calling for purposeful shifts in voice, tone, level of formality, design, medium, and/or structure.** | 1a, "Moving between social and academic writing," asks students to reflect on the different choices they make in different writing contexts.<br><br>Chapter 2, "Rhetorical Situations," discusses making appropriate decisions for all aspects of the situation.<br><br>Chapter 19, "Academic Work in Any Discipline," discusses responding to assignments beyond the composition classroom.<br><br>Chapter 26, "Writing to Make Something Happen in the World," discusses public writing for a purpose.<br><br>Chapter 27, "Writing to the World," talks about purposeful shifts for global audiences.<br><br>Chapter 29, "Language Variety," discusses using different kinds of English (and other languages) effectively.<br><br>LaunchPad media: Student writing activities on formal and informal reflective writing ask students to analyze language choices in a portfolio cover letter and in a blog post reflecting on a college writing assignment. |
| **Understand and use a variety of technologies to address a range of audiences.** | 1a, "Moving between social and academic writing," discusses social media writing.<br><br>2f, "Thinking about genres and media," asks students to consider appropriate media for any writing.<br><br>Chapter 17, "Presentations," discusses various kinds of in-person and online presentations.<br><br>Chapter 18, "Communicating in Other Media," addresses using digital technology as well as low-tech multimedia. |

| WPA Outcomes | Relevant Features of *The St. Martin's Handbook* |
|---|---|
| | LaunchPad media: Tutorials on audio editing and photo editing |
| | (The book never assumes that today's student writing projects are only print-based, so examples appear throughout.) |
| **Match the capacities of different environments (e.g., print and electronic) to varying rhetorical situations.** | 1a, "Moving between social and academic writing" |
| | 2f, "Thinking about genres and media" |
| | Chapter 16, "Design for Print and Digital Writing" |
| | Chapter 17, "Presentations" |
| | Chapter 18, "Communicating in Other Media" |
| | 19g, "Using conventional patterns and formats" |
| | Chapter 26, "Writing to Make Something Happen in the World" |
| **Critical Thinking, Reading, and Composing** | |
| **Use composing and reading for inquiry, learning, thinking, and communicating in various rhetorical contexts.** | 1d, "Becoming an engaged reader and active listener," identifies skills needed for academic work. |
| | Part 2 (Chapters 7–9), "Critical Thinking and Argument," gives students a step-by-step approach to reading both verbal and visual texts critically and to analyzing and composing persuasive texts. |
| | Part 3 (Chapters 10–15), "Doing Research and Using Sources," offers advice on finding, evaluating, and integrating texts composed by others. |
| | Part 5 (Chapters 19–26), "Academic, Professional, and Public Writing," addresses reading and writing in school, work, and community contexts. |

| WPA Outcomes | Relevant Features of *The St. Martin's Handbook* |
|---|---|
| **Read a diverse range of texts, attending especially to relationships between assertion and evidence, to patterns of organization, to interplay between verbal and nonverbal elements, and how these features function for different audiences and situations.** | Chapter 7, "Reading Critically," includes advice on previewing, annotating, summarizing, and analyzing verbal and visual texts.<br><br>Chapter 8, "Analyzing Arguments," helps students focus on cultural and rhetorical contexts for argument and on what makes arguments effective.<br><br>Chapter 9, "Constructing Arguments," explains the choices students must make so that their own arguments will work in specific contexts.<br><br>12d, "Evaluating usefulness and credibility," asks students to consider sources in the context of their own purposes.<br><br>12e, "Reading and interpreting sources," suggests questions to help students interpret texts they read for their research.<br><br>Chapter 19, "Academic Work in Any Discipline"; 20a, "Reading texts in the humanities"; 21a, "Reading texts in the social sciences"; 22a, "Reading texts in the natural and applied sciences"; and 23a, "Reading texts for business," explain the basics of reading discipline-specific texts.<br><br>Chapter 25, "Portfolios," asks students to read their own work critically and present it effectively. |
| **Locate and evaluate primary and secondary research materials, including journal articles, essays, books, databases, and informal Internet sources.** | Chapter 11, "Conducting Research," explains how to find and evaluate sources from library, Internet, and field research. |

| WPA Outcomes | Relevant Features of *The St. Martin's Handbook* |
| --- | --- |
| Use strategies—such as interpretation, synthesis, response, critique, and design or redesign—to compose texts that integrate the writer's ideas with those from appropriate sources. | Chapter 4, "Reviewing, Revising, Editing, and Reflecting," offers advice on peer reviewing (as writer and reviewer) and revising with peer and instructor comments.<br><br>Chapter 12, "Evaluating Sources and Taking Notes," discusses evaluating sources in the context of the rhetorical situation and synthesizing others' work into texts.<br><br>Chapter 16, "Design for Print and Digital Writing," helps students think about how to make texts readable and inviting. |
| **Processes** | |
| **Develop a writing project through multiple drafts.** | Part 1 (Chapters 1–6), "The Art and Craft of Writing," works through the process of becoming a college writer, from understanding expectations and rhetorical contexts to revising, editing, and reflecting on work. |
| **Develop flexible strategies for reading, drafting, reviewing, collaborating, revising, rewriting, rereading, and editing.** | Chapter 3, "Exploring, Planning, and Drafting"; Chapter 4, "Reviewing, Revising, Editing, and Reflecting"; Chapter 5, "Developing Paragraphs"; and Chapter 6, "Working with Others," suggest multiple strategies for composing and collaborating effectively. |
| **Use composing processes and tools as a means to discover and reconsider ideas.** | Chapter 3, "Exploring, Planning, and Drafting," offers many ideas for exploring topics alone and with others, on paper and online.<br><br>Chapter 10, "Preparing for a Research Project," and Chapter 11, "Conducting Research," discuss focusing on a topic of interest and finding out more about it. |

| WPA Outcomes | Relevant Features of **The St. Martin's Handbook** |
|---|---|
| **Experience the collaborative and social aspects of writing processes.** | 1a, "Moving between social and academic writing"<br><br>Chapter 6, "Working with Others"<br><br>19i, "Collaborating and communicating"<br><br>Chapter 26, "Writing to Make Something Happen in the World," discusses using texts to engage with communities |
| **Learn to give and act on productive feedback to works in progress.** | 4b, "Reviewing peer writers' work"<br><br>4c, "Getting the most from peer reviewers' comments"<br><br>4d, "Learning from instructor comments"<br><br>4e, "Revising with peer and instructor comments"<br><br>LaunchPad media: Videos, exercises, and student writing activities in the Chapter 4 resources |
| **Adapt composing processes for a variety of technologies and modalities.** | 1a, "Moving between social and academic writing," asks students to reflect on differences between formal and informal composing.<br><br>2f, "Thinking about genres and media," discusses how genres and media affect composing.<br><br>Chapter 16, "Design for Print and Digital Writing," asks students to consider rhetorical questions of presenting work.<br><br>Chapter 17, "Presentations," discusses writing for reading and listening audiences.<br><br>Chapter 18, "Communicating in Other Media," analyzes rhetorical questions of multimodal composing beyond presentations.<br><br>19g, "Using conventional patterns and formats," addresses the need to consider conventions in context. |

| WPA Outcomes | Relevant Features of *The St. Martin's Handbook* |
|---|---|
| Reflect on the development of composing practices and how those practices influence their work. | 4m, "Reflecting on your writing," discusses the importance of reflection for learning.<br><br>"Connect, Create, Reflect" modules at the beginning of most chapters suggest reflection activities.<br><br>"Thinking Critically" exercises at the end of most chapters ask students to reflect on their own and others' writing.<br><br>LaunchPad media includes 26 video prompts for reflecting on writing (see the Resources tab for a complete list). |
| **Knowledge of Conventions** | |
| Develop knowledge of linguistic structures, including grammar, punctuation, and spelling, through practice in composing and revising. | Part 8 (Chapters 36–43), "Grammar"<br><br>Part 9 (Chapters 44–49), "Clarity"<br><br>Part 10 (Chapters 50–53), "Style"<br><br>Part 11 (Chapters 54–59), "Punctuation"<br><br>Part 12 (Chapters 60–63), "Mechanics" |
| Understand why genre conventions for structure, paragraphing, tone, and mechanics vary. | Part 5 (Chapters 19–26), "Academic, Professional, and Public Writing"<br><br>Part 6 (Chapters 27–31), "Effective Language" |
| Gain experience negotiating variations in genre conventions. | Part 1 (Chapters 1–6), "The Art and Craft of Writing"<br><br>Part 5 (Chapters 19–26), "Academic, Professional, and Public Writing" |
| Learn common formats and/or design features for different kinds of texts. | 2f, "Thinking about genres and media"<br><br>Chapter 16, "Design for Print and Digital Writing"<br><br>19g, "Using conventional patterns and formats" |

| WPA Outcomes | Relevant Features of *The St. Martin's Handbook* |
|---|---|
| **Explore the concepts of intellectual property (such as fair use and copyright) that motivate documentation conventions.** | Chapter 14, "Acknowledging Sources and Avoiding Plagiarism," discusses citation issues with attention to both copyright and academic integrity.<br><br>32a, "Understanding the basics of MLA style"; 33a, "Understanding the basics of APA style"; and 34a, "Understanding the basics of *Chicago* style," address reasons that academic and popular citations differ. |
| **Practice applying citation conventions systematically in their own work.** | Part 7 (Chapters 32–35), "Documenting Sources," covers MLA, APA, *Chicago*, and CSE style documentation, with plentiful models and advice on citing sources when no model is exactly the same. |

# The
# St. Martin's
# Handbook

EIGHTH EDITION

# The St. Martin's Handbook

## Andrea A. Lunsford
Stanford University

A section for multilingual writers and a section on genre with

**Paul Kei Matsuda**
Arizona State University

**Christine M. Tardy**
University of Arizona

A section on academic and professional writing with

**Lisa Ede**
Oregon State University

**Bedford/St. Martin's**     Boston ◆ New York

## For Bedford/St. Martin's

*Vice President, Editorial, Macmillan Higher Education Humanities:* Edwin Hill
*Editorial Director for English and Music:* Karen S. Henry
*Publisher for Composition, Business and Technical Writing, and Developmental Writing:*
   Leasa Burton
*Executive Editor for Handbooks:* Brendan Baruth
*Executive Editor:* Carolyn Lengel
*Editorial Assistants:* Leah Rang and Kathleen Wisneski
*Senior Production Editor:* Ryan Sullivan
*Senior Production Supervisor:* Steven Cestaro
*Marketing Manager:* Emily Rowin
*Copy Editor:* Wendy Polhemus-Annibell
*Indexer:* Ellen Kuhl Repetto
*Director of Rights and Permissions:* Hilary Newman
*Senior Art Director:* Anna Palchik
*Text Design:* Claire Seng-Niemoeller
*Cover Design:* William Boardman
*Composition:* Graphic World, Inc.
*Printing and Binding:* RR Donnelley and Sons

9   8   7   6   5   4
f   e   d   c   b   a

*For information, write:* Bedford/St. Martin's, 75 Arlington Street, Boston, MA 02116 (617-399-4000)

ISBN 978-1-4576-6726-8 (Student Edition, paperback)
ISBN 978-1-4576-6724-4 (Student Edition, hardcover)
ISBN 978-1-4576-6725-1 (Instructor's Edition)

## Acknowledgments

# PREFACE

For *decades* now, it seems, I have been saying, "These are exciting times for writers and teachers of writing." And they have been exciting. But today, the word *exciting* scarcely begins to convey the wealth of opportunities at hand. Student writers are engaging with new literacies and with multimodality, creating arguments not simply as academic essays but as documentaries, videos, podcasts, visual collages, and much, much more. In fact, many teachers and researchers today regard all writing as multimodal: even a print text that relies only on words engages not only that linguistic mode but also the visual mode through layout, fonts, use of white space, and so on. Colleges and universities increasingly reflect this focus on multimodality, as Writing Centers become Writing and Speaking Centers or Writing, Media, and Speaking Centers. And writing teachers are working with a whole new range of media and genres as well, learning how to teach and assess the products of "new literacies" — while still holding on to the best of the "old" literacy, with its emphasis on carefully structured argument and analysis, academic essays, and traditional print texts.

Are student writers and their teachers up to the challenges and opportunities offered today? Absolutely. Research I (and lots of others) have done shows that student writers are already far ahead of us in terms of engaging new literacies outside of school, that they are thinking in sophisticated ways about the worldwide audiences they may now address, and that they are keenly aware of the need to adjust their messages according to audience, purpose, and context. In such an atmosphere of excitement and change, taking a rhetorical perspective is particularly important. In the first place, rhetoric has always been a multimodal art, one that attended to speaking as well as writing, to body language and illustration. In addition, a rhetorical perspective is particularly important today because it rejects either/or, right/wrong, black/white approaches to writing in favor of asking what choices will be most appropriate, effective, and ethical in any given writing situation, using any genre, any medium, any mode.

*The St. Martin's Handbook* has always taken such a perspective, and the numerous changes to the eighth edition reflect this tradition. Throughout, this book invites student writers to take each choice they make as an opportunity for critical engagement with ideas, audiences, texts, media, and genre. But as I've incorporated new material, I've been careful not to lose sight of the mission of any handbook: to be a relevant and accessible reference for students and instructors alike.

## Research for *The St. Martin's Handbook*

From the beginning, *The St. Martin's Handbook* has been informed by research on student writing. The late Robert J. Connors and I first began work on *The*

*St. Martin's Handbook* in 1983, when we realized that most college handbooks were based on research into student writing conducted almost fifty years earlier. Our own historical studies had convinced us that student writing and what teachers think of as "good" writing change over time, so we began by gathering a nationwide sample of more than twenty-one thousand marked student essays and carefully analyzing a stratified sample to identify the twenty surface errors most characteristic of contemporary student writing.

Our analysis of these student essays revealed the twenty errors that most troubled students and teachers in the 1980s (spelling was by far the most prevalent error then) as well as the organizational and other global issues of greatest concern to teachers. Our findings on the twenty most common errors led to sections in *The St. Martin's Handbook* that attempt to put error in its place, presenting the conventions of writing as rhetorical choices a writer must make rather than as a series of rules that writers must obey.

Every subsequent edition of *The St. Martin's Handbook* has been informed by research, from a national survey of student writers on how they are using technology, to a series of intensive interviews with students and focus group sessions with first-year writing instructors, to a nationwide study for which Karen Lunsford and I replicated the research Connors and I did twenty-five years ago. Our "'Mistakes Are a Fact of Life': A National Comparative Study" appeared in the June 2008 issue of *College Composition and Communication*. In sum, this study found that students are writing much longer essays than they were twenty-five years ago; that they are tackling more cognitively demanding topics and assignments, usually focusing on argument; *and* that the ratio of errors per one hundred words has not gone up but has remained almost constant during the last one hundred years (according to every national study we could find). While students are not making more mistakes, however, we found that they are making different ones — especially having to do with the use of and documentation of sources. And in an ironic note, we found that while spelling errors have decreased dramatically with the use of spell checkers, the number of "wrong word" mistakes has risen — partly because of spell checkers suggesting that wrong word! Finally, in the midst of national hand-wringing over the damage texting, chatting, and blogging are doing to writing, our study showed that students in first-year writing classes, at least, know perfectly well when to write "LOL" or "GTG" or a host of other shortcuts and when such Internet lingo is inappropriate for their audience, purpose, and context. (You can find articles detailing my research with Bob Connors and with Karen Lunsford in *From Theory to Practice: A Selection of Essays* by Andrea A. Lunsford, available free from Bedford/St. Martin's.)

These findings are borne out by a five-year longitudinal study of both in-class and out-of-class writing (in any medium or genre) I have conducted, analyzing the writing of 189 writers. Again I saw longer pieces of writing and more analytical topics along with extracurricular writing of all kinds, from blog postings and emails to multimedia presentations and even a three-hour "hip-hopera." These student writers were aware of themselves as writers and rhetors, conscious that they could reach worldwide audiences at the click of a mouse; intrigued by new concepts of textual ownership and knowledge production brought about by collaborative programs like Google Docs and file sharing of all kinds; and convinced that good writing is, as they told me over and over, "writing that makes something happen in the world." They see writing, then, as active and performative, as something that gets up off the page or screen and marches out into the world to do some good. In addition, they report that their best breakthroughs in terms of writing development tend to occur during what researcher Paul Rogers calls "dialogic interaction." That is, they learned most and best from interactions with knowledgeable others, whether peers, parents, or instructors — in the kind of give-and-take during which they could talk through ideas and get an immediate response.

In my most recent research project, I surveyed writing teachers across the country, asking them whether they gave multimodal writing assignments and, if so, what they were like. Some 80 percent of the teachers surveyed said that they do give multimodal assignments, and they sent in a dizzying array of such projects, from blogs to vlogs and everything in between: wikis, illustrated storybooks, podcasts and other audio essays, video, film, Twitter contests, animated smartphone mini-lessons, "pitch" proposals for new apps, PechaKuchas, and digital research projects, to name just a few. So while traditional academic print texts are probably still the most common assignment across the disciplines on college campuses today, that scene is rapidly changing.

So today, nearly thirty years after I started working on *The St. Martin's Handbook*, I am more optimistic about students and student writing than ever. That optimism and the findings of my most recent research inform this eighth edition of the text. As always, this book seeks to serve students as a ready reference that will help them make appropriate grammatical, syntactical, and rhetorical choices. Beyond this immediate goal, though, I hope to guide students in understanding and experiencing for themselves the multiple ways in which truly good writing always means more than just following any set of rules. Truly good writing, as the students in the longitudinal study of writing insisted, means applying those rules in specific rhetorical situations for specific purposes and with specific audiences in ways that will bring readers and writers, teachers and students, to spirited conversation as well as to mutual understanding and respect.

## New to this edition

*A new approach to U.S. academic English.* International students and Generation 1.5 English speakers aren't the only students puzzled by English structures and academic genres. Following best practices in the field of composition and rhetoric, coverage of these topics in *The St. Martin's Handbook* is integrated throughout this edition so that the information is accessible to students from all language and educational backgrounds. Students can benefit from learning more about academic genres and formal English structures, and from understanding more about other Englishes used by their classmates, co-workers, and neighbors. The advice for multilingual writers comes from expert contributors Paul Kei Matsuda and Christine Tardy. Look for the "Multilingual" icon to find content of particular use to multilingual writers, or see the directory on p. 814.

**An awareness that today's academic writing goes beyond print.** My conversations with instructors nationwide show that students engage eagerly with the many new kinds of academic projects they are asked to create — from blogs and wikis to presentations and PechaKuchas — but that they still need help composing such work for academic audiences. Advice in *The St. Martin's Handbook* never assumes that students are producing only traditional print projects for their coursework. Updated chapters (in the new part "Designing and Performing Writing") help students make decisions about design, functionality, and style to create rhetorically effective multimodal texts. Model student writing in the print book and in the accompanying LaunchPad media includes presentations, Web pages, essays with live links, and other digital-first texts as well as print-based genres such as essays, research projects, and analyses.

**An explicit focus on reflection to make learning stick.** Most chapters begin with a "Connect, Create, Reflect" box that teachers can incorporate into their classroom activities or assignments and that students can use on their own. In each box, the "Connect" question makes explicit connections between the material in the chapter and material elsewhere in *The St. Martin's Handbook*, encouraging students to become familiar with the handbook and use it to answer their writing questions. The "Create" suggestion asks students to produce some kind of text, and the "Reflect" prompt asks students to think about their own writing processes. Most chapters also end with "Thinking Critically" exercises that encourage additional reflection. And throughout the "Writing Process" chapters (Chapters 1–6), I've included explicit reminders to reflect — see, for instance, section 4m, "Reflecting on your writing," on p. 92.

**More help with academic reading.** Because reading in print isn't the same as reading online, I've added a new section 7a, "Reading print and digital texts," to give students tools to understand and adapt to the differences. And because reading scholarly work, such as an article in a journal, will be necessary for most students throughout their academic years, I've worked with two students who modeled the critical reading process — previewing, annotating, summarizing, and analyzing an assigned journal article (7b–e).

*A focus on the "why" as well as the "how" of documenting sources.* New coverage of the basics of various documentation styles helps students understand why academic work calls for more specific citation than popular writing, how to tell the difference between a work from a database and a work online, why medium matters, and more. And additional visual help (including color-coding) with documentation models makes it easy to see what information writers should include in citations.

*Integrated, interactive, assignable digital content.* The LaunchPad for *The St. Martin's Handbook* takes advantage of all the Web can do. You'll find videos of student writers talking about their work, with prompts asking students to reflect on their own processes; texts by student writers in multiple genres with activities for analysis and reflection; tutorials and visual exercises; and LearningCurve adaptive quizzing activities that students can use to practice on their own. LaunchPad for *The St. Martin's Handbook* is available free with the purchase of a new book. See pp. xi–xiii for details.

## Features of *The St. Martin's Handbook*

*Attention to good writing, not just to surface correctness.* *The St. Martin's Handbook* helps students understand that effective texts in every genre and medium follow conventions that always depend on their audience, situation, and discipline.

*Help solving the most common writing problems.* A nationwide study that I conducted with Karen Lunsford — revisiting the original 1980s research that Bob Connors and I did on student writing — shows the problems U.S. college students are most likely to have in their writing today. In this book, a special section on pp. 1–11 presents a quick guide to troubleshooting the Top Twenty — with examples, explanations, and information on where to turn in the book for more detailed information.

*A focus on bridging social and academic writing.* My recent research shows that students today are writing more than any generation ever has, and that they often make well-informed decisions in their social writing. *The St. Martin's Handbook* helps students recognize and use the rhetorical strategies that they employ in their extracurricular writing to create more effective academic writing.

*A focus on helping students produce as well as consume texts.* Many students define good writing as active and participatory; they tell me that their most important writing aims to "make something happen in the world." Sample student writing in *The St. Martin's Handbook* reflects the writing students are doing today, both in and out of class — from tweets and fundraising pages to reports and literary analyses. And I encourage students throughout the book to engage with issues and ideas that interest them and put their growing media savvy and rhetorical smarts to good use!

***Up-to-date advice on research and documentation.*** As best practices for research continue to evolve, *The St. Martin's Handbook* continues to offer excellent coverage of library and online research to help students find authoritative and credible information in any medium, plus advice on integrating sources, avoiding plagiarism, and citing sources in MLA, APA, *Chicago*, and CSE documentation styles.

***Comprehensive coverage of critical thinking and argument.*** Because first-year writing assignments increasingly call for argument, *The St. Martin's Handbook* provides all the information student writers need to respond effectively to their writing assignments, including practical advice on critical reading and analysis of all kinds of texts, instruction on composing arguments, and two complete student projects.

***Essential help for writing in the disciplines.*** Student writers will find strategies for understanding discipline-specific assignments, vocabulary, style, and use of evidence, along with student writing assignments, including research projects in MLA, APA, *Chicago*, and CSE styles; first-year writing assignments in the humanities, social sciences, and natural sciences; and business documents, including traditional and creative résumés.

***Unique coverage of language and style.*** Unique chapters on language help students think about language in context and about the consequences that language choices have on writers and readers. Boxed tips throughout the book help students communicate effectively across cultures — and use varieties of language both wisely and well.

***A user-friendly, all-in-one index.*** Entries include both everyday words (such as *that* or *which*) and grammatical terms (such as *pronoun*, which is defined in the index), so students can find what they're looking for quickly and easily.

## Get the most out of your course with *The St. Martin's Handbook*

Bedford/St. Martin's offers resources and format choices that help you and your students get even more out of your book and course. To learn more about or to order any of the following products, contact your Bedford/St. Martin's sales representative, email sales support (**sales_support@bfwpub.com**), or visit the Web site at **macmillanhighered.com/smh/catalog**.

## ☐ LaunchPad for *The St. Martin's Handbook*: Where students learn

**LaunchPad** provides engaging media content and new ways to get the most out of your course. Get an **interactive e-book**, and combine it with **unique, book-specific materials** in a fully customizable course space; then assign and mix our resources with yours.

- **Multimedia selections.** *The St. Martin's Handbook* offers videos of student writers talking about their own processes, with reflective prompts for low-stakes writing; student writing in many genres with activities; and tutorials on topics like citing sources and using tools to create multimodal projects.

- **Prebuilt units** — including readings, videos, quizzes, discussion groups, and more — are **easy to adapt and assign** by adding your own materials and mixing them with our high-quality multimedia content and ready-made assessment options, such as **LearningCurve** adaptive quizzing.

- LaunchPad also provides access to a **gradebook** that provides a clear window on the performance of your whole class, individual students, and even individual assignments.

- A **streamlined interface** helps students focus on what's due, and social commenting tools let them **engage** with content, make connections, and learn from each other. Use LaunchPad on its own or integrate it with your school's learning management system so that your class is always on the same page.

To get the most out of your course, order LaunchPad for *The St. Martin's Handbook* packaged with the print book free for a limited time. (LaunchPad for *The St. Martin's Handbook* can also be purchased on its own.) An activation code is required. To order LaunchPad for *The St. Martin's Handbook* with the print book, use the following ISBN:

- with paperback book: **ISBN 978-1-319-02137-5**
- with hardcover book: **ISBN 978-1-319-02136-8**

## ☐ LaunchPad media contents for *The St. Martin's Handbook*

To see a detailed list of the media activities that are available with this book, go to **macmillanhighered.com/smh8e**, and click on the Resources tab.

**STUDENT WRITING MODELS**

Annotated bibliography: Chan

Annotated bibliography (reflective): Sriram

Annotations of scholarly article: Sanchez and Lum

APA research project: Bell

Blog post: Nguyen

*Chicago* research project: Rinder

Close reading (literature): Sillay

Cover letter: Kung

Critical reading: Song

CSE research project: Hays

Early draft: Lesk

Final draft: Lesk

Lab report (chemistry): Goldberg

MLA research project: Craig

Pitch package: Jane and Burke

Presentation: Song

Researched argument project: Mercer-Golden

Résumés: Lange

Review of literature (biology): Hays

Review of literature (psychology): Redding

Review of literature (public health): Bell

Rhetorical analysis: Ateyea

Synthesis project: Warner

Web site: Dart

**VIDEOS OF STUDENT WRITERS**

Brain mapping [on clustering]: Nguyen

Correctness in context: Bridgewater, Chen, Cuervels, Murray, Quarta, Vanjani

Developing a sense of audience: Chen, Garry, Harris, Lima, Matalucci, McElligott, Murray, Sherman, Vanjani

Facing a challenging argument: Chilton

Filling in the gaps [on drafting]: Chilton

Getting ideas from social media: Chilton

If I were in the audience [on presenting]: Chilton

Improving with practice: Ly

It's hard to delete things: Song

Lessons from being a peer reviewer: Edwards, Nguyen

Lessons from informal writing: Edwards, Mercer-Golden

Lessons from peer review: Mercer-Golden

Looking for the essential points [on genres and media]: Song

Pay attention to what you're interested in: Song

Presentation is performance: Song

Researching something exciting: Chilton

Revision happens: Cuervels, Diaz, Harris, Mackler, Murray, Ramirez

Something to learn from each other: Nguyen

This will take longer than I thought [on planning]: Mercer-Golden

When to stop researching: Song

Working with other people: Edwards, Ly

Writing for the real world: Song

Writing processes: Bridgewater, Chen, Murray, Quarta, Ramirez, Sherman, Vanjani

You just have to start: Nguyen

You want them to hear you [on slide design]: Song

### QUIZZES, VISUAL EXERCISES, TUTORIALS, AND LEARNINGCURVE ADAPTIVE QUIZZING

Top Twenty contextualized editing quizzes

Storyboard visual exercises on rhetorical situations, creating a working thesis, being a peer reviewer, getting help from peer reviewers, revising and editing, critical reading, and synthesis

Tutorials on active reading, word processing, reading visuals, online research tools, citation, presentations, audio editing, photo editing, and job search

LearningCurve adaptive quizzing on twenty-nine topics (for a complete list, see p. 818)

## ☐ Choose from alternative formats of *The St. Martin's Handbook*

Bedford/St. Martin's offers a range of affordable formats, allowing students to choose the one that works best for them. For details, visit **macmillanhighered .com/smh/formats**.

- **Hardcover or paperback.** To order the paperback book with free LaunchPad media access, use **ISBN 978-1-319-02137-5**. To order the hardcover book with free LaunchPad media access, use **ISBN 978-1-319-02136-8**. (If you prefer the paperback without free LaunchPad access, use ISBN 978-1-4576-6726-8; for the hardcover without LaunchPad, use ISBN 978-1-4576-6724-4.)

- **Bedford e-Book to Go.** A portable, downloadable e-book is available at about half the price of the print book.

- **Other popular e-book formats.** For details, visit **macmillanhighered .com/ebooks**.

## ☐ Instructor resources

You have a lot to do in your course. Bedford/St. Martin's wants to make it easy for you to find the support you need — and to get it quickly.

*Teaching with Lunsford Handbooks* is available as a PDF that can be downloaded from the Bedford/St. Martin's online catalog at **macmillanhighered .com/smh/catalog**. In addition to chapter overviews and teaching tips, the instructor's manual includes several sample syllabi, correlations to the Council of Writing Program Administrators' Outcomes Statement, and classroom activities. If you prefer a print copy, use ISBN 978-1-4576-8170-7.

*Teaching Central* offers the entire list of Bedford/St. Martin's print and online professional resources in one place. You'll find landmark reference works, sourcebooks on pedagogical issues, award-winning collections, and practical advice for the classroom — all free for instructors. Visit **macmillanhighered .com/teachingcentral**.

## ☐ Be a part of Andrea's teaching community

- **Andrea Lunsford's "Teacher to Teacher" channel** on the award-winning *Bits* blog brings you new suggestions for the classroom and invites you to discuss ideas and events that are important to teachers of writing. When classes are in session, look for multimodal composition ideas on Andrea's **"Multimodal Mondays" channel**. Join the *Bits* community to discuss revision, research, grammar and style, technology, peer review, and much more. Take, use, adapt, and pass the ideas around. Then come back to the site to comment or share your own suggestion. Visit **bedfordbits.com**.

- Andrea is on **Twitter**! Follow **@Lunsfordhandbks** to keep up with Andrea's tweets.

- Andrea Lunsford's **author page on Facebook** also offers regular updates and links. Find Andrea at **facebook.com/AndreaALunsford**.

# Acknowledgments

*The St. Martin's Handbook* remains a collaborative effort in the best and richest sense of the word. For this edition, I am enormously indebted to Carolyn Lengel, whose meticulous care, tough-minded editing, great good humor, and sheer hard work are everywhere apparent. Carolyn is ever the consummate professional — and a very good friend. Leasa Burton, Karen Henry, and Erica Appel have provided support, encouragement, and good advice, and my former editor, Marilyn Moller, continues to provide support and friendship.

Ryan Sullivan has managed the entire book from manuscript to bound book with skill and grace — and together with Steve Cestaro has made an enormously complex project run smoothly. Wendy Polhemus-Annibell, the *Handbook*'s talented copyeditor, and Allison Hart, the new media production editor, have also provided much-needed support. Thanks also to editor Adam Whitehurst, who has offered advice on the media content and developed tutorials, and to Leah Rang and Kathleen Wisneski, who have guided ancillary development and taken care of countless other details. For the truly snazzy interior design, I am indebted to Claire Seng-Niemoeller; for the cool cover, to William Boardman; for the endlessly fascinating part opener images, to photographer Mike Enright and photo stylist Barbara Lipp; and for sage advice on all design-related matters, to Anna Palchik. I am fortunate indeed to have had Jane Helms and Emily Rowin on the marketing team; in my experience, they set the standard. And, as always, I am grateful to the entire Bedford/St. Martin's sales force, on whose wisdom and insights and energy I always depend.

## ☐ Contributors

For this edition, I owe special thanks to Keith Walters and to Christine Tardy, both of whom provided extremely helpful advice on integrating the content for multilingual writers. Special thanks also go to Alyssa O'Brien, Lisa Dresdner, and Michael Moore for their work on *Teaching with Lunsford Handbooks*; to Mike Hennessy for his tutorial in the *Handbook*; to Adam Banks, with whom I taught a course at Bread Loaf during summer 2014 that taught me as much as it did our students; and to Karen Lunsford, Paul Rogers, Jenn Fishman, Laurie Stapleton, Erin Krampetz, and Warren Liew, my partners in ongoing research on student writing.

As always, I am extremely fortunate to have had the contributions of very fine student writers, whose work appears throughout this text or in its accompanying media: Michelle Abbott, Carina Abernathy, Milena Ateyea, Martha Bell, Deborah Burke, Tony Chan, David Craig, Justin Dart, Allyson Goldberg, Tara Gupta, Joanna Hays, James Kung, Megan Lange, Nastassia Lopez, Sarah Lum, Benjy Mercer-Golden, Alicia Michalski, Jenny Ming, Thanh Nguyen, Stephanie Parker, Tawnya Redding, Amanda Rinder, Fernando Sanchez, Bonnie Sillay, Nandita Sriram, and Caroline Warner. I am especially grateful to Emily Lesk, whose imaginative and carefully researched essay appears in Chapters 2–6, and to Shuqiao Song, whose essay and multimedia presentation on Alison Bechdel's *Fun Home* enliven Chapters 7 and 16. And for this edition, I am also indebted to students who agreed to talk on video about their writing processes: Jamie Bridgewater, Yishi Chen, Cyana Chilton, Matteo Cuervels, Ayadhiri Diaz, Halle Edwards, John Garry, Ashley Harris, Isaias Lima, Brandon Ly, Keith Mackler, Luisa Matalucci, Liz McElligott, Benjy Mercer-Golden, William Murray, Thanh Nguyen, Rachel Quarta, Rachel Ramirez, David Sherman, Shuqiao Song, and Apeksha Vanjani.

## ☐ Reviewers

For *The St. Martin's Handbook*, we have been blessed with a group of very special reviewers whose incisive comments, queries, criticisms, and suggestions have improved this book immeasurably: Joann Allen, Oral Roberts University; Shan Ayers, Berea College; Paul Baggett, South Dakota State University; Rachael Bailey, Purdue University; Paula Barnes, Hampton University; Andrew Baskin, Berea College; Tanya Bennett, University of North Georgia; Curtis Bobbitt, University of Great Falls; Michelle Boucher, Southwestern College; Erin Breaux, South Louisiana Community College; Ellie Bunting, Florida SouthWestern State College; Mary Jo Caruso, Manhattanville College and Vaughn College of Aeronautics and Technology; P.J. Colbert, Marshalltown Community College; Rick Cole, Boston University; Elizabeth Devore, Kent State University at Ashtabula; Lisa Diehl, University of North Georgia; Dianne Donnelly, University of South Florida; Darrell Fike, Valdosta State University; Nathan Fink, DePaul University; Sherry Forkum, Santa Rosa Junior College; Wanda Fries, Somerset Community College; Chad Fulwider, Centenary College of Louisiana; Royce Grubic, Western New Mexico University; Jeff Harris, Somerset Community College; Holly French Hart, Bossier Parish Community College; Deana Holifield, Pearl River Community College; Matt Hurwitz, University of Massachusetts Lowell; Lutfi Hussein, Mesa Community College; Guillemette Johnston, DePaul University; Jean-Marie Kauth, Benedictine University; Casey Kayser, University of Arkansas; Michael Keller, South Dakota State University; Marsha Kruger, University of Nebraska Omaha; Alexander Kurian, North Lake College; Susan Lang, Texas Tech University; John Levine, University of California–Berkeley; Brooke Lopez, University of Texas at San Antonio; Kevin Lyon, DePaul University; Cynthia Marshall, Wright State University; Angela Miss, Belmont Abbey College; Dhrubaa Mukherjee, Texas A&M University; Courtney Mustoe, University of Nebraska Omaha; Beverly Neiderman, Kent State University; William Quirk, Rider University; Matthew Parfitt, Boston University; Charlene Pate, Point Loma Nazarene University; Sabrina Peters-Whitehead, University of Toledo; Karen Roop, University of North Georgia; Nathan Serfling, South Dakota State University; Marilyn Seymour, Newberry College; Erin Smith, University of Arkansas; Jimmy Smith, Union College; Wes Spratlin, Motlow State Community College; Matthew Stewart, Boston University; Linda Van Buskirk, Cornell University; Bobby Vasquez, University of Nebraska Omaha; and Nicole Wilson, Bowie State University.

Finally, I wish to offer very special thanks to the extraordinary community of teacher-researchers at the Bread Loaf Graduate School of English, whose responses to this text have helped to shape and refine its goals.

I could go on and on in praise of the support and help I have received, for I am fortunate to be part of a unique scholarly community, one characterized by compassion as well as passionate commitment to students and to learning. I remain grateful to be among you.

*Andrea A. Lunsford*

# HOW TO USE THIS BOOK

The main goal of *The St. Martin's Handbook* is to help you become a more effective writer, throughout and beyond your student years. To reach that goal, take a few minutes to learn what's in your handbook and how to find it quickly. If you learn to use this tool, it will serve you well any time you need reliable answers to your questions about writing for years to come.

## Finding help

Depending on what information or advice you're looking for, you may want to consult any or all of the following:

- **BRIEF CONTENTS** Inside the front cover is a brief table of contents, which lists general contents. Start here if you're looking for advice on a broad topic, and then just flip to the chapter. The tabs at the top of each page tell you where you are.

- **CONTENTS** If you're looking for specific information, the detailed table of contents inside the back cover lists chapter titles and major headings.

- **THE TOP TWENTY** On pp. 1–11 is advice on the twenty common problems teachers are most likely to identify in academic writing by first-year students. The Top Twenty provides examples and brief explanations to guide you toward recognizing, understanding, and editing these common errors. Cross-references point to other places in the book where you'll find more detailed information.

- **MEDIA CONTENT** In the preface and in the directory at the back of the book, you can find a list of all the integrated media — videos about writing issues, exercises, adaptive quizzing, student writing models, tutorials, and more. Cross-references at the bottom of a page direct you to **macmillanhighered .com/smh8e** for media content related to that section of the book.

- **DOCUMENTATION NAVIGATION** Each documentation section has its own color-tabbed pages; look for directories within each section to find models for citing your sources. Color-coded source maps walk you through the process of citing sources.

- **GLOSSARY OF USAGE** This glossary, on the pages before the index, gives help with commonly confused words.

- **GLOSSARY/INDEX** The index lists everything covered in the book. You can find information by looking up a topic or, if you're not sure what your topic is called, by looking up the word you need help with. The index doubles as a glossary that defines important terms.

- DIRECTORY   The directory at the end of the book (after the index) lists types of content you may need to find quickly in the print book and identifies the complete contents of the digital media for *The St. Martin's Handbook.*

| FOR CONTENT IN THE PRINT BOOK | FOR CONTENT IN LAUNCHPAD MEDIA |
|---|---|
| For Multilingual Writers content (boxed tips and sections of special interest to multilingual students) | model student writing with activities |
| | videos of student writers |
| Talking the Talk boxes | tutorials |
| Considering Disabilities boxes | quizzes and visual exercises |
| | LearningCurve adaptive quizzing |

- REVISION SYMBOLS   The symbols at the end of the directory can help you understand markings an instructor or a reviewer may make on your draft.

## Page navigation help

These descriptions correspond to the numbered elements on p. xix.

1 GUIDES ON EVERY PAGE   Headings on the left-hand page tell you what **part and chapter** you're in, while headings on the right identify the **section**. Red tabs identify the **chapter number and section letter**. The **page number** appears at the outside edge of the page.

2 MULTILINGUAL WRITERS ICONS   Help for speakers of all kinds of English, and from all educational backgrounds, is integrated throughout the book. Content that may be of particular interest to international students and other English language learners is identified with the "Multilingual" icon. **Boxed tips for multilingual writers** set off additional help. A directory to all content for multilingual writers appears on p. 814.

3 HAND-EDITED EXAMPLES   **Example sentences** are hand-edited in blue, allowing you to see an error or nonstandard usage and its revision at a glance. Pointers and boldface type make examples easy to spot on the page.

4 QUICK HELP AND BOXED TIPS   Many chapters include **Quick Help content** that provides an overview of important information. Look under "Quick Help" in the index to find a list. **Talking the Talk boxes** offer help with academic language and concepts. **Considering Disabilities boxes** offer tips on making your work accessible to audiences with different abilities.

5 CROSS-REFERENCES TO MEDIA CONTENT   Cross-references at the end of a page point to videos, LearningCurve quizzing, student writing models, and more.

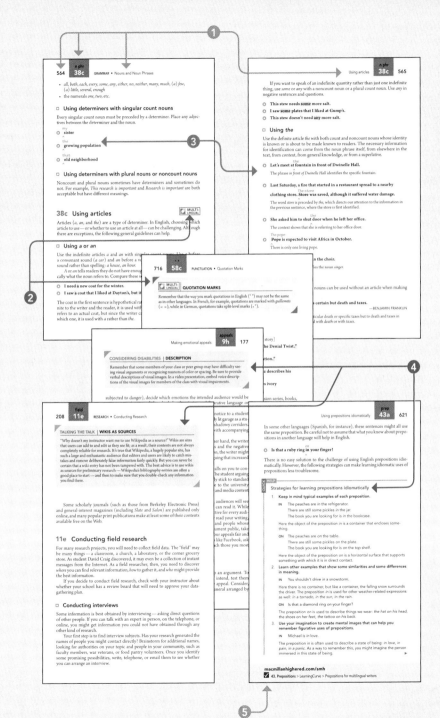

- *all, both, each, every, some, any, either, no, neither, many, much, (a) few, (a) little, several, enough*
- the numerals *one, two,* etc.

□ **Using determiners with singular count nouns**

Every singular count noun must be preceded by a determiner. Place any adjectives between the *determiner* and the noun.

  *my*
  sister

  *the*
  growing population

  *that*
  old neighborhood

□ **Using determiners with plural nouns or noncount nouns**

Noncount and plural nouns sometimes have determiners and sometimes do not. For example, *This research is important* and *Research is important* are both acceptable but have different meanings.

## 38c  Using articles [MULTI-LINGUAL]

Articles (*a, an,* and *the*) are a type of determiner. In English, choosing which article to use—or whether to use an article at all—can be challenging. Although there are exceptions, the following general guidelines can help.

□ **Using a or an**

Use the indefinite articles *a* and *an* with singular count nouns. Use *a* before a consonant sound (*a car*) and *an* before a v... sound rather than spelling: *a house, an hour.*

*A* or *an* tells readers they do not have enoug... cally what the noun refers to. Compare these s...

○ I need a new coat for the winter.
○ I saw a coat that I liked at Dayton's, but it...

The coat in the first sentence is hypothetical ra... nite to the writer and the reader, it is used with... refers to an actual coat, but since the writer ca... which one, it is used with *a* rather than *the.*

If you want to speak of an indefinite quantity rather than just one indefinite thing, use *some* or *any* with a noncount noun or a plural count noun. Use *any* in negative sentences and questions.

○ This stew needs some more salt.
○ I saw some plates that I liked at Gump's.
○ This stew doesn't need any more salt.

□ **Using the**

Use the definite article *the* with both count and noncount nouns whose identity is known or is about to be made known to readers. The necessary information for identification can come from the noun phrase itself, from elsewhere in the text, from context, from general knowledge, or from a superlative.

○ Let's meet at *the* fountain in front of Dwinelle Hall.

The phrase *in front of Dwinelle Hall* identifies the specific fountain.

○ Last Saturday, a fire that started in a restaurant spread to a nearby clothing store. *The store* Store was saved, although it suffered water damage.

The word *store* is preceded by *the,* which directs our attention to the information in the previous sentence, where the store is first identified.

○ She asked him to shut *the* door when he left her office.

The context shows that she is referring to her office door.

○ *The pope* Pope is expected to visit Africa in October.

There is only one living pope.

... in the choir. ... the noun *singer.*

... nouns can be used without an article when making ...

... certain but death and taxes.
—BENJAMIN FRANKLIN

... particular death or specific taxes but to death and taxes in ... with *death* or with *taxes.*

[MULTI-LINGUAL]  **QUOTATION MARKS**

Remember that the way you mark quotations in English (" ") may not be the same as in other languages. In French, for example, quotations are marked with *guillemets* (« »), while in German, quotations take split-level marks („ ").

**CONSIDERING DISABILITIES | DESCRIPTION**

Remember that some members of your class or peer group may have difficulty seeing visual arguments or recognizing nuances of color or spacing. Be sure to provide verbal descriptions of visual images. In a video presentation, embed voice descriptions of the visual images for members of the class with visual impairments.

subjected to danger), decide which emotions the intended audience would be ... rative language on...

... story|
... the Denial Twist."
... tion."
... z describes his
... s ivory

**TALKING THE TALK | WIKIS AS SOURCES**

"Why doesn't my instructor want me to use Wikipedia as a source?" Wikis are sites that users can add to and edit as they see fit; as a result, their contents are not always completely reliable for research. It's true that Wikipedia, a hugely popular site, has such a large and enthusiastic audience that editors and users are likely to catch mistakes and remove deliberately false information fairly quickly. But you can never be certain that a wiki entry has not been tampered with. The best advice is to use wikis as sources for preliminary research—Wikipedia's bibliography entries are often a good place to start—and then to make sure that you double-check any information you find there.

Some scholarly journals (such as those from Berkeley Electronic Press) and general-interest magazines (including *Slate* and *Salon*) are published only online, and many popular print publications make at least some of their contents available free on the Web.

## 11e  Conducting field research

For many research projects, you will need to collect field data. The "field" may be many things—a classroom, a church, a laboratory, or the corner grocery store. As student David Craig discovered, it may even be a collection of instant messages from the Internet. As a field researcher, then, you need to discover *where* you can find relevant information, *how* to gather it, and *who* might provide the best information.

If you decide to conduct field research, check with your instructor about whether your school has a review board that will need to approve your data-gathering plan.

□ **Conducting interviews**

Some information is best obtained by interviewing—asking direct questions of other people. If you can talk with an expert in person, on the telephone, or online, you might get information you could not have obtained through any other kind of research.

Your first step is to find interview subjects. Has your research generated the names of people you might contact directly? Brainstorm for additional names, looking for authorities on your topic and people in your community, such as faculty members, war veterans, or food pantry volunteers. Once you identify some promising possibilities, write, telephone, or email them to see whether you can arrange an interview.

notice to a student ... ly lit garage as a stu- ... shadowy corridors ... with accompanying ...

her hand, the writer ... s and the negative ... on, the writer might ... using that increased ...

alls on you to con- ... he student arguing ... ly stick to standard ... e to the university ... and media content ...

audiences will see ... can read it. While ... tive for every audi- ... read your writing, ... and people whose ... ument public, take ... our appeals fair and ... like Facebook, ask- ... ch those you most ...

an argument. To ... intend, test them ... appeal. Consider, ... neral arranged by ...

In some other languages (Spanish, for instance), these sentences might all use the same preposition. Be careful not to assume that what you know about prepositions in another language will help in English.

○ Is that a ruby ring *on* in your finger?

There is no easy solution to the challenge of using English prepositions idiomatically. However, the following strategies can make learning idiomatic uses of prepositions less troublesome.

**HELP**

**Strategies for learning prepositions idiomatically**

1. **Keep in mind typical examples of each preposition.**

   IN   The peaches are in the refrigerator.
        There are still some pickles in the jar.
        The book you are looking for is in the bookcase.

   Here the object of the preposition *in* is a container that encloses something.

   ON   The peaches are on the table.
        There are still some pickles on the plate.
        The book you are looking for is on the top shelf.

   Here the object of the preposition *on* is a horizontal surface that supports something with which it is in direct contact.

2. **Learn other examples that show some similarities and some differences in meaning.**

   IN   You shouldn't drive in a snowstorm.

   Here the object of *in* is not a container, but like a container, the falling snow surrounds the driver. The preposition *in* is used for other weather-related expressions as well: *in a tornado, in the sun, in the rain.*

   ON   Is that a diamond ring on your finger?

   The preposition *on* is used to describe things we wear: *the hat on his head, the shoes on her feet, the tattoo on his back.*

3. **Use your imagination to create mental images that can help you remember figurative uses of prepositions.**

   IN   Michael is in love.

   The preposition *in* is often used to describe a state of being: *in love, in pain, in a panic.* As a way to remember this, you might imagine the person immersed in this state of being.  ▶

macmillanhighered.com/smh
☑ 43. Prepositions > LearningCurve > Prepositions for multilingual writers

# A tutorial on using *The St. Martin's Handbook,* Eighth Edition

For this book to serve you well, you need to get to know it — to know what's inside and how to find it. The following tutorial is designed to help you familiarize yourself with *The St. Martin's Handbook.*

## GETTING STARTED WITH *THE ST. MARTIN'S HANDBOOK*

1. Where will you find advice on identifying the top twenty issues that instructors are most likely to consider problems in student writing?

2. Where will you find advice on revising a rough draft of an essay?

3. Where can you find out what a comma splice is and how to fix one?

4. Where will you find guidelines on how to include quotations in your project without plagiarizing?

## PLANNING AND DRAFTING

5. Where in the *Handbook* can you find advice on brainstorming to explore a topic?

6. Where can you find general guidelines for developing effective paragraphs?

7. Your instructor wants you to adapt your print essay into a multimodal presentation. Where would you find an example of this kind of presentation?

## DOING RESEARCH

8. You have a topic for your research project, but your instructor asks you to narrow it down. What help can you find in the *Handbook*?

9. Your midterm assignment is a group research project, and you've been assigned to a group with students who have very different majors and live on and off campus. Where in your handbook can you find advice for planning and conducting research as a group?

10. What information can you find in the *Handbook* for keeping track of your research?

11. Your instructor has reviewed your bibliography and has asked you to replace some popular sources with scholarly sources, but you're not sure how to identify the differences. Where can you find help in distinguishing them?

12. You are unsure whether you need to cite a paraphrase from a magazine article. Where can you find the answer in the *Handbook*?

13. Your instructor has asked you to use MLA style. Where can you find guidelines for documenting information from an article on a Web site?

## REVIEWING, REVISING, AND EDITING

14. Your instructor asks your class to work in small groups to review each others' drafts of a writing project. You aren't sure where to begin or what kinds of issues to comment on. Where can you find guidelines for peer review?

15. You need advice on using appropriate prepositions in academic writing—either because you grew up speaking a language other than English at home or because you are used to different informal idioms. Where can you look?

16. Your instructor has written *wrdy* next to this sentence: *The person who wrote the article is a scientist who makes the argument that it seems as though the scientific phenomenon of global warming is becoming a bigger issue at this point in time.* Where do you look in your handbook for help responding to your instructor's comment?

17. As you edit a final draft, you stop at the following passage: *Because the actor had a reputation for delivering Oscar-worthy performances. He received the best roles.* How do you find out if this is a sentence fragment and what you should do if it is?

18. You have finished your essay and decide to use an unusual font to make your essay more visually appealing. Is it a good idea to use this font? What information does the *Handbook* provide?

## MEETING YOUR INSTRUCTOR'S EXPECTATIONS

19. You are required to turn in a portfolio of writing samples at the end of the semester, but you're not sure what to include. What advice can your handbook give you about building a portfolio?

20. Your instructor returns a draft to you and says that your paper contains mostly summary and that you need to do more critical thinking and analysis. Where can you look for information on how to read and write critically?

21. You've learned a lot by looking at the samples of good writing that your instructor has shared with the class. Where in the *Handbook* can you find more sample student work?

22. Your professor has created a blog with a discussion forum, and you are required to comment on the week's discussion topic. You're not sure how to write online as part of a class requirement. Where in the *Handbook* can you look for help?

## WRITING IN ANY DISCIPLINE

23. You need to write a paper for your sociology class, but you've never written a sociology paper before, and you're unsure what kind of evidence to use. Where can you look for help in the *Handbook*?

24. For a chemistry course, you're writing a lab report, and your instructor wants you to include a table to detail the results of your experiment. Where can you look in your handbook for help incorporating visuals?

25. You're used to writing online for social media sites, but you aren't sure what "normal" academic writing should look like. Where can you look in your handbook to help you figure out how to write for an academic audience?

## USING MULTIMEDIA RESOURCES IN YOUR LAUNCHPAD

26. The tutor at your school's writing center suggested that you work on using active verbs in your writing. Where can you find quizzes that will help you?

27. Your instructor assigned a research project, but you can't decide on a topic. Where can you find a video that might help you figure out what topic would work for you?

28. Before you write a research essay, you want to see how another student has incorporated sources. Where can you find an interactive activity that will help you analyze how a student uses evidence?

☐ **Answer key**

1. "The Top Twenty" on pp. 1–11. (Searching for *common errors* in the index also points students toward "The Top Twenty.")

2. Chapter 4, "Reviewing, Revising, Editing, and Reflecting."

3. Chapter 46, "Comma Splices and Fused Sentences" (*comma splice* in the index also helps you find this information quickly). Or look at "The Top Twenty" — "comma splice" is item 16.

4. Chapter 13, on integrating sources into your writing, gives advice on how to use quotations correctly to strengthen your writing. Chapter 14 focuses on using sources ethically and avoiding plagiarism.

5. Looking up *brainstorming* in the index leads you to section 3a, on exploring a topic. A cross-reference in this section directs you to videos of students talking about their writing processes, accessible by logging in at **macmillanhighered .com/smh8e**.

6. Looking up *paragraphs* in the index leads you to Chapter 5, on developing paragraphs. (Check the Quick Help box at the beginning of the chapter for a list of questions that will help you compose effective paragraphs and direct you to other sections in Chapter 5 where you can get more help.)

7. Looking for *presentations* in the index will lead you to Chapter 17 on presentations. The LaunchPad media at **macmillanhighered.com/smh8e** includes both the print essay Shuqiao Song wrote about *Fun Home* and the multimodal presentation she created from her essay.

8. Searching for *narrowing a topic* in the index will lead you to 3b, "Narrowing a topic."

9. Chapter 6, "Working with Others," can help you plan collaborative projects in college, divide work effectively, and accommodate your group members' talents and needs.

10. Skimming the brief table of contents under the header "Doing Research and Using Sources" leads you to Chapter 12; section 12c explains how to keep a working bibliography, and 12g covers taking notes and annotating sources.

11. Consulting the index under either *popular sources* or *scholarly sources* leads you to 11a, "Differentiating kinds of sources," where you can find information on identifying the two types of sources.

12. For guidance on whether to cite the article, use the index to find *acknowledgment required for* under *paraphrases*, which points you to section 14b, "Knowing which sources to acknowledge." To be sure you've paraphrased acceptably, look under *paraphrases* in the index for *acceptable and unacceptable*. This will lead you to section 12g, which shows you how to paraphrase without inadvertently plagiarizing your source.

13. The table of contents leads you to the green-tipped pages in Chapter 32, which provide a full discussion of MLA documentation conventions. The directory to MLA style for a list of works cited in 32d points you to the models for documenting Web site sources on a works-cited page. The source map on pp. 432–33 provides a visual guide to locating the information you need.

14. Looking up *peer review* in the index will lead you to the Quick Help box in 4b that provides guidelines for reviewers.

15. In Chapter 43, "Prepositions and Prepositional Phrases," a Quick Help box gives strategies for using prepositions idiomatically. A cross-reference in Chapter 43 also lets you know that there is a LearningCurve activity on prepositions for multilingual writers at **macmillanhighered .com/smh8e**. To find help especially suited for multilingual writers, consult the directory of content for multilingual writers at the back of the book.

16. A list of revision symbols appears in the directory at the back of the *Handbook*. Consulting this list tells you that *wrdy* refers to "wordy" and that wordy writing is addressed in Chapter 50, on conciseness.

17. The table of contents leads you to Chapter 47, "Fragments," where you will find examples of sentence fragments and several options for revising them.

18. Looking up *fonts* or *type* in the index will take you to an entry on choosing appropriate formats in 16c, on formatting print and digital texts. The information under "Choosing type sizes and fonts" in section 16c points out that most college writing requires a standard font and that unusual fonts may be difficult to read.

19. Scanning the table of contents or searching for *portfolios* in the index will lead you to Chapter 25, which includes information on creating portfolios as well as examples of a student's portfolio cover letter and a student's portfolio home page.

20. Part 2 (Chapters 7–9) addresses critical thinking and argument, and Chapter 7, "Reading Critically," includes sections on summarizing texts (7d) and analyzing texts (7e). These include instructions and student writing samples to help you distinguish between summarizing and analyzing.

21. Student writing is listed in small capital letters in the table of contents. Searching for *student writing* in the index will also lead you to the directory of student writing in the back of your book. This lists all the samples you can find in your text, as well as those available in the LaunchPad media at **macmillanhighered.com /smh8e**.

22. Chapter 1, "Expectations for College Writing," has helpful advice you can use for any college writing. In particular, section 1f on using media effectively provides guidelines for writing in online discussion lists, forums, and comments.

23. Part 5 (Chapters 19–26) covers writing in the disciplines. Section 19f focuses on using appropriate evidence in all academic work, and Chapter 21 is dedicated to writing for the social sciences. Searching for *social sciences* in the index will also lead you to this chapter. Check the orange-tipped pages of Chapter 33 for instruction in using APA style, which includes examples of the types of evidence you might cite in a social science project.

24. Check the index for *tables* or *visuals and media* to find section 16d on considering visuals and media. A Quick Help box in this section will remind you to check Chapters 32–35 on documentation. Chapter 35 gives you guidelines for using tables and other visuals in a CSE-style formatted document. In addition, the LaunchPad media at **macmillanhighered.com /smh8e** includes a student's chemistry lab report that can serve as a model for your own writing.

25. Browsing the table of contents, you'll see that Chapter 1 covers expectations for college writing — section 1a discusses moving between social and academic writing. For more help thinking about writing for a

specific audience, check the index for *audience*.

26. Check the directory at the back of the book to find a list of topics for LearningCurve adaptive quizzes (you can also look in the Resources tab of the LaunchPad media at **macmillanhighered.com/smh8e**). The LearningCurve activities on "Active and passive voice" and "Verbs" can both help you practice.

27. If you navigate to LaunchPad at **macmillanhighered.com/smh8e**, clicking on the Resources tab and then on "Content by type" will lead you to a list of videos of student writers discussing relevant topics, including "Pay attention to what you're interested in" and "Researching something exciting." In the print *Handbook*, topics with accompanying videos are indicated with a cross-reference at the bottom of the page.

28. Go to **macmillanhighered.com /smh8e**, and look for student writing in the Resources tab. You'll find several models that ask you to consider a student research project, including an analysis activity that allows you to evaluate Benjy Mercer-Golden's use of sources in his argument paper.

# The
# St. Martin's
# Handbook

# A Quick Guide to Troubleshooting Your Writing

ALTHOUGH MANY PEOPLE THINK of correctness as absolute, based on unchanging rules, instructors and students know that there are rules, but they change with time. "Is it okay to use *I* in essays for this class?" asks one student. "My high school teacher wouldn't let us." In the past, use of first person was discouraged by instructors, sometimes even banned. But today, most fields accept such usage in moderation. Such examples show that rules clearly exist but that they are always shifting and that they thus need our ongoing attention.

The conventions involving surface errors — grammar, punctuation, word choice, and other small-scale matters — are a case in point. Surface errors don't always disturb readers. Whether your instructor marks an error in any particular assignment will depend on his or her judgment about how serious and distracting it is and what you should be giving priority to at the time. In addition, not all surface errors are consistently viewed as errors: some of the patterns identified in the research for this book are considered errors by some instructors but as stylistic options by others.

Shifting standards do not mean that there is no such thing as correctness in writing — only that *correctness always depends on some context*. Correctness is not so much a question of absolute right or wrong as of the way the choices a writer makes are perceived by readers. As writers, we all want to be considered competent and careful. We know that our readers judge us by our control of the conventions we have agreed to use, even if the conventions change from time to time.

To help you in producing writing that is conventionally correct, you should become familiar with the twenty most common error patterns among U.S. college students today, listed on the next page in order of frequency. These twenty errors are the ones most likely to result in negative responses from your instructors and other readers. A brief explanation and examples of each error are provided in the following sections, and each error pattern is

1

cross-referenced to other places in this book where you can find more detailed information and additional examples.

---

**QUICK HELP**

## The Top Twenty

1. Wrong word
2. Missing comma after an introductory element
3. Incomplete or missing documentation
4. Vague pronoun reference
5. Spelling (including homonyms)
6. Mechanical error with a quotation
7. Unnecessary comma
8. Unnecessary or missing capitalization
9. Missing word
10. Faulty sentence structure
11. Missing comma with a nonrestrictive element
12. Unnecessary shift in verb tense
13. Missing comma in a compound sentence
14. Unnecessary or missing apostrophe (including *its/it's*)
15. Fused (run-on) sentence
16. Comma splice
17. Lack of pronoun-antecedent agreement
18. Poorly integrated quotation
19. Unnecessary or missing hyphen
20. Sentence fragment

## 1 Wrong word

▶ **Religious texts, for them, take ~~prescience~~ precedence over other kinds of sources.**

*Prescience* means "foresight," and *precedence* means "priority of importance."

▶ **The child suffered from a severe ~~allegory~~ allergy to peanuts.**

*Allegory,* which refers to a symbolic meaning, is a spell checker's replacement for a misspelling of *allergy.*

▶ **The panel discussed the ethical implications ~~on~~ of the situation.**

Wrong-word errors can involve using a word with the wrong shade of meaning, a word with a completely wrong meaning, or a wrong preposition or word in an idiom. Selecting a word from a thesaurus without being certain of its meaning or allowing a spell checker to correct your spelling automatically can lead to wrong-word errors, so use these tools with care. If you have trouble with prepositions and idioms, memorize the standard usage. (See Chapter 30 on choosing the correct word, 31f on using spell checkers wisely, and Chapter 43 on using prepositions and idioms.)

## 2 Missing comma after an introductory element

▷ **Determined to get the job done, we worked all weekend.**

▷ **In German, nouns are always capitalized.**

Readers usually need a small pause between an introductory word, phrase, or clause and the main part of the sentence, a pause most often signaled by a comma. Try to get into the habit of using a comma after every introductory element. When the introductory element is very short, you don't always need a comma after it. But you're never wrong if you do use a comma. (See 54a.)

## 3 Incomplete or missing documentation

▷ **Satrapi says, "When we're afraid, we lose all sense of analysis and reflection." (263).**

The writer is citing a print source using MLA style and needs to include the page number where the quotation appears.

▷ **According to one source, James Joyce wrote two of the five best novels of all time. ("100 Best Novels").**

The writer must identify the source. Because "100 Best Novels" is an online source, no page number is needed.

Be sure to cite each source as you refer to it in the text, and carefully follow the guidelines of the documentation style you are using to include all the information required (see Chapters 32–35). Omitting documentation can result in charges of plagiarism (see Chapter 14).

# 4 Vague pronoun reference

POSSIBLE REFERENCE TO MORE THAN ONE WORD

▶ Transmitting radio signals by satellite is a way of overcoming the

*the airwaves*

problem of scarce airwaves and limiting how ~~they~~ are used.

Does *they* refer to the signals or the airwaves? The editing clarifies what is being limited.

REFERENCE IMPLIED BUT NOT STATED

*a policy*

▶ The company prohibited smoking, ~~which~~ many employees resented.

What does *which* refer to? The editing clarifies what employees resented.

A pronoun — a word such as *she, yourself, her, it, this, who,* or *which* — should refer clearly to the word or words it replaces (called the *antecedent*) elsewhere in the sentence or in a previous sentence. If more than one word could be the antecedent, or if no specific antecedent is present in the sentence, edit to make the meaning clear. (See 41h.)

# 5 Spelling (including homonyms)

*bear*

▶ No one came forward to ~~bare~~ witness to the crime.

*Reagan*

▶ Ronald ~~Regan~~ won the election in a landslide.

*Everywhere*

▶ ~~Every where~~ we went, we saw crowds of tourists.

*until*

▶ The wolves stayed ~~untill~~ the pups were able to leave the den.

The most common kinds of misspellings today are those that spell checkers cannot identify. The categories that spell checkers are most likely to miss include homonyms (words that sound alike but have different meanings); compound words incorrectly spelled as two separate words; and proper nouns, particularly names. Proofread carefully for errors that a spell checker cannot catch — and be sure to run the spell checker to catch other kinds of spelling mistakes. (See 31f.)

# 6 Mechanical error with a quotation

▶ "I grew up the victim of a disconcerting confusion,"/Rodriguez says (249).

The comma should be placed *inside* the quotation marks.

▶ **Captain Renault (Claude Rains) says that he is shocked — shocked!**

**to find gambling going on in here" (*Casablanca*).**

> Both the beginning and the end of the quotation (from the film *Casablanca*) should be marked with quotation marks.

Follow conventions when using quotation marks with commas (54i), semicolons (55c), question marks (56b), and other punctuation (58e). Always use quotation marks in pairs, and follow the guidelines of your documentation style for block quotations and poetry (58a). Use quotation marks to mark titles of short works (58b), but use italics for titles of long works (62a).

## 7 Unnecessary comma

### BEFORE CONJUNCTIONS IN COMPOUND CONSTRUCTIONS THAT ARE NOT COMPOUND SENTENCES

▶ **This conclusion applies to the United States/ and to the rest of the world.**

> No comma is needed before *and* because it is joining two phrases that modify the same verb, *applies*.

### WITH RESTRICTIVE ELEMENTS

▶ **Many parents/ of gifted children/ do not want them to skip a grade.**

> No comma is needed to set off the restrictive phrase *of gifted children*; it is necessary to indicate which parents the sentence is talking about.

Do not use commas to set off restrictive elements — those necessary to the meaning of the words they modify. Do not use a comma before a coordinating conjunction (*and, but, for, nor, or, so, yet*) when the conjunction is not joining two parts of a compound sentence. Do not use a comma before the first or after the last item in a series, and do not use a comma between a subject and verb, between a verb and its object or complement, or between a preposition and its object. (See 54k.)

## 8 Unnecessary or missing capitalization

▶ **Some ~~Traditional Chinese Medicines~~ containing ~~Ephedra~~ remain legal.**
<br>traditional · medicines · ephedra

Capitalize proper nouns and proper adjectives, the first words of sentences, and important words in titles, along with certain words indicating directions and family relationships. Do not capitalize most other words, and proofread to make sure your word processor has not automatically added unnecessary capitalization (after an abbreviation ending with a period, for example). When in doubt, check a dictionary. (See Chapter 60.)

## 9 Missing word

◉ The site foreman discriminated ^against^ women and promoted men with less

experience.

◉ Christopher's behavior becomes ^so^ bizarre that his family asks for help.

Be careful not to omit little words, including prepositions (43a), parts of two-part verbs (43b), and correlative conjunctions (36g). Proofread carefully for any other omitted words, and be particularly careful not to omit words from quotations.

## 10 Faulty sentence structure

◉ ~~The information which~~ ^High^ high school athletes are presented with ~~mainly~~

~~includes information on what credits~~ ^they^ needed to graduate, ~~and thinking about~~

^colleges to try^ ^how to^
~~the college which athletes are trying~~ to play for, ~~and apply.~~

◉ People who use marijuana may build up a tolerance for it ^and^ ~~will~~ want a

stronger drug.

When a sentence starts out with one kind of structure and then changes to another kind, it confuses readers. If readers have trouble following the meaning of your sentence, read the sentence aloud and make sure that it contains a subject and a verb (37a and b). Look for mixed structures (49a), subjects and predicates that do not make sense together (49b), and comparisons with unclear meanings (49e). When you join elements (such as subjects or verb phrases) with a coordinating conjunction — *and, but, for, nor, or, so,* or *yet* — make sure that the elements have parallel structures (45b).

## 11 Missing comma with a nonrestrictive element

◉ Marina ^,^ who was the president of the club ^,^ was first to speak.

The reader does not need the clause *who was the president of the club* to know the basic meaning of the sentence: Marina was first to speak.

A nonrestrictive element is not essential to the basic meaning of a sentence. If you remove a nonrestrictive element, the sentence would still make sense.

Use commas to set off any nonrestrictive elements from the rest of a sentence. (See 54d.)

## 12 Unnecessary shift in verb tense

▶ A few countries produce almost all of the world's illegal drugs, but
  *affects*
  addiction ~~affected~~ many countries.
               ^

▶ Priya was watching the great blue heron. Then she ~~slips~~ and ~~falls~~ into
                                                   *slipped*   *fell*
                                                      ^          ^
  the swamp.

Verb tenses tell readers when actions take place: saying *Ron went to school* indicates a past action whereas saying *he will go* indicates a future action. Verbs that shift from one tense to another with no clear reason can confuse readers. (See 44a.)

## 13 Missing comma in a compound sentence

▶ The words "I do" may sound simple, but they mean a life commitment.
                                   ^

▶ Meredith waited for Samir, and her sister grew impatient.
                          ^
  Without the comma, a reader may think at first that Meredith waited for Samir and her sister.

A compound sentence consists of two or more parts that could each stand alone as a sentence. When the parts are joined by a coordinating conjunction — *and, but, so, yet, or, nor,* or *for* — use a comma before the conjunction to indicate a pause between the two thoughts. In very short sentences, the comma is optional if the sentence can be easily understood without it. Including the comma, however, will never be wrong. (See 54c.)

## 14 Unnecessary or missing apostrophe (including *its / it's*)

▶ Overambitious parents can be very harmful to a ~~childs~~ well-being.
                                                *child's*
                                                   ^

▶ Matt Harvey has been one of the ~~Met's~~ most electrifying pitchers.
                                  *Mets'*
                                    ^

　　　　　　　　*its*　　　　　　　*It's*
▶ **The car is lying on it's side in the ditch. Its a white 2004 Passat.**
　　　　　　　　　　　　　　　　　^　　　　　　　^

　　　　　　　　　　　　　　　　*hers.*
▶ **She passed the front runner, and the race was her's.**
　　　　　　　　　　　　　　　　　　　　　　　^

To make a noun possessive, add either an apostrophe and an *-s* (*Ed's book*) or an apostrophe alone (*the boys' gym*). Do *not* use an apostrophe with the possessive pronouns *ours, yours, hers, its,* and *theirs.* Use *its* to mean *belonging to it*; use *it's* only when you mean *it is* or *it has.* (See Chapter 57.)

## 15　Fused (run-on) sentence

　　　　　　　　　　　　*He*
▶ **The current was swift. he could not swim to shore.**
　　　　　　　　　　　　　^

　　　　　　　　　　　　　　　*but*
▶ **Klee's paintings seem simple, they are very sophisticated.**
　　　　　　　　　　　　　　　　^

　*Although she*
▶ **She doubted the value of meditation, she decided to try it once.**
　^　　　　　　　　　　　　　　　　　　　　　　　^

A fused sentence (also called a run-on sentence) is created when clauses that could each stand alone as a sentence are joined with no punctuation or words to link them. Fused sentences must either be divided into separate sentences or joined by adding words, punctuation, or both. (See Chapter 46.)

## 16　Comma splice

▶ **Westward migration had passed Wyoming by,/; even the discovery of gold**
　　　　　　　　　　　　　　　　　　　　　　　　^

　　**in nearby Montana failed to attract settlers.**

　　　　　　　　　　　　　　　*for*
▶ **I was strongly drawn to her, she had special qualities.**
　　　　　　　　　　　　　　　　^

　　　　　　　　　　　　　*that*
▶ **We hated the meat loaf,/ the cafeteria served it every Friday.**
　　　　　　　　　　　　　　^

A comma splice occurs when only a comma separates clauses that could each stand alone as a sentence. To correct a comma splice, you can insert a semicolon or period, connect the clauses clearly with a word such as *and* or *because,* or restructure the sentence. (See Chapter 46.)

# 17 Lack of pronoun-antecedent agreement

▶ Each of the puppies thrived in ~~their~~ new home.
    *its*

Many indefinite pronouns, such as *everyone* and *each*, are always singular.

▶ Either Nirupa or Selena will be asked to give ~~their~~ speech to the graduates.
    *her*

When antecedents are joined by *or* or *nor*, the pronoun must agree with the closer antecedent.

▶ The team frequently changed ~~its~~ positions to get varied experience.
    *their*

A collective noun can be either singular or plural, depending on whether the people are seen as a single unit or as multiple individuals.

▶ Every student must provide his own uniform.
    *or her*

With a singular antecedent that can refer to either a man or a woman, you can use *his or her, he or she,* and so on. You can also rewrite the sentence to make the antecedent and pronoun plural or to eliminate the pronoun altogether.

Pronouns must agree with their antecedents in gender (for example, using *he* or *him* to replace *Abraham Lincoln* and *she* or *her* to replace *Queen Elizabeth*) and in number. (See 41f.)

# 18 Poorly integrated quotation

▶ A 1970s study of what makes food appetizing "Once it became apparent
    *showed how color affects taste:*

that the steak was actually blue and the fries were green, some people

became ill" (Schlosser 565).

▶ "Dumpster diving has serious drawbacks as a way of life" (~~Eighner~~ 383).
    *According to Lars Eighner,*

Finding edible food is especially tricky.

Quotations should fit smoothly into the surrounding sentence structure. They should be linked clearly to the writing around them (usually with a signal phrase) rather than dropped abruptly into the writing. (See 13b.)

# 19 Unnecessary or missing hyphen

▶ **This paper looks at fictional and real-life examples.**

A compound adjective modifying a following noun may require a hyphen.

▶ **Some of the soldiers were only eleven/years/old.**

A complement that follows the noun it modifies should not be hyphenated.

▶ **The buyers want to fix/up the house and resell it.**

A two-word verb should not be hyphenated.

A compound adjective that appears before a noun often needs a hyphen (63a). However, be careful not to hyphenate two-word verbs or word groups that serve as subject complements (63c).

# 20 Sentence fragment

**NO SUBJECT**

▶ **Marie Antoinette spent huge sums of money on herself and her favorites.**
Her extravagance
**And helped bring on the French Revolution.**

**NO COMPLETE VERB**

was
▶ **The old aluminum boat sitting on its trailer.**

*Sitting* cannot function alone as the verb of the sentence. The auxiliary verb *was* makes it a complete verb.

**BEGINNING WITH A SUBORDINATING WORD**

where
▶ **We returned to the drugstore/, Where we waited for our buddies.**

A sentence fragment is part of a sentence that is written and punctuated as if it were a complete sentence. A fragment may lack a subject, a complete verb, or both. Fragments may also begin with a subordinating word (such as *because*) that makes the fragment depend on another sentence for its meaning. Reading your draft out loud, backwards, sentence by sentence, will help you spot sentence fragments easily. (See Chapter 47.)

## Taking a writing inventory

One way to learn from your mistakes is to take a writing inventory. It can help you think critically and analytically about how to improve your writing skills.

1.  Collect two or three pieces of your writing to which either your instructor or other students have responded.

2.  Read through this writing, adding your own comments about its strengths and weaknesses. How do your comments compare with those of others?

3.  Group all the comments into three categories—*broad content issues* (use of evidence and sources, attention to purpose and audience, overall impression), *organization and presentation* (overall and paragraph-level organization, sentence structure and style, formatting), and *surface errors* (problems with spelling, grammar, punctuation, and mechanics).

4.  Make an inventory of your own strengths in each category.

5.  Study your errors. Mark every instructor and peer comment that suggests or calls for an improvement and put them all in a list. Consult the relevant part of this handbook or speak with your instructor if you don't understand a comment.

6.  Make a list of the top problem areas you need to work on. How can you make improvements? Then note at least two strengths that you can build on in your writing. Record your findings in a writing log that you can add to as the class proceeds.

# PART 1
# The Art and Craft of Writing

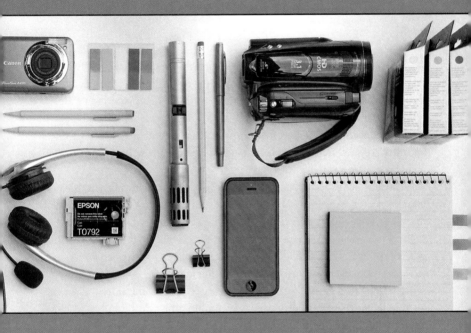

# CHAPTER 1

# Expectations for College Writing

YOU MAY HAVE THOUGHT of college primarily as a step on the way to a career, but in today's unpredictable working world, learning the specific skills you need to get a particular job may be less useful than acquiring a wide range of abilities that will serve you well in any position you hold. The abilities a college education can help you develop—such as critical reading and writing and effective speaking—will help you succeed in college and beyond, no matter where your career path leads.

Making your expectations for your college education match up with what your instructors expect of you will be one of your most significant challenges in college. Your college instructors—as well as your future colleagues and supervisors—will expect you to demonstrate your ability to think critically, to consider ethical issues, to find as well as solve problems, to do effective research, to work productively with people of widely different backgrounds, and to present the knowledge you construct in a variety of ways and in a variety of genres and media. Your success will depend on communicating clearly and on making appropriate choices for the context.

> **CONNECT:** How does your academic work relate to writing you want to do? **1a, Chapter 26**
>
> **CREATE:** Make a written or video response to **Exercise 1.1.**
>
> **REFLECT:** Go to **macmillanhighered.com/smh**, and respond to **1. Expectations > Video > Lessons from informal writing**.

## 1a Moving between social and academic writing

As Clive Thompson noted in *Wired* magazine in 2009, "Before the Internet came along, most Americans never wrote anything, ever, that wasn't a school assignment. Unless they got a job that required producing text . . . , they'd leave school and virtually never construct a paragraph again." Times have indeed changed. Digital tools have ensured that writing is not only important for school, but it is also essential for most jobs and (thanks to texting and social media) is a key part of social life for most people, a way to share information with everyone from close friends to total strangers. Social connection today involves so much writing that you probably write more out of class than in class. In fact, social writing has opened doors for writers like never before. Writing on social networking sites allows writers to get almost instant feedback, and anticipating responses from an audience often has the effect of making online writers very savvy: they know the importance of analyzing the audience and of using an appropriate style, level of formality, and tone to suit the online occasion.

Writers on Twitter, for example, compose in short bursts of no more than 140 characters. By tagging content, tweeting at groups and individuals, and pointing toward links, they can start discussions, participate in ongoing conversations, and invite others to join in. Here are two representative tweets from the Twitter feed of Stephanie Parker, a college student whose interests include technology and Korean pop culture.

© STEPHANIE PARKER

### sparker2

Rain's over, going to Trader Joe's to buy some healthy stuff to fight this cold . . . suggestions?

Watching Queen Seon Duk/선덕여왕 on @**dramafever**, love it so far! **http://www.dramafever.com/drama/56/ #nowplaying**

In these tweets, Stephanie shows a keen awareness both of the audiences she is trying to reach on Twitter and of two very common purposes for this kind of informal writing—to seek information (in the first tweet, about foods to fight off a cold) and to share information (in the second tweet, about her view of a popular Korean drama, with a link so readers can check it out for themselves).

Like Stephanie, many young writers today are adept at informal social writing across a range of genres and media. You may not think consciously about the audience you'll reach in a Facebook post or a tweet, or about your purpose for writing in such spaces, but you are probably more skilled than you give yourself credit for when it comes to making appropriate choices for your informal writing.

Of course, informal writing is not the only writing skill a student needs to master. You'll also need to move back and forth between informal social writing and formal academic writing, and to write across a whole range of genres and media. Take time to reflect on your informal writing: What do you assume about your audience? What is your purpose? How do you achieve a particular tone? In short, why do you write the way you do in these situations? Analyzing the choices you make in a given writing context will help you develop the ability to make good choices in other contexts as well—an ability that will allow you to move between social and academic writing.

### EXERCISE 1.1

Choose a sample of your own informal writing from a social networking site to reflect on: a status update, text message, or tweet, for example. Why did you write the post? What did you assume about your readers, and why? Why did you choose the words, images, links, or other parts of the text, and how do these choices contribute to the way the writing comes across to an audience? Does the writing do what you want it to do? Why, or why not?

## 1b Preparing to meet expectations for U.S. academic writing

If you're like most students, you probably have less familiarity with academic writing contexts than you do with informal contexts. You may not have written formal academic papers much more than five pages long before coming to college, and you may have done only minimal research. The contexts for your college writing will require you to face new challenges and even new definitions of *writing*; you may be asked, for example, to create a persuasive Web site or to research, write, and deliver a multimedia presentation. If you grew up speaking and writing in other languages, the transition to producing effective college work can be especially complicated. Not only do you have to learn new information and new ways of thinking and arguing in unfamiliar rhetorical situations, but you also have to do it in a language that may not come naturally to you.

Instructors sometimes assume that students are already familiar with their expectations for college writing. To complicate the matter further, there is no single "correct" style of communication in any country, including the United States. Effective oral styles differ from effective written styles, and what is considered good writing in one field of study is not necessarily appropriate in another. Within a field, different rhetorical situations and genres may require different ways of writing. In business, for example, memos are usually short and simple, while a market analysis report may require complex paragraphs with tables, graphs, and diagrams. Even the variety of English often referred to as "standard"

---

**TALKING THE TALK | CONVENTIONS**

"Aren't conventions just rules with another name?" Not entirely. Conventions—agreed-on language practices of grammar, punctuation, and style—convey shorthand information from writer to reader. In college writing, you will generally want to follow the conventions of standard academic English unless you have a good reason to do otherwise. But unlike hard and fast rules, conventions are flexible; a convention appropriate for one time or situation may be inappropriate for another. You may also choose to ignore conventions at times to achieve a particular effect. (You might, for example, write a sentence fragment rather than a full sentence, such as the *Not entirely* at the beginning of this box.) As you become more experienced and confident in your writing, you will develop a sense of which conventions to apply in different writing situations.

---

covers a wide range of styles (see Chapter 29). In spite of this wide variation, several features are often associated with U.S. academic English in general:

- conventional grammar, spelling, punctuation, and mechanics
- organization that links ideas explicitly (4g)
- an easy-to-read type size and typeface, conventional margins, and double spacing
- explicitly stated claims supported by evidence (Chapter 9)
- careful documentation of all sources (Chapters 32–35)
- consistent use of an appropriate level of formality (27c and 30a)
- conventional use of idioms (Chapter 43)
- use of conventional academic formats, such as literature reviews, research essays, lab reports, and research proposals

This brief list suggests features of the genre often described as U.S. academic writing. Yet these characteristics can lead to even more questions: What does *conventional* mean? How can you determine what is appropriate in any given rhetorical situation? New contexts often require the use of different sets of conventions, strategies, and resources, so ask your instructor for advice, or check with your writing center, local library, or friends for examples of the kind of text you need to create.

## 1c Positioning yourself as an academic writer

### ☐ Establishing authority

In the United States, most instructors expect student writers to begin to establish their own authority—to become constructive critics who can analyze and interpret the work of others and can eventually create new knowledge based on their own thinking and on what others have said. But what does establishing your authority mean in practice?

- Assume that your opinions count (as long as they are informed rather than tossed out with little thought) and that your audience expects you to present them in a well-reasoned manner. In class discussion, for example, you can build authority by stating an opinion clearly and then backing it up with evidence.

- Draw conclusions based on what you have heard, observed, and read, and then offer those conclusions in a clear and straightforward way.

- Build your authority by citing the works of others, both from the reading you have done for class and from good points your instructor and classmates have made.

## ☐ Being direct

Your instructors will often expect you to get to your main point quickly and to be direct throughout your project. Good academic writing prepares readers for what is coming next, provides definitions, and identifies clear topics and transitions. Research for this book confirms that readers depend on writers to organize and present their material in ways that aid understanding. To achieve directness in your writing, try the following strategies:

- State your main point early and clearly; don't leave anything to the reader's imagination.

- Avoid overqualifying your statements. Instead of writing *I think the facts reveal*, come right out and say *The facts reveal*.

- Avoid digressions. If you use an anecdote or example from personal experience, be sure it relates directly to your main point.

- Make sure to use examples and concrete details to help support your main point. Choose evidence that helps readers understand and offers proof that what you are saying is sensible and worthy of attention (9f).

- Make your transitions from point to point obvious and clear. The first sentence of a new paragraph should reach back to the paragraph before and then look forward to what is to come (5f).

- Guide readers through your writing by using effective and varied sentences that link together smoothly (Chapters 50–53).

- If your project is long or complex, consider brief summary statements between sections, but be careful to avoid unnecessary repetition.

- Design the project appropriately for the audience and purpose you have in mind (Chapter 16).

# 1d Becoming an engaged reader and active listener

Expect to engage actively with the texts you read and with the people in your class, whether you meet in person or online.

## ☐ Reading actively

Your instructors expect you to offer informed opinions in response to your reading. Keep in mind that instructors are not asking you to be negative or combative; rather, they want to know that you are engaged with the text and with the class. Here are some expectations many instructors have about what good readers do:

- Carefully note the name of the author or creator and the date and place of publication; these items can give you clues to purpose, audience, and context.

- Understand the overall content of a piece, and be able to summarize it in your own words.

- Formulate informed and critical questions about the text.

- Understand each sentence, and make direct connections among sentences and paragraphs.

- Keep track of the use of sources as well as of repeated themes or images, and figure out how they contribute to the entire piece.

- Note the creator's attitude toward and assumptions about the subject. Then you can speculate on how the attitude and assumptions may have affected the creator's thinking.

- Distinguish between the creator's stance and how the creator reports on the stances of others. Keep an eye open for the key phrases a writer uses to signal an opposing argument: *while some have argued that, in the past,* and so on.

For more detailed advice on reading critically, see Chapter 7.

## ☐ Participating actively in class

Speaking up in class is viewed as inappropriate or even rude in some cultures. In U.S. academic settings, however, doing so is expected and encouraged. Indeed, some instructors assign credit for participation in class discussions. The challenge is to contribute without losing track of the overall conversation or aims of the class and without monopolizing the discussion. These guidelines can help:

- Listen purposefully, jotting down related points and following the flow of the conversation.

- If you think you might lose track of your ideas while speaking, jot down key words to keep you on track.

- Make your comments count by asking a key question to clarify a point, by taking the conversation in a more productive direction, or by analyzing or summarizing what has been said.

- Respond to questions or comments by others as specifically as possible (*The passage on p. 42 supports your point* rather than *I agree*).

- If you have trouble participating in class discussions, try making one comment a day. You might also speak with your instructor about ways to contribute to the conversation.

- Remember that there is no direct correlation between talking in class and being intellectually engaged: many students are participating actively, whether or not they are speaking.

## 1e  Preparing for college research

The reading and writing you do in college are part of what we broadly think of as research. In fact, much of the work you do in college may turn an informal search into various kinds of more formal research: you might start by wondering how many students on your campus are vegetarians, for example, and end up with a research project for your sociology class that then becomes part of a multimedia presentation for a campus organization.

Many of your writing assignments will require extensive or formal research with a wide range of print, online, and media sources as well as information drawn from observations, interviews, or surveys. Research can help you find important information you didn't know, even if you know a topic very well. And no matter what you discover, your research will be an important tool for establishing credibility with your audience members and thus gaining their confidence in you as a writer. Often, what you write will be only as good as the research on which it is based. (For more on research, see Chapters 10–15.)

## 1f  Using media effectively

Increasingly, your instructors may expect you to produce texts using a variety of media. You may be asked to create Web content; post your work to course management systems, lists, blogs, wikis, or social networking sites; and respond to the work of others on such sites. In addition, you will probably write email and text messages to your instructors and other students. You may use sound, video, or other multimedia content as part or all of the texts you create. As always, in writing such texts, remember to consider your audience and your context in deciding what is appropriate. Research for this book indicates that many student writers are already adept at making such calls: you probably know, for example, that using informal Internet abbreviations and emoticons in academic writing is seldom appropriate. But because electronic communication is so common, it's easy to fall into the habit of writing very informally. If you forget to adjust style and voice for different occasions and readers, you may undermine your own intentions.

## □ Following best practices for formal messages and posts

When writing most academic and professional messages, or when posting to a public list that may be read by people you don't know well, follow the conventions of standard academic English (1b), and be careful not to offend or irritate your audience—remember that jokes may be read as insults and that ALL CAPS may look like shouting. Finally, proofread to make sure your message is clear and free of errors, and that it is addressed to your intended audience, before you hit send.

### DISCUSSION LISTS, FORUMS, AND COMMENTS

- Avoid unnecessary criticism of others' spelling or language. If a message is unclear, ask politely for a clarification. If you disagree with an assertion, offer what you believe to be the correct information, but don't insult the writer.
- If you think you've been insulted, give the writer the benefit of the doubt. Replying with patience establishes your credibility and helps you appear mature and fair.
- For email discussion lists, decide whether to reply off-list to the sender of a message or to the whole group, and be careful to use REPLY or REPLY ALL accordingly to avoid potential embarrassment.
- Keep in mind that more people than you think may be reading your messages.

### EMAIL

- Use a subject line that states your purpose clearly.
- Use a formal greeting and closing (*Dear Ms. Aulie* rather than *Hey*).
- Keep messages as concise as possible.
- Conclude your message with your name and email address.
- Ask for permission before forwarding a sensitive message from someone else.

- Consider your email messages permanent and always findable, even if you delete them. Many people have been embarrassed (or worse, prosecuted) because of email trails.

- Make sure that the username on the email account you use for formal messages does not present a poor impression. If your username is *Party2Nite*, consider changing it, or use your school account for academic and professional communication.

## ☐ Following best practices for informal situations

Sometimes audiences expect informality. When you write in certain situations—Twitter posts, for example, and most text messages—you can play with (or ignore) the conventions you would probably follow in formal writing. Many people receiving text messages expect shorthand such as *u* for "you," but be cautious about using such shortcuts with an employer or instructor. You may want to stick to a more formal method of contact if your employer or instructor has not explicitly invited you to send text messages—or texted you first. And if you initiate a text conversation with someone you don't know well, be sure to identify yourself in your first message!

Even when you think the situation calls for an informal tone, be attuned to your audience's needs and your purpose for writing. And when writing for any online writing space that allows users to say almost anything about themselves or to comment freely on the postings of others, bear in mind that anonymity sometimes makes online writers feel less inhibited than they would be in a face-to-face discussion. Don't say anything you want to remain private, and even if you disagree with another writer, avoid personal attacks.

▼ ▼ ▼ ▼ ▼ ▼ ▼ ▼ ▼ ▼ ▼ ▼ ▼ ▼ ▼ ▼ ▼ ▼ ▼ ▼ ▼ ▼ ▼ ▼ ▼ ▼

### THINKING CRITICALLY ABOUT YOUR EXPECTATIONS FOR COLLEGE WRITING

How do you define good college writing? Make a list of the characteristics you come up with. Then make a list of what you think your instructors' expectations are for good college writing, and note how they may differ from yours. (Research suggests that many students today define good writing as "writing that makes something happen in the world." Would that match your definition or that of your instructors?) What might account for the differences—and the similarities—in the definitions and lists? Do you need to alter your ideas about good college writing to meet your instructors' expectations? Why, or why not?

# CHAPTER 2
# Rhetorical Situations

**W**HAT DO A DOCUMENTED ESSAY on global warming research, a Facebook post objecting to a change in the site's privacy policy, a tweet to other students in your sociology class, a comment on a blog post, a letter to the editor of your local newspaper, and a Web site about energy conservation all have in common? To communicate successfully, the writers of all these texts must analyze their particular rhetorical situation and then respond to it in appropriate ways.

---

**CONNECT:** How can you reach audiences beyond your teacher? **2e, 9f–h on argument, 17a on presentations**

**CREATE:** Make a written or video response to **Exercise 2.3**.

**REFLECT:** Go to **macmillanhighered.com/smh**, and respond to **2. Rhetorical Situations > Video > Developing a sense of audience**.

---

## 2a  Making good choices for your situation

A *rhetorical situation* is the full set of circumstances surrounding any communication. To communicate effectively, you need to make careful choices about all of the elements of your situation.
The rhetorical situation is often depicted as a triangle to present the idea that three important elements are closely connected — your *text*, including your topic and the message you want to convey (2c); your role as the *communicator*, including your purpose and stance, or attitude toward the text (2d); and your *audience* (2e). If all the pieces making up the larger triangle don't work together, the communication will not be effective. But important

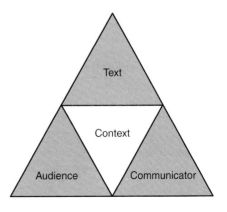

as these elements are, they are connected to a *context* that shapes all the angles of the triangle. Considering context fully requires you to answer many other questions about the rhetorical situation, such as what kind of text you should create (2f) and what conventions you should follow to meet audience expectations for creating and delivering the text (2g).

### ☐ Looking at the big picture

As the triangle suggests, you'll benefit from thinking about audience, topic, and purpose together — as part of a whole — rather than as separate parts. Although one context may require you to begin by analyzing your audience, another may work better if you start by picking a topic or considering your purpose. The important point is that wherever you begin, you need to make all the elements of your rhetorical situation fit together into a comprehensible big picture.

### ☐ Deciding to write

Because elements of the rhetorical situation are such important considerations in effective writing, you should start thinking about them at an early stage, as soon as you make the decision to write. In a general sense, of course, this decision is often made for you when employers and instructors set deadlines and due dates. But even in such situations, consciously deciding to write is important. Experienced writers report that making up their minds to begin a writing task represents a big step toward getting the job done.

### ☐ Considering informal and formal rhetorical situations

You may well be accustomed to writing in some rhetorical situations that you don't analyze closely. When you post something on a friend's Facebook page, for example, you probably spend little time pondering what your friend values or finds amusing, how to phrase your words, which links or photos would best emphasize your point, or why you're taking the time to post.

However, academic and other formal rhetorical situations may seem considerably less familiar than the social writing you share with friends. Until you understand clearly what such situations demand of you, you should allow additional time to analyze the topic, purpose, audience, and other elements of your context with care.

### ☐ Seizing the opportune moment

In ancient Greece, Kairos (youngest son of Zeus), the god of opportunity, was depicted as running, with a prominent lock of hair on his forehead but a bald head in back. Seizing the opportune moment meant grabbing the hair as Kairos approached; once he passed, the opportune moment was gone. Considering rhetorical situations means thinking hard about *kairos*, the appropriate time and the most opportune ways to get your point across. Just as you understand that re-tweeting should happen soon after the original tweet or not at all, take advantage of *kairos* to choose appropriate timing and current examples and evidence for your rhetorical situation.

## 2b Understanding academic assignments

Most formal on-the-job writing addresses specific purposes, audiences, and topics: a nurse documents patient care for other members of a health care team; an accountant creates a plain-English summary of the pros and cons of an investment option; a team of psychologists prepares video scripts to help companies deal with employee stress. These writers all have one thing in common: specific goals. They know why, for whom, and about what they are writing.

College writing assignments, in contrast, may seem to appear out of the blue, with no specific purpose, audience, or topic. In extreme cases, they may be only one word long, as in a theater examination that consisted of the word *Tragedy*! At the opposite extreme come the fully developed, very specific cases often assigned in business and engineering courses. In between the one-word exam and the fully developed case, you may get assignments that specify purpose but not audience — to write an essay arguing for or against Internet censorship, for example. Or you may be given an organizational pattern to use — say, to compare and contrast two novels read in a course — but no specific topic. Make every effort to comprehend an assignment accurately and fully so you can respond to it successfully.

---

**QUICK HELP**

### Analyzing an assignment

- What exactly does the assignment ask you to do? Look for such words as *analyze, classify, compare, contrast, describe, discuss, define, explain,* and *survey.* Remember that the meaning of these words may differ among disciplines — *analyze* might mean one thing in literature, another in biology.
- What knowledge or information do you need? What kinds of research or exploration will you need to do, and where are you most likely to find the information you need? **(3a and d)**
- Do you need to find or create visual or media content? What purpose should it serve? **(3d and e)**
- How can you limit — or broaden — the topic or assignment to make it more interesting? Do you have interest in or knowledge about any particular aspect of the topic? Be sure to check with your instructor if you wish to redefine the assignment. **(3b)**
- What problem(s) does the topic suggest to you? How might the problem(s) give you an interesting angle on the topic? **(2c)**  ▶

Analyzing an assignment, continued

- What are the assignment's specific requirements? Consider genre, length, format, organization, and deadline—all of which will help you know the scope expected. If no length is designated, ask for guidelines. **(2b)**
- What is your purpose? Do you need to demonstrate knowledge of certain material, or show your ability to express certain ideas clearly? **(2d)**
- Who is the audience for this writing? Does the task imply that you will assume a particular readership besides your instructor? **(2e)**

### Emily Lesk's assignment

In this and the next several chapters, you can follow the writing process of Emily Lesk as she developed an essay for her first-year English course. Her class was given the following assignment:

> Explore the ways in which one or more media (television, print advertising, and so on) have affected an aspect of American identity, and discuss the implications of your findings for you and your readers.

Emily saw that the assignment was broad enough to allow her to focus on something that interested her, and she knew that the key word *explore* invited her to examine — and analyze — an aspect of American identity that was of special interest to her. Her instructor said to assume that she and members of the class would be the primary audience for this essay. Emily felt comfortable having her instructor and classmates as the primary audience: she knew what their expectations were and how to meet those expectations. But Emily also hoped to post her essay on the class Web site, thus reaching a wider audience — in fact, her essay might be read by anyone with access to the Internet. With this broad and largely unknown audience in mind, Emily determined to be as clear as possible

---

TALKING THE TALK | **ASSIGNMENTS**

"How do instructors come up with these assignments?" Assignments, like other kinds of writing, reflect particular rhetorical contexts that vary from instructor to instructor, and they change over time. The assignment for an 1892 college writing contest was to write an essay "On Coal"; in research conducted for this textbook in the 1980s, the most common writing assignment was a personal narrative. Assignments also reflect changing expectations for college students and the needs of society. Competing effectively in today's workforce calls for high-level thinking, for being able to argue convincingly, and for knowing how to do the research necessary to support a claim. It's no surprise, then, that a recent study of first-year college writing in the United States found that by far the most common assignment today asks students to compose a researched argument. (See Chapters 8 and 9.)

and to take nothing for granted in terms of explaining her point of view and supporting her thesis.

### ◢ EXERCISE 2.1

The following assignment was given to an introductory business class: "Discuss in an essay the contributions of the Apple and Microsoft companies to the personal computing industry." What would you need to know about the assignment in order to respond successfully? Using the questions in the Quick Help box on pp. 25–26, analyze this assignment.

### ◢ EXERCISE 2.2

Think back to a recent academic writing assignment. What helped you finally decide to write? Once you made that decision, what exactly did you do to get going? In a paragraph or two, describe your situation and answer these questions. Then compare your description with those of two or three classmates.

## 2c Thinking about your topic and message

When a topic is left open, many writers put off getting started because they can't decide what to write about. Experienced writers say that the best way to choose a topic is literally to let it choose you. The subjects that compel you — that confuse, puzzle, irritate, or in some way pose a problem for you — are likely to engage your interests and hence evoke your best writing. You can begin to identify a topic or problem by thinking through the following questions:

- What topics do you wish you knew more about?
- What topics are most likely to get you fired up?
- What about one of these topics is most confusing to you? most exciting? most irritating? most tantalizing?
- What person or group might this topic raise problems for?

Deciding on a broad topic is an essential step before beginning to write, but you need to go further than that to decide what you want to say about your topic and how you will shape what you want to say into a clear, powerful message. Remember that regardless of the topic you choose, it must be manageable for the time you have to write and the constraints of your project (length limits, expectations of audience, and so on). For help with limiting a topic, see 3b and 10c.

---

**macmillanhighered.com/smh**

 2. Rhetorical Situations > Video > Pay attention to what you're interested in

## 2d  Considering your purpose and stance as a communicator

In ancient Rome, the great orator Cicero noted that a good speech generally fulfills one of three major purposes: to delight, to teach, or to move. Today, our purposes when we communicate with one another remain pretty much the same: we seek to *entertain* (delight), to *inform or explain* (teach), and to *persuade or convince* (move).

Whether you choose to communicate for purposes of your own or have that purpose set for you by an instructor or employer, you should consider the purpose for any communication carefully. For the writing you do that is not connected to a class or work assignment, your purpose may be very clear to you: you may want to convince neighbors to support a community garden, get others in your office to help keep the kitchen clean, or tell blog readers what you like or hate about your new phone. Even so, analyzing what you want to accomplish and why can make you a more effective communicator.

### ☐  Considering purposes for academic writing

Academic work requires particular attention to your reasons for writing. On one level, you are writing to establish your credibility with your instructor, to demonstrate that you are a careful thinker and an effective communicator. On another level, though, you are writing to achieve goals of your own, to say as clearly and forcefully as possible what you think about a topic.

For most college writing, consider purpose in terms of the assignment, the instructor's expectations, and your own goals.

- What is the primary purpose of the assignment — to entertain? to explain? to persuade? some other purpose? What does this purpose suggest about the best ways to achieve it? If you are unclear about the primary purpose, talk with your instructor. Are there any secondary purposes to keep in mind?

- What are the instructor's purposes in giving this assignment — to make sure you have read certain materials? to determine your understanding? to evaluate your thinking and writing? How can you fulfill these expectations?

- What are your goals in carrying out this assignment — to meet expectations? to learn? to communicate your ideas? How can you achieve these goals?

### ☐  Considering your rhetorical stance

Thinking about your own position as a communicator and your attitude toward your text — your *rhetorical stance* — has several advantages. It will help you examine where your opinions come from and thus help you address the topic fully; it will help you see how your stance might differ from the stances held by members of your audience; and it will help you establish your credibility with that audience. This part of your rhetorical stance — your *ethos* or credibility — helps determine how well your message will be received. To be credible, you will need to do your homework on your subject, present your information fairly and honestly, and be respectful of your audience.

A student writing a proposal for increased services for people with disabilities, for instance, knew that having a brother with Down syndrome gave her an intense interest that her audience might not have in this topic. She needed to work hard, then, to get her audience to understand — and share — her stance.

- What is your overall attitude toward the topic? How strong are your opinions?
- What social, political, religious, personal, or other influences have contributed to your attitude?
- How much do you know about the topic? What questions do you have about it?
- What interests you most about the topic? Why?
- What interests you least about it? Why?
- What seems important — or unimportant — about the topic?
- What preconceptions, if any, do you have about it?
- What do you expect to conclude about the topic?
- How will you establish your credibility (*ethos*)? That is, how will you show that you are knowledgeable and trustworthy? (See 8d and 9e.)

### Purpose and stance of visuals and media

Images and media you choose to include in your writing can help establish credibility. But remember that they, too, always have a point of view or perspective. The postcard on p. 30, for example, illustrates two physical perspectives — a photo of the Carquinez Bridge and a road map showing the bridge's location. It also shows a time perspective from 1927, when the bridge was new. This postcard, captioned "America's Greatest Highway Bridge," presents the construction of the bridge (now demolished) as a triumph of modern technology. So when you choose an image, think hard about its perspective and about how well it fits in with your topic and purpose. Does the image have an attitude — and does that attitude serve the purpose of your writing?

### Emily Lesk's purposes

As she considered the assignment (see p. 26), Emily Lesk saw that her primary purpose was to explain the significance and implications of her topic to herself and her readers, but she recognized some other purposes as well. Because this essay was assigned early in the term, she wanted to get off to a good start; thus,

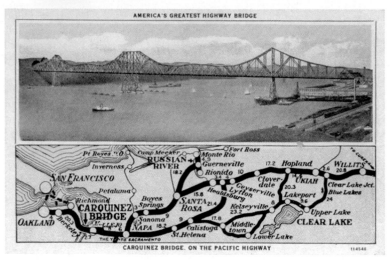

Consider the purpose and stance of each visual and media file you use.

one of her purposes was to write as well as she could to demonstrate her ability to her classmates and instructor. In addition, she decided that she wanted to find out something new about herself and to use this knowledge to get her readers to think about themselves.

For the first draft of Emily Lesk's essay, see 3g. For the final draft of her essay, see 4l.

## 2e Analyzing audiences

Every writer can benefit from thinking carefully about who the audience is, what the audience already knows or thinks, and what the audience needs and expects to find out. One of the characteristic traits of an effective writer is the ability to write for a variety of audiences, using language, style, and evidence appropriate to particular readers. The key word here is *appropriate*: just as you would be unlikely to sprinkle jokes through a PTA presentation on child abuse, neither would you post a detailed and academic argument in response to a blog filled with funny cat pictures. Such behavior would be wildly inappropriate given the nature of your audience.

Thinking systematically about your audience can help you make decisions about a writing assignment. For example, it can help you decide what sort of organizational plan to follow, what information to include or exclude, and even what specific words to use. If you are writing an article for a journal for nurses about a drug that prevents patients from developing infections from intravenous feeding tubes, you will not need to give much information about how such tubes work or to define many terms. But if you are writing about the same topic in a pamphlet for patients, you will have to give a great deal of background information and define (or avoid) technical terms.

- What person or group do you most want to reach? Is this audience already sympathetic to your views?
- How much do you know about your audience? In what ways may its members differ from you? from one another? Consider education, geographic region, age, gender, occupation, social class, ethnic and cultural heritage, politics, religion, marital status, sexual orientation, disabilities, and so on. (See Chapter 28.)
- What assumptions can you make about your audience members? What might they value — brevity, originality, conformity, honesty, wit, seriousness, thrift, generosity? What goals and aspirations do they have? Take special care to examine whether distant readers will understand references, allusions, and so on.
- What do members of the audience already know about your topic? Do you need to provide background information or define terms?
- What kind of information and evidence will the audience find most compelling — quotations from experts? personal experiences? photographs? statistics?
- What stance do your audience members have toward your topic? What are they likely to know about it? What views might they already hold?
- What is your relationship to the audience?
- What is your attitude toward the audience?

☐ **Imagining audiences for informal writing**

For some informal writing — a Facebook message to a friend, for example — you know exactly who your audience is, and communicating appropriately may be a simple matter. It's still worth remembering that when you post informal writing in a public space — whether on a friend's Facebook page, in a blog's comment section, or on Twitter — you may not be aware of how large and varied your online audience can be. Can your friend's parents, or her employer, see your posts? (The answer depends on how she manages her privacy settings.) Who's reading the blogs you comment on or following your tweets?

In a famous cartoon by Peter Steiner, one dog tells another, "On the Internet, nobody knows you're a dog." However, as online privacy becomes less common — and as online writers become more likely to grant large audiences access to their thoughts, including everyone from old high school classmates and former co-workers to beer buddies and members of their church — maintaining distinct identities is more difficult. On the Internet today, some writers have suggested, *everyone* knows you're a dog, whether you want them to or not!

☐ **Imagining audiences for formal and academic writing**

Even if you write with intuitive ease in tweets and texts to friends, you may struggle when asked to write for an instructor or for a general audience. You may wonder, for example, why you need to define terms in your writing that your instructor has used in class, or what you can assume a general audience knows about your topic. When you are new to academic writing, making such assumptions can be tricky. If you can identify samples of writing that appeal to an audience similar to the one you are writing for, look for clues about what level of knowledge you can assume; if still in doubt, check with your instructor.

Members of your class will also usually be part of your audience, especially if you are responding to one another's drafts in peer review. You may also have a chance to identify an audience for your assignment — perhaps a business proposal addressed to a hypothetical manager or a Web presentation posted for an online audience that is potentially global. In each case, it pays to consider carefully how your audience(s) may respond to the words, images, and other elements you choose.

**EXERCISE 2.3**

Describe one of your courses to three audiences: your best friend, your parents, and a group of high school students attending an open house at your college. Then describe the differences in content, organization, and wording that the differences in audience led you to make.

☐ **Appealing to your whole audience**

All writers need to pay very careful attention to the ways in which their writing can either invite readers to be part of the audience or leave them out. Look at the following sentence: *As every schoolchild knows, the world is losing its rain forests at the rate of one acre per second.* The writer here gives a clear message about who is — and who is not — part of the audience: if you don't know this fact or suspect it may not be true, you are not invited to participate and, as a result, may feel insulted.

You can help make readers feel they are part of your audience. Be especially careful with the pronouns you use, the assumptions you make, and the kinds of support you offer for your ideas.

- **Use appropriate pronouns.** The pronouns you use (see Chapter 41) can include or exclude readers. When bell hooks says "The most powerful resource any of us can have as we study and teach in university settings is full understanding and appreciation of the richness, beauty, and primacy of our familial and community backgrounds," she uses "us" and "we" to connect with her audience — those who "study and teach in university settings."

## CONSIDERING DISABILITIES | YOUR WHOLE AUDIENCE

Remember that considering your whole audience means thinking about members with varying abilities and special needs. If you are writing to veterans in a VA hospital or to a senior citizens' group, for example, you can be sure that many audience members will be living with some form of disability. But it's very likely that any audience will include members with disabilities — from anorexia to dyslexia, multiple sclerosis, or attention deficit disorder — and that there may be significant differences within disabilities. Approximately one in five Americans are living with a disability. All writers need to think carefully about how their words reach out and connect with such very diverse audiences.

Using "us" and "we" to speak directly to your audience, however, can sometimes be dangerous: those who do not see themselves as fitting into the "we" group can feel left out — and they may resent it. So take special care with the pronouns you use to refer to your readers.

- **Avoid unfounded assumptions.** Be careful what you assume about your readers and their views, and avoid language that may unintentionally exclude readers. Use words like *naturally* and *of course* carefully, for what seems natural to you — that English should be the official U.S. language, for instance, or that smoking should be outlawed — may not seem at all natural to some members of your audience. Try to take nothing about your audience for granted.

- **Offer appropriate evidence.** The evidence you use to support your arguments can help draw in your readers. A student writing about services for people with disabilities might ask readers who have no personal experience with the topic to imagine themselves in a wheelchair, trying to enter a building with steps but no ramp. Inviting them to be part of her audience would help them accept her ideas. On the other hand, inappropriate evidence can leave readers out. Complex statistical evidence might well appeal to public-policy planners but may bore or irritate ordinary citizens. (For more on building common ground with readers, see Chapter 28.)

### Emily Lesk's audiences

In addition to her instructor, Emily Lesk's audience included the members of her writing class and her potential online readers. Emily saw that her classmates were mostly her age, that they came from diverse ethnic backgrounds, and that they came from many areas of the country. Her online readers could be almost anyone.

## 2f Thinking about genres and media

You no doubt are familiar with the word *genre* in terms of movies (comedy, action, horror) or music (hip-hop, folk, punk rock). But *genre* is also used to describe forms of writing, such as research projects, personal narratives, and lab reports. Genres and media are not the same — the genre of a research project or promotional flyer might be created using either digital or print media, for example — but some genres are tied closely to specific media, so the two categories are related.

### ▫ Understanding genre conventions

A genre is a form of communication used to achieve a particular purpose. An annotated bibliography, for example, lists and comments on potential sources for a research project. Over time, genres develop conventions — such as the types of content, rhetorical strategies, and kinds of language used. Most audiences begin to expect those conventional features in the genre. But genres are not cookie-cutter templates. They are flexible and develop over time.

As an academic writer, you'll encounter genres both familiar and new. Even when a genre at first seems familiar, you may find new expectations or conventions at different levels of education, in different academic disciplines, or even in different classrooms, so you'll want to look closely at any genre you are considering for a writing project.

### ◢ EXERCISE 2.4

Consider some of the genres that you have encountered as a student, jotting down answers to the following questions and bringing them to class for discussion.

1. What are some genres that you read but don't usually write?
2. What are some genres that you write for teachers?
3. What are some genres that you write to or with other students?
4. What are some genres that you will likely encounter in your major or in your career?
5. How are some of the genres you listed different from those you encountered in high school?

### ▫ Analyzing features of genres

If you are not sure what kind of text you are supposed to write, ask your instructor for clarification and examples. (Some examples may also be available at your school's writing center.) You may want to find multiple examples so that you can develop a sense of how different writers approach the same writing task.

## TALKING THE TALK | GENRE NAMES

"What does my instructor mean by 'essay'?" Writing assignments often mention a specific genre, such as *essay* or *report*, but genre names can be confusing. The same genre may work differently in different contexts, or people may use the same term in various ways. Depending on the field, an essay might be a personal narrative, a critical analysis, or even a journal article. Even when the name of the genre sounds familiar to you, look for specific instructions for each assignment or analyze examples provided by the instructor.

Another strategy is to discuss the assignment with a few classmates or a writing center tutor. You may find the help you need, and you may see that you are not the only one struggling to understand the assignment. Look carefully at the samples to make sure you understand the conventional expectations, and ask questions like these about the genre's typical features.

- What does the genre look like? How is the text laid out? How are headings, sidebars, footnotes, and other elements incorporated into the main text? If visuals or media elements are included, how and why are they used? (See Chapter 16.)

- How long is typical work in this genre? How long is each paragraph or unit?

- What topics are usually found in this genre? What type of content is rare?

- How does the text introduce the topic? How and where does it present the main point? Is the main point stated explicitly or implicitly?

- How does each section contribute to the main point? How is the main point of each section supported?

- How are the key terms defined? How much and what kind of background information is provided?

- What kind of sentence structure is common in this genre? Are sentences short, long, simple, complicated? Is passive voice common?

- What is the level of formality? Does the text use contractions such as *he's* and *can't* instead of *he is* and *cannot*? (57c)

- Does the text take a personal stance (*I, we*), address the audience directly (*you*), or talk about the subject without explicitly referring to the writer or the reader?

- Does the genre use technical terms (jargon)? If so, how common are they? Does the genre use slang or other common conversational expressions?

- How many sources are used in the text? How are they introduced? Are sources mentioned in the text, cited in parentheses, or both? Which documentation style — such as MLA or APA — is followed (Chapters 32–35)?

- What medium is typically used for this genre? Are visual images or audio commonly used? If so, for what purposes?
- Who reads this genre, and why? Does the genre usually aim to inform, to persuade, to entertain, or to serve some other purpose?
- How are the characteristics of the text similar to or different from similar genres that you have encountered elsewhere?
- How much latitude do you have in ignoring or stretching some of the boundaries of the genre?

## ☐ Preparing to work in a genre

Think carefully about what you'll need to do to write successfully in this genre. Plan ahead to allow the amount of time necessary for composing your text, and make sure that you understand limitations — such as delivery time (for a presentation) or word count — for the length of the final product. Consider the media you will need to use, and make sure you have access to any technology required — and any training necessary to use it well. If the genre will require you to conduct interviews, seek permissions, or otherwise contact or collaborate with other people, allow time to find appropriate people and work with them effectively. Do you need to make any other preparations to create a text that fulfills the demands of the genre?

## ☐ Choosing multimodal genres and media for academic work

Much college writing is still done on paper in traditional genres, but this is changing. You may be asked, or may be able to choose, to create multimodal writing using audio, video, images, and words as well as written-word projects. When you are able to make decisions about media for a project, make sure that your choices are appropriate for your topic, purpose, audience, and genre. You may start off planning to write a traditional print-based academic essay and then discover as you proceed that a different genre or medium may offer more effective ways to communicate your point. One student, Will Rogers, who had been assigned to write an essay about something on campus that most students and faculty took for granted, focused on a giant crane being used in the construction of a new building complex. His research involved finding out all he could about the crane. When he interviewed the crane's operator, he got hooked: the operator was eighteen and had left his first year in college to take this job. The student found the operator's story so compelling that he decided that it would work better — and be more powerful — as a video. That way, viewers could actually see the crane operator and hear his voice as he described the decisions he had made. The result: a three-minute documentary called "Crane Man" for which the student did all the writing, filming, and editing.

### ☐ Translating work from one genre or medium to another

You may be asked to create a work in one genre or medium, such as a print-based research project, and translate it to another type of writing, such as a multimedia presentation, podcast, or scrapbook. Such translations may not be as straightforward as they seem. Just as filmmakers may omit content, streamline plot, and conflate characters when they create a movie version of a book, developing a solid thesis and supporting it effectively may require different strategies if you are turning a paper-based work into a video, a PowerPoint presentation, or some digital form.

Go to **macmillanhighered.com/smh** and click on **17. Presentations > Student Writing** to see an essay converted into a multimedia presentation.

## 2g Considering language and style

Although most of your college writing will be completed in standard academic English, some of it may demand that you use specialized occupational or professional varieties of English — those characteristic of medicine, say, or computer science or law or music. Similarly, you may wish to use regional, communal, or other varieties of English to connect with certain audiences or to catch the sound of someone's spoken words. You may even need to use words from a language other than English — in quoting someone, perhaps, or in using certain technical terms. In considering your use of language, think about what languages and varieties of English will be most appropriate for reaching your audience and accomplishing your purposes (see Chapter 29).

You will also want to think carefully about style: should you be casual and breezy, somewhat informal, formal, or extremely formal? The style you choose will call for certain kinds of sentence structures, organizational patterns, and word choices. And your style will be important in creating the tone you want, one that is appropriate to your assignment, audience, topic, purpose, and genre.

### Style in visual and audio elements

Remember that visual and audio elements can influence the tone of your writing as much as the words you choose. Such elements create associations in viewers' minds: one reader may react much more positively than another to a rap or heavy metal soundtrack, for example — and a presentation with a heavy metal accompaniment will make a far different impression than the same presentation with an easy-listening soundtrack. Writers can influence the way their work is perceived by carefully analyzing their audience and choosing audio and visual elements that set a mood appropriate to the point they want to make.

**BRINGING IN OTHER LANGUAGES**

If you are familiar with languages other than English, you may want or need to include words, phrases, or whole passages in another language. When you do so, consider whether your readers will understand that language and whether you need to provide a translation, as in this example from John (Fire) Lame Deer's "Talking to the Owls and Butterflies":

> Listen to the air. You can hear it, feel it, smell it, taste it.
> *Woniya waken* — the holy air — which renews all by its breath.
> *Woniya, woniya waken* — spirit, life, breath, renewal — it means all that.

In this instance, translation is necessary because the phrase that Lame Deer is discussing has multiple meanings in English. (See 29e for more on bringing in other languages.)

 **EXERCISE 2.5**

Consider a writing assignment you are currently working on. What is its genre? What medium or media does it use? How would you describe the style and tone? Finally, what visuals are you going to include and how well do they work to create the appropriate style and tone?

▼ ▼ ▼ ▼ ▼ ▼ ▼ ▼ ▼ ▼ ▼ ▼ ▼ ▼ ▼ ▼ ▼ ▼ ▼ ▼ ▼ ▼ ▼

## THINKING CRITICALLY ABOUT RHETORICAL SITUATIONS

### Reading with an eye for purpose, audience, and context

Advertisements provide good examples of writing that is tailored carefully for specific audiences. Find two ads for the same product in contexts that suggest that the ads aim to appeal to different audiences—for example, men and women. What differences do you see in the messages and photography? What conclusions can you draw about ways of appealing to specific audiences?

### Thinking about your own attention to purpose, audience, and context

Analyze a text you have written or are working on right now for an academic course.

- Can you state its purpose(s) clearly and succinctly? If not, what can you do to clarify its purpose(s)?
- What other purposes for this piece of writing can you imagine? How would fulfilling some other purpose change the writing?
- Can you tell from reading the piece who the intended audience is? If so, what in your text clearly relates to that audience? If not, what can you add that will strengthen your appeal to this audience?

- What other audiences can you imagine? How would the writing change if you were to address a different audience? How would it change if you were writing to a largely unknown audience, such as people on the Web?

- What changes would you have to make to create the work in a different genre or medium?

- Does your writing follow the conventions of standard academic English — and if not, should you revise it so that it will? Note your conclusions about purpose and audience in your own writing.

# CHAPTER 3

# Exploring, Planning, and Drafting

**P**ERHAPS, LIKE SOME WRITERS, you just plunge right into your work, thinking about and developing ideas as you go along. Or perhaps you find that you can work more effectively by producing detailed blueprints or storyboards before you ever begin drafting. You may even draw pictures to help you find something new and compelling to say. If you haven't found an effective way to get started, you may want to try out different methods.

> **CONNECT:** What kind of thesis will your audience want or need to see? **3c, 10d–h**
>
> **CREATE:** Draft a thesis for a piece of writing that you are doing either for school or for fun.
>
> **REFLECT:** Go to **macmillanhighered.com/smh**, and respond to **3. Exploring, Planning, Drafting > Exercise > Storyboards on working thesis**.

## 3a  Exploring a topic

The point is so simple that it's easy to forget: you write best about topics you know well. One of the most important parts of the entire writing process, therefore, is choosing a topic that will engage your strengths and your interests, surveying what you know about it, and determining what you need to find out.

### ☐  Brainstorming

Used widely in business and industry, brainstorming involves tossing out your ideas — either orally or in writing — to discover new ways to approach a topic. You can brainstorm with others or by yourself.

1. Within five or ten minutes, list every word or phrase that comes to mind about the topic. Jot down key words and phrases, not sentences. No one has

CONSIDERING DISABILITIES | **FREESPEAKING**

If you are better at talking out than writing out your ideas, try freespeaking. Begin by speaking into a recording device or into a computer with voice-recognition software, and just keep talking about your topic for at least seven to ten minutes. Say whatever comes to your mind, and don't stop talking. You can then listen to or read the results of your freespeaking and look for an idea to pursue at greater length.

to understand the list but you. Don't worry about whether or not something will be useful — just list as much as you can in this brief span of time.

2. If little occurs to you, try calling out or writing down thoughts about the opposite side of your topic. If you are trying, for instance, to think of reasons to raise tuition and are coming up blank, try concentrating on reasons to reduce tuition. Once you start generating ideas in one direction, you'll find that you can usually move back to the other side fairly easily.

3. When the time is up, stop and read over the lists you've made. If anything else comes to mind, add it to the list. Then reread the list. Look for patterns of interesting ideas or for one central idea.

### Emily Lesk's brainstorming

Emily Lesk, the student whose work appears in Chapters 2–4, did some brainstorming with her classmates on the general topic the class was working on: an aspect of American identity affected by one or more media. Here are some of the notes Emily made during the brainstorming session:

- "American identity" — Don't Americans have more than one identity?
- Picking a kind of media could be hard. I like clever ads. Maybe advertising and its influence on us?
- Wartime advertising; recruiting ads that promote patriotic themes.
- Look at huge American companies like Walmart and McDonald's and how their ads affect the way we view ourselves. Not sure what direction to take. . . .

☐ **Freewriting and looping**

Freewriting is a method of exploring a topic by writing about it for a period of time *without stopping*.

1. Write for ten minutes or so. Think about your topic, and let your mind wander freely. Write down everything that occurs to you — in complete

sentences as much as possible — but don't worry about spelling or grammar. If you get stuck, write anything — just don't stop.

2. When the time is up, look at what you have written. Much of this material will be unusable, but you may still discover some important insights and ideas.

If you like, you can continue the process by looping: find the central or most intriguing thought from your freewriting, and summarize it in a single sentence. Freewrite for five more minutes on the summary sentence, and then find and summarize the central thought from the second "loop." Keep this process going until you discover a clear angle or something about the topic that you can pursue.

### Emily Lesk's freewriting

Here is a portion of the freewriting Emily Lesk did to focus her ideas after the brainstorming session:

> Media and effect on American identity. What media do I want to write about? That would make a big difference — television, radio, Internet — they're all different ways of appealing to Americans. TV shows that say something about American identity? What about magazine or TV advertising? Advertising tells us a lot about what it means to be American. Think about what advertising tells us about American identity. What ads make me think "American"? And why?

### □ Clustering

Clustering is a way of generating ideas using a visual scheme or chart. It is especially helpful for understanding the relationships among the parts of a broad topic and for developing subtopics. You may have a software program for clustering. If not, follow these steps:

1. Write your topic in the middle of a piece of paper, and circle it.

2. In a ring around the topic circle, write what you see as the main parts of the topic. Circle each part, and draw a line from it to the topic.

3. Think of more ideas, examples, facts, or other details relating to each main part. Write each of these near the appropriate part, circle each one, and draw a line from it to the part.

4. Repeat this process with each new circle until you can't think of any more details. Some trails may lead to dead ends, but you will still have many useful connections among ideas.

## Emily Lesk's clustering

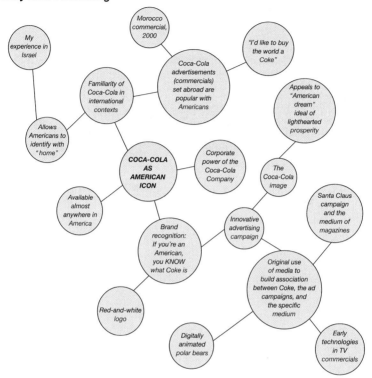

*Emily Lesk's clustering*

When Emily Lesk asked herself what things made her think "American," one of her first answers was "Coca-Cola." So later in her planning and exploring process, she decided to work on the topic of Coca-Cola advertising and American identity (3b and c). After finding a large Coca-Cola advertising archive, Emily used clustering to help focus her emerging ideas. Her clustering appears here. (Remember that you may want to explore aspects of your ideas more than once — and exploring may be helpful at any stage as you plan and draft a piece of writing.)

□ **Drawing or making word pictures**

If you're someone who prefers visual thinking, you might either create a drawing about the topic or use figurative language — such as similes and metaphors — to describe what the topic resembles. Working with pictures or verbal imagery can sometimes also help illuminate the topic or uncover some of your unconscious ideas or preconceptions about it.

1. If you like to draw, try sketching your topic. What images do you come up with? What details of the drawing attract you most? What would you most like to expand on? A student planning to write an essay on her college experience began by thinking with pencils and pen in hand. Soon she found that she had drawn a vending machine several times, with different products and different ways of inserting money to extract them (one of her drawings appears here). Her sketches led her to think about what it might mean to see an education as a product.

Even abstract doodling can lead you to important insights about the topic and to focus your topic productively.

2. Look for figurative language — metaphors and similes — that your topic resembles. Try jotting down three or four possibilities, beginning with "My subject is _____" or "My subject is like _____." A student working on the subject of genetically modified crops came up with this simile: "Genetically modified foods are like empty calories: they do more harm than good." This exercise made one thing clear to this student writer: she already had a very strong bias that she would need to watch out for while developing her topic.

Play around a bit with your topic. Ask, for instance, "If my topic were a food (or a song or a movie or a video game), what would it be, and why?" Or write a Facebook status update about your topic, or tweet a friend or an interested group saying — within 140 characters — why this topic appeals to you. Such exercises can get you out of the rut of everyday thinking and help you see your topic in a new light.

## □ Looking at images and videos

Searching images or browsing videos may spark topic ideas or inspire questions that you want to explore. If you plan to create a highly visual project — a video essay or slide presentation, for instance — you will probably need to decide what you want to show your audience before you plan the words that will accompany the images.

## ☐ Keeping a reflective journal or private blog

Writers often get their best ideas by jotting down or recording thoughts that come to them randomly. You can write in a notebook, record audio notes on a phone, store pictures and video files on a private blog — some writers even keep a marker and writing board on the shower wall so that they can write down the ideas that come to them while bathing! As you begin thinking about your assignment, taking time to record what you know about your topic and what still puzzles you may lead you to a breakthrough or help you articulate your main idea.

## ☐ Asking questions

Another basic strategy for exploring a topic and generating ideas is simply to ask and answer questions. Here are several widely used sets of questions to get you started, either on your own or with one or two others.

### Questions to describe a topic

Originally developed by Aristotle, the following questions can help you explore a topic by carefully and systematically describing it:

- **What is it?** What are its characteristics, dimensions, features, and parts? What do your senses tell you about it?
- **What caused it?** What changes occurred to create your topic? How is it changing? How will it change?
- **What is it like or unlike?** What features differentiate your topic from others? What analogies can you make about your topic?
- **What larger system is the topic a part of?** How does your topic relate to this system?
- **What do people say about it?** What reactions does your topic arouse? What about the topic causes those reactions?

### Questions to explain a topic

The well-known questions *who, what, when, where, why,* and *how,* widely used by news reporters, are especially helpful for explaining a topic.

- **Who** is doing it?
- **What** is at issue?
- **When** does it take place?
- **Where** is it taking place?
- **Why** does it occur?
- **How** is it done?

**MULTI-LINGUAL**   **USING YOUR BEST LANGUAGE TO EXPLORE IDEAS**

For generating and exploring ideas — the work of much brainstorming, freewriting, looping, clustering, and questioning — consider using your best language; it may help you come up with good ideas quickly and spontaneously. Later in the process of writing, you can choose the best of these ideas and begin working with them in English.

*Questions to persuade*

When your purpose is to persuade or convince, the following questions, developed by philosopher Stephen Toulmin, can help you think analytically about your topic (8e and 9j):

- What **claim** are you making about your topic?
- What **good reasons** support your claim?
- What valid **underlying assumptions** support the reasons for your claim?
- What **backup evidence** can you find for your claim?
- What **refutations** of your claim should you anticipate?
- In what ways should you **qualify** your claim?

☐ **Consulting sources**

At the library and on the Internet, browse for a topic you want to learn more about. If you have a short list of ideas, follow links from one interesting article to another to see what you can find, or do a quick check of reference works to get overviews of the topics. You can begin with a general encyclopedia or a specialized reference work that focuses on a specific area, such as music or psychology (11b). You can also use Wikipedia as a starting point: take a look at entries that relate to your topic, especially noting the sources they list. While you should not rely on Wikipedia alone, it is a highly accessible way to begin your research.

☐ **Collaborating**

As you explore your topic, remember that you can gain valuable insights from others. Many writers say that they get their best ideas in conversation with other people. If you talk with friends or roommates about your topic, at the very least you will hear yourself describe the topic and your interest in it; this practice will almost certainly sharpen your understanding of what you are doing. You can also seek out Facebook groups, Web forums, or other networking sites as places to share your thinking on a topic and find inspiration.

# 3b Narrowing a topic

After exploring ideas, you may have found a topic that interests you and would also be interesting to your audience. The topic, however, may be too large to be manageable. If this is the case, narrow your topic to focus on a more work-able idea. You might consider your personal connections to the topic and why it interests you, or think about the most controversial or intriguing aspects of the topic. (For help crafting a thesis from your narrowed topic, see 3c.)

### Emily Lesk's work on narrowing her topic

Emily Lesk planned to discuss how advertising affects American identity, but she knew that her topic was far too broad. She began to think about possible types of advertising and then about products that are pitched as particularly "American" in their advertising. When she got stuck, she posted a Facebook status update asking her friends to "name products that seem super-American." She quickly got seventeen responses with answers ranging from Hummer and Winchester rifles to "soft toilet paper," Spam, Wheaties, and maple syrup. One friend identified Coca-Cola and Pepsi-Cola, two products that Emily associated with many memorable and well-documented advertising campaigns.

### EXERCISE 3.1

Choose a topic that interests you, and explore it by using two of the strategies described in 3a. When you have generated some material, you might try comparing your results with those of other members of the class to see how effective or helpful each strategy was. If you have trouble choosing a topic, use one of the preliminary working theses in Exercise 3.2.

# 3c Drafting a working thesis

Academic and professional writing in the United States often contains an ex-plicit thesis statement. The thesis functions as a promise to readers, letting them know what the writer will discuss. Your readers may (or may not) expect you to craft the thesis as a single sentence near the beginning of the text. If you want to suggest a thesis implicitly rather than stating one explicitly, if you plan to con-vey your main argument somewhere other than in your introduction, or if you prefer to make your thesis longer than a single sentence, consider whether the rhetorical situation allows such flexibility. For an academic project, also consult with your instructor about how to meet expectations.

Whether you plan to use an implicit or explicit thesis statement in your text, you should establish a tentative working thesis early in your writing process.

The word *working* is important here because your thesis may well change as you write — your final thesis may be very different from the working thesis you begin with. Even so, a working thesis focuses your thinking and research, and helps keep you on track.

A working thesis should have two parts: a topic, which indicates the subject matter the writing is about, and a comment, which makes an important point about the topic.

> ● In the graphic novel *Fun Home*, illustrations and words combine to make meanings that are more subtle than either words alone or images alone could convey.

A successful working thesis has three characteristics:

1. It is potentially *interesting* to the intended audience.
2. It is as *specific* as possible.
3. It limits the topic enough to make it *manageable*.

You can evaluate a working thesis by checking it against each of these characteristics, as in the following examples:

> ● **Graphic novels combine words and images.**
>
> INTERESTING?    The topic of graphic novels could be interesting, but this draft of a working thesis has no real comment attached to it — instead, it states a bare fact, and the only place to go from here is to more bare facts.

> ● **In graphic novels, words and images convey interesting meanings.**
>
> SPECIFIC?    This thesis is not specific. What are "interesting meanings," exactly? How are they conveyed?

> ● **Graphic novels have evolved in recent decades to become an important literary genre.**
>
> MANAGEABLE?    This thesis would not be manageable for a short-term project because it would require research on several decades of history and on hundreds of texts from all over the world.

### Emily Lesk's working thesis

Emily Lesk wrote this preliminary thesis: "Coca-Cola and Pepsi-Cola have shaped our national identity." When she analyzed this thesis, she concluded

## STATING A THESIS EXPLICITLY

In some cultures, stating the main point explicitly may be considered rude or inelegant. In U.S. academic and business practices, however, readers often expect the writer to make key points and positions explicit. Unless your main point is highly controversial or hard for the reader to accept (such as a rejection letter), state your main point early — before presenting the supporting details.

that it was indeed interesting; however, she decided that the two brands were not trying to do exactly the same thing, so her thesis was probably not specific enough. In addition, both Coke and Pepsi had existed for over a century, and she realized that just investigating the advertising for the two brands would probably take more time than she had available — so the thesis was probably not manageable. After talking with her instructor, Emily decided to focus on a single advertising icon, the world-famous Coca-Cola logo. Her revised working thesis became "Coca-Cola is a cultural icon that shapes American identity."

For Emily Lesk's first draft, see 3g. For her final draft, see 4l.

### EXERCISE 3.2

Choose one of the following preliminary working theses, and after specifying an audience, evaluate the thesis in terms of its interest, specificity, and manageability. Revise the working thesis as necessary to meet these criteria.

1. The benefits of standardized testing are questionable.
2. Vaccinations are dangerous.
3. Too many American parents try to micromanage their children's college education.
4. Many people are afraid to fly in a plane, although riding in a car is statistically more dangerous.
5. An educated public is the key to a successful democracy.

### EXERCISE 3.3

Write a preliminary working thesis for your chosen topic. Evaluate the thesis in terms of its interest, specificity, and manageability. Revise it as necessary to create a satisfactory working thesis.

# 3d Gathering information

Writing often calls for research. Your curiosity may be triggered by a found object or image that you want to learn more about. An assignment may specify that you conduct research on your topic and cite your sources. Even if you're writing about a topic on which you're an expert, you may find that you don't know enough about some aspect of the topic to write about it effectively without doing research.

You may need to do research at various stages of the writing process — early on, to help you understand or define your topic, and later on, to find additional examples and illustrations to support your thesis. Once you have developed a working thesis, consider what additional information, opinions, visuals, and media you might need.

Basically, you can do three kinds of research to support your thesis: library research, which includes books, periodicals, and databases (and perhaps archives of other kinds of sources, such as music, films, posters, photographs, and so on); online research, which gives you access to texts, visuals, media, and people on the Internet; and field research, which includes personal observation, interviews, surveys, and other means of gathering information directly. (For more information on conducting research, see Chapter 11.)

# 3e Organizing verbal and visual information

While you're finding information on your topic, think about how you will group or organize that information to make it accessible and persuasive to readers. At the simplest level, writers most often group information in their writing projects according to four principles — space, time, logic, and association.

## ☐ Organizing spatially

Spatial organization of texts allows the reader to "walk through," beginning at one point and moving around in an organized manner — say, from near to far, left to right, or top to bottom. It can be especially useful when you want the audience to understand the layout of a structure or the placement of elements and people in a scene: texts such as a museum visitors' audio guide, a written-word description of a historic battlefield, or a video tour of a new apartment might all call for spatial organization. Remember that maps, diagrams, and other graphics may help readers visualize your descriptions more effectively.

## ☐ Organizing chronologically (by time)

Organization can also indicate *when* events occur, usually chronologically from first to last. Chronological organization is the basic method used in cookbooks, lab reports, instruction manuals, and many stories and narrative films. You may find it useful to organize information by describing or showing the sequence of events or the steps in a process.

## ☐ Organizing logically

Organizing according to logic means relating pieces of information in ways that make sense. Following is an overview of some of the most commonly used logical patterns: *illustration, definition, division and classification, comparison and contrast, cause and effect, problem and solution, analogy,* and *narration.* For examples of paragraphs organized according to these logical patterns, see 5d.

### Illustration

You will often gather examples to illustrate a point. If you write an essay discussing how one novelist influenced another, you might cite examples from the second writer's books that echo themes or characters from the first writer's works. For a pamphlet appealing for donations to the Red Cross, you might use photographs showing situations in which donations helped people in trouble, along with appropriate descriptions. For maximum effect, you may want to arrange examples in order of increasing importance unless your genre calls for an attention-grabbing initial illustration.

### Definition

Often a topic can be developed by definition — by saying what something is (or is not) and perhaps by identifying the characteristics that distinguish it from things that are similar or in the same general category. If you write about poverty in your community, for example, you would have to define very carefully what level of income, assets, or other measure defines a person, family, or household as "poor." In an essay about Pentecostalism, you might explain what characteristics separate Pentecostalism from related religious movements.

### Division and classification

Division means breaking a single topic into separate parts; classification means grouping many separate items of information about a topic according to their similarities. An essay about military recruiting policies might divide the military into different branches — army, navy, air force, and so on — and examine how each recruits volunteers. For a project on women's roles in the eighteenth century, you could organize your notes by classification: information related to women's education, occupations, legal status, and so on.

### Comparison and contrast

Comparison focuses on the similarities between two things, whereas contrast highlights their differences, but the two are often used together. If you were asked to analyze two case studies in an advertising text (one on Budweiser ads and the other on ads for the latest iPhone), you might well organize the response by presenting all the information on Budweiser advertising in one section and all on iPhone ads in another (block comparison) or by alternating between Budweiser and iPhone ads as you look at particular characteristics of each (alternating comparison).

### Cause and effect

Cause-effect analysis may deal with causes, effects, or both. If you examine why something happens or happened, you are investigating causes. If you explain what has occurred or is likely to occur from a set of conditions, you are discussing effects. An environmental-impact study of the probable consequences of building a proposed dam, for instance, would focus on effects. On the other hand, a video essay on the breakdown of authority in inner-city schools might begin with the effects of the breakdown and trace them back to their causes.

### Problem and solution

Moving from a problem to a solution is a natural way to organize certain kinds of information. For example, a student studying motorcycle parking on campus decided to organize his writing in just this way: he identified a problem (the need for more parking) and then offered two possible solutions, along with visuals to help readers imagine the solutions (his outline appears on p. 55). Many assignments in engineering, business, and economics call for a similar organizational strategy.

### Analogy

An analogy establishes connections between two things or ideas. Analogies are particularly helpful in explaining something new in terms of something very familiar. Likening the human genome to a map, for example, helps explain the complicated concept of the genome to those unfamiliar with it.

### Narration

Narration involves telling a story of some kind. You might, for example, tell the story of how deer ravaged your mother's garden as a way of showing why you support population control measures for wildlife. Narrating calls on the writer to set the story in a context readers can understand, providing any necessary background and descriptive details as well as chronological markers and transitions (*later that day, the following morning,* and so on) to guide readers through the story.

## ☐ Organizing by association

Some writers organize information through a series of associations that grow directly out of their own experiences and memories. In doing so, they may rely on a sensory memory, such as an aroma, a sound, or a scene. Thus, associational organization is common in personal narrative, where the writer follows a chain of associations to render an experience vividly for readers, as in this description:

> Flying from San Francisco to Atlanta, I looked down to see the gentle roll of the Smoky Mountains begin to appear. Almost at once, I was transported back to my granny's porch, sitting next to her drinking iced tea and eating peaches. Those fresh-picked peaches were delicious — ripened on the tree, skinned, and eaten with no regard for the sticky juice trickling everywhere. And on special occasions, we'd make ice cream, and Granny would empty a bowl brimming with chopped peaches into the creamy dish. Now — that was the life!

 **QUICK HELP**

### Organizing visuals and media in academic writing

- Use video and still images to capture your readers' attention and interest in a vivid way, to emphasize a point you make in words, to present information that is difficult to convey in words, or to communicate with audiences with different language skills.
- Consider whether you want to use images alone to convey your message, or whether words are also needed to help readers understand.
- For presentations, consider what your audience should look at as they listen to you. Make sure that the visuals enhance rather than compete with what you say. **(Chapter 17)**
- If you are using visuals and words together, consider both the way each image or video works on its own and the way it works in combination with the words you use.
- If you are using visuals to illustrate a written-word text, place each visual as near as possible to the words it illustrates. Introduce each visual clearly (*As the map to the right depicts . . .* ). Comment on the significance or effect of the visual (*Figure 1 corroborates the firefighters' statements . . .* ). Label each visual appropriately, and cite the source. **(Chapters 32–35)**

## ☐ Combining organizational patterns

In much of your writing, you will want to use two or more principles of organization. You might, for example, combine several passages of narration with vivid examples to make a striking comparison, as one student did in an essay about the dramatic differences between her life in her Zuñi community and her life as a teacher in Seattle. In addition, you may want to include not only visuals but sound and other multimedia effects as well.

**ORGANIZING INFORMATION**

You may know ways of organizing information that differ markedly from those discussed in this section. A Navajo teacher notes, for example, that explicit linear organization, through chronology or other strictly logical patterns, doesn't ever sound quite right to her. As she puts it, "In traditional Navajo, it's considered rude to get right to the point. Polite conversation or writing between two engaged people always takes a while to get to the point." Although effective organization depends largely on the reader's expectations, it may sometimes make sense to deviate from those expectations. If you choose to organize your writing differently from what your teacher or classmates might expect, consider explaining the reason for your choice — for example, in a cover letter or a footnote.

### Emily Lesk's organizational patterns

Emily Lesk begins the final draft of her essay (4l) with what she calls a "confession": *I don't drink Coke.* She follows this opening with an anecdote about a trip to Israel during which she nevertheless bought a T-shirt featuring the Coca-Cola logo. She goes on to explore what lies behind this purchase, relating it to the masterful advertising campaigns of the Coca-Cola Company and illustrating the way that the company's advertising "sells" a certain kind of American identity along with its products. She closes her draft by reflecting on the implications of this relationship between corporate advertising and national identity. Thus her essay, which begins with a personal experience, combines the patterns of narrative with cause-effect and comparison.

 **EXERCISE 3.4**

Identify the most effective means of organizing information for a project you are currently working on. Write a brief paragraph explaining why you chose this particular method (or these methods) of organization.

## 3f Planning

At this point, you will find it helpful to write out an organizational plan, outline, or storyboard. To do so, simply begin with your thesis; review your exploratory notes, research materials, and visual or multimedia sources; and then list all the examples and other good reasons you have to support the thesis. (For information on paragraph-level organization, see Chapter 5.)

## ☐ Creating an informal plan

One informal way to organize your ideas is to figure out what belongs in your introduction, body paragraphs, and conclusion. A student who was writing about solutions to a problem used the following plan:

**WORKING THESIS**

▶ **Increased motorcycle use demands the reorganization of campus parking lots.**

**INTRODUCTION**

give background and overview (motorcycle use up dramatically), and include photograph of overcrowded lot

state purpose — to fulfill promise of thesis by offering solutions

**BODY**

describe current situation (tell of my research at area parking lots)

describe problem in detail (report on statistics; cars vs. cycles), and graph my findings

present two possible solutions (enlarge lots or reallocate space)

**CONCLUSION**

recommend against first solution because of cost and space

recommend second solution, and summarize advantages

## ☐ Writing a formal outline

Even if you have created an informal written plan before drafting, you may wish (or be required) to prepare a more formal outline, which can help you see exactly how the parts of your writing will fit together — how your ideas relate, where you need examples, and what the overall structure of your work will be. Even if your instructor doesn't ask you to make an outline or you prefer to use some other method of sketching out your plans, you may want to come back to an outline later: doing a retrospective outline — one you do after you've already drafted your project — is a great way to see whether you have any big logical gaps or whether parts of the essay are in the wrong place.

Most formal outlines follow a conventional format of numbered and lettered headings and subheadings, using roman numerals, capital letters, arabic numerals, and lowercase letters to show the levels of importance of the various ideas and their relationships. Each new level is indented to show its subordination to the preceding level.

Thesis statement
I. First main idea
   A. First subordinate idea
      1. First supporting detail or idea
      2. Second supporting detail or idea
      3. Third supporting detail
   B. Second subordinate idea
      1. First supporting detail or idea
      2. Second supporting detail or idea
II. Second main idea
   A. (continues as above)

Note that each level contains at least two parts, so there is no A without a B, no 1 without a 2. Comparable items are placed on the same level — the level marked by capital letters, for instance, or arabic numerals. Keep in mind that headings should be stated in parallel form — either all sentences or all grammatically parallel topics.

Formal outlining requires a careful evaluation of your ideas, and this is precisely why it is valuable. (A full-sentence outline will reveal the relationships between ideas — or the lack of relationships — most clearly.) Remember, however, that an outline is at best a means to an end, not an end in itself. Whatever form your plan takes, you may want or need to change it along the way. (For an example of a formal outline, see 15e.)

## ☐ Making a storyboard

The technique of storyboarding — working out a narrative or argument in visual form — can be a good way to come up with an organizational plan, especially if you are developing a video essay, Web site, or other media project. You can find storyboard templates online to help you get started, or you can create your own storyboard by using note cards or sticky notes. Even if you're writing a more traditional word-based college essay, however, you may find storyboarding helpful; take advantage of different colors to keep track of threads of argument, subtopics, and so on. Flexibility is a strong feature of storyboarding: you can move the cards and notes around, trying out different arrangements, until you find an organization that works well for your writing situation.

Here are some possible organizational patterns for a storyboard.

Use linear organization when you want readers to move in a particular order through your material. An online report might use the following linear organization:

**Linear organization**

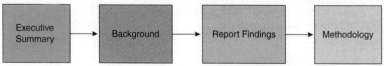

Executive Summary → Background → Report Findings → Methodology

A hierarchy puts the most important material first, with subtopics branching out from the main idea. A Web site on dog bite prevention might be arranged like this:

**Hierarchical organization**

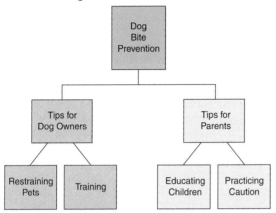

A spoke-and-hub organization allows readers to move from place to place in no particular order. Many portfolio Web sites are arranged this way:

**Spoke-and-hub organization**

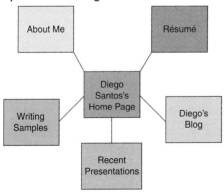

Whatever form your plan takes, you may want or need to change it along the way. Writing has a way of stimulating thought, and the process of drafting may generate new ideas. Or you may find that you need to reexamine some data or information or gather more material.

**EXERCISE 3.5**

Write out or sketch a plan for a piece of writing supporting your working thesis.

# 3g Drafting

In some sense, drafting begins the moment you start thinking about a topic. At some point, however, you attempt an actual written draft.

No matter how good your planning, investigating, and organizing have been, chances are you will need to return to these activities as you draft. This fact of life leads to the first principle of successful drafting: be flexible. If you see that your organizational plan is not working, do not hesitate to alter it. If some information or medium now seems irrelevant, leave it out, even if you went to great lengths to obtain it. Throughout the drafting process, you may need to refer to points you have already written about. You may learn that you need to do more research, that your whole thesis must be reshaped, or that your topic is still too broad and should be narrowed further.

## QUICK HELP

### Guidelines for drafting

- **Set up a computer folder or file for your essay.** Give the file a clear and relevant name, and save to it often.
- **Save and name your files to distinguish among drafts.** Since you will likely change your text over time, save a copy of each version. If you are sending a copy to classmates for review, give the file a new but related name. For example, for a first draft saved as *religion essay d1*, save a copy as *religion essay d2*. Then, when you receive responses, you can leave the copy of your first draft as is and make revisions on *religion essay d2*.
- **Track changes within a document file to try out new versions.** Most writing software allows you to track changes you make within a draft, seeing how new material would look and deciding later whether to keep or discard the changes. This function is useful when you are working on a piece of writing with another writer or when you aren't sure which version of your draft you like best.
- **Have all your information close at hand and arranged according to your organizational plan.** Stopping to search for a piece of information can break your concentration or distract you.
- **Keep track of any sources you plan to include.** Keep a working bibliography **(12c)**, and make notes in your draft of any information that comes from your research. If you find useful information online, you can cut and paste it into a document to ensure that you have the information exactly as you found it; however, highlight or save it in a different color so that you don't mistakenly borrow writing that is not your own. **(Chapters 13 and 14)**
- **Try to write in stretches of at least thirty minutes.** Writing can provide momentum, and once you get going, the task becomes easier.

▶

---

CONSIDERING DISABILITIES | **A TALKING DRAFT**

Using a word processor with voice-recognition software will allow you to speak your ideas, which will then appear onscreen. A "talking" draft of this kind can be a very good way to get your initial draft done, especially if you have difficulty with the physical act of writing. If voice-recognition software isn't available, try to find another student who will work with you to produce talking drafts: as one of you talks, the other types in what is being said. Your school's office of disability services should be able to provide scribes or notetakers as well.

## Guidelines for drafting, continued

- **Don't let small questions bog you down.** Just make a note of them in brackets—or in all caps—or make a tentative decision and move on.
- **Remember that first drafts aren't perfect.** Concentrate on getting all your ideas written down, and don't worry about anything else.
- **Stop writing at a place where you know exactly what will come next.** Doing so will help you start easily when you return to the draft.

### Emily Lesk's first draft

Here is Emily Lesk's first draft. She uses brackets and highlighting here to identify questions and sources she will need to cite.

STUDENT WRITING

### All-Powerful Coke

I don't drink Coke. Call me picky for disliking the soda's 1 saccharine aftertaste. Call me cheap for choosing a water fountain over a twelve-ounce aluminum can that costs a dollar from a vending machine but only pennies to produce. Even call me unpatriotic for rejecting the potable god that over the last century has come to represent all the enjoyment and ease to be found in our American way of life. But don't call me a hypocrite when I admit that I still identify with Coke and the Coca-Cola culture.

I have a favorite T-shirt that says "Drink Coca-Cola Classic" in Hebrew. It's 2 Israel's standard tourist fare, like little nested dolls in Russia or painted horses in Scandinavia, and before setting foot in the Promised Land three years ago, I knew where I could find one. The T-shirt shop in the central block of a Jerusalem shopping center did offer other shirt designs ("Maccabee Beer" was a favorite), but that Coca-Cola shirt was what drew in most of the dollar-carrying tourists. I waited almost

**macmillanhighered.com/smh**

▶ 3. Exploring, Planning, Drafting > Video > It's hard to delete things

3. Exploring, Planning, Drafting > Video > You just have to start

twenty minutes for mine, and I watched nearly everyone ahead of me say "the Coke shirt" (and "thanks" in Hebrew).

At the time, I never asked why I wanted the shirt. I do know, though, that the reason I wear it often, despite a hole in the right sleeve, has to do with its power as a conversation piece. Few people notice it without asking something like, "Does that say Coke?" I usually smile and nod. They mumble a compliment and we go our separate ways. But rarely does anyone want to know what language the world's most famous logo is written in. And why should they? Perhaps because Coca-Cola is a cultural icon that shapes American identity.  3

Throughout the company's history, marketing strategies have centered on putting Coca-Cola in scenes of the happy, carefree American life we never stop striving for. What 1950s teenage girl wouldn't long to see herself in the soda shop pictured in a Coca-Cola ad appearing in a 1958 issue of *Seventeen* magazine? A clean-cut, handsome man flirts with a pair of smiling girls as they laugh and drink Coca-Colas. And any girls who couldn't put themselves in that perfect, happy scene could at least buy a Coke for consolation. The malt shop — complete with a soda jerk in a white jacket and paper hat — is a theme that, even today, remains a symbol of Americana. [Use ad? Source is *'50s American Magazine Ads* edited by Ikuta.]  4

But while countless campaigns with this general strategy have together shaped the Coca-Cola image, presenting a product as key to a happy life represents a fairly typical approach to advertising everything from Fords to Tylenol. Coca-Cola's advertising is truly unique, however, for the original way the beverage giant has utilized specific advertising media — namely magazines and television — to drive home this message.  5

One of the earliest and best-known examples of this strategy is artist Haddon Sundblom's masterpiece of Santa Claus. In December 1931, Coca-Cola introduced an advertising campaign featuring Sundblom's depiction of a jolly, Coke-drinking Santa. [Cite Coca-Cola Web site.] [Look for a picture of this original Coke Santa.] But the success of Santa Claus goes far beyond Sundblom's magazine advertisements depicting a warm, happy grandfather figure delighting in an ice-cold Coke after a tiring night of delivering presents. The way in which Coca-Cola advertisers presented that inviting image represents Coca-Cola's brilliant manipulation of the medium itself. [Need to cite Pendergrast book here.]  6

In today's world of CNN, e-journals, and *Newsweek.com*, it is often easy to forget how pervasive a medium the magazine was prior to the advent of television. Until the late 1950s, American households of diverse backgrounds and geographic locations subscribed loyally to general-subject weeklies and monthlies such as *Life* and the *Saturday Evening Post*. These publications provided the primary source of  7 news, entertainment, and other cultural information to families nationwide. This large and constant group of subscribers enabled Coca-Cola to build a perennial Christmastime advertising campaign that used an extremely limited number of ads ["designs" better word?] [add source], which Americans soon came to look forward to and seek out each holiday season. The marketing strategy was not to capture consumers with a few color drawings, but rather to make them wait eagerly by the mailbox each December so that they could flip through the *Saturday Evening Post* to find the latest scene featuring Santa gulping a Coke. For this strategy to be successful, the advertisements had to be seen by many, but also be just hard enough to come by to be exciting. What better location for this than the December issue of an immensely popular magazine?

There is no denying that this strategy worked brilliantly, as this inviting image 8 of Santa Claus graduated from the pages of the *Saturday Evening Post* to become the central figure of the most celebrated and beloved season of the year. Travel to any strip mall in the United States during December (or even November — that's how much we love Christmas!) and you will no doubt run into Santa clones left and right, punched out of cardboard and sculpted in tinsel hung atop lampposts, all in Coca-Cola red and white. And while, in today's nonmagazine world, Coca-Cola must celebrate Christmas with specially designed Diet Coke cans and television commercials, the Coca-Cola Santa Claus will forever epitomize the former power of magazine advertising in America. [Getting off track here?]

In other words, Coca-Cola has hammered itself into our perceptions — both 9 conscious and subconscious — of an American cultural identity by equating itself with media that define American culture. When the omnipresent general magazine that marked the earlier part of the century fell by the wayside under television's power, Coke was there from the beginning. In its 1996 recap of the previous fifty years in industry history, the publication *Beverage Industry* [need to cite] cites Coca-Cola as a frontrunner in the very first form of television advertising: sponsorship of entire programs such as, in the case of Coke, *The Bob Dixon Show* and *The Adventures of Kit Carson*. Just as today we associate sports stadiums with their corporate sponsors, viewers of early television programs will forever equate them with Coke.

When networks switched from offering sponsorships to selling exclusive commercial 10 time in short increments (a format modeled after magazine advertisements), Coca-Cola strove to distinguish itself again, this time by producing new formats and technologies for these commercials. [This sentence is way too long!] Early attempts at this — such as choppy "stop motion" animation, where photographs of objects such as Coke bottles move without the intervention of actors — attracted much attention, according to the Library of Congress Motion Picture Archives [need to cite]. Coca-Cola also experimented with color advertisements early enough that the excitement of color advertising technology drew additional attention to these commercials.

But the Coke advertising campaign that perhaps best illustrates the ability 11
of Coca-Cola advertisers to equate their product with a medium / technology
[reword!] did not appear until 1993. In the holiday Coke ad that year, completely
digitally animated polar bears rolled, swam, snuggled, slid on ice, and gurgled
about in a computerized North Pole and finished off the playful experience with
a swig of Coke. This campaign captured America's attention and held if for six
separate commercials, and not because or at least not just because the bears were
cute and cuddly. Their main draw was the groundbreaking technology used to
create them. In 1993, two years before the release of the first *Toy Story*, these
were some of the very first widely viewed digital films [cite Library of Congress
here]. With these bears, as with other campaigns, Coke didn't just utilize the
latest technology — Coke *introduced* the latest technology.

As a result of this brilliant advertising, a beverage which I do not even let 12
enter my mouth [reword!] is a significant part of my American cultural identity.
That's why I spent thirty Israeli shekels and twenty minutes in a tourist trap
I would ordinarily avoid buying my Hebrew Coca-Cola shirt. That shirt — along
with the rest of the Coca-Cola collectibles industry — demonstrates the power of
[something about Coke connecting itself with the American ideal of a life of diversion
and lightheartedness]. Seeing the logo that embodies all of this halfway around
the world gave me an opportunity to affirm a part of my American identity.

The red-and-white logo's ability to appeal to Americans even in such a foreign 13
context speaks to Coke advertisers' success at creating this association. A 1999
American television commercial described by the Library of Congress archive [need
to cite] as highly successful is set in Kenya, with dialogue in a local dialect and
English subtitles. In it, two Kenyan boys taste their first Cokes and comment that
the experience is much like the way they imagine kissing a girl will be. This image
appeals to Americans because it enables us to use the symbol of Coca-Cola to make
ourselves comfortable even in the most unfamiliar situations. And if that can't
sell your product, nothing can.

(For the works-cited page that Emily Lesk submitted with her final paper, which
includes the sources indicated in her notes in this draft, see 4l.)

▼ ▼ ▼ ▼ ▼ ▼ ▼ ▼ ▼ ▼ ▼ ▼ ▼ ▼ ▼ ▼ ▼ ▼ ▼ ▼ ▼ ▼ ▼ ▼ ▼ ▼ ▼ ▼ ▼

## THINKING CRITICALLY ABOUT YOUR WRITING PROCESS

Using the following guidelines, reflect on the process you went through as you prepared for and wrote your draft. Make your answers an entry in your writing log if you
are keeping one.

1. How did you arrive at your specific topic?
2. When did you first begin to think about the assignment?

3. What kinds of exploring or planning did you do? What kinds of research did you need to do?

4. How long did it take to complete your draft (including the time spent gathering information)?

5. Where did you write your draft? Briefly describe the setting.

6. How did awareness of your audience help shape your draft?

7. What have you learned from your draft about your own rhetorical stance on your topic?

8. What did you learn about your ideas for this topic by exploring, planning, and talking with others about it?

9. What do you see as the major strengths of your draft? What is your favorite sentence, and why?

10. What do you see as the major weaknesses of your draft? What are you most worried about, and why?

11. What would you like to change about your process of exploring, planning, and drafting?

# CHAPTER 4

# Reviewing, Revising, Editing, and Reflecting

THE ANCIENT ROMAN POET HORACE advised aspiring writers to get distance from their work by putting it away for *nine years*. Although impractical, to say the least, Horace's advice holds a nugget of truth: putting your draft aside even for a short while will help clear your mind and give you more objectivity about your writing.

Make time to review and reflect on your work (by yourself or with others) and to revise, edit, and proofread. Reviewing calls for reading your draft with a critical eye and asking others to look over your work. Revising involves reworking your draft on the basis of the review, making sure that the draft is clear, effective, complete, and well organized. Editing involves fine-tuning, attending to all the details. Of course, you also need to format and proofread your writing carefully to make it completely ready for public presentation.

> **CONNECT:** What kind of advice from other people is most useful for your writing? **4c and d, 19i**
>
> **CREATE:** Make a checklist to guide a friend who is responding to your writing.
>
> **REFLECT:** Go to **macmillanhighered.com/smh**, and respond to **4. Reviewing > Video > Lessons from peer review**.

## 4a Rereading your draft

After giving yourself — and your draft — a rest, review the draft by rereading it carefully for meaning, recalling your purpose, reconsidering your rhetorical stance, considering your audience, and evaluating your organization and use of visuals.

### ☐ Reading for meaning

At this point, don't sweat the small stuff. Instead, concentrate on your message and on whether you have expressed it clearly. Note any places where the meaning seems unclear.

## ☐ Reflecting on purpose

Does your draft achieve its purpose? If you wrote for an assignment, make sure that you have produced what was asked for. If you set out to prove something, make sure you have succeeded. If you intended to propose a solution to a problem, make sure you have set forth a well-supported solution rather than just an analysis of the problem.

## ☐ Reflecting on rhetorical stance

Take time to look at your draft with one central question in mind: where are you coming from in this draft? That is, articulate the rhetorical stance you take, and ask yourself what factors or influences have led you to that position. (For more on rhetorical stance, see 2d.)

## ☐ Reflecting on audience

How appropriate is the text for your audience? Think carefully about your audience members' experiences and expectations. Will they be interested in and able to follow your discussion? Is the language formal or informal enough for these readers? Have you defined any terms they may not know? What objections might they raise? (For more on audience, see 2e.)

When Emily Lesk reread her draft (3g), she noticed that she sounded a bit like a know-it-all, especially in the opening of her essay. After reflection, she decided that her tone was inappropriate, perhaps because she was trying too hard to get her audience's attention, and that she needed to work on this problem in her revision.

**EXERCISE 4.1**

Take twenty to thirty minutes to look critically at a draft you have written recently. Reread it carefully, check to see how well the purpose is accomplished, and consider how appropriate the draft is for the audience. Then write a paragraph about how you would go about revising the draft.

**EXERCISE 4.2**

To prepare for a peer review, write a description of your purpose, rhetorical stance, and audience for your reviewer(s) to consider. For example, Emily Lesk might write, "I want to figure out why Coca-Cola seems so American and how the company achieves this effect. My audience is primarily college students like me, learning to analyze their own cultures. I want to sound knowledgeable, and I want this essay to be fun and interesting to read." This type of summary statement can help your reviewers keep your goals in mind as they give you feedback.

## ☐ Checking organization

Look through your draft, paying attention to the way one idea flows into another. Note particularly the first sentence of each new paragraph, and ask yourself how it relates to the paragraph that came before. If you can't immediately see the connection, you probably need to strengthen the transition (5f).

Another good way to check your organization is to number the paragraphs in the draft, and then read through each one, jotting down the main idea or topic. Do the main ideas clearly relate to the thesis and to each other? Can you identify any confusing leaps from point to point? Have you left out any important points? Does any part of your essay go off track?

## ☐ Reflecting on genre and media

You decided to write in a particular genre, so think again about why you made that choice. Is writing in this genre the best way to achieve your purpose and reach your audience? Does the draft fulfill the requirements of the genre? Would any content in your draft be more effective presented in another medium — for example, as a print handout instead of a PowerPoint slide? Should you consider "translating" your work into another medium (17a and b)? Do you need to take any additional steps to make your work as effective as it can be in this medium?

### Visuals and media

Look closely at the images, audio, and video you have chosen to use. How do they contribute to your draft? Make sure that all visuals and media files are labeled with captions and sources, and remember to refer to visuals and media and to comment on their significance to the rest of your text. Would any information in your draft work better in visual than in verbal form?

## 4b Reviewing peer writers' work

Whether you are part of a small peer-review group in your writing class or you are assigned a peer reviewer in a MOOC (massive open online course) with hundreds or even thousands enrolled, you can use reviewers to your advantage — and you should do your best to help peers when you review their work as well. (For help with peer review, see the Quick Help guidelines on pp. 69–70.)

## ◻ Understanding the role of the peer reviewer

The most helpful reviewers are interested in the topic and the writer's approach to it. They ask questions, make concrete suggestions, report on what is confusing and why, and offer encouragement. Good reviewers give writers a new way to see their drafts so that they can revise effectively. After reading an effective review, writers should feel confident about taking the next step in the writing process.

Peer review is difficult for two reasons. First, offering writers a way to imagine their next draft is just hard work. Unfortunately, there's no formula for giving good writing advice. But you can always do your best to offer your partner a careful, thoughtful response to the draft and a reasonable sketch of what the next version might contain. Second, peer review is challenging because your job as a peer reviewer is not to grade the draft or respond to it as an instructor would. As a peer reviewer, you will have a chance to think alongside writers whose writing you may consider much better or far worse than your own. Don't dwell on these comparisons. Instead, remember that a thesis is well supported by purposefully arranged details, not by punctuation or impressive vocabulary. Your goal is to read the writer's draft closely enough to hear what he or she is trying to say and to suggest a few strategies for saying it better.

Being a peer reviewer should improve your own writing as you see how other writers approach the same assignment. So make it a point to tell writers what you learned from their drafts; as you express what you learned, you'll be more likely to remember their strategies. Also, you will likely begin reading your own texts in a new way. Although all writers have blind spots when reading their own work, you will gain a better sense of where readers expect cues and elaboration.

 **UNDERSTANDING PEER REVIEWS**

If you are not used to giving or receiving criticisms directly, you may find it disturbing when some or most of your classmates take a questioning or even challenging stance toward your work. As long as the questions and suggestions are constructive, however, they are appropriate to peer-review collaboration. Your peers will expect you to join in the critical collaboration, too, so be sure to offer your questions, suggestions, and insights.

## ☐ Working with peer reviewers in an online course

If you are taking an online writing class or MOOC, you can still take advantage of peer reviews. In an online course, you may be assigned to a peer-review group and given guidelines to follow. But if you are not assigned to a peer-review group, organize one for yourself. Post a note to the class, asking those interested in forming a group to contact you. Then talk through the purpose of the group in a collaborative space (in your course management site, if you have one, or even via email): what is it you want each member to contribute? It's best to be explicit and straightforward when you're working with people you don't know and won't meet face to face. Then, as with any peer group, agree on what each of you will do (such as comment on specific aspects of a draft, identify confusing parts or passages, provide specific advice for improvement, and so on) and set a timeline. Give the group a test drive on your first drafts: you are looking for members who are as trustworthy, reliable, and smart as you are!

## ☐ Using tools for peer review

Remember that one of your main goals as a peer reviewer is to help the writer see his or her draft differently. You want to *show* the writer what does and doesn't work about particular aspects of the draft. Visually marking a draft can help the writer know at a glance what revisions the reviewer suggests. (Remember that visual mark-ups can be useful for drafts of all kinds of texts. If you are reviewing a slide presentation or video draft, for instance, you may be able to mark up a printout or transcript as part of your review.)

### Marking up a print draft

If you are reviewing a hard copy of a draft, write compliments in the left margin and critiques, questions, and suggestions in the right margin. As long as you explain what your symbols mean, you can also use circles, underlining, highlighting, or other visual annotations to point out patterns to the writer. If an idea is mentioned in several paragraphs, for example, you can circle those sentences and suggest that the writer use them to form a new paragraph.

### Marking up a digital draft

If the draft comes to you as a digital file, save the document in a folder under a name you will recognize. It's wise to include the writer's name, the assignment, the number of the draft, and your initials. For example, Ann G. Smith might name the file for the first draft of Javier Jabari's first essay *jabari essay1 d1 ags.doc.*

    You can use the TRACK CHANGES function of your word-processing program to add comments and suggestions and to revise the text of written-word documents. Insert a comment explaining each revision and suggesting how the writer can build on it in the next draft. (If you prefer, you can use footnotes for comments instead.)

For media drafts that are difficult to annotate visually, ask the writer about preferred ways to offer suggestions — audio annotations? written notes? comments on a posted file? face-to-face discussion? something else?

You should also consider using highlighting in written-word texts. If you explain to the writer what the colors mean and use only a few colors, highlighting can make a powerful visual statement about what needs to be revised. Here is an example of a color key for the writer:

| Color | Revision Suggestion |
|---|---|
| Yellow | Read this sentence aloud, and then revise for clarity. |
| Green | This material seems out of place. Reorganize? |
| Blue | This idea isn't clearly connected to your thesis. Cut? |

## ☐ Conducting a peer review

Whenever you respond to a piece of writing, think of the response you are giving — whether orally or in writing — as a letter to the writer of the draft. Your written response should usually have two parts: (1) a personal letter to the writer, and (2) visual markings or other annotations on the text.

Before you read the draft, ask the writer for any feedback instructions. Take the writer's requests seriously. If, for example, the writer asks you to look at specific aspects of his or her writing and to ignore others, be sure to respond to that request.

To begin your review, read straight through the project and think about the writer's specific instructions as well as the following general guidelines.

---

**QUICK HELP**

Guidelines for peer review

- **Overall thoughts.** What are the main strengths and weaknesses of the draft? What might be confusing to the audience? What is the single most important thing the writer says in the draft? What will the audience want to know more about?
- **Assignment.** Does the draft carry out the assignment?
- **Title and introduction.** Does the title tell the audience what the draft is about? How does it catch their interest? Does the opening make the audience want to continue reading? In what other ways might the draft begin? **(4h)**
- **Thesis and purpose.** Paraphrase the thesis as a promise: *In this project, the writer will. . . .* Does the draft fulfill that promise? Why, or why not? Does it carry out the writer's purposes? **(2d)**
- **Audience.** How does the draft interest and appeal to its intended audience? **(2e)**

▶

### Guidelines for peer review, continued

- **Rhetorical stance.** Where does the writer stand? What words or phrases indicate the stance? What influences have likely contributed to that stance? **(2d)**
- **Major points.** List the main points, and review them one by one. Do any points need to be explained more or less fully? Do any seem confusing or boring? Should any points be eliminated or added? How well is each major point supported? **(4f)**
- **Visuals and media.** Do the visuals, if any, add to the key points? Do your media files play properly, and do they serve their intended purpose? Are all images and media files clearly referred to in the draft? Are they appropriately identified? **(4a and j)**
- **Organization and flow.** Is the writing easy to follow? Are the ideas presented in an order that will make sense to the audience? **(3e)** Do effective transitions ease the flow between paragraphs and ideas? **(5f)**
- **Paragraphs or sections.** Which paragraphs or sections are clearest and most interesting? Which need further development, and how might they be improved? **(Chapter 5)**
- **Sentences.** Are any sentences particularly effective and well written? Are any sentences weak—confusing, awkward, or uninspired? Are the sentences varied in length and structure? Are the sentence openings varied? **(Chapter 52)**
- **Words.** Which words draw vivid pictures or provoke strong responses? Which words are weak, vague, or unclear? Do any words need to be defined? Are the verbs active and vivid? **(53b)** Are any words potentially offensive? **(Chapter 28)**
- **Tone.** What dominant impression does the draft create—serious, humorous, persuasive, something else? Where, specifically, does the writer's attitude come through most clearly? Is the tone appropriate to the topic and the audience? Is it consistent throughout? **(Chapter 30)**
- **Conclusion.** Does the draft conclude in a memorable way, or does it seem to end abruptly or trail off into vagueness? How else might it end? **(4h)**

## A summary of the draft

After reading the draft, begin by summarizing the main idea(s) of the piece of writing. You might begin by writing *I think the main argument is . . .* or *In this draft, you promise to. . . .* Then outline the main points that support the thesis (3e and f).

Once you prepare the outline, your most important work as a peer reviewer can begin. You need to think alongside the writer about how to support the thesis and arrange details most effectively for the audience. Ask yourself the following questions and make notes that you can include in the letter to the writer:

- If I heard this topic mentioned in another situation, what would I expect the conversation to include? Would any of those ideas strengthen this writing?

- If I had not read this draft, what order would I expect these ideas to follow?
- Are any ideas or connections missing?

### Your mark-up of the draft

Next, as you reread the draft, use the mark-up strategies discussed earlier to give the writer specific feedback. As you use these strategies, always think about how you would respond to the same mark-ups in your own draft. Avoid an overwhelming number of comments or changes, for example, and don't highlight too extensively. In addition, remember that your job in marking up the text is to point out the problems, not to solve them (though you should certainly offer suggestions).

Unlike in the personal letter, where you try to help the writer imagine the next draft, your comments, annotations, and other markings should respond to what is already written. Aim for a balance between compliments and constructive criticism. If you think the author has stated something well, comment on why you like it. If you have trouble understanding or following the writer's ideas, comment on what you think may be causing problems. The chart here provides several examples of ways to frame effective marginal comments.

| Compliments | Constructive Criticism |
|---|---|
| • I'd never thought of it that way. Really smart insight. | • Here I expected _____ instead of _____. |
| • Your strongest evidence is _____. | • I think you need more evidence to support your claim that _____. |
| • You got my attention here by _____. | • You might consider adding _____. |
| • This example is great because _____. | • What about _____? There are other perspectives on this topic. |
| • I like the way you use _____ to tie all these ideas together. | • I think you need to say this sooner. |
| • I like this sentence because _____. | • I had to read this sentence twice to get what you mean. Simplify it. |
| • I think this approach and your tone are perfect for the audience because _____. | • Your tone shifts here. Try to sound more _____. |

### A letter to the writer

Begin by addressing the writer by name (*Dear Javier*). Using your outline, identify the main points of the draft, and write your suggestions in the letter. You might use sentences like *I didn't understand _____. Could you explain it differently? I think _____ is your strongest point, and I recommend you move _____.* This portion of the letter will help the writer make the most significant changes to the argument and supporting evidence.

---

| ◆ MULTI-LINGUAL | **REVIEWING A DRAFT** |
| --- | --- |

Your knowledge of and experience with multiple languages or cultures may give you special insights that help you point out unclear or confusing ideas in your peers' work. Your peers may find questions or comments from your unique perspective helpful in expanding their ideas. Even if you are not used to speaking up in class, remember that you have a lot to offer!

---

After you have added all your mark-ups to the draft, conclude your letter by adding two or three brief paragraphs addressing the following points:

- **The strengths of the current draft.**  Refer to the outline you developed and your compliments.

- **Two or three things you think will significantly improve the draft's effectiveness.**  Refer to your constructive criticism.

- **Areas on which the writer asked you to focus** (if any).

Read over your comments once more, checking your tone and clarity. Close by signing your name. Save your response, and send it to the writer using the method recommended by your instructor.

## ▢  Basing responses on the stage of the draft

You may be asked to review your peers' work at any stage of the writing — after the first draft, during an intermediate stage, or when the paper is close to a final draft. Different stages in the writing process call for different strategies and areas of focus on the part of the peer reviewer.

### Early-stage drafts

Writers of early-stage drafts need direction and options, not editing that focuses on grammar or punctuation. Your goal as a peer reviewer of an early draft is to help the writer think of ways to expand on the ideas. Pose questions and offer examples that will help the writer think of new ways to approach the topic. Try to help the writer imagine what the final draft might be like.

Approach commenting on and marking up an early draft with three types of questions in mind:

- **Fit.**  How does this draft fit the assignment? In what areas might the writer struggle to meet the criteria? How does this draft fit the audience? What else does the writer need to remember about the audience's expectations and needs?

- **Potential.** What ideas in this draft are worth developing more? What other ideas or details could inform the argument? Are there other viewpoints on this topic that the writer should explore?
- **Order.** Considering only the parts that are worth keeping, what sequence do you recommend? What new sections do you think need to be added?

### Intermediate-stage drafts

Writers of intermediate-stage drafts need to know where their claims lack sufficient evidence, what ideas confuse readers, and how their approach misses its target audience. They also need to know which parts of their drafts are clear and well written.

Approach commenting on and marking up an intermediate draft with these types of questions in mind:

- **Topic sentences and transitions.** Topic sentences introduce the idea of a paragraph, and transitions move the writing smoothly from one paragraph or section or idea to the next (5b, e, and f). How well does the draft prepare readers for the next set of ideas by explaining how they relate to the overall claim? Look for ideas or details that don't seem to fit into the overall structure of the draft. Is the idea or detail out of place because it is not well integrated into this paragraph? If so, recommend a revision or a new transition. Is it out of place because it doesn't support the overall claim? If so, recommend deletion.
- **Supporting details.** Well-developed paragraphs and arguments depend on supporting details (5c and d). Does the writer include an appropriate number and variety of details? Could the paragraph be improved by adding another example, a definition, a comparison or contrast, a cause-effect relationship, an analogy, a solution to a problem, or a personal narrative?

### Late-stage drafts

Writers of late-stage drafts need help with first and last impressions, sentence construction, word choice, tone, and format. Their next step is proofreading (4l), and your job as a peer reviewer is to call attention to the sorts of problems writers need to solve before submitting their final work. Your comments and markings should identify the overall strengths of the draft as well as one or two weaknesses that the writer can reasonably improve in a short amount of time.

### Reviews of Emily Lesk's draft

On the following pages are the first paragraphs of Emily Lesk's draft, as reviewed by two students, Beatrice Kim and Nastassia Lopez. Beatrice and Nastassia reviewed the draft separately and combined their comments on the draft they returned to Emily. As this review shows, Nastassia and Bea agreed on some of the major

**MULTI-LINGUAL** | **ASKING AN EXPERIENCED WRITER TO REVIEW YOUR DRAFT**

One good way to make sure that your writing is easy to follow is to have someone else read it. You might find it especially helpful to ask someone who is experienced in the kind of writing you are working on to read over your draft and to point out any words or patterns that are unclear or ineffective.

problems — and good points — in Emily's draft. Their comments on the draft, however, revealed some different responses. You, too, will find that different readers do not always agree on what is effective or ineffective. In addition, you may find that you simply do not agree with their advice. In examining responses to your writing, you can often proceed efficiently by looking first for areas of agreement (*everyone was confused by this sentence — I'd better revise it*) or strong disagreement (*one person said my conclusion was "perfect," and someone else said it "didn't conclude" — better look carefully at that paragraph again*).

### All-Powerful Coke

I don't drink Coke. Call me picky for disliking the soda's saccharine aftertaste. Call me cheap for choosing a water fountain over a twelve-ounce aluminum can that costs a dollar from a vending machine but only pennies to produce. Even call me unpatriotic for rejecting the potable god that over the last century has come to represent all the enjoyment and ease to be found in our American way of life. But don't call me a hypocrite when I admit that I still identify with Coke and the Coca-Cola culture.

I have a favorite T-shirt that says "Drink Coca-Cola Classic" in Hebrew. It's Israel's standard tourist fare, like little nested dolls in Russia or painted horses in Scandinavia, and before setting foot in the Promised Land three years ago, I knew where I could find one. The T-shirt shop in the central block of a Jerusalem shopping center did offer other shirt designs ("Maccabee Beer" was a favorite), but that Coca-Cola shirt was what drew in most of the dollar-carrying tourists. I waited almost twenty minutes for mine, and I watched nearly everyone ahead of me say "the Coke shirt" (and "thanks" in Hebrew).

At the time, I never asked why I wanted the shirt. I do know, though, that the reason I wear it often, despite a hole in the right sleeve, has to do with its power as

**Comment (NL):** I'm not sure the title says enough about your argument.

**Comment (NL):** The first sentence is a good attention-getter.

**Comment (BK):** The beginning seems kind of abrupt.

**Comment (BK):** What does this mean? Will other members of your audience know?

**Comment (NL):** The style of repeating "call me" is good, but I'm not sure the first three have much to do with the rest of the essay.

**Comment (NL):** Do you need these details? Will any of this be important later?

**Comment (NL):** One of what? A doll or a horse?

**Comment (BK):** Saying it in Hebrew would be cool here.

**Comment (NL):** This transition works really well. I wasn't sure where this was going, but here you are starting to clue the reader in.

a conversation piece. Few people notice it without asking something like, "Does that say Coke?" I usually smile and nod. They mumble a compliment and we go our separate ways. But rarely does anyone want to know what language the world's most famous logo is written in. And why should they? Perhaps because Coca-Cola is a cultural icon that shapes American identity.

> **Comment (NL):** Good detail! Lots of people can relate to a "conversation piece" shirt.

> **Comment (NL):** Good question! But I don't think the next sentence really answers it.

> **Comment (BK):** Is this the thesis? It kind of comes out of nowhere.

Throughout the company's history, marketing strategies have centered on putting Coca-Cola in scenes of the happy, carefree American life we never stop striving for. What 1950s teenage girl wouldn't long to see herself in the soda shop pictured in a Coca-Cola ad appearing in a 1958 issue of *Seventeen* magazine? A clean-cut, handsome man flirts with a pair of smiling girls as they laugh and drink Coca-Colas. And any girls who couldn't put themselves in that perfect, happy scene could at least buy a Coke for consolation. The malt shop — complete with a soda jerk in a white jacket and paper hat — is a theme that, even today, remains a symbol of Americana.

> **Comment (BK):** OK, here I am beginning to understand where your argument is going.

> **Comment (NL):** Maybe this is a little too broad?

> **Comment (BK):** Any girls? Really?

The following is the text of an email message that Emily's two peer-review partners wrote to her, giving her some overall comments to accompany those they had written in the margins of her draft.

Hi Emily:

We're attaching your draft with our comments. Good luck on revising!

First, we think this is a great draft. You got us interested right away with the story about your T-shirt and we just wanted to keep on reading. So the introduction seems really good. But the introduction goes on for a while — several paragraphs, we think, and we were beginning to wonder what your point was and when you were going to get to it. And when you get to your thesis, could you make it a little more specific or say a little more about what it means that Coca-Cola is an icon that shapes identity? This last idea wasn't clear to us.

Your stance, though, is very clear, and we liked that you talked about how you were pulled into the whole Coke thing even though you don't particularly like the soda. Sometimes we got bogged down in a ton of details, though, and felt like maybe you were telling us too much.

We were impressed with some of the words you use — we had to look up what "potable" meant! But sometimes we weren't sure a word was the very best one — we marked some of these words on your draft for you.

See you in class.

Nastassia and Bea

P.S. Could you add a picture of your T-shirt? It would be cool to see what it looks like.

Emily also got advice from her instructor, who suggested that Emily do a careful outline of this draft to check for how one point led to another and to see if the draft stayed on track.

 Based on her own review of her work as well as all of the responses she received, Emily decided to (1) make her thesis more explicit, (2) delete some extraneous information and examples, (3) integrate at least one visual into her text, and (4) work especially hard on the tone and length of her introduction and on word choice.

## 4c Getting the most from peer reviewers' comments

Remember that your reviewers should be acting as coaches, not judges, and that their job is to help you improve your essay as much as possible. Listen to and read their comments carefully. If you don't understand a particular suggestion, ask for clarification, examples, and so on. Remember, too, that reviewers are commenting on your writing, not on *you*, so be open and responsive to what they recommend. But you are the final authority on your essay; you will decide which suggestions to follow and which to disregard.

## 4d Learning from instructor comments

Instructor comments on any work that you have done can help you identify mistakes, particularly ones that you make repeatedly, and can point you toward larger issues that prevent your writing from being as effective as it could be. Whether or not you will have an opportunity to revise a particular piece of writing, you should look closely at the comments from your instructor.

**macmillanhighered.com/smh**

**4. Reviewing** > Exercise > Storyboard on getting help from peer reviewers

**4. Reviewing** > Video > Lessons from peer review

In responding to student writing, however, instructors will sometimes use phrases or comments that are a kind of shorthand — comments that are perfectly clear to the instructor but may be less clear to the students reading them. The instructor comments in the following chart, culled from over a thousand first-year student essays, are among those that you may find most puzzling. If your paper includes a puzzling comment that is not listed here, be sure to ask your instructor what the comment means and how you can fix the problem.

| Instructor Comment | Actions to Take in Response |
|---|---|
| "thesis not clear" | Make sure that you have a main point, and state it directly. **(4f)** The rest of the paper will need to support the main point, too—this problem cannot be corrected by adding a sentence or two. |
| "trying to do too much"<br>"covers too much ground" | Focus your main point more narrowly so that you can say everything that you need to in a project of the assigned length. You may need to cut back on some material and then expand what remains. |
| "hard to follow"<br>"not logical"<br>"incoherent"<br>"jumps around"<br>"parts not connected"<br>"transition" | If overall organization is unclear, try mapping or outlining and rearranging your work. **(3e)** See if transitions and signals **(5e)** or additional explanation will solve the problem. |
| "too general"<br>"vague" | Use concrete language and details, and make sure that you have something specific and interesting to say. **(30c)** If not, reconsider your topic. |
| "underdeveloped"<br>"thin"<br>"sparse" | Add examples and details, and be as specific as possible. **(30c)** You may need to do more research. **(Chapters 10–12)** |
| "what about the opposition?"<br>"one-sided"<br>"counterarguments?" | Add information on why some people disagree with you, and represent their views fairly and completely before you refute them. Recognize that reasonable people may hold views that differ from yours. **(9f)** ▶ |

| Instructor Comment | Actions to Take in Response |
|---|---|
| "repetitive"<br>"you've already said this" | Revise any parts of your writing that repeat an argument, point, word, or phrase; avoid using the same evidence over and over. |
| "awk"<br>"awkward" | Ask a peer or your instructor for suggestions about revising awkward sentences. **(Chapters 44–49)** |
| "syntax"<br>"awkward syntax"<br>"convoluted" | Read the sentence aloud to identify the problem; revise or replace the sentence. **(Chapters 44–49)** |
| "unclear" | Find another way to explain what you mean; add any background information or examples that your audience may need to follow your reasoning. |
| "tone too conversational"<br>"not an academic voice"<br>"too informal"<br>"colloquial"<br>"slang" | Look for overly informal words and phrasing you can revise. Consider your audience, and revise material that addresses or refers to that group too familiarly or informally. **(Chapter 30)** |
| "pompous"<br>"stilted"<br>"stiff" | Make sure you understand the connotations of the words you use, and revise any that contribute to a pompous, excessively old-fashioned, or inappropriate tone. **(30a and b)** |
| "set up quotation"<br>"integrate quotation" | Read the sentence containing the quotation aloud; revise it if it does not make sense as a sentence. Introduce every quotation with information about the source. Explain each quotation's importance to your work. **(Chapter 13)** |
| "your words?"<br>"source?"<br>"cite" | Mark all quotations clearly. Cite paraphrases and summaries of others' ideas. Give credit for help from others, and remember that you are responsible for your own work. **(Chapters 13 and 14)** |

| Instructor Comment | Actions to Take in Response |
|---|---|
| "doc" | Check the citations to be sure that you include all of the required information, that you punctuate correctly, and that you omit information not required by the documentation style. **(Chapters 32–35)** |

## 4e Revising with peer and instructor comments

Approach comments from peer reviewers or from your instructor in several stages. First, read straight through the comments. Take a few minutes to digest the feedback and get some distance from your work (4a). Then make a revision plan — as elaborate or as simple as you want — that prioritizes the changes needed in your next draft.

If you have comments from more than one reviewer, you may want to begin by making two lists: (1) areas in which reviewers agree on needed changes, and (2) areas in which they disagree. You will then have to make choices about which advice to heed and which to ignore from both lists. Next, rank the suggestions you've chosen to address.

Focus on comments about your purpose, audience, stance, thesis, and support. Leave any changes to sentences, words, punctuation, and format for later in the process; your revision of bigger-picture issues comes first.

Prepare a file for your revised draft. Use your previous draft as a starting point, renaming it to indicate that it is a revision. (For example, Javier Jabari might rename his file *jabari essay1 d2*, using his name, assignment number, and draft number.)

In the new file, make the changes you identified in your revision plan. Be prepared to revise heavily, if necessary; if comments suggest that your thesis isn't working, for example, you may need to change the topic or the entire direction of your text. Heavy revision is not a sign that there's something wrong with your writing; on the contrary, major revision is a common feature of serious, goal-oriented writing.

Once you are satisfied that your revisions adequately address major concerns, make corrections to sentences, words, and punctuation.

### EXERCISE 4.3

Using the Quick Help guidelines on pp. 69–70, analyze your own draft.

## 4f Revising thesis and support

Once you have sufficient advice on your draft and have studied all the responses, reread the draft once more, paying special attention to your thesis and its support. If the kind of writing you are doing calls for an explicit thesis, make sure that you have one and that it contains both a clear statement of the topic and a comment explaining what is particularly significant about the topic (3c). As you read, ask yourself how each paragraph relates to or supports the thesis and how each sentence develops the paragraph topic. Such careful rereading can help you eliminate irrelevant material and identify sections needing further details or examples.

Be particularly careful to note what kinds of evidence, examples, or good reasons you offer in support of your major points. If some points are off topic, look back at your exploratory work (3a). Emily Lesk found, for example, that an entire paragraph in her draft (paragraph 8) did nothing to support her thesis. Thus she deleted the entire paragraph.

### ◢ EXERCISE 4.4

After rereading your draft, evaluate the revised working thesis. Then evaluate its support in the draft. Identify points that need further support, and list those things you must do to provide that support.

## 4g Rethinking organization

One good way to check the organization of a draft is to outline it (3f). After numbering the paragraphs in the draft, read through each one, jotting down its main idea or topic. Then examine your outline, and ask yourself the following questions:

- What overall organizational strategies do you use? spatial? chronological? logical? associational?
- Do the main points clearly relate to the thesis and to one another? Are any of them irrelevant? Should any sections or paragraphs be moved to another part of the draft?
- Can you identify any confusing leaps from point to point? Do you need to provide additional or stronger transitions?
- Do you leave out any important points?

## 4h Revising title, introduction, and conclusion

Readers remember the first and last parts of a piece of writing better than anything else. For this reason, it is wise to pay careful attention to three important elements — the title, the introduction, and the conclusion.

---

**CONSIDERING DISABILITIES | TECHNOLOGY FOR REVISING**

Many students with dyslexia and other language-processing disabilities can benefit from the use of assistive technologies. Today, reading and writing software offers active spell checking, word-predictor functions, audio and visual options, and help with mechanics, punctuation, and formatting. You may want to make these technologies a regular part of your revising process.

## ☐ Revising the title

A good title gives readers information, draws them into the piece of writing, and may even indicate the writer's view of the topic. The title of Emily Lesk's draft, "All-Powerful Coke," did not provide the link Emily wanted to establish between Coca-Cola and American identity. During the review process, she titled her new draft "Red, White, and Everywhere." This title piques readers' curiosity and suggests that the familiar "red, white, and blue" would be linked to something that is everywhere.

## ☐ Revising the introduction

A good introduction accomplishes two important tasks: first, it attracts readers' interest, and, second, it presents the topic and makes some comment on it. It contains, in other words, a strong lead, or hook, and often an explicit thesis as well. Many introductions open with a general statement about the topic and then go into more detail, leading up to a specific thesis at the end. A writer can also begin an introduction effectively with a vivid statement of the problem that led to the thesis or with an intriguing quotation, an anecdote, a question, or a strong opinion. The rest of the introduction then moves from this beginning to a presentation of the topic and the thesis. (For more on introductions, see 5g.)

In many cases, especially when a writer begins with a quotation or an anecdote, the introduction consists of two or three paragraphs: the first provides the hook, while the next paragraph or two explain the significance of the hook. Emily Lesk used this pattern in her introduction. Her first paragraph contains such a hook, which is followed by a two-paragraph narrative anecdote about a trip to Israel that links Coca-Cola advertising and Americans' sense of identifying with the product. After considering the responses of her peers and analyzing her opening, Emily decided that the introduction took too long to get to the point and that it didn't lead to a clearly articulated thesis. She decided to shorten the introduction and to make her thesis more explicit and detailed.

## ☐ Revising the conclusion

An effective conclusion leaves readers satisfied that a full discussion has taken place. Many conclusions begin with a restatement of the thesis and end with more general statements that grow out of it: this pattern reverses the common general-to-specific pattern of the introduction. Writers also use other approaches to conclude effectively, including a provocative question, a quotation, a vivid image, a call for action, or a warning.

Emily Lesk's draft features a two-paragraph conclusion emphasizing the main point of her essay, that the Coke logo now represents America, but it then goes on to discuss the impact of such advertising in other countries, such as Kenya. On reflection, however, Emily decided to cut the paragraph on Kenya because it didn't really draw her essay to a close but rather went off in a different direction. (For more on conclusions, see 5g.)

### ◢ EXERCISE 4.5

Review Emily Lesk's draft (3g), and compose an alternative conclusion. Then write a paragraph commenting on the strengths and weaknesses of the two conclusions.

## 4i   Revising paragraphs, sentences, words, and tone

In addition to examining the larger issues of logic, organization, and development, effective writers look closely at the smaller elements: paragraphs, sentences, and words. Many writers, in fact, look forward to this part of revising and editing because its results are often dramatic. Turning a weak paragraph into a memorable one — or finding exactly the right word to express a thought — can yield great satisfaction and self-confidence.

### ☐  Revising paragraphs

Paragraphing serves the reader by visually breaking up long expanses of writing and signaling a shift in focus. Readers expect a paragraph to develop an idea, a process that usually requires several sentences or more. These guidelines can help you revise your paragraphs:

- Look for the topic or main point of each paragraph, whether it is stated or implied. Does every sentence expand, support, or otherwise relate to the topic?
- Check to see how each paragraph is organized — spatially, chronologically, associationally, or by some logical relationship (3e). Is this organization appropriate to the topic of the paragraph?
- Note any paragraphs that have only a few sentences. Do these paragraphs sufficiently develop the topic of the paragraph?

For additional guidelines on editing paragraphs, see p. 95.

Paragraph 5 in Emily Lesk's draft (3g) contains only two sentences, and they don't lead directly into the next paragraph. In her revision, Emily lengthened (and strengthened) the paragraph by adding a sentence that points out the result of Coca-Cola's advertising campaign:

> But while countless campaigns with this general strategy have together shaped the Coca-Cola image, presenting a product as key to a happy life represents a fairly typical approach to advertising everything from Fords to Tylenol. Coca-Cola's advertising is unique, however, for the original way the beverage giant has utilized specific advertising media — namely magazines and television — to drive home this message. As a result, Coca-Cola has come to be associated not only with the images of Americana portrayed in specific advertisements but also with the general forms of advertising media that dominate American culture.

### EXERCISE 4.6

Choose two other paragraphs in Emily Lesk's draft in 3g, and evaluate them using the Quick Help guidelines on pp. 69–70. Write a brief paragraph suggesting ways to improve the development or organization of these paragraphs.

## ☐ Revising sentences

As with life, variety is the spice of sentences. You can add variety to your sentences by looking closely at their length, opening patterns, and structure. (See the guidelines for editing sentences in Chapter 52.)

### Sentence length

Too many short sentences, especially one after another, can sound like a series of blasts on a car horn, whereas a steady stream of long sentences may tire or confuse readers. Most writers aim for some variety of length.

Emily Lesk found that all the sentences in one paragraph were fairly long:

> In other words, Coca-Cola has hammered itself into our perceptions — both conscious and subconscious — of an American cultural identity by equating itself with media that define American culture. When the omnipresent general magazine that marked the earlier part of the century fell by the wayside under television's power, Coke was there from the beginning. In its 1996 recap of the previous fifty years in industry history, the publication *Beverage Industry* cites Coca-Cola as a frontrunner in the very first form of television advertising: sponsorship of entire programs such as, in the case of Coke, *The Bob Dixon Show* and *The Adventures of Kit Carson*. Just as today we associate sports stadiums with their corporate sponsors, viewers of early television programs will forever equate them with Coke.

In an early revision of her draft, Emily decided to shorten the second sentence, thereby inserting a short, easy-to-read sentence between two long sentences:

> In other words, Coca-Cola has hammered itself into our perceptions — both conscious and subconscious — of an American cultural identity by equating itself with media that define American culture. As the print magazine gave way to television, Coke was there. In its 1996 recap of the previous fifty years in industry history, the publication *Beverage Industry* cites Coca-Cola as a frontrunner in the very first form of television advertising: sponsorship of entire programs such as, in the case of Coke, *The Bob Dixon Show* and *The Adventures of Kit Carson*. Just as we now associate sports stadiums with their corporate sponsors, viewers of early television programs will forever equate them with Coke.

### Sentence openings

Most sentences in English follow subject-predicate order and hence open with the subject of an independent clause, as does the sentence you are now reading. But opening sentence after sentence this way results in a jerky, abrupt, or choppy rhythm. You can vary sentence openings by beginning with a dependent clause, a phrase, an adverb, a conjunctive adverb, or a coordinating conjunction (52b).

Emily Lesk's second paragraph (see pp. 59–60) tells the story of how she got her Coke T-shirt in Israel. Before she revised her draft, every sentence in this paragraph opened with the subject: *I have a favorite T-shirt, It's Israel's standard tourist fare, I waited. . . .* In her revision, Emily deleted some examples and varied her sentence openings for a dramatic and easy-to-read paragraph:

> Even before setting foot in Israel three years ago, I knew exactly where I could find the Coke T-shirt. The tiny shop in the central block of Jerusalem's Ben Yehuda Street did offer other designs, but the one with a bright white "Drink Coca-Cola Classic" written in Hebrew cursive across the chest was what drew in most of the dollar-carrying tourists. While waiting almost twenty minutes for my shirt, I watched nearly every customer ahead of me ask for "the Coke shirt, *todah rabah* [thank you very much]."

### Sentences opening with *it* or *there*

As you go over the sentences of your draft, look especially at those beginning with *it is, it was, there is, there was, there are,* or *there were*. Sometimes these words can create a special emphasis, as in "It was a dark and stormy night." But they can also cause problems (50b). A reader doesn't know what *it* means, for instance, unless the writer has already pointed out exactly what the word stands for. A more subtle problem with these openings, however, is that they may allow a writer to avoid taking responsibility for a statement:

~~The chancellor believes~~
**~~It is believed~~ that fees must increase next semester.**
^
The original sentence avoids responsibility by failing to tell us who believes that fees must increase.

### Sentence structure

Using only simple sentences can be very dull, but overusing compound sentences may result in a singsong or repetitive rhythm. At the same time, strings of complex sentences may sound, well, overly complex. Try to vary your sentence structure (see Chapter 52).

◢ **EXERCISE 4.7**

Find a paragraph in your own writing that lacks variety in sentence length, sentence openings, or sentence structure. Then write a revised version.

## ☐ Revising words

Maybe even more than paragraphs and sentences, word choice — or diction — offers writers an opportunity to put their personal stamp on a piece of writing (see Chapter 30).

- Do you use too many abstract and general nouns rather than concrete and specific ones? Saying that you bought a car is much less memorable than saying you bought a used Mini Cooper (30c).

- Are there too many nouns in relation to the number of verbs? The *effect* of the *overuse* of *nouns* in *writing* is the *placing* of too much *strain* on the inadequate *number* of *verbs* and the resultant *prevention* of *movement* of the *thought.* In the preceding sentence, the verb *is* carries the entire weight of all those nouns (in italics). The result is a heavy, boring sentence. Why not say instead, *Overusing nouns places a big strain on the verbs and slows down the prose*?

- How many verbs are forms of *be* — *be, am, is, are, was, were, being, been*? If *be* verbs account for more than about a third of your total verbs, you are probably overusing them. (See 36a, 37c, Chapter 39, and 53b.)

- Are most of your verbs *active* rather than passive? Although the passive voice has many uses (39g), your writing will generally be stronger and more energetic if you use active verbs.

- Are your words *appropriate*? Check to be sure they are not too fancy — or too casual (30a).

Emily Lesk made a number of changes in word choice. She decided to change *Promised Land* to *Israel* since some of her readers might not regard these two as synonymous. She also made her diction more lively, changing *from Fords to Tylenol* to *from Allstate insurance to Ziploc bags* to take advantage of the A-to-Z reference.

### ☐ Revising for tone

Word choice is closely related to tone, the attitude that a writer's language carries toward the topic and the audience. In examining the tone of your draft, think about the nature of the topic, your own attitude toward it, and that of your intended audience. Check for connotations of words as well as for slang, jargon, emotional language, and your level of formality. Does your language create the tone you want to achieve (humorous, serious, impassioned, and so on)? Is that tone appropriate, given your audience and topic? (For more on creating an appropriate tone through word choice, see Chapter 30.)

Although Emily Lesk's peer reviewers liked the overall tone of her essay, one reviewer had found her opening sentence abrupt. To make her tone friendlier, she decided to preface *I don't drink Coke* with another clause, resulting in *America, I have a confession to make: I don't drink Coke.* Emily also shortened her first paragraph considerably, in part to eliminate the know-it-all attitude she herself had detected.

## 4j   Checking visuals, media, and design

As you check what you've written about your topic, you also need to take a close look at the way your text looks and works.

- Do your visuals, audio, and video (if any) appear in appropriate places and play properly?
- Do your reviewers think the visuals and media help you make your points? How can you make this content more effective?
- Do you use design effectively for your genre and medium? Is your text readable and inviting? (See Chapter 16.)

### Emily Lesk's visuals and media

Emily Lesk originally planned to include an early Coke ad or the original Coca-Cola Santa Claus in her draft. Since she was planning to post her essay on a class Web site that was open to the public, her instructor told her that she would need to obtain permission for these images, which proved difficult to do on her deadline. As a result, she looked for other images. Emily's peer reviewers had also wanted to see her T-shirt, so she took a photo of that for use in her text. She also decided to include live links to some of her Web sources in the version of the essay she posted online.

## 4k Editing

Because readers expect a final copy that is clean and correct in every way, you need to make time for careful final editing — checking your use of grammar, punctuation, mechanics, and spelling. If you have not run your spell checker yet, do so now, and check every word the spell checker flags. Remember, however, that spell checkers are limited and that relying too heavily on them can introduce new errors (31f).

To improve your editing of future assignments, keep a personal checklist of the patterns of editing problems you find. Here again, your computer can help: if you notice that you often misuse a certain word, find every instance of that word, and then check the usage carefully.

### An editing checklist

To begin a checklist, jot down all the errors or corrections marked on the last piece of writing you did. Then note the context in which each error appeared, and indicate what you should look for in the future. You can add to this inventory every time you write and edit a draft. Here is an example of one student's checklist:

| ERRORS MARKED | IN CONTEXT | I NEED TO LOOK AT |
|---|---|---|
| fragment | starts with *when* | sentences beginning with *when* |
| missing comma | after *however* | sentences that include *however* |
| missing apostrophe | *company's* | all possessive nouns |
| tense shift | *go* for *went* | my use of the present tense |
| wrong word | *defiantly* for *definitely* | the spell checker's suggestions |
| incomplete documentation | no page number | the guidelines for documenting sources |

This writer has begun to isolate patterns, such as her tendency to accept the spell checker's suggestions too readily.

 **EXERCISE 4.8**

Using several essays you have written, establish your own editing checklist.

---

### EXERCISE 4.9

Using the guidelines in 4a–k, reread a recent draft with an eye for revising. Try to do this at least one day after you completed the draft. List the things you need or want to address in your revision. At this point, you may want to exchange drafts with one or two classmates and share responses.

---

## 4l Proofreading the final draft

Take time for one last, careful proofreading, which means reading to correct any typographical errors or other slips, such as inconsistencies in spelling and punctuation. Remember that running the spell checker, while necessary, is *not* the equivalent of thorough proofreading (31f). To proofread most effectively, read through the copy aloud, making sure that you have used punctuation marks correctly and consistently, that all sentences are complete, and that no words are missing. Then go through the copy again, this time reading backward so that you can focus on each word and its spelling.

### *Emily Lesk's final draft*

STUDENT WRITER
Emily Lesk

You have already seen and read about a number of the revisions Emily Lesk made to her first draft. On the following pages is the edited and proofread version she turned in to her instructor. If you compare her final draft with her first draft (3g), you will notice a number of additional changes she made in editing and proofreading. What corrections and improvements can you spot? To see and work with the Web version with embedded links that Emily posted on her class site, go to **macmillanhighered.com/smh** and click on **4. Reviewing, Revising, Editing, Reflecting > Student Writing**. (Photo © Emily Lesk)

Emily Lesk
Professor Arraéz
Electric Rhetoric
November 15, 2013

Red, White, and Everywhere

America, I have a confession to make: I don't drink Coke. But don't call me     1
a hypocrite just because I am still the proud owner of a bright red shirt that
advertises it. Just call me an American.

Even before setting foot in Israel three years ago, I knew exactly where I     2
could find the Coke T-shirt. The tiny shop in the central block of Jerusalem's Ben

---

Yehuda Street did offer other designs, but the one with a bright white "Drink Coca-Cola Classic" written in Hebrew cursive across the chest was what drew in most of the dollar-carrying tourists. While waiting almost twenty minutes for my shirt (depicted in Fig. 1), I watched nearly every customer ahead of me ask for "the Coke shirt, *todah rabah* [thank you very much]."

At the time, I never thought it strange that I wanted one, too. After having     3
absorbed sixteen years of Coca-Cola propaganda through everything from NBC's Saturday morning cartoon lineup to the concession stand at Camden Yards (the Baltimore Orioles' ballpark), I associated the shirt with singing along to the "Just for the Taste of It" jingle and with America's favorite pastime, not with a brown fizzy beverage I refused to consume. When I later realized the immensity of Coke's corporate power, I felt somewhat manipulated, but that didn't stop me from wearing the shirt. I still don it often, despite the growing hole in the right sleeve, because of its power as a conversation piece. Few Americans notice it without asking something like "Does that say Coke?" I usually smile and nod. Then they mumble a one-word compliment, and we go our separate ways. But rarely do they want to know what language the internationally recognized logo is written in. And why should they? They are interested in what they can relate to as Americans: a familiar red-and-white logo, not a foreign language. Through nearly a century of brilliant advertising strategies, the Coca-Cola Company has given Americans not only a thirst-quenching beverage but a cultural icon that we have come to claim as our own.

Throughout the company's history, its marketing strategies have centered     4
on putting Coca-Cola in scenes of the happy, carefree existence Americans are supposedly striving for. What 1950s teenage girl, for example, wouldn't long to see herself in the Coca-Cola ad that appeared in a 1958 issue of *Seventeen* magazine? A clean-cut, handsome man flirts with a pair of smiling girls as they laugh and drink Cokes at a soda-shop counter. Even a girl who couldn't picture herself in that idealized role could at least buy a Coke for consolation. The malt shop, complete with a soda jerk in a white jacket and paper hat and a Coca-Cola fountain, is a theme that, even today, remains a piece of Americana (Ikuta 74).

Fig. 1. Hebrew Coca-Cola T-shirt. Personal photograph by author.
(© Emily Lesk)

But while countless campaigns with     5
this general strategy have together shaped the Coca-Cola image, presenting a product as key to a happy life is a fairly typical approach to advertising everything from Allstate insurance to Ziploc bags. Coca-Cola's advertising strategy is unique, however, for the original way the beverage giant has used the specific advertising media

of magazines and television to drive home this message. As a result, Coca-Cola has become associated not only with the images of Americana portrayed in specific advertisements but also with the general forms of advertising media that dominate American culture.

One of the earliest and best-known examples of this strategy is artist Haddon  6
Sundblom's rendering of Santa Claus. Using the description of Santa in Clement Moore's poem "A Visit from St. Nicholas" — and a friend's rosy-cheeked face as a model — Sundblom contributed to the round, jolly image of this American icon, who just happens to delight in an ice-cold Coke after a tiring night of delivering presents ("The True History of the Modern-Day Santa Claus"). Coca-Cola utilized the concept of the magazine to present this inviting image in a brilliant manipulation of the medium (Pendergrast 181).

Today, it's easy to forget how pervasive a medium the magazine was before  7
television became readily available to all. Well into the 1960s, households of diverse backgrounds all across America subscribed loyally to general-subject weeklies and monthlies such as *Life* and the *Saturday Evening Post*, which provided news and entertainment to families nationwide. This large and constant group of subscribers enabled Coca-Cola to build an annual Christmastime campaign that used an extremely limited number of advertisements. According to the Coca-Cola Company's Web site, Sundblom created only around forty images of Santa Claus during the campaign's duration from 1931 to 1964 ("The True History of the Modern-Day Santa Claus"). As a result, Americans soon began to seek out the ads each holiday season. The marketing strategy was to make consumers wait eagerly by the mailbox each December to see the latest *Saturday Evening Post* ad featuring Santa gulping a Coke. For this strategy to succeed, the advertisements had to be seen by many, but they also had to be just hard enough to come by to seem special. What better way to achieve these goals than to place an advertisement in the December issue of an immensely popular magazine?

Effective magazine advertising is just one example of the media strategies  8
Coca-Cola has used to encourage us to equate Coke with the "happy life" element of American identity. As the print magazine gave way to television, Coke was there. In its 1996 recap of the previous fifty years in industry history, the publication *Beverage Industry* cites Coca-Cola as a frontrunner in the very first form of television advertising: sponsorship of entire programs such as *The Bob Dixon Show* and *The Adventures of Kit Carson* ("Fabulous Fifties" 16). Just as we now associate sports stadiums with their corporate sponsors, viewers of early television programs will forever equate those programs with Coke.

When networks switched from offering sponsorships to selling exclusive  9
commercial time in short increments, Coca-Cola strove to distinguish itself once

again, this time by experimenting with new formats and technologies for those commercials. Early attempts — such as choppy "stop motion" animation, where photographs of objects such as Coke bottles move without the intervention of actors — attracted much attention, according to the Library of Congress Motion Picture Archives Web site. Coca-Cola was also a pioneer in color television; after a series of experimental reels, the company produced its first color commercial in 1964 ("Highlights"). While the subject matter of these original commercials was not particularly memorable (Coca-Cola cans and bottles inside a refrigerator), the hype surrounding the use of new technologies helped draw attention to the product.

But the advertising campaign that perhaps best illustrates the ability of Coca-Cola advertisers to tie their product to a groundbreaking technology did not appear until 1993. For the 1994 Winter Olympics, Coke created six television commercials featuring digitally animated polar bears rolling, swimming, snuggling, and sliding about in a computerized North Pole — and finishing off the playful experience with a swig of Coke. In 1993, two years before the release of *Toy Story*, these commercials were some of the very first widely viewed digital films ("Highlights"). As with Sundblom's Santa Clauses, television viewers looked forward to their next sighting of the cute, cuddly, cutting-edge bears, who created a natural association between Coca-Cola and digital animation. Once again, Coke didn't just use the latest technology — Coke defined it.

10

As a result of all of this brilliant advertising, a beverage I never even drink is a significant part of my American cultural identity. That's why I spent thirty Israeli shekels and twenty minutes in a tourist trap I would ordinarily avoid buying my Hebrew Coca-Cola shirt. That shirt, along with the rest of the enormous Coca-Cola collectibles industry, demonstrates Coke's power to identify itself with the American ideal of a lighthearted life of diversion and pleasure. Standing in line halfway around the world for the logo that embodies these values gave me an opportunity to affirm a part of my American identity.

11

## Works Cited

"The Fabulous Fifties." *Beverage Industry* 87.6 (1996): 16. *General OneFile*. Web. 2 Nov. 2013.

Hebrew Coca-Cola T-shirt. Personal photograph by the author. 8 Nov. 2013.

"Highlights in the History of Coca-Cola Television Advertising." *Fifty Years of Coca-Cola Television Advertisements: Highlights from the Motion Picture Archives at the Library of Congress*. Motion Picture, Broadcasting, and Recorded Sound Div., Lib. of Cong., 29 Nov. 2000. Web. 5 Nov. 2013.

Ikuta, Yasutoshi, ed. *'50s American Magazine Ads*. Tokyo: Graphic-Sha, 1987. Print.

Pendergrast, Mark. *For God, Country, and Coca-Cola: The Definitive History of the Great American Soft Drink and the Company That Makes It.* 2nd ed. New York: Basic, 2000. Print.

"The True History of the Modern-Day Santa Claus." *The Coca-Cola Company: Holidays.* The Coca-Cola Company, 2012. Web. 3 Nov. 2013.

## 4m  Reflecting on your writing

Research demonstrates a strong connection between careful reflection and learning: thinking back on what you've learned and assessing it help make that learning stick. As a result, first-year college writing courses are increasingly encouraging students to take time for such reflection, both during the writing process and after the final draft is done. Whenever you finish a major piece of writing or a writing course, make time to reflect on the experience and see what lessons you can learn from it.

- What lessons have you learned from writing — from an individual piece of writing or an entire course?
- From what you have learned, what can you apply to the work you will do for other classes?
- What about your writing do you feel most confident about — and why do you feel this way?
- What about your writing do you think needs additional work, and what plans do you have for improving?
- What confusions did you have while writing, and what did you do to resolve them?
- What major questions do you still have?
- How has writing helped you clarify your thinking, extend your knowledge, or deepen your understanding?
- Identify a favorite passage in your writing, and then try to articulate what you like about it. Can you apply what you learn from this analysis to other pieces of writing?
- How would you describe your development as a writer?
- What goals do you have for yourself as a writer?

**macmillanhighered.com/smh**

**e** **4. Reviewing, Revising, Editing, Reflecting** > Student Writing > Reflective blog post (Nguyen)

**4. Reviewing, Revising, Editing, Reflecting** > Student Writing > Reflective cover letter (Kung)

▼ ▼ ▼ ▼ ▼ ▼ ▼ ▼ ▼ ▼ ▼ ▼ ▼ ▼ ▼ ▼ ▼ ▼ ▼ ▼ ▼ ▼ ▼ ▼ ▼ ▼ ▼ ▼

## THINKING CRITICALLY ABOUT YOUR REVIEWING AND REVISING PROCESS

1. How did you begin reviewing your draft?

2. What kinds of comments on or responses to your draft did you have? How helpful were they, and why?

3. How long did revising take? How many drafts did you produce?

4. What kinds of changes did you tend to make? in organization, paragraphs, sentence structure, wording, adding or deleting information? in the use of visuals?

5. What gave you the most trouble as you were revising?

6. What pleased you most? What is your very favorite sentence or passage in the draft, and why?

7. What would you most like to change about your process of revising, and how do you plan to go about doing so?

# CHAPTER 5

# Developing Paragraphs

**A** **PARAGRAPH IS A GROUP OF SENTENCES** or a single sentence set off as a unit. All the sentences in a paragraph usually relate to one main idea, but within this general guideline, paragraph structure is highly flexible, allowing you to create many different effects. For instance, the first paragraph of an article may aim to get your attention and convince you to read on, while subsequent paragraphs may indicate a new point or a shift in focus or tone.

## 5a Creating strong paragraphs

Most readers of English come to any piece of formal or academic writing with certain expectations about paragraphs:

- Paragraphs will begin and end with important information.
- The topic sentence will often let readers know what a paragraph is about.
- A paragraph will make sense as a whole; its words and sentences will be clearly related.
- A paragraph will relate to the paragraphs around it.

Let us look now at the elements in a well-written paragraph — one that is easy for readers to understand and follow.

> I never knew anyone who'd grown up in Jackson without being afraid of Mrs. Calloway, our librarian. She ran the Library absolutely by herself, from the desk where she sat with her back to the books and facing the stairs, her dragon eye on the front door, where who knew what kind of person might come in from the public? SILENCE in big black letters was on signs tacked up everywhere. She herself spoke in her normally commanding voice; every word could be heard all over the Library above a steady seething sound coming from her electric fan; it was the only fan in the Library and stood on her desk, turned directly onto her streaming face. —EUDORA WELTY, *One Writer's Beginnings*

This paragraph begins with a general statement of the main idea: that everyone who grew up in Jackson feared Mrs. Calloway. All the other sentences then give specific details about why she inspired such fear. This example demonstrates the three qualities essential to most academic paragraphs: unity, development, and coherence. It focuses on one main idea (unity); its main idea is supported with specifics (development); and its parts are clearly related (coherence).

**Editing the paragraphs in your writing**

- What is the topic sentence of each paragraph? Is it stated or implied? If stated, where in the paragraph does it fall? Should it come at some other point? Would any paragraph be improved by deleting or adding a topic sentence? **(5b)**
- Within each paragraph, how does each sentence relate to the main idea? **(5b)**
- How completely does each paragraph develop its topic? What details and methods of development are used? Are they effective? Do any paragraphs need more detail? **(5c)** What other methods of development might be used? **(5d)**
- Are paragraphs varied in length? Does any paragraph seem too long or too short? **(Quick Help box, p. 107)**
- Is each paragraph organized in a way that is easy for readers to follow? Are sentences within each paragraph clearly linked? Do any of the transitional expressions try to create links between ideas that do not really exist? **(5e and f)**
- Are the paragraphs clearly linked? Do more links need to be added? **(5f)**
- How does the introductory paragraph catch readers' interest—with a quotation? an anecdote? a question? a strong opinion? How else might it open? **(5g)**
- How does the last paragraph draw the essay to a conclusion? What lasting impression will it leave with readers? How else might it conclude? **(5g)**

## 5b Writing unified paragraphs

An effective paragraph generally focuses on one main idea. A good way to achieve paragraph unity is to state the main idea clearly in one sentence — the topic sentence — and relate all other sentences in the paragraph to that idea. Like the thesis for an essay (3c), the topic sentence includes a topic and a comment on that topic. In the paragraph by Eudora Welty in 5a, the topic sentence opens the paragraph. Its topic is Mrs. Calloway; its comment, that those who grew up in Jackson were afraid of her.

### ☐ Positioning a topic sentence

A topic sentence often appears at the beginning of a paragraph, but it can come at the end — or it may be implied rather than stated directly.

*Topic sentence at the beginning*

If you want readers to see your point immediately, open with the topic sentence. This strategy can be particularly useful in letters of application (23b) or in argumentative writing (Chapter 9). The following paragraph opens with a clear topic sentence (highlighted), on which subsequent sentences build:

Our friendship was the source of much happiness and many memories. We grooved to every new recording from Beyoncé. We sweated together in the sweltering summer sun, trying to win the championship for our softball team. I recall the taste of pepperoni pizza as we discussed the highlights of our team's victory. Once we even became attracted to the same person, but luckily we were able to share his friendship.

### Topic sentence at the end

When specific details lead up to a generalization, putting the topic sentence at the end of the paragraph makes sense, as in the following paragraph about Alice Walker's "Everyday Use":

During the visit, Dee takes the pictures, every one of them, including the one of the house that she used to live in and hate. She takes the churn top and dasher, both whittled out of a tree by one of Mama's uncles. She tries to take Grandma Dee's quilts. Mama and Maggie use these inherited items every day, not only appreciating their heritage but living it too. Dee, on the other hand, wants these items only for decorative use, thus forsaking and ignoring their real heritage.

### Topic sentence at the beginning and end

Sometimes you will want to state a topic sentence at the beginning of a paragraph and then refer to it in a slightly different form at the end. Such an echo of the topic sentence adds emphasis to the main idea. In the following paragraph, the writer begins with a topic sentence announcing a problem:

Many of the difficulties we experience in relationships are caused by the unrealistic expectations we have of each other. Think about it. Women are expected to feel comfortable doing most of the sacrificing. They are supposed to stay fine, firm, and forever twenty-two while doing double duty, in the home and in the workplace. The burden on men is no easier. They should be tall, handsome, and able to wine and dine the women. Many women go for the glitter and then expect these men to calm down once in a relationship and become faithful, sensitive, supportive, and loving. Let's face it. Both women and men have been unrealistic. It's time we develop a new sensitivity toward each other and ask ourselves what it is we need from each other that is realistic and fair.

The last sentence restates the topic sentence as a proposal for solving the problem. This approach is especially appropriate here, for the essay goes on to specify how the problem might be solved.

### Topic sentence implied but not stated

Occasionally a paragraph's main idea is so obvious that it does not need to be stated explicitly in a topic sentence. Here is such a paragraph, from an essay about working as an airport cargo handler:

> In winter the warehouse is cold and damp. There is no heat. The large steel doors that line the warehouse walls stay open most of the day. In the cold months, wind, rain, and snow blow across the floor. In the summer the warehouse becomes an oven. Dust and sand from the runways mix with the toxic fumes of fork lifts, leaving a dry, stale taste in your mouth. The high windows above the doors are covered with a thick, black dirt that kills the sun. The men work in shadows with the constant roar of jet engines blowing dangerously in their ears.  —PATRICK FENTON, "Confessions of a Working Stiff"

Here the implied topic sentence might be stated as *Working conditions in the warehouse are uncomfortable, dreary, and hazardous to one's health*. But the writer does not have to state this information explicitly because we can infer it easily from the specific details he provides.

Though implied topic sentences are common in descriptions, many instructors prefer explicit topic sentences in college writing.

---

◢ **EXERCISE 5.1**

Choose an essay you have written, and identify the topic sentence of each paragraph, noting where in the paragraph the topic sentence appears or whether it is implied rather than stated. Experiment with one paragraph, positioning its topic sentence in at least two different places. What difference does the change make? If you have any implied topic sentences, try stating them explicitly. Does the paragraph become easier to read?

---

## □  Relating each sentence to the main idea

Whether the main idea of a paragraph is stated in a topic sentence or is implied, each sentence in the paragraph should contribute to the main idea. Look, for example, at the following paragraph, which opens an essay about African American music:

**BEING EXPLICIT**

In U.S. academic contexts, readers often expect paragraphs to be organized around a clearly defined topic, and they expect the relationship among ideas to be signaled by transitional devices (5e). Such step-by-step explicitness may strike you as unnecessary or ineffective, but it helps ensure that the reader understands your point.

> When I was a teenager, there were two distinct streams of popular music: one was black, and the other was white. The former could only be heard way at the end of the radio dial, while white music dominated everywhere else. This separation was a fact of life, the equivalent of blacks sitting in the back of the bus and "whites only" signs below the Mason-Dixon line. Satchmo might grin for days on "The Ed Sullivan Show" and certain historians hold forth ad nauseam on the black contribution to American music, but the truth was that our worlds rarely twined.
>
> —MARCIA GILLESPIE, "They're Playing My Music, but Burying My Dreams"

The first sentence announces the topic (there were two streams of popular music: black and white), and all of the other sentences back up this idea. The result is a unified paragraph.

### EXERCISE 5.2

Choose one of the following topic sentences, and spend some time exploring the topic (3a). Then write a paragraph that includes the topic sentence. Make sure that each of the other sentences relates to it. Assume that the paragraph will be part of a letter you are writing to an acquaintance.

1. I found out quickly that college life was not quite what I had expected.
2. Being part of the "in crowd" used to be essential to me.
3. My work experience has taught me several important lessons.
4. Until recently, I never appreciated my parents fully.
5. One of my high school teachers helped prepare me for life as an adult.

### EXERCISE 5.3

Choose an essay you have written recently, and examine the second, third, and fourth paragraphs. Does each have a topic sentence or strongly imply one? Do all the other sentences in the paragraph focus on its main idea? Would you now revise any of these paragraphs—and, if so, how?

## 5c Developing paragraphs with supporting details

In addition to being unified, a paragraph should hold readers' interest and explore its topic fully, using whatever details, evidence, and examples are necessary. Without such development, a paragraph may seem lifeless and abstract.

Most good academic writing not only presents general ideas but also backs them up with specifics. This balance, the shifting between general and specific, is especially important at the paragraph level. If a paragraph contains nothing but details, readers may have trouble following the writer's meaning. If, on the other hand, a paragraph contains only general statements, readers may grow bored or may not be convinced.

#### A POORLY DEVELOPED PARAGRAPH

No such thing as human nature compels people to behave, think, or react in certain ways. From the time of our infancy to our death, we are constantly being taught by the society that surrounds us, the customs, norms, and mores of our distinct culture. Everything in culture is learned, not genetically transmitted.

This paragraph is boring. Although its main idea is clear, it fails to gain our interest or hold our attention because it lacks any examples or details. Now look at the paragraph revised to include needed specifics.

#### THE SAME PARAGRAPH, REVISED

A child in Los Angeles decorates a Christmas tree with shiny red ornaments and sparkling tinsel. A few weeks later, a child in Beijing celebrates the Chinese New Year with feasting, firecrackers, and gift money in lucky red envelopes. It is not by instinct that one child knows how to decorate the tree while the other knows how to celebrate the New Year. No such thing as human nature compels people to behave, think, or react in certain ways. Rather, from the time of our infancy to our death, we are constantly being taught by the society that surrounds us the customs, norms, and mores of one or more distinct cultures. Everything in culture is learned, not genetically transmitted.

Though both paragraphs make the same point, the second one comes to life by bringing in specific details.

### Details in visual texts

Details are important in both written and visual texts. If you decide to use an image because of a particular detail, make sure your readers will notice what you want them to see. Crop out any unnecessary information, and clarify

what's important about the image, either in your text or with a caption. The first image above shows the original photograph. The cropped second image, which appeared on a blog about street food, makes the sandwich the center of the frame.

## 5d Following patterns of development

The patterns shown in 3e for organizing essays can also help you develop and arrange paragraphs.

### ☐ Developing with narration

Narration tells a story in order to develop a main idea. Although writers usually arrange narrative paragraphs in chronological order, they sometimes use such variations as flashbacks and flash-forwards. Some narratives include dialogue; some gradually lead to a climax, the most dramatic point in the story. Here is one student's narrative paragraph that tells a personal story in order to support a point about the dangers of racing bicycles with flimsy alloy frames. Starting with a topic sentence, the paragraph proceeds chronologically and builds to a climax.

> People who have been exposed to the risk of dangerously designed bicycle frames have paid too high a price. I saw this danger myself in the 1984 Putney Race. An expensive Stowe-Shimano graphite frame failed, and the rider was catapulted onto Vermont pavement at fifty miles per hour. The pack of riders behind him was so dense that most other racers crashed into a tangled, sliding heap. The aftermath: four hospitalizations. I got off with some stitches, a bad road rash, and severely pulled tendons. My Italian racing bike was pretzeled, and my racing was over for that summer. Others were not so lucky. An Olympic hopeful, Brian Stone of the Northstar team, woke up in a hospital bed to find that his cycling was over — and not just for that summer. His kneecap had been surgically removed. He couldn't even walk.

## ☐ Developing with description

Description uses specific details to create a clear impression. In the following descriptive paragraph, the writer includes details about an old schoolroom where "time had taken its toll." Although a topic sentence may be unnecessary in such a paragraph (5b), sometimes a topic sentence at the beginning helps set the scene. The paragraph below shows the writer using spatial organization (3e), moving from the ceiling to the floor.

> The professor's voice began to fade into the background as my eyes wandered around the classroom in the old administration building. The water-stained ceiling was cracked and peeling, and the splitting wooden beams played host to a variety of lead pipes and coils. My eyes followed these pipes down the walls and around corners until I eventually saw the electric outlets. I thought it was strange that they were exposed, not built in, until I realized that there probably had been no electricity when the building was built. Below the outlets the sunshine was falling in bright rays across the hardwood floor, and I noticed how smoothly the floor was worn. Time had taken its toll on this building.

## ☐ Developing with illustration

Illustration makes a point with concrete examples or good reasons. To support the topic sentence in the following illustration paragraph, Mari Sandoz uses one long example about her short hair and short stature.

A SINGLE EXAMPLE

> The Indians made names for us children in their teasing way. Because our very busy mother kept my hair cut short, like my brothers', they called me Short Furred One, pointing to their hair and making the sign for short, the right hand with fingers pressed close together, held upward, back out, at the height intended. With me this was about two feet tall, the Indians laughing gently at my abashed face. I am told that I was given a pair of small moccasins that first time, to clear up my unhappiness at being picked out from the dusk behind the fire and my two unhappy shortcomings made conspicuous.  —MARI SANDOZ, "The Go-Along Ones"

In the following excerpt, John Rickford offers several reasons that underlie linguists' argument that Ebonics is not "poor grammar" but a legitimate and powerful dialect of English.

SEVERAL REASONS

> Why do linguists see the issue so differently from most other people? A founding principle of our science is that we describe *how* people talk; we don't judge how language should or should not be used. A second principle

is that all languages, if they have enough speakers, have dialects — regional or social varieties that develop when people are separated by geographic or social barriers. And a third principle, vital for understanding linguists' reactions to the Ebonics controversy, is that all languages and dialects are systematic and rule-governed. Every human language and dialect that we have studied to date — and we have studied thousands — obeys distinct rules of grammar and pronunciation.

—JOHN RICKFORD, "Suite for Ebony and Phonics"

## □ Developing with definition

When you write a paragraph to define a word or concept, you will often want to combine definition with other patterns of development. In the following paragraph, Timothy Tregarthen starts with a definition of economics and then uses examples to support it:

> Economics is the study of how people choose among the alternatives available to them. It's the study of little choices ("Should I take the chocolate or the strawberry?") and big choices ("Should we require a reduction in energy consumption in order to protect the environment?"). It's the study of individual choices, choices by firms, and choices by governments. Life presents each of us with a wide range of alternative uses of our time and other resources; economists examine how we choose among those alternatives.

—TIMOTHY TREGARTHEN, *Economics*

## □ Developing with division and classification

Division breaks a single item into parts. Classification groups many separate items according to their similarities. A paragraph evaluating one history course might divide the course into several segments — textbooks, lectures, assignments — and examine each one in turn. A paragraph giving an overview of many history courses at your college might classify, or group, the courses in a number of ways — by time periods, by geographic areas, and so on. In the following paragraph, note how Aaron Copland divides the listening process into three parts:

**DIVISION**

> We all listen to music according to our separate capacities. But, for the sake of analysis, the whole listening process may become clearer if we break it up into its component parts, so to speak. In a certain sense, we all listen to music on three separate planes. For lack of a better terminology, one might name these (1) the sensuous plane, (2) the expressive plane, (3) the sheerly musical plane. The only advantage to be gained from mechanically splitting up the listening process into these hypothetical planes is the clearer view to be had of the way in which we listen.

—AARON COPLAND, *What to Listen for in Music*

In this paragraph, the writer classifies, or separates, fad dieters into two groups:

CLASSIFICATION

Two types of people are seduced by fad diets. Those who have always been overweight turn to them out of despair; they have tried everything, and yet nothing seems to work. The second group to succumb appear perfectly healthy but are baited by slogans such as "look good, feel good." These slogans prompt self-questioning and insecurity — do I really look good and feel good? — and, as a direct result, many healthy people fall prey to fad diets. With both types of people, however, the problems surrounding such diets are numerous and dangerous. In fact, these diets provide neither intelligent nor effective answers to weight control.

## ☐ Developing with comparison and contrast

Comparing two things means looking at their similarities; contrasting means focusing on the differences. You can structure paragraphs that compare and contrast in two different ways. The block method presents all the information about one item and then all the information about the other item. The alternating method switches back and forth between the two items.

BLOCK METHOD

You could tell the veterans from the rookies by the way they were dressed. The knowledgeable ones had their heads covered by kerchiefs, so that if they were hired, tobacco dust wouldn't get in their hair; they had on clean dresses that by now were faded and shapeless, so that if they were hired they wouldn't get tobacco dust and grime on their best clothes. Those who were trying for the first time had their hair freshly done and wore attractive dresses; they wanted to make a good impression. But the dresses couldn't be seen at the distance that many were standing from the employment office, and they were crumpled in the crush. — MARY MEBANE, "Summer Job"

ALTERNATING METHOD

Malcolm X emphasized the use of violence in his movement and employed the biblical principle of "an eye for an eye and a tooth for a tooth." King, on the other hand, felt that blacks should use nonviolent civil disobedience and employed the theme of "turning the other cheek," which Malcolm X rejected as "beggarly" and "feeble." The philosophy of Malcolm X was one of revenge, and often it broke the unity of black Americans. More radical blacks supported him, while more conservative ones supported King. King thought that blacks should transcend their humanity. In contrast, Malcolm X thought they should embrace it and reserve their love for one another, regarding whites as "devils" and the "enemy." King's politics were those of a rainbow, but Malcolm X's rainbow was insistently one color — black. The distance between Martin Luther King Jr.'s thinking and Malcolm X's was the distance between growing up in the seminary and growing up on the streets, between the American dream and the American reality.

## EXERCISE 5.4

Outline the preceding paragraph on Martin Luther King Jr. and Malcolm X, noting its alternating pattern. Then rewrite the paragraph using block organization: the first part of the paragraph devoted to King, the second to Malcolm X. Finally, write a brief analysis of the two paragraphs, explaining which seems more coherent and easier to follow—and why.

## □ Developing with cause and effect

You can often develop paragraphs by detailing the causes of something or the effects that something brings about. The following paragraph discusses the causes that led pediatrician Phil Offit to study science and become a physician:

> To understand exactly why Offit became a scientist, you must go back more than half a century, to 1956. That was when doctors in Offit's home-town of Baltimore operated on one of his legs to correct a club foot, requiring him to spend three weeks recovering in a chronic care facility with 20 other children, all of whom had polio. Parents were allowed to visit just one hour a week, on Sundays. His father, a shirt salesman, came when he could. His mother, who was pregnant with his brother and hospitalized with appendi-citis, was unable to visit at all. He was five years old. "It was a pretty lonely, isolating experience," Offit says. "But what was even worse was looking at these other children who were just horribly crippled and disfigured by polio." That memory, he says, was the first thing that drove him toward a career in pediatric infectious diseases.          —AMY WALLACE, "An Epidemic of Fear"

## □ Developing with process

You may need to develop a paragraph to explain a process — that is, to describe how something happens or is done, usually in chronological order, as this para-graph illustrates.

> In July of 1877, Eadweard Muybridge photographed a horse in motion with a camera fast enough to capture clearly the split second when the horse's hooves were all off the ground — a moment never before caught on film. His next goal was to photograph a sequence of such rapid images. In June of 1878, he set up twelve cameras along a track, each connected to a tripwire. Then, as a crowd watched, a trotting horse raced down the track pulling a two-wheeled carriage. The carriage wheels tripped each camera in quick succession, snapping a dozen photographs. Muybridge developed the

negatives and displayed them to an admiring public that same morning. His technical achievement helped to pave the way for the first motion pictures a decade later.

## Developing from problem to solution

A paragraph developed in the problem-solution pattern opens with a topic sentence that states a problem or asks a question about a problem; then it offers a solution or an answer to the question, as in the following example from a review of Ted Nordhaus and Michael Shellenberger's book *Break Through: From the Death of Environmentalism to the Politics of Possibility*:

> Unfortunately, at the moment growth means burning more fossil fuel. . . . How can that fact be faced? How to have growth that Americans want, but without limits that they instinctively oppose, and still reduce carbon emissions? [Nordhaus and Shellenberger's] answer is: investments in new technology. Acknowledge that America "is great at imagining, experimenting, and inventing the future," and then start spending. They cite examples ranging from the nuclear weapons program to the invention of the Internet to show what government money can do, and argue that too many clean-energy advocates focus on caps instead.
> —BILL McKIBBEN, "Can Anyone Stop It?"

## Developing with analogy

Analogies (comparisons that explain an unfamiliar thing in terms of a familiar one) can also help develop paragraphs.

> Since the advent of Hollywood editing, back in the earliest days of cinema, the goal of filmmakers has been for us to feel the movement of the camera but not to be aware of it, to look past the construction of the media, to ignore the seams in the material. Just as an Olympic diver smiles and hides the effort as she catapults skyward and manages to pull off multiple flips while seemingly twisting in both directions, good storytelling — whether oral, in print, or visual — typically hides the construction and the hard work that go into making it. Both the medal-winning dives and the best stories are more intricate than they appear.
> —STEPHEN APKON, *The Age of the Image: Redefining Literacy in a World of Screens*

## Developing with reiteration

Reiteration is a method of development that you may recognize from political speeches or some styles of preaching. In this pattern, the writer states the main point of a paragraph and then restates it, hammering home the point and often building in intensity as well. In the following passage from Barack Obama's 2004 keynote speech at the Democratic National Convention, Obama contrasts what he identifies as the ideas of "those who are preparing to divide us" with memorable references to common ground and unity, including repeated references to the United States as he builds to his climactic point:

> Now even as we speak, there are those who are preparing to divide us — the spin masters, the negative ad peddlers who embrace the politics of anything goes. Well, I say to them tonight, there is not a liberal America and a conservative America — there is the United States of America. There is not a black America and a white America and Latino America and an Asian America — there's the United States of America. The pundits like to slice and dice our country into Red States and Blue States: Red States for Republicans, Blue States for Democrats. But I've got news for them, too. We worship an awesome God in the Blue States, and we don't like federal agents poking around in our libraries in the Red States. We coach Little League in the Blue States and yes, we've got some gay friends in the Red States. There are patriots who opposed the war in Iraq and there are patriots who supported the war in Iraq. We are one people, all of us pledging allegiance to the stars and stripes, all of us defending the United States of America.　　　　—BARACK OBAMA

☐ **Combining patterns**

Most paragraphs combine patterns of development. In the following paragraph, the writer begins with a topic sentence and then divides his topic (the accounting systems used by American companies) into two subtopics (the system used to summarize a company's overall financial state and the one used to measure internal transactions). Next he develops the second subtopic through illustration (the assessment of costs for a delivery truck shared by two departments) and cause and effect (the system produces some disadvantages).

> Most American companies have basically two accounting systems. One system summarizes the overall financial state to inform stockholders, bankers, and other outsiders. That system is not of interest here. The other system, called the managerial or cost accounting system, exists for an entirely different reason. It measures in detail all of the particulars of transactions between departments, divisions, and key individuals in the organization, for the purpose of untangling the interdependencies between people. When, for example, two departments share one truck for deliveries, the cost accounting system charges each department for part of the cost of maintaining the truck and driver, so that at the end of the year, the performance of each department can be individually assessed, and the better department's manager can receive a larger raise. Of course, all of this information processing costs money, and furthermore may lead to arguments between the departments over whether the costs charged to each are fair.
> 　　　　—WILLIAM OUCHI, "Japanese and American Workers: Two Casts of Mind"

**EXERCISE 5.5**

Choose two of the following topics or two others that interest you, and brainstorm or freewrite about each one for ten minutes (3a). Then use the information you have produced to determine what method(s) of development would be most appropriate for each topic.

1. the pleasure a hobby has given you

2. the different images of two noted athletes

3. how to prepare for a storm

4. why wearing a seat belt should (or should not) be mandatory

5. the best course you've ever taken

**EXERCISE 5.6**

Take an assignment you have written recently, and study the ways you developed each paragraph. For one of the paragraphs, write a brief evaluation of its development. How would you expand or otherwise improve the development?

---

QUICK HELP

## Determining paragraph length

Though writers must keep their readers' expectations in mind, paragraph length is determined primarily by content and purpose. Paragraphs should develop an idea, create any desired effects (such as suspense or humor), and advance the larger piece of writing. Fulfilling these aims sometimes requires short paragraphs, sometimes long ones. For example, if you are writing a persuasive essay, you may put all your evidence into one long paragraph to create the impression of a solid, overwhelmingly convincing argument. In a narrative about an exciting event, on the other hand, you may use a series of short paragraphs to create suspense, to keep the reader rushing to each new paragraph to find out what happens next.

Remember that a new paragraph often signals a pause in thought. Just as timing is crucial in telling a joke, so the pause signaled by a paragraph helps readers anticipate what is to follow or gives them a moment to think about the previous paragraph.

**REASONS TO START A NEW PARAGRAPH**

- to turn to a new idea
- to emphasize something (such as a point or an example)
- to change speakers (in dialogue)
- to lead readers to pause
- to take up a subtopic
- to start the conclusion

Examine the paragraph breaks in something you have written recently. Explain briefly in writing why you decided on each of the breaks. Would you change any of them now? If so, how and why?

## 5e  Making paragraphs coherent

A paragraph has coherence — or flows — if its details fit together clearly in a way that readers can easily follow. You can achieve paragraph coherence by organizing ideas, by repeating key terms or phrases, and by using parallel structures and transitional devices.

### □ Organizing ideas

When you arrange information in a particular order, you help readers move from one point to another. There are a number of ways to organize details — you might use spatial, chronological, or associational order (3e) or one or more logical patterns, such as illustration, definition, or comparison and contrast (5d). Two other patterns commonly used in paragraphs are general to specific and specific to general.

Paragraphs organized in a general-to-specific pattern usually open with a topic sentence that presents a general idea. The topic sentence is then followed by specific points that support the generalization. In the following paragraph, the topic sentence presents a general idea about the Black Death, which is then backed up by specific examples:

**GENERAL TO SPECIFIC**

A massive epidemic, the Black Death of the fourteenth century, brought loss of life in the tens of millions of people and catastrophic debilitation to commerce and agriculture across Eurasia and North Africa. The bubonic plague seems to have initially irrupted into Chinese populations beginning in the 1320s. It spread in many parts of China until the 1350s with great loss of life. At the same time, it appears to have been carried into Mongolia and across the steppes into Crimea. Two Central Asian areas, one inhabited by the Nestorian Christians and the other by the Uzbek Muslims, were devastated by the plague before it struck in Europe, Southwest Asia, and Northwest Africa. Travel along Chinese and Central Asian trade routes facilitated the spread of this deadly disease.

—LANNY B. FIELDS, RUSSELL J. BARBER, AND CHERYL A. RIGGS, *The Global Past*

Paragraphs can also follow a specific-to-general organization, first providing a series of specific examples or details and then tying them together with a topic sentence that provides a conclusion. The following paragraph begins with specific details about two people's reactions to an event and ends with a topic sentence:

SPECIFIC TO GENERAL

I remember one afternoon as I was sitting on the steps of our monastery in Nepal. The monsoon storms had turned the courtyard into an expanse of muddy water and we had set out a path of bricks to serve as stepping-stones. A friend of mine came to the edge of the water, surveyed the scene with a look of disgust, and complained about every single brick as she made her way across. When she got to me, she rolled her eyes and said, "Yuck! What if I'd fallen into that filthy muck? Everything's so dirty in this country!" Since I knew her well, I prudently nodded, hoping to offer her some comfort through my mute sympathy. A few minutes later, Raphaèle, another friend of mine, came to the path through the swamp. "Hup, hup, hup!" she sang as she hopped, reaching dry land with the cry "What fun!" Her eyes sparkling with joy, she added: "The great thing about the monsoon is that there's no dust." Two people, two ways of looking at things; six billion human beings, six billion worlds.
—MATTHIEU RICARD, *Happiness*

## ☐ Repeating key words and phrases

A good way to build coherence in paragraphs is through repetition. Weaving in repeated key words and phrases — or pronouns that refer to them — not only links sentences but also alerts readers to the importance of those words or phrases in the larger piece of writing. Notice in the following example how the repetition of highlighted key words and the pronoun *they* helps hold the paragraph together:

Over the centuries, shopping has changed in function as well as in style. Before the Industrial Revolution, most consumer goods were sold in open-air markets, customers who went into an actual shop were expected to buy something, and shoppers were always expected to bargain for the best possible price. In the nineteenth century, however, the development of the department store changed the relationship between buyers and sellers. Instead of visiting several market stalls or small shops, customers could now buy a variety of merchandise under the same roof; instead of feeling expected to buy, they were welcome just to look; and instead of bargaining with several merchants, they paid a fixed price for each item. In addition, they could return an item to the store and exchange it for a different one or get their money back. All of these changes helped transform shopping from serious requirement to psychological recreation.

## ☐ Creating parallel structures

Parallel structures — structures that are grammatically similar — are another effective way to bring coherence to a paragraph. Readers are pulled along by the force of the parallel structures in the following example:

William Faulkner's "Barn Burning" tells the story of a young boy trapped in a no-win situation. If he betrays his father, he loses his family. If he betrays justice, he becomes a fugitive. In trying to free himself from his trap, he does both.

For more on parallel structures, see Chapter 45.

## □ Using transitions

Transitional words and phrases, such as *after all, for example, indeed,* and *finally,* signal relationships between and among sentences and paragraphs. (For information on linking paragraphs together coherently, see 5f.) Transitions bring coherence to a paragraph by helping readers follow the progression of one idea to the next. To understand how important transitions are in guiding readers, try reading the following paragraph, from which all transitions have been removed:

**A PARAGRAPH WITH NO TRANSITIONS**

In "The Fly," Katherine Mansfield tries to show us the "real" personality of "the boss" beneath his exterior. The fly helps her to portray this real self. The boss goes through a range of emotions and feelings. He expresses these feelings to a small but determined fly, whom the reader realizes he unconsciously relates to his son. The author basically splits up the story into three parts, with the boss's emotions and actions changing quite measurably. With old Woodifield, with himself, and with the fly, we see the boss's manipulativeness. Our understanding of him as a hard and cruel man grows.

We can, if we work at it, figure out the relationship of these ideas to one another, for this paragraph is essentially unified by one major idea. But the lack of transitions results in an abrupt, choppy rhythm; the paragraph lurches from one detail to the next, dragging the confused reader behind. See how much easier the passage is to read and understand with transitions added.

**THE SAME PARAGRAPH, WITH TRANSITIONS**

In "The Fly," Katherine Mansfield tries to show us the "real" personality of "the boss" beneath his exterior. The fly in the story's title helps her to portray this real self. In the course of the story, the boss goes through a range of emotions and feelings. At the end, he finally expresses these feelings to a small but determined fly, whom the reader realizes he unconsciously relates to his son. To accomplish her goal, the author basically splits up the story into three parts, with the boss's emotions and actions changing quite measurably throughout. First with old Woodifield, then with himself, and last with the fly, we see the boss's manipulativeness. With each part, our understanding of him as a hard and cruel man grows.

Note that transitions can only clarify connections between thoughts; they cannot create connections. As a writer, you should not expect a transition to provide meaning.

## Commonly used transitions

**TO SIGNAL SEQUENCE**
again, also, and, and then, besides, finally, first . . . second . . . third,
furthermore, last, moreover, next, still, too

**TO SIGNAL TIME**
after a few days, after a while, afterward, as long as, as soon as, at last, at that
time, before, earlier, immediately, in the meantime, in the past, lately, later,
meanwhile, now, presently, simultaneously, since, so far, soon, then, thereafter,
until, when

**TO SIGNAL COMPARISON**
again, also, in the same way, likewise, once more, similarly

**TO SIGNAL CONTRAST**
although, but, despite, even though, however, in contrast, in spite of, instead,
nevertheless, nonetheless, on the contrary, on the one hand . . . on the other
hand, regardless, still, though, yet

**TO SIGNAL EXAMPLES**
after all, even, for example, for instance, indeed, in fact, of course, specifically,
such as, the following example, to illustrate

**TO SIGNAL CAUSE AND EFFECT**
accordingly, as a result, because, consequently, for this purpose, hence, so,
then, therefore, thus, to this end

**TO SIGNAL PLACE**
above, adjacent to, below, beyond, closer to, elsewhere, far, farther on, here,
near, nearby, opposite to, there, to the left, to the right

**TO SIGNAL CONCESSION**
although it is true that, granted that, I admit that, it may appear that, naturally,
of course

**TO SIGNAL SUMMARY, REPETITION, OR CONCLUSION**
as a result, as has been noted, as I have said, as mentioned earlier, as we have
seen, in any event, in conclusion, in other words, in short, on the whole,
therefore, to summarize

# 5f  Linking paragraphs together

The same methods that you use to link sentences and create coherent paragraphs
can be used to link paragraphs themselves so that a whole piece of writing flows
smoothly. You should include some reference to the previous paragraph, either
explicit or implied, in each paragraph after the introduction. As with sentences,
you can create this link by repeating or paraphrasing key words and phrases and
by using parallel structures and transitional expressions.

**REPEATING KEY WORDS**

In fact, human offspring remain dependent on their parents longer than the young of any other species.

    Children are dependent on their parents or other adults not only for their physical survival but also for their initiation into the uniquely human knowledge that is collectively called culture. . . .

**USING PARALLEL STRUCTURES**

Kennedy made an effort to assure non-Catholics that he would respect the separation of church and state, and most of them did not seem to hold his religion against him in deciding how to vote. Since his election, the church to which a candidate belongs has become less important in presidential politics.

    The region from which a candidate comes remains an important factor. . . .

**USING TRANSITIONAL EXPRESSIONS**

While the Indian, in the character of Tonto, was more positively portrayed in *The Lone Ranger*, such a portrayal was more the exception than the norm.

    Moreover, despite this brief glimpse of an Indian as an ever-loyal side-kick, Tonto was never accorded the same stature as the man with the white horse and silver bullets. . . .

### ◢ EXERCISE 5.8

Look at a recent draft and identify the ways your paragraphs are linked together. Identify each use of repetition, parallel structures, and transitional expressions, and then evaluate how effectively you have joined the paragraphs.

## 5g Writing special-purpose paragraphs

Some kinds of paragraphs deserve special attention: opening paragraphs, concluding paragraphs, transitional paragraphs, and dialogue paragraphs.

### ☐ Writing strong opening paragraphs

Even a good piece of writing may remain unread if it has a weak opening paragraph. In addition to announcing your topic (usually in a thesis statement), an introductory paragraph must engage readers' interest and focus their attention on what is to follow. At their best, introductory paragraphs serve as hors d'oeuvres, whetting the appetite for the following courses.

    One common kind of opening paragraph follows the general-to-specific pattern (5e), in which the writer opens with a general statement and then gets more and more specific, ultimately concluding with the thesis.

Throughout Western civilization, places such as the ancient Greek agora, the New England town hall, the local church, the coffeehouse, the village square, and even the street corner have been arenas for debate on public affairs and society. Out of thousands of such encounters, "public opinion" slowly formed and became the context in which politics was framed. Although the public sphere never included everyone, and by itself did not determine the outcome of all parliamentary actions, it contributed to the spirit of dissent found in a healthy representative democracy. Many of these public spaces remain, but they are no longer centers for political discussion and action. They have largely been replaced by television and other forms of media — forms that arguably isolate citizens from one another rather than bringing them together. —MARK POSTER, "The Net as a Public Sphere"

In this paragraph, the opening sentence introduces a general subject — sites of public debate throughout history; subsequent sentences focus more specifically on political discussion; and the concluding sentence presents the thesis, which the rest of the essay will develop.

Other effective ways of opening an essay include using quotations, anecdotes, questions, or strong opinions.

### Opening with a quotation

There is a bumper sticker that reads, "Too bad ignorance isn't painful." I like that. But ignorance is. We just seldom attribute the pain to it or even recognize it when we see it. Take the postcard on my corkboard. It shows a young man in a very hip jacket smoking a cigarette. In the background is a high school with the American flag waving. The caption says, "Too cool for school. Yet too stupid for the real world." Out of the mouth of the young man is a bubble enclosing the words "Maybe I'll start a band." There could be a postcard showing a jock in a uniform saying, "I don't need school. I'm going to the NFL or NBA." Or one showing a young man or woman studying and a group of young people saying, "So you want to be white." Or something equally demeaning. We need to quit it. —NIKKI GIOVANNI, "Racism 101"

### Opening with an anecdote

I first met Angela Carter at a dinner in honor of the Chilean writer José Donoso at the home of Liz Calder, who then published all of us. My first novel was soon to be published; it was the time of Angela's darkest novel, "The Passion of New Eve." And I was a great fan. Mr. Donoso arrived looking like a Hispanic Buffalo Bill, complete with silver goatee, fringed jacket and cowboy boots, and proceeded, as I saw it, to patronize Angela terribly. His apparent ignorance of her work provoked me into a long expostulation in which I informed him that the woman he was talking to was the most brilliant writer in England. Angela liked that. By the end of the evening, we liked each other, too. That was almost 18 years ago. She was the first great writer I ever met, and she was one of the best, most loyal, most truth-telling, most inspiring friends anyone could ever have. I cannot bear it that she is dead. —SALMAN RUSHDIE, "Angela Carter"

### Opening with a question

When will international phone calls be free? Not anytime soon, bub. But when you eventually get your iPhone 4G, they should be included in your rate plan. Which is weird, because it's probably been a long time since you nervously eyed the clock while on the phone with your granny in Smallville. Long distance has been all-you-can-eat since cell phones and voice-over IP conquered the universe. But international telephony — whether landline, cellular, or Internet-based — is still a piggybank-rattling affair: Providers just can't offer dirt-cheap calls across borders. —CLIFF KUANG, "Burning Question"

### Opening with a strong opinion

I have not always loved Dr. King. In the sixties I could not understand his reaching beyond race to stand on principle. I could not understand, or support, his own example of "nonviolence." There was so much I didn't know! —JUNE JORDAN, *Some of Us Did Not Die*

## ◻ Writing satisfying concluding paragraphs

A good conclusion wraps up a piece of writing in a satisfying and memorable way. It reminds readers of the thesis of the essay and leaves them feeling that their expectations have been met. The concluding paragraph is also your last opportunity to get your message across.

A common strategy for concluding uses the specific-to-general pattern (5e), often beginning with a restatement of the thesis (but not word for word) and moving to more general statements. The following paragraph moves in such a way, opening with a final point of comparison between Generals Grant and Lee, specifying it in several sentences, and then ending with a much more general statement:

Lastly, and perhaps greatest of all, there was the ability, at the end, to turn quickly from war to peace once the fighting was over. Out of the way these two men behaved at Appomattox came the possibility of a peace of reconciliation. It was a possibility not wholly realized, in the years to come, but which did, in the end, help the two sections to become one nation again . . . after a war whose bitterness might have seemed to make such a reunion wholly impossible. No part of either man's life became him more than the part he played in this brief meeting in the McLean house at Appomattox. Their behavior there put all succeeding generations of Americans in their debt. Two great Americans, Grant and Lee — very different, yet under everything very much alike. Their encounter at Appomattox was one of the great moments of American history.

— BRUCE CATTON, "Grant and Lee: A Study in Contrasts"

Other effective strategies for concluding include using questions, quotations, vivid images, calls for action, or warnings.

### Concluding with a question

The training students receive in reading is one of our oldest and most powerful experiences, the first mark of a capacity to perform in a literate culture. In the process of learning how to read, every literate person absorbs, at a young age, a broad and potentially confusing range of cultural, ethical, and social lessons. As much as gender, race, religion, class, or national identity, one's literacy defines one's place in society. But like these other givens, literacy need not mean only one thing. Just as one can be male, female, or transgendered, one race or multiracial, a member of more than one religious or ethnic identity, so also one can read in different ways. Why assume that literacy is the simple answer to a complex question?

— WYN KELLEY AND HENRY JENKINS, *Reading in a Participatory Culture*

### Concluding with a quotation

Despite the celebrity that accrued to her and the air of awesomeness with which she was surrounded in her later years, Miss Keller retained an unaffected personality, certain that her optimistic attitude toward life was justified. "I believe that all through these dark and silent years God has been using my life for a purpose I do not know," she said. "But one day I shall understand and then I will be satisfied."

— ALDEN WHITMAN, "Helen Keller: June 27, 1880–June 1, 1968"

### Concluding with a vivid image

At the time the Web was born, in the early 1990s, a popular trope was that a new generation of teenagers, reared in the conservative Reagan years, had turned out to be exceptionally bland. The members of "Generation X" were characterized as blank and inert. The anthropologist Steve Barnett saw in them the phenomenon of pattern exhaustion, in which a culture runs out of variations in their pottery and becomes less creative. A common rationalization in the fledgling world of digital culture back then was that we were entering a transitional lull before a creative storm — or were already in the eye of one. But we were not passing through a momentary calm. We had, rather, entered a persistent somnolence, and I have come to believe that we will escape it only when we kill the hive. — JARON LANIER, *You Are Not a Gadget*

*Concluding with a call for action*

Do we have cause for hope? Many of my friends are pessimistic when they contemplate the world's growing population and human demands colliding with shrinking resources. But I draw hope from the knowledge that humanity's biggest problems today are ones entirely of our own making. Asteroids hurtling at us beyond our control don't figure high on our list of imminent dangers. To save ourselves, we don't need new technology: we just need the political will to face up to our problems of population and the environment.  —JARED DIAMOND, "The Ends of the World as We Know Them"

*Concluding with a warning*

Because propaganda is so effective, it is important to track it down and understand how it is used. We may eventually agree with what the propagandist says because all propaganda isn't necessarily bad; some advertising, for instance, urges us not to drive drunk, to have regular dental checkups, to contribute to the United Way. Even so, we must be aware that propaganda is being used. Otherwise, we will have consented to handing over our independence, our decision-making ability, and our brains.

—ANN McCLINTOCK, "Propaganda Techniques in Today's Advertising"

## ☐ Using transitional paragraphs

On some occasions, you may need to alert your readers to a major transition between ideas. To do so in a powerful way, you might use an entire short paragraph, as in the following example from a book on Web site design. The one-sentence transitional paragraph arrests our attention, announcing that the people who create Web sites expect certain responses from site users — but, as the next paragraph reveals, the users don't often behave the way a site's creator might hope.

When we're creating sites, we act as though people are going to pore over each page, reading our finely crafted text, figuring out how we've organized things, and weighing their options before deciding which link to click.

What they actually do most of the time (if we're lucky) is *glance* at each new page, scan *some* of the text, and click on the first link that catches their interest or vaguely resembles the thing they're looking for. There are usually large parts of the page that they don't even look at.

—STEVE KRUG, *Don't Make Me Think*

## ☐ Using paragraphs to signal dialogue

Dialogue can add life to almost any sort of writing. To set up written dialogue, simply start a new paragraph each time the speaker changes, no matter how short each bit of conversation is. Here is an example:

Whenever I brought a book to the job, I wrapped it in newspaper — a habit that was to persist for years in other cities and under other circumstances. But some of the white men pried into my packages when I was absent and they questioned me.

"Boy, what are you reading those books for?"

"Oh, I don't know, sir."

"That's deep stuff you're reading, boy."

"I'm just killing time, sir."

"You'll addle your brains if you don't watch out."

—RICHARD WRIGHT, *Black Boy*

## THINKING CRITICALLY ABOUT PARAGRAPHS

### Reading with an eye for paragraphs

Read something by a writer you admire. Find one or two paragraphs that impress you in some way, and analyze them, using the guidelines in the Quick Help box on p. 95. Try to decide what makes them effective paragraphs.

### Thinking about your own use of paragraphs

Examine two or three paragraphs you have written, using the guidelines on p. 95, to evaluate the unity, coherence, and development of each one. Identify the topic of each paragraph, the topic sentence (if one is explicitly stated), any patterns of development, and any means used to create coherence. Decide whether or not each paragraph successfully guides your readers, and explain your reasons. Then choose one paragraph, and revise it.

# CHAPTER 6

# Working with Others

I N A MEMORABLE STATEMENT, philosopher Hannah Arendt confirms what many people feel about collaboration: "For excellence, the presence of others is always required." The old maxim that two heads are better than one seems to be especially true in today's world of digital communication. Feedback is more visible than ever; today's writers expect and want reactions to their posts, messages, and updates. And thanks to collaborative tools that allow writers anywhere to work on a single document, working on a group project has never been more feasible. Still, successful collaboration requires special attention.

> **CONNECT:** When is collaborating helpful? **6a, 19i**
>
> **CREATE:** Work with team members to create a space where you can meet physically or share work virtually.
>
> **REFLECT:** Go to **macmillanhighered.com/smh**, and respond to **6. Working with Others** > **Video** > **Working with other people**.

## 6a Collaborating in college

Although you will find yourself working together with many people on or off campus, your most immediate collaborators will probably be the members of your writing class. You can learn a great deal by comparing ideas with these class-mates and by using them as a first audience for your writing (4b). As you talk and write, you will find the ideas they contribute making their way into your writing, and your ideas into theirs. In short, the texts you write are shaped in part by conversations with others. This exchange is one reason citing sources and help from others is so important (see Chapter 14).

In online communication, especially, the roles of "writer" and "reader" and "text" are often interchangeable, as readers become writers and then readers again, and texts constantly change as multiple voices contribute to them. A blog post, for example, may carry with it a long discussion in the comments section that has accumulated as people have replied to one

---

**TALKING THE TALK | COLLABORATING OR CHEATING?**

"When is asking others for help and opinions acceptable, and when is it cheating?" In academic work, the difference between collaborating and cheating depends almost entirely on context. There will be times — during exams, for example — when instructors will expect you to work alone. At other times, working with others — for a team project, perhaps, or peer review — may be required, and getting others' opinions on your writing is always a good habit. You draw the line, however, at having another person do your work for you. Submitting material under your name that you did not write is unacceptable in college writing. But collaboration is a key fact of life in today's digital world, so it's important to think carefully about how to collaborate effectively — and ethically.

---

another. Or a document being drafted in Google Drive or another software program designed to facilitate collaboration will carry the voices of multiple authors. These examples paint a portrait of how meaning is made collaboratively.

# 6b Working on group projects

You may often be asked to work as part of a team to produce a group project such as a print report, an oral presentation, or a Web document or site. Since group projects are collaborative from the outset, they require additional planning and coordination.

## ☐ Planning a collaborative project

Planning goes a long way toward making any group collaboration work well. Although you will probably do much of your group work online, keep in mind that face-to-face meetings can accomplish some things that virtual meetings cannot.

Many college instructors now routinely integrate online work into their classes. If your course has a Web site, it probably offers space for extending the collaborative work of the classroom. Your writing class may already have an email discussion list, chat space, blog, or wiki; if not, you may want to set up such a space for yourself and your collaborators. You may also want to use a space such as Google Drive to create a collaborative project; if so, make sure that every member of your group knows where to find the project and has the appropriate level of access — the ability to edit, for example — to any document posted there.

---

**macmillanhighered.com/smh**

 6. Working with Others > Video > Working with other people

6. Working with Others > Tutorial > Word processing

## Guidelines for group projects

- Establish a regular meeting time and space (whether in person or online), and exchange contact information.
- During your first meeting, discuss the overall project and establish ground rules. For example, you might agree that everyone has a responsibility to participate and to meet deadlines, and that all members will be respectful toward others in the group.
- Establish clear duties for each participant.
- With final deadlines in mind, create an overall agenda to organize the project. At each group meeting, take turns writing up notes on what was discussed and review them at the end of the meeting.
- Use group meetings to work together on difficult problems. If an assignment is complex, have each member explain one section to the others. Check with your instructor if part of the task is unclear or if members don't agree on what is required.
- Express opinions politely. If disagreements arise, try paraphrasing to see if everyone is hearing the same thing.
- Remember that the goal is not for everyone just to get along; constructive conflict is desirable. Get a spirited debate going, and discuss all available options.
- If your project requires a group-written document, assign one member to get the writing project started. Set deadlines for each part of the project. Come to an agreement about how you will edit and change each other's contributions to avoid offending any member of the group.
- Assess the group's effectiveness periodically. Should you make changes as you go forward? What has been accomplished? What has the group done best? What has it done less successfully? What has each member contributed? What have you learned about how to work more effectively with others on future projects?

## ◻ Considering models for collaboration

Experienced collaborative writers often use one of three models for setting up the project: an expertise model, a division-of-labor model, or a process model.

---

CONSIDERING DISABILITIES | **ACCOMMODATING DIFFERENCES**

When you are working with other members of your class to share files for peer review or other group activities, remember to consider differences group members may have. Think of such differences not only in terms of computer compatibility but also in terms of the sensory, physical, or learning abilities of yourself and your classmates. You may have colleagues who wish to receive printouts in a very large type size, for example, in order to read them with ease. Similarly, you may have a peer who prefers to share files early to read the material or avoid the stress of last-minute preparation. You may have a peer who uses a voice screen reader. Help your group get off to a good start by making a plan to accommodate everyone's needs.

| **CONSTRUCTIVE CRITICISM**

When you collaborate with your peers, criticizing each other's work is often necessary, but different cultures have different ways of expressing criticisms that are appropriate. Observe how your peers communicate their suggestions and comments, and how others respond to them. If you feel uncomfortable with strong criticisms from peers, you can ask them to "put it more gently."

**Expertise model.** This model plays to the strengths of each team member. The person who knows the most about graphics and design, for example, takes on all jobs that require those skills, while the person who knows most about the topic takes the lead in drafting.

**Division-of-labor model.** In this model, each group member becomes an expert on one aspect of the project. For example, one person might agree to do Internet research, while another searches library resources, and still another conducts interviews. This model is particularly helpful if a project is large and time is short.

**Process model.** You can also divide up the project in terms of its chronology: one person gets the project going, presenting an outline for the group to consider and carrying out any initial research; then a second person takes over and begins a draft for the group to review; a third person designs and illustrates the project; and another person takes the job of revising and editing. This model can work well if members are unable to participate equally throughout the entire project. Once the project is completely drafted, however, the whole group needs to work together to create a final version.

## 6c Making presentations

Some collaborative projects may call for oral or multimedia presentations. If your group is to make such a presentation, follow these guidelines:

- Find out exactly how much time you will have for the presentation, and stick to that time limit.

- Divide the preparatory work fairly. For example, who will revise the written text for oral presentation? Who will prepare the slides or other visuals? Who will do the necessary research?

- Decide how each group member will contribute to the presentation. Make sure that everyone has an obvious role.

- Leave time for at least two practice sessions. During the first session, time yourselves carefully, and make a sound or video recording of the presentation. Then view or listen to the recording, and make any necessary adjustments. If you can't videotape your group presentation, then practice it in front of several friends: feedback is very important, so ask them to summarize what they got out of the presentation and to comment on how easy it was to understand the major points, how effective body language and eye contact were, and how well you used visual or multimedia support.

- If your presentation will be available online, remember that it's very hard to know who may see it. Try for a presentation that will be easily understood by people beyond your own class or university — or even your own culture. Also, remember that you *must* label all visuals and cite their sources.

- Make sure that your audience will be able to read any accompanying handouts, slides, or posters, and revise any that fail this test. Use your visuals as you rehearse, and try to do so in a room similar in size and lighting to the room in which you will make the presentation.

- After your presentation, try to have a debriefing with your instructor so that you can get pointers on improving future presentations.

For more on oral and multimedia presentations, see Chapter 17.

▼ ▼ ▼ ▼ ▼ ▼ ▼ ▼ ▼ ▼ ▼ ▼ ▼ ▼ ▼ ▼ ▼ ▼ ▼ ▼ ▼ ▼ ▼ ▼ ▼

## THINKING CRITICALLY ABOUT YOUR COLLABORATIVE WORK

Begin by making a list of all the ways in which you collaborate with others. Then reflect on the kinds of collaboration you find most effective. Finally, take an example of a recent collaboration you have been part of, and examine how well it worked by answering the following questions: What did I contribute to the collaboration? What worked well, and what did not work well? What could I have done to improve the collaboration?

# PART 2
# Critical Thinking and Argument

# CHAPTER 7

# Reading Critically

**I**F YOU TAKE TIME to list all the reading you do in the course of a day, you will no doubt find that you are reading a lot — and that you are reading both in print and onscreen. For a long time, most people have thought of reading as, well, just plain *reading*. But the digital revolution has helped us see that we actually read in many different ways for many different reasons — and using different tools and media. Being a strong reader today means understanding these differences and learning to use them to your advantage.

In addition to thinking carefully about *how* you read, reading critically means questioning, commenting, analyzing, and reflecting thoughtfully on a text — whether it's a white paper for a psychology class, a graphic novel, a Super Bowl ad, a business email, or a YouTube video. Any method you use to keep track of your questions and make yourself concentrate on a text can help you become a better critical reader.

> **CONNECT:** How can you evaluate a text you are assigned to read? **7a, 12d and e**
>
> **CREATE:** Preview an assigned text, finding out what you can about the creator's authority on the subject and how this text fits into a conversation with others on the same topic.
>
> **REFLECT:** Go to **macmillanhighered.com/smh**, and respond to **7. Reading Critically > Student Writing > Annotations of scholarly article (Sanchez, Lum)**.

## 7a Reading print and digital texts

You're probably used to reading a lot onscreen — posting and responding to updates in your social networks, checking email, browsing the Web, and so on. Onscreen reading is often social and collaborative, allowing you to connect with other readers, discuss what you've read, and thus turn reading into writing.

In addition to changing reading from a solitary to a group activity, digital reading can be useful for finding information quickly. Research suggests that onscreen readers tend to take shortcuts, scanning and skimming and jumping from link to link. Because screen reading can help you find content that relates to what you're looking for, it can be a powerful tool that you can use effectively in your college work.

Given these obvious advantages, you might think that readers would prefer to do most of their reading onscreen. But current research suggests that this is not yet the case. Students today tell researchers that they prefer to read print works when the reading needs to be absorbed and remembered. Like many students, you may find it easier to navigate and be in control of a print text — you know just where you are, how much you have read, and how much you have left to read; you can flip back and forth looking for something more easily than you can online. Reading on the Internet can often be distracting: with so much information on hand, it can be hard to concentrate on one text. Reading onscreen for long periods can also be tiring. Perhaps most importantly, psychologists find that students reading onscreen don't do nearly as much "metacognitive learning" — that is, learning that reflects on what has been learned and makes connections among the things learned — as readers of print texts do. So it turns out that print still holds some major advantages for readers.

If you have a choice of media when you're asked to read a text, then, consider whether reading onscreen or in print will work better for your purposes. And if you must read a complex text onscreen rather than in print, be aware that you may need to try harder than usual to focus. Get in the habit of working through the steps described in this chapter — previewing (7b), annotating (7c), summarizing (7d), and analyzing (7e and f) — to ensure that you are reflecting and making appropriate connections, whether you're reading a printed page or a digital text.

## 7b Previewing a text

Find out all you can about a text before beginning to look closely at it, considering its context, author, subject, genre, and design.

### PREVIEWING THE CONTEXT

- Where have you encountered the work? Are you encountering it in its original context? For example, an essay in a collection of readings may have been previously published in a magazine; a speech you watch on YouTube may have been delivered to a live or televised audience; a painting on a museum wall may have been created for a wealthy patron in a distant country centuries earlier.

- What can you infer from the original or current context of the work about its intended audience and purpose?

## TALKING THE TALK | CRITICAL THINKING

"Are criticizing and thinking critically the same thing?" *Criticize* can sometimes mean "find fault with," and you certainly do not have to be relentlessly negative when you think critically. Instead, critical thinking means, first and foremost, asking good questions — and not simply accepting what you see at face value. By asking not only what words and images mean, but also how meaning gets across, critical thinkers consider why an author makes a particular claim, what he or she may be leaving out or ignoring, and how to tell whether evidence is accurate and believable. If you're asking and answering questions like these, then you're thinking critically.

### LEARNING ABOUT THE AUTHOR OR CREATOR

- What information can you discover about the author or creator of the text?
- What purpose, expertise, and possible agenda might you expect this person to have? Where do you think the author or creator is coming from in this text?

### PREVIEWING THE SUBJECT

- What do you know about the subject of the text?
- What opinions do you have about the subject, and on what are your opinions based?
- What would you like to learn about the subject?
- What do you expect the main point to be? Why?

### CONSIDERING THE TITLE, MEDIUM, GENRE, AND DESIGN

- What does the title (or caption or other heading) indicate?
- What do you know about the medium in which the work appears? Is it a text on the Web, a printed advertising brochure, a speech stored in iTunes, or an animated cartoon on television? What role does the medium play in achieving the purpose and connecting to the audience?
- What is the genre of the text — and what can it help illuminate about the intended audience or purpose? Why might the authors or creators have chosen this genre?
- How is the text presented? What do you notice about its formatting, use of color, visuals or illustrations, overall design, general appearance, and other design features?

## Student preview of an assigned text

STUDENT WRITER
Fernando Sanchez

STUDENT WRITER
Sarah Lum

Fernando Sanchez and Sarah Lum, students in a first-year writing class, read and analyzed an academic article, "'Mistakes Are a Fact of Life': A National Comparative Study," by Andrea A. Lunsford and Karen J. Lunsford. Some of the preview notes they made before reading the article appear below. (See 7c–e for additional steps in the critical reading from these students.) (Photos © Fernando Sanchez and Sarah Lum)

This essay was published in *College Composition and Communication* in June 2008. According to the journal's Web site, "*College Composition and Communication* publishes research and scholarship in rhetoric and composition studies that supports college teachers in reflecting on and improving their practices in teaching writing and that reflects the most current scholarship and theory in the field." So the original audience was probably college writing teachers.

*Information on context*

The essay begins with these words from poet and essayist Nikki Giovanni: "Mistakes are a fact of life. It is the response to the error that counts." The introduction explains that the article will talk about a study of first-year college writing and compare it to "a similar study conducted over twenty years ago."

Andrea A. Lunsford was an English professor and the director of the Program in Writing and Rhetoric at Stanford University when this article appeared in 2008. She is also the author of the book we are using in our writing class. Karen J. Lunsford is an associate professor of writing at the University of California, Santa Barbara.

*About the author*

It was easy to find a lot of information on these authors on the Internet. According to Google Scholar, both have published many articles and conducted a lot of research on writing, so they have experience that relates to this article.

The authors will study writing from students across the country and see whether problems are increasing or whether mistakes are just "a fact of life." I am the subject of this study without even knowing it! My high school

*Subject of article*

teachers used to tell me to be careful not to include any "Internet lingo" in my writing. . . . I wonder if students really are losing the ability to write because of technology?

I see that the authors are replicating a study done by Andrea Lunsford and Robert Connors in 1984, and they will give a detailed comparison between the two studies. This essay may say that making mistakes in writing may not be such a bad thing.

The title includes a quotation from the epigraph that opens the essay and that sets the theme for the whole article, indicating that the authors will focus on the mistakes that others point out in this generation of student writing.

The genre of this essay is a scholarly article published in a journal. This journal requires MLA documentation style for endnotes and for the list of works cited. The essay also uses headings to signal changes in topics within the essay. Eight tables provide data to back up what the authors are saying.

*Other preview information*

 **EXERCISE 7.1**

Following the guidelines in 7b, preview a text you have been assigned to read.

## 7c  Reading and annotating a text

The first time you read a text, mark it up (if the medium allows) or take notes. Consider content, author, intended audience, and genre and design.

**READING FOR CONTENT**

- What do you find confusing or unclear about the text? Where can you look for explanations or more information? Do you need background information?
- What key terms, ideas, or patterns do you see? What images stay with you?
- What sources or other works does this text cite, refer to, or allude to?
- How does the content fit with what you already know?
- Which points do you agree with? Which do you disagree with? Why?

**READING FOR AUTHOR/CREATOR AND AUDIENCE**

- Do the authors or creators present themselves as you anticipated?
- For what audience was this text created? Are you part of its intended audience?
- What underlying assumptions can you identify in the text?
- Are the medium and genre appropriate for the topic, audience, and purpose?

READING FOR DESIGN, COMPOSITION, AND STYLE

- Is the design appropriate for the subject and genre?
- Does the composition serve a purpose — for instance, does the layout help you see what is more and less important in the text?
- Do words, images, sound, and other media work together well?
- How would you describe the style of the text? What contributes to this impression — word choice? references to research or popular culture? formatting? color? something else?

### Student annotation of an assigned text

Following is an excerpt from Andrea A. Lunsford and Karen J. Lunsford's essay "'Mistakes Are a Fact of Life': A National Comparative Study," with annotations made by Sarah Lum and Fernando Sanchez. To read the full article with Sarah and Fernando's annotations, go to **macmillanhighered.com/smh** and click on **7. Reading Critically > Student Writing**.

## "Mistakes Are a Fact of Life": A National Comparative Study

BY ANDREA A. LUNSFORD AND KAREN J. LUNSFORD

> Mistakes are a fact of life. It is the response to the error that counts.
> —NIKKI GIOVANNI, *Black Feeling, Black Talk, Black Judgment*

Perhaps it is the seemingly endless string of what have come to be called "Bushisms" ("We shouldn't fear a world that is more interacted") and the complex response to them from both right and left. Perhaps it is the hype over Instant Messaging lingo cropping up in formal writing and the debate among teachers over how to respond (Farmer 48). Perhaps it is the long series of attempts to loosen the grip of "standard" English on the public imagination, from the 1974 special issue of *College Composition and Communication* (*Students' Right to Their Own Language*) to a 2006 special issue of *College English* devoted to *Cross-Language Relations in Composition*. Or perhaps it is the number of recent reports, many of them commissioned by the government, that have bemoaned the state of student literacy and focused attention on what they deem significant failures at the college level (see especially the recent reports from the Spellings Commission and Derek Bok's *Our Underachieving Colleges*).

**Fernando Sanchez:** To an older audience, this is a good reference. To a much younger audience reading and researching this, "Bushisms" might not be a word in their vocabulary.

**Sarah Lum:** Perhaps text message lingo is not the main problem of student writing; rather it is the subjects students are currently interested in. They are reading less formal texts and are more engaged in social media. In the past, I read an essay in which a student had quoted the lyrics of a rapper rather than an author.

Whatever the reasons, and they are surely complex and multilayered, forms of language use have been much in the news, with charges of what student writers can and cannot (or should and should not) do all around us. The times seemed ripe, then, for taking a close look at a national sample of student writing to see what it might tell us about the current state of affairs. With that goal in mind, we drew up plans to conduct a national study of first-year college student writing and to compare our findings to those of a similar study conducted over twenty years ago.

### "The Frequency of Formal Errors," or Remembering Ma and Pa Kettle

But we are getting a bit ahead of ourselves here. For now, flash back to the mid-1980s. Some readers may remember receiving a letter from Robert Connors and Andrea Lunsford asking them to participate in a national study of student writing by submitting a set of marked student papers from a first-year composition course. That call brought in well over 21,000 papers from 300 teachers around the country, and in fairly short order Andrea and Bob

> **FS:** This article will contain much content that older readers are already familiar with. It also includes phrases like "for now, flash back to the mid-1980s," implying the audience can easily remember those times.

drew a random sample of 3,000 student papers stratified to be representative in terms of region of the country, size of institution, and type of institution. While they later analyzed patterns of teacher response to the essays as well as the particular spelling patterns that emerged (in that study, spelling was the most frequent student mistake by some 300 percent), they turned first to an analysis of which formal errors (other than spelling) were most common in this sample of student writing.

> **SL:** As frequent as misspelling is, I would expect that percentage to decrease in this age because we rely on computers to autocorrect our mistakes.

Why the focus on error in the Lunsford and Connors study? Bob and Andrea's historical research had led each of them to caches of student papers with teacher comments focusing on errors that sometimes seemed very out of date if not downright odd ("stringy" syntax, for example, or obsessive comments on how to distinguish between the use of "shall" and "will"), and they wondered what teachers in the 1980s would focus on instead. In addition, the 1938–39 research into student patterns of formal error carried out by John C. Hodges, author of the *Harbrace Handbook of English*, piqued their curiosity — and led to a review of earlier studies. As Connors and Lunsford put it:

> Beginning around 1910 . . . teachers and educational researchers began trying to taxonomize errors and chart their frequency. The great heyday of error-frequency seems to have occurred between 1915 and

1935. . . . Our historical research indicates that the last large-scale research into student patterns of formal error was conducted in 1938–39 by John C. Hodges. . . . Hodges collected 20,000 student papers, . . . using his findings to inform the 34-part organization of his *Harbrace Handbook*. (396)

As Connors and Lunsford noted, Hodges did not publish any results of his study in contemporary journals, though in a footnote to the preface of the first edition of his *Handbook*, he did list the top ten errors he found. Connors and Lunsford's research turned up two other "top ten" lists, one by Roy Ivan Johnson in 1917, the other by Paul Witty and Roberta Green in 1930. The three lists are presented in Table 1.2.

[*Table 1: Historical Top Ten Errors Lists appeared here.*]

Increasingly intrigued to see how formal error patterns might have shifted in the sixty-odd years since these earlier research reports, Connors and Lunsford set out to discover the most common patterns of student errors characteristic of the mid-1980s and which of those patterns were marked most consistently by teachers. Table 2 presents their findings.

[*Table 2: Connors and Lunsford List of Most Frequent Formal Errors appeared here.*]

As noted above, Table 2 omits spelling errors, which constituted such a large number of the formal errors that Andrea and Bob decided to study them separately (see "Exercising Demonolatry"). In analyzing the other most frequent patterns of formal error and teacher marking of them, Bob and Andrea drew some intriguing conclusions: First, teachers vary widely in their thinking about what constitutes a "markable" error. Second, teachers do not mark as many errors as the popular stereotype might have us believe, perhaps because of the difficulty of explaining the error or because the teacher is focusing on only a few errors at any one time.

**SL:** Some teachers are more lenient and some are more constructive—students learn most from constructive criticism.

**FS:** What is that popular stereotype?

Finally, they concluded that error patterns had indeed shifted since the time of Hodges's *Harbrace Handbook*, especially in terms of a "proliferation of error patterns that seem to suggest declining familiarity with the visual look of a written page" (406).

While Andrea and Bob found errors aplenty in the 3,000 papers from 1984, they also found reason for optimism:

**FS:** Good wording to keep the reader's mind on the idea of mistakes being a fact of life!

> One very telling fact emerging from our research is our realization that college students are *not* making more formal errors in writing than they used to. The numbers of errors made by students in earlier studies and the numbers we found in the 1980s agree remarkably. (406)

Table 3 presents their comparison of the findings of the three studies.

[*Table 3: Comparison of Three Studies' Findings appeared here.*]

Given the consistency of these numbers, Connors and Lunsford concluded that "although the length of the average paper demanded in freshman composition has been steadily rising, the formal skills of students have not declined precipitously" (406)....

**FS:** Although I did not know about the Lunsford and Connors study in 1984, this first section really gave me a good summary and base to start to understand the statistics and studies of today.

**SL:** Since this is a scholarly article, I expected it to be hard to read and understand, but it is pretty clear so far.

### EXERCISE 7.2

Following is the full text of Abraham Lincoln's Gettysburg Address. Using the guidelines in 7b, preview the speech to understand the context. Then use the guidelines in 7c to read and annotate Lincoln's speech.

Four score and seven years ago our fathers brought forth on this continent a new nation, conceived in Liberty, and dedicated to the proposition that all men are created equal.

Now we are engaged in a great civil war, testing whether that nation, or any nation so conceived and so dedicated, can long endure. We are met on a great battlefield of that war. We have come to dedicate a portion of that field, as a final resting place for those who here gave their lives that that nation might live. It is altogether fitting and proper that we should do this.

But, in a larger sense, we can not dedicate — we can not consecrate — we can not hallow — this ground. The brave men, living and dead, who struggled here, have consecrated it, far above our poor power to add or detract. The world will little note, nor long remember what we say here, but it can never forget what they did here. It is for us the living, rather, to be dedicated here to the unfinished work which they who fought here have thus far so nobly advanced. It is rather for us to be here dedicated to the great task remaining before us — that from these honored dead we take increased devotion to that cause for which they gave the last full measure of devotion — that we here highly resolve that these dead shall not have died in vain — that this nation, under God, shall have a new birth of freedom — and that government of the people, by the people, for the people, shall not perish from the earth.       —ABRAHAM LINCOLN, *Gettysburg Address*

## 7d Summarizing a text

When you feel that you have read and understood the text, summarize the contents in your own words. A summary *briefly* captures the main ideas of a text and omits information that is less important. Try to identify the key points in the text, find the essential evidence supporting those points, and explain the contents concisely and fairly, so that a reader unfamiliar with the original can make sense of it all. Deciding what to leave out can make summarizing a tricky task — but mastering this skill can serve you well in all the reading you do in your academic, professional, and civic life. (For more information on writing a summary, see 13d.)

### Student summary of an assigned text

Students Fernando Sanchez and Sarah Lum, whose critical reading notes appear in this chapter, summarized the "Mistakes" article. Here is Sarah's summary:

> In "'Mistakes Are a Fact of Life': A National Comparative Study," Andrea and Karen Lunsford investigate the claim that students today can't write as well as students in the past. To determine how writing has changed over time, they replicated the 1984 Connors and Lunsford study of errors in student writing to find similarities and differences between the formal errors made by first-year writing students in 2006. Their findings reveal that the number of mistakes made two decades ago are consistent with the number of errors made today and that actually the rate of mistakes has stayed stable for a hundred years. The authors found that slang and shorthand commonly used by young adults do not interfere with college writing. The major difference between writing then and now is that students are writing more argument essays as opposed to personal narratives and that typical papers are two-and-a-half times longer now. We can't avoid making mistakes, but we can document them and figure out means of improvement.

*Begins by identifying authors, title, and date of article, and by stating main goal of study*

*Summarizes major findings*

*Closes with comment that captures main point of article*

## 7e   Analyzing and reflecting on a text

When you feel that you understand the meaning of the text, move on to your analysis by asking additional questions about the text.

**ANALYZING IDEAS AND EXAMPLES**

- What are the main points in this text? Are they implied or explicitly stated?
- Which points do you agree with? Which do you disagree with? Why?
- Does anything in the text surprise you? Why, or why not?
- What kinds of examples does the text use? What other kinds of evidence does the text offer to back up the main points? Can you think of other examples or evidence that should have been included?
- Are viewpoints other than those of the author or creator included and treated fairly?
- How trustworthy are the sources the text cites or refers to?

- What assumptions does the text make? Are those assumptions valid? Why, or why not?

**ANALYZING FOR OVERALL IMPRESSION**

- Do the authors or creators achieve their purpose? Why, or why not?
- What intrigues, puzzles, or irritates you about the text? Why?
- What else would you like to know?

## Student analysis of an assigned text

After previewing, reading, annotating, and summarizing the article, students Sarah Lum and Fernando Sanchez analyzed the text. Here is Fernando's analysis:

Reading the first page gives the audience a good overview of what they are about to dive into. Andrea and Karen Lunsford clearly imply what side of the argument they will defend and expand on — that student errors have not increased over time. As I read, I noticed that the title quotation slowly and eloquently ties in with the argument. The authors' word choice (*positivity*, *optimism*, etc.) reminded me of this, and the phrase "mistakes are a fact of life" is also repeated several times to underline the main point.

States major finding of article

Shows how title quotation guides argument of entire essay

While a lot of people today think that students just can't write as well as we used to, this study proves the fear to be false. I am convinced by the results, which are based on careful analysis of a large number of student essays. One factor that did surprise me was an increase in student essay length. What happened between 1986 and 2006 that caused such a huge change in length? The authors suggest that the change is related to use of technology, and this explanation makes sense to me.

Notes surprising aspect of essay and speculates on causes

Explains why he agrees with major point of essay

The authors use clear and direct examples from other studies over a century, and the tables they use really help readers understand the differences between the studies. In fact, this was a major goal: the authors want readers to see for themselves the similarities and differences in student errors that studies have shown over the past hundred years. They have done a lot of research in order to find similar studies of error. In addition, one of the authors, Andrea Lunsford, was a researcher on a previous study. In my estimation, the authors achieved their purpose and have the evidence to support their conclusion. This article was well written, well explained, and well researched.

Notes effect of good examples and of tables representing findings

Notes how authors establish credibility

# 7f  Analyzing visual texts

You can use the steps given in 7b–e to read any kind of text created by human beings, from a scholarly article for a research project to a prehistoric cave painting or an Instagram image. You may be at least as accustomed to reading visual texts as you are to reading words, whether or not you take time to make a formal analysis of what you see. But pausing to look closely and reflect on how a visual text works is a useful exercise that can make you more aware of how visuals convey information.

Following is a Pulitzer Prize–winning photograph (by Craig F. Walker of the *Denver Post*) and its caption. This image appeared as part of a series documenting the experiences of a Colorado teenager, Ian Fisher, who joined the U.S. Army to fight in Iraq.

*During a weekend home from his first assignment at Fort Carson, Colorado, Ian walked through a Denver-area mall with his new girlfriend, Kayla Spitzlberger, on December 15, 2007, and asked whether she wanted to go ring shopping. She was excited, but working out the financing made him nervous. They picked out the engagement ring in about five minutes, but Ian wouldn't officially propose until Christmas Day in front of her family. The couple had met in freshman math class but never really dated until now. She wrote to him during basic training and decided to give Ian a chance. The engagement would end before Valentine's Day.*

An analysis of this photograph made the following points:

The couple are in the center of the photo — and at the center of our attention. But at this moment of choosing an engagement ring, they do not look "engaged" with each other. Kayla looks excited but uncertain, as if she knows that Ian feels doubts, but she hopes he will change his mind. She is looking right at him, with her

Notes what is foregrounded in image and relates it to "main point" of visual

body leaning toward him but her head leaning away: she looks very tentative. Ian is looking away from Kayla, and the expression on his face suggests that he's already having second thoughts about the expense of the ring (we see his wallet on the counter by his elbow) and perhaps even about asking Kayla to marry him. The accompanying caption helps us interpret the image, telling us about the couple's brief history together and noting that the engagement will last less than two months after this moment. But the message comes through pretty clearly without words.

*Analyzes why they "do not look 'engaged' with each other"*

*Shows how caption underscores image's main point*

Ian and Kayla look as if they're trying on roles in this photograph. She looks ready to take the plunge, and he is resisting. These attitudes conform to stereotypical gender roles for a man and woman considering marriage (or going shopping, for that matter). The woman is expected to want the marriage and the ring; the man knows that he shouldn't show too much enthusiasm about weddings and shopping. It's hard for the reader to tell whether Ian and Kayla really feel that they are making good or careful choices for their situation at this moment or whether they're just doing what they think they're supposed to do under the circumstances.

*Analysis suggests that people in the image conform to stereotypical gender roles*

The reader also can't tell how the presence of the photographer, Craig F. Walker, affected the couple's actions. The photo is part of a series of images documenting Ian Fisher's life after joining the military, so Walker had probably spent a lot of time with Ian before this photo was taken. Did Ian want to give a particular impression of himself on this day? Were he and Kayla trying on "adult" roles in this situation? Were they feeling pressure to produce a memorable moment for the camera? And what was Walker thinking when he accompanied them to the mall and took this photograph? Did he foresee the end of their engagement when he captured this revealing moment? What was his agenda?

*Notes that photographer's perspective may affect readers' understanding of image*

*Raises questions for further analysis*

 **EXERCISE 7.3**

Write a two- to three-paragraph analysis of a text you have read or seen.

"How can an image be a text?" In its traditional sense, a *text* involves words on paper. But we spend at least as much time reading and analyzing images — including moving images — as we spend on printed words. So it makes sense to broaden the definition of "text" to include anything that sends a message. That's why images are often called *visual texts*.

# 7g A student's critical reading of a text

STUDENT WRITER
Shuqiao Song

Following is an abridged version of a student essay by Shuqiao Song based on her critical reading of Alison Bechdel's graphic novel *Fun Home: A Family Tragicomic*. Shuqiao's critical reading involved looking closely at the words, at the images, and at how the words and images together create a very complex story. For Shuqiao Song's PowerPoint presentation of this essay, see 17f. (Photo © Shuqiao Song)

Song 1

Shuqiao Song

Dr. Andrea Lunsford

English 87N

13 March 2014

Residents of a Dys*FUN*ctional *HOME*

In a 2008 online interview, comic artist Alison Bechdel remarked, "I love words, and I love pictures. But especially, I love them together — in a mystical way that I can't even explain" ("Interview"). Indeed, in her graphic novel memoir, *Fun Home: A Family Tragicomic,* text and image work together in a mystical way: text *and* image. But using both image and text results not in a simple summation but in a strange relationship — as strange as the relationship between Alison Bechdel and her father. These strange pairings have an alluring quality that

Introduces author of the work she is discussing, along with her major topic

Song 3

*First example in support of thesis*

The Bechdels' elaborately restored house is the gilded, but tense, context of young Alison's familial relationships and a metaphor for her father's deceptions. "He used his skillful artifice not to make things, but to make things appear to be what they were not," Bechdel notes alongside an image of her father taking a photo of their family, shown in Fig. 2 (*Fun* 16). The scene represents the nature of her father's artifice; her father is *posing* a photo, an image of their family.

Fig. 2. Alison's father posing a family photo (Bechdel, *Fun* 16).

*Second example in support of thesis*

In that same scene, Bechdel also shows her own sleight of hand; she manipulates the scene and reverses her father's role and her own to show young Alison taking the photograph of the family and her father posing in Alison's place (Fig. 3). In the image, young Alison symbolizes Bechdel in

Fig. 3. Alison and her father trade places (Bechdel, *Fun* 17).

the present — looking back through the camera lens to create a portrait of her family. But unlike her father, she isn't using false images to deceive. Bechdel overcomes the treason of images by confessing herself as an "artificer" to her audience (*Fun* 16). Bechdel doesn't villainize the illusory nature of images; she repurposes their illusory power to reinterpret her memories. . . .

Song 8

Works Cited

Bechdel, Alison. *Fun Home: A Family Tragicomic*. Boston: Houghton
Mifflin, 2006. Print.

---. Interview with Eva Sollberger. "Stuck in Vermont 109: Alison
Bechdel." *YouTube*. YouTube, 13 Dec. 2008. Web. 6 Feb. 2014.

Chabani, Karim. "Double Trajectories: Crossing Lines in *Fun Home*." *GRAAT*
1 Mar. 2007: 1-14. Print.

Chute, Hillary. "An Interview with Alison Bechdel." *MFS Modern Fiction
Studies* 52.4 (2006): 1004-13. *Project Muse*. Web. 30 Jan. 2014.

Gardner, Jared. "Autography's Biography, 1972-2007." *Biography* 31.1
(Winter 2008). *Project Muse*. Web. 11 Feb. 2014.

Magritte, René. *The Treason of Images*. 1929. Los Angeles County Museum
of Art. *lacma.org*. Web. 11 Feb. 2014.

Uses MLA style
appropriately

## THINKING CRITICALLY ABOUT READING

Choose a text you have been assigned to read for a class. Read it over carefully,
annotating the material, and then write a one- or two-paragraph summary of the
contents. Then analyze your summary. Did your annotations help you summarize?
Why, or why not? Does your summary interpret the material or aim for an objective
stance? What does your summary omit from the original material, and how did you
decide what to leave out?

# CHAPTER 8

# Analyzing Arguments

IN **ADVERTISEMENTS,** news stories, textbooks, reports, and media of all kinds, language competes for our attention and argues for our agreement. Since argument so pervades all our lives, you need to be able to recognize and use it effectively — and to question your own arguments as well as those put forth by others.

> **CONNECT:** How does an argument get your attention? **5g on written-word texts, 8d, 17b on presentations**
>
> **CREATE:** Write or record a brief analysis of how a text you are reading appeals to its intended audience.
>
> **REFLECT:** Go to **macmillanhighered.com/smh,** and respond to **8. Analyzing Arguments > Student Writing > Rhetorical analysis (Ateyea).**

## 8a  Recognizing and contextualizing argument

In one important sense, all language use has an argumentative edge. When you greet friends warmly, you wish to convince them that you are genuinely glad to see them, that you value their presence. Even apparently objective news reporting has strong argumentative overtones. By putting a particular story on the front page, for example, a newspaper argues that this subject is more important than others; by using emotional language or by focusing on certain details, a newscaster tries to persuade the audience to view an event in a particular way.

Emily Lesk's primary purpose in her essay "Red, White, and Everywhere" is to reflect on her own identification with one particular American icon, Coca-Cola (4l). But her essay clearly has an argumentative edge, asking readers to examine their cultural identifications and to understand the power of advertising in creating and sustaining such identifications.

It's possible, then, to read any message or text, verbal or visual, as an argument, even if argument is not its primary purpose. In much academic writing, however, *argument* is more narrowly defined as a text that makes a claim (usually in the form of an arguable statement) and supports it fully.

## Guidelines for analyzing an argument

Here are some questions that can help you judge the effectiveness of an argument:

- What conclusions about the argument can you reach by playing both the believing and the doubting game? **(8b)**
- What cultural contexts inform the argument, and what do they tell you about where the writer is coming from? **(8b and c)**
- What emotional, ethical, and logical appeals is the writer making in support of the argument? **(8d)**
- How has the writer established credibility to write about the topic? **(8d)**
- What is the claim (or arguable statement)? Is it qualified in any way? **(8e)**
- What reasons and assumptions support and underlie the claim? **(8e)**
- What additional evidence backs up the assumption and claim? How current and reliable are the sources? **(8e)**
- How does the writer use images, graphics, or other visuals to support the argument? **(8e)**
- What fallacies can you identify, and what effect do they have on the argument's persuasiveness? **(8f and g)**
- What is the overall impression you get from analyzing the argument? Are you convinced?

## 8b Thinking critically about argument

Although critical thinking has a number of complex definitions, it is essentially the process by which you make sense of all the information around you. As such, critical thinking is a crucial component of argument, for it guides you in recognizing, formulating, and examining arguments.

Several elements of critical thinking are especially important.

**Playing the believing — and the doubting — game.** Critical thinkers are able to shift stances as they take in an argument, allowing them to gain different perspectives. One good way to begin is to play the *believing game*: that is, put yourself in the position of the person creating the argument, see the topic from that person's point of view as much as possible, and think carefully about how and why that person arrived at the claim(s). Once you have given the argument your sympathetic attention, listening very carefully to its point of view, play the *doubting game*: revisit the argument, looking skeptically at each claim and examining each piece of evidence to see how well, or if, it supports the claim. Eventually, this process of believing and doubting will become natural.

**Asking pertinent questions.** Concentrate on getting to the heart of the matter. Whether you are thinking about others' ideas or about your own, you will want to ask the following kinds of questions:

- What is the writer or speaker's agenda — his or her unstated purpose?
- Why does this person hold these ideas or beliefs? What larger social, economic, political, or other factors may have influenced him or her?
- What does he or she want the audience to do — and why?
- What are the writer or speaker's qualifications for making this argument?
- What reasons does he or she offer to support the ideas? Are they good reasons?
- What are the underlying values or unstated assumptions of the argument? Do you accept them — and why, or why not?
- What sources does the writer or speaker rely on? How current and reliable are they? What agendas do these sources have? Are any perspectives left out?
- What objections do you have to the argument?
- What individual or organization is responsible for publishing or promoting the argument? (See 12d.)
- How do media and design appeal to the audience? Study the visual and audio aspects of the argument, including the use of color, graphics, and multimedia techniques. What do they contribute to the argument?

**Getting information.** To help you decide whether to accept an argument, often you will need to find more information on the topic as well as other perspectives.

**Interpreting and assessing information.** No information that comes to us in language or visuals is neutral; all of it has a perspective — a spin. Your job as a critical thinker is to identify the perspective and to assess it, examining its sources and finding out what you can about its context. Asking pertinent questions will help you examine the interpretations and conclusions drawn by others.

**Making and assessing your own arguments.** The ultimate goal of all critical thinking is to construct your own ideas and reach your own sound and fair conclusions. These, too, you must question and assess. The rest of this chapter will guide you in the art of assessing arguments.

## 8c  Considering cultural contexts

If you want to understand as fully as possible the arguments of others, remember that writers come from an astonishing variety of cultural and linguistic backgrounds. Pay attention to clues to cultural context, and be open to the many ways of thinking you will encounter. In short, practice the believing game before you play the doubting game — especially when analyzing an argument influenced by a culture different from your own. In addition, remember that within any given culture there are great differences among individuals. So don't expect that every member of a culture will argue in any one way.

Above all, watch your own assumptions very closely as you read. Just because you assume that the use of statistics as support for your argument holds more water than, say, precedent drawn from religious belief, you can't assume that all writers agree with you. Take a writer's cultural beliefs into account before you begin to analyze an argument. (See Chapter 27.)

# 8d  Reading emotional, ethical, and logical appeals

Aristotle categorized argumentative appeals into three types: emotional appeals that speak to our hearts and values (known to the ancient Greeks as *pathos*), ethical appeals that appeal to character (*ethos*), and logical appeals that involve factual information and evidence (*logos*).

## ☐  Analyzing emotional appeals

Emotional appeals stir our emotions and remind us of deeply held values. When politicians argue that the country needs more tax relief, they almost always use examples of one or more families they have met, stressing the concrete ways in which a tax cut would improve the quality of their lives. Doing so creates a strong emotional appeal. Some have criticized the use of emotional appeals in argument, claiming that they are a form of manipulation intended to mislead an audience. But emotional appeals are an important part of almost every argu-

© RICK FRIEDMAN/CORBIS

ment. Critical readers "talk back" to such appeals by analyzing them, deciding which are acceptable and which are not.

The accompanying photo shows gun-rights advocates rallying in Boston. To what emotions are the protesters appealing here? Do you find this appeal effective, manipulative, or both? Would you accept this argument? On what grounds would you do so?

## ☐  Analyzing ethical appeals

Ethical appeals support the credibility, moral character, and goodwill of the argument's creator. These appeals are especially important for critical readers to recognize and evaluate. Should a respected baseball manager's credibility in the clubhouse convince you to invest in mutual funds he promotes? Should an actress respected for her award-winning roles convince you to give to a particular charity? To identify ethical appeals in arguments, ask yourself these questions: What is the creator of the argument doing to show that he or she is knowledgeable and credible about the subject — has really done the homework on it? What sort of character does he or she build, and how? More important, is that character trustworthy? What does the creator of the argument do to show that he or she has the best interests of an audience in mind? Do those best interests match your own, and, if not, how does that alter the effectiveness of the argument? Try to identify the ethical appeals that documentary filmmaker Joshua Oppenheimer makes in this excerpt from his "Director's Statement" for the *The Act of Killing*, a film in which the perpetrators of massacres in 1960s Indonesia reenact the murders they committed:

> When I began developing *The Act of Killing* in 2005, I had already been filming for three years with survivors of the 1965–66 massacres. I had lived for a year in a village of survivors in the plantation belt outside Medan. I had become very close to several of the families there. During that time, Christine Cynn and I collaborated with a fledgling plantation workers' union to make *The Globalization Tapes,* and began production on a forthcoming film about a family of survivors that begins to confront (with tremendous dignity and patience) the killers who murdered their son. Our efforts to record the survivors' experiences — never before expressed publicly — took place in the shadow of their torturers, as well as the executioners who murdered their relatives — men who, like Anwar Congo, would boast about what they did.
> —JOSHUA OPPENHEIMER

☐ **Analyzing logical appeals**

Logical appeals are often viewed as especially trustworthy: "The facts don't lie," some say. Of course, facts are not the only type of logical appeals, which also include firsthand evidence drawn from observations, interviews, surveys and questionnaires, experiments, and personal experience; and secondhand evidence drawn from authorities, the testimony of others, statistics, and other print and online sources. Critical readers need to examine logical appeals just as carefully as emotional and ethical ones. What is the source of the logical appeal — and is that source trustworthy? Are all terms defined clearly? Has the logical evidence presented been taken out of context, and, if so, does that change the meaning of the data? Look, for example, at the following brief passage:

---

 **MULTI-LINGUAL** | **RECOGNIZING APPEALS IN VARIOUS SETTINGS**

You may be familiar with emotional, ethical, or logical appeals that are not discussed in this chapter. If so, consider describing them — and how they work — to your class. Doing so would deepen the entire class's understanding of what appeals carry the most power in particular settings.

[I]t is well for us to remember that, in an age of increasing illiteracy, 60 percent of the world's illiterates are women. Between 1960 and 1970, the number of illiterate men in the world rose by 8 million, while the number of illiterate women rose by 40 million.[1] And the number of illiterate women is increasing.  — ADRIENNE RICH, "What Does a Woman Need to Know?"

As a critical reader, you would question these facts and hence check the footnote to discover the source, which in this case is the UN *Compendium of Social Statistics*. At this point, you might accept this document as authoritative — or you might look further into the United Nations' publications policy, especially to find out how that body defines *illiteracy*. You would also no doubt wonder why Rich chose the decade from 1960 to 1970 for her example and, as a result, check to see when this essay was written. As it turns out, the essay was written in 1979, so the most recent data available on literacy would have come from the decade of the sixties. That fact might make you question the timeliness of these statistics: Are they still meaningful more than forty years later? How might these statistics have changed?

If you attend closely to the emotional, ethical, and logical appeals in any argument, you will be on your way to analyzing — and evaluating — it.

## ☐ Analyzing appeals in a visual argument

The poster on p. 146, from TurnAround, an organization devoted to helping victims of domestic violence, is "intended to strike a chord with abusers as well as their victims." The dramatic combination of words and image builds on an analogy between a child and a target and makes strong emotional and ethical appeals.

The bull's-eye that draws your attention to the center of the poster is probably the first thing you notice when you look at the image. Then you may observe that the "target" is, in fact, a child's body; it also has arms, legs, and a head with wide, staring eyes. The heading at the upper left, "A child is not a target," reinforces the bull's-eye/child connection.

This poster's stark image and headline appeal to viewers' emotions, offering the uncomfortable reminder that children are often the victims of domestic violence. The design causes viewers to see a target first and only afterward recognize that the target is actually a child — an unsettling experience. But the poster also offers ethical appeals ("TurnAround can help") to show that the organization is credible and that it supports the worthwhile goal of ending "the cycle of domestic violence" by offering counseling and other support services. Finally, it uses the logical appeal of a statistic to support this ethical appeal, noting that TurnAround has served "more than 10,000 women, children and men each year" and giving specific information about where to get help.

**macmillanhighered.com/smh**

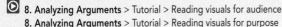 **8. Analyzing Arguments** > Tutorial > Reading visuals for audience
**8. Analyzing Arguments** > Tutorial > Reading visuals for purpose

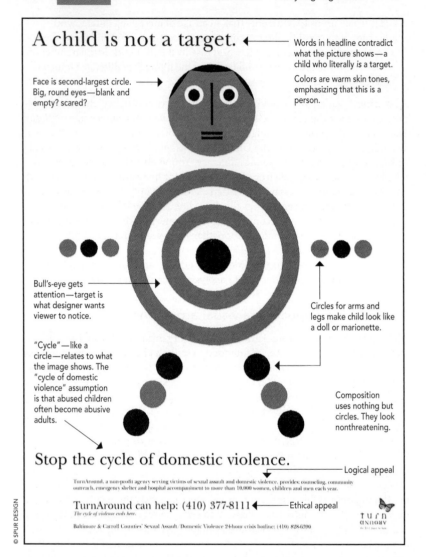

A child is not a target. ← Words in headline contradict what the picture shows—a child who literally *is* a target.

Face is second-largest circle. Big, round eyes—blank and empty? scared? →

Colors are warm skin tones, emphasizing that this is a person.

Bull's-eye gets attention—target is what designer wants viewer to notice.

Circles for arms and legs make child look like a doll or marionette.

"Cycle"—like a circle—relates to what the image shows. The "cycle of domestic violence" assumption is that abused children often become abusive adults.

Composition uses nothing but circles. They look nonthreatening.

Stop the cycle of domestic violence. ── Logical appeal

TurnAround, a non-profit agency serving victims of sexual assault and domestic violence, provides counseling, community outreach, emergency shelter and hospital accompaniment to more than 10,000 women, children and men each year.

TurnAround can help: (410) 377-8111 ← Ethical appeal
*The cycle of violence ends here.*

turn around

Baltimore & Carroll Counties' Sexual Assault/Domestic Violence 24-hour crisis hotline: (410) 828-6390

© SPUR DESIGN

## 8e Identifying elements of an argument

According to philosopher Stephen Toulmin's framework for analyzing arguments, most arguments contain common features: a *claim* or *claims*; *reasons* for the claim; *assumptions*, whether stated or unstated, that underlie the argument (Toulmin calls these *warrants*); *evidence* or *backing*, such as facts,

## Elements of a Toulmin argument

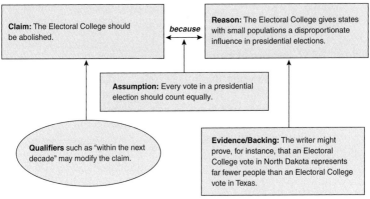

authoritative opinions, examples, and statistics; and *qualifiers* that limit the claim in some way.

## ☐ Identifying claims

Claims (also referred to as arguable statements) are statements that the writer wants to prove. In longer essays, you may detect a series of linked claims or even several separate claims that you need to analyze before you agree to accept them. Claims worthy of arguing are those that are debatable: to say "Ten degrees Fahrenheit is cold" is a claim, but it is probably not debatable — unless you are describing northern Alaska, where ten degrees might seem balmy. If a movie review you are reading has as its claim "Great movie!" is that claim debatable? Probably not if the reviewer is basing the claim solely on personal taste. But if the reviewer goes on to offer good reasons to admire the movie, along with strong evidence to support the reasons, he or she could present a debatable — and therefore arguable — claim. In the example shown above, the claim that the Electoral College should be abolished is certainly arguable; a Google search will turn up numerous arguments for and against this claim.

## ☐ Considering reasons

In fact, a claim is only as good as the reasons attached to it. If a student claims that course portfolios should be graded pass or fail because so many students in the class work full-time jobs, critical readers may question whether that reason is sufficient to support the claim. In the example above, the writer gives a reason — that states with small populations have too much influence over the

Electoral College — to support the claim of abolishing the institution. As you analyze claims, test each reason by asking how directly it supports the claim, how timely it is, and what counter-reasons you could offer to question it.

## □ Identifying assumptions

Putting a claim and reasons together often results in what Aristotle called an *enthymeme*, an argument that rests on an assumption the writer expects the audience to hold. These assumptions (which Toulmin calls *warrants*) that connect claim and reasons are often the hardest to detect in an argument, partly because they are often unstated, sometimes masking a weak link. As a result, it's especially important to identify the assumptions in arguments you are analyzing. Once the assumption is identified, you can test it against evidence and your own experience before accepting it. If a writer argues that the Electoral College should be abolished because states with small populations have undue influence on the outcome of presidential elections, what is the assumption underlying this claim and reason? It is that *presidential elections should give each voter the same amount of influence*. As a critical reader, remember that such assumptions are deeply affected by culture and belief: ask yourself, then, what cultural differences may be at work in your response to any argument.

## □ Analyzing evidence or backing

Evidence, which Toulmin calls *backing*, also calls for careful analysis in arguments. In an argument about abolishing the Electoral College, the writer may offer as evidence a statistical analysis of the number of voters represented by an Electoral College vote in the least populous states and in the most populous states; a historical discussion of why the Founding Fathers developed the Electoral College system; or psychological studies showing that voters in states where one political party dominates feel disengaged from presidential elections. As a critical reader, you must evaluate each piece of evidence the writer offers, asking specifically how it relates to the claim, whether it is appropriate and timely, and whether it comes from a credible source.

## □ Considering qualifiers

Qualifiers offer a way of limiting or narrowing a claim so that it is as precise as possible. Words or phrases that signal a qualification include *many, sometimes, in these circumstances*, and so on. Claims having no qualifiers can sometimes lead to overgeneralizations. For example, the statement *The Electoral College should be abolished* is less precise than *The Electoral College should be abolished by 2024*. Look carefully for qualifiers in the arguments you analyze, since they will affect the strength and reach of the claim.

◻ **Analyzing elements of a visual argument**

Visual arguments, too, can be analyzed using Toulmin's methods. Look closely at the advertisement to the right. If you decide that this advertisement is claiming that people should adopt shelter pets, you might word a reason like this: *Dogs and cats need people, not just shelter.* You might note that the campaign assumes that people make pets happier (and that pets deserve happiness) — and that the image backs up the overall message that this inquisitive, well-cared-for dog is happier living in a home with a human than in a shelter. Considering unstated qualifiers (should *every* person consider adopting a shelter pet?) and thinking about potential evidence for the claim would help you complete an analysis of this visual argument.

## 8f   Identifying fallacies

Fallacies have traditionally been viewed as serious flaws that damage the effectiveness of an argument. But arguments are ordinarily fairly complex in that they always occur in some specific rhetorical situation and in some particular place and time; thus what looks like a fallacy in one situation may appear quite different in another. The best advice is to learn to identify fallacies but to be cautious in jumping to quick conclusions about them. Rather than thinking of them as errors you can root out and use to discredit an arguer, you might think of them as barriers to common ground and understanding, since they so often shut off rather than engender debate. If a letter to the editor argues *If this newspaper thinks additional tax cuts are going to help the middle-class family, then this newspaper is run by imbeciles*, it clearly indulges in a fallacy — in this case, an argument ad hominem or argument against character. But the more important point is that this kind of argument shuts down debate: few are going to respond reasonably to being called imbeciles.

## ☐ Identifying verbal fallacies

### Ad hominem

Ad hominem charges make a personal attack rather than focusing on the issue at hand.

▶ **Who cares what that fat loudmouth says about the nation's health care system?**

### Guilt by association

Guilt by association attacks someone's credibility by linking that person with a person or activity that the audience will consider bad, suspicious, or untrustworthy.

▶ **She does not deserve reelection; her husband has had extramarital affairs.**

### False authority

False authority is often used by advertisers who show famous actors or athletes testifying to the greatness of a product about which they may know very little.

▶ **He's today's greatest NASCAR driver — and he banks at National Mutual!**

### Bandwagon appeal

Bandwagon appeal suggests that a great movement is under way and the reader will be a fool or a traitor not to join it.

▶ **This new smartphone is everyone's must-have item. Where's yours?**

### Flattery

Flattery tries to persuade readers by suggesting that they are thoughtful, intelligent, or perceptive enough to agree with the writer.

▶ **You have the taste to recognize the superlative artistry of Bling diamond jewelry.**

### In-crowd appeal

In-crowd appeal, a special kind of flattery, invites readers to identify with an admired and select group.

▶ **Want to know a secret that more and more of Middletown's successful young professionals are finding out about? It's Mountainbrook Manor condominiums.**

### Veiled threat

Veiled threats try to frighten readers into agreement by hinting that they will suffer adverse consequences if they don't agree.

▶ **If Public Service Electric Company does not get an immediate 15 percent rate increase, its services to you may be seriously affected.**

### False analogy

False analogies make comparisons between two situations that are not alike in important respects.

▶ **The volleyball team's sudden descent in the rankings resembled the sinking of the *Titanic*.**

### Begging the question

Begging the question is a kind of circular argument that treats a debatable statement as if it had been proved true.

▶ **Television news covered that story well; I learned all I know about it by watching TV.**

### Post hoc fallacy

The post hoc fallacy (from the Latin *post hoc, ergo propter hoc*, which means "after this, therefore caused by this") assumes that just because B happened *after* A, it must have been *caused* by A.

▶ **We should not rebuild the town docks because every time we do, a big hurricane comes along and damages them.**

### Non sequitur

A non sequitur (Latin for "it does not follow") attempts to tie together two or more logically unrelated ideas as if they were related.

▶ **If we can send a spaceship to Mars, then we can surely discover a cure for cancer.**

### Either-or fallacy

The either-or fallacy insists that a complex situation can have only two possible outcomes.

▶ **If we do not build the new highway, businesses downtown will be forced to close.**

### Hasty generalization

A hasty generalization bases a conclusion on too little evidence or on bad or misunderstood evidence.

◑ **I couldn't understand the lecture today, so I'm sure this course will be impossible.**

### Oversimplification

Oversimplification claims an overly direct relationship between a cause and an effect.

◑ **If we prohibit the sale of alcohol, we will get rid of binge drinking.**

### Straw man

A straw-man argument misrepresents the opposition by pretending that opponents agree with something that few reasonable people would support.

◑ **My opponent believes that we should offer therapy to the terrorists. I disagree.**

## ☐ Identifying visual fallacies

Fallacies can also take the form of misleading images. The sheer power of images can make them especially difficult to analyze — people tend to believe what they see. Nevertheless, photographs and other visuals can be manipulated to present a false impression.

### Misleading photographs

Faked or altered photos have existed since the invention of photography, and fakes continue to surface. Here, for example, are an original photograph of an Iranian missile launch and the doctored image, showing a fourth launching missile, that Iran released to demonstrate its military might.

Today's technology makes such photo alterations easier than ever, if also easier to detect. But photographs need not be altered to try to fool viewers.

Think of all the photos that make a politician look misleadingly bad or good. In these cases, you should closely examine the motives of those responsible for publishing the images.

### Misleading charts and graphs

Facts and statistics, too, can be presented in ways that mislead readers. For example, the following bar graph purports to deliver an argument about how differently Democrats, on the one hand, and Republicans and Independents, on the other, felt about an issue:

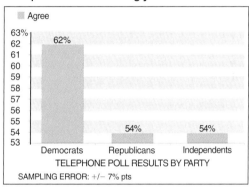

Look closely and you'll see a visual fallacy at work: the vertical axis starts not at zero but at 53 percent, so the visually large difference between the groups is misleading. In fact, a majority of all respondents agree about the issue, and only eight percentage points separate Democrats from Republicans and Independents (in a poll with a margin of error of +/− seven percentage points). Here's how the graph would look if the vertical axis began at zero:

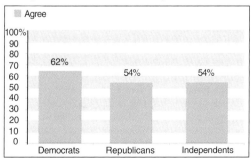

### EXERCISE 8.1

Read the following brief essay by Derek Bok, which argues that college administrators should seek to educate and persuade rather than censor students who use
speech or symbols that others find deeply offensive. Then carry out an analysis of
the argument, beginning with identifying the audience and the author's purpose,
and moving to identifying the claim, reason(s), assumption(s), evidence, and qualifiers (if any). As you work, be sure also to identify the emotional, ethical, and logical
appeals as well as any fallacies put forward by Bok. You may want to compare your
own analysis to the one written by Milena Ateyea in 8g.

For several years, universities have been struggling with the problem of trying to reconcile the rights of free speech with the desire to avoid racial tension.
In recent weeks, such a controversy has sprung up at Harvard. Two students hung
Confederate flags in public view, upsetting students who equate the Confederacy
with slavery. A third student tried to protest the flags by displaying a swastika.

These incidents have provoked much discussion and disagreement. Some
students have urged that Harvard require the removal of symbols that offend
many members of the community. Others reply that such symbols are a form of
free speech and should be protected.

Different universities have resolved similar conflicts in different ways. Some
have enacted codes to protect their communities from forms of speech that are
deemed to be insensitive to the feelings of other groups. Some have refused to
impose such restrictions.

It is important to distinguish between the appropriateness of such communications and their status under the First Amendment. The fact that speech is protected by the First Amendment does not necessarily mean that it is right, proper,
or civil. I am sure that the vast majority of Harvard students believe that hanging a Confederate flag in public view—or displaying a swastika in response—is
insensitive and unwise because any satisfaction it gives to the students who display these symbols is far outweighed by the discomfort it causes to many others.

I share this view and regret that the students involved saw fit to behave in
this fashion. Whether or not they merely wished to manifest their pride in the
South—or to demonstrate the insensitivity of hanging Confederate flags, by
mounting another offensive symbol in return—they must have known that they
would upset many fellow students and ignore the decent regard for the feelings of
others so essential to building and preserving a strong and harmonious community.

To disapprove of a particular form of communication, however, is not enough
to justify prohibiting it. We are faced with a clear example of the conflict between
our commitment to free speech and our desire to foster a community founded
on mutual respect. Our society has wrestled with this problem for many years.
Interpreting the First Amendment, the Supreme Court has clearly struck the balance in favor of free speech.

While communities do have the right to regulate speech in order to uphold
aesthetic standards (avoiding defacement of buildings) or to protect the public
from disturbing noise, rules of this kind must be applied across the board and cannot be enforced selectively to prohibit certain kinds of messages but not others.

Under the Supreme Court's rulings, as I read them, the display of swastikas
or Confederate flags clearly falls within the protection of the free-speech clause

of the First Amendment and cannot be forbidden simply because it offends the feelings of many members of the community. These rulings apply to all agencies of government, including public universities.

Although it is unclear to what extent the First Amendment is enforceable against private institutions, I have difficulty understanding why a university such as Harvard should have less free speech than the surrounding society—or than a public university.

One reason why the power of censorship is so dangerous is that it is extremely difficult to decide when a particular communication is offensive enough to warrant prohibition or to weigh the degree of offensiveness against the potential value of the communication. If we begin to forbid flags, it is only a short step to prohibiting offensive speakers.

I suspect that no community will become humane and caring by restricting what its members can say. The worst offenders will simply find other ways to irritate and insult.

In addition, once we start to declare certain things "offensive," with all the excitement and attention that will follow, I fear that much ingenuity will be exerted trying to test the limits, much time will be expended trying to draw tenuous distinctions, and the resulting publicity will eventually attract more attention to the offensive material than would ever have occurred otherwise.

Rather than prohibit such communications, with all the resulting risks, it would be better to ignore them, since students would then have little reason to create such displays and would soon abandon them. If this response is not possible—and one can understand why—the wisest course is to speak with those who perform insensitive acts and try to help them understand the effects of their actions on others.

Appropriate officials and faculty members should take the lead, as the Harvard House Masters have already done in this case. In talking with students, they should seek to educate and persuade, rather than resort to ridicule or intimidation, recognizing that only persuasion is likely to produce a lasting, beneficial effect. Through such effects, I believe that we act in the manner most consistent with our ideals as an educational institution and most calculated to help us create a truly understanding, supportive community.     —DEREK BOK, "Protecting Freedom of Expression at Harvard"

## 8g  A student's rhetorical analysis of an argument

STUDENT WRITER
Milena Ateyea

For a class assignment, Milena Ateyea was asked to analyze Derek Bok's essay by focusing on the author's use of emotional, ethical, and logical appeals. Her rhetorical analysis follows. (Photo © Milena Ateyea)

### A Curse and a Blessing

*Provocative title suggests mixed response to Bok*

*Connects article to her own experience to build credibility (ethical appeal)*

In 1991, when Derek Bok's essay "Protecting Freedom of Expression at Harvard" was first published in the *Boston Globe*, I had just come to America to escape the oppressive Communist regime in Bulgaria. Perhaps my background explains why I support Bok's argument that we should not put arbitrary limits on freedom of expression. Bok wrote the essay in response to a public display of Confederate flags and a swastika at Harvard, a situation that created a heated controversy among the students. As Bok notes, universities have struggled to achieve a balance between maintaining students' right of free speech and avoiding racist attacks. When choices must be made, however, Bok argues for preserving freedom of expression.

*Brief overview of Bok's argument*

*Identifies Bok's central claim*

*Links Bok's claim to strategies he uses to support it*

*Direct quotations show appeals to emotion through vivid description*

In order to support his claim and bridge the controversy, Bok uses a variety of rhetorical strategies. The author first immerses the reader in the controversy by vividly describing the incident: two Harvard students had hung Confederate flags in public view, thereby "upsetting students who equate the Confederacy with slavery" (51). Another student, protesting the flags, decided to display an even more offensive symbol — the swastika. These actions provoked heated discussions among students. Some students believed that school officials should remove the offensive symbols, whereas others suggested that the symbols "are a form of free speech and should be protected" (51). Bok establishes common ground between the factions: he regrets the actions of the offenders but does not believe we should prohibit such actions just because we disagree with them.

*Bok establishes common ground between two positions*

*Emphasizes Bok's credibility (ethical appeal)*

*Links Bok's credibility to use of logical appeals*

The author earns the reader's respect because of his knowledge and through his logical presentation of the issue. In partial support of his position, Bok refers to U.S. Supreme Court rulings, which remind us that "the display of swastikas or Confederate flags clearly falls within the protection of the free-speech clause of the First Amendment" (52). The author also emphasizes the danger of the slippery slope of censorship when he warns the reader, "If we begin to forbid flags, it is only a short step to prohibiting offensive speakers" (52). Overall, however, Bok's work lacks the kinds of evidence that statistics, interviews with students, and other representative examples of controversial conduct could provide. Thus, his essay may not be strong enough to persuade all readers to make the leap from this specific situation to his general conclusion.

Throughout, Bok's personal feelings are implied but not stated directly. As a lawyer who was president of Harvard for twenty years, Bok knows how to present his opinions respectfully without offending the feelings of the students. However, qualifying phrases like "I suspect that" and "Under the Supreme Court's rulings, as I read them" could weaken the effectiveness of his position. Furthermore, Bok's attempt to be fair to all seems to dilute the strength of his proposed solution. He suggests that one should either ignore the insensitive deeds in the hope that students might change their behavior, or talk to the offending students to help them comprehend how their behavior is affecting other students.

Nevertheless, although Bok's proposed solution to the controversy does not appear at first reading to be very strong, it may ultimately be effective. There is enough flexibility in his approach to withstand various tests, and Bok's solution is general enough that it can change with the times and adapt to community standards.

In writing this essay, Bok faced a challenging task: to write a short response to a specific situation that represents a very broad and controversial issue. Some people may find that freedom of expression is both a curse and a blessing because of the difficulties it creates. As one who has lived under a regime that permitted very limited, censored expression, I am all too aware that I could not have written this response in 1991 in Bulgaria. As a result, I feel, like Derek Bok, that freedom of expression is a blessing, in spite of any temporary problems associated with it.

---

*Marginal annotations:*

Comments critically on kinds of evidence Bok's argument lacks

Reiterates Bok's credibility

Identifies qualifying phrases that may weaken claim

Analyzes weaknesses of Bok's proposed solution

Raises possibility that Bok's imperfect solution may work

Summarizes Bok's task

Ties conclusion back to title

Returns to experience with censorship, which argues for accepting Bok's solution

Work Cited

Bok, Derek. "Protecting Freedom of Expression at Harvard." *Boston
Globe* 25 May 1991. Rpt. in *Current Issues and Enduring Questions*.
Ed. Sylvan Barnet and Hugo Bedau. 6th ed. Boston: Bedford, 2002.
51–52. Print.

 **EXERCISE 8.2**

Working with one or two classmates, analyze a brief argumentative text—an essay, an advertisement, or an editorial cartoon—by playing the believing and doubting game; identifying emotional, ethical, and logical appeals; and listing claims, reasons, assumptions, evidence, and qualifiers. Then work together to create a collaborative critical response to the text you've chosen.

▼ ▼ ▼ ▼ ▼ ▼ ▼ ▼ ▼ ▼ ▼ ▼ ▼ ▼ ▼ ▼ ▼ ▼ ▼ ▼ ▼ ▼ ▼ ▼ ▼ ▼ ▼

## THINKING CRITICALLY ABOUT ANALYZING ARGUMENTS

In the following brief review for *Rolling Stone*, music critic James Hunter recaps five CDs that reissue ten Merle Haggard albums from early in the country star's career. What central claim(s) does Hunter make? What emotional, ethical, and logical appeals does he present in support of his claim, and how effective are these appeals?

### Outlaw Classics: The Albums That Kept Nashville Real in the Sixties and Seventies

[Review of *Merle Haggard* (Capitol Nashville / EMI)]

**BY JAMES HUNTER**

Merle Haggard wasn't the first outsider to rebuke Nashville prissiness in the Sixties—Johnny Cash, who arrived from Sun Records in Memphis, deserves that honor—but Hag was the most down-to-earth soul that the Music City had seen for some time when he loped onto the scene in the mid- to late Sixties. An ex-con from California with Oklahoma roots, he sang eloquently about booze and prison life. His beginnings were in honky-tonk Bakersfield, where he learned first-class musical directness from guys like the great Buck Owens and Wynn Stewart.

For years, Haggard's Sixties and early-Seventies work has been represented chiefly on compilations. This bunch of reissues restores ten of those albums, all with interesting bonus tracks; four of the ten albums have never appeared before on CD. Each showcases Haggard's awesome gifts and inextricable orneriness: There is no Tennessee gothic or flashy Texas ego to this outsider; Haggard was more about subtlety and West Coast calm. A hummable, elastic honky-tonk tune can convey everything he wants to say. His melodies carry a broad range of topics, from cranky love songs ("I'm Gonna Break Every Heart I Can") to prison tunes ("Bring Me Back Home") to perfectly wrought whiskey-and-wine songs, to looks back at his parents' lives. Sometimes, as on the scarily good "I Can't Be Myself," Haggard seems to want to jump out of his own skin; other times, as on "I Threw Away the Rose," he's as centered in his own smooth, crusty tenor as any singer has ever been. In all cases, Haggard sounds like country's coolest customer.

These reissues underscore how Haggard's music far exceeds "Okie from Muskogee," the anti-hippie 1969 smash that made him internationally famous. Cash rocked country up and then went on to become his world's black-clad cultural ambassador. George Jones showed how the field needs at least one opera star, and Willie Nelson yoked local songwriting to American poetry. Haggard proved how crucial it was for a country guy to say what was on his mind—and because he was such a sublime recording artist, he was able to make it stick, right from the start.

# CHAPTER 9

# Constructing Arguments

Y OU SEE AND RESPOND to arguments all the time. When you see a stop sign and come to a halt, you've accepted the argument that stopping at such signs is a sensible thing to do. But constructing an effective argument of your own isn't as easy as putting up a stop sign — or obeying its command to stop. Creating a thorough and convincing argument requires careful reasoning and appropriate attention to your audience, purpose, and other aspects of the rhetorical situation. It also calls for remembering *kairos* — recognizing the most suitable time and place for making your argument and for the most opportune way to make it.

---

**CONNECT:** What audience(s) do you want your argument to reach? **2e, 9f–h**

**CREATE:** Sketch or write a description showing what you know about your audience(s).

**REFLECT:** Go to **macmillanhighered.com/smh**, and respond to **9. Constructing Arguments > Student Writing > Argument project (Mercer-Golden)**.

---

## 9a  Understanding contexts for argument

Remember that writing in general, and arguments in particular, exist in relationship to a larger conversation that surrounds the topic or subject and helps create the context for a particular argument. When you begin to think about making an argument of your own, then, it's important to see what other people are saying and thinking about the topic. Doing so often means doing some early research about your topic and learning about how others have approached the topic and what they have contributed to it. Then you can consider how your argument fits into this larger conversation and how it can make its own distinct contributions to it. You can then put your argument out in the world and see how others will respond — and how you might become a part of an ongoing intellectual conversation.

**Checklist for constructing an argument**

- What is the context of your argument? How much do you know about other arguments related to the one you are making? **(9a)**
- What is the purpose of your argument—to convince others? to make a good decision? to change yourself? **(9b)**
- Is the point you want to make arguable? **(9c)**
- Have you formulated a clear claim and given good reasons for it? **(9d and e)**
- Have you formulated a strong working thesis, and have you qualified it sufficiently? **(9d)**
- How have you established your own credibility in the argument? **(9f)**
- Have you respectfully considered, and addressed, counterarguments? **(9f)**
- How have you incorporated logical appeals into your argument? **(9g)**
- How have you used emotional appeals in your argument? **(9h)**
- How have you used verbal and visual sources in your argument, and how effectively are they integrated into your argument? **(9i)**
- Is your argument clearly organized? **(9j)**
- How will you deliver your argument to audiences? How effective is your design for your purpose? **(9k)**

# 9b Arguing for a purpose

Since all language is in some sense argumentative, the purposes of argument vary widely. For many years, however, traditional notions of argument tended to highlight one purpose — winning. Although winning is still one important purpose of argument, studies of the argument strategies of people from groups historically excluded from public debate — including women and people of color — have demonstrated that it is by no means the only purpose. Researchers Sonja Foss and Cindy Griffin describe an *invitational argument* whose purpose is to invite others to join in mutual exploration based on careful listening and respect. In addition, *Rogerian argument* (named after psychologist Carl Rogers) seeks to find common ground and establish trust among those who disagree about issues. Writers who take either of these approaches try to see where the other person is coming from, looking for "both/and" or "win/win" solutions when possible. You will probably find that your own arguments will serve several different purposes. For instance, if you are trying to decide whether to major in business or in chemistry, you may want to consider, or "argue," all sides of the issue. Your purpose is hardly to win out over someone else; instead, it is to understand your choices in order to make a wise decision.

## ☐ Arguing to win

The most traditional purpose of academic argument, arguing *to win*, is used in campus debating societies, in political debates, in trials, and often in business.

---

TALKING THE TALK | **ARGUMENTS**

"Argument seems so negative — I don't want to attack anybody or contradict what someone else says." In some times and places — law courts, for example — argument may call for attacking the credibility of the opponent. Or you may have used the word *argument* in childhood to describe a conversation in which you voiced nothing more than "I did not!" or "You did too!" But in college writing, you have a chance to reject this narrow definition and to use argument in a much broader way. Instead of attacking or contradicting, you will be expected to explore ideas and to work toward convincing yourself as well as others that these ideas are valuable.

---

The writer or speaker aims to present a position that prevails over or defeats the positions of others. Presidential debates and trials, for example, focus most often not on changing the opponent's mind but on defeating him or her in order to appeal to someone else — the voting public, the judge, and so on.

## ☐ Arguing to convince

More often than not, out-and-out defeat of another is not only unrealistic but also undesirable. Rather, the goal is *to convince* other persons that they should change their minds about an issue. A writer must provide reasons so compelling that the audience willingly agrees with the writer's conclusion. Such is the goal of advocates of assisted suicide: they well know that they cannot realistically hope to defeat or conquer those who oppose such acts. Rather, they understand that they must provide reasons compelling enough to change people's minds.

## ☐ Arguing to understand

Often, a writer must enter into conversation with others and collaborate in seeking the best possible understanding of a problem, exploring all possible approaches and choosing the best alternative. The Rogerian and invitational forms of argument both call for understanding as a major goal of arguing. Argument *to understand* does not seek to conquer or control others or even to convince them. Your purpose in many situations — from trying to decide which job to pursue to exploring with your family the best way to care for an elderly relative — will be to share information and perspectives in order to make informed political, professional, and personal choices.

## ☐ Arguing to change yourself

Sometimes you will find yourself arguing primarily with yourself, and those arguments often take the form of intense meditations on a theme, or even of prayer. In such cases, you may be hoping *to transform something in yourself* or to reach peace of mind on a troubling subject. If you know a familiar mantra or prayer, for example, think of what it "argues" for and how it uses quiet meditation to help achieve that goal.

## 9c  Determining whether a statement can be argued

An early step in an argument intended to convince or decide is to make a statement about a topic and then check to see that the statement can, in fact, be argued. An arguable statement has three characteristics:

1. It attempts to convince readers of something, change their minds about something, or urge them to do something — or it explores a topic in order to make a wise decision.

2. It addresses a problem for which no easily acceptable solution exists or asks a question to which no absolute answer exists.

3. It presents a position that readers might realistically have varying perspectives on.

ARGUABLE STATEMENT  Advertising that features very thin models contributes to the poor self-image that afflicts many young women.

The statement here seeks to convince, addresses a problem — poor self-image among young women — that has no clear-cut solution, and takes a position many could disagree with.

UNARGUABLE STATEMENT  Advertisers earn millions of dollars every year.

This statement does not present a position; it states a fact that can easily be verified and thus offers a poor basis for argument.

### ◢ EXERCISE 9.1

Using the three characteristics just listed, decide which of the following statements are arguable and which are not.

1. *American Hustle* was the best movie of the last decade.
2. The climate of the earth is gradually getting warmer.
3. The United States must further reduce social spending in order to balance the budget.
4. Shakespeare died in 1616.
5. President Roosevelt knew that the Japanese were planning to bomb Pearl Harbor in December 1941.

6. Water boils at 212 degrees Fahrenheit.

7. Van Gogh's paintings are the work of a madman.

8. The incidence of breast cancer has risen in the last ten years.

9. The Federal Emergency Management Agency's response to disasters must be radically improved.

10. A fifty-five-mile-per-hour speed limit lowers accident rates.

## 9d Formulating a working thesis

Once you have an arguable statement, you need to develop it into a working thesis (3c). One way to do so — often called the Toulmin system — is to identify the elements of an argument (8e and 9j), which include the following: the claim or arguable statement; one or more reasons for the claim; and assumptions — sometimes unstated — that underlie the claim and reasons. Let's apply these elements to a specific topic — the use of pesticides.

**Begin with an arguable statement (or initial claim).** The following statement is arguable because it aims to convince, it addresses an issue with no one identifiable answer, and it can realistically be disputed.

| | |
|---|---|
| ARGUABLE STATEMENT (OR INITIAL CLAIM) | Pesticides should be banned. |

**Attach a good reason.** Although the preceding statement does make a claim — that pesticides should be banned — it offers no reason for doing so. To turn a claim into a working thesis for an argument, you need to include at least one good reason to support the arguable statement.

| | |
|---|---|
| REASON | They endanger the lives of farmworkers. |
| WORKING THESIS (CLAIM WITH REASON ATTACHED) | Because they endanger the lives of farmworkers, pesticides should be banned. |

**Develop or identify assumptions underlying the claim and reasons.** Once you have a working thesis, examine your assumptions to help test your reasoning and strengthen your argument. Begin by identifying underlying assumptions that support the working thesis.

| | |
|---|---|
| WORKING THESIS | Because they endanger the lives of farmworkers, pesticides should be banned. |
| ASSUMPTION 1 | Workers have a right to a safe working environment. |
| ASSUMPTION 2 | Substances that endanger the lives of workers deserve to be banned. |

Once you have a working thesis, you may want to use qualifiers to make it more precise and thus less susceptible to criticism. The preceding thesis might be qualified in this way:

 **Because they *may* endanger the lives of farmworkers, *most* pesticides should be banned.**

 **EXERCISE 9.2**

Find or create two arguable statements. Then formulate two working theses based on these statements, identifying the claim, reason(s), and assumption(s) for each thesis.

**EXERCISE 9.3**

Formulate an arguable statement, and create a working thesis, for two of the following general topics.

1. legalizing marijuana
2. creating an amnesty program for illegal immigrants
3. lowering college tuition
4. reinstating a military draft
5. downloading music

**EXERCISE 9.4**

Working with two other members of your class, find two current advertisements you consider particularly eye-catching and persuasive. Then work out what central claim each ad is making, and identify reasons and assumptions in support of the claim. Finally, prepare a brief collaborative report of your findings for the class.

## 9e Finding good reasons

In his *Rhetoric*, Aristotle discusses various ways that one can support a claim. Torture, he notes, makes for a very convincing argument but not one that reasonable people will resort to. In effecting real changes in minds and hearts, we need instead to rely on *good reasons* — reasons that establish our credibility, that appeal to logic, and that appeal to emotion (9f–h). You can use these appeals to analyze the arguments of others (8d) as well as to construct arguments of your own.

## 9f Making ethical appeals

To make your argument convincing, you must first gain the respect and trust of your readers, or establish your credibility with them. The ancient Greeks called this particular kind of character appeal *ethos*, often known today as an ethical appeal (8d). You can establish credibility by demonstrating your knowledge of the topic, by showing that you and your audience share at least some common ground, and by showing yourself to be fair and evenhanded. Visuals can strengthen your ability to make such ethical appeals.

## ☐ Demonstrating knowledge about the topic

A writer can establish credibility first by demonstrating knowledge about the topic at hand. You can show that you have some personal experience with the subject: for example, if you are a former preschool teacher, you could mention your teaching background as part of an argument for increased funding of universal pre-K programs. In addition, showing that you have thought about and researched the subject carefully can help you establish a confident tone.

To determine whether you can effectively present yourself as knowledgeable enough to argue about an issue, consider the following questions:

- Can you provide information about your topic from sources other than your own knowledge?
- How reliable are your sources?
- Do any sources contradict one another? If so, can you account for or resolve the contradictions?
- If you have personal experience relating to the issue, would telling about this experience help support your claim?

These questions may help you see what other work you need to do to establish credibility: perhaps you should do more research, resolve contradictions, refocus your working thesis, or even change your topic.

## ☐ Finding common ground

Many arguments between people or groups are doomed to end without resolution because the two sides occupy no common ground, no starting point of agreement. They are, to use an informal phrase, coming from completely different places. Such has often been the case, for example, in India-Pakistan talks, in which the beginning positions of each party have directly conflicted with those of the other side, leaving no room for a settlement that appeases both nations.

Lack of common ground also dooms many arguments that take place in our everyday lives. If you and your roommate cannot agree on how often to clean your apartment, for instance, the difficulty may well be that your definition of a clean apartment conflicts radically with your roommate's. You may find, in fact, that you will not be able to resolve such issues until you can establish common definitions, ones that can turn futile quarrels into constructive arguments. (For more on establishing common ground, see Chapter 28.)

Common ground is just as important in written arguments as it is in diplomatic negotiations or personal disputes. The following questions can help you find common ground in presenting an argument:

- What are the differing perspectives on this issue?
- What common ground can you find — aspects of the issue on which all sides agree?
- How can you express such agreement clearly to all sides?
- How can you discover — and consider — opinions on this issue that differ from your own?
- How can you use language — occupational, regional, or ethnic varieties of English or languages other than English (29c–e) — to establish common ground with those you address?

## ☐ Showing fairness toward counterarguments

Being fair and reasonable in arguments you make calls for considering counterarguments and alternative points of view. When you begin work on an argument, you need to look not only for sources and evidence that support your point of view but also for those that take different or even opposing points of view. Only when you have considered those counterarguments carefully and tried to look at your topic from their vantage point can you go on to address them in your own argument. Addressing alternate points of view goes a long way to convince readers that you are fair, credible, and ethical. To do so, ask questions like these:

- How can you show that you are taking into account all significant points of view?
- How can you demonstrate that you understand and sympathize with points of view other than your own?
- What can you do to show that you have considered evidence carefully, even when it does not support your position?

Some writers, instead of demonstrating fairness, may make unjustified attacks on an opponent's credibility. In your writing, avoid such attacks, which are known as fallacies (8f).

## ☐ Making ethical appeals with visuals

In arguments and other kinds of writing, visuals can combine with text to help present a writer or an organization as trustworthy and credible. Like businesses, many institutions and individuals are using logos and other images to brand themselves as they wish the public to see them. The Sustainable Food Laboratory logo, seen here, suggests the organization is concerned about food production as well as the environment.

© SUSTAINABLE FOOD LAB

Visuals that make ethical appeals add to your credibility and fairness as a writer. Just as you consider the impression your LinkedIn profile image makes on your audience, you should think about what kind of case you're making for yourself when you choose images and design elements for your argument.

### EXERCISE 9.5

List the ways in which the Sustainable Food Laboratory's logo demonstrates knowledge, establishes common ground, and shows fairness. Do you think the visual is helpful in convincing you of the organization's credibility? Why, or why not?

### EXERCISE 9.6

Using a working thesis you have drafted for a current project, write a paragraph or two describing how you would go about establishing your credibility in arguing that thesis.

## 9g Making logical appeals

While the character a writer presents in writing always exerts a strong appeal (or lack of appeal) in an argument, credibility alone cannot and should not carry the full burden of convincing readers. Indeed, many are inclined to think that the logic of the argument — the reasoning behind it — is as important as its ethos. Logical appeals (8d), known to the ancient Greeks as *logos*, can thus be very effective; particularly useful types of logical appeals include examples, precedents, and narratives; authority and testimony; causes and effects; and inductive and deductive reasoning. In addition, visuals can help you enhance your logical appeals.

### ☐ Using examples, precedents, and narratives

Just as a picture can sometimes be worth a thousand words, so can a well-conceived example be extremely valuable in arguing a point. Examples are used most often to support generalizations or to bring abstractions to life. In an argument about American mass media and body image, for instance, you might make the general statement that popular media send the message that a woman must be thin to be attractive; you might then illustrate your generalization with these examples:

> At the supermarket checkout, a tabloid publishes unflattering photographs of a young singer and comments on her apparent weight gain in shocked captions that ask "What happened?!?" Another praises a starlet for quickly shedding "ugly pounds" after the recent birth of a child. The cover of *Cosmopolitan* features a glamorously made-up and airbrushed actress in an outfit that reveals her remarkably tiny waist and flat stomach. Every woman in every advertisement in the magazine is thin — and the context makes it clear that we're supposed to think that she is beautiful.

The generalization would mean far less without the examples.

Examples can also help us understand abstractions. Poverty, for instance, may be difficult for us to think about in the abstract, but a description of several residents of a poverty-stricken community, vying for low-paying jobs, visiting local food pantries and soup kitchens, or facing homelessness, speaks directly to our understanding.

Precedents are particular kinds of examples taken from the past. The most common use of precedent occurs in law, where an attorney may ask for a certain ruling based on a similar earlier case. Precedent appears in everyday arguments as well. If, as part of a proposal for increasing lighting in the library garage, you point out that the university has increased lighting in four other garages in the past year, you are arguing on the basis of precedent.

In research writing (see Chapters 10–15), you must identify your sources for any examples or precedents not based on your own knowledge.

The following questions can help you check any use of example or precedent:

- How representative are the examples?
- Are they sufficient in strength or number to lead to a generalization?
- In what ways do they support your point?
- How closely does the precedent relate to the point you're trying to make? Are the situations really similar?
- How timely is the precedent? (What would have been applicable in 1980 is not necessarily applicable today.)

Because storytelling is universal, narratives can be very persuasive in helping readers understand and accept the logic of an argument. Narratives that use video and audio to capture the faces and voices of the people involved are often particularly compelling. In *As We Sow*, a documentary arguing against corporate pork production methods, the farmers shown on p. 170 told of their struggle to continue raising animals as their families had for generations — ultimately urging their children not to follow in their footsteps.

*Farmers tell their story in the documentary* As We Sow. (Source: Jan Weber / As We Sow)

Stories drawn from your own experience can appeal particularly to readers, for they not only help make your point in true-to-life, human terms but also help readers know you better and therefore identify with you more closely. In arguing for a stronger government campaign against smoking, for example, former President Clinton often drew on personal stories of his own family's experience with lung cancer.

When you include stories in your argument, ask yourself the following questions:

- Does the narrative support your thesis?
- Will the story's significance to the argument be clear to your readers?
- Is the story one of several good reasons or pieces of evidence — or does it have to carry the main burden of the argument?

In general, do not rely solely on the power of stories to carry your argument, since readers usually expect writers to state and argue their reasons more directly and abstractly as well. An additional danger if you use only your own experiences is that you can seem focused too much on yourself (and perhaps not enough on your readers).

As you develop your own arguments, keep in mind that while narratives can provide effective logical support, they may be used equally effectively for ethical or emotional appeals as well.

**MULTI-LINGUAL** | **COUNTING YOUR OWN EXPERIENCE**

You may have learned that stories based on your own personal experience don't count in academic arguments. If so, reconsider this advice, for showing an audience that you have personal experience with a topic can carry strong persuasive appeal with many English-speaking audiences. As with all evidence used in an argument, however, narratives based on your own experience must be pertinent to the topic, understandable to the audience, and clearly related to your purpose.

## ☐ Citing authority and testimony

Another way to support an argument logically is to cite an authority. For nearly fifty years, the use of authority has figured prominently in the controversy over smoking. Since the U.S. surgeon general's 1964 announcement that smoking is hazardous to health, millions of Americans have quit smoking, largely persuaded by the authority of the scientists offering the evidence.

But as with other strategies for building support for an argumentative claim, citing authorities demands careful consideration. Ask yourself the following questions to be sure you are using authorities effectively:

- Is the authority timely? (The argument that the United States should pursue a policy just because it was supported by Thomas Jefferson will probably fail because Jefferson's time was so radically different from ours.)

- Is the authority qualified to judge the topic at hand? (To cite a movie star in an essay on linguistics, an appeal to false authority, would not strengthen your argument [8f].)

- Is the authority likely to be known and respected by readers? (To cite an unfamiliar authority without some identification will lessen the impact of the evidence.)

- Are the authority's credentials clearly stated and verifiable? (Especially with Web-based sources, it is crucial to know whose authority guarantees the reliability of the information.)

Authorities are commonly cited in research writing (see Chapters 10–15), which often relies on the findings of other people. In addition, you may cite authorities in an assignment that asks you to review the literature of any field.

Testimony — the evidence an authority presents in support of a claim — is a feature of much contemporary argument. If testimony is timely, accurate, representative, and provided by a respected authority, then it, like authority itself, can add powerful support to an argument. In an essay for a literature class, for example, you might argue that a new edition of a literary work will open up many new areas of interpretation. You could strengthen this argument by adding

## BRINGING IN OTHER VOICES

Sometimes quoting authorities will prompt you to use language other than standard academic English. For instance, if you're writing about political relations between Mexico and the United States, you might quote a leader of a Mexican American organization; using that person's own words — which may be partly or entirely in Spanish or a regional variety of English — can carry extra power, calling up a voice from a pertinent community. See Chapter 29 for advice about using varieties of English and other languages.

a quotation from the author's biographer, noting that the new edition carries out the author's intentions much more closely than the previous edition did.

In research writing (Chapters 10–15), you should cite your sources for authority and testimony not based on your own knowledge.

## ☐ Showing causes and effects

Showing that one event is the cause — or the effect — of another can sometimes help support an argument. Suppose you are trying to explain, in a petition to change your grade in a course, why you were unable to take the final examination. In such a case, you would probably try to trace the causes of your failure to appear (the death of your grandmother followed by the theft of your car, perhaps) so that the committee reading the petition would reconsider the effect (your not taking the examination).

Tracing causes often lays the groundwork for an argument, particularly if the effect of the causes is one we would like to change. In an environmental science class, for example, a student may argue that a national law regulating smokestack emissions from utility plants is needed because (1) acid rain on the East Coast originates from emissions at utility plants in the Midwest, (2) acid rain kills trees and other vegetation, (3) utility lobbyists have prevented midwestern states from passing strict laws controlling emissions from such plants, and (4) in the absence of such laws, acid rain will destroy a high percentage of eastern forests. In this case, the first point is that the emissions cause acid rain; the second, that acid rain causes destruction in eastern forests; and the third, that states have not acted to break the cause-effect relationship established by the first two points. The fourth point ties all of the previous points together to provide an overall argument from effect: unless a national law is passed, most eastern forests are doomed.

In fact, a cause-effect relationship is often extremely difficult to establish. Scientists and politicians continue to disagree, for example, over the extent to which acid rain is responsible for the so-called dieback of many eastern forests. If you can show strong evidence that a cause produces an effect, though, you will have a powerful argument at your disposal.

## □ Using inductive and deductive reasoning

Traditionally, logical arguments are classified as using either inductive or deductive reasoning, but in practice, the two types of reasoning usually appear together. Inductive reasoning is the process of making a generalization based on a number of specific instances. If you find you are ill on ten occasions after eating shellfish, for example, you will likely draw the inductive generalization that shellfish makes you ill. It may not be an absolute certainty that shellfish was the culprit, but the probability lies in that direction.

Deductive reasoning, on the other hand, reaches a conclusion by assuming a general principle (known as a major premise) and then applying that principle to a specific case (the minor premise). In practice, this general principle is usually derived from induction. The inductive generalization *Shellfish makes me ill*, for instance, could serve as the major premise for the deductive argument *Since all shellfish makes me ill, the shrimp on this buffet is certain to make me ill*.

Deductive arguments have traditionally been analyzed as syllogisms — three-part statements that contain a major premise, a minor premise, and a conclusion.

| | |
|---|---|
| MAJOR PREMISE | All people die. |
| MINOR PREMISE | I am a person. |
| CONCLUSION | I will die. |

Syllogisms, however, are too rigid and absolute to serve in arguments about questions that have no absolute answers, and they often lack any appeal to an audience. Aristotle's simpler alternative, the enthymeme (8e), calls on the audience to supply the implied major premise. Consider the following example:

Because children who are bullied suffer psychological harm, schools should immediately discipline students who bully others.

You can analyze this enthymeme by restating it in the form of two premises and a conclusion.

| | |
|---|---|
| MAJOR PREMISE | Schools should immediately discipline students who harm other children. |
| MINOR PREMISE | Being bullied causes psychological harm to children. |
| CONCLUSION | Schools should immediately discipline students who bully other children. |

Note that the major premise is one the writer can count on an audience agreeing with or supplying: safety and common sense demand that schools should discipline children who harm other students. As such, this premise is *assumed* rather than stated in the enthymeme. By implicitly asking the audience to supply this premise to the argument, the writer engages the audience's participation.

Note that a deductive conclusion is only as strong as the premises on which it is based. The citizen who argues that *Ed is a crook and shouldn't be elected to public office* is arguing deductively, based on an implied major premise: *No crook should be elected to public office*. Most people would agree with this major premise. So the issue in this argument rests on the minor premise that Ed is a crook. Satisfactory proof of that premise will make us likely to accept the deductive conclusion that Ed shouldn't be elected.

At other times, the unstated premise may be more problematic. The person who says *Don't bother to ask for Ramon's help with physics — he's a jock* is arguing deductively on the basis of an implied major premise: *Jocks don't know anything about physics*. In this case, careful listeners would demand proof of the unstated premise. Because bigoted or prejudiced statements often rest on this kind of reasoning — a type of fallacy (8f) — writers should be particularly alert to it.

A helpful variation on the syllogism and the enthymeme is the Toulmin system (8e, 9d, and 9j), which looks for claims, reasons, and assumptions rather than major and minor premises.

| CLAIM | Schools should immediately discipline students who bully other children. |
|---|---|
| REASON(S) | Being bullied causes psychological harm to children. |
| ASSUMPTION | Schools should discipline students who harm other children. |

Note that in this system the assumption — which may be unstated — serves the same function as the assumed major premise in an enthymeme.

 **EXERCISE 9.7**

The following sentences contain deductive arguments based on implied major premises. Identify each of the implied premises.

1. The recreational use of marijuana should be legal if it is regulated the same way alcoholic beverages are.
2. Women soldiers should not serve in combat positions because doing so exposes them to a much higher risk of death.
3. Animals can't talk; therefore they can't feel pain as humans do.

□ **Making logical appeals with visuals**

Charts, graphs, tables, maps, photographs, and so on can be especially useful in arguments because they present factual information that can be taken in at a glance. *Mother Jones* used the following simple chart to carry a big message about income distribution in the United States. Consider how long it would take to explain all the information in this chart with words alone.

### A visual that makes a logical appeal

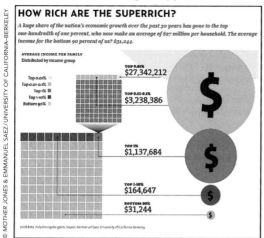

**HOW RICH ARE THE SUPERRICH?**

*A huge share of the nation's economic growth over the past 30 years has gone to the top one-hundredth of one percent, who now make an average of $27 million per household. The average income for the bottom 90 percent of us? $31,244.*

AVERAGE INCOME PER FAMILY
Distributed by income group

Top 0.01%
Top 0.01-0.1%
Top 1%
Top 1-10%
Bottom 90%

TOP 0.01%
$27,342,212

TOP 0.01-0.1%
$3,238,386

TOP 1%
$1,137,684

TOP 1-10%
$164,647

BOTTOM 90%
$31,244

---

**◢ EXERCISE 9.8**

Write a paragraph describing the logical appeals you would use to support the thesis of a project you are currently working on.

---

## 9h  Making emotional appeals

Most successful arguments appeal to our hearts as well as to our minds; in fact, current research suggests that people make decisions based on emotion rather than logic alone. Thus, good writers supplement appeals to logic and reason with emotional appeals to their readers. This principle is vividly demonstrated by the campaign to curb the AIDS epidemic in Africa. Facts and figures — logical appeals — convince us that the problem is serious. What elicits an outpouring of support, however, is the arresting emotional power of stories and images of a people living with the disease. An effective emotional appeal (*pathos,* to the ancient Greeks) can be made with description and concrete language, with figurative language, and with visuals — as well as by shaping an appeal to a particular audience.

### ☐  Using description and concrete language

Like photographs, vivid, detailed description can bring a moving immediacy to any argument. A student may amass facts and figures, including diagrams and maps, to illustrate the problem of wheelchair access to the library. But only when the student asks a friend who uses a wheelchair to accompany her to the library does the student writer discover the concrete details necessary to move readers

(30c). The student can then write, "Marie inched her wheelchair up the steep entrance ramp, her face pinched with the sheer effort."

## ☐ Using figurative language

Figurative language, or figures of speech (30d), paints detailed pictures that build understanding. It does so by relating something new or unfamiliar to something the audience knows well and by making striking comparisons between something you are writing about and something else that helps a reader visualize, identify with, or understand it.

Figures of speech include metaphors, similes, and analogies. Metaphors compare two things directly: *Richard the Lion-Hearted; old age is the evening of life; the defensive players are pit bulls on pork chops.* Similes make comparisons using *like* or *as*: *Richard was as brave as a lion; old age is like the evening of life; the defensive players are like pit bulls on pork chops.* Analogies are extended metaphors or similes that compare an unfamiliar concept or process to a more familiar one to help the reader understand the unfamiliar concept.

> I see the Internet as a city struggling to be built, its laws only now being formulated, its notions of social order arising out of the needs of its citizens and the demands of their environment. Like any city, the Net has its charlatans and its thieves as well as its poets, engineers, and philosophers. . . . Our experience of the Internet will be determined by how we master its core competencies. They are the design principles that are shaping the electronic city. —PAUL GILSTER, *Digital Literacy*

A student arguing for a more streamlined course-registration process may find good use for an analogy, saying that the current process makes students feel like laboratory rats in a maze. This analogy, which suggests manipulation, frustration, and a clinical coldness, creates a vivid description and adds emotional appeal to the argument. For the analogy to work effectively, however, the student would have to show that the current registration process has a number of similarities to a laboratory maze, such as confused students wandering through complex bureaucratic channels and into dead ends.

As you use analogies or other figurative language to bring emotion into an argument, be careful not to overdo it. Emotional appeals that are unfair or overly dramatic — known as fallacies (8f) — may serve only to cloud your readers' judgment and ultimately diminish your argument.

## ☐ Shaping your appeal to your audience

As with appeals to credibility and logic, appealing to emotions is effective only insofar as it moves your particular audience. A student arguing for increased lighting in campus parking garages, for instance, might consider the emotions such a discussion might raise (fear of attack, for example, or anger at being

---

**CONSIDERING DISABILITIES | DESCRIPTION**

Remember that some members of your class or peer group may have difficulty seeing visual arguments or recognizing nuances of color or spacing. Be sure to provide verbal descriptions of visual images. In a video presentation, embed voice descriptions of the visual images for members of the class with visual impairments.

---

subjected to danger), decide which emotions the intended audience would be most responsive to, and then look for descriptive and figurative language or appropriate visuals to carry out such an appeal.

In a leaflet to be distributed on campus or in an online notice to a student list, for example, the writer might describe the scene in a dimly lit garage as a student parks her car and then has to walk to an exit alone down shadowy corridors. Or she might make a short video in the garage and post it with accompanying music from a horror film.

In a proposal to the university administration, on the other hand, the writer might describe past attacks on students in campus garages and the negative publicity and criticism these provoked. For the administration, the writer might compare the lighting in the garages to high-risk gambling, arguing that increased lighting would lower the odds of future attacks.

Notice that shaping your appeal to a specific audience calls on you to consider very carefully the genre, media, and language you use. The student arguing for better lighting in campus parking garages would probably stick to standard academic English in a print letter or formal email message to the university administration but might well want to use informal language and media content when writing for students.

Remember, however, that you can't always know which audiences will see your work — especially if it is posted online where anyone can read it. While there is no foolproof way to shape an appeal that will be effective for every audience everywhere, bear in mind that a variety of people may read your writing, including people from cultures very different from yours and people whose ideas or actions you are criticizing. Before making your argument public, take the time to imagine the response from such audiences. Are your appeals fair and civil? In addition, if you are writing on social media networks like Facebook, ask how you might limit or shape your audience so that you reach those you most want to talk with.

## ☐ Making emotional appeals with visuals

Visuals that make emotional appeals can add substance to an argument. To make sure that visual appeals will serve the purpose you intend, test them with some potential readers to see how they interpret the appeal. Consider, for example, the photograph on p. 178, which shows a funeral arranged by

## A visual that makes an emotional appeal

© JOE RAEDLE / GETTY IMAGES

*Funeral for homeless veterans*

an American Legion post in Florida to honor U.S. military veterans who died homeless. Some readers might see this image as an indictment of the government, which allowed soldiers who had fought for their country to end up without a place to live — but others might view it instead (or also) as confirmation that patriots come from every walk of life or that veterans honor their own even when others fail to do so.

### EXERCISE 9.9

Make a list of common human emotions that might be attached to each of the following topics, and suggest appropriate ways to appeal to those emotions in a specific audience you choose to address.

1. banning drinking on campus
2. airport security
3. birth control
4. health care reform
5. steroid use among athletes

### EXERCISE 9.10

Using a working thesis you have formulated for a project you are working on, make a list of the emotional appeals most appropriate to your topic and audience. Then spend ten to fifteen minutes brainstorming, looking for descriptive and figurative language, images, or videos to carry out the appeals.

## 9i   Using sources in an argument

In constructing a written argument, it is often essential to use sources. The key to persuading people to accept your argument is good reasons; and even if your assignment doesn't specify that you must consult outside sources, they are often the most effective way of finding and establishing these reasons. Sources can help you to do the following:

- provide background information on your topic
- demonstrate your knowledge of the topic to readers
- cite authority and testimony in support of your thesis
- find opinions that differ from your own, which can help you sharpen your thinking, qualify your thesis if necessary, and demonstrate fairness to opposing arguments

For a more thorough discussion of finding, gathering, and evaluating sources, see Chapters 10–15.

Be sure to give appropriate credit for any sources, including images and media files, that you use in your argument. Follow the conventions of your genre and medium for citing sources; a Web site may use links to indicate the source of information, for example, but academic arguments almost always call for following the guidelines of a specific documentation style (see Chapters 32–35).

## 9j   Organizing an argument

Once you have assembled good reasons and evidence in support of an argumentative thesis, you must organize your material to present the argument convincingly. Although there is no universally favored, one-size-fits-all organizational framework, you may find it useful to try one of the following patterns.

### ☐   Organizing with the classical system

In the classical system of argument — followed by ancient Greek and Roman orators and still in widespread use today, some twenty-five hundred years later — the speaker begins with an introduction, which states the thesis and then gives background information. Next come the different lines of argument and then the consideration of alternative arguments. A conclusion both sums up the argument and makes a final appeal to the audience. You can adapt this format to arguments in many genres and media.

1. Introduction
   - Gain readers' attention and interest.
   - Establish your qualifications to write about your topic.

- Establish common ground with readers.
- Demonstrate fairness.
- State or imply your thesis.

2. Background
   - Present any necessary background information, including pertinent personal narrative.

3. Lines of argument
   - Present good reasons and evidence (including logical and emotional appeals) in support of your thesis.
   - Generally present reasons in order of importance.
   - Demonstrate ways that your argument may be in readers' best interest.

4. Consideration of alternative arguments
   - Examine alternative points of view.
   - Note advantages and disadvantages of alternative views.
   - Explain why one view is better than others.

5. Conclusion
   - Summarize the argument if you choose.
   - Elaborate on the implication of your thesis.
   - Make clear what you want readers to think or do.
   - Make a strong ethical or emotional appeal.

## ☐ Organizing with Toulmin's elements of argument

The simplified and systematic form of argument developed by Stephen Toulmin (8e and 9d) can help you organize an argumentative essay:

1. Make your claim or (arguable statement).

   **The federal government should ban smoking.**

2. Qualify your claim, if necessary.

   **The ban would be limited to public places.**

3. Present good reasons to support your claim.

   **Smoking causes serious diseases in smokers.**
   **Nonsmokers are endangered by secondhand smoke.**

4. Explain the underlying assumptions that connect your claim and your reasons. Also provide additional explanations of any controversial assumptions.

| ASSUMPTION | The Constitution was established to "promote the general welfare." |
|---|---|
| ASSUMPTION | Citizens are entitled to protection from harmful actions by others. |
| ADDITIONAL EXPLANATION | The federal government is supposed to serve the basic needs of the American people, including safeguarding their health. |

5. Provide additional evidence to support your claim (facts, statistics, testimony, and other ethical, logical, or emotional appeals).

| STATISTICS | Cite the incidence of deaths attributed to secondhand smoke. |
|---|---|
| FACTS | Cite lawsuits won against large tobacco companies. |
| FACTS | Cite bans on smoking already imposed in many municipalities and states. |
| AUTHORITY | Cite the surgeon general. |
| EMOTIONAL APPEAL | Show images or video of nonsmokers suffering from tobacco-related illnesses. |

6. Acknowledge and respond to possible counterarguments.

| COUNTER-ARGUMENTS | Smoking is legal. Smokers have rights, too. |
|---|---|
| RESPONSE | The suggested ban applies only to public places; smokers would be free to smoke in private. A nonsmoker's right not to have to inhale smoke in public places counts for more than a smoker's right to smoke. |

7. State your conclusion in the strongest way possible.

## ☐ Organizing with Rogerian or invitational argument

The psychologist Carl Rogers (9b) argued that people should not enter into disputes until they can thoroughly and fairly understand the other person's (or persons') perspectives. From Rogers's theory, rhetoricians Richard Young, Alton Becker, and Kenneth Pike adapted a four-part structure that is now known as "Rogerian argument":

- The introduction describes the issue, problem, or conflict in enough detail to demonstrate that the writer fully grasps and respects alternative points of view.

- The writer then fairly describes the contexts in which such alternative positions might be valid.

- The writer offers his or her position on the issue and explains in what circumstances and why that position would be valid.

- Finally, the writer explains how those who hold alternative positions can benefit from adopting the writer's position.

Invitational rhetoric has as its goal getting people to work together effectively and to identify with each other; it aims for connection and collaboration. Such arguments call for structures that are closer to good two-way conversations or freewheeling dialogues than a linear march from thesis to conclusion. If you try developing such a conversational structure, you may find that it opens up a space in your argument for new perceptions and fresh ideas.

## 9k Delivering an argument

When someone asked the ancient orator Demosthenes to name the three most important parts of rhetoric, he said: *delivery, delivery, delivery.* In short, while what speakers said was important, the way they said it was of even greater importance. Today, Demosthenes's words have special meaning: we live in a time of information overload, when many powerful messages are vying for our attention. In such a time, getting and keeping an audience's attention is paramount — and doing so is all about delivery. Figuring out the medium of delivery (print? digital? in-person?) and the appropriate genre is important, and so is designing the argument to appeal to your target audience. As a writer in the digital age, then, you will need to think carefully about how to deliver your message.

- What medium will best get and hold your audience's attention? print? video? in-person or Web presentation? social media site? Choosing just the right one is important to your success. (2f)

- What genre is most appropriate for your message? a report? a narrative? an essay? a brochure? (2f)

- What word choice, style, and tone will be most successful in delivering your message?

- Are any conventions expected in the kind of argument you are writing? Look for examples of similar arguments, or ask your instructor for information. (2f)

- What visual style will appeal to your intended readers, set a clear tone for your argument, and guide readers through your text? Spend time thinking about how the argument will look, and aim for a consistent visual design and for appealing fonts and colors. (Chapter 16)

- Are visual and media elements clearly integrated into your argument? Place images close to the text they illustrate, and label each one clearly. Make sure that audio and video files appear in appropriate places and are identified for users.

After you have a rough plan for delivering your argument, test it on friends and classmates, asking them what you need to change to make it more effective.

### EXERCISE 9.11

Using the guidelines in this chapter, draft an argument in support of the working thesis for a project you are working on.

▼ ▼ ▼ ▼ ▼ ▼ ▼ ▼ ▼ ▼ ▼ ▼ ▼ ▼ ▼ ▼ ▼ ▼ ▼ ▼ ▼ ▼ ▼ ▼ ▼

### THINKING CRITICALLY ABOUT CONSTRUCTING ARGUMENTS

Using the checklist in section 9a, analyze a draft of an argument you've recently written. Decide what you need to do to revise your argument, and write out a brief plan for revision.

## 9l A student's argument essay

STUDENT WRITER
Benjy Mercer-Golden

In this argument essay, Benjy Mercer-Golden argues that socially conscious businesses and traditional for-profit businesses can learn from each other in ways that benefit businesses, consumers, and the environment. His essay has been annotated to point out the various parts of his argument as well as his use of good reasons, evidence, and appeals to logic and emotion. For activities related to this argument, go to **macmillanhighered.com/smh** and click on **9. Constructing Arguments > Student Writing**. (Photo © Benjy Mercer-Golden)

Mercer-Golden 1

Benjy Mercer-Golden

28 Nov. 2012

Provocative word choice for title

Lessons from Tree-Huggers and Corporate Mercenaries:

A New Model of Sustainable Capitalism

Emotional appeals through use of vivid imagery

Televised images of environmental degradation — seagulls with oil coating their feathers, smokestacks belching gray fumes — often seem designed to shock, but these images also represent very real issues: climate change, dwindling energy resources like coal and oil, a scarcity of clean drinking water. In response, businesspeople around the world are thinking about how they can make their companies greener or more socially beneficial to ensure a brighter future for humanity. But progress in the private sector has been slow and inconsistent. To accelerate the move to sustainability, for-profit businesses need to learn from the hybrid model of social entrepreneurship to ensure that the company is efficient and profitable while still working for social change, and more investors need to support companies with long-term, revolutionary visions for improving the world.

Thesis establishing purpose

Claim related to thesis

Opposing viewpoint to establish writer's credibility

Rebuttal

In fact, both for-profit corporations and "social good" businesses could take steps to reshape their strategies. First, for-profit corporations need to operate sustainably and be evaluated for their performance with long-term measurements and incentives. The conventional argument against for-profit companies deeply embedding environmental and social goals into their corporate strategies is that caring about the world does not go hand in hand with lining pockets. This morally toxic case is also problematic from a business standpoint. A 2012 study of 180 high-profile companies by Harvard Business School professors Robert G. Eccles and George Serafeim and London Business School professor Ioannis Ioannou shows that "high sustainability companies," as defined by environmental and social variables, "significantly outperform their counterparts over the long term, both in terms of stock market and accounting performance." The study argues that the better financial returns of these companies are especially evident in sectors where "companies' products significantly depend upon extracting large amounts of natural resources" (Eccles, Ioannou, and Serafeim).

Mercer-Golden 2

Such empirical financial evidence to support a shift toward using energy from renewable sources to run manufacturing plants argues that executives should think more sustainably, but other underlying incentives need to evolve in order to bring about tangible change. David Blood and Al Gore of Generation Investment Management, an investment firm focused on "sustainable investing for the long term" ("About Us"), wrote a groundbreaking white paper that outlined the perverse incentives company managers face. For public companies, the default practice is to issue earnings guidances — announcements of projected future earnings — every quarter. This practice encourages executives to manage for the short term instead of adding long-term value to their company and the earth (Gore and Blood). Only the most uncompromisingly green CEOs would still advocate for stricter carbon emissions standards at the company's factories if a few mediocre quarters left investors demanding that they be fired. Gore and Blood make a powerful case against requiring companies to be subjected to this "What have you done for me lately?" philosophy, arguing that quarterly earnings guidances should be abolished in favor of companies releasing information when they consider it appropriate. And to further persuade managers to think sustainably, companies need to change the way the managers get paid. Currently, the CEO of ExxonMobil is rewarded for a highly profitable year but is not held accountable for depleting nonrenewable oil reserves. A new model should incentivize thinking for the long run. Multiyear milestones for performance evaluation, as Gore and Blood suggest, are essential to pushing executives to manage sustainably.

But it's not just for-profit companies that need to rethink strategies. Social good–oriented leaders also stand to learn from the people often vilified in environmental circles: corporate CEOs. To survive in today's economy, companies building sustainable products must operate under the same strict business standards as profit-driven companies. Two social enterprises, Nika Water and Belu, provide perfect examples. Both sell bottled water in the developed world with the mission of providing clean water to impoverished communities through their profits. Both have visionary leaders who define the lesson that all environmental and social

Transition referring to ideas in previous paragraph

Details of claim

Logical appeals using information and evidence in white paper

Ethical appeal to companies

Partial solution proposed

Claim extended to socially responsible businesses

Logical appeals

Mercer-Golden 3

entrepreneurs need to understand: financial pragmatism will add far more value to the world than idealistic dreams. Nika Water founder Jeff Church explained this in a speech at Stanford University:

> Social entrepreneurs look at their businesses as nine parts cause, one part business. In the beginning, it needs to be nine parts business, one part cause, because if the business doesn't stay around long enough because it can't make it, you can't do anything about the cause.

**Additional logical appeals**

When U.K.-based Belu lost £600,000 ($940,000) in 2007, it could only give around £30,000 ($47,000) to charity. Karen Lynch took over as CEO, cutting costs, outsourcing significant parts of the company's operations, and redesigning the entire business model; the company now donates four times as much to charity (Hurley). The conventional portrayal of do-gooders is that they tend to be terrible businesspeople, an argument often grounded in reality. It is easy to criticize the Walmarts of the world for caring little about sustainability or social good, but the idealists with big visions who do not follow through on their promises because their businesses cannot survive are no more praiseworthy.

**Return to thesis: businesses should learn from one another**

Walmart should learn from nonprofits and social enterprises on advancing a positive environmental and social agenda, but idealist entrepreneurs should also learn from corporations about building successful businesses.

**Transition to second part of thesis signaled**

The final piece of the sustainable business ecosystem is the investors who help get potentially world-changing companies off the ground. Industries that require a large amount of money to build complex products with expensive materials, such as solar power companies, rely heavily on investors — often venture capitalists based in California's Silicon Valley (Knight).

**Problem explained**

The problem is that venture capitalists are not doing enough to fund truly groundbreaking companies. In an oft-cited blog post titled "Why Facebook Is Killing Silicon Valley," entrepreneur Steve Blank argues

**Reasons in support of claim**

that the financial returns on social media companies have been so quick and so outsized that the companies with the *really* big ideas — like providing efficient, cheap, scalable solar power — are not being backed: "In the past, if you were a great [venture capitalist], you could make $100 million on an investment in 5–7 years. Today, social media startups can

Mercer-Golden 4

return hundreds of millions or even billions in less than 3 years." The point Blank makes is that what is earning investors lots of money right now is not what is best for the United States or the world.

There are, however, signs of hope. Paypal founder Peter Thiel runs his venture capital firm, the Founders Fund, on the philosophy that investors should support "flying cars" instead of new social media ventures (Packer). While the next company with the mission of making photo-sharing cooler or communicating with friends easier might be both profitable and valuable, Thiel and a select few others fund technology that has the potential to solve the huge problems essential to human survival.

The world's need for sustainable companies that can build products from renewable energy or make nonpolluting cars will inevitably create opportunities for smart companies to make money. In fact, significant opportunities already exist for venture capitalists willing to step away from what is easy today and shift their investment strategies toward what will help us continue to live on this planet tomorrow — even if seeing strong returns may take a few more years. Visionaries like Blank and Thiel need more allies (and dollars) in their fight to help produce more pioneering, sustainable companies. And global warming won't abate before investors wise up. It is vital that this shift happen now.

When we think about organizations today, we think about nonprofits, which have long-term social missions, and corporations, which we judge by their immediate financial returns like quarterly earnings. That is a treacherous dichotomy. Instead, we need to see the three major players in the business ecosystem — corporations, social enterprises, and investors — moving toward a *single* model of long-term, sustainable capitalism. We need visionary companies that not only set out to solve humankind's biggest problems but also have the business intelligence to accomplish these goals, and we need investors willing to fund these companies. Gore and Blood argue that "the imperative for change has never been greater." We will see this change when the world realizes that sustainable capitalism shares the same goals as creating a sustainable environment. Let us hope that this realization comes soon.

*Margin annotations:*

Transition signaling reason for optimism

Reason presented

Emotional appeal

Logical appeal

Thesis revisited

Quotation, restatement of thesis, and emotional appeal close argument

Mercer-Golden 5

Works Cited

"About Us." *Generation*. Generation Investment Management LLC, 2012.
    Web. 26 Nov. 2012.

Blank, Steve. "Why Facebook Is Killing Silicon Valley." *Steveblank.com*.
    N.p., 21 May 2012. Web. 23 Nov. 2012.

Church, Jeff. "The Wave of Social Entrepreneurship." Entrepreneurial
    Thought Leaders Seminar. NVIDIA Auditorium, Stanford U, Stanford,
    CA. 11 Apr. 2012. Lecture.

Eccles, Robert G., Ioannis Ioannou, and George Serafeim. "The Impact
    of a Corporate Culture of Sustainability on Corporate Behavior and
    Performance." Working Paper 12-035. Harvard Business School, 9 May
    2012. PDF file.

Gore, Al, and David Blood. "A Manifesto for Sustainable Capitalism."
    *Generation*. Generation Investment Management, 14 Dec. 2011. PDF
    file.

Hurley, James. "Belu Boss Shows Bottle for a Turnaround." *Daily
    Telegraph*. Telegraph Media Group, 28 Feb. 2012. Web. 26 Nov. 2012.

Knight, Eric R. W. "The Economic Geography of Clean Tech Venture
    Capital." Oxford University Working Paper Series in Employment,
    Work, and Finance, 13 Apr. 2010. *Social Science Research Network*.
    Web. 23 Nov. 2012.

Packer, George. "No Death, No Taxes: The Libertarian Futurism of a Silicon
    Valley Billionaire." *New Yorker*. New Yorker, 28 Nov. 2011. Web. 24
    Nov. 2012.

# PART 3
# Doing Research and Using Sources

# CHAPTER 10

# Preparing for a Research Project

Y OUR EMPLOYER ASKS YOU to recommend the best software for a particular project. You want to plan a trip during your spring break. You need to find an inexpensive source for your dog's heartworm medication. Once you begin to think about it, you'll find that many of your day-to-day activities call for research. Preparing to do research means taking a long look at what you already know, the best way to proceed, and the amount of time you have to find the information you need.

> **CONNECT:** How can you tell if your research topic is manageable and interesting? **3b, 10c**
>
> **CREATE:** Create a brief oral or written description of your topic, and get feedback on it from three people who might be part of your target audience.
>
> **REFLECT:** Go to **macmillanhighered.com/smh**, and respond to **10. Preparing for Research** > **Video** > **Researching something exciting**.

## 10a Considering the research process

If you have little experience doing research for academic projects, you may feel some anxiety about a major research assignment. Bear the following tips in mind to turn yourself into an expert researcher:

- **You already know something about doing research.** You act as a researcher whenever you try to find out more about anything that interests you. If you are researching coffee options, you may look up information online about the trade practices of coffee suppliers or talk with friends about coffee shops with the best atmosphere, the lowest prices, or the tastiest coffee.

- **Research projects that interest you are easier and more enjoyable to complete.** Researchers usually seek out information and opinions for a reason. Your main purpose in college research may be to fulfill an assignment, but if you can also find a purpose with which you make a personal connection, your research task will be more rewarding.

- **Research rarely progresses in a neat line from start to finish.** When you begin any research, you don't know exactly what you will discover. You begin with a question that may lead you to other sources. Additional research may narrow your idea — or cause you to change directions entirely. If you set out to find information on the development of the multiplayer online game *World of Warcraft* and end up interested in how players work together to succeed in the game, your new purpose will require you to take another look at the research you need to do.

- **Good research calls for careful reflection.** While you may often begin research by skimming to identify useful sources, once you have found key sources, stop skimming! Read carefully, taking notes and reflecting on what a particular source offers you in terms of the major point or argument you are making. What makes this source useful to you? How reliable is it? What does it suggest you may need more information on?

- **Good research can make you a genuine expert.** If you approach your research seriously and follow all the leads that you can, you may eventually become an expert on a topic that interests you — a Korean soap opera, homeopathic allergy treatments, or low-cost early childhood services in your neighborhood.

College research may range from a couple of hours spent gathering background information on a topic for a brief essay to weeks or months of full-scale exploration for a term project.

## 10b Analyzing the assignment

For an introductory writing course, David Craig (whose final project appears in 32e) received the following assignment:

Choose a subject of interest to you, and use it as the basis for a research essay of approximately 2,500 words that makes and substantiates a claim. You should use a minimum of five sources, including at least three scholarly sources.

### ☐ Considering requirements and limits

Before you begin any research assignment, make sure you understand what you need to do.

- How many sources should you use?
- Does your instructor require certain kinds of sources? If so, what kinds?
- What genre and medium will be appropriate for this project? Are you expected to write a traditional print essay or slide presentation? Should you consider another genre or medium, such as a Web report or video essay?

- Will you use images, sound, or video in your assignment?
- Should you work independently or collaborate with others on the project?
- What kind of documentation style does your instructor want you to use? (See Chapters 32–35.)
- Do you understand what your instructor expects you to do? If not, ask for clarification.

## ☐ Considering the rhetorical situation

Be sure to consider the rhetorical situation of any research project.

### Purpose

- Do you have a choice about the purpose of your assignment? If you can choose the purpose, what would you like to accomplish?
- What do you need to do in this project — explain a situation? weigh opposing viewpoints and make a claim about which is correct? convince the audience to do something? explore the causes or effects of a particular phenomenon? Your purpose will affect the kinds of sources you need to find.
- If you have been assigned a specific research project, keep in mind the key words in that assignment. Does the assignment ask that you *describe*, *survey*, *analyze*, *persuade*, *explain*, *classify*, *compare*, or *contrast*? What do such words mean in this field (2b)?

### Audience

- Who will be the audience for your research project (2e)? Why will they be interested in the information you gather?
- What do you know about their backgrounds? What assumptions might they hold about the topic? What do they already know, and what do they need to know?
- What genre and medium will be the best way to reach your audience (2f)?
- What response do you want to elicit from them?
- What kinds of evidence will you need to convince them?
- What will your instructor expect?

### Rhetorical stance

What is your attitude or stance toward your topic (2d)? Are you curious about it? critical of it? Do you like it? dislike it? find it confusing? What influences have shaped your stance?

## Scope

How many and what kinds of sources should you use? What kinds of visuals — charts, maps, photographs, and so on — will you need to include? Will you use sound or video files? Will you do any field research — interviewing, surveying, or observing? (For more on kinds of sources, see 11a.)

## Length

How long is your project supposed to be? You will need far less research and writing time for a 1,000-word essay or a two-minute presentation than for a 3,000-word essay or a ten-minute presentation.

## Deadlines

When is the project due? Are any preliminary materials — a working bibliography, a thesis, an outline, a first draft — due before this date? Create a schedule for your project (a sample schedule is shown here).

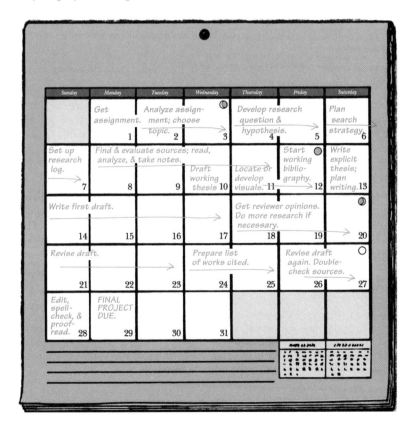

---

TALKING THE TALK | **REACHING AN AUDIENCE**

"Isn't my audience just my teacher?" To write effectively, you must think of your writing as more than just an assignment you go through to get a grade. Recognize that you have something to say — and that in order to get others to pay attention, you have to think about who they are and how to reach them. Of course, your instructor is part of your audience. But who else will be interested in your topic and the unique perspective you bring to it? What does that audience need from you?

---

## ☐ Choosing a topic

If your assignment does not specify a topic, consider the following questions:

- What subjects do you already know something about? Which of them would you like to explore more fully?
- What subjects do you care about? What might you like to become an expert on?
- What subjects evoke a strong reaction from you — intense puzzlement, skepticism, affirmation?

Be sure to get responses about your possible topic from your instructor, classmates, and friends. Ask them whether they would be interested in reading about the topic, whether it seems manageable, and whether they know of any good sources for information on the topic.

### David Craig's topic

David Craig hit on his topic one evening after spending several hours exchanging texts and messages with several friends. Like most of the people his age that he knew, David had considered texting and messaging a regular part of his writing experience for years, so he expected his classmates to find the subject intriguing. (To read his essay, see 32e.)

---

▰ **EXERCISE 10.1**

Using the questions in 10b, come up with at least two topics you would like to carry out research on. Then write a brief response to some key questions about each topic: How much information do you think is available on this topic? What sources on this topic do you know about or have access to? Who would know about this topic — historians, doctors, filmmakers, psychologists, others?

---

## 10c Narrowing a topic

Any topic you choose to research must be manageable — it should suit the scope, audience, length, and time limits of your assignment. Making a topic manageable often requires narrowing it, but you may also need to find a particular slant and look for a question to guide your research. To arrive at such a question, you might first generate a series of questions about your topic. You can then evaluate them and choose one or two that are both interesting and manageable.

### David Craig's narrowed topic

David Craig knew that he had to zero in on some aspect of texting or messaging and take a position on it. He considered researching "the prevalence of messaging worldwide," but since he didn't know where to begin, he realized that this topic was vague and unmanageable. He spoke with two instructors about his topic, and both of them criticized messaging for its negative influence on students' writing. Intrigued by this reaction, David decided to focus on messaging language and its harmful effects on youth literacy.

## 10d Moving from research question to hypothesis

The result of the narrowing process is a research question that can be tentatively answered by a hypothesis, a statement of what you anticipate your research will show. Like a working thesis (3c, 9d), a hypothesis must be manageable, interesting, and specific. In addition, it must be arguable, a debatable proposition that you can prove or disprove with a reasonable amount of research evidence (9c). For example, a statement like this one is not arguable since it merely states a fact: "Senator Joseph McCarthy attracted great attention with his anti-Communist crusade during the 1950s." On the other hand, this statement is an arguable hypothesis because evidence for or against it can be found: "Roy Cohn's biased research while he was an assistant to Senator Joseph McCarthy was partially responsible for McCarthy's anti-Communist crusade."

In moving from your general topic of interest, such as Senator Joseph McCarthy's anti-Communist crusade of the 1950s, to a useful hypothesis, such as the one in the previous paragraph, you first narrow the topic to a single manageable issue: Roy Cohn's role in the crusade, for instance. After background reading, you then raise a question about that issue ("To what extent did Cohn's research contribute to McCarthy's crusade?") and devise a possible answer, your hypothesis.

## David Craig's hypothesis

| | |
|---|---|
| TOPIC | Texting and messaging |
| NARROWED TOPIC | Texting and messaging slang |
| ISSUE | The effect of messaging slang on youth literacy |
| RESEARCH QUESTION | How has the popularity of messaging affected literacy among today's youth? |
| HYPOTHESIS | Messaging seems to have a negative influence on the writing skills of young people. |

David's hypothesis, which tentatively answers his research question, is precise enough to be either supported or challenged by a manageable amount of research.

## 10e  Determining what you know

Once you have formulated a hypothesis, determine what you already know about your topic. Here are some strategies for doing so:

- **Brainstorming.** Take five minutes to list everything you think of or wonder about your hypothesis (3a). You may find it helpful to do this in a group with other students.

- **Freewriting about your hypothesis.** For five minutes, write about every reason for believing your hypothesis is true. Then for another five minutes, write down every argument you can think of, no matter how weak, that someone opposed to your hypothesis might make.

- **Freewriting about your audience.** Write for five minutes about your readers, including your instructor. What do you think they currently believe about your topic? What sorts of evidence will convince them to accept your hypothesis? What sorts of sources will they respect?

- **Tapping your memory for sources.** List everything you can remember about *where* you learned about your topic: Web sites, emails, books, magazines, courses, conversations, television. What you know comes from somewhere, and that "somewhere" can serve as a starting point for research.

### EXERCISE 10.2

Using the tips in 10e, write down as much as you can about a topic that interests you. Then take some time to reread your notes, and jot down the questions you still need to answer as well as the sources you need to find.

## 10f Making a preliminary research plan

Once you've considered what you already know about your topic, you can develop a research plan. To do so, answer the following questions:

- What kinds of sources (books, journal articles, databases, Web sites, government documents, specialized reference works, images, videos, and so on) will you need to consult? How many sources should you consult? (For more on different kinds of sources, see Chapter 11.)

- How current do your sources need to be? (For topical issues, current sources are usually most important. Older sources are often useful for historical research.)

- How can you determine the location and availability of the kinds of sources you need?

- Do you need to consult sources contemporary with an event or a person's life? If so, how will you get access to those sources?

One goal of your research plan is to begin building a strong working bibliography (see 12c). Carrying out systematic research and keeping careful notes on your sources will make developing your works-cited list or bibliography (Chapters 32–35) easier later on.

## 10g Keeping a research log

Keeping a research log will make the job of writing and documenting your sources more efficient and accurate. You can use your log to jot down ideas about your topic and possible sources — and to keep track of print and online materials.

- A private blog or other online site can be a good place to record your thoughts on the reading you are doing and to add links to Web sites, documents, and articles that you find online. (For more on blogs, see 18c.)

- If you are keeping a computer research log, create a new folder and label it with a name that will be easy to identify, such as *Research Log for Project on Messaging*. Within this folder, create subfolders that will help you manage your project, such as *Assignment info, Working bibliography, Image ideas, Drafts*, and so on.

- If you prefer to keep a print research log, set up a binder with dividers similar to the subfolders listed above.

Be sure to carefully distinguish the notes and comments you make from quoted passages you record (see Chapter 12).

> CONSIDERING DISABILITIES | **DICTATION**
>
> If you have difficulty taking notes either on a computer or in a notebook, consider dictating your notes. You might dictate into a handheld recorder for later playback, into a word processor with voice-recognition capability, or into a phone for podcasting on a Web site.

## 10h  Moving from hypothesis to working thesis

As you gather more information and begin reading and evaluating sources, you will probably refine your research question and change your hypothesis significantly. You may find that your interest shifts, that a whole line of inquiry is unproductive, or that your hypothesis is simply wrong. In each case, the process of research pushes you to learn more about your hypothesis, to make it more precise, to become an expert on your topic. Only after you have explored your hypothesis, tested it, and sharpened it by reading, writing, and talking with others does it become a working thesis.

### David Craig's working thesis

David Craig did quite a bit of research on messaging language, youth literacy, and the possible connection between the two. The more he read, the more he felt that the hypothesis suggested by his discussion with instructors — that texting and messaging had contributed to a decline in youth literacy — did not hold up. Thus, he shifted his attention to the positive effects of texting and messaging on communication skills, and he developed the following working thesis: "Although some educators criticize messaging, it may aid literacy by encouraging young people to use words and to write — even if messaging requires a different kind of writing." (His final project appears in 32e.)

▼ ▼ ▼ ▼ ▼ ▼ ▼ ▼ ▼ ▼ ▼ ▼ ▼ ▼ ▼ ▼ ▼ ▼ ▼ ▼ ▼ ▼ ▼ ▼ ▼ ▼

**THINKING CRITICALLY ABOUT YOUR OWN RESEARCH**

If you have done research for an essay or research project before, go back and evaluate the work you did as a researcher and as a writer in light of the principles developed in this chapter. What was the purpose of the research? Who was your audience? How did you narrow and focus your topic? What kinds of sources did you use? Did you use a research log? What about your research and your essay pleased you most? What pleased you least? What would you do differently if you were to revise the essay now?

# CHAPTER 11

# Conducting Research

WHETHER YOU ARE RESEARCHING Heisenberg's uncertainty principle or haircuts, you need to be familiar with the kinds of sources you are likely to use, the searches you are likely to perform, and the three main types of research you will most often be doing: library, Internet, and field research.

> **CONNECT:** How can talking to real people help you with your research project? **11e, 29c–e**
>
> **CREATE:** Draft an email invitation to a person you would like to interview for your project.
>
> **REFLECT:** Record a brief audio or video reflection explaining what you did to find and contact the interview subject, what response (if any) you received, what you learned from the interview (if anything), and what you would do differently the next time.

## 11a   Differentiating kinds of sources

Sources can include data from interviews and surveys, books and articles in print and online, Web sites, films, video and audio content, images, and more.

### ☐  Using primary and secondary sources

Primary sources provide firsthand knowledge; secondary sources report on or analyze the research of others. Primary sources are basic sources of raw information, including your own field research; films, works of art, or other objects you examine; literary works you read; and eyewitness accounts, photographs, news reports, and historical documents such as letters and speeches. Secondary sources are descriptions or interpretations of primary sources, such as researchers' reports, reviews, biographies, and encyclopedia articles. Often what constitutes a primary or secondary source depends on the purpose of your research. A critic's review of a film, for instance, serves as a secondary source if you are writing about the film but as a primary source if you are studying the critic's writing.

Most research projects draw on both primary and secondary sources. For example, a research-based project on the effects of steroid use on Major League Baseball might draw on primary sources, such as players' testimony to Congress, as well as secondary sources, such as articles or books by baseball experts.

## ☐ Using scholarly and popular sources

While nonacademic sources like magazines and personal Web sites can help you get started on a research project, your college writing will often call for you to depend more heavily on authorities in a field, whose work generally appears in scholarly journals in print or online.

SCHOLARLY

POPULAR

| | |
|---|---|
| Title often contains the word *Journal* | *Journal* usually does not appear in title |
| Available mainly through libraries and library databases | Available at newsstands or from a home Internet connection |
| Print periodicals have matte (not glossy) pages with few commercial advertisements | Print periodicals have glossy pages with many advertisements |
| Little or no color; few illustrations | Full color; many illustrations |
| Authors identified with academic credentials | Authors are usually journalists or reporters hired by the publication, not academics or experts |

| SCHOLARLY | POPULAR |
|---|---|
| Summary or abstract appears before beginning of article; articles are fairly long | No summary or abstract; articles are fairly short |
| Articles cite sources and provide bibliographies | Articles may include quotations but do not cite sources or provide bibliographies |
| Examples: *Public Opinion Research Quarterly, Journal of the American Medical Association, Ecology and Society* | Examples: *Scientific American, The New Yorker, Salon* |

Many (but not all) scholarly sources are *peer reviewed*, which means that experts in the discipline read and approve every article before it is published in the journal.

## ☐ Using older and more current sources

Most projects can benefit from both older, historical sources and more current ones. Some older sources are classics in their fields, essential for understanding the scholarship that follows them. Others are simply dated, though even these works can be useful to researchers who want to see what people wrote and read about a topic in the past. Depending on your purpose, you may rely primarily on recent sources (for example, if you are writing about a new scientific discovery), primarily on historical sources (for instance, if your project discusses a nineteenth-century industrial accident), or on a mixture of both. Whether a source appeared hundreds of years ago or this morning, evaluate it carefully to determine how useful it will be for you (Chapter 12).

# 11b Using the library to get started

Even when you have a general idea of what kinds of sources exist and which kinds you need for your research project, you still have to locate these sources. Many beginning researchers are tempted to assume that all the information they could possibly need is readily available on the Internet from a home connection. However, it is a good idea to begin almost any research project with the sources available in your college library.

## ☐ Asking reference librarians

You might start by getting to know one particularly valuable resource, your library staff — especially reference librarians. You can make an appointment to talk with a librarian about your research project and get specific recommendations about databases and other helpful places to begin your research. In addition, many libraries have online chat environments where students can

---

CONSIDERING DISABILITIES | **WEB SITE ACCESSIBILITY**

While the Americans with Disabilities Act stipulates that all government Web sites must be accessible to those with disabilities, these rules have now been expanded to cover educational and other Web sites. If you encounter sites that are not accessible to you, ask a reference librarian to help you identify similar sites that may be more accessible. Also consider clicking on the CONTACT US button, if there is one, and letting the sponsors of the site know that some potential users can't get ready access to the information.

---

ask questions about their research and have them answered, in real time, by a reference librarian. To get the most helpful advice, whether online or in person, pose *specific* questions — not "Where can I find information about computers?" but "Where can I find information on the history of messaging technologies?" If you are having difficulty asking precise questions, you probably need to do some background research on your topic and formulate a sharper hypothesis. A librarian may be helpful in this regard as well.

☐ **Using catalogs and databases**

Your library's computers hold many resources not available on the Web or not accessible to students except through the library's system. One of these resources is the library's own catalog of books and other holdings, but most college libraries also subscribe to a large number of databases — electronic collections of information, such as indexes to journal and magazine articles, texts of news stories and legal cases, lists of sources on particular topics, and compilations of statistics — that students can access for free. Many of these databases have been screened or compiled by editors, librarians, or other scholars. Your library may also have metasearch software that allows you to search several databases at once.

☐ **Consulting general reference works**

Consulting general reference works, such as encyclopedias, biographical dictionaries, and almanacs, is another good way to get started on a research project. These works are especially helpful for getting an overview of a topic, identifying subtopics, finding more specialized sources, and identifying useful keywords for electronic searches.

## 11c  Finding library resources

The library is one of a researcher's best friends, especially in an age of digital communication. Your college library may seem daunting at first. Experienced student researchers will tell you that the best way to make the library a friend is to get to know it: a good starting place is its Web site, where you can find useful information, including its hours of operation, its floor plan, its collections, and so on; many libraries also have a virtual tour and other tutorials on their Web sites that give you a first-rate introduction to the available resources.

## ☐ Searching databases and catalogs

The most important tools your library offers are its online databases and catalogs. Searching these tools will always be easier and more efficient if you use carefully chosen words to limit the scope of your research.

### Keyword search

Searches using keywords make use of the computer's ability to look for any term in any field of the electronic record, including not just subject but also author, title, series, and notes. In article databases, a keyword search will look in abstracts and summaries of articles as well. Keyword searching requires you to put some thought into choosing your search terms in order to get the best results.

### Subject word search

Library holdings usually index their contents not only by author and title, but also by subject headings — standardized words and phrases used to classify the subject matter of books and articles. Most U.S. academic libraries classify their material using the *Library of Congress Subject Headings*, or LCSH. When you find a library source that seems especially relevant, you can use the subject headings for that source as search terms to browse for related titles.

### Advanced search options

Many library search engines offer advanced search options (sometimes on a separate page) to help you combine keywords, search for an exact phrase, or exclude items containing particular keywords. Often they can limit your search in other ways as well, such as by date or language. If you don't see a way to conduct an advanced search, note that simply entering terms in the search box may bring up advanced search options. Note, too, that search engines vary in the exact terms they use to refine searches; for instance, some use phrases such as "all these words," while others may use the word AND or something else. Most search tools offer tips on how to use the tool effectively, but these general tips can help:

- Enter at least two keywords in an "all these words" search box (or use AND) to limit your results. Entering *messaging* and *language* would bring up only results that include both terms.
- Search for an exact phrase, usually by putting the phrase in quotation marks, to limit your results. Searching for *"messaging language"* would include results containing "text messaging language" but not those containing "messaging as a language."

- Enter at least two keywords in an "any of these words" search box (or use OR) to expand your results. Entering *messaging* or *language* would bring up every result that included either term.

- Enter unwanted keywords in a "none of these words" search box (or use NOT) to exclude irrelevant results. Searching for *messaging* and *language* but not *popular* would omit results focusing on popular messaging slang.

## ▢ Finding articles

Some libraries use discovery tools that allow you to search all available materials at once, but if your library does not, you will need to use a periodical index to find articles. Ask a reference librarian for guidance about the most likely index for the subject of your research.

### General and specialized indexes

Different indexes cover different groups of periodicals; articles written before 1990 may be indexed only in a print volume. General indexes of periodicals list articles from general-interest magazines (such as *Time*), newspapers, and perhaps some scholarly journals. General indexes are useful for finding current sources on a topic. Specialized indexes, which tend to include mainly scholarly periodicals, may focus on one discipline (as the education index ERIC does) or on a group of related disciplines (as Social Sciences Abstracts does).

### Full text and abstracts

Some periodical indexes offer the full text of articles, and some offer abstracts (short summaries) of the articles. Be sure not to confuse an abstract with a complete article. Full-text databases can be extremely convenient — you can read and print out articles directly from the computer, without the extra step of tracking down the periodical in question. However, don't limit yourself to full-text databases, which may not contain graphics and images that appeared in the print version of the periodical — and which may not include the sources that would benefit your research most. Take advantage of abstracts, which give you a very brief overview of the article's contents so you can decide whether you need to spend time finding and reading the full text.

To locate a promising article that is not available in a full-text version, check to see whether a print version is available in your library's periodicals room.

### David Craig's library research

David Craig's research on instant messaging required research on educators' opinions on this technology's effect on youth literacy. His search on the keywords *text message* and *literacy* gave him the results you see on p. 205. After clicking on an entry that looked like it might pertain to his subject, he was able to read an abstract, and, based on the summary, David thought the article would be helpful. He found the full text in his library's journals collection. Full articles are sometimes accessible in online databases, but you may have to consult your library's periodicals section for a hard copy of the article.

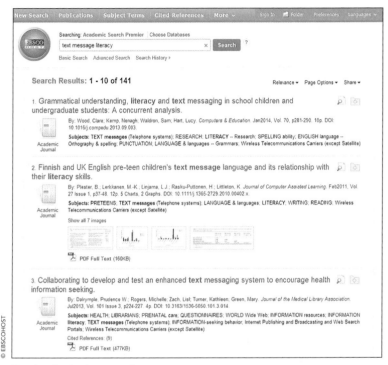

*Results of a database search*

## ☐ Finding books

Libraries categorize books by the *author's name*, by the *title*, and by one or more *subjects*. If you can't find a particular source under any of these headings, you can search by using a combination of subject headings and keywords. Such searches may turn up other useful titles as well.

More and more library holdings are digitized, but many books are available only in print. Catalog entries for print books list not only the author, title, subject, and publication information but also a call number that indicates how the book is classified and where it is shelved. (Many also indicate whether a book has been checked out and, if so, when it is due.)

Once you have the call number for a book, look for a library map or shelving plan to tell you where the book is housed. Take the time to browse through the books near the call number you are looking for — often you will find other books related to your topic in the immediate area.

Another strategy for finding books is to check a review index, which will help you find reviews so that you can check the relevance of a book to your project or get a thumbnail sketch of its contents before you track it down. Ask a reference librarian for guidance on review indexes.

## ☐ Using bibliographies

Look at any bibliographies (lists of sources) in books or articles you are using for your research; they can lead you to other valuable resources. In addition, check with a reference librarian to find out whether your library has more extensive bibliographies devoted to the area of your research.

## ☐ Using other library resources

In addition to books and periodicals, libraries give you access to many other useful materials that might be appropriate for your research.

- **Special collections and archives.** Your library may house archives (collections of valuable papers) and other special materials that are often available to student researchers. One student, for example, learned that her university owned a vast collection of twentieth-century posters. With help from a librarian, she was able to use some of these posters as primary sources for her research project on German culture after World War II.

- **Audio, video, multimedia, and art collections.** Many libraries have areas devoted to media and art, where they collect films, videos, paintings, and sound recordings.

- **Government documents.** Many libraries have collections of historical documents produced by local or state government offices. Check with a librarian if government publications would be useful sources for your topic. You can also look at the online version of the U.S. Government Printing Office, known as the Federal Digital System (FDsys), for electronic versions of government publications.

- **Interlibrary loans.** To borrow books, videos, or audio materials from another library, use an interlibrary loan. You can also request copies of journal articles from other libraries. Some loans — especially of books — can take time, so plan ahead.

## 11d Conducting Internet research

The Internet is many college students' favorite way of accessing information, and it's true that much information — including authoritative sources identical to those your library provides — can be found online, sometimes for free. However, information in library databases comes from identifiable and professionally edited sources; because no one is responsible for regulating information on the Web, you need to take special care to find out which information online is reliable and which is not. (See Chapter 12 for more on evaluating sources.)

## ☐ Searching the Internet

Research using a search tool such as Google usually begins with a keyword search (11c). Choose keywords carefully to improve the odds of finding what you're looking for. For example, if you're searching for information on legal issues regarding the Internet and enter *Internet* and *law* as keywords in a Google search, you will get over three million possible sources. You may find what you need on the first page or two of results, but if not, choose new keywords that lead to more specific sources. Look for a search engine's search tips or advanced search options for help with refining and limiting a keyword search.

Many people begin and end Internet searches with Google. However, every search tool has unique properties. If you try other search engines or a metasearch tool that searches multiple search engines simultaneously, you may find that one of them has capabilities that are particularly helpful for your purposes.

## ☐ Using bookmarking tools

Today's powerful bookmarking tools can help you browse, sort, and track resources online. Social bookmarking sites allow users to tag information and share it with others. If you find a helpful site, you can check to see how others have tagged it and quickly browse similar tags to find related information. You can sort and group information according to your tags. Users whose tagged sites you like and trust can become part of your network so that you can follow their sites of interest.

Web browsers can also help you bookmark and return to online resources. However, unlike the bookmarking tools in a Web browser, which are tied to one machine, you can use social bookmarking tools wherever you have an Internet connection.

## ☐ Finding authoritative sources online

You can find many authoritative and credible sources online. You can browse collections in virtual libraries, for example, or collections housed in government sites such as the Library of Congress, the National Institutes of Health, and the U.S. Census Bureau. For current national news, consult online versions of reputable newspapers such as the *New York Times* or the *Washington Post* or electronic sites for news services such as C-SPAN. Google Scholar can help you limit searches to scholarly works.

TALKING THE TALK | **WIKIS AS SOURCES**

"Why doesn't my instructor want me to use Wikipedia as a source?" Wikis are sites that users can add to and edit as they see fit; as a result, their contents are not always completely reliable for research. It's true that Wikipedia, a hugely popular site, has such a large and enthusiastic audience that editors and users are likely to catch mistakes and remove deliberately false information fairly quickly. But you can never be certain that a wiki entry has not been tampered with. The best advice is to use wikis as sources for preliminary research — Wikipedia's bibliography entries are often a good place to start — and then to make sure that you double-check any information you find there.

Some scholarly journals (such as those from Berkeley Electronic Press) and general-interest magazines (including *Slate* and *Salon*) are published only online, and many popular print publications make at least some of their contents available free on the Web.

## 11e Conducting field research

For many research projects, you will need to collect field data. The "field" may be many things — a classroom, a church, a laboratory, or the corner grocery store. As student David Craig discovered, it may even be a collection of instant messages from the Internet. As a field researcher, then, you need to discover *where* you can find relevant information, *how* to gather it, and *who* might provide the best information.

If you decide to conduct field research, check with your instructor about whether your school has a review board that will need to approve your data-gathering plan.

### ☐ Conducting interviews

Some information is best obtained by interviewing — asking direct questions of other people. If you can talk with an expert in person, on the telephone, or online, you might get information you could not have obtained through any other kind of research.

Your first step is to find interview subjects. Has your research generated the names of people you might contact directly? Brainstorm for additional names, looking for authorities on your topic and people in your community, such as faculty members, war veterans, or food pantry volunteers. Once you identify some promising possibilities, write, telephone, or email them to see whether you can arrange an interview.

When you have identified someone to interview, prepare your questions. You need to know your topic well, and you need to know a fair amount about your interviewee. You will probably want to ask several kinds of questions. Questions about facts and figures (*How many employees do you have?*) elicit specific answers and don't invite expansion or opinion. You can lead the interviewee to think out loud and to give additional details by asking open-ended questions: *What was the atmosphere like at the company just before the union went on strike? How do you feel now about deciding to enlist in the military after 9/11?*

Avoid questions that would encourage vague answers (*What do you think of youth today?*) or yes/no answers (*Should the laws governing corporate accounting practices be changed?*). Instead, ask questions that must be answered with supporting details (*Why should the laws governing corporate accounting practices be changed?*).

**QUICK HELP**

### Conducting an interview

- Determine your exact purpose, and be sure it relates to your research question and hypothesis.
- Set up the interview well in advance. Specify how long it will take, and if you wish to record the session, ask permission to do so.
- Prepare a written list of factual and open-ended questions. Brainstorming or freewriting can help you come up with questions. (3a) Leave plenty of space for notes after each question. If the interview proceeds in a direction that seems fruitful, do not feel that you have to ask all of your prepared questions.
- Record the subject, date, time, and place of the interview.
- Even if you are taping, take notes. Ask your interviewee for permission to use video, audio, or quotations that will appear in print.
- Thank those you interview, either in person or in a letter or email.

### ☐ Conducting observations

"What," you might ask, "could be easier than observing something? You just choose a subject, look at it closely, and record what you see and hear." Yet trained observers tell us that making a faithful record of an observation requires intense concentration and mental agility.

Moreover, observation is never neutral. Just as a photographer has a particular angle on a subject, so an observer always has an angle on what he or she is looking at. If, for instance, you decide to conduct a formal observation of your writing class, the field notes you take will reflect your status as an insider. Consequently, you will need to check your observations to see what your participation in the class may have obscured or led you to take for granted. In other instances, when you are not an insider, you still need to aim for optimal objectivity, altering as little as possible the phenomena you are looking at.

Before you conduct any observation, decide exactly what you want to find out, and anticipate what you are likely to see. Are you going to observe an action repeated by many people (such as pedestrians crossing a street), a sequence of actions (such as a medical procedure), or the interactions of a group (such as a church congregation)? Also decide exactly what you want to record and how. In a grocery store, for instance, decide whether to observe shoppers or store employees and what you want to note about them — what they say, what they buy, how they are dressed, how they respond to one another, and so on.

### Conducting an observation

- Determine the purpose of the observation, and be sure it relates to your research question and hypothesis.
- Brainstorm about what you are looking for, but don't be rigidly bound to your expectations. **(3a)**
- If necessary, make appointments and gain permission to observe.
- Develop an appropriate system for recording data. Consider using a "split" notebook or screen: on one side, record your observations directly; on the other, record your thoughts and interpretations.
- Record the date, time, and place of the observation.

## ☐ Conducting surveys

Although surveys can take the form of interviews, they usually depend on questionnaires. To do survey research, all you need is a representative sample of people and a questionnaire that will elicit the information you need.

How do you choose the people you will survey? In some cases, you might want to survey all members of a small group, such as everyone in one of your classes. More often, however, you'll aim for a random sample of a large group — the first-year class at your university, for example. While a true random sample is probably unattainable, you can aim for a good cross section by, say, emailing every fifth person in the class directory.

On any questionnaire, the questions should be clear and easy to understand and designed so that you will be able to analyze the answers easily. For example, questions that ask respondents to say yes or no or to rank items on a five-point scale are particularly easy to tabulate.

As you design your questionnaire, think about ways your respondents might misunderstand you or your questions. Adding a category called "other" to a list of options you are asking people about, for example, allows them to fill in information you would not otherwise get.

Because tabulating the responses takes time and because people often resent answering long questionnaires, limit the number of questions to no more than twenty. After tabulating your results, put them in an easily readable format, such as a chart or spreadsheet.

### Designing a survey questionnaire

- Write out your purpose, and review your research question and hypothesis to determine the kinds of questions to ask.
- Figure out how to reach respondents.
- Draft questions that call for short, specific answers.
- Test the questions on several people, and revise questions that seem unfair, ambiguous, too hard to answer, or too time consuming.
- Draft a cover letter or invitation email. Be sure to state your deadline.
- If you are using a print questionnaire, leave adequate space for answers.
- Proofread the questionnaire carefully.

## ☐ Analyzing, synthesizing, and interpreting data

To make sense of the information you have gathered, first try to identify what you want to look at: kinds of language? comparisons between men's and women's responses? The point is to find a focus, since you can't pay equal attention to everything. This step is especially important in analyzing results from observations or survey questionnaires. If you need assistance, see if your instructor can recommend similar research so that you can see how it was analyzed.

Next, synthesize the data by looking for recurring words or ideas that fall into patterns (12f). Establish a system for coding your information, labeling each pattern you identify — a plus sign for every positive response on a questionnaire, for example. If you ask classmates to review your notes or data, they may notice other patterns.

Finally, interpret your data by summing up the meaning of what you have found. What is the significance of your findings? Be careful not to make large generalizations.

### David Craig's field research

A large part of David Craig's essay (32e) rests on analyzing the data he collected on messaging language. To determine whether the phrases used in online discussions constitute a language, David obtained and analyzed actual IM conversations from U.S. residents aged twelve to seventeen. After examining over eleven thousand lines of text, David identified four common kinds of messaging language and was able to use his field research to support his thesis.

▼ ▼ ▼ ▼ ▼ ▼ ▼ ▼ ▼ ▼ ▼ ▼ ▼ ▼ ▼ ▼ ▼ ▼ ▼ ▼ ▼ ▼ ▼ ▼ ▼

## THINKING CRITICALLY ABOUT CONDUCTING RESEARCH

Begin to analyze the research project you are now working on by examining the ways in which you conducted your research: What use did you make of primary and secondary sources? What library, online, and field research did you carry out? What aspect of the research process was most satisfying? What was most disappointing or irritating? How could you do research more efficiently? Bring your answers to these questions to class.

# CHAPTER 12

# Evaluating Sources and Taking Notes

W ITH MOST TOPICS, your problem will not be so much finding sources as figuring out *which* sources to consult in the limited time you have available. The difference between a useful source and a poor one depends to a great extent on your topic, purpose, and audience. Learning how to tell which sources are best for you allows you to use your time wisely. Once you've found good sources, taking effective notes allows you to use the insights you find to your greatest advantage.

> **CONNECT:** What source do you need to summarize for your research project? **12c, 13d**
>
> **CREATE:** Draft a summary of your source.
>
> **REFLECT:** Go to **macmillanhighered.com/smh**, and respond to **12. Evaluating Sources > Student Writing > Annotated bibliography (Chan)** or **12. Evaluating Sources > Reflective annotated bibliography (Sriram)**.

## 12a Using sources for a purpose

Why do writers decide to use one source rather than another? Sources serve different purposes, so part of evaluating sources involves deciding what you need the source to provide for your research project. You may need background information or context that your audience will need to follow your writing; explanations of concepts unfamiliar to your audience; verbal and visual emphasis for your points; authority or evidence for your claims, which can help you create your own authority; other perspectives on your topic; or counter-examples or counter-evidence that you need to consider.

As you begin to work with your sources, make notes in your research log about why you plan to use a particular source. At the same time, you should also begin your working bibliography (12c).

## 12b Moving beyond previewing a source

Researchers examining research writing by first-year college students report that student writers often seem to use a quotation or paraphrase from the very beginning of a source — and then set that source aside and go on to something else. By skimming or even skipping the rest of the source, such writers may well miss information that could be useful to them. In addition, this research project strongly suggests that student writers often have not read a source carefully, or have misinterpreted or misunderstood it. Again, once you identify a source that seems particularly useful to you, you need to read it carefully — and make sure that you have grasped its meaning. That means reading most or all of the source, not just the first page.

## 12c Keeping a working bibliography

A working bibliography is a list of sources that you may ultimately use for your project. As you find and begin to evaluate research sources — articles, books, Web sites, and so on — you should record source information for every source you think you might use. (Relevant information includes everything you need to find the source again and cite it correctly; the information you will need varies based on the type of source, whether you found it in a library or not, and whether you consulted it in print or online.) The emphasis here is on *working* because the list will probably include materials that end up not being useful. For this reason, you don't absolutely need to put all entries into the documentation style you will use (see Chapters 32–35). If you do follow the required documentation style, however, that part of your work will be done when you prepare the final draft.

The following chart will help you keep track of the sorts of information you should try to find:

| Type of Source | Information to Collect (if applicable) |
| --- | --- |
| Print book | Library call number, author(s) or editor(s), title and subtitle, place of publication, publisher, year of publication, any other information (translator, edition, volume) |
| Part of a book | Call number, author(s) of part, title of part, author(s) or editor(s) of book, title of book, place of publication, publisher, year of publication, inclusive page numbers for part |
| Print periodical article | Call number of periodical, author(s) of article, title of article, name of periodical, volume number, issue number, date of issue, inclusive page numbers for article |

| Type of Source | Information to Collect (if applicable) |
|---|---|
| Digital source | Author(s), title of document, title of site, editor(s) of site, sponsor of site, publication information for print version of source, name of database or online service, date of electronic publication or last update, date you accessed the source, URL |

For other kinds of sources (films, recordings, visuals), you should also list the information required by the documentation style you are using (see Chapters 32–35) and note where you found the information.

## ☐ Creating an annotated bibliography

You might wish to annotate your working bibliography to include a summary of the source's contents as well as publishing information (whether or not annotations are required) because annotating can help you understand and remember what the source says, as in this excerpt from Tony Chan's annotated bibliography.

ANNOTATED BIBLIOGRAPHY ENTRY

Diamond, Edwin, and Stephen Bates. *The Spot: The Rise of Political Advertising on Television.* 3rd ed. Cambridge, MA: MIT Press, 1992. Diamond and Bates illustrate the impact of television on political strategy and discourse. The two argue that Lyndon Johnson's "Daisy Girl" ad succeeded by exploiting the advantages provided by the nascent television medium, using violent images and sounds and the words "nuclear bomb" to sway the audience's emotions. Emphasizing Johnson's direct control over the production of the ad, the authors illustrate the crucial role the ad played in portraying Goldwater as a warmonger.

## ☐ Customizing an annotated bibliography

Some annotated bibliographies can be very detailed — going beyond a summary of the main points in a source to examine research methods, evaluate the credibility of the source, reflect on its usefulness for a particular project, and more. Writing professor Mark McBeth asks his students to include new vocabulary and potential quotations from the source as part of a reflective annotated bibliography assignment for his course. Annotations that go beyond summaries can help you think critically about your sources and their place in your overall research project. Consider the kind of annotations that will be most useful for

TALKING THE TALK | **RESEARCH WITH AN OPEN MIND**

"What's wrong with looking for sources that back up what I want to say?" When you start researching a topic, keep an open mind: investigate every important source, even if you think you won't agree with it. If all your sources take the same position you take, you may be doing some pretty selective searching — and you may be missing a big part of the picture. Who knows? You may change your position after learning more about the topic. Even if you don't, ignoring counterarguments and other points of view harms your credibility, suggesting that you haven't done your homework.

your annotated bibliography. Student Nandita Sriram's annotated bibliography, in the integrated media at **macmillanhighered.com/smh**, includes summaries, descriptions of research methods, and evaluations.

## 12d Evaluating usefulness and credibility

Since you want the information and ideas you glean from sources to be reliable and persuasive, you must evaluate each potential source carefully. Use these guidelines to help you assess the sources you are considering:

- **Your purpose.** What will this source add to your research project? Does it help you support a major point, demonstrate that you have thoroughly researched your topic, or help establish your own credibility through its authority?

- **Relevance.** How closely related is the source to the narrowed topic you are pursuing? You may need to read beyond the title and opening paragraph to check for relevance.

- **Level of specialization and audience.** General sources can be helpful as you begin your research, but you may then need the authority or currency of more specialized sources. On the other hand, extremely specialized works may be very hard to understand. Who was the source originally written for — the general public? experts in the field? advocates or opponents? How does this fit with your concept of your own audience?

- **Credentials of the publisher or sponsor.** What can you learn about the publisher or sponsor of the source you are using? For example, is it a major newspaper known for integrity in reporting, or is it a tabloid? Is it a popular source, or is it sponsored by a professional or governmental organization or academic institution (11a)? If you're evaluating a book, is the publisher one you recognize or can find described on its own Web site? No hard and fast rules exist for deciding what kind of source to use. But knowing the sponsor's or publisher's credentials can help you determine whether a source is appropriate for your research project.

- **Credentials of the author.** As you do your research, note names that come up from one source to another, since these references may indicate that the author is influential in the field. An author's credentials may also be presented in the article, book, or Web site, or you can search the Internet for information about the author. In U.S. academic writing, experts and those with significant experience in a field have more authority on the subject than others.

- **Date of publication.** Recent sources are often more useful than older ones, particularly in the sciences or other fields that change rapidly. However, in some fields — such as the humanities — the most authoritative works may be older ones. The publication dates of Internet sites can often be difficult to pin down. And even for sites that include dates of posting, remember that the material posted may have been composed some time earlier. Sites that list recent updates may be more reliable.

- **Accuracy of the source.** How accurate and complete is the information in the source? How thorough is the bibliography or list of works cited that accompanies the source? Can you find other sources that corroborate what your source is saying?

- **Stance of the source.** Identify the source's point of view or rhetorical stance, and scrutinize it carefully. Does the source present facts, or does it interpret or evaluate them? If it presents facts, what is included and what is omitted, and why? If it interprets or evaluates information that is not disputed, the source's stance may be obvious, but at other times, you will need to think carefully about the source's goals (12e). What does the author or sponsoring group want? to convince you of an idea? sell you something? call you to action in some way?

- **Cross-references to the source.** Is the source cited in other works? If you see your source cited by others, notice how they cite it and what they say about it to find additional clues to its credibility.

For more on evaluating Web sources and periodical articles, see the source maps on pp. 218–21.

### EXERCISE 12.1

Choose two sources that seem well suited to your topic, and evaluate their usefulness and credibility using the criteria presented in this chapter. If possible, analyze one print source and one digital source. Bring the results of your analysis to class for discussion.

## 12e  Reading and interpreting sources

For those sources that you want to analyze more closely, reading with a critical eye can make your research process more efficient. Use the following tips to guide your critical reading.

## ☐ Keeping your research question in mind

As you read, ask yourself the following questions:

- How does this material address your research question and support your hypothesis?
- What quotations from this source might help support your thesis?
- Does the source include counterarguments to your hypothesis that you will need to answer? If so, what answers can you provide?

## ☐ Noting the author's stance and tone

Even a seemingly factual report, such as an encyclopedia article, is filled with judgments, often unstated. Read with an eye for the author's overall rhetorical stance, or perspective, as well as for facts or explicit opinions. Also pay attention to the author's tone, the way his or her attitude toward the topic and audience is conveyed. The following questions can help:

- Is the author a strong advocate or opponent of something? a skeptical critic? a specialist in the field?
- Are there any clues to why the author takes this stance (2d)? Is professional affiliation a factor?
- How does this stance affect the author's presentation and your reaction to it?
- What facts does the author include? Can you think of any important fact that is omitted?
- What is the author's tone? Is it cautious, angry, flippant, serious, impassioned? What words indicate this tone?

## ☐ Considering the argument and evidence

Every piece of writing takes a position. Even a scientific report implicitly "argues" that we should accept it and its data as reliable. As you read, look for the main point or the main argument the author is making. Try to identify the reasons the author gives to support his or her position. Then try to determine *why* the author takes this position.

- What is the author's main point, and what evidence supports it?
- How persuasive is the evidence? Can you think of a way to refute it?
- Can you detect any questionable logic or fallacious thinking (8f)?
- Does this author disagree with arguments you have read elsewhere? If so, what causes the disagreements — differences about facts or about how to interpret facts?

For more on argument, see Chapters 7–9.

# Evaluating Web Sources

### Is the sponsor credible?

1. Who is the **sponsor or publisher** of the source? See what information you can get from the URL. The domain names for government sites may end in *.gov* or *.mil* and for educational sites in *.edu*. The ending *.org* may—but does not always—indicate a nonprofit organization. If you see a tilde (~) or percent sign (%) followed by a name, or if you see a word such as *users* or *members*, the page's creator may be an individual, not an institution. In addition, check the header and footer, where the sponsor may be identified. The Web page and downloaded PDF article shown here come from a site sponsored by the nonprofit Nieman Foundation for Journalism at Harvard University.

2. Look for an ***About*** page or a link to a home page for background information on the sponsor. Is a mission statement included? What are the sponsoring organization's purpose and point of view? Does the mission statement seem balanced? What is the purpose of the site (to inform, to persuade, to advocate for a cause, to advertise, or something else)? Does the information on the site come directly from the sponsor, or is the material reprinted from another source? If it is reprinted, check the original.

### Is the author credible?

3. What are the **author's credentials**? Look for information accompanying the material on the page. You can also run a search on the author to find out more. Does the author seem qualified to write about this topic?

### Is the information credible and current?

4. When was the information **posted or last updated**? Is it recent enough to be useful?

5. Does the page document sources with **footnotes or links**? If so, do the sources seem credible and current? Does the author include any additional resources for further information? Look for ways to corroborate the information the author provides.

**1** Sponsor or Publisher  **2** About Page

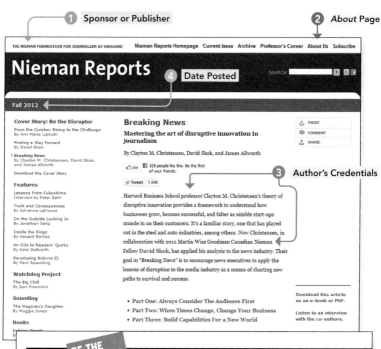

THE NIEMAN FOUNDATION FOR JOURNALISM AT HARVARD   Nieman Reports Homepage   Current Issue   Archive   Professor's Corner   About Us   Subscribe

# Nieman Reports

**4** Date Posted

SEARCH

Fall 2012

**Cover Story: Be the Disruptor**
From the Curator: Rising to the Challenge
By Ann Marie Lipinski

Finding a Way Forward
By David Skok

> Breaking News
By Clayton M. Christensen, David Skok, and James Allworth

Download the Cover Story

**Features**
Lessons From Fukushima
Interview by Peter Behr

Truth and Consequences
By Adrienne LaFrance

On the Outside Looking In
By Jonathan Seitz

Inside the Rings
By Howard Berkes

An Ode to Readers' Quirks
By Kate Galbraith

Developing Notions
By Pam Spaulding

**Watchdog Project**
The Big Chill
By Dan Froomkin

**Sounding**
The Magician's Daughter
By Maggie Jones

**Books**

## Breaking News
### Mastering the art of disruptive innovation in journalism

By Clayton M. Christensen, David Skok, and James Allworth

Like  529 people like this. Be the first of your friends.

Tweet  1,946

**3** Author's Credentials

Harvard Business School professor Clayton M. Christensen's theory of disruptive innovation provides a framework to understand how businesses grow, become successful, and falter as nimble start-ups muscle in on their customers. It's a familiar story, one that has played out in the steel and auto industries, among others. Now Christensen, in collaboration with 2012 Martin Wise Goodman Canadian Nieman Fellow David Skok, has applied his analysis to the news industry. Their goal in "Breaking News" is to encourage news executives to apply the lessons of disruption to the media industry as a means of charting new paths to survival and success.

- Part One: Always Consider The Audience First
- Part Two: When Times Change, Change Your Business
- Part Three: Build Capabilities For a New World

PRINT
COMMENT
SHARE

Download this article as an e-book or PDF.

Listen to an interview with the co-authors.

---

COVER STORY  **BE THE DISRUPTOR**

# Breaking News

Mastering the art of disruptive innovation
in journalism

**BY CLAYTON M. CHRISTENSEN, DAVID SKOK, AND JAMES ALLWORTH**

OLD HABITS DIE HARD.

Four years after the 2008 financial crisis, traditional news organizations continue to see their newsrooms shrink or close. Those that survive remain mired in the innovator's dilemma: A false choice between today's revenues and tomorrow's digital promise. The problem is a profound one: A study in March by the Pew Research Center's Project for Excellence in Journalism showed that newspapers have been, on average, losing print advertising dollars at seven times the rate they have been growing digital ad revenue.

Journalism institutions play a vital role in the democratic process and we are

This has happened before. Eighty-nine years ago, Henry Luce started Time as a weekly magazine summarizing the news. All 28 pages of the black-and-white weekly were filled with advertisements and aggregation. This wasn't just rewrites of the week's news; it was rip-and-read copy from the day's major publications—The Atlantic Monthly, The Christian Science Monitor, and the New York World, to name a few.

Today Time, with its print and online properties, confronts the challenges posed by the digital age, but reaches a global audience of 25 million.

With history as our guide, it shouldn't be a surprise when new entrants like

It happened with Japanese automakers: They started with cheap subcompacts that were widely considered a joke. Now they make Lexuses that challenge the best of what Europe can offer.

It happened in the steel industry, where minimills began as a cheap, lower-quality alternative to established integrated mills, then moved their way up, pushing aside the industry's giants.

In the news business, newcomers are doing the same thing: delivering a product that is faster and more personalized than that provided by the bigger, more established news organizations. The newcomers aren't burdened by the expensive overheads of legacy organiza-

Photos © Nieman Foundation for Journalism at Harvard

219

# Evaluating Articles

**Determine the relevance of the source.**

**1** Look for an **abstract**, or article summary. Is this source directly related to your research? Does it provide useful information and insights? Will your readers consider it persuasive support for your thesis?

**Determine the credibility of the publication.**

**2** Consider the publication's **title**. Words in the title such as *Journal*, *Review*, and *Quarterly* may indicate that the periodical is a scholarly source. Most research projects rely on authorities in a particular field, whose work usually appears in scholarly journals. For more on distinguishing between scholarly and popular sources, see 11a.

**3** Try to determine the **publisher or sponsor**. This journal is published by the University of Illinois Press. Academic presses such as this one generally review articles carefully before publishing them and bear the authority of their academic sponsors.

**Determine the credibility of the author.**

**4** Evaluate the **author's credentials**. In this case, they are given in a note, which indicates that the author is a college professor.

**Determine the currency of the article.**

**5** Look at the **publication date**, and think about whether your topic and your credibility depend on your use of very current sources.

**Determine the accuracy of the article.**

**6** Look at the **sources cited** by the author of the article. Here, they are documented in a reference list. Ask yourself whether the works the author has cited seem credible and current. Are any of these works cited in other articles you've considered?

**In addition, consider the following questions:**

- What is the article's stance or point of view? What are the author's goals? What does the author want you to know or believe?

- How does this source fit in with your other sources? Does any of the information it provides contradict or challenge other sources?

ELIZABETH TUCKER

# Changing Concepts of Childhood: Children's Folklore Scholarship since the Late Nineteenth Century

*This essay examines children's folklore scholarship from the late nineteenth century to the present, tracing key concepts from the Gilded Age to the contemporary era. These concepts reflect significant social, cultural, political, and scientific changes. From the "savage child" to the "secret-keeping child," the "magic-making child," the "cerebral child," the "taboo-breaking child," the "monstrous child," and others, scholarly representations of young people have close connections to the eras in which they developed. Nineteenth-century children's folklore scholarship relied on evolutionism; now evolutionary biology provides a basis for children's folklore research, so we have re-entered familiar territory.*

SINCE 1977, WHEN THE American Folklore Society decided to form a new section for scholars interested in young people's traditions, I have belonged to the Children's Folklore Section. It has been a joy to contribute to this dynamic organization, which has significantly influenced children's folklore scholarship and children's book authors' focus on folk tradition. This essay examines children's folklore scholarship from the late nineteenth century to the contemporary era in the English language. These concepts reflect significant social, cultural, political, and scientific changes that have occurred since William Wells Newell, the first secretary of the American Folklore Society and the first editor of the *Journal of American Folklore*, published *Games and Songs of American Children* in 1883. They also reveal some very interesting commonalities. Those of us who pursue children's folklore scholarship today may consider ourselves to be light years away from nineteenth-century scholars' research but may find, when reading nineteenth-century works, that we have stayed fairly close to our scholarly "home base."

Before examining concepts of childhood that folklorists have developed, I will offer a working definition of this life stage and briefly explain the beginning of childhood studies. I will also summarize the Children's Folklore Section's work during the past thirty-four years. According to the *Oxford English Dictionary*, childhood consists of "the state or stage of life of a child; the time during which one is a child; the time from birth to puberty" (2011). Scholars of childhood tend to draw a line between childhood that begins at puberty and follows pre-adolescence. The folklore

ELIZABETH TUCKER is Professor of English at Binghamton University

*Journal of American Folklore* 125(498):389–410
Copyright © 2012 by the Board of Trustees of the University of Illinois

*and Humanities* 3:145–60.

Carpenter, Carole H. 2011. Why Children's Studies? *Centre for Young People's Texts and Cultures*. crytc.uwinnipeg.ca/pdf/papers/Carole.Carpenter.pdf.
Chamberlain, Alexander Francis. 1896. *The Child and Childhood in Folk-Thought*. New York: Macmillan.
Cline, Foster W., and Jim Fay. 1990. *Parenting with Love and Logic: Teaching Children Responsibility*. Colorado Springs, CO: Pinon Press.
Conrad, JoAnn. 2002. The War on Youth: A Modern Oedipal Tragedy. *Children's Folklore Review* 24(1–2):33–42.
Crandall, Bryan Ripley. 2009. *Cow Project*. bryanripleycrandall.files.wordpress.com/2009/05/slbscow-project.pdf.
Darwin, Charles. 1859. *On the Origin of Species by Means of Natural Selection, or the Preservation of Favoured Races in the Struggle for Life* (1st edition). London: John Murray.
Dégh, Linda. 2001. *Legend and Belief*. Bloomington: Indiana University Press.
Dorson, Richard M. 1968. *The British Folklorists: A History*. Chicago: University of Chicago Press.
Douglas, Norman. [1916] 1968. *London Street Games*. Detroit: Singing Tree Press.

# 12f  Synthesizing sources

When you read and interpret a source — for example, when you consider its purpose and relevance, its author's credentials, its accuracy, and the kind of argument it is making — you are analyzing the source. Analysis requires you to take apart something complex (such as an article in a scholarly journal) and look closely at the parts to understand the whole better. For academic writing you also need to *synthesize* — group similar pieces of information together and look for patterns — so you can put your sources (and your own knowledge and experience) together in an original argument. Synthesis is the flip side of analysis: you already understand the parts, so your job is to assemble them into a new whole.

To synthesize sources for a research project, try the following tips:

- **Read the material carefully.**  Don't just grab a quotation and move on — make sure you really understand. For tips on reading with a critical eye, see Chapter 7.

- **Understand the purpose of each source.**  Make sure the source is relevant and necessary to your argument.

- **Determine the important ideas in each source.**  Take notes on each source (12g). Identify and summarize the key ideas of each piece.

- **Formulate a position.**  Review the key ideas of each source and figure out how they fit together. Look for patterns: discussions of causes and effects, specific parts of a larger issue, background information, and so on. After considering multiple perspectives, decide what you have to say.

- **Summon evidence to support your position.**  You might use paraphrases, summaries, or direct quotations from your sources as evidence (13b–d), or your personal experience or prior knowledge. Integrate quotations properly (see Chapter 13), and keep your ideas central to the piece of writing.

- **Deal with counterarguments.**  You don't have to use every idea or every source available — some will be more useful than others. However, ignoring evidence that opposes your position makes your argument weaker. You should acknowledge the existence of valid opinions that differ from yours, and try to understand them well before explaining why they are incorrect or incomplete.

- **Combine your source materials effectively.**  Be careful to avoid simply summarizing or listing your research. Think carefully about how the ideas in your reading support your argument. Try to weave the various sources together rather than discussing your sources one by one.

Using sources effectively can pose challenges (12b). Even after you have evaluated a source, take time to look at how well it works in your specific situation.

And if you change the focus of your work after you have begun doing research, be especially careful to check whether your sources still fit.

## A student's synthesis project

STUDENT WRITER
Caroline Warner

Caroline Warner's full research-based essay on "Hydration and Sports Drinks in Competitive Cycling" appears online at **macmillanhighered.com/smh**. In this excerpt, she identifies important ideas from her research on hydration for athletes, formulates a position, and supports her argument, effectively synthesizing her sources. (Photo © Caroline Warner)

There is little controversy as to the seriousness of dehydration. However, experts recommend varied methods for dealing with it. The *British Journal of Sports Medicine* outlines two general approaches. One method is for athletes to hydrate, using only water, whenever they are thirsty during exercise. The athlete, after his workout, is then free to use sports drinks for recovery and electrolyte replacement. While this method does result in some degree of dehydration, exercise-associated hyponatremia (EAH) — overdrinking — is no longer a danger, and this method may better prepare athletes for any competitive situation in which they will not be able to rehydrate until after performing. This method has been adopted by USA Track & Field, as well as the International Marathon Medical Directors Association. The other approach to hydration maintains that an athlete should attempt to replace 100 percent of body weight lost during exercise. The athlete should drink every fifteen to twenty minutes, preferably consuming supplemental sodium like that found in sports drinks; the sodium allows the athlete to retain water and allows for better nervous system communication. In this scenario, the athlete does not wait to become thirsty (the assumption is that a thirsty athlete is already dehydrated); instead, he drinks small amounts consistently, and his body weight losses are less than 1 percent.

> Source identifies two main methods of hydration for athletes

Summary of journal source

This approach has been adopted by the American College of Sports Medicine as well as the National Athletic Trainers Association (Beltrami, Hew-Butler, and Noakes).

Reasons for cyclists' preference for second method

Synthesis of findings from a number of sources that establish a clear pattern in favor of appeal

Most cyclists are believers in the second method. In a sport that both requires alertness and demands performance for extended amounts of time, it makes sense to stay up on hydration. As for what to drink, online communities at both www.bikeforums.com and www.cyclingforums .com are filled with advocates for sports drinks rather than water. There is some debate over which drink is most effective — Heed, Cytomax, Pro-Opti, Accelerade, GU$_2$0, and Gatorade are among the most popular — and over how much to use (many people dilute or mix their drinks), but everyone seems to advocate one drink or another. Arielle Filiberti, a three-time junior national champion cyclist and the favorite for women's U23s this year, says that her most horrific crash came at the end of a long ride when she ran out of both water and her preferred energy drink. Filiberti had been experiencing dizziness and light-headedness for some time, and as she was rounding a corner, she misjudged the turn and swung out too far into the road. She then swerved to avoid oncoming traffic, lost her balance, and skidded sideways off the road. Doctors found that Filiberti had lost about 3.5 percent of her body weight over a four-hour ride — almost five pounds of water. Furthermore, her reflexes were slow and she was unable to focus her eyes either close up or far away — a result of electrolyte and sodium loss. She was put on a saline drip and hospitalized overnight (Filiberti). This kind of story is much more common than is safe or necessary. Thus for the competitive cyclist, it makes most sense to hydrate continuously through training.

Note the way Caroline identifies important information from a journal and expands on the significance of the information in her discussion of sources from two Web sites for cyclists and a personal interview. All of these sources are synthesized to support her own claim that continuous hydration with sports drinks is the best way for cyclists to combat the threat of dehydration. (For more on synthesizing sources, see Chapter 13 and 15d.)

# 12g Taking notes and annotating sources

Note-taking methods vary greatly from one researcher to another, so you may decide to use a digital file, a notebook, or index cards. Regardless of the method, however, you should (1) record enough information to help you recall the major points of the source; (2) put the information in the form in which you are most likely to incorporate it into your research essay, whether a summary, a paraphrase, or a quotation; and (3) note all the information you will need to cite the source accurately, including the author's name, the shortened title, and, for print sources, the page number(s) on which the quotation appears. Make sure you have a corresponding working-bibliography entry with complete source information (12c).

The following example shows the major items a note should include:

### Elements of an accurate note

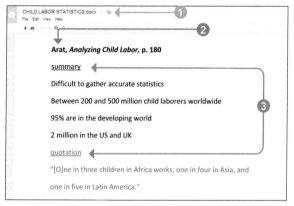

CHILD LABOR STATISTICS.docx
File   Edit   View   Help

**Arat, *Analyzing Child Labor*, p. 180**

summary

Difficult to gather accurate statistics

Between 200 and 500 million child laborers worldwide

95% are in the developing world

2 million in the US and UK

quotation

"[O]ne in three children in Africa works, one in four in Asia, and

one in five in Latin America."

① **Use a subject heading.** Label or title each note with a brief, descriptive heading so that you can group similar subtopics together.

② **Identify the source.** List the author's name and a shortened title of the source, and a page number, if available. Your working-bibliography entry (12c) for the source will contain the full bibliographic information, so you don't need to repeat it in each note.

③ **Indicate whether the note is a direct quotation, paraphrase, or summary.** Make sure quotations are copied accurately. Put square brackets around any change you make, and use ellipses if you omit material.

Taking complete notes will help you digest the source information as you read and incorporate the material into your text without inadvertently plagiarizing the source (see Chapter 14). Be sure to reread each note carefully, and recheck it against the source to make sure quotations, statistics, and specific facts are accurate. (For more information on working with quotations, paraphrases, and summaries, see Chapter 13.)

## ☐ Using quotations

Some of the notes you take will contain quotations, which give the *exact words* of a source.

---

**QUICK HELP**

### Guidelines for quotation notes

- Copy quotations carefully, with punctuation, capitalization, and spelling *exactly* as in the original.
- Use quotation marks; don't rely on your memory to distinguish your own words from those of the source. Identify the note as a quotation.
- Use square brackets if you introduce words of your own into a quotation or make changes in it, and use ellipses if you omit material. If you later incorporate the quotation into your essay, copy it faithfully — brackets, ellipses, and all. **(13b)**
- If the quotation appears on more than one page of a print source, use a slash ( / ) to indicate where one page ends and another begins.

---

Here is a note with a quotation that student Benjy Mercer-Golden used in his research paper (9l):

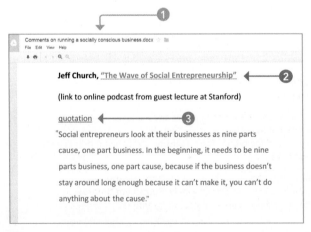

Comments on running a socially conscious business.docx
File  Edit  View  Help

**Jeff Church,** <u>"The Wave of Social Entrepreneurship"</u> ← ②

**(link to online podcast from guest lecture at Stanford)**

<u>quotation</u> ← ③
"Social entrepreneurs look at their businesses as nine parts cause, one part business. In the beginning, it needs to be nine parts business, one part cause, because if the business doesn't stay around long enough because it can't make it, you can't do anything about the cause."

① Name of document indicates subject

② Author and short title of source (no page number for electronic source)

③ Direct quotation

## □ Using paraphrases

A paraphrase accurately states all the relevant information from a passage *in your own words and sentence structures*, without any additional comments or elaborations. A paraphrase is useful when the main points of a passage, their order, and at least some details are important but — unlike passages worth quoting — the particular wording is not. Unlike a summary, a paraphrase always restates *all* the main points of a passage in the same order and often in about the same number of words.

---

**QUICK HELP**

### Guidelines for paraphrase notes

- Include all main points and any important details from the original source, in the same order in which the author presents them.
- State the meaning in your own words and sentence structures (without looking at the original). If you want to include especially memorable language from the original, enclose it in quotation marks. Identify your work as a paraphrase.
- Save your comments, elaborations, or reactions on another note.

---

To paraphrase without plagiarizing inadvertently, do not simply substitute synonyms, and do not imitate an author's style. If you wish to cite some of an author's words within a paraphrase, enclose them in quotation marks. The following examples of paraphrases resemble the original either too little or too much:

**ORIGINAL**

Language play, the arguments suggest, will help the development of pronunciation ability through its focus on the properties of sounds and sound contrasts, such as rhyming. Playing with word endings and decoding the syntax of riddles will help the acquisition of grammar. Readiness to play with words and names, to exchange puns and to engage in nonsense talk, promotes links with semantic development. The kinds of dialogue interaction illustrated above are likely to have consequences for the development of conversational skills. And language play, by its nature, also contributes greatly to what in recent years has been called *metalinguistic awareness*, which is turning out to be of critical importance in the development of language skills in general and of literacy skills in particular. —DAVID CRYSTAL, *Language Play* (180)

**UNACCEPTABLE PARAPHRASE: STRAYING FROM THE AUTHOR'S IDEAS**

Crystal argues that playing with language — creating rhymes, figuring out how riddles work, making puns, playing with names, using invented words, and so on — helps children figure out a great deal about language, from the basics of pronunciation and grammar to how to carry on a conversation. Increasing their understanding of how language works in turn helps them become more interested in learning new languages and in pursuing education (180).

This paraphrase starts off well enough, but it moves away from paraphrasing the original to inserting the writer's ideas; Crystal says nothing about learning new languages or pursuing education.

UNACCEPTABLE PARAPHRASE: USING THE AUTHOR'S WORDS

Crystal suggests that language play, including rhyme, helps children improve pronunciation ability, that looking at word endings and decoding the syntax of riddles allows them to understand grammar, and that other kinds of dialogue interaction teach conversation. Overall, language play may be of critical importance in the development of language and literacy skills (180).

Because the highlighted phrases are either borrowed from the original without quotation marks or changed only superficially, this paraphrase plagiarizes.

UNACCEPTABLE PARAPHRASE: USING THE AUTHOR'S SENTENCE STRUCTURES

Language play, Crystal suggests, will improve pronunciation by zeroing in on sounds such as rhymes. Having fun with suffixes and analyzing riddle structure will help a person acquire grammar. Being prepared to play with language, to use puns and talk nonsense, improves the ability to use semantics. These playful methods of communication are likely to influence a person's ability to talk to others. And language play inherently adds enormously to what has recently been known as *metalinguistic awareness*, a concept of great magnitude in developing speech abilities generally and literacy abilities particularly (180).

Although this paraphrase does not rely explicitly on the words of the original, it does follow the sentence structures too closely. Substituting synonyms while keeping the original paragraph structure is not enough to avoid plagiarism. The paraphrase must represent your own interpretation of the material and thus must show your own thought patterns.

Here are two paraphrases of the same passage that express the author's ideas accurately and acceptably, the first completely in the writer's own words and the second, from David Craig's notes (32e), including a quotation from the original.

ACCEPTABLE PARAPHRASE: IN THE STUDENT WRITER'S OWN WORDS

Crystal argues that playing with language — creating rhymes, figuring out riddles, making puns, playing with names, using invented words, and so on — helps children figure out a great deal, from the basics of pronunciation and grammar to how to carry on a conversation. This kind of play allows children to understand the overall concept of how language works, a concept that is key to learning to use — and read — language effectively (180).

ACCEPTABLE PARAPHRASE: QUOTING SOME OF THE AUTHOR'S WORDS

Crystal argues that playing with language — creating rhymes, figuring out riddles, making puns, playing with names, using invented words, and so on — helps children figure out a great deal, from the basics of pronunciation and grammar to how to carry on a conversation. This kind of play allows children to understand the overall concept of how language works, or "meta-linguistic awareness," a concept that Crystal sees as "of critical importance in the development of language skills in general and of literacy skills in particular" (180).

## ☐ Using summaries

A summary is a significantly shortened version of a passage or even of a whole chapter or work that captures main ideas *in your own words.* Unlike a paraphrase, a summary uses just the main points of a source. Your goal is to keep the summary as brief as possible without distorting the author's meaning.

---

**QUICK HELP**

### Guidelines for summaries

- To summarize a short passage, read it carefully and, without looking at the text, write a one- or two-sentence summary.
- To summarize a long passage or an entire chapter, skim the headings and topic sentences, making notes; then write your summary in a paragraph or two. For a whole book, you may want to refer to the preface and introduction as well as chapter titles, headings, and topic sentences — and your summary may take a page or more. In general, try to identify the thesis or claim being made, and then look for the subtopics or supports for that claim.
- Use your own words. If you include any language from the original, enclose it in quotation marks. Identify your work as a summary.

---

Here is David Craig's note recording a summary of the Crystal passage. The note states the author's main points selectively — without using his words.

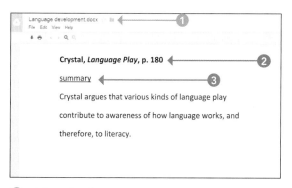

1. Subject heading
2. Author, title, page reference
3. Summary of source

## □ Taking other kinds of notes

Many researchers take notes that don't fall into the categories of quotations, paraphrases, or summaries. Those who work with media sources, especially, need alternatives. Some researchers take key-term notes, which might include the topic addressed in the source along with names or short statements to jog their memories when they begin drafting. Others record personal or critical notes — questions, criticisms, or other ideas that come to mind as they read. In fact, an exciting part of research occurs when the materials you are reading spark new ideas in your mind, ideas that may become part of your thesis or argument. Don't let them get away. While you may later decide not to use these ideas, you need to make notes about them just in case.

### David Craig's notes

As part of his study on messaging language and youth literacy, David Craig analyzed messaging conversations and kept notes on each occurrence of nonstandard English spellings and words and their frequencies. Since he was attempting to categorize these occurrences as well as quantify them, he labeled each note with the type of change that he was noticing. David's notes not only helped him synthesize his data; they also made it easier for him to present the data in a clear, concise chart (32e). Researchers also take field notes, which record their firsthand observations or the results of their surveys or interviews (11e).

Whatever form your notes take, be sure to list the source's title, author, and a way to find the information again, such as page number(s), links, or time codes. In addition, check that you have carefully distinguished your own thoughts and comments from those of the source itself.

## □ Annotating source material

Sometimes you may photocopy or print out a source you intend to use. In such cases, you can annotate the photocopies or printouts with your thoughts and questions and highlight interesting quotations and key terms. You can also use video or audio annotation tools to take notes on media sources.

If you take notes in a computer file, you may be able to copy online sources electronically, paste them into the file, and annotate them there. Try not to rely too heavily on copying or printing out whole pieces, however; you still need to read the material very carefully. Also resist the temptation to treat copied material as notes, an action that could lead to inadvertent plagiarizing. (In a computer file, using a different color for text pasted from a source will help prevent this problem.)

**EXERCISE 12.2**

Choose an online source you are sure you will use in your research project. Then download and print out the source, record all essential publication information for it, and annotate it as you read it.

▼ ▼ ▼ ▼ ▼ ▼ ▼ ▼ ▼ ▼ ▼ ▼ ▼ ▼ ▼ ▼ ▼ ▼ ▼ ▼ ▼ ▼ ▼ ▼ ▼ ▼ ▼ ▼

## THINKING CRITICALLY ABOUT YOUR EVALUATION OF SOURCES

Take a careful look at the sources you have gathered for your research project. How many make points that support your point of view? How many provide counter-arguments to your point of view? Which sources are you relying on most — and why? Which sources seem most credible to you — and why? Which sources, if any, are you suspicious of or worried about? Bring the results of this investigation to class for discussion.

# CHAPTER 13

# Integrating Sources into Your Writing

THE PROCESS OF ABSORBING your sources and then integrating them gracefully into your own writing is one of the challenges but also the pleasures of successful research. As you work with sources and make plans to use them in your own writing, they become *yours*. When you integrate sources appropriately into your work, they don't take over your writing or drown out your voice. Instead, they work in support of your own good ideas.

---

**CONNECT:** How should you introduce a source in your own writing? **13a and 32c (MLA), 33c (APA), 34c (*Chicago*), or 35b (CSE)**

**CREATE:** Make a brief video, or write a paragraph introducing the source to your readers as if it were a teacher or an acquaintance.

**REFLECT:** Go to **macmillanhighered.com/smh**, and respond to **13. Integrating Sources > Student Writing > Synthesis project (Warner)**.

---

## 13a Deciding whether to quote, paraphrase, or summarize

You tentatively decided to quote, paraphrase, or summarize material when you took notes on your sources (12g). As you choose which sources to use in your research project and how to use them, however, you may begin to reevaluate those decisions.

---

**HELP**

Deciding to quote, paraphrase, or summarize

**QUOTE**
- wording that is so memorable or powerful, or expresses a point so perfectly, that you cannot change it without weakening the meaning
- authors' opinions you wish to emphasize

▶

> **Deciding to quote, paraphrase, or summarize, continued**
>
> - authors' words that show you are considering varying perspectives
> - respected authorities whose opinions support your ideas
> - authors whose opinions challenge or vary greatly from those of others in the field
>
> **PARAPHRASE**
> - passages in which the details, but not the exact words, are important to your point
>
> **SUMMARIZE**
> - long passages in which the main point is important to your point but the details are not

## 13b  Working with quotations

Quoting involves using a source's exact words. You might use a direct quotation to catch readers' attention or make an introduction memorable. Quotations from respected authorities can help establish your credibility by showing that you've sought out experts in the field. In addition, quoting authors who disagree with your opinions helps demonstrate your fairness (9f).

Finally, well-chosen quotations can broaden the appeal of your project by drawing on emotion as well as logic (8d and 9g–h). A student writing on the ethics of bullfighting, for example, might quote Ernest Hemingway's striking comment that "the formal bullfight is a tragedy, not a sport, and the bull is certain to be killed."

Although quotations can add interest and authenticity to an essay, be careful not to overuse them: your research project is primarily your own work, meant to showcase your ideas and your argument.

### ☐  Integrating brief quotations

Short prose quotations should be run in with your text, enclosed in quotation marks that mark where someone else's words begin and end. When you include such quotations — or other source material — use both signal phrases and parenthetical references or notes, depending on the requirements of the documentation style you are using (see Chapters 32–35). Signal phrases introduce the material, often including the author's name. Parenthetical references and notes direct your readers to full bibliographic entries included elsewhere in your text.

The following brief quotation uses Modern Language Association (MLA) style (32c):

In Miss Eckhart, Welty recognizes a character who shares with her "the love of her art and the love of giving it, the desire to give it until there is no more left" (10).

In this example, the signal phrase that introduces the quotation (*In Miss Eckhart, Welty recognizes*) includes the author's name, so MLA style requires only the page number in parentheses for this print source.

## ☐ Integrating long quotations

If you are following MLA style, set off a prose quotation longer than four lines. If you are following the style of the American Psychological Association (known as APA style), set off a quotation of more than forty words or more than one paragraph. If you are following *Chicago* style, set off a quotation of more than one hundred words or more than one paragraph. Begin such a quotation on a new line. For MLA style, indent every line one inch; for APA style, five to seven spaces; for *Chicago* style, indent the text or use a smaller font (check your instructor's preference). Quotation marks are unnecessary. Introduce long quotations with a signal phrase or a sentence followed by a colon.

The following long quotation follows MLA style:

> A good seating arrangement can prevent problems; however, "withitness," as defined by Woolfolk, works even better:
>> Withitness is the ability to communicate to students that you are aware of what is happening in the classroom, that you "don't miss anything." With-it teachers seem to have "eyes in the back of their heads." They avoid becoming too absorbed with a few students, since this allows the rest of the class to wander. (359)
> This technique works, however, only if students actually believe that their teacher will know everything that goes on.

Note that the parenthetical citation comes after the period at the end of the quotation and does not have a period after it.

Though long quotations are often necessary in research projects, use them cautiously. Too many of them may make your writing seem choppy — or suggest that you have not relied enough on your own thinking.

## ☐ Using signal phrases

Carefully integrate quotations into your text so that they flow smoothly and clearly into the surrounding sentences by using a signal phrase or signal verb.

### Signal verbs

| | | | |
|---|---|---|---|
| acknowledges | concludes | emphasizes | replies |
| advises | concurs | expresses | reports |
| agrees | confirms | interprets | responds |
| allows | criticizes | lists | reveals |
| answers | declares | objects | says |
| asserts | describes | observes | states |
| believes | disagrees | offers | suggests |
| charges | discusses | opposes | thinks |
| claims | disputes | remarks | writes |

Remember that the signal verb must be appropriate to the idea you are expressing. In the following example, the verb *notes* tells us that the writer probably agrees with what Welty is saying. If that were not the case, the writer might have chosen a different verb, such as *asserts* or *contends*.

> As Eudora Welty notes, "learning stamps you with its moments. Childhood's learning," she continues, "is made up of moments. It isn't steady. It's a pulse" (9).

In the next example, the signal phrase *Some instructors claim* indicates that other authorities might disagree with the teacher's opinion or that the writer of this example disagrees. To support a point, the writer might have used entirely different wording, such as *Many instructors agree*.

> Some instructors claim that the new technology damages students' ability to compose academic work. "Abbreviations commonly used in online instant messages are creeping into formal essays that students write for credit," said Debbie Frost, who teaches language arts and social studies to sixth-graders ("Young Messagers").

Notice that these examples also feature neutral signal verbs — *continues* and *said* — where appropriate. The signal verbs you choose allow you to characterize the author's viewpoint or perspective as well as your own, so choose them with care.

## ☐ Marking changes with square brackets and ellipses

Sometimes you may wish to alter a direct quotation in some way — to make a verb tense fit smoothly into your text, to replace a pronoun with a noun, to eliminate unnecessary detail, to change a capital letter to lowercase or vice versa.

Enclose any changed or added words or letters in square brackets (59b), and indicate any deletions with ellipsis points (59f). Do not use ellipses at the beginning or end of a quotation unless the last sentence as you cite it is incomplete.

Here are two examples of quotations that have been altered with bracketed information or ellipsis points and integrated smoothly into the surrounding text.

> "There is something wrong in the [Three Mile Island] area," one farmer told the Nuclear Regulatory Commission after the plant accident ("Legacy" 33).

The brackets indicate that this information was added by the writer and is not part of the original quotation.

> Economist John Kenneth Galbraith pointed out that "large corporations cannot afford to compete with one another. . . . In a truly competitive market someone loses" (qtd. in Key 17).

Whenever you change a quotation, be careful not to alter its meaning. In addition, use brackets and ellipses sparingly; too many of them make for difficult reading and might suggest that you have removed some of the context for the quotation.

---

### EXERCISE 13.1

Take a source-based piece of writing you have done recently or a research project you are working on now, and examine it to see how successfully you have integrated quotations. Have you used accurate signal verbs and introduced the sources of the quotations? Have you used square brackets and ellipses accurately to indicate changes in quotations?

---

## 13c Paraphrasing

Introduce paraphrases clearly in your text, usually with a signal phrase that includes the author of the source, as the highlighted words in this example indicate:

> Professor of linguistics Deborah Tannen says that she offers her book *That's Not What I Meant!* to "women and men everywhere who are trying their best to talk to each other" (19). Tannen goes on to illustrate how communication between women and men breaks down and then to suggest that an awareness of "genderlects" improves relationships (297).

In the preceding passage, notice how the student writer brings authority to the point she makes in the first sentence. She introduces the author by title and name and then paraphrases her work, including quotations for important words and phrases. Note also that a page number is included in parentheses at the end of each paraphrase.

**IDENTIFYING SOURCES**

While some language communities and cultures expect audiences to recognize the sources of important documents and texts, thereby eliminating the need to cite them directly, conventions for writing in North America call for careful attribution of any quoted, paraphrased, or summarized material. When in doubt, explicitly identify your sources.

## 13d Summarizing

Summaries, too, need to be carefully integrated into your text, with the source identified. Benjy Mercer-Golden integrated this summary into his researched argument (91):

> David Blood and Al Gore of Generation Investment Management, an investment firm focused on "sustainable investing for the long term" ("About Us"), wrote a groundbreaking white paper that outlined the perverse incentives company managers face. For public companies, the default practice is to issue earnings guidances — announcements of projected future earnings — every quarter. Gore and Blood argue that this practice encourages executives to manage for the short term instead of adding long-term value to their company and the earth.

Note that the writer introduces his sources (Gore and Blood), establishes the sources' expertise by identifying their connection to the field, and uses the signal verb *argue* to characterize the summary as making a case, not simply offering information.

Whenever you include summaries, paraphrases, or quotations in your own writing, it is crucially important that you identify the sources of the material; even unintentional failure to cite material that you drew from other sources constitutes plagiarism. Be especially careful with paraphrases and summaries, where there are no quotation marks to remind you that the material is not your own. For more information on acknowledging sources and avoiding plagiarism, see Chapter 14.

## 13e Working with visuals and media

Choose visuals and media wisely, whether you use video, audio, photographs, illustrations, charts and graphs, or other kinds of images. Integrate all visuals and media smoothly into your text.

## ☐ Choosing appropriate visuals and media

Choose visuals and media that will enhance your research project and pique the interest of your readers.

- **Does each visual or media file make a strong contribution to the message?** Tangential or purely decorative visuals and media may weaken the power of your writing.
- **Is each visual or media file appropriate and fair to your subject?** An obviously biased perspective may seem unfair or manipulative to your audience.
- **Is each visual or media file appropriate for and fair to your audience?** Visuals and media should appeal to various members of your likely audience.

Whenever you post documents containing visuals or media to the Web, make sure you check for copyright information. While it is considered "fair use" to use such materials in an essay or other project for a college class, once that project is published on the Web, you might infringe on copyright protections if you do not ask the copyright holder for permission to use the visual or media file. U.S. copyright law considers the reproduction of works for purposes of teaching and scholarship to be "fair use" not bound by copyright, but the law is open to multiple interpretations. If you have questions about whether your work might infringe on copyright, ask your instructor for help.

## ☐ Integrating visuals and media

Like quotations, paraphrases, and summaries, visuals and media need to be introduced and commented on in some way.

- Refer to the visual, audio, or video in the text *before* it appears (*As Fig. 3 demonstrates . . .*).
- Explain or comment on the relevance of the visual or media file. This can appear *after* the visual or media file.
- Check the documentation system you are using to make sure you label visuals and media appropriately; MLA, for instance, asks that you number and title tables and figures (*Table 1: Average Amount of Rainfall by Region*).
- If you are posting your document or essay on a Web site, make sure you have permission to use any visuals or media files that are covered by copyright.

For more on using visuals and media in your work, see 2f and Chapter 16.

### David Craig's charts

David Craig integrated a chart about SAT scores into his research essay (32e). The chart, which he found in a report published by the College Board, illustrated the point that youth literacy is declining. He added his own trend lines to the chart to make the visual more effective. Following MLA style, David labeled the chart *Fig. 1* and included a descriptive title and enough source information to refer readers to the works-cited page. In the text of his paper, he included a reference to the chart and a detailed discussion of its data.

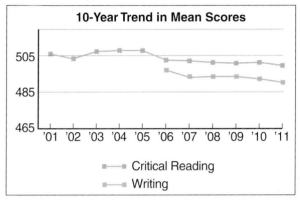

Fig. 1. Ten-year trend in mean SAT reading and writing scores (2001-2011). Source: College Board, "2011 SAT Trends."

## 13f   Checking for excessive use of source material

Your text needs to synthesize your research in support of your own argument; it should not be a patchwork of quotations, paraphrases, and summaries from other people (see 14c). You need a rhetorical stance that represents you as the author. If you cite too many sources, your own voice will disappear, a problem the following passage demonstrates:

TALKING THE TALK | **SAYING SOMETHING NEW**

"What can I say about my topic that experts haven't already said?" All writers — no matter how experienced — face this problem. As you read more about your topic, you will soon see areas of disagreement among experts, who may not be as expert as they first appear. Notice what your sources say and, especially, what they don't say. Consider how your own interests and experiences give you a unique perspective on the topic. Slowly but surely you will identify a claim that you can make about the topic, one related to what others say but taking a new angle or adding something different to the discussion.

The United States is one of the countries with the most rapid population growth. In fact, rapid population increase has been a "prominent feature of American life since the founding of the republic" (Day 31). In the past, the cause of the high rate of population growth was the combination of large-scale immigration and a high birth rate. As Day notes, "Two facts stand out in the demographic history of the United States: first, the single position as a receiver of immigrants; second, our high rate of growth from natural increase" (31).

Nevertheless, American population density is not as high as in most European countries. Day points out that the Netherlands, with a density of 906 persons per square mile, is more crowded than even the most densely populated American states (33).

Most readers will think that the source is much too prominent here and that the author of the essay is only secondary. The quotations and paraphrases overwhelm the writer's voice and may leave readers wondering what the writer's own argument is.

▼ ▼ ▼ ▼ ▼ ▼ ▼ ▼ ▼ ▼ ▼ ▼ ▼ ▼ ▼ ▼ ▼ ▼ ▼ ▼ ▼ ▼ ▼ ▼ ▼ ▼ ▼

## THINKING CRITICALLY ABOUT YOUR INTEGRATION OF SOURCES

From a research project you have finished or are drafting now, choose three passages that cite sources. Then examine how well these sources are integrated into your text. Consider how you can make that integration smoother, and try your hand at revising one of them.

# CHAPTER 14

# Acknowledging Sources and Avoiding Plagiarism

WHATEVER WRITING YOU DO has in some way been influenced by what you have already read and experienced and is part of a much larger conversation that includes other writers and thinkers. As a writer today, you need to understand current definitions of plagiarism, which have changed over time and vary from culture to culture, as well as the concept of intellectual property — those works protected by copyright or by alternatives such as a Creative Commons license — so you can give credit where credit is due. It seems likely that an age of instant copying and linking will someday lead to revised understandings about who can "own" a text and for how long. But in college today, it is still important to cite the sources you use (whether written, oral, or visual) carefully and systematically and hence to avoid plagiarism, the use of someone else's words and ideas as if they were your own.

## 14a Understanding reasons to acknowledge sources

Acknowledging the sources you use offers a polite "thank you" for the work of others. In addition, the sources you acknowledge tell your reader that you have tried to gain expertise on your topic, that you are credible, and that you have been fair enough to consider several points of view. Similarly, your sources can help place your research in the context of other thinking. Most of all, you should acknowledge sources in order to help your readers follow your thoughts, understand how your ideas relate to the thoughts of others, and know where to go to find more information.

Acknowledging sources fully and generously, then, is a way to establish your trustworthiness as a researcher. Failure to credit sources can destroy both your own credibility and that of your research.

### Avoiding plagiarism

- Maintain an accurate and thorough working bibliography. **(12c)**
- Establish a consistent note-taking system, listing sources and page numbers and clearly identifying all quotations, paraphrases, summaries, statistics, and visuals. **(12g)**
- Identify all quotations with quotation marks—both in your notes and in your essay. **(13b)**
- Be sure your paraphrases and summaries use your own words and sentence structures. **(13c and d)**
- Give a citation or note for each quotation, paraphrase, summary, arguable assertion or opinion, statistic, and visual from a source, including an online source. **(To understand what sources to cite, see 14b; for in-text documentation, see 32c, 33c, 34c, and 35b.)**
- Prepare an accurate and complete list of sources cited according to the required documentation style. **(32d, 33d, 34c, and 35c)**
- Plan ahead on writing assignments so that you can avoid the temptation to take shortcuts.

## 14b Knowing which sources to acknowledge

You should understand the distinction between source materials that require acknowledgment and those that do not. Now that huge amounts of reliable information are available online, conventions regarding acknowledgment, fair use, and source citation are shifting. It is still important, however, to be as careful as possible in providing citations so that your readers will know where you got your information.

### Materials that do not require acknowledgment

- **Common knowledge.** If most readers know a fact, you probably do not need to cite a source for it. You do not need to credit a source to say that Barack Obama was reelected president in 2012, for example.

- **Facts available in a wide variety of sources.** If a number of encyclopedias, almanacs, reputable Web sites, or textbooks include a certain piece of information, you usually need not cite a specific source for it. For instance, you would not need to cite a source if you write that the Japanese bombed Pearl Harbor on December 7, 1941.

- **Findings from field research.** If you conduct observations or surveys, announce your findings as your own. Acknowledge people you interview as individuals rather than as part of a survey.

If you are not sure whether a fact, an observation, or a piece of information requires acknowledgment, err on the side of safety, and cite the source.

**macmillanhighered.com/smh**

▶ 14. Acknowledging Sources > Tutorial > Do I need to cite that?

## Materials that require acknowledgment

For material that does not fall under the preceding categories, credit sources as fully as possible. Follow the conventions of the citation style you are using (see Chapters 32–35), and include each source in a bibliography or list of works cited.

- **Quotations, paraphrases, and summaries.** Whenever you use another person's words, ideas, or opinions, credit the source. Even though the wording of a paraphrase or summary is your own, you should still acknowledge the source (12g and 13b–d).

- **Facts that aren't widely known or claims that are arguable.** If your readers would be unlikely to know a fact, or if an author presents as fact a claim that may or may not be true, cite the source. To claim, for instance, that Switzerland is amassing an offensive nuclear arsenal would demand a source citation because Switzerland has long been an officially neutral state. If you are not sure whether a fact will be familiar to your readers or whether a statement is arguable, go ahead and cite the source.

- **Images, statistics, charts, tables, graphs, and other visuals from any source.** Credit all visual and statistical material not derived from your own field research, even if you create your own graph or table from the data provided in a source.

- **Help provided by others.** If an instructor gave you a good idea or if friends responded to your draft or helped you conduct surveys, give credit — usually in a footnote that says something like "Thanks to Kiah Williams, who first suggested this connection."

Here is a quick-reference chart to guide you in deciding whether or not you need to acknowledge a source:

| NEED TO ACKNOWLEDGE | DON'T NEED TO ACKNOWLEDGE |
|---|---|
| • quotations | • your own ideas expressed in your own words |
| • paraphrases or summaries of a source | |
| • ideas you glean from a source | • your own observations, surveys, and findings from field research you conduct yourself |
| • little-known or disputed facts | |
| • graphs, tables, and other statistical information from a source | • common knowledge — facts known to most readers |
| • photographs, visuals, video, or sound taken from sources | • drawings and other visuals, audio recordings, video, and any other materials you create on your own |
| • experiments conducted by others | |

▶

| NEED TO ACKNOWLEDGE | DON'T NEED TO ACKNOWLEDGE |
|---|---|
| • interviews that are not part of a survey | • facts available in many reliable sources, whether or not they are common knowledge |
| • organization or structure taken from a source | |
| • help or advice from an instructor or another student | |

## 14c Recognizing patchwriting

Integrating sources into your writing can be a significant challenge. In fact, as a beginning researcher, you might do what Professor Rebecca Howard calls "patchwriting"; that is, rather than integrate sources smoothly and accurately, you patch together words, phrases, and even structures from sources into your own writing, sometimes without citation. The author of this book remembers doing such "patchwriting" for a middle-school report on her hero, Dr. Albert Schweitzer. Luckily, she had a teacher who sat patiently with her, showing her how to paraphrase, summarize, and quote from sources correctly and effectively. So it takes time and effort — and good instruction — to learn to integrate sources appropriately rather than patchwriting, which is sometimes considered plagiarism even if you didn't mean to plagiarize.

## 14d Adapting structures and phrases from a genre without plagiarizing

If you are not accustomed to writing in a particular academic genre, you may find it useful to borrow and adapt transitional devices and pieces of sentence structure from other people's writing in the genre you are working in. Be careful to borrow only structures that are generic and not ideas or sentences that come from a particular, identifiable writer. You should not copy any whole sentences or sentence structures verbatim, or your borrowing may seem plagiarized.

| ORIGINAL ABSTRACT FROM A SOCIAL SCIENCE PAPER | EFFECTIVE BORROWING OF STRUCTURES FROM A GENRE |
|---|---|
| Using the interpersonal communications research of J. K. Brilhart and G. J. Galanes, and W. Wilmot and J. Hocker, along with T. Hartman's personality assessment, I observed and | Drawing on the research of Deborah Tannen on men's and women's conversational styles, I analyzed the conversational styles of six first-year students at DePaul University. Based on ▶ |

| ORIGINAL ABSTRACT FROM A SOCIAL SCIENCE PAPER | EFFECTIVE BORROWING OF STRUCTURES FROM A GENRE |
|---|---|
| analyzed the leadership roles and group dynamics of my project collaborators in a communications course. Based on results of the Hartman personality assessment, I predicted that a single leader would emerge. However, complementary individual strengths and gender differences encouraged a distributed leadership style, in which the group experienced little confrontation and conflict. Conflict, because it was handled positively, was crucial to the group's progress. | Tannen's research, I expected that the three men I observed would use features typical of male conversational style and the three women would use features typical of female conversational style. In general, these predictions were accurate; however, some exceptions were also apparent. |

The example above illustrates effective borrowing. The student writer borrows phrases (such as "drawing on" and "based on") that are commonly used in academic writing in the social sciences to perform particular functions. Notice how the student also modifies these phrases to suit her needs.

## 14e Maintaining academic integrity and avoiding plagiarism

The principle of academic integrity in intellectual work allows you to trust the sources you use and to demonstrate that your own work is equally trustworthy. While there are many ways to damage your ethos and academic integrity, two that are especially important are the inaccurate or incomplete citation of sources — also called unintentional plagiarism — and plagiarism that is deliberately intended to pass off one writer's work as another's.

Whether intentional or not, plagiarism can bring serious consequences. At some colleges, students who plagiarize fail the course automatically; at others, they are expelled. Academics who plagiarize, even inadvertently, have had their degrees revoked and their books withdrawn from publication. And outside academic life, eminent political, business, and scientific leaders have been stripped of candidacies, positions, and awards because of plagiarism.

### ☐ Avoiding inaccurate or incomplete citation of sources

If your paraphrase is too close to the original wording or sentence structure of the source (even if you identify the source); if you do not identify the source of a quotation (even if you include the quotation marks); or if you fail to indicate clearly the source of an idea that you obviously did not come up with on your own, you may be accused of plagiarism even if your intent was not to plagiarize. Inaccurate or incomplete acknowledgment of sources often results either from carelessness or from not learning how to borrow material properly in the first place.

Academic integrity calls for you to be faithful not only to the letter of the material you are drawing on but also to its spirit: you need to honor the intention of the original source. For example, if your source says that an event *may* have happened in a particular way, then it isn't ethical to suggest that the source says that the event *absolutely* happened that way.

Because the costs of even unintentional plagiarism can be severe, it's important to understand how it can happen and how you can guard against it. In a January 2002 article published in *Time* magazine, historian Doris Kearns Goodwin explains how she made acknowledgment errors in one of her books. The book in question, nine hundred pages long and with thirty-five hundred footnotes, took Goodwin ten years to write. During this time, she says, she took most of her notes by hand, organized them, and later checked her sources to make sure all the material she was using was correctly cited. "Somehow in this process," Goodwin goes on to say, "a few books were not fully rechecked," and thus she omitted some acknowledgments and some quotation marks by mistake. Discovering such carelessness in her own work was very troubling to Goodwin since, as she puts it, "the writing of history is a rich process of building on the work of the past. . . . Through footnotes [and citations] you point the way to future historians."

Goodwin certainly paid a steep price for her carelessness: she had to leave Harvard's Board of Overseers and also resigned from the committee that awards Pulitzer Prizes. In addition, she was put on indefinite leave from a television program to which she had contributed regularly, was asked not to give a planned commencement address at the University of Delaware, and had to negotiate at least one settlement with a person whose work she had used without proper citation. Perhaps most seriously, this event called into question all of Goodwin's work.

As a writer of academic integrity, you will want to take responsibility for your research and for acknowledging all sources accurately. One easy way to keep track is to keep photocopies, printouts, or unaltered digital copies of every source as you conduct your research; then you can identify needed quotations by highlighting them on each source.

□ **Avoiding deliberate plagiarism**

Deliberate plagiarism — handing in an essay written by a friend or purchased (or simply downloaded) from an essay-writing company; cutting and pasting

---

 **PLAGIARISM AS A CULTURAL CONCEPT**

Many cultures do not recognize Western notions of plagiarism, which rest on a belief that language and ideas can be owned by writers. Indeed, in many countries outside the United States, and even within some communities in the United States, using the words and ideas of others without attribution is considered a sign of deep respect as well as an indication of knowledge. In academic writing in the United States, however, you should credit all materials except those that are common knowledge, that are available in a wide variety of sources, or that are your own creations (photographs, drawings, and so on) or your own findings from field research.

---

passages directly from source materials without marking them with quotation marks and acknowledging your sources; failing to credit the source of an idea or concept in your text — is what most people think of when they hear the word *plagiarism*. This form of plagiarism is particularly troubling because it represents dishonesty and deception: those who intentionally plagiarize present the hard thinking and hard work of someone else as their own, and they deceive readers by claiming knowledge they don't really have.

Deliberate plagiarism is also fairly simple to spot: your instructor will be well acquainted with your writing and likely to notice any sudden shifts in the style or quality of your work. In addition, by typing a few words from an essay into a search engine such as Google, your instructor can identify "matches" very easily.

### EXERCISE 14.1

Read the brief original passage that follows, and then look closely at the five attempts to quote or paraphrase it. Decide which attempts are acceptable and which plagiarize, prepare notes on what supports your decision in each case, and bring your notes to class for discussion.

> The strange thing about plagiarism is that it's almost always pointless. The writers who stand accused, from Laurence Sterne to Samuel Taylor Coleridge to Susan Sontag, tend to be more talented than the writers they lift from.
> —MALCOLM JONES, "Have You Read This Story Somewhere?"

1. According to Malcolm Jones, writers accused of plagiarism are always better writers than those they are supposed to have plagiarized.

2. According to Malcolm Jones, writers accused of plagiarism "tend to be more talented than the writers they lift from."

3. Plagiarism is usually pointless, says writer Malcolm Jones.

4. Those who stand accused of plagiarism, such as Vice President Joseph Biden, tend to be better writers than those whose work they use.

5. According to Malcolm Jones, "plagiarism is . . . almost always pointless."

## 14f Considering your intellectual property

Although you may not have thought too much about it, all of your work in college — including all the research and writing you do, online and off — represents a growing bank of intellectual property. In fact, such original work is automatically copyrighted, even if it lacks the © symbol. But remember that the open source movement is gaining momentum and that sharing your ideas and writing freely with others is a way to perpetuate them and to gain an audience for your views.

For work that you want to protect, here are some tips for making sure that others respect your intellectual property just as you respect theirs:

- Realize that your text and email messages, blog posts and comments, and posts to social networking sites and discussion groups are essentially public. If you don't want your thoughts and ideas repeated or forwarded, keep them offline. Let recipients know specifically when you do not want your email messages passed on to any third parties. In turn, remember that you should not use material from email, discussion groups, or other online forums without first asking for permission.

- Be careful with your passwords, and use a secure storage method so that only you can give someone access to your work.

- Save all your drafts and notes so that you can show where your work has come from should anyone ask you.

## 14g Collaborating

With so much focus on plagiarism and with the advent of online paper mills, you may feel reluctant to share or discuss your work with anyone else. That would be a very unfortunate result, however, since much of our knowledge comes from talking with and learning from others. Indeed, many college projects now require some form of collaboration or teamwork, whether it involves commenting on someone else's draft, preparing a group presentation of research findings, or composing a text with many others on a wiki or on Google Drive.

Collaborative writing projects call for the same kind of acknowledgments you use in a paper or other project you prepare by yourself. In general, cite all sources used by the group, and acknowledge all assistance provided by others. In some cases, you may decide to do this in an endnote rather than in your bibliography or list of works cited.

▼ ▼ ▼ ▼ ▼ ▼ ▼ ▼ ▼ ▼ ▼ ▼ ▼ ▼ ▼ ▼ ▼ ▼ ▼ ▼ ▼ ▼ ▼ ▼ ▼

## THINKING CRITICALLY ABOUT YOUR OWN ACKNOWLEDGMENT OF SOURCES

Look at a recent piece of your writing that incorporates material from sources, and try to determine how completely and accurately you acknowledged them. Did you properly cite every quotation, paraphrase, and summary? every opinion or other idea from a source? every source you used to create visuals? Did you unintentionally plagiarize someone else's words or ideas? Make notes, and bring them to class for discussion.

# CHAPTER 15

# Writing a Research Project

WHEN YOU ARE WORKING on an academic research project, there comes a time to draw the strands of research together and articulate your conclusions in writing.

---

**CONNECT:** Would outlining your draft help you see what to do next? **3f, 15b**

**CREATE:** Use sticky notes to outline your draft, and try different ways of arranging them.

**REFLECT:** Go to **macmillanhighered.com/smh**, and respond to **3. Exploring, Planning, Drafting > Video > Filling the gaps**.

---

## 15a Refining your plans

You should by now have notes containing facts, opinions, paraphrases, summaries, quotations, and other material; you probably have images or media to integrate as well. You may also have ideas about how to synthesize these many pieces of information. And you should have some sense of whether your hypothesis has sufficient support. Now is the time to reconsider your purpose, audience, stance, and working thesis.

- What is your central purpose? What other purposes, if any, do you have?
- What is your stance toward your topic (2d)? Are you an advocate, a critic, a reporter, an observer?
- What audience(s) are you addressing (2e and 10b)?
- How much background information or context does your audience need?
- What supporting information will your readers find most convincing?
- Should your tone be that of a colleague, an expert, a friend?

- How can you establish common ground with your readers and show them that you have considered points of view other than your own? (See 9f and Chapter 28.)
- What is your working thesis trying to establish? Will your audience accept it?

## ☐ Moving from working thesis to explicit thesis

Writing out an explicit thesis statement allows you to articulate your major points and to see how well they carry out your purpose and appeal to your audience. Depending on the purpose, audience, and genre of your project, you may or may not decide to include the explicit thesis in your final draft — but developing your working thesis into an explicit statement can still be very useful.

David Craig, the student whose research appears throughout Part 3, developed the following explicit thesis statement (see Chapter 32):

> Instant messaging seems to be a positive force in the development of youth literacy because it promotes regular contact with words, the use of a written medium for communication, and the development of an alternative form of literacy.

## ☐ Asking questions about your thesis

Although writing out an explicit thesis will often confirm your research, you may find that your hypothesis is invalid, inadequately supported, or insufficiently focused. In such cases, you need to rethink your original research question and perhaps do further research. To test your thesis, consider the following questions:

- How can you state your thesis more precisely or more clearly (3c)? Should the wording be more specific? Could you use more specific, concrete nouns (30c) or stronger verbs (53b)? Should you add qualifying adjectives or adverbs (Chapter 42)?
- In what ways will your thesis interest your audience? What can you do to increase that interest (2e)?
- Will your thesis be manageable, given your limits of time and knowledge? If not, what can you do to make it more manageable?
- What evidence from your research supports each aspect of your thesis? What additional evidence do you need?

### ◢ EXERCISE 15.1

Take the thesis from your current research project, and test it against the questions provided in 15a. Make revisions if your analysis reveals weaknesses in your thesis.

**ASKING EXPERIENCED WRITERS TO REVIEW A THESIS**

You might find it helpful to ask one or two classmates who have more experience with the particular type of academic writing to look at your explicit thesis. Ask if the thesis is as direct and clear as it can be, and revise accordingly.

## ☐ Planning design

As you move toward producing a draft, take some time to think about how you want your research project to look. What font will you use? Should you use color? Do you plan to insert text boxes and visuals? Will you need headings and subheadings? Will you incorporate audio, video, or other media? (For more on design, see Chapter 16.)

## 15b Organizing information

Experienced writers differ considerably in the ways they go about organizing ideas and information, and you will want to experiment until you find a method that works well for you. (For more on organizational strategies, see 3e.) This section will discuss two organizing strategies — grouping material by subject and outlining.

## ☐ Grouping by subject

You may find it useful to have physical notes to arrange — note cards or sticky notes, for example, or printouts of your slides or of notes you have been keeping online that you mark in some way to make the subject categories easy to identify. You can group the pieces around subject headings and reorder the parts until they seem to make sense. Shuqiao Song, the student who wrote the critical analysis in 7g, organized the plans for her PowerPoint presentation (17f) by moving sticky notes around on her window, as shown in her photo on p. 253.

Grouping your notes will help you see how well you can support your thesis and help you see if you have missed any essential points. Do you need to omit any ideas or sources? Do you need to find additional evidence for a main or supporting point? Once you have gathered everything together and organized your materials, you can see how the many small pieces of your research fit together. Make sure that your evidence supports your explicit thesis; if not, you may need to revise it or do additional research — or both.

Once you have established initial groups, skim through the notes and look for ways to organize your draft. Figure out what background your audience needs, what points you need to make first, how much detail and support to offer for each point, and so on.

© SHUQIAO SONG

*Sticky notes can help you figure out your project's organization.*

## □ Making an outline

You can use outlines in various ways and at various stages. Some writers group their notes, write a draft, and then outline the draft to study its tentative structure. Others develop an informal working outline from their notes and revise it as they go along. Still other writers prefer to plot out their organization early on in a formal outline. (For more on outlines, see 3f.)

### David Craig's working outline

David Craig drew up a working outline of his ideas while he was still doing research on his topic, thinking that this simple structure would help him focus on the information he still needed to find. Here is his informal outline:

> Decline of youth literacy
> > Lower test scores, other proof (statistics)
> > How instant messaging fits in, examples from critics
> My research
> > Can I show that IM is a language?
> > How widespread is it?
> Comments from linguists — tie-in to IM language
> What is the real cause of declining youth literacy?

Because he knew he was required to submit a formal outline with his essay, David Craig kept revising this informal outline as his research and writing progressed. He did not complete his formal outline until after his essay was drafted (see "Outlining Your Draft" in 15e). At that point, the formal outline helped him analyze and revise the draft.

## 15c   Drafting

For most college research projects, drafting should begin *at least* two weeks before the instructor's deadline in case you need to gather more information or do more drafting. Set a deadline for having a complete draft, and structure your work with that date in mind. Gather your notes, outline, and sources, and read through them, getting involved in your topic. Most writers find that some sustained work (two or three hours at a time) pays off at this point. Begin drafting a section that you feel confident about. For example, if you are not sure how you want to introduce the draft but do know how you want to approach a particular point, begin with that, and return to the introduction later. The most important thing is to get started.

The drafting process varies considerably among researchers (3g), and no one else can determine what will work best for you. No matter what approach you take, remember to include sources (for quotations, paraphrases, summaries, and media) as you draft; doing so will save time later and help you produce your list of works cited.

### ◻ Creating a working title and introduction

The title and introduction (4h) play special roles, for they set the context for what is to come. Ideally, the title announces your subject in an intriguing or memorable way. To accomplish these goals, Emily Lesk, the student writer whose work appears in Part 1, revised the title of her essay from "All-Powerful Coke" (p. 74) to "Red, White, and Everywhere" (4l). David Craig began with the title "Messaging and Texting," but he later added the more specific and intriguing subtitle "The Language of Youth Literacy."

The introduction should draw readers in and provide any background they will need to understand the discussion. Here are some tips for drafting an introduction to a research project:

- You may want to open with a *question*, especially your research question, or with a *strong or arresting statement* of some kind. Next, you might explain what you will do to answer the question or to elaborate on the statement. For academic projects, instructors may expect you to end with your *explicit thesis statement* — in essence, the answer to the question or the response to the strong statement.

- Help readers get their bearings by *forecasting your main points.*

- *Establish your own credibility* by revealing how you have become knowledgeable about your topic.

- You may use a *quotation* to get attention, but singling out one source in this way can give that source too much emphasis.

### David Craig's introduction

David Craig begins his essay with a strong statement (*The English language is under attack*) that immediately gets readers' attention. He then presents a brief overview of what the critics are saying about youth literacy and brings up messaging language — the general subject of his essay — before ending the introduction with his explicit thesis statement.

## ☐ Crafting a conclusion

A good conclusion helps readers know what they have learned (4h and 5g). Its job is not to persuade — the body of the essay or project should already have done that — but to contribute to the overall effectiveness of your writing. The following strategies may be helpful:

- Refer to your thesis, and then expand to a more general conclusion that reminds readers of the significance of your discussion.

- If you have covered several main points, you may want to remind readers of them. Be careful, however, to provide more than a summary.

- Try to end with something that will have an impact — a provocative quotation or question, a vivid image, a call for action, or a warning. But guard against sounding preachy.

### David Craig's conclusion

In his conclusion, David Craig briefly recaps his thesis and then summarizes the main point of his argument (pp. 448–49). He ends with a strong assertion: *Although messaging may expose literacy problems, it does not create them.*

## 15d Incorporating source materials

When you reach the point of drafting your research project, a new task awaits: weaving your source materials into your writing. The challenge is to use your sources yet remain the author — to quote, paraphrase, and summarize other voices while remaining the major voice in your work. (Because learning how to effectively integrate source material is so important, Chapter 13 is devoted entirely to this process.)

## 15e Reviewing and getting responses to your draft

Because a research project involves a complex mix of your thoughts and materials from outside sources, it calls for an especially careful review. You should examine the draft yourself as well as seek the comments of other readers. Ask friends and classmates to read and respond to your draft, and get a response from your instructor if possible.

### ▢ Reviewing your own draft

As with most kinds of writing, taking a break after drafting is important so that when you reread the draft, you can bring a fresh eye to the task. When you do return to the draft, read it straight through without stopping. Then read the draft again slowly, reconsidering your purpose, audience, stance, thesis, and support.

- From your reading of the draft, what do you now see as its *purpose*? How does this compare with your original purpose? Does the draft do what your assignment requires?
- What *audience* does your essay address?
- What is your *stance* toward the topic?
- What is your *thesis*? Is it clearly stated?
- What *evidence* supports your thesis? Is the evidence sufficient?

Answer these questions as best you can, since they are the starting point for revision. If you notice a problem but are unsure how to solve it, write down your concerns so that you can ask readers if they notice the same problem and have ideas about solving it.

### ▢ Outlining your draft

You might find that outlining your draft (3f and 15b) helps you analyze it at this point: an outline will reveal the bare bones of your argument and help you see what may be missing or out of place. Here is the formal outline that David Craig prepared after drafting his research paper on instant messaging (32e).

> **Thesis statement:** Messaging seems to be a beneficial force in the development of youth literacy because it promotes regular contact with words, the use of a written medium for communication, and the development of an alternative form of literacy.
> I. Decline of youth literacy — overview
>    A. What many parents, librarians, educators believe
>    B. Messaging as possible cause

1. Definition of messaging
2. Example of IM conversation
3. Messaging as beneficial to youth literacy

II.  Two background issues
   A.  Current state of literacy
       1. Decline in SAT scores
       2. Decline in writing ability
   B.  Prevalence of messaging
       1. Statistics indicating widespread usage
       2. Instant messagers and texters using new vocabulary

III.  My field research to verify existence of messaging language
   A.  Explanation of how research was done
   B.  Results of research
       1. Four types of messaging language: phonetic replacements, acronyms, abbreviations, inanities
       2. Frequency of messaging language use
       3. Conclusions about vocabulary

IV.  What critics of messaging say
   A.  Many problems with student writing, such as incomplete sentences, grammar, and spelling
   B.  Students using online abbreviations (smileys) in formal papers

V.  What linguists and other supporters of messaging say
   A.  Traditional literacy not harmed by messaging
   B.  Messaging indicative of advanced literacy
       1. Crystal's explanation of metalinguistics and wordplay
       2. Human ability to write in many styles, messaging style being only one alternative
       3. Messaging helping students shift from language to language

VI.  Other possible causes of decline in youth literacy
   A.  Lower enrollment in English composition and grammar classes
   B.  Messaging exposing literacy problems but not causing them

## □ Seeking responses from peers

You should seek responses from friends and classmates as your draft evolves. Your reviewers will be best prepared to give you helpful advice and to ask questions specific to your project if they have background information about your writing task.

Tell your reviewers the purpose of your draft, the assignment's criteria, and your target audience. Ask them to explain their understanding of your stance on the topic. Also ask for feedback on your thesis and its support. If you are unsure about whether to include a particular point, how to use a certain quotation, or where to add more examples, ask your reviewers specifically what they think you should do. You should also ask them to identify any parts of your draft that confuse them. Even if you are writing to a target audience with more expertise in the topic than your peer reviewers, you should carefully consider revising the parts they identify as confusing: you may be making too many assumptions about what concepts need to be explained. (For more on peer review, see 4b.)

## 15f   Revising and editing

When you have considered your reviewers' responses and your own analysis, you can turn to revising and editing.

**QUICK HELP**

### Guidelines for revising a research project

- **Take responses into account.** Look at specific problems that reviewers think you need to solve or strengths you might capitalize on. For example, if they showed great interest in one point but no interest in another, consider expanding the first and deleting the second.
- **Reconsider your original purpose, audience, and stance.** Have you achieved your purpose? How well have you appealed to your readers? Make sure you satisfy any special concerns of your reviewers. If your rhetorical stance toward your topic has changed, does your draft need to change, too?
- **Assess your research.** Think about whether you have investigated the topic thoroughly and consulted materials with more than one point of view. Have you left out any important sources? Are the sources you use reliable and appropriate for your topic? Have you synthesized your research findings and drawn warranted conclusions?
- **Assess your use of visuals and media.** Make sure that each one supports your argument, is clearly labeled, and is cited appropriately.
- **Gather additional material.** If you need to strengthen any points, first check your notes to see whether you already have the necessary information. In some instances, you may need to do more research.
- **Decide what changes you need to make.** List everything that you must do in order to perfect your draft. With your deadline in mind, plan your revision.
- **Rewrite your draft.** Many writers prefer to revise first on paper rather than on a computer. However you revise, be sure to save copies of each draft. Begin with the major changes, such as adding content or reorganizing. Then turn to sentence-level problems and word choice. Can you sharpen the work's dominant impression? ▶

Guidelines for revising a research project, continued

- **Reevaluate the title, introduction, and conclusion.** Is your title specific and engaging? Does the introduction capture readers' attention and indicate what the work discusses? Does your conclusion help readers see the significance of your argument?
- **Check your documentation.** Make sure you've included a citation in your text for every quotation, paraphrase, summary, visual, and media file you incorporated, and that you've followed your documentation style consistently.
- **Edit your draft.** Check grammar, usage, spelling, punctuation, and mechanics. Consider the advice of computer spell checkers **(31f)** and grammar checkers carefully before accepting it.

## 15g   Preparing a list of sources

Once your final draft and source materials are in place, you are ready to prepare a list of sources. Follow the guidelines for your documentation style carefully (see Chapters 32–35), creating an entry for each source used. Double-check your work to make sure that you have listed every source mentioned in your draft and (unless you are listing all the sources you consulted) that you have not listed any sources not cited. Most word-processing programs can help you alphabetize and format lists of sources as well as prepare endnotes and footnotes.

## 15h   Proofreading your final copy

Your final rough draft may look very rough indeed, so your next step is to create a final, perfectly clean copy. You will submit this version, which represents all your work and effort, to your instructor. At this point, run the spell checker but do not stop there. To make sure that this final version puts your best foot forward, proofread extremely carefully. It's best to work with a hard copy, since reading onscreen often leads to missed typos. Read the copy aloud for content and for the flow of the argument, making sure you haven't mistakenly deleted words, lines, or whole sections. Then read the copy backward from the last sentence to the first, looking for small mistakes such as punctuation problems or missing words. If you are keeping an editing checklist (4k), look for the types of editing problems you have had in the past.

Once you are sure your draft is free of errors, check the design one last time to be sure you are using effective margins, type size, color, boldface and italics, headings, and so on. You want your final copy to be as attractive and readable as possible (see Chapter 16).

After your manuscript preparation and proofreading are complete, celebrate your achievement: your research and hard work have produced a project that you can, and should, take pride in.

▼ ▼ ▼ ▼ ▼ ▼ ▼ ▼ ▼ ▼ ▼ ▼ ▼ ▼ ▼ ▼ ▼ ▼ ▼ ▼ ▼ ▼ ▼ ▼ ▼ ▼ ▼

## THINKING CRITICALLY ABOUT RESEARCH PROJECTS

Reflect on the research project you have completed. How did you go about organizing your information? What would you do to improve this process? What problems did you encounter in drafting? How did you solve these problems? How many quotations did you use, and how did you integrate them into your text? When and why did you use summaries and paraphrases? If you used visuals, how effective were they in supporting your points? What did you learn from revising?

# PART 4
# Designing and Performing Writing

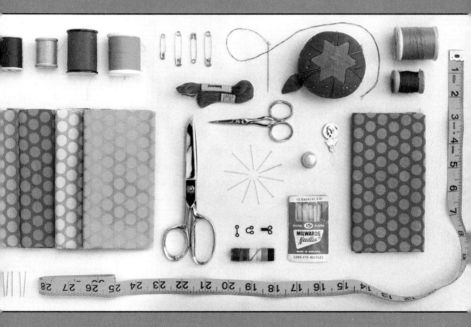

# CHAPTER 16

# Design for Print and Digital Writing

I N THE ANCIENT GREEK WORLD, a speaker's delivery (known as *actio*) was an art every educated person needed to master: how a speaker delivered a speech — tone, pace, volume, use of gestures, and so on — had a great impact on the message and how it would be received. In the age of (mountains of) information, as Professor Richard Lanham points out, it's increasingly difficult to get and hold people's attention. As a result, we are returning to the ancient art of delivery. But writers now have many tools that writers and speakers in the ancient world did not have to help them get and hold an audience's attention, from font options to color and video. All these tools help bring the dimension of *visual rhetoric* to today's writing.

---

**CONNECT:** How can peer reviewers help you revise the visual structure of your project? **4b, 16b**

**CREATE:** Draft the overall look of your first slide, your home page, or another key part of your multimodal project, and set up a peer-review session with friends or classmates to collect responses.

**REFLECT:** Go to **macmillanhighered.com/smh**, and respond to **4. Reviewing > Exercise > Storyboard on getting help from peer reviewers**.

---

## 16a Choosing a type of text

A text can be anything that you might "read" — not just words but also images, data, audio, video, or combinations of media. A print book, for example, may include words alone or words and visuals. Texts that go online can grow much richer with the ability to include animations, video, audio, links, and interactive features. As a result, college writers today have choices that were almost unimaginable until quite recently.

## ☐  Considering the rhetorical context for your design

Ultimately, the organization and look of any text you design should depend on what you are trying to achieve. You should make decisions about layout, formatting, color, fonts (for written words), nonalphabetic elements such as images or video, and other aspects of design based on rhetorical needs — your audience, purpose, topic, stance, genre conventions, and so on — and on practical constraints, such as the time and tools available.

## ☐  Making design choices for different genres

While you still will probably be assigned to compose traditional texts such as academic essays, you may also be asked to create coursework in other genres. Research conducted for this textbook found that today's students are encountering assignments that range from newsletters and poster presentations to PechaKuchas and video essays — and that multimodal assignments are increasingly characteristic of first-year writing courses. Whatever genre you choose for your assignment, familiarize yourself with conventions of design for that genre, and think carefully about the most appropriate and compelling design choices for your particular context.

## ☐  Choosing print or digital delivery

One of your first design decisions will be choosing between print delivery and digital delivery (or deciding to create both print and digital versions). In general, print documents are easily portable, easy to read without technical assistance, and relatively fast to produce. In addition, the tools for producing print texts are highly developed and stable. Digital texts, on the other hand, can include sound, animation, and video; updates are easy to make; distribution is fast and efficient; and feedback can be swift. Design decisions may have similar goals, such as clarity and readability, no matter what medium you are working in, but the specific choices you make to achieve those goals may differ in print and digital texts.

# 16b  Planning a visual structure

Today, all writers need to think carefully about the look of any text they create and plan a visual structure for it. The design decisions you make will help guide readers by making the texts easier on the eyes and easier to understand.

## ☐  Following design principles

Designer Robin Williams, in her *Non-Designer's Design Book*, points out four simple principles for designing effective texts — contrast, alignment, repetition, and proximity. These principles are illustrated here with the familiar Wikipedia page design.

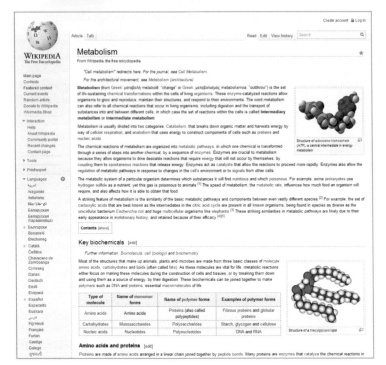

*Chances are that most readers will look first at either the heading or the images on this Wikipedia page. The site uses large black type against a white background for the title of each page at the upper left. On this page, color images of molecular models also draw the eye.*

## Contrast

Contrast attracts your eye to elements on a page and guides you around it, helping you follow an argument or find information. You may achieve contrast through the use of color, icons, boldface or large type size, headings, and so on. Begin with a focus point — the dominant point, image, or words where you want your reader's eye to go first — and structure the flow of your visual information from this point.

## Alignment

Alignment refers to the way visuals and text on a page are lined up, both horizontally and vertically. The overall guideline is not to mix alignments arbitrarily. That is, if you begin with a left alignment, stick with it for the major parts of your page. The result will be a cleaner and more organized look. For example, the title, text, and subheadings of a Wikipedia article align with the left margin, and images align with the right margin.

### Repetition

Readers are guided by the repetition of key words and elements. Use a consistent design throughout your document for such elements as color, typeface, and images. Every Wikipedia page uses the same fonts and the same layout, so readers know what to expect.

### Proximity

Parts of a text that are closely related should appear together (proximate to one another). Your goal is to position related points, text, and visuals near one another and to use clear headings to identify these clusters, as the Wikipedia page does.

### Consistent overall impression

Aim for a visual structure and design that create the appropriate overall impression or mood for your text. For an academic essay, whether print or digital, you will probably make conservative choices that strike a serious scholarly note. In a newsletter for a campus group, you might choose attention-getting images. In a Web site designed to introduce yourself to future employers, you might favor a mix of material drawn from your current résumé, including writing, embedded video or links to digital content that relates to your skills and career goals, and at least one image of yourself — all in a carefully organized and easy-to-comprehend structure.

## ☐ Using templates

If designing your writing yourself seems intimidating, consider using a template. Templates are basic models that show you how to lay out a particular type of text. You may have used templates in a word-processing program to create a document such as a memo or report, in PowerPoint to create slides, or in a blog-publishing service to design your content. Templates are readily available for many genres of texts in both print and digital media. Before you create a text in a genre that is new to you, it's a good idea to look for available design templates. You can use them to familiarize yourself with conventional elements and layouts for the genre, even if you decide not to follow the template's settings for color, fonts, and other details of formatting.

## 16c  Formatting print and digital texts

With so many options available, you should always spend some time thinking about appropriate formatting for elements of your text. Although the following guidelines often apply, remember that print documents, Web pages, slide shows, videos, and so on all have their own formatting conventions. (To learn more about formatting requirements for academic research projects in MLA style, see 32b; in APA style, see 33b; in *Chicago* style, see 34b; in CSE style, see 35a.)

**READING PATTERNS**

In documents written in English and other Western languages, information tends to flow from left to right and top to bottom — since that is the way English texts are written. In some languages, which may be written from right to left or vertically, documents may be arranged from top right to bottom left. Understanding the reading patterns of the language you are working in will help you design your documents most effectively.

## ◻ Using white space (negative space)

The parts of a page or screen left intentionally blank are called *white space* or *negative space*, and they emphasize content and direct readers' eyes. Too little white space makes a page look crowded, while too much can make it seem empty or unfinished. Think about the amount of white space at the page level (top and side margins), paragraph level (the space between paragraphs), and sentence level (the space between sentences). Within the page, you can also use white space around particular content, such as an image, an embedded video, or a list, to make it "pop" or stand out.

## ◻ Using color

As you design your documents, keep in mind that some colors can evoke powerful responses, so take care that the colors you use match the message you are sending. Color can enliven texts that are mainly alphabetic, but using color poorly can also make a text seem less readable and inviting.

- Use color to draw attention to elements you want to emphasize: headings, text boxes, or graphs, for example.
- Be consistent in your use of color; use the same color for all of your subheads, for example, or the same background color for all of your PowerPoint slides.
- Keep the color palette fairly small for most projects; too many colors can create a jumbled or confused look.
- Choose color combinations that are easy to read. Ask a few peers or colleagues whether your text is legible against the background before presenting, submitting, or posting your work for a wider audience.
- Make sure all color visuals and text are legible in the format where they will be read. Colors can be sharper on a computer monitor than in a print document, and slides may look dramatically different when you project them.

CONSIDERING DISABILITIES | **COLOR FOR CONTRAST**

Remember when you are using color that not everyone will see it as you do. Some individuals do not perceive color at all; others perceive color in a variety of ways, especially colors like blue and green, which are close together on the color spectrum. When putting colors next to one another, then, use those on opposite sides of the color spectrum, such as purple and gold, in order to achieve high contrast. Doing so will allow readers to see the contrast, if not the nuances, of color.

## ☐ Choosing type sizes and fonts

For words in the body of a traditional report, essay, or Web posting, an 11- or 12-point type size is conventional. (A 12-point type size is larger than an 11-point type size of the same font, but type size in different fonts can vary considerably, so aim for a size that seems neither unreadably small nor surprisingly large.)

Choose a readable font, either a serif font (used in this sentence) or a sans serif font (used in headings on this page). Although unusual fonts might seem attractive at first glance, readers may find such styles distracting and hard to read over long stretches of material. Remember that fonts help you create the tone of a document, so consider your audience and purpose when selecting type.

*Different fonts convey different feelings.*
**Different fonts convey different feelings.**
**DIFFERENT FONTS CONVEY DIFFERENT FEELINGS.**
Different fonts convey different feelings.

Most important, be consistent in the size and style of typeface you use, especially for the main part of your text. Unless you are striving for some special effect, shifting sizes and fonts within a document can give an appearance of disorderliness. But purposeful use of special fonts can signal imagination, humor, and even spontaneity. One student who wanted to go into graphic design created a new font and then animated it in a three-minute video that really captured her audience's attention.

## ☐ Using margin and line spacing

For traditional print projects, you will probably use a single column of text with standard one-inch margins for your writing, but many other kinds of projects call for text columns of variable widths or for multiple columns. Both very short and very long text lines can be difficult to read. Online readers generally prefer short, manageable chunks of text rather than long paragraphs; consider breaking up a long online piece with headings or visuals.

Computers allow you to decide whether or not you want left and right margins justified, or squared off — as they are on typical book pages (including this one). Readers will often expect you to justify the left margin, except in posters and other texts where you are trying to achieve a distinctive visual effect. However, most readers — and many instructors — prefer the right margin to be "ragged," or unjustified, as it is in the Wikipedia entry on p. 264.

For college writing assignments that are submitted in print, you will usually use double-spaced type with the first line of each paragraph indented one-half inch. Letters, memorandums, and online texts are usually single-spaced and may use spaces between paragraphs instead of paragraph indentation. Check the conventions of the genre, or ask about your instructor's preference.

## ☐ Using headings

For brief essays and reports, you may need no headings at all. For longer texts, however, headings call attention to the organization and thus help readers understand. Headings can help break long Web texts into the short, manageable chunks that online readers expect. Some kinds of reports require conventional headings (such as *Abstract* and *Summary*), which writers must provide; see p. 484 for an example.

You can distinguish headings by type size and font as well as by color, as this book does — for example, by using capital letters, boldface type, italics, and so on. Position each level of heading consistently throughout the text. And remember that headings need to appear above the text they introduce; be careful, for example, not to put a heading at the bottom of a printed page.

For formal academic work, look for the most succinct and informative way to word headings. In general, state a topic in a single word, usually a noun (*Toxicity*); in a phrase, usually a noun phrase (*Levels of Toxicity*) or a gerund phrase (*Measuring Toxicity*); in a question that will be answered in the text (*How Can Toxicity Be Measured?*); or in an imperative that tells readers what steps to take (*Measure the Toxicity*). Informal texts might use more playful headings. For both informal and formal texts, use the same structure consistently for all headings of the same level.

## 16d Considering visuals and media

Choose visuals and other media that will help make a point more vividly and succinctly than written words alone. In some cases, visuals and media may even be your primary text.

---

**QUICK HELP**

### Using visuals and media effectively

- Choose visual and media elements that will make your text more effective for your audience. If they don't help you accomplish your purpose, look for better options. ▶

**Using visuals and media effectively, continued**

- Consider design principles for placement of visual and media files within a text, and aim to make your media files accessible to as many readers as possible. **(16b)**
- Tell the audience explicitly what a visual demonstrates, especially if it presents complex information. Do not assume readers will "read" the visual the way you do; your commentary on it is important.
- Follow established conventions for documenting visual and media sources. **(Chapters 32–35)** Ask permission for use if someone else controls the rights. **(Chapter 14)**
- Get responses to your visuals and media in an early draft. If readers can't follow them or are distracted by them, revise accordingly.
- If you alter or edit visuals, audio, or video to include them in your writing, be sure to do so ethically. **(8f)**

## ☐ Selecting visuals and media

Consider carefully what you want visuals, audio, or video to do for your writing. What will your audience want or need you to show? Try to choose visuals and media that will enhance your credibility, allow you to make your point more emphatically, and clarify your overall text. (See the following examples for advice on which visuals work best for particular situations.)

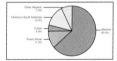

Use *pie charts* to compare parts to the whole.

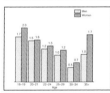

Use *bar graphs* and *line graphs* to compare one element with another, to compare elements over time, or to show correlations and frequency.

| Table 10: Commuter Rail Schedule: Reading/ Haverhill Line, Boston 2004 | | |
| --- | --- | --- |
| | Train 223 | Train 227 | Train 231 |
| North Station | 3:00 pm | 4:36 pm | 5:15 pm |
| Reading | 3:38 pm | 4:54 pm | 5:42 pm |
| Haverhill | 4:04 pm | 5:31 pm | 6:21 pm |

Use *tables* to draw attention to detailed numerical information.

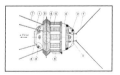

Use *diagrams* to illustrate textual information or to point out details of objects or places described.

Use *maps* to show geographical locations and to emphasize spatial relationships.

Use *cartoons* to illustrate a point dramatically or comically.

Use *photographs* or *illustrations* to show particular people, places, objects, and situations described in the text or to help readers find or understand types of content.

(BOTTOM) © MICHAEL ENRIGHT/WWW.MENRIGHT.COM

Effective media content can come from many sources — your own drawings or photographs, charts or graphs you create, or recordings you make, as well as materials created by others. If you are using media from another source, be sure to give appropriate credit and to get permission before making it available to the public as part of your work.

## ☐ Positioning and identifying visuals and media

Make sure to position visuals and media clips alongside or after the text that refers to them. In formal texts, number figures and tables separately and give them informative titles. Some documentation styles ask that you include source information in a caption (see Chapters 32–35).

### *Making media texts accessible*

As you create media texts, take steps to make sure that all your readers can access your content — for example, by providing alternative text for all visuals so that they will make sense when read by a screen reader, and by providing captions for sound files and transcripts of longer audio content. For details on designing accessible texts, visit the Americans with Disabilities Act site at www.ada.gov.

## ☐ Using visuals and media ethically

Technical tools available to writers and designers today make it relatively easy to manipulate and edit visuals, audio, and video. As you would with any source material, carefully assess any visuals you find for effectiveness, appropriateness, and validity, and identify the source for any media files you use that you have not created yourself.

- Check the context in which the visual, video, or audio appears. Is it part of an official government, school, or library site or otherwise from a credible source (12d)?
- If the visual is a photograph, is the information about the photo believable?
- If the visual is a chart, graph, or diagram, are the numbers and labels explained? Are the sources of the data given? Will the visual representation help readers make sense of the information, or could it mislead them (8e and f)?
- Can you find contact information for the creator or rightsholder?

At times, you may make certain changes to visuals that you use, such as cropping an image to show the most important detail, digitally brightening a dark image, or using a short clip from a longer audio or video file. You can make digital changes as long as you do so ethically, telling your audience what you have done and making no attempt to mislead readers.

### EXERCISE 16.1

Take an essay or other writing assignment you have done recently, one that makes little use of the design elements discussed in this chapter. Reevaluate the effectiveness of your text, and make a note of all the places where visuals and other design elements (color, different type size, and so on) would help you get your ideas across more effectively.

▼ ▼ ▼ ▼ ▼ ▼ ▼ ▼ ▼ ▼ ▼ ▼ ▼ ▼ ▼ ▼ ▼ ▼ ▼ ▼ ▼ ▼ ▼ ▼ ▼

## THINKING CRITICALLY ABOUT DESIGN FOR WRITING

Look at a print text you have recently completed. Using the advice in this chapter, assess your use of visual structure, consistent use of conventions for guiding readers through your text, and use of visuals. Then take a look at an online text that you have composed—a Web page or a blog posting or an invitation or announcement of some kind—and make the same kind of assessment. Then write a brief analysis of how well each text is designed and how you could improve either or both.

## CHAPTER 17

# Presentations

WHEN THE GALLUP POLL reports on what U.S. citizens say they fear most, the findings are always the same: public speaking is apparently even scarier than an attack from outer space. Nevertheless, many writing courses may require you not only to compose written texts but also to give presentations in front of an audience, and it's safe to say that most jobs require you to present information orally in front of audiences of all kinds. People who are successful presenters point to four elements crucial to their effectiveness: a thorough knowledge of the subject at hand, careful attention to the interactive nature of speaking and thus to the needs of the audience, careful integration of verbal and visual information, and practice, practice, and more practice.

---

**CONNECT:** How should you organize your presentation? **3e, 17c**

**CREATE:** Sketch or write out a draft outline for your presentation. Show your work to a friend, and ask for feedback.

**REFLECT:** Write or record a brief reflection on the response to your plan, and explain what you need to do next to create a well-organized presentation.

---

## 17a  Considering assignment, purpose, and audience for presentations

You'll be wise to begin preparing for a class presentation as soon as you get the assignment. Think about how much time you have to prepare; how long the presentation is to be; whether you will use written-out text or note cards or some other kind of cue; what kind of posters, handouts, slides, or other materials you may need; and what equipment you will need. If you are making a group presentation, you will need time to divide duties and practice (6b). Make sure that you understand the criteria for evaluation — how will the presentation be graded or assessed?

Consider the purpose of your presentation (2d). Are you to lead a discussion? teach a lesson? give a report? engage a group in an activity? Also consider the audience (2e). If your instructor is a member of the audience, what will he or she expect you to do — and do well? What do audience members know about your topic? What opinions do they already hold about it? What do they need to know to follow your presentation and perhaps accept your point of view? If your presentation will be posted online, how much can you know about the audience? In a webinar format, you may have a list of all participants; but in other settings you may not be able to know who your words will reach. In these cases, you may want to shape or limit the audience who will have access to your presentation. Finally, consider your own stance toward your topic and audience. Are you an expert? novice? well-informed observer? peer?

---

**QUICK HELP**

### Guidelines for presentations

- How can your presentation accomplish the specifications of the assignment? **(17a)**
- How will your presentation achieve your purpose? How will it appeal to your audience's experiences and interests? **(2d and e)**
- What do you know about your audience, and how will you get the audience's attention? What background information do you need to provide? **(17b)**
- What organizational structure informs your presentation? **(17b)**
- Check for signposts that can guide listeners. Are there explicit transitions? Do you repeat key words or ideas? **(17b)**
- Have you used mostly straightforward sentences? Consider revising any long or complicated sentences to make your talk easier to follow. Substitute concrete words for abstract ones as often as you can. **(17b)**
- How should you mark your script or notes for pauses and emphasis? Have you marked material that you can omit if you find yourself short of time? **(17b)**
- What should your audience see and hear during your presentation? How will your slides and media contribute to your presentation? **(17c)**
- Have you followed principles of good design for your visuals? **(16b)**
- Have you practiced your presentation so that you will appear confident and knowledgeable? **(17d)**

---

### *Shuqiao Song's analysis of a presentation assignment*

Shuqiao Song's assignment for her writing class on graphic narratives featured two major parts: first, she had to write a ten- to fifteen-page argument based on research on a graphic narrative, and then she had to turn that information

**macmillanhighered.com/smh**

 **17. Presentations** > Tutorial > Presentations

**17. Presentations** > Video > If I were in the audience

into a script for a twelve-minute oral presentation accompanied by slides. After some brainstorming and talking with her instructor, Shuqiao chose her favorite graphic memoir, Alison Bechdel's *Fun Home*, as her topic.

As she thought about her assignment and topic, Shuqiao realized that she had more than one purpose. Certainly she wanted to do well on the assignment and receive a good grade. But she also wanted to convince her classmates that Bechdel's book was a complex and important one and that its power lay in the relationship of words and images. She also had to admit to at least one other purpose: it would be great to turn in a truly *impressive* performance. Her audience — the other students in the class — seemed smart, and some were apparently experienced presenters. Shuqiao knew she had her work cut out for her.

## 17b  Writing to be heard and remembered

Getting and keeping the attention of listeners may require you to use different strategies than the ones you generally employ when writing for a reading audience. To be *remembered* rather than simply heard, write a memorable introduction and conclusion, and use explicit structures, helpful signpost language, straightforward syntax, and concrete diction throughout the presentation.

### ☐  Planning your introduction and conclusion

Remember that listeners, like readers, tend to remember beginnings and endings most readily, so work extra hard to make these elements memorable (4h). Consider, for example, using a startling statement, opinion, or question; a dramatic anecdote; a powerful quotation; or a vivid image. Shifting language, especially into a variety of language that your audience will identify with, is another effective way to catch their attention (see Chapter 29). Whenever you can link your subject to the experiences and interests of your audience, do so.

#### Shuqiao Song's introduction

Shuqiao Song began her presentation this way:

> Welcome, everyone. I'm Shuqiao Song and I'm here today to talk about residents of a dys*FUN*ctional *HOME*.
> We meet these residents in a graphic memoir called *Fun Home*.

## CONSIDERING DISABILITIES | **ACCESSIBLE PRESENTATIONS**

Remember that some members of your audience may not be able to see your presentation or may have trouble hearing it, so do all you can to make your presentation accessible.

- Be sure to face any audience members who rely on lip-reading to understand your words. For a large audience, request an ASL (American Sign Language) interpreter.
- Do not rely on color or graphics alone to get across information — some audience members may be unable to pick up these visual cues.
- For presentations you publish on the Web, provide brief textual descriptions of your visuals.
- If you use video, provide labels for captions to explain any sounds that won't be audible to some audience members, and embed spoken captions to explain images to those who cannot see them. Be sure that the equipment you'll be using is caption capable.
- Remember that students have very different learning styles and abilities. You may want to provide a written overview of your presentation or put the text of your presentation on slides or transparencies for those who learn better by reading *and* listening.

(Here, Shuqiao showed a three-second video clip of author Alison Bechdel saying, "I love words, and I love pictures. But especially, I love them together — in a mystical way that I can't even explain.")

> That was Alison Bechdel, author of *Fun Home*. In that clip, she conveniently introduces the topics of my presentation today: Words. Pictures. And the mystical way they work together.

Note that this presentation opened with a play on words ("dys*FUN*ctional *HOME*"), to which Shuqiao returned later on, and with a short, vivid video clip that perfectly summed up the main topic of the presentation. Also note the use of short sentences and fragments, special effects that act like drumbeats to get and hold the attention of the audience.

## ☐ Using signpost language

Organize your presentation clearly and carefully, and give an overview of your main points toward the beginning of your presentation. (You may wish to recall these points again toward the end of the talk.) Throughout your presentation, pause between major points, and use signpost language as you move from one topic to the next. Such signposts act as explicit transitions in your talk and should be clear and concrete: *The second crisis point in the breakup of the Soviet Union occurred hard on the heels of the first* instead of *The breakup of the Soviet Union came to another crisis point.* . . . In addition to such explicit transitions (5e) as *next, on the contrary,* and *finally,* you can offer signposts to your listeners by carefully repeating key words and ideas as well as by sticking to concrete topic sentences to introduce each new idea.

### Shuqiao Song's signpost language

At the end of Shuqiao's introduction, she set forth the structure of her presentation in a very clear, straightforward, and simple way to help her audience follow what came next:

> So, to outline the rest of my presentation: first, I'll show how *text* is insufficient — but also why it is necessary to Bechdel's story. Second, I'll show how *images* can't be trusted, but again, why they are still necessary for Bechdel's purposes. Third and finally, I'll show how the interplay of text and image in *Fun Home* creates a more complex and comprehensive understanding of the story.

## ☐ Using simple syntax and memorable language

Avoid long, complicated sentences, and use straightforward sentence structure (subject-verb-object) as much as possible. Listeners prefer action verbs and concrete nouns to abstractions. You may need to deal with abstract ideas, but try to provide concrete examples for them (30c). Memorable presentations often call on the power of figures of speech and other devices of language, such as careful repetition, parallelism, and climactic order.

### Shuqiao Song's example

Shuqiao Song's presentation script included the following example:

> Now, to argue my second point, I'll begin with an image. This is a René Magritte painting. The text means, *"This is not a pipe."* Is this some surrealist Jedi mind trick? Not really. Now listen to the title of the painting to grasp Magritte's point. The painting is called *The Treason of Images.* Here Magritte is showing us that "this is not a pipe" because it is an *image* of a pipe.

Shuqiao's short sentences, vivid word choice ("surrealist Jedi mind trick"), and straightforward subject-verb-object syntax all help to make the passage easy on listeners.

© SHUQIAO SONG

## □ Turning writing into a script

Even though you will probably rely on some written material, you will need to adapt it for speech. Depending on the assignment, the audience, and your personal preferences, you may even speak from a full script. If so, double- or triple-space it, and use fairly large print so that it will be easy to refer to. Try to end each page with the end of a sentence so that you won't have to pause while you turn a page. In addition, you may decide to mark spots where you want to pause and to highlight words you want to emphasize.

### A paragraph from Shuqiao Song's print essay

Finally, we can see how image and text function together. On the one hand, image and text support each other in that each highlights the subtleties of the other; but on the other hand, the more interesting interaction comes when there is some degree of distance between what is written and what is depicted. In *Fun Home*, there is no one-to-one closure that mentally connects text and image. Rather, Bechdel pushes the boundaries of mental closure between image and text. If the words and pictures match exactly, making the same point, the story would read like a children's book, and that would be too simple for what Bechdel is trying to accomplish. However, text and image can't be so mismatched that meaning completely eludes the readers. Bechdel crafts her story deliberately, leaving just enough mental space for the reader to solve the rest of the puzzle and resolve the cognitive dissonance. The reader's mental closure, which brings coherence to the text and images and draws together loose ends, allows for a more complex and sophisticated understanding of the story.

### Shuqiao Song's paragraph revised for oral presentation

Finally, image and text can work together. They support each other: each highlights the subtleties of the other. But they are even more interesting when there's a gap — some distance between the story the words tell and the story the pictures tell. In *Fun Home,* text and image are never perfectly correlated. After all, if the words and pictures matched up exactly, the story would read like a kids' book. That would be way too simple for Bechdel's purposes. But we wouldn't want a complete disconnect between words and images either, since we wouldn't be able to make sense of them.

Still, Bechdel certainly pushes the boundaries that would allow us to bring closure between image and text. So what's the take-home point here? That in Bechdel's *Fun Home,* image and text are not just supporting actors of each other. Instead, each offers a *version* of the story. It's for us — the readers. We take these paired versions and weave them into a really rich understanding of the story.

Note that the revised paragraph presents the same information, but this time it is written to be heard. The revision uses helpful signpost language, some repetition, simple syntax, and informal varieties of English to help listeners follow along and keep them interested.

### ☐ Speaking from notes

If you decide to speak from notes rather than from a full script, here are some tips for doing so effectively:

- In general, use one note card for each point in your presentation, beginning with the introduction and ending with the conclusion.
- Number the cards so that you can quickly find the next part of your presentation if your cards are out of order.
- On each card, include the major point you want to make in large bold text. Include subpoints in a bulleted list below the main point, again printed large enough for you to see easily. You can use full sentences or phrases, as long as you include enough information to remind you of what you have planned to say.
- Include signpost language on each note so that you will be sure to use it to guide your listeners.
- Practice your presentation using the notes at least twice.

- Time your presentation very carefully so that you will be sure not to go overtime. If you think you may run out of time, use color or brackets to mark material in your notes that you can skip. If your presentation is too long, move past the marked material so that you can end with your planned conclusion.

The following note card for the introduction to Shuqiao's presentation reminds the student to emphasize her title and her three points about the origins of graphic novels. Notice how she has highlighted her signpost language as well as the card's number.

**Notecard for an oral presentation**

[Card 3]

Overview of the rest of the presentation

- **First,** text is insufficient but necessary

- **Second,** images can't be trusted but are necessary

- **Finally,** interplay of text and image creates complex, comprehensive understanding

# 17c   Creating a presentation

Visuals are often an integral part of a presentation, carrying a lot of the message the speaker wants to convey. So think of your visuals not as add-ons but as a major means of getting your points across. Many speakers use slides created in presentation software to help keep themselves on track and to guide the audience. In addition, posters, flip charts, chalkboards, or interactive whiteboards can also help you make strong visual statements.

Presentation software such as PowerPoint or Prezi allows you to prepare slides you want to display and even to enhance the images with sound. PowerPoint presentations move in a linear fashion from beginning to end, while Prezi software allows presenters to move in more circular paths (and to show the circling in the slides). To choose software for a presentation, consider what the software allows you to do and how much time you will need to learn to use it effectively. Before you begin designing your presentation, make sure that the equipment you need will be available, and keep simple design principles in mind (16b).

**HELP**

**QUICK**

Guidelines for slide presentations

- Audiences can't read and listen to you at the same time, so make the slides support what you are saying as clearly and visually as possible. Just one or two words — or a visual without words — may back up what you are saying more effectively than a list of bullet points.   ▶

### Guidelines for slide presentations, continued

- Avoid reading from your slides. Your audience can read faster than you can talk, and you are guaranteed to bore them with this technique.

- Use your media wisely, and respect your audience's time. If you feel that you need to include more than three or four bullet points (or more than fifty words of text) on a slide, you may be trying to convey information in a slide show that would make more sense in a report. Rethink your presentation so that what you say and what you show work together to win over your audience.

- Use text on your slides to guide your audience—not as a teleprompter. Be familiar enough with your material so that you don't have to rely on your slides to know what comes next.

- Make sure any text you show is big enough to read, and create a clear contrast between text or illustration and background. In general, light backgrounds work better in a darkened room, and dark backgrounds in a lighted one.

- Be careful not to depend too heavily on slide templates. The choices of color, font, and layout offered by such templates may not always match your goals or fit with your topic.

- Choose visuals that will reproduce sharply, and make sure they are large enough to be clearly visible.

- Make sure that sound or video clips are audible and that they relate directly to your topic. If you want to use sound as background, make sure it does not distract from what you are trying to say.

- Although there are no firm rules about how many slides you should use or how long each slide should be made visible, plan length and timing with your audience's needs and your purpose in mind.

- Most important, make sure your slides engage and help your listeners rather than distract them from your message.

#### Shuqiao Song's slides

For her presentation, "Residents of a Dys*FUN*ctional *HOME*: Text and Image," Shuqiao Song developed a series of very simple slides aimed at underscoring her points and keeping her audience focused on them. She began by introducing the work, showing the book cover on an otherwise black slide. Throughout the presentation, she used very simple visuals — a word or two, or a large image from the book she was discussing — to keep her audience focused on what she was saying.

## 17d Practicing the presentation

In oral presentations, as with many other things in life, practice makes perfect. Prepare a draft of your presentation and slides or other media far enough in advance to allow for workshopping the slides with friends or classmates — just as you would workshop an essay — and for several run-throughs. If possible, make a video of yourself, and then examine the video in detail. You can also practice in front of a mirror or in front of friends. Do whatever works for you — just as long as you practice!

If you are using slides or other visuals to accompany your presentation (and today, most students do so), make sure your use of the visuals is smooth and on track with your script. Some student speakers like to embed all visuals or slides into their scripts so that they can coordinate easily, using a clicker to advance the slides. Others prefer to use the slides to guide them through the presentation, though to do so they must know their material so well that they don't leave awkward gaps as they move from slide to slide.

Make sure you can be heard clearly. If you are soft-spoken, concentrate on projecting your voice. If your voice tends to rise when you are in the spotlight, practice lowering your pitch. If you speak rapidly, practice slowing down and enunciating words clearly. Remember that tone of voice affects listeners, so aim for a tone that conveys interest in and commitment to your topic and listeners. If you practice with friends or classmates, ask them how well they can hear you and what advice they have for making your voice clearer and easier to listen to.

Once you are comfortable giving the presentation, make sure you will stay within the allotted time. One good rule of thumb is to allow roughly two and a half minutes per double-spaced 8½" x 11" page of text or script. The only way to be sure about your time, however, is to time yourself as you practice. Knowing that your presentation is neither too short nor too long will help you relax and gain self-confidence; and when the members of your audience sense your self-confidence, they will become increasingly receptive to your message.

## 17e Delivering the presentation

Experienced speakers always expect to feel at least some anxiety before delivering a presentation — and they develop strategies for dealing with it. Remember that a little nervousness can act to your advantage: adrenaline, after all, can help you perform well.

Having confidence in your own knowledge will go a long way toward making you a confident presenter. In addition to doing your homework, however, you may be able to use the following strategies to good advantage:

- Consider how you will dress and how you will move around. In each case, your choices should be appropriate for the situation. Most experienced speakers like to dress simply and comfortably for easy movement. But dressing up a little signals your pride in your appearance and your respect for your audience.

- Go over the scene of your presentation in your mind, and think it through completely, in order to feel more comfortable during it. In addition, check out the presentation room and double-check to make sure you have all the equipment you might need.

- If you are using handouts (of bibliographies or slide notes, for example), decide when to distribute them. Unless they include material you want your audience to use while you speak, distribute them after the presentation.
- Get some rest before the presentation, and avoid consuming too much caffeine.
- Try to relax while you wait to begin. You might want to do some deep-breathing exercises.

If possible, stand up for your presentation. Most speakers make a stronger impression standing than sitting. Move around the room if you are comfortable doing so. If you are more comfortable in one spot, then keep both feet flat on the floor. If you are behind a lectern, rest your hands lightly on it. Many speakers find that this stance keeps them from fidgeting.

Pause before you begin your presentation, concentrating on your opening lines. During your presentation, interact with your audience as much as possible. You can do so by facing the audience at all times and making eye contact as often as possible. You may want to choose two or three people to look at and "talk to," particularly if you are addressing a large group. In any case, make sure you are looking at your audience during the entire presentation, not at your laptop or at the screen behind you. Allow time for the audience to ask questions. Try to keep your answers short so that others may participate in the conversation. When you conclude, remember to thank your audience.

### EXERCISE 17.1

Attend a lecture or watch a presentation online (such as a TEDtalk), and analyze its effectiveness. How does the speaker capture and hold your interest? What signpost language and other guides to listening can you detect? How well are visuals integrated into the presentation? How do the speaker's tone of voice, dress, and eye contact affect your understanding and appreciation (or lack of it)? What is most memorable about the presentation, and why? Bring your analysis to class and report your findings.

## 17f   A student's presentation

To see Shuqiao Song's presentation, "Residents of a DysFUNctional *HOME*: Text and Image," go to the integrated media page at **macmillanhighered.com/smh**.

## 17g   Considering other kinds of presentations

You may want or need to think about other kinds of presentations for school or work, including poster presentations, online presentations, or PechaKuchas.

## ☐ Giving a poster presentation

Many college courses and conferences now call on students to make poster presentations. During the class or conference session, the presenter will use a poster board as background while talking through the presentation and answering questions. Remember the following tips if you are preparing a poster presentation:

- Create a board that can be read from at least three feet away.
- Include a clear title (at least two inches high) at the top of the board.
- Include your name and other appropriate information: course title and number, name of instructor, conference title or session, and so on.
- Use a series of bullets or boxes to identify your major points and to lead the audience through the presentation.
- Include an arresting image or an important table or figure if it illustrates your points in a clear and memorable way.
- Consider using a provocative question toward the bottom of the poster to focus attention and anticipate your conclusion.
- Remember that simple, uncluttered posters are usually easier to follow and therefore more effective than overly complex ones.
- Practice the oral part of the presentation until you are comfortable referring to the poster while keeping your full attention on the audience.

## ☐ Presenting online

A Webcast is essentially a presentation that is broadcast on the Internet, using streaming media to distribute the presentation to viewers, who might be anywhere in the world.

As you learn to adapt to online presentation environments, remember these commonsense guidelines:

- Practice is very important, since you need to make sure that you can immediately access everything you need online — a set of slides, for example, or a document or video clip, as well as any names, dates, or sources that you might be called on to provide during the presentation.
- Because you cannot make eye contact with audience members, you should remember to look into the camera, if you are using one. If you are using a stationary Webcam, practice staying still enough to remain in the frame without looking stiff.
- Even though your audience may not be visible to you, assume that if you are on camera, the audience can see you quite well; if you slouch, they'll notice. Also assume that your microphone is always live — don't say anything that you don't want your audience to hear.

□ **Presenting a PechaKucha**

PechaKucha — from Japanese: ペチャクチャ, for "chit chat" — is a special form of presentation with a set structure: twenty slides, each of which advances automatically after twenty seconds, for a total time of 6:40. Astrid Klein and Mark Dytham, architects in Tokyo, invented PechaKucha in 2003 because they felt that "architects talk too much" about their own work; they wanted to design a way to keep the presentations succinct and crisp. From this professional presentation format grew "PechaKucha nights" where people can share their work in a relaxed and supportive, if sometimes also competitive, atmosphere. Some college instructors are now inviting students to try their hands at constructing a PechaKucha as a way of presenting ideas to classmates. If you have an opportunity to create a PechaKucha, here are a few tips:

- Choose your topic carefully. The best PechaKuchas feature an element of surprise; many use humor to great effect. Think of a topic you can tell a story or weave a narrative about, one that will allow you to be creative.

- Choose images that will help tell your story. These images should be simple to grasp and easy to see. Many PechaKucha experts use just one image per slide, and few use more than two on any slide.

- Use PowerPoint, Prezi, or other presentation software to develop slides of your images, and set the slides to auto-advance after twenty seconds.

- Create a script to accompany each slide, making sure that the script lasts precisely twenty seconds and includes a segue to the next slide.

- Practice, practice, practice — then practice some more!

▼ ▼ ▼ ▼ ▼ ▼ ▼ ▼ ▼ ▼ ▼ ▼ ▼ ▼ ▼ ▼ ▼ ▼ ▼ ▼ ▼ ▼ ▼ ▼ ▼ ▼

## THINKING CRITICALLY ABOUT ORAL AND MULTIMODAL PRESENTATIONS

Study the text of an oral or multimodal presentation you've prepared or given. Using the advice in this chapter, see how well your presentation appeals to your audience. Look in particular at how well you catch and hold their attention. How effective is your use of signpost language or other structures that help guide your listeners? How helpful are the visuals (PowerPoint slides, posters) in conveying your message? What would you do to improve this presentation?

# CHAPTER 18

# Communicating in Other Media

A RECENT SURVEY conducted for this book identified over forty kinds of multimodal or multimedia projects that writing instructors across the country are assigning to their students: not just PowerPoint and Prezi presentations but annotated playlists, blogs, comics, product pitches, live tweets, video essays, wikis, and more. Student writers seem to like and appreciate such assignments, saying that they provide room for creative control and for self-expression. As communicating with media becomes more common and even more necessary in your life, it's important to think carefully about your goals and your audiences — as well as about how to accomplish and reach them most effectively, no matter what kind of project you are creating.

---

**CONNECT:** How can you work well with others on a wiki or other collaborative project? **6a and b, 18b and c**

**CREATE:** Working with friends or classmates, choose a wiki entry that you know about and are interested in, and revise or add to it to make it more useful to others.

**REFLECT:** Go to **macmillanhighered.com/smh**, and respond to **6. Working with Others > Video > Working with other people**.

---

## 18a  Considering your rhetorical context

As with any college assignment, you will want to make sure you consider time and technical constraints. Many online projects take much more time than a traditional writing assignment: one student, for example, told us that she spent ninety hours creating a three-minute animated video. So you need to plan carefully to make sure you have both the access to any tools you will need and the time to carry out the project (and to learn about the tools, if necessary).

As with any writing project, you will want to think about rhetorical concerns, such as your purpose for creating the text, the needs of your audience, and the main point or message you want to get across.

---

**QUICK HELP**

**Rhetorical contexts for multimodal writing**

- Why are you creating this text, document, or project? How do you want viewers to use it? Considering purpose will help you determine what features you want to highlight.
- What potential audience(s) can you identify? Thinking about the audience for your project will help you make strong rhetorical choices about tone, word choice, graphic style and design, level of detail, and many other factors. If your intended audience is limited to people you know (such as a wiki for members of your class), you may be able to make some assumptions about their background, knowledge, and likely responses. If you are covering a particular topic, you may have ideas about the type of audience you think you'll attract. Plan your project to appeal to readers you expect — but remember that an online text may reach other, unanticipated audiences.
- What is the subject or topic of your project? The topic will certainly affect the content and design of the project. If you want to focus on the latest Hong Kong film releases, for example, you might create a blog that always places your most recent posts at the top; if you want to explore the works of 1940s detective writers, you might produce a Web site with pages devoted to particular writers or themes. If you prefer to show information on your topic, you might consider creating an infographic or a video essay that you can post to an existing site.
- How do you relate to your subject matter? Your rhetorical stance determines how your audience will see you. Will you present yourself as an expert, a fan, a novice seeking input from others? What information will make you seem credible and persuasive to your audience(s)?

---

## 18b Planning Web-based texts

Use organization, interactivity, and links to make your Web text work as effectively as possible.

### ☐ Organizing content

Whether you are creating a layout for a Web page or storyboarding a video essay, you should develop a clear structure for your text. Some types of online texts are organized in standard ways — most blogs and social media sites, for example, put the newest posts at the top. Others allow you to make choices about how to arrange materials. Choose a structure that makes sense for your purpose, audience, topic, and rhetorical stance. Arrange your text to allow readers to find what they are looking for as quickly and intuitively as possible. (For more on organizing and planning your text, see 3e, 3f, and 4g.)

## ◻ Allowing interaction

The possibility of interaction with readers is one of the great opportunities of online writing, but you can consider different levels of interactivity. While wikis are full-scale collaborative efforts and frequently allow contribution from users, you might also include something as simple as a thumbs-up / thumbs-down or LIKE button to allow users to register their reaction to a text. Online texts can incorporate polls, comments, and links for contacting writers.

## ◻ Linking

Academic and formal writing follows guidelines that tell readers the sources of other people's ideas and research through notes and bibliographic references (see Chapters 32–35). Some less formal online writing includes links to external sites. You can also link to content that helps prove a point — complex explanations, supporting statistics, bibliographies, referenced Web sites, or additional readings. Links also help readers navigate from one part of a text to another.

Each link should have a clear rhetorical purpose and be in an appropriate location. If you put a link in the middle of a paragraph, be aware that readers may go to the linked content before finishing what's before them — and if that link takes them to an external site, they may never come back! If it's important for users to read the whole paragraph, you may want to move the link to the end of it.

# 18c   Creating Web-based texts

Among the common types of digital assignments in college writing courses are Web pages, blogs and microblogs, wikis, and audio and video projects.

## ◻ Creating Web sites and Web pages

A Web site can consist of multiple individual Web pages. The hypertext that makes up a Web site allows the writer to organize elements as a cluster of associations. Each page may cover a single topic within a larger pool of content; a menu on the page typically lets readers find related information on the site. A Web site is relatively easy to change in order to accommodate new information.

Keep your purpose in mind as you create, embed, or link to content for your site, and workshop your layout and navigation plan with friends or classmates. Is

---

**CONSIDERING DISABILITIES | ACCESSIBLE WEB TEXTS**

Much on the Web remains hard to access and read for persons with disabilities. The Web site for the Americans with Disabilities Act provides guidelines on designing accessible sites, which include offering textual descriptions of any visuals and captions for any sound files. For details, visit www.ada.gov.

the layout clear and easy to navigate? Do users find what they are looking for, or are you missing content that readers need? If your instructor does not require you to follow a particular plan for a Web site or Web page, consider following a template design, or use a site or page that you admire as a model for your own work.

## ☐ Blogging

Some blogs resemble journals or diaries, giving personal perspectives on issues of importance in the life of the blogger. Other blogs may report on a particular topic, such as technology, travel, or politics. Some bloggers write short posts or comment on links to other sites; others write essay-length analyses of issues that interest them. There are as many varieties of blogs as there are reasons for writing them. Therefore, you won't find any hard and fast rules about how informal your tone should be when you write (or comment on) a blog post. Many bloggers adopt a conversational tone, but blogs aimed at a general audience tend to follow the conventions of standard edited English unless the writer wants to achieve a special effect.

Readers expect blog content to be refreshed frequently, so blog posts are often time-stamped, and the newest content appears first. Blogs also usually invite readers to comment publicly on each post. If you are creating a blog, consider whether you want to be able to moderate comments before they appear.

- When you create or contribute to a blog, consider how you want to represent yourself to readers. Will they expect humor, careful reasoning, personal anecdotes, expertise? What level of formality will produce the results you want from your audience?

- To comment on a blog, follow the same conventions you would for a discussion-list posting. Become familiar with the conversation before you add a comment of your own, and in general, avoid commenting on entries that are several days old.

## ☐ Microblogging

Social media sites that encourage you to write very short updates, such as Twitter and Tumblr, have some additional conventions.

- In microblog posts — particularly Twitter, which limits your posts to 140 characters — brevity is more important than conventionally correct grammar and spelling. As always, however, remember your audience. Posts on such sites *do* follow conventions, even though they don't resemble those for academic writing. So learn the current standards of the community you are trying to reach — especially the conventions for sharing other users' posts.

- Use punctuation appropriately to organize posts and help others find information they want. For instance, to communicate with a particular group, you can add the symbol # (hashtag) and an identifying label to your tweets to make it easier for group members to find your posts; your Hindi study group might use a tag such as *#hin101*.

### ☐ Contributing to a wiki

Wikis, such as Wikipedia, are collaborative online texts that empower all users of the site to contribute content, although this content may be moderated before being posted. Wikis create communities where all content is peer reviewed and evaluated by other members; they are powerful tools for sharing a lot of information because they draw on the collective knowledge of many contributors.

Wiki organization is largely left up to contributors, so you can decide when to link to existing content, create new pages, and so on. If the wiki you are working on allows you to annotate your work, you may want to explain your reasons for changing or correcting content others have posted. Many wikis allow users to add citations and create bibliographies; if you add content, you will help others by including links or identifying sources for your information.

### ☐ Creating audio and video projects

Today's technology makes it easy for users to record, edit, and upload audio and video files to the Web. Audio and video content can vary as widely as the content found in written-word media — audiobooks, video diaries, pop-culture mash-ups and remixes, radio shows, short documentaries, fiction films, and so on. Writers who create podcasts (which can be downloaded for playback) and streaming media (which can be played without downloading) may produce episodic content united by a common host or theme.

Creating audio and video may be a somewhat greater technical challenge than adding words and images to a blog post or Web site, but your school may have media experts who can help, or you may be able to turn to friends or classmates for technical advice — so don't assume that video or audio projects are necessarily too difficult. If you have the opportunity to create audio or video essays in response to an assignment, consider the following as you make choices about your project:

- Audio and video files can stand alone as online texts on sites like YouTube, but they can also be embedded on a Web page or blog or included in a presentation to add dimension to still images and written words. If only part of your text needs audio or video, consider embedding a short clip instead of making the entire project a media file.

**macmillanhighered.com/smh**

 18. Communicating in Other Media > Tutorial > Photo editing with GIMP

 18. Communicating in Other Media > Tutorial > Audio editing with Audacity

- Do you need to record your own audio or video? If so, make a plan for getting the content you need, which might include creating a script or interview questions, finding locations, and so on. Will you appear in the project? Will others also need to participate?

- Will you need sound or images from other sources? If so, where can you acquire what you need? If you use the work of others in a project that will be posted for the public, you may need to seek permission from the rightsholders (see Chapter 14). However, critiquing or analyzing someone else's work in your own project is often considered a "fair use" that does not require permission. You may also want to look for images and sounds distributed under a Creative Commons license, which allows others to use them freely.

# 18d  Creating nondigital multimodal projects

If the idea of having to use technology to create a writing project seems intimidating, remember that you can make a multimodal or multimedia project without digital tools. To be "multimodal" or "multimedia," a project simply needs to go beyond words — but you can use pens and scissors and any other resources at hand to add images, shapes, and other features to your texts.

Comics, scrapbooks, posters, and collages are just a few of the multimodal genres that you can create with or without digital help. Projects like these may incorporate words, or they may let images do most or all of the communicating. However, your instructor will still expect you to consider the rhetorical features of your projects and to convey your purpose and stance effectively to your audience, no matter what genres you choose or what tools you use.

### ◢ EXERCISE 18.1

Use a search engine to find a Web site that you haven't visited before but that addresses a topic you know something about. What is the purpose of the text? Who is its intended audience? What rhetorical stance does it take? What overall impression does the text create — and how does it do so?

▼ ▼ ▼ ▼ ▼ ▼ ▼ ▼ ▼ ▼ ▼ ▼ ▼ ▼ ▼ ▼ ▼ ▼ ▼ ▼ ▼ ▼ ▼ ▼

## THINKING CRITICALLY ABOUT MULTIMODAL TEXTS

Take some time to reflect on a multimodal text you have created, whether it's an assignment posted to a course Web site, a blog post or comment, a YouTube video, or a poster presentation. Evaluate the work you've created. For what purpose did you create the text? Did you achieve your goals? What audience did you anticipate, and did that audience see your work? Who else saw it? What was your topic, and what stance did you take? Finally, what kind of feedback did you get? Conclude by drawing up a list of tips for making future online texts, noting what aspects of your text were successful and what you would do differently.

# PART 5
# Academic, Professional, and Public Writing

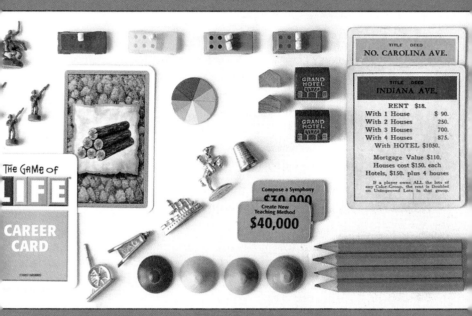

# CHAPTER 19

# Academic Work in Any Discipline

A RECENT SURVEY CONFIRMED that good writing plays an important role in almost every profession. As one MBA wrote, "Those who advance quickly in my company are those who write and speak well — it's as simple as that." But while writing is always a valuable skill, writing works in different ways in different disciplines. As you prepare written assignments for various courses, then, you will need to become familiar with the expectations, vocabularies, styles, methods of proof, and conventional formats used in each field.

## 19a Writing in any discipline

You may feel that writing will be of secondary importance after you complete your composition courses. Yet professionals working not just in the humanities, but in natural and applied sciences, social sciences, business, and other areas have a different understanding:

> Is writing important in chemistry? Don't chemists spend their time turning knobs, mixing reagents, and collecting data? They still get to do those things, but professional scientists also make presentations, prepare reports, publish results, and submit proposals. Each of these activities involves writing. If you remain skeptical about the need for writing skills, then ask your favorite professor, or any other scientist, to track the fraction of one workday spent using a word-processing program. You (and they) may be surprised at the answer. —OREGON STATE UNIVERSITY, *Writing Guide for Chemistry*

A student pursuing an education major agrees: "Writing is the key to just about everything I do, from constructing lesson plans to writing reviews of literature to learning to respond — in writing — to the students I will eventually teach."

Writing is central to learning regardless of the discipline; in addition, writing plays a major role in the life of every working professional. So whether you are preparing a case history in a nursing program, writing up the results of a psychology study, or applying for an internship, writing well will help you achieve your goals.

# 19b Reading in any discipline

As you already know, reading isn't a "one size fits all" activity: you need to adjust your reading strategies to fit the task at hand (see Chapter 7). Most instructors probably won't give you specific instruction in how to read texts; they will simply assume that you know how.

The more you read in any discipline, the easier you will find it to understand — and to write in that discipline. So read a lot, and pay attention to the texts you are reading. To get started, choose an article in an important journal in the field you plan to major in and then answer the following questions:

- How does a journal article in this discipline begin?
- How is the article organized? Does it have specific sections with subheads?
- What sources are cited, and how are they used — as backup support, as counter-examples, or as an argument to refute?
- What audience does the text seem to address? Is it a narrow technical or disciplinary audience, or is it aimed at a broader reading public? Is it addressed to readers of a specific journal? Is it published in print, online, or both? Is it intended for an international readership?
- How is the text formatted, and what citation style does it use?
- How are visuals such as charts or graphs used?

Finally, make sure you know whether articles you are reading are from juried or nonjuried journals (11a). Juried journals use panels of expert readers to analyze proposed articles and recommend publication (or not) to the journal editor, so articles in juried journals have been examined and accepted by experts in the field. Nonjuried journals can also offer valuable information, but they may bear the stamp of the editor and that person's biases more strongly than a juried journal would.

# 19c Understanding academic assignments

Since academic assignments vary widely from course to course and from professor to professor, the tips this section offers can only be general. For any discipline, make sure you are in control of the assignment rather than letting the assignment be in control of you. To take control, try to understand the assignment fully and understand what professors in the particular discipline expect in response.

**QUICK HELP**

Analyzing an assignment

- **What is the purpose of the assignment?** Are you expected to start or join a discussion, demonstrate mastery of a topic, or something else? **(2d)**
- **Who is the audience?** The instructor will be one audience, but are there others? If so, who are they? **(2e)** ▶

Analyzing an assignment, continued

- **What does the assignment ask of you?** Look for key terms such as *summarize*, *explain*, *evaluate*, *interpret*, *illustrate*, and *define*.
- **Do you need clarification of any terms?** If so, ask your instructor.
- **What do you need to know or find out to complete the assignment?** You may need to do background reading, develop a procedure for analyzing or categorizing information, or carry out some other kind of preparation.
- **What does the instructor expect in response?** How will you use sources (both written and visual)? How should you organize and develop the assignment? What is the expected format and length?
- **Can you find a model of an effective response to a similar assignment?**
- **What do other students think the assignment requires?** Talking over an assignment with classmates is one good way to test your understanding.

### EXERCISE 19.1

Analyze the following assignment from a communications course using the questions in 19c.

Assignment: Distribute a questionnaire to twenty people (ten male, ten female) asking these four questions: (1) What do you expect to say and do when you meet a stranger? (2) What don't you expect to say and do when you meet a stranger? (3) What do you expect to say and do when you meet a very close friend? (4) What don't you expect to say and do when you meet a very close friend?

When you have collected the responses, read them over and answer the following questions:

- What, if any, descriptions were common to all respondents' answers?
- How do male and female responses compare?
- What similarities and differences did you find between the responses to the stranger and to the very close friend?
- What factors (environment, time, status, gender, and so on) do you think had an impact on these responses?

Discuss your findings, using concepts and theories explained in your text.

## 19d Learning specialized vocabulary

As philosopher Kenneth Burke has noted, entering into an academic discipline is like going to a party where you do not know anyone. At first you feel like an outsider, and you may not understand much of what you hear or see. Before you enter the conversation, you have to listen and observe carefully. Eventually, however, you will be able to join in — and if you stay long enough, participating in the conversation becomes easy and natural.

To learn the routines, practices, and ways of knowing in a new field, you must also make an effort to enter into the conversation, and that means taking action. One good way to get started is to study the vocabulary of the field you are most interested in.

Highlight the key terms in your reading or notes to learn how much specialized or technical vocabulary you will be expected to know. If you find only a small amount of specialized vocabulary, try to master the new terms quickly by reading your textbook carefully, looking up key words or phrases, and asking questions. If you find a great deal of specialized vocabulary, however, you may want to familiarize yourself with it methodically. Any of the following procedures may help:

- Keep a log of unfamiliar or confusing words *in context*. Check definitions in your textbook's glossary or index, or consult a specialized dictionary; ask your instructor or a librarian for help finding appropriate reference works.

- Review your class notes each day. Underline important terms, review definitions, and identify anything that is unclear. Use your textbook or ask questions to clarify anything confusing before the class moves on to a new topic.

- Try to use and work with key concepts. Even if they are not yet entirely clear to you, working with them will help you understand them. For example, in a statistics class, try to work out (in words) how to do an analysis of *covariance*, step by step, even if you are not sure of the precise definition of the term. Or try to plot the narrative progression in a story even if you are still not entirely sure of the definition of *narrative progression*.

Whatever your techniques for learning a specialized vocabulary, begin to use the new terms whenever you can — in class, in discussions with instructors and other students, and in your assignments. This ability to use what you learn in speaking and writing is crucial to your full understanding of and participation in the discipline.

## 19e Following disciplinary style

Another important way to learn about a discipline is to identify its stylistic features. Study some pieces of writing in the field with the following in mind:

- **Genres and media.** What kinds of texts do people in the discipline typically create? (See 19g.) Are typical texts in print or digital formats (or both)?

- **Design and visuals.** Do writers typically use elements such as graphs, tables, maps, or photographs? How are visuals integrated into the text? How are they labeled? What role, if any, do headings and other formatting elements play in the writing? (See Chapter 16.)

---

**TALKING THE TALK** | **THE FIRST PERSON**

"Is it true that I should never use *I* in college writing?" In much writing in college, using the first-person *I* is perfectly acceptable to most instructors. As always, think about the context — if your own experience is relevant to the topic, you are better off saying *I* than trying too hard not to. But don't overdo it, especially if the writing isn't just autobiographical. And check with your instructor if you aren't sure: in certain academic disciplines, such as the natural sciences, using *I* may be seen as inappropriate.

---

- **Overall tone.** How would you describe the tone of the writing? (See 4i.)
- **Stance.** To what extent do writers in the field strive for distance and objectivity? What strategies help them to achieve this stance? (See 2d.)
- **Titles.** Are titles generally descriptive ("Findings from a Double-Blind Study of the Effect of Antioxidants"), persuasive ("Antioxidants Proven Effective"), or something else? How do each of the titles shape your expectations?
- **Sentence length.** Are sentences long and complex? Simple and direct?
- **Voice.** Are verbs generally active or passive? Why? (See 39g.)
- **Person.** Do writers use the first-person *I* or third-person terms such as *the investigator*? What is the effect of this choice? (See box above.)
- **Documentation style.** Do writers use MLA, APA, *Chicago*, or CSE style? (See Chapters 32–35.) Are sources cited in some other way?

## 19f  Using appropriate evidence

What is acceptable and persuasive evidence in one discipline may be less so in another. Observable, quantifiable data may constitute the best evidence in experimental psychology, but similar data may be less appropriate — or impossible to come by — in a historical study. An engineering proposal will be backed up with drawings, maps, and detailed calculations. A case study in cultural anthropology, on the other hand, may depend almost entirely on interview data. As you grow familiar with an area of study, you will develop a sense of what it takes to prove a point in that field. You can speed up this process, however, by investigating and questioning. The following questions will help you think about the use of evidence in materials you read:

- How do writers in the field use precedent and authority? What or who counts as an authority in this field? How are the credentials of an authority established? (See 9g.)

- What kinds of quantitative data (countable or measurable items) are used, and for what purposes? How are the data gathered and presented?
- How are qualitative data (systematically observed items) used?
- How are statistics used and presented? Are tables, charts, graphs, or other visuals important, and why?
- How is logical reasoning used? How are definition, cause and effect, analogy, and example used?
- Do writers in the field include any personal information, use first person, or provide evidence intended to stir emotions?
- How does the field use primary and secondary sources? (See 11a.) What are the primary and secondary materials? How is each type of source presented?
- What kinds of textual evidence are cited?
- How are quotations and other references to sources used and integrated into the text? (See Chapter 13.)

In addition to carrying out your own investigation, ask your instructor how you can best go about making a case in this field.

### EXERCISE 19.2

Read a few journals associated with your prospective major or a discipline of particular interest to you, using the preceding questions to study the use of evidence in that discipline. If you are keeping a writing log, make an entry summarizing what you have learned.

## 19g  Using conventional patterns and formats

To produce effective writing in a discipline, you need to know the field's generally accepted formats for organizing and presenting evidence. A typical laboratory report, for instance, follows a fairly standard organizational framework and usually has a certain look (see 22c for an example). A case study in sociology or education or anthropology likewise follows a typical organizational plan.

Ask your instructor to recommend some excellent examples of the kind of writing you will do in the course. Then analyze these examples in terms of format and organization. You might also look at major scholarly journals in the field to see what types of formats seem most common and how each is organized. Consider the following questions about organization and format:

- What types of articles, reports, or documents are common in this field? What is the purpose of each?
- What can a reader expect to find in each type of writing? What does each type assume about its readers?

- Do articles or other documents typically begin with an abstract? If so, does the abstract describe the parts of the article to come, or does it provide substantive information such as findings or conclusions? (See 21c.)
- How is each type of text organized? What are its main parts? How are they labeled?
- How does a particular type of essay, report, or document show the connections among ideas? What assumptions does it take for granted? What points does it emphasize?

Remember that there is a close connection between the writing patterns and formats a particular area of study uses and the work that scholars in that field undertake.

## 19h  Making ethical decisions

Writers in all disciplines face ethical questions. Those who plan and carry out research on living people, for example, must be careful to avoid harming their subjects. Researchers in all fields must be scrupulous in presenting data to make sure that others can replicate research and test claims. In whatever discipline or field you are working, you should take into consideration your own interests, those of your collaborators, and those of your employers — but you must also responsibly safeguard the interests of the general public.

Fortunately, a growing number of disciplines have adopted guidelines for ethics. The American Psychological Association has been a pioneer in this area, and many other professional organizations and companies have their own codes or standards of ethics. These guidelines can help you make decisions about day-to-day writing. Even so, you will no doubt encounter situations where the right or ethical decision is murky at best. In such situations, consult your own conscience first and then talk your choices over with colleagues you respect before coming to a decision on how to proceed.

## 19i  Collaborating and communicating

In contemporary academic and business environments, working with others is not just a highly valued skill — it is a necessity. Such collaboration happens when peers work together on a shared document, when classmates divide research and writing duties to create a multimedia presentation, when reviewers share advice on a draft, or when colleagues in an office offer their views on appropriate revisions for a companywide document.

Because people all over the world now have the ability to research, study, write, and work together, you must be able to communicate effectively within and across cultures. Conventions for academic writing (or for forms of digital communication) can vary from culture to culture, from discipline to discipline, and from one form of English to another. What is considered polite in one culture may seem rude in another, so those who communicate globally must take care to avoid giving offense — or taking it where none was intended. (For more information on writing across cultures, see Chapter 27.)

▼ ▼ ▼ ▼ ▼ ▼ ▼ ▼ ▼ ▼ ▼ ▼ ▼ ▼ ▼ ▼ ▼ ▼ ▼ ▼ ▼ ▼ ▼ ▼ ▼ ▼

## THINKING CRITICALLY ABOUT READING AND WRITING IN A DISCIPLINE

### Reading with an eye for disciplinary discourse

When you take your first course in any new discipline, ask a librarian to recommend an important journal in that discipline, and then choose two abstracts of articles in the journal. What can you infer about the discourse of the discipline—about its characteristic vocabulary, style, use of evidence, and so on—from the information in the abstracts?

### Thinking about your own writing in a discipline

Choose a piece of writing you have produced for a class in a particular discipline—a blog or discussion post, a laboratory report, a review of the literature, or any other written assignment. Examine your writing closely for its use of that discipline's vocabulary, style, methods of proof, and conventional formats. How comfortable are you writing a piece of this kind? In what ways are you using the conventions of the discipline easily and well? What conventions give you difficulty, and why? You might talk with an instructor in this field about the conventions and requirements for writing in the discipline. Make notes about what you learn about being a better writer in the field.

# CHAPTER 20

# Writing for the Humanities

I N HUMANITIES DISCIPLINES, the interpretation and creation of texts are central. The nature of texts can vary widely, from poems and plays to novels, articles, philosophical treatises, films, advertisements, paintings, and so on. But whether the text being studied is ancient or modern, literary or historical, verbal or visual, textual analysis plays a critical role in the reading and writing that people in the humanities undertake.

---

**CONNECT:** What kinds of genres will your writing in the humanities require? **2f, 19g**

**CREATE:** On your own or in collaboration with another writer, analyze the features of a print and a digital example of a genre you may be asked to create in a humanities course.

**REFLECT:** Use the questions in Exercise 2.4 on p. 34 to reflect on genres in the humanities.

---

## 20a Reading texts in the humanities

To read critically in the humanities, you will need to pose questions and construct hypotheses as you read. You may ask, for instance, why a writer might make some points or develop some examples but omit others. Rather than finding meaning only in the surface information that texts or artifacts convey, you should use your own questions and hypotheses to create fuller meanings — to construct the significance of what you read.

To successfully engage texts, you must recognize that you are not a neutral observer, not an empty cup into which the meaning of a work is poured. If such were the case, writing would have exactly the same meanings for all of us, and reading would be a fairly boring affair. If you have ever gone to see a movie with a friend and each come away with a completely different under-standing or response, you already have ample evidence that a text never has just one meaning.

Nevertheless, you may in the past have been willing to accept the first meaning to occur to you — to take a text at face value. Most humanities courses, however, will expect you to exercise your interpretive powers. The following guidelines can help you build your strengths as a close reader of humanities texts.

---

### Guidelines for reading texts in the humanities

- **Be clear about the purpose of the text.** The two most common purposes for works in the humanities are to provide information and to argue for a particular interpretation. Pay attention to whether the text presents opinions or facts, to what is included and omitted, and to how facts are presented to the audience. **(12d)**
- **Get an overall impression.** What does the work make you think about — and why? What is most remarkable or memorable? What confuses you?
- **Annotate the text.** Be prepared to "talk back," ask questions, note emerging patterns or themes, and point out anything out of place or ineffective. **(Chapter 7)**
- **Look at the context.** Consider the time and place represented in the work as well as when and where the writer lived. You may also consider social, political, or personal forces that may have affected the writer.
- **Think about the audience.** Who are the readers or viewers the writer seems to address? Do they include you?
- **Pay attention to genre.** What category does the work fall into (graphic novel, diary, political cartoon, sermon, argumentative essay, Hollywood western)? What is noteworthy about the form? How does it conform to, stretch, or even subvert your expectations about the genre? **(2f)**
- **Pay attention to visual elements and design.** How does the text look? What visual elements does it include? What contribution do these make to the overall effect or argument?
- **Note the point of view.** Whose point of view is represented? How does it affect your response?
- **Notice the major themes.** Are specific claims being advanced? How are these claims supported?
- **Understand the difference between primary and secondary sources.** Primary sources provide firsthand knowledge, while secondary sources report on or analyze the research of others. **(11a)**

---

## 20b Writing texts in the humanities

As a writer in the humanities, you will use the findings from close examination of a text or artifact to develop an argument or to construct an analysis.

## ☐ Understanding assignments

Common assignments that make use of the skills of close reading, analysis, and argument include summaries, response pieces, position papers, critical analyses of primary and secondary sources, and research-based projects. In philosophy, for example, you might need to summarize an argument, critique a text's logic and effectiveness, or discuss a moral issue from a particular philosophical perspective. A literature assignment may ask you to look very closely at a particular text ("Examine the role of chocolate in Toni Morrison's *Tar Baby*") or to go well beyond a primary text ("Discuss the impact of agribusiness on modernist novels"). Other disciplines may ask you to write articles, primary source analyses, or research papers.

For texts in literature, modern languages, and philosophy, writers often use the documentation style of the Modern Language Association; see Chapter 32 for advice on using MLA style. For projects in history and other areas of the humanities, writers often use the documentation style of the University of Chicago Press; see Chapter 34 for advice on using *Chicago* style.

## ☐ Developing a critical stance

To analyze a text, you need to develop a critical stance — the approach you will take to the work — that can help you develop a thesis or major claim (see 3c and 9d). To evaluate the text and present a critical response to it, you should look closely at the text itself, including its style; at the context in which it was produced; and at the audience the text aims to reach, which may or may not include yourself.

To look closely at the text itself, consider its genre, form, point of view, and themes, and look at the stylistic features, such as word choice, use of imagery, visuals, and design. Then consider context: ask why the text was created, note its original and current contexts, and think about how attitudes and ideas of its era may have influenced it. Consider who the intended audience might be, and think about how people outside this intended group might respond to the text. Finally, think about your personal response to the text as well. (See also Chapters 7 and 8.)

Carrying out these steps should provide you with plenty of material to work with as you begin to shape a critical thesis and write your analysis. You can begin by grounding your analysis in one or more important questions you have about the work.

## ☐ Writing a literary analysis

When you analyze or interpret a literary work, think of your thesis as answering a question about some aspect of the work. The guiding question you bring to the literary work will help you decide on a critical stance toward the work. For example, a student writing about Shakespeare's *Macbeth* might find her curiosity piqued by the many comic moments that appear in this tragedy. She might turn the question of why Shakespeare uses so much comedy in *Macbeth* into the following thesis statement, which proposes an answer to the question: "The many unexpected comic moments in *Macbeth* emphasize how disordered the world becomes for murderers like Macbeth and his wife."

## 20c A student's close reading of poetry

**STUDENT WRITER**
**Bonnie Sillay**

Following is an excerpt from student Bonnie Sillay's close reading of two poems by E. E. Cummings. This essay follows MLA style (see Chapter 32). Bonnie is creating her own interpretation, so the only works she cites are the poems she analyzes. To read the full essay, work with annotations, and do other activities related to writing about literature, go to **macmillanhighered.com/smh**. (Photo © Bonnie Sillay)

Sillay 1

Bonnie Sillay

Instructor Angela Mitchell

English 1102

December 4, 2010

"Life's Not a Paragraph"

Throughout his poetry, E. E. Cummings leads readers deep into a thicket of scrambled words, missing punctuation, and unconventional structure. Within Cummings's poetic bramble, ambiguity leads the reader through what seems at first a confusing and winding maze. However, this confusion actually transforms into a path that leads the reader to the center of the thicket where Cummings's message lies: readers should not allow their experience to be limited by reason and rationality. In order to communicate his belief that emotional experience should triumph over reason, Cummings employs odd juxtapositions, outlandish metaphors, and inversions of traditional grammatical structures that reveal the illogic of reason. Indeed, by breaking down such formal boundaries, Cummings's poems "since feeling is first" and "as freedom is a breakfastfood" suggest that emotion, which provides the compositional fabric for our experience of life, should never be defined or controlled.

In "since feeling is first," Cummings urges his reader to reject attempts to control emotion, using English grammar as one example of the restrictive conventions present in society. Stating that "since feeling is first / who pays any attention / to the syntax of things" (lines 1-3), Cummings suggests that emotion should not be forced to fit into some preconceived framework or mold. He carries this message throughout the poem by juxtaposing images of the abstract and the concrete — images of emotion and of English grammar. Cummings's word choice enhances his intentionally strange juxtapositions, with the poet using grammatical terms that suggest regulation or confinement. For example, in the line "And death i think is no parenthesis" (16), Cummings uses the idea that parentheses confine the words they surround in order to warn the reader not to let death confine life or emotions.

*Annotations indicate effective choices or MLA-style formatting.*

---

**Margin annotations:**

- Name, instructor, course, date on left margin
- Title centered
- Present tense used to discuss poetry
- Foreshadows discussion of work to come
- Introductory paragraph ends with thesis statement
- Quotation cited parenthetically
- Double spacing throughout
- 1"

Sillay 4

Works Cited

Cummings, E. E. "as freedom is a breakfastfood." *E. E. Cummings: Complete Poems 1904-1962*. Ed. George J. Firmage. New York: Liveright, 1991. 511. Print.

---. "since feeling is first." *E. E. Cummings: Complete Poems 1904-1962*. Ed. George J. Firmage. New York: Liveright, 1991. 291. Print.

Second work by same author uses three hyphens in place of name

▼ ▼ ▼ ▼ ▼ ▼ ▼ ▼ ▼ ▼ ▼ ▼ ▼ ▼ ▼ ▼ ▼ ▼ ▼ ▼ ▼ ▼ ▼ ▼ ▼

## THINKING CRITICALLY ABOUT WRITING IN THE HUMANITIES

Choose at least two projects or assignments you have written for different disciplines in the humanities—say, history and film. Reread these papers with an eye to their similarities. What features do they have in common? Do they use similar methods of analysis and value similar kinds of evidence, for instance? In what ways do they differ? Based on your analysis, what conclusions can you draw about these two disciplines?

# CHAPTER 21

# Writing for the Social Sciences

THE SOCIAL SCIENCES SHARE with the humanities an interest in what it means to be human. But the social sciences also share with the sciences the goal of engaging in a systematic, observable study of human behavior. When you write in the social sciences, you will attempt to identify, understand, and explain patterns of human behavior.

> **CONNECT:** What kinds of genres will your writing in the social sciences require? **2f, 21b**
>
> **CREATE:** On your own or in collaboration with another writer, analyze the features of a print and a digital example of a genre you may be asked to create in a social-science course.
>
> **REFLECT:** Use the questions in Exercise 2.4 on p. 34 to reflect on genres in the social sciences.

## 21a  Reading texts in the social sciences

When you read in the social sciences, you ask questions, analyze, and interpret as you read, whether you are reading an academic paper that sets forth a theoretical premise or overall theory and defends it, a case study that describes a particular case and draws out inferences and implications from it, or a research report that presents the results of an investigation into an important question in the field. Most of what you read in the social sciences will attempt to prove a point, and you will need to evaluate how well that particular point is supported.

The social sciences, like other disciplines, often use specialized vocabulary as shorthand for complex ideas that otherwise would take paragraphs to explain.

## ☐ Understanding qualitative and quantitative studies

Different texts in the social and natural sciences may call for different methods and strategies. Texts that report the results of *quantitative* studies collect data represented with numerical measurements drawn from surveys, polls, experiments, and tests. For example, a study of voting patterns in southern states might rely on quantitative data such as statistics. Texts that report the results of *qualitative* studies rely on non-numerical methods such as interviews and observations to reveal social patterns. A study of the way children in one kindergarten class develop rules of play, for instance, would draw on qualitative data — observations of social interaction, interviews with students and teachers, and so on. Of course, some work in the social and behavioral sciences combines quantitative and qualitative data and methods: an educational report might begin with statistical data related to a problem and then move to a qualitative case study to exemplify what the statistics reveal.

In the social sciences, both quantitative and qualitative researchers must determine what they are examining and measuring in order to get answers to research questions. A researcher who studies childhood aggression must first define and measure *aggression*. If the research is qualitative, a researcher may describe types of behavior that indicate aggression and then discuss observations of children and interviews with teachers and peers about those behaviors. A quantitative researcher, on the other hand, might design an experiment that notes how often children hit a punching bag or that asks children to rate their peers' aggression on a scale of one to ten.

Be sure to recognize that both quantitative and qualitative studies have points of view, and that researchers' opinions influence everything from the hypothesis and the design of the research study to the interpretation of findings. You must consider whether researchers' views are sensible and solidly supported by evidence, and pay close attention to the kind of data the writer is using and what those data can — and cannot — prove. For example, if researchers of childhood aggression define *aggression* in a way that you find unpersuasive, or if they observe behaviors that you consider playful rather than aggressive, then you will likely not accept their interpretation of the findings.

## ☐ Recognizing conventional formats

Make use of conventional disciplinary formats to help guide your reading in the social sciences. Many such texts conform to the format and documentation style of the American Psychological Association (APA). In addition, articles often include standard features — an abstract that gives an overview of the findings, followed by an introduction, review of literature, methods, results, discussion, and references. Become familiar with standard formats so that you can easily find the information you need. (For more on APA style, see Chapter 33.)

# 21b Writing texts in the social sciences

Perhaps because the social sciences share concerns with both the humanities and the sciences, the forms of writing within the social sciences are particularly varied, including summaries, abstracts, literature reviews, reaction pieces, position papers, radio scripts, briefing notes, book reviews, briefs, research papers, quantitative research reports, case studies, ethnographic analyses, and meta-analyses. You may find such an array of writing assignments overwhelming, but in fact these assignments can be organized under five main categories:

- Writing that encourages student learning, such as reaction pieces and position papers
- Writing that demonstrates student learning, such as summaries, abstracts, and research papers
- Writing that reflects common on-the-job communication tasks for members of a discipline, such as radio scripts, briefing notes, and informational reports
- Writing that requires students to analyze and evaluate the writings of others, such as literature reviews, book reviews, and briefs
- Writing that asks students to replicate the work of others or to engage in original research, such as quantitative research reports, case studies, and ethnographic analyses

Many forms of writing in the social sciences call either explicitly or implicitly for argument (see Chapter 9). If you write an essay that reports on the results of a survey you developed about attitudes toward physician-assisted suicide among students on your campus, you will make an explicit argument about the significance of your data. But even with other forms of writing, such as summaries and book reports, you will implicitly argue that your description and analysis provide a clear, thorough overview of the text(s) you have read.

## ☐ Using style in the social sciences

Writing in the social sciences need not be dry and filled with jargon. While you need to understand the conventions, concepts, and habits of mind typical of a discipline, you can still write clear prose that engages readers.

When discussing research sources in a paper conforming to APA style, use the past tense or the present perfect tense (39e) for the verbs: *Raditch showed* or *Raditch has shown*. Make sure that any writing you do is as clear and grammatically correct as possible so that readers see you as capable and credible.

☐ **Writing a literature review**

Students of the social sciences carry out literature reviews to find out the most current thinking about a topic, to learn what research has already been carried out on that topic, to evaluate the work that has been done, and to set any research they will do in context. The following guidelines are designed to help you explore and question sources, looking for flaws or gaps. Such a critical review could then lead to a discussion of how your own research will avoid such flaws and advance knowledge.

- What is your topic or dependent variable (item or characteristic studied)?
- What is already known about this topic? What characteristics does the topic or dependent variable have? How have other researchers measured the item or characteristic being studied? What other factors are involved, and how are they related to each other and to your topic or variable? What theories are used to explain the way things are now?
- How has research been done so far? Who or what has been studied? How have measurements been taken?
- Has there been change over time? What has caused any changes?
- What problems do you find in the new research? What questions have not been answered? Have researchers drawn unwarranted conclusions?
- What gaps will your research fill? How is it new? What problems do you want to correct?

◢ **EXERCISE 21.1**

Identify a literature review in a social-science field you are interested in (ask your instructor or a librarian for help in finding one), and read it carefully, noting how it addresses the questions above. Bring your notes to class for discussion.

## 21c   A student's psychology literature review

STUDENT WRITER
Tawnya Redding

Following is an excerpt from a psychology literature review by Tawnya Redding that adheres to the conventions for social science writing in this genre and follows the guidelines of APA style (see Chapter 33) to document sources. To read the full text, annotate and highlight, and do other activities related to writing in the social sciences, go to **macmillanhighered .com/smh**. (Photo © Tawnya Redding)

Running head
(fifty characters
or fewer) appears
flush left on first
line of title page

Page number
appears flush
right on first line
of every page

Title, name,
and affiliation
centered and
double-spaced

Mood Music: Music Preference and the Risk for Depression

and Suicide in Adolescents

Tawnya Redding

Psychology 480

Professor Ede

February 23, 2009

Annotations indicate effective choices or APA-style formatting.

MOOD MUSIC                                                                           2

### Abstract

There has long been concern for the effects that certain genres of music (such as heavy metal and country) have on youth. While a correlational link between these genres and increased risk for depression and suicide in adolescents has been established, researchers have been unable to pinpoint what is responsible for this link, and a causal relationship has not been determined. This paper will begin by discussing correlational literature concerning music preference and increased risk for depression and suicide, as well as the possible reasons for this link. Finally, studies concerning the effects of music on mood will be discussed. This examination of the literature on music and increased risk for depression and suicide points out the limitations of previous research and suggests the need for new research establishing a causal relationship for this link as well as research into the specific factors that may contribute to an increased risk for depression and suicide in adolescents.

Heading centered

No indentation

Use of passive voice appropriate for social sciences

Clear, straightforward description of literature under review

Text is double-spaced

Conclusions indicated

Full title centered

Mood Music: Music Preference and the Risk for Depression and
Suicide in Adolescents

Paragraphs indented

Music is a significant part of American culture. Since the explosion
of rock and roll in the 1950s there has been a concern for the effects
that music may have on listeners, and especially on young people.

Background information about review supplied

The genres most likely to come under suspicion in recent decades have
included heavy metal, country, and blues. These genres have been
suspected of having adverse effects on the mood and behavior of young
listeners. But can music really alter the disposition and create self-

Questions focus reader's attention

destructive behaviors in listeners? And if so, which genres and aspects
of those genres are responsible? The following review of the literature
will establish the correlation between potentially problematic genres of
music such as heavy metal and country and depression and suicide risk.
First, correlational studies concerning music preference and suicide risk
will be discussed, followed by a discussion of the literature concerning
the possible reasons for this link. Finally, studies concerning the effects
of music on mood will be discussed. Despite the link between genres such
as heavy metal and country and suicide risk, previous research has been
unable to establish the causal nature of this link.

Boldface headings help organize review

**The Correlation Between Music and Depression and Suicide Risk**

Studies over the past two decades have set out to answer this
question by examining the correlation between youth music preference
and risk for depression and suicide. A large portion of these studies have
focused on heavy metal and country music as the main genre culprits

Parenthetical references follow APA style

associated with youth suicidality and depression (Lacourse, Claes, &
Villeneuve, 2001; Scheel & Westefeld, 1999; Stack & Gundlach, 1992).
Stack and Gundlach (1992) examined the radio airtime devoted to
country music in 49 metropolitan areas and found that the higher the
percentages of country music airtime, the higher the incidence of suicides
among whites. The researchers hypothesized that themes in country music
(such as alcohol abuse) promoted audience identification and reinforced
a preexisting suicidal mood, and that the themes associated with country
music were responsible for elevated suicide rates. Similarly, Scheel and

MOOD MUSIC                                                                        9

### References

Baker, F., & Bor, W. (2008). Can music preference indicate mental
    health status in young people? *Australasian Psychiatry, 16*(4),
    284 – 288. Retrieved from http://www3.interscience.wiley.com
    /journal/118565538/home

George, D., Stickle, K., Rachid, F., & Wopnford, A. (2007). The association
    between types of music enjoyed and cognitive, behavioral, and
    personality factors of those who listen. *Psychomusicology, 19*(2),
    32 – 56.

Lacourse, E., Claes, M., & Villeneuve, M. (2001). Heavy metal music and
    adolescent suicidal risk. *Journal of Youth and Adolescence, 30*(3),
    321 – 332.

Lai, Y. (1999). Effects of music listening on depressed women in
    Taiwan. *Issues in Mental Health Nursing, 20,* 229 – 246. doi:
    10.1080/016128499248637

Martin, G., Clark, M., & Pearce, C. (1993). Adolescent suicide: Music
    preference as an indicator of vulnerability. *Journal of the American
    Academy of Child and Adolescent Psychiatry, 32,* 530 – 535.

Scheel, K., & Westefeld, J. (1999). Heavy metal music and adolescent
    suicidality: An empirical investigation. *Adolescence, 34*(134).
    253 – 273.

Siedliecki, S., & Good, M. (2006). Effect of music on power, pain,
    depression and disability. *Journal of Advanced Nursing, 54*(5),
    553 – 562. doi: 10.1111/j.1365-2648.2006.03860.x

Smith, J. L., & Noon, J. (1998). Objective measurement of mood change
    induced by contemporary music. *Journal of Psychiatric & Mental
    Health Nursing, 5,* 403 – 408.

Stack, S. (2000). Blues fans and suicide acceptability. *Death Studies, 24,*
    223 – 231.

Stack, S., & Gundlach, J. (1992). The effect of country music on suicide.
    *Social Forces, 71*(1), 211 – 218. Retrieved from http://socialforces.unc
    .edu/

References begin
on new page

Journal article
from a database,
no DOI

Print journal
article

Journal article
from a database
with DOI

▼ ▼ ▼ ▼ ▼ ▼ ▼ ▼ ▼ ▼ ▼ ▼ ▼ ▼ ▼ ▼ ▼ ▼ ▼ ▼ ▼ ▼ ▼ ▼ ▼ ▼ ▼ ▼ ▼ ▼ ▼

## THINKING CRITICALLY ABOUT WRITING IN THE SOCIAL SCIENCES

### Reading with an eye for writing in the social sciences

Choose two readings from a social-science discipline, and read them with an eye toward issues of style. Does the use of disciplinary terms and concepts seem appropriate? In what ways do the texts attempt to engage readers and establish the authority of the writer? If the texts are not clear and understandable, how might they be improved?

### Thinking about your own writing in the social sciences

Choose a text you like that you have written for a social-science discipline. Then examine your style in this paper to see how well you have engaged your readers. Note variation in sentence length and type (do you, for example, use any questions?), number of active and passive verbs, use of concrete examples and everyday language, and so on. How would you rate your writing as a social scientist?

# CHAPTER 22

# Writing for the Natural and Applied Sciences

NATURAL SCIENCES SUCH AS BIOLOGY, chemistry, and physics study the natural world and its phenomena; applied sciences such as nanotechnology and the various fields of engineering apply knowledge from the natural sciences to practical problems. Whether you are working in the lab or the field, writing will play a key role in your courses in the natural and applied sciences.

---

**CONNECT:** What kinds of genres will your writing in the natural or applied sciences require? **2f, 22b**

**CREATE:** On your own or in collaboration with another writer, analyze the features of a print and a digital example of a genre you may be asked to create in a natural or applied sciences course.

**REFLECT:** Use the questions in Exercise 2.4 on p. 34 to reflect on genres in the natural and applied sciences.

---

## 22a Reading texts in the natural and applied sciences

Scientists and engineers work with evidence that can be observed, verified, and controlled. Though they cannot avoid interpretation, they still strive for objectivity by using the scientific method — observing or studying phenomena, formulating a hypothesis about the phenomena, and testing that hypothesis through controlled experiments and observations. Scientists and engineers aim to generate precise, replicable data; they develop experiments to account for extraneous factors. In this careful, precise way, scientists and engineers identify, test, and write persuasively about theoretical and real-world problems.

## ☐ Identifying argument

As you read in the sciences, try to become familiar with disciplinary terms, concepts, and formats, and practice reading — and listening — for detail. If you are reading a first-year biology textbook, you can draw upon general critical-reading strategies. In addition, charts, graphs, illustrations, models, and other visuals often play an important role in scientific writing, so your ability to read and comprehend these visual displays of knowledge is particularly important. (See Chapter 7.)

When you read a science or engineering textbook, you can assume that the information presented there is authoritative and as objective as possible. When you read specialized materials, however, recognize that although scholarly reports undergo significant peer review, they nevertheless represent arguments (see Chapter 8). The connection between facts and claims in the sciences, as in all subject areas, is created by the author rather than simply revealed by the data. So read both facts and claims with a questioning eye: Did the scientist choose the best method to test the hypothesis? Are there other reasonable interpretations of the experiment's results? Do other studies contradict the conclusions of this experiment? When you read specialized texts in the sciences with questions like these in mind, you are reading — and thinking — like a scientist. (For additional information on assessing a source's credibility, see 12d.)

## ☐ Recognizing conventional formats

As you advance in your course work, you will need to develop reading strategies for increasingly specialized texts. Many scientific texts conform to the format and documentation style of the Council of Science Editors (CSE); for more on CSE style, see Chapter 35. (However, you should be prepared to follow an instructor's guidelines for citation and references if another style is used in your discipline or in a particular course.) In addition, articles often include standard features — an abstract that gives an overview of the findings, followed by an introduction, literature review, materials and methods, results, discussion, and references.

You might expect to read a journal article for a science or engineering course from start to finish, giving equal weight to each section. However, an experienced reader in sciences and engineering might skim an abstract to see if an article warrants further reading. If it does — and this judgment is based on the reader's own research interest — he or she might then read the introduction to understand the rationale for the experiment and then skip to the results. A reader with a specific interest in the methods will read that section with particular care.

**EXERCISE 22.1**

Choose a respected journal in a discipline in the natural or applied sciences that interests you. (Ask your instructor or a reference librarian if you need help identifying a journal.) Then read quickly through two articles, taking notes on the author's use of any headings and subheadings, specialized vocabulary, visuals, and evidence. Bring the results of your investigation to class for discussion.

## 22b Writing texts in the natural and applied sciences

In the sciences and engineering, you must be able to respond to a diverse range of writing and speaking tasks. Often, you must maintain lab or engineering notebooks that include careful records of experiments. You will also write memos, papers, project proposals and reports, literature reviews, and progress reports; in addition, you may develop print and Web-based presentations for both technical and lay audiences (see Chapter 17). Particularly common writing assignments in the sciences are the literature review, research proposal, and research report.

### ☐ Understanding assignments

Writing a literature review enables you to keep up with and evaluate developments in your field. Literature reviews are an essential first step in any research effort, for they enable you to discover what research has already been completed and how you might build on earlier efforts. Successful literature reviews demonstrate your ability to identify relevant research on a topic and to summarize and in some instances evaluate that research.

Most scientists spend a great deal of time writing research or grant proposals aimed at securing funds to support their research. As an undergraduate, you may have an opportunity to make similar proposals to an office of undergraduate research or to a science-based firm that supports student research, for instance. Funding agencies often have guidelines for preparing a proposal. Proposals for research funding generally include the following sections: title page, introduction, purpose(s) and significance of the study, methods, timeline, budget, and references. You may also need to submit an abstract.

Research reports, another common writing form in the sciences, may include both literature reviews and discussions of primary research, most often experiments. Like journal articles, research reports generally follow this form: title, author(s), abstract, introduction, literature review, materials and methods, results, discussion, and references. Many instructors will ask you to write lab reports (22c), which are briefer versions of research reports and may not include a literature review.

Today, most scientific writing is collaborative. As you move from introductory to advanced courses and then to the workplace, you will increasingly find yourself working as part of a team or group. Indeed, in such areas as engineering, collaborative projects are the norm (see Chapter 6).

## ☐ Using style in the natural and applied sciences

In general, use the present tense for most writing you do in the natural and applied sciences. Use the past tense, however, when you are describing research already carried out (by you or others) or published in the past.

As a writer in the sciences, you will need to produce complex figures, tables, images, and models and use software designed to analyze data or run computer simulations. In addition, you must present data carefully. If you create a graph, you should provide headings for columns, label axes with numbers or units, and identify data points. Caption figures and tables with a number and descriptive title. And avoid orphan data — data that you present in a figure or table but don't comment on in your text.

Finally, make sure that any writing you do is as clear, concise, and grammatically correct as possible to ensure that readers see you as capable and credible.

## 22c   A student's chemistry lab report

**STUDENT WRITER**
Allyson Goldberg

Following is an excerpt from a lab report on a chemistry experiment by student Allyson Goldberg. To read the full text, annotate and highlight (or read others' annotations), and do other activities related to writing in the natural and applied sciences, go to **macmillanhighered.com/smh**. (Photo © Allyson Goldberg)

Goldberg 2

## Introduction

The purpose of this investigation was to experimentally determine the value of the universal gas constant, R. To accomplish this goal, a measured sample of magnesium (Mg) was allowed to react with an excess of hydrochloric acid (HCl) at room temperature and pressure so that the precise amount and volume of the product hydrogen gas ($H_2$) could be determined and the value of R could be calculated using the ideal gas equation, PV=nRT.

*Introduction explains purpose of lab and gives overview of results*

## Materials & Methods

Two samples of room temperature water, one about 250mL and the other about 400mL, were measured into a smaller and larger beaker respectively. 15.0mL of HCl was then transferred into a side arm flask that was connected to the top of a buret (clamped to a ringstand) through a 5/16" diameter flexible tube. (This "gas buret" was connected to an adjacent "open buret," clamped to the other side of the ringstand and left open to the atmosphere of the laboratory at its wide end, by a 1/4" diameter flexible tube. These two burets were adjusted on the ringstand so that they were vertically parallel and close together.) The HCl sample was transferred to the flask such that none came in contact with the inner surface of the neck of the flask. The flask was then allowed to rest, in an almost horizontal position, in the smaller beaker.

*Materials and methods section explains lab setup and procedure*

*Passive voice throughout is typical of writing in natural sciences*

The open buret was adjusted on the ringstand such that its 20mL mark was horizontally aligned with the 35mL mark on the gas buret. Room temperature water was added to the open buret until the water level of the gas buret was at about 34.00mL.

A piece of magnesium ribbon was obtained, weighed on an analytical balance, and placed in the neck of the horizontal side arm flask. Next, a screw cap was used to cap the flask and form an airtight seal. This setup was then allowed to sit for 5 minutes in order to reach thermal equilibrium.

After 5 minutes, the open buret was adjusted so that the menisci on both burets were level with each other; the side arm flask was then tilted

Goldberg 3

vertically to let the magnesium ribbon react with the HCl. After the brisk reaction, the flask was placed into the larger beaker and allowed to sit for another 5 minutes.

Next, the flask was placed back into the smaller beaker, and the open buret was adjusted on the ringstand such that its meniscus was level with that of the gas buret. After the system sat for an additional 30 minutes, the open buret was again adjusted so that the menisci on both burets were level.

This procedure was repeated two more times, with the exception that HCl was not again added to the side arm flask, as it was already present in enough excess for all reactions from the first trial.

Results and calculations show measurements and calculations of final value of R

## Results and Calculations

| Trial # | Lab Temp. (°C) | Lab Pressure (mbar) | Mass of Mg Ribbon Used (g) | Initial Buret Reading (mL) | Final Buret Reading (mL) |
|---|---|---|---|---|---|
| 1 | 24.4 | 1013 | 0.0147 | 32.66 | 19.60 |
| 2 | 24.3 | 1013 | 0.0155 | 33.59 | N/A* |
| 3 | 25.0 | 1013 | 0.0153 | 34.35 | 19.80 |

*See note in Discussion section.

| Trial # | Volume of $H_2$ (L) | Moles of $H_2$ Gas Produced | Lab Temp. (K) | Partial Pressure of $H_2$ (atm) | Value of R (L atm/ mol K) | Mean Value of R (L atm/ mol K) |
|---|---|---|---|---|---|---|
| 1 | 0.01306 | $6.05 \times 10^{-4}$ | 298 | 0.970 | 0.0704 | 0.0728 |
| 2 | N/A | N/A | N/A | N/A | N/A | |
| 3 | 0.01455 | $6.30 \times 10^{-4}$ | 298 | 0.968 | 0.0751 | |

Table 1 Experimental results

(Sample Calculations — see Table 1)

Volume of $H_2$ gas = final buret reading − initial buret reading

Volume of $H_2$ gas = 32.66mL − 19.60mL = 13.06mL = 0.01306 L

▼ ▼ ▼ ▼ ▼ ▼ ▼ ▼ ▼ ▼ ▼ ▼ ▼ ▼ ▼ ▼ ▼ ▼ ▼ ▼ ▼ ▼ ▼ ▼ ▼ ▼ ▼ ▼

## THINKING CRITICALLY ABOUT WRITING FOR THE SCIENCES

### Reading with an eye for writing in the sciences

Identify one or more features of scientific texts, and consider their usefulness. Why, for instance, does an abstract precede the actual article? How do scientific nomenclatures, classification systems, and other features of scientific writing aid the work of scientists? Try to identify the functions that textual elements such as these play in the ongoing work of science. Finally, research the scientific method to see how it is served by the features of scientific writing discussed in this chapter.

### Thinking about your own writing in the sciences

Choose a piece of writing you did for a natural or applied science class—a lab report, a research report, a proposal—and read it carefully. Note the format and headings you used, how you presented visual data, what kinds of evidence you used, and what citation system you used. Compare your piece of writing with a similar piece of writing published in a journal in the field. How well does your writing compare? What differences are most noticeable between your writing and that of the published piece?

# CHAPTER 23

# Writing for Business

I N TODAY'S BUSINESS WORLD, the global economy is now a commonplace concept, and both corporate giants and home-office eBay operations conduct business worldwide. Yet in the midst of these changes, one constant remains: written communication is still essential in identifying and solving the complex problems of today's companies.

> **CONNECT:** How can you best represent yourself on a professional networking site? **2a, 23b**
>
> **CREATE:** Draft a profile that shows off your skills, experience, and education for a prospective employer.
>
> **REFLECT:** Reflect on your draft using the "Thinking about Your Own Business Writing" prompt on p. 330.

## 23a Reading texts for business

In business today, you and your colleagues may have almost unlimited access to information and to people whose expertise can be of use to your projects. Somehow, you will need to negotiate and evaluate a huge stream of information.

General strategies for effective reading (Chapter 7) can help. One such strategy — keeping a clear purpose in mind when you read — is particularly important for work-related reading. Are you reading to solve a problem? to gather and synthesize information? to make a recommendation? Knowing why you are reading will increase your productivity. Time constraints and deadlines will also affect your decisions about what and how to read; the ability to identify important information quickly is a skill you should cultivate as a business reader.

## 23b Writing texts for business

Writing assignments in business classes serve two related functions. While their immediate goal is to help you master the theory and practice of business, these assignments also prepare you for the kinds of writing that you will face in the world of work. For this reason, students in *every* discipline need to know how to write effective business documents such as memos, emails, letters, résumés, and reports.

Business writing tends to use conventional formats and to follow the conventions of standard written English. When you write to employers or prospective employers, stick to more formal communication unless you have a very good reason to do otherwise.

Remember that much or all of the writing you do at work is essentially public and that employers have easy access to email written by employees. (For more about email, see 1f.) As always, it's best to use discretion and caution in all on-the-job communication.

## ☐ Writing a business memo

Memos are a common form of print or electronic correspondence sent within and between organizations. Memos tend to be brief, often dealing with only one subject.

As with any writing, consider the audience for your memo carefully. Make sure to include everyone who might need the information, but be cautious about sharing it too widely, especially when the information in your document may be sensitive.

---

**QUICK HELP**

### Guidelines for writing more effective memos and business email

- Clearly identify the subject.
- Begin with the most important information: depending on the memo's purpose, you may have to provide background information, define the task or problem, or clarify the goal.
- Use your opening paragraph to focus on how the information you convey affects your readers.
- Focus each of your subsequent paragraphs on one idea pertaining to the subject.
- Relate your information concisely and present it from the readers' perspective.
- Emphasize exactly what you want readers to do and when.
- Use attachments for detailed supporting information.
- Adjust your style and tone to fit your audience.
- Attempt to build goodwill in your conclusion.

STUDENT WRITER
Michelle Abbott

STUDENT WRITER
Carina Abernathy

Following is a memo, written by student writers Michelle Abbott and Carina Abernathy, that presents an analysis and recommendation to help an employer make a decision. (Photos © Michelle Abbott and Carina Abernathy)

## Memo

TO:         ROSA DONAHUE, SALES MANAGER

FROM:    MICHELLE ABBOTT & CARINA ABERNATHY

SUBJECT:   TAYLOR NURSERY BID

Opening provides background

As you know, Taylor Nursery has requested bids on a 25,000-pound order of private-label fertilizer. Taylor Nursery is one of the largest distributors of our Fertikil product.

Most important information put in bold

**The total cost for manufacturing 25,000 pounds of the private-label brand for Taylor Nursery is $44,075.** This cost includes direct material, direct labor, and variable manufacturing overhead. Although our current equipment and facilities provide adequate capacity for processing this special order, the job will require overtime labor, which has been factored into our costs.

Options presented

The minimum price that Jenco could bid for this product without losing money is $44,075 (our cost). Applying our standard markup of 40% results in a price of $61,705. You could reasonably establish a price anywhere within that range.

Final recommendation

Taylor Nursery has requested bids from several competitors. One rival, Eclipse Fertilizers, is submitting a bid of $60,000 on this order. Therefore, our recommendation is to slightly underbid Eclipse with a price of $58,000, representing a markup of approximately 32%.

Closing builds goodwill by offering further help

Please let us know if we can be of further assistance in your decision on the bid.

## ☐ Writing a cover letter or letter of inquiry

When you send a business or professional letter, you are writing either as an individual or as a representative of an organization. In either case, and regardless of your purpose, a business letter should follow certain conventions.

A cover letter often accompanies a résumé. The purpose of a cover letter is to demonstrate how the experiences and skills you outline in your résumé have prepared you for a particular job. (A letter of inquiry does similar work, but the writer typically asks more generally about openings or job leads.) Remember to focus, then, on how you can benefit the company, not how the company can help you. A well-written letter can help you stand out from a pile of applications and inquiries, even if you are new to the field and don't yet have impressive qualifications, so craft your words carefully.

If you are posting a cover letter to accompany an online application, you will probably provide your contact information elsewhere, and you may not know the address (or name or title) of the person who will ultimately read the letter. The basic contents, however, will be the same whether you print and mail a letter or post it online.

**QUICK HELP**

### Guidelines for effective business correspondence

- Use a conventional format unless you have a specific reason to do otherwise.
- Whenever possible, write to a specific person (*Dear Mr. Robinson* or *Dear Ms. Otuteye*) rather than to a general *Dear Sir or Madam*.
- Open cordially and be polite—even if you have a complaint.
- Clearly state your reason for writing. Include whatever details will help your reader see your point and respond.
- If appropriate, make clear what you hope your reader will do.
- Express appreciation for your reader's attention.
- Make it easy for your reader to respond by including your contact information. If you are mailing a print letter and expect a reply, include a self-addressed, stamped envelope.

STUDENT WRITER
Nastassia Lopez

The following cover letter was written (for print) by student Nastassia Lopez. (Photo © Nastassia Lopez)

## Cover letter

Contact
information

**Nastassia Rose Lopez**

523 Brown Avenue
Stanford, CA 94305
650-326-5555 / nrl91@mail.com

February 1, 2014

Inside address
with full name,
title, and address

Mr. Price Hicks
Director of Educational Programs and Services
Academy of Arts and Sciences
5220 Lankersheim Blvd.
North Hollywood, CA 91601

Salutation to
specific person

Dear Mr. Hicks:

Opening
provides
information and
lists major goals

I am an enthusiastic student who believes that a Development Internship at the
Academy of Arts and Sciences would greatly benefit both the Academy and me.
A Los Angeles native in my first year at Stanford, I'm a serious student who is a
hard worker. My current goal is to comprehend the full scope of the entertainment industry and to learn the ropes of the craft.

As an experienced writer, I am attracted to the Development Department
because I am curious to learn the process of television production from paper
to screen. In high school, I was enrolled in Advanced Placement Writing, and
I voluntarily took a creative writing class. At Stanford, I received High Honors
for maintaining an excellent grade-point average across all my classes, including
several writing-intensive courses.

Background
information
illustrates skills
and strength of
interest

My passion for writing, producing, directing, and learning is real. If my application is accepted, I will bring my strong work ethic, proficiency, and creativity to
the Academy.

Thank you very much for your time and consideration. My résumé is enclosed,
and I look forward to hearing from you.

Sincerely yours,

Four line spaces
for signature

*Nastassia Rose Lopez*

Nastassia Rose Lopez

# ☐ Writing a résumé

While a cover letter usually emphasizes specific parts of the résumé, telling how your background is suited to a particular job, a résumé summarizes your experience and qualifications and provides support for your letter. An effective résumé is brief, usually one or two pages.

Research shows that employers generally spend less than a minute reading a résumé. Remember that they are interested not in what they can do for you but what you can do for them. They expect a résumé to be formatted neatly, and your aim is to use clear headings and adequate spacing that will make it easy to read.

A well-written résumé with a standard format and typefaces is still, in many cases, the best way to distinguish yourself, but in certain contexts, a creative résumé that includes media links, images, and other nontraditional content may help you succeed. As with any writing situation, consider your context and purpose.

Your résumé may be arranged chronologically (from most to least recent) or functionally (based on skill or expertise). Include the following information:

**Name, address, phone number, email address.** You may also want to include links to a career profile page or personal Web site, and, if the content is professionally appropriate, to social media content such as a Twitter feed.

**Educational background.** Include degrees, diplomas, majors, and special programs or courses that pertain to your field of interest.

**Work experience.** Identify each job — whether a paying job, an internship, or military experience — with dates and names of organizations. Describe your duties by carefully selecting strong action verbs.

**Skills, personal interests, activities, awards, and honors.**

**References.** Most writers simply say that references are available on request.

Some applicants also include images in their résumés (see p. 329). Make choices that seem appropriate for your specific situation.

Increasingly, job seekers are uploading résumés to a company Web site when applying for a position. In such cases, take special care to make sure that you have caught any errors or typos before submitting the form.

**STUDENT WRITER**
Megan N. Lange

The following pages show student Megan N. Lange's résumé in two formats, one in traditional print style and the other in a creative format optimized for digital presentation. Like many recent college graduates, she is considering possible career paths, and having two very different résumés prepared allows her to present herself appropriately to either traditional or more creative potential employers. To do a résumé activity, go to **macmillanhighered.com/smh**. (Photo © Megan N. Lange)

## Standard résumé

Name in boldface and larger type size

**Megan N. Lange**
1234 Kingston Pike • Knoxville, TN 37919
Phone: 865.643.xxxx • Email: mlange1@utk.edu

### Education

Educational background

Exp. May 2014 **The University of Tennessee**, Knoxville. B.A. in Technical Writing
and Business Editing, Classical Studies

May 2009 **Lenoir City High School**

Relevant work experience

### Work Experience

• **The Yankee Candle Company** – Store 433     August 2010 – present
Sales Associate: assists guests in-store, answers phones,
restocks floor, operates cash register

• **Holston Conference of the United Methodist Church**    June 2011 – August 2011
Youth and Young Adult Intern: worked in-office with team,
out-of-office with local youth workers, planned and facilitated
youth retreats and events

• **Megan Lange Photography**     January 2011 – present
Head Photographer: senior portraiture, weddings, maternity

Courses relevant to position being sought

### Relevant Courses

• **Technical Writing 360**     Fall 2011
Focused on proper formatting of different professional
documents, teamwork, creative thinking

• **Technical Writing 460**     Spring 2012
Proofreading and formatting of professional documents,
email etiquette, international communication

### Affiliations/Memberships

Affiliations and experience not listed above

• **Society for Technical Communication**, East Tennessee Chapter    Spring 2012

### Other Experience

• **Great Smoky Mountain Chrysalis Board**     August 2010 – present
• **University of Tennessee Singers**     August 2009 – May 2011
• **Cedar Springs Presbyterian Church Choir**     August 2011 – present

*References available upon request.

*Megan Lange uses this résumé to apply for most jobs. The clean, inviting, businesslike look presents the expected content in expected ways — her name and contact information, educational background, work experience, courses she has taken in the field she hopes to enter, and other information that may help prospective employers know more about the kind of person she is.*

## Creative résumé

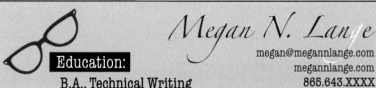

**Megan N. Lange**
megan@megannlange.com
megannlange.com
865.643.XXXX

**Education:**

**B.A., Technical Writing**
University of Tennessee, Knoxville
Exp. graduation: May 2014

**Work Experience:**

**Celeris Networks Consulting Group**    May 2013-Present
Email campaigns, graphic design for website & marketing,
website redesign (in-progress), social media, press releases

**EventBooking.com, LLC**    May 2012-Sept 2013
Email campaigns, maintain social media, client relations,
website redesign/maintenance, press releases, newsletter

**Other Experience:**

**Photographer:** The International Biscuit Festival, May 2013
**Freelance Photographer:** University of Tennessee's **The Daily Beacon**, Fall 2013
**Media/Entertainment:** Sertoma Center's All That Jazz Dinner and Auction, 2011-2012
**Co-Chair/Entertainment:** Sertoma Center's All That Jazz Dinner and Auction, 2012-2013
**Event Chair:** Sertoma Center's All That Jazz Dinner and Auction, 2013-2014
**Fundraising Chair:** Artistic Spectrum, 2013-2014

**Social Media:**

**Skillset:**

Standard HTML Coding
Twitter Bootstrap Website Scaffolding
Adobe Photoshop/Illustrator
WordPress.org site management/basic development
Microsoft Word/Excel/PowerPoint
Photography (DSLR — manual shooting)
Zift.com/Contactology Email Clients

**Things I like:**

*Megan Lange uses this résumé to apply for positions for which her creativity would be an asset. The design is still easy to read, but reveals more of her personality. Icons under "Social Media" are live links to her feeds on various sites. (Source: © Megan N. Lange)*

**macmillanhighered.com/smh**

 23. **Writing for Business** > Student Writing > Résumés (Lange)

 23. **Writing for Business** > Tutorial > Job search and personal branding

▼ ▼ ▼ ▼ ▼ ▼ ▼ ▼ ▼ ▼ ▼ ▼ ▼ ▼ ▼ ▼ ▼ ▼ ▼ ▼ ▼ ▼ ▼ ▼ ▼ ▼ ▼ ▼

## THINKING CRITICALLY ABOUT BUSINESS WRITING

### Reading with an eye for writing in business

Monitor your mail, email, text messages, and targeted ads on social media sites for a few days, saving everything that tries to sell a product, provide a service, or solicit information or money. Then go through these pieces of business writing and advertising, and choose the one you find most effective. What about the writing appeals to you or gets and holds your attention? What might lead you to buy the product, choose the service, or make a contribution? What might make the piece of writing even more effective? Bring the results of your investigation to class for discussion.

### Thinking about your own business writing

Chances are, you have written a cover letter for a job, completed a résumé, or sent some business-related letters or email messages. Choose a piece of business-related writing that is important to you or that represents your best work, and then analyze it carefully. How clear is the writing? How well do you represent yourself in the writing? Do you follow the conventions for business letters, résumés, memos, and so on? Make notes on what you could do to improve this piece of writing.

# CHAPTER 24

# Essay Examinations

**T**HE SKILLS YOU NEED to perform well on a written exam can also serve you in your nonacademic life. Being prepared to present information effectively is always useful, such as when you are asked to submit a personal statement to accompany an application for insurance, an internship, or a loan.

## 24a Preparing for an essay examination

Nothing can take the place of knowing the subject well, so you can start preparing for an essay examination by taking careful notes on lectures and readings. You may want to outline a reading assignment, list its main points, list and define its key terms, or briefly summarize its argument. A particularly effective method is to divide your notes into two categories, labeling the left-hand side *Summaries and Quotations* and the right-hand side *Questions and Comments*. Then, as you read, use the left side to record summaries of major points and noteworthy quotations. On the right, record questions that your reading has not answered, puzzling ideas, and your own comments. This note-taking encourages active, critical reading and, combined with careful class notes, will do much to prepare you. Here are one student's notes:

| Summaries and Quotations | Questions and Comments |
|---|---|
| Rhetoric — "the art of discovering, in any particular case, all available means of persuasion." (Aristotle, on p. 3) | Maybe all language is persuasive, but if I greet people warmly, I don't consciously try to persuade them that I'm glad to see them. I just respond naturally. |
| All language is essentially argumentative — purpose is to persuade | |

In addition to taking careful, detailed notes, you can prepare by writing out essay answers to questions you think are likely to appear on the exam. Practicing ahead of time is much more effective than last-minute cramming. On the day of the exam, do ten to fifteen minutes of writing just before you go into the examination to warm up your thinking muscles.

 **EXERCISE 24.1**

Create a question you think you might be likely to encounter on an essay examination in a class you are currently taking. Then write a paragraph or two about what you would need to know in order to write an exceptional answer.

## ☐ Analyzing essay questions

Before you begin writing, read the question carefully several times, and analyze what it asks you to do. Most essay examination questions contain two kinds of terms, strategy terms that describe your task in writing the essay and content terms that define the scope and limits of the topic.

| STRATEGY | CONTENT |
| --- | --- |
| Analyze | Jesus's Sermon on the Mount. |

| STRATEGY | CONTENT |
| --- | --- |
| Describe | the major effects of Reconstruction. |

| STRATEGY | CONTENT |
| --- | --- |
| Explain | the advantages of investing in government securities. |

Words like *analyze*, *describe*, and *explain* tell what logical strategy to use and often set the form your answer takes. Since not all terms mean the same thing in every discipline, be sure you understand exactly what the term means in context of the material covered on the examination. In general, however, the most commonly used strategy terms have standard meanings. Don't hesitate to ask your instructor to clarify terms you're unsure of.

---

**QUICK HELP**

### Common strategy terms

- **Analyze:** Divide an event, idea, or theory into its component elements, and examine each one in turn.

    Analyze Milton Friedman's theory of permanent income.

- **Compare and/or contrast:** Demonstrate similarities or dissimilarities between two or more events or topics.

    Compare the portrayal of women in *Beloved* with that in *Their Eyes Were Watching God*.

- **Define:** Identify and state the essential traits or characteristics of something, differentiating it clearly from other things.

    Define *osmosis*.

- **Describe:** Tell about an event, person, or process in detail, creating a clear and vivid image of it.

    Describe the dress of a medieval knight. ▶

Common strategy terms, continued

- **Evaluate:** Assess the value or significance of the topic.

  Evaluate the contributions of jazz musicians to American music.

- **Explain:** Make a topic as clear and understandable as possible by offering reasons, examples, and so on.

  Explain the functioning of the circulatory system.

- **Summarize:** State the major points concisely and comprehensively. **(7d)**

  Summarize the major arguments against using animals in laboratory research.

If strategy terms are not explicitly stated in an essay question, you need to infer a strategy from the content terms. For example, a question that mentions two groups working toward the same goal may imply comparison and contrast, and a question referring to events in a given time period may imply summary.

## ☐ Thinking through your answer

You may be tempted to begin writing your essay examination at once. Time is precious — but so are organizing and planning. So spend some time (about 10 percent of the allotted time is a good rule of thumb) thinking through your answer.

Begin by deciding which major points you need to make and in what order to present them. Jot down support for each point. Craft a clear, succinct thesis that satisfies the strategy term of the exam question. In most writing situations, you start from a working thesis, but when writing under pressure you will probably find it more efficient to outline (or simply jot down) your ideas and craft your thesis from your outline. For example, if you were asked to define the three major components of personality according to Freud, you might write a brief informal outline as a framework for your answer.

Id

basic definition — what it is and is not
major characteristics
functions

Ego

basic definition — what it is and is not
major characteristics
functions

Superego

basic definition — what it is and is not
major characteristics
functions

┌─────────────────────────────────────────┐
│ **MULTI-LINGUAL** │ **WRITING NOTES IN YOUR OWN LANGUAGE** │
└─────────────────────────────────────────┘

Before writing an essay answer in English, consider making some notes in whatever language you are most comfortable writing in. Writing down key words and main points in your native language may help you organize your answer more quickly and ensure that you don't leave out something important.

From this outline, you can develop a thesis: *According to Freud, the human personality consists of three major and interconnected elements: the id, the ego, and the superego.*

## 24b  Writing an essay examination response

Your goal in producing an essay examination answer is twofold: to demonstrate that you have mastered the course material and to communicate your ideas and information clearly, directly, and logically.

### ☐ Drafting

During the drafting stage, use your outline to keep yourself on track: if you depart from it, you will lose time and perhaps have trouble returning to the main discussion. As a general rule, develop each of your major points into at least one paragraph. Be sure to make clear the connections among your main points by using transitions. *The last element of the human personality, according to Freud, is the superego.*

Besides referring to your outline for guidance, pause and read what you have written before going on to a new point. Rereading may remind you of other ideas while you still have time to include them and should also help you establish a clear connection with whatever follows. If you are asked to write your essay on paper, write neatly, skip lines, and leave ample margins so that you have space for changes or additions when you revise. If you are writing your essay exam on a computer, use double spacing and paragraph indentations.

### ☐ Revising and editing

Leave enough time (a minimum of five minutes) to read through your essay answer carefully. Consider the following questions:

- Is the thesis clearly stated? Does it answer the question?
- Are all the major points covered?
- Are the major points adequately developed and supported?

- Is each sentence complete?
- Are spelling, punctuation, and syntax as correct as you can make them? Have you checked for missing words?
- Is the handwriting legible? If you are using a computer, take time to run your spell checker.

## 24c Writing take-home exams

You may sometimes be asked to do an essay exam at home. If so, make sure to clarify any guidelines about how much time you should spend working on the exam, how long your answer should be, and how you should submit the exam (for example, through email or to the instructor's campus mailbox).

You probably won't have as much time to write a take-home essay exam as you would a regular academic essay, so set a reasonable time line and stick to it. Be direct in your response, starting right in with your thesis, and use a straightforward beginning-middle-conclusion organizational sequence. Most important, as you plan for your take-home exam, bring in ways to show that you know the subject matter of the course and that you can provide concrete, detailed examples to support the main points you are making. As with any essay exam, look closely at the question itself and make sure that you are responding to the question in appropriate ways.

## 24d A student's essay exam response

A student in a first-year American history course had fifty-five minutes to answer two of three essay questions and three of five short-answer questions. She chose to answer the following question first.

> Between 1870 and 1920, African Americans and women both struggled to establish certain rights. What did each group want? Briefly analyze the strategies each group used, and indicate how successful they were.

This student began her exam with this question because she knew the most about this topic. With another essay and three short answers to write, she decided to devote no more than twenty minutes to this essay.

First, she analyzed what the question asked her to do, noting the strategy terms. She decided that the first sentence of the question strongly implied comparison and contrast of the two struggles. The second sentence asked for an explanation of the goals of each group, and in the third sentence, she took *analyze* and *indicate* to mean "explain what each group did and how well it succeeded." (As it turned out, this was a very shrewd reading of the question; the instructor later remarked that those who had included a comparison and contrast produced better answers than those who did not.) Note that, in this instance, the strategy the instructor expected is not stated explicitly in the question. Instead, class members were expected to read between the lines to infer the strategy.

The student identified content terms around which to develop her answer: the groups — African Americans and women — and their actions, goals, strategies, and degrees of success. Using these terms, she spent about three minutes producing the following informal outline:

Introduction

goals, strategies, degree of success

African Americans

want equality
two opposing strategies: DuBois and Washington
even with vote, great opposition

Women

many goals (economic, political, educational), but focus on vote
use men's arguments against them
use vote to achieve other goals

Conclusion

educational and economic differences between groups

From this outline, the student crafted the following thesis: *In the years between 1870 and 1920, African Americans and women were both fighting for equal rights but in significantly different ways.* She then wrote a brief answer that compared the strategies and successes of each group's struggle.

▼ ▼ ▼ ▼ ▼ ▼ ▼ ▼ ▼ ▼ ▼ ▼ ▼ ▼ ▼ ▼ ▼ ▼ ▼ ▼ ▼ ▼ ▼ ▼ ▼ ▼ ▼

## THINKING CRITICALLY ABOUT ESSAY EXAMINATIONS

Choose an essay exam that you have recently written. Use the guidelines in 24a to analyze what the exam question asked you to do. Then reread your answer carefully. Did you do what the question asked? If not, how should you have responded? Then, referring to 24b, reconstruct how you answered the question. How could you improve the content and presentation of your answer? Note any new strategies that might help you improve your success in taking essay exams.

# CHAPTER 25

# Portfolios

A PORTFOLIO IS A SELECTION OF YOUR WORK — whether for class, for a job, or for some other purpose — that you think shows off your skills to best advantage. Many college writing classes require portfolios from students at the end of the course, but putting together a portfolio can also help you develop real-world skills. Applicants for jobs and internships in many fields can make an impact with a carefully chosen portfolio of work that shows off relevant expertise or training.

> **CONNECT:** What kind of portfolio would help you achieve your current goal? **Chapter 16, 25a**
>
> **CREATE:** Draft an introduction (such as a letter or a video script) for the portfolio you need.
>
> **REFLECT:** Go to **macmillanhighered.com/smh**, and respond to **25. Portfolios > Student Writing > Reflective cover letter (Kung)**.

## 25a Planning a portfolio

Depending on your purpose, audience, and the type of work that you plan to include, you may want to create a traditional paper portfolio in a folder or binder, an electronic portfolio online, or some other specialized kind of portfolio. Your concept of what the portfolio should accomplish will affect the form it takes.

### ☐ Thinking about your purpose

Some possible purposes for a writing portfolio include fulfilling course requirements, showing work to a prospective employer, entering a competition, and keeping a record of your college (or artistic) work. Each of these purposes will lead to different decisions about what to include, how to arrange the material, and whether to make work available online, in print, or in some other format.

## ☐ Considering your audience

Your audience will also affect what materials you include. If, for example, your audience is a writing instructor, you will need to demonstrate what you've learned; if it is a prospective employer, you may need to focus on what you can do. In some cases, the primary audience for a portfolio may be yourself.

## ☐ Organizing your work

Your audience and purpose should guide you in deciding how to organize the material. If you are presenting a portfolio as the final component of a course, your instructor may designate an organizational arrangement. If not, you may decide to arrange the portfolio in chronological order and comment on your progress throughout the course. Other methods of organization include arranging material by theme, by importance, or by some other category that makes sense for your work. If you are creating a digital portfolio, you can include a text in more than one category if it makes sense to do so.

## ☐ Creating an appealing design

Think carefully about how you want your portfolio to look. What impression do you want to give? Choose color, fonts, typefaces, images, and other graphic elements that will enhance the appeal of your portfolio and make the content inviting and accessible. Make sure the design is helpful for your audience, too, with clear navigation such as a table of contents. If you are creating a Web portfolio, you may want to follow a template or model your portfolio on a site that works to show off the kinds of texts you will include. For more on design, see Chapter 16.

## ☐ Selecting contents

How many entries should you include in a portfolio? The answer depends on your purpose. If you are developing a personal portfolio to post online, for example, you may include materials in several categories — essays, audio recordings, photos, presentations, a résumé, or anything else that seems relevant — because those reviewing your portfolio will click on only those items that interest them. If you are developing a portfolio for a writing class, however, you should probably limit yourself to five to seven examples of your writing because readers will look at every item you include. Here are some kinds of texts — which may take either print or digital form — that you might include in a portfolio:

- an academic essay demonstrating your ability to argue a claim
- a personal essay that shows insight and demonstrates your ability to communicate vividly
- a piece of writing that reflects on your learning over the college years
- a brief report for a class or community project

- a writing project showing your ability to analyze and solve a problem
- your favorite piece of writing
- writing based on field research, library research, or both
- a piece of writing for a group, club, or campus publication
- an example of a collaboratively written text, accompanied by a description of how the team worked and what you contributed
- an example of your best writing on an essay examination
- correspondence, such as a letter of inquiry or a job application

You should also include the assignments for your work, whenever applicable. If your portfolio is for a writing course, you may be expected to include examples of your notes and early drafts as well as any responses you got from other readers.

One student who had done spoken-word performances throughout his college years decided to assemble a portfolio of those performances. To do so, he compiled a DVD with video clips that he could distribute when applying for scholarships and for admission to graduate school — and that he could keep as a record of his writing and performing. Given his purpose and potential audiences, he organized the portfolio chronologically and made each piece easily accessible for future use.

### ◢ EXERCISE 25.1

Make a list of the times you have organized some of your work — to apply for a job, to create a record of your writing from middle through high school, or for some other reason. What spurred you on to carry out these tasks? Did you have an audience other than yourself in mind? What criteria did you use in choosing pieces? Bring your list to class to compare with those of other students.

## 25b Completing a portfolio

To complete a portfolio, you will need to prepare a reflective statement, assemble your material, obtain feedback from others, and prepare the final revised copy.

### ☐ Reflecting on your work

You should introduce a portfolio with a written statement that explains and reflects on your work. This statement might be in the form of a memo, cover letter, personal essay, or video, depending on what works best for your portfolio. Think carefully about the overall impression you want the portfolio to create, and make sure that the tone and style of your statement set the stage for the entire portfolio. The statement should include the following:

- **a description of what is in the portfolio:** what was the purpose of each work (or of the portfolio as a whole)?

- **an explanation of your choices:** how did you decide that these pieces represent your best work?
- **a reflection on your strengths and abilities:** What have you learned by completing the work for the portfolio? What problems have you encountered, and how have you solved them?

## ☐ Assembling the portfolio

For a print portfolio, number all pages in consecutive order, and prepare a table of contents. Label and date each piece of writing if you haven't done so previously. Put a cover sheet on top with your name and the date; if the portfolio is for a class, include the course title and number. Assemble everything in a folder.

For a digital portfolio, arrange the works in a way that makes sense to you and that allows your readers to find what they are looking for easily. Add any links that seem necessary to help users move from place to place within the portfolio or at external sites — and check that the links work.

## ☐ Getting responses

Once you have assembled your portfolio, seek responses to it from several classmates or friends and, if possible, from at least one instructor. (You may want to refer your reviewers to the guidelines on reviewing a draft in 4b.) Revise accordingly.

If this portfolio is part of your work in a course, ask your instructor whether a few corrections are acceptable. If you intend to use it as part of a job search, you should make each piece as final, professional, and functional as possible. Either way, the time and effort you spend revising and editing the contents of your portfolio will be time well spent.

## 25c A student's reflective cover letter for a portfolio

STUDENT WRITER
James Kung

Here is the cover letter that James Kung wrote to reflect on the print portfolio he submitted at the conclusion of his first-year writing course. To do an activity on reflective writing, go to **macmillanhighered.com/smh**. (Photo © James Kung)

December 6, 2014

Dear Professor Ashdown:

Addresses audience directly

"Writing is difficult and takes a long time." You have uttered this simple yet powerful statement so many times in our class that it has essentially become our motto. In just ten weeks, my persuasive writing skills have improved dramatically, thanks to many hours spent writing, revising, polishing, and (when I wasn't writing) thinking about my topic. The various drafts, revisions, and other materials in my course portfolio show this improvement.

Reflects on improvement

I entered this first-quarter Writing and Rhetoric class with both strengths and weaknesses. I was strong in the fundamentals of writing: logic and grammar. I have always written fairly well-organized essays. However, despite this strength, I struggled throughout the term to narrow and define the various aspects of my research-based argument.

Analyzes overall strengths and weaknesses

The first aspect of my essay that I had trouble narrowing and defining was my major claim, or my thesis statement. In my first writing assignment for the class, the "Proposal for Research-Based Argument" (1A), I proposed to argue about the case of Wen Ho Lee, the Los Alamos scientist accused of copying restricted government documents, but most of the major claims I made were too broad. I stated, "The Wen Ho Lee incident deals with the persecution of not only one man, but a whole ethnic group." You commented that the statement was a "sweeping claim" that would be "hard to support."

Analyzes first piece included in portfolio

After seeing the weaknesses in my claims, I spent weeks trying to rework them to make them more specific and debatable. I came up with so many claims that I almost lost interest in the Wen Ho Lee trial. Finally, as seen in my "Writer's Notebook 10/16" (5A), I analyzed my argument and decided that I had chosen the Lee case as my topic in the first place because of my belief that the political inactivity of Asian Americans contributed to the case against Wen Ho Lee. Therefore, I decided to focus on this issue in my thesis.

Explains process of revising and strengthening claim

While my new major claim was more debatable than previous claims, it was still problematic because I had established a cause-effect claim, one of the most difficult types of claims to argue. Therefore, I once again revised my claim, stating that the political inactivity did not cause but rather contributed to racial profiling in the Wen Ho Lee case. In 6C, 6D, and the final draft, I tempered the claim to make it more feasible: "Although we can't possibly prove that the political inactivity of Asian Americans was the sole cause of the racial profiling of Wen Ho Lee, we can safely say that it contributed to the whole fiasco."

Explains process of defining audience

I also had trouble defining my audience. I briefly alluded to the fact that my audience was a "typical American reader." However, I later decided to address my paper to an Asian American audience for two reasons. First, it would establish a greater ethos for myself as a Chinese American. Second, it would enable me to target the people the Wen Ho Lee case directly affects: Asian Americans. As a result, in my final research-based argument, I was much more sensitive to the needs and concerns of my audience, and my audience trusted me more.

The actual process of writing the essay was also important. For instance, when I wrote my first informal outline for the "Structure and Appeals" assignment, I had not yet put much of the research-based argument down on

Reflects on how ideas changed with inclusion of research

paper. Although the informal outline made perfect sense on paper, as I began to actually write my research project, I found that many of the ideas that were stressed heavily in the informal outline had little relevance to my thesis and that issues I had not included in the informal outline suddenly seemed important.

I hope to continue to improve my writing of research-based arguments. The topic that I am currently most interested in researching is Eastern medicine—a controversial topic, and one that interests a diverse audience. I

Concludes with future plans

plan to apply for undergraduate research funds to work on this project, and I will be able to use all of the argumentative firepower that I have learned in this class.

Sincerely,
James Kung

## 25d A student's portfolio home page

Jenny Ming composed the following home page for her digital portfolio in her senior year, as she was preparing to look for a job. She wanted to get her work out for others to see, and so she created an eye-catching graphic as background for her name along with a menu of her work on the left side of the page. Her welcome text introduces herself clearly and simply and invites viewers to take a look at her work and to contact her with comments or questions. Note that she includes a link to her résumé at the bottom of the page.

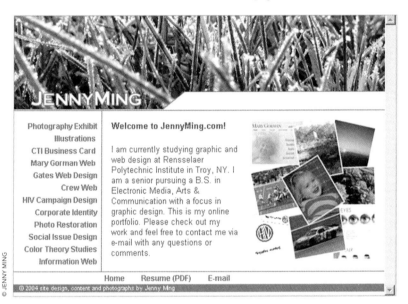

### THINKING CRITICALLY ABOUT PORTFOLIOS

Choose a portfolio cover letter or home page that you have recently created. Ask first how your portfolio introduces your work to readers. How does the cover letter or home page represent your strengths as a communicator? How well do you present the portfolio physically? What could you change, add, or delete to make your portfolio more effective?

# CHAPTER 26

# Writing to Make Something Happen in the World

COLLEGE STUDENTS PARTICIPATING in a research study were asked, "What is good writing?" The researchers expected fairly straightforward answers like "writing that gets its message across," but the students kept coming back to one central idea: good writing "makes something happen in the world." They felt particular pride in the writing they did for family, friends, and community groups — and for many extracurricular activities that were meaningful to them. They produced newsletters for community action groups, nature guides for local parks, and Web sites for local emergency services. Furthermore, once these students graduated from college, they continued to create — and to value — these kinds of public writing. The writing that matters most to many students and citizens, then, is writing that has an effect in the world: writing that gets up off the page or screen, puts on its working boots, and marches out to get something done!

> **CONNECT:** What would you like your writing to do, and how can you reach your audience? **2c–e, 26b**
>
> **CREATE:** Write a draft, sketch a plan, or create a storyboard for a writing project that will help make something good happen in your community.
>
> **REFLECT:** Go to **macmillanhighered.com/smh**, and respond to **26. Writing to Make Something Happen > Student Writing > Fundraising Web page (Dart)**.

## 26a Deciding to make something happen

During your college years or soon after, you are highly likely to create writing that is not just something that you turn in for a grade, but writing that you do because you want to make a difference. You may already have found reasons for communicating with a public audience — perhaps you have invited others to an event, advertised your expertise, reported on a project you were involved in, or advocated for a cause. Often the purpose for doing this kind of writing may seem obvious to you — you have a clear idea of *what* the writing needs to accomplish. Now take the time to consider *how* to get the results that you want. Get feedback from friends and others who may be affected by your plan.

---

**QUICK HELP**

**Characteristics of writing that makes something happen**

- Public writing has a very clear *purpose* (to promote a local cause or event; to inform or explain an issue or problem; to persuade others to act; sometimes even to entertain). **(26a)**
- It is intended for a specific *audience* and addresses those people directly. **(26b)**
- It uses the *genre* most suited to its purpose and audience—a poster to alert people to an upcoming fund drive, a newsletter to inform members of a group, a brochure to describe the activities of a group, a letter to the editor to argue for an issue, a video to promote an upcoming musical performance—and it appears in a *medium* (print, online, or both) where the intended audience will see it. **(26b)**
- It generally uses straightforward, everyday *language*.
- It generally uses *design* to get and hold the audience's attention.

---

## 26b  Connecting with your audience

When you have clarified the actions you want your readers to take in response to your writing, think about the people you most want to reach — audiences today can be as close as your immediate neighbors or as dispersed as global netizens. Who will be interested in the topic you are writing about? For example, if you are trying to encourage your elementary school to plant a garden, you might try to interest parents, teachers, and PTA members; if you are planning a voter registration drive, you might start with eighteen-year-olds.

Once you have a target audience in mind, you'll need to think carefully about where and how you are likely to find them, how you can get their attention, and what you can say to achieve your purpose.

### ☐  Appealing to an audience

What do you know about your audience's interests? Why should they appreciate what you want to communicate? If you want to convince your neighbors to contribute their time, effort, and resources to build a local playground, then you may have a head start: knowing the neighbors and their children, and understanding local concerns about safety, can help you think of effective appeals to get their attention and convince them to join in this project. If you want to create a flash mob to publicize ineffective security at chemical plants near your city, on the other hand, you will need to reach as many people as possible, most of whom you will not know. Finding ways to reach appropriate audiences and convince them to join your project will probably require you to do some research.

### ☐ Choosing genre and media

Even if you know the members of your audience, you still need to think about the genre and media that will be most likely to reach them. To get neighbors involved in the playground project mentioned above, you might decide that a colorful print flyer delivered door to door and posted at neighborhood gathering places would work best, or you may put together a neighborhood Facebook page or email list in order to share information digitally. To gather a flash mob, an easily forwarded message — text, tweet, or email — will probably work best.

### ☐ Using appropriate language

For all public writing, think carefully about the audience you want to reach — as well as *unintended* audiences your message might reach. Doing so can help you craft writing that will be persuasive without being offensive.

### ☐ Considering timing

Making sure your text will appear in a timely manner is crucial to the success of your project. If you want people to plan to attend an event, present your text to them at least two weeks ahead of time. If you are issuing a blog or newsletter, make sure that you create content frequently enough to keep people interested (but not so often that readers can't or won't bother to keep up). If you are reporting information based on something that has already happened, make it available as soon as possible so that your audience won't consider your report "old news."

## 26c   Sample writing that makes something happen in the world

On the following pages are some examples of the forms that public writing can take.

## Fundraising Web page

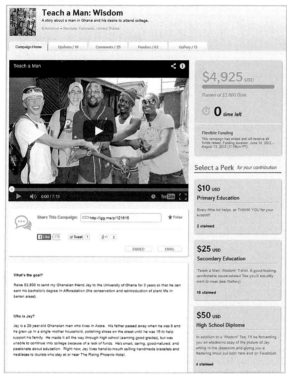

COURTESY JUSTIN B. DART

This fundraising Web page, created by student Justin Dart, has a very clear purpose: to crowd-source the funding to help Jey, a young street vendor in Accra, Ghana, get a college education. Justin, who was studying marketing at the University of Colorado, aimed this fundraising campaign, "Teach a Man: Wisdom," at friends and acquaintances and urged them to share it on social media outlets. Using the Indiegogo template, Justin posted a video spelling out the background and purpose of the Indiegogo fundraiser (you can watch it at **macmillanhighered.com/smh**); a short written description of the project, broken into easily digestible chunks with boldface headings; and a list of perks for donors at various levels. Other tabs offered updates that Justin posted over the course of the fundraising project, comments from donors, photos, and more. Justin and his team ended up raising enough to pay for Jey's university tuition for his college career, housing, and incidentals.

## Advocacy flyer

**El Boletin de Trabajadores Temporales**

Local 715
SEIU

Volume 1: Issue 3

### Servicios educativos para sus hijos:

Necesitan mas ayuda sus niños con la tarea? ó Quieren hacer algo despues de la escuela para divertirse? Informece sobre los varios programas que ofrece Stanford para niños que viven en la area cercana. Hay programas para niños de todos años desde la escuela primaria hasta la preparatoria. Ofrecen apoyo academico como ayuda con la tarea y tambien actividades Los programas son durante y despues de la escuela. Para aprender como puede inscribir sus hijos en uno de estos programas, llame a Leticia Rodriguez en la oficina de SEIU Local 715 al (650) 723-3680.

### OPORTUNIDADES PARA TRABAJOS PERMANENTES

Según el acuerdo en el nuevo contracto de la unión, Stanford va a crear 40 posiciones permanentes en los próximos 4 años. Adicionalmente, trabajadores temporales que han trabajado 20 horas por semana por más de cuatro

### Preocupado por dinero?

Esta endeudado con tarjetas de credito? Quiere saber como obtener su reporte de credito? Nosotros podemos ayudarle a crear un presupuesto mensual, mejorar su puntuacion en su reporte de credito, reducir los interes que paga en tarjetas de credito, y ahorrar dinero. Para citas gratuitas comuniquese con Araceli Rodriguez o Nancy Villareal a la oficina de SEIU, Local 715 al (650) 723-3680.

**CUENTO PERSONAL**

Student Anna Mumford created and posted copies of this flyer advocating for pay raises for campus workers. Her purpose is clear: to raise awareness on her campus of what she views as highly inequitable salaries and working conditions for temporary workers. Her audience in this case is a local one that includes the temporary workers as well as the students, faculty, and administrators on her campus. Anna did not have an easy way to distribute the information electronically to temporary workers, nor was she certain that all of them had access to computers, so she chose to produce a print flyer that would be easy to distribute across campus. She wrote in Spanish (on an English-speaking campus), the home language of most of the temporary workers, to reach her target audience more effectively.

## Pitch package

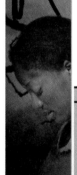

### AMERICA LOVES MUSICALS!!!

With hit shows like *Glee* and *Smash,* musicals are becoming a bigger phenomenon and more popular than ever. Now more gritty and raw, musicals are used to explore many different elements of life. *Strange Fruit* is no exception. Using the most popular musical art form today, hip-hop, *Strange Fruit* bravely goes into uncharted territory through innovative means. *Strange Fruit* is a film that digs up the deep roots of our American past, discovering how slavery affects interracial relationships today. It's a powerful and poignant film, full of music, drama, humor, and passion. It's aimed to be a musical sensation.

### SAMPLE BOX OFFICE GROSS COMPARISONS

| MOVIE | COST | GROSS |
|---|---|---|
| The Help | 25 million | 169 million |
| Dreamgirls | 70 million | 100 million |
| The Color Purple | 15 million | 98 million |
| Chicago | 45 million | 306 million |
| Back to the Future | 19 million | 350 million |
| Precious | 10 million | 47 million |

PHOTOS © DEBORAH JANE AND JAMIE BURKE

Deborah Jane and Jamie Burke collaborated to create this pitch package, to encourage backers to invest in a film based on Deborah's play *Strange Fruit: The Hip-Hopera.* The pitch package includes a synopsis, individual character breakdowns, character relationship dynamics, brief biographies of the production team, and the financial analysis seen here. Deborah and Jamie created the pitch package digitally for easy distribution. To see the entire package, go to **macmillanhighered.com/smh**.

## Newsletter

### Videos are up!
### Joelle on About.com

I spent Memorial Day sequestered in Go Yoga shooting instructional videos for About.com. It was a hot day and my first time on film. (Second time was also this summer in a poet-bike messenger murder mystery set in NY--I play the role of a "senior editor." More about this next month!)

Some of the videos are now live. Take a look. Here's bow pose.

Thank you, Ann Pizer, former student, and current yoga adviser and blogger at About.com, for inviting me to do these videos. Read her blog post about the videos here.

### After Labor Day
### Back to Normal Teaching Schedule

I was fortunate to go on several retreats this summer. Thanks for your patience as I subbed out my classes. I'm now back to my normal schedule.

Curious about where I went?
I was at the Himalayan Institute, learning the magic of Tantra (it's not what you think!)--studies I'll continue over the next year. I was also in upstate New York at an inspired gathering of women called the Goddess Retreat, run by Kula teacher Alison Sinatra. Super heart-filled--and fun! And finally I attended Omega's Being Yoga conference in Rhinebeck, NY, to interview young PhD and yoga dynamo, Kelly McGonigal, who's developing compassion-based protocols sanctioned by the Dalai Lama.

### My Recent Articles & Blog Posts

RECENT ARTICLES & BLOG POSTS:

**YogaCityNYC**
Interview with my teacher Gary Kraftsow Last Labor Day and again this summer, I interviewed Gary about his life as a student, teacher, and trainer of thousands. He was destined to become a great teacher--the stars foretold it--and has pioneered the field of yoga therapy in the US.

Anatomy Studies for Yoga Teachers: Jason R. Brown took the hard road to learn anatomy, but his new program (ASYT) makes the way much easier for the rest of us.

**JOELLE'S YOGA**
**teaching & writing**
**NEWSLETTER**

**TEACHING SCHEDULE**
Sunday, 10am open
Monday, 8:15pm basics

at Go Yoga
N6th at Berry, Williamsburg

Privates available by
appointment or for trade

yoganation gmail com

**INFO**
If you have any questions,
comments, or suggestions
don't hesitate to get in touch.

Namaste!

photos of me by
timknoxphotography.com

© JOELLE HANN

As with the writers of the Web page, flyer, and pitch package, yoga teacher Joelle Hann has a clear purpose in mind for her newsletter: to provide information to her audience — students and others interested in her yoga classes and developments in the yoga community. Emailing the newsletter to her subscribers allows her to reach an interested audience quickly and to provide links to more of the content she's discussing. This format also means she can include photos, illustrations, and color to enhance her document's design impact.

## Online report

### Less Trash, More Compost!
### A report on a community partnership to reduce trash and promote composting and recycling at a summer camp

*Funded in part by the New England Grassroots Environmental Fund*

*...When campers have something in their hand, they are very likely to ask where is the compost, where is the recycling...and that is exciting...*

Counselor, Athol Area YMCA Day Camp

Deb Habib and Kaitlin Doherty
Seeds of Solidarity
November, 2007

**Project Background and Goals**

"Gross, but fun!" exclaims an eight-year old compost enthusiast, one of over 200 campers, plus counselors and staff at the Athol Area YMCA day camp in Orange, Massachusetts who worked together to successfully divert over one ton of their breakfast and lunch waste from the landfill to compost. And they won't mind telling you that they had fun doing it.

Seeds of Solidarity, a non-profit organization based in Orange, partnered with the summer food service director, the Athol Area YMCA, and a local hauler to implement a composting and recycling initiative, diverting the waste from approximately 3,600 meals at two sites over an eight-week period in the summer of 2007. This pilot project was inspired by success using biodegradable and compostable utensils and plates at the annual North Quabbin Garlic and Arts Festival, also sponsored by Seeds of Solidarity, which results in only two bags of trash for 10,000 people.

Athol and Orange are located in the North Quabbin region, where 20% of the children live below the federal poverty line. Food service director Sherry Fiske runs a state and

This excerpt from a report created by Deb Habib and Kaitlin Doherty of the non-profit group Seeds of Solidarity provides information about a successful experimental recycling and composting program at a Massachusetts camp. (Only the first part of the twenty-six-page PDF is shown.) Other sections include "Project Description," "Voices of Campers," "Successes and Challenges," "Summary of Key Considerations," and an appendix with additional documents. The report appears on the organization's Web site, which notes that Seeds of Solidarity "provid[es] people of all ages with the inspiration and practical tools to use renewable energy and grow food in their communities." While the report offers information about an experiment that has already taken place, the document also serves to encourage and inform others who might want to create a similar program.

▼ ▼ ▼ ▼ ▼ ▼ ▼ ▼ ▼ ▼ ▼ ▼ ▼ ▼ ▼ ▼ ▼ ▼ ▼ ▼ ▼ ▼ ▼ ▼ ▼ ▼ ▼ ▼ ▼

## THINKING CRITICALLY ABOUT WRITING THAT MAKES SOMETHING HAPPEN IN THE WORLD

You have probably done quite a bit of writing to make something happen in the world, though you might not have thought of it as official "writing." Yet as this chapter shows, such writing is important to those who do it—and to those affected by it. Think about the groups you belong to—informal or formal, home- or community- or school-based—and choose a piece of writing you have done for the group, whether on your own or with others. Then take a careful look at it: Looking at it with a critical eye, is its purpose clear? What audience does it address, and how well does it connect to that audience? Are the genre (newsletter, poster, flyer, brochure, report, etc.) and the medium (print, electronic) appropriate to achieving the purpose and reaching the audience? How might you revise this text to make it even more effective?

# PART 6
# Effective Language

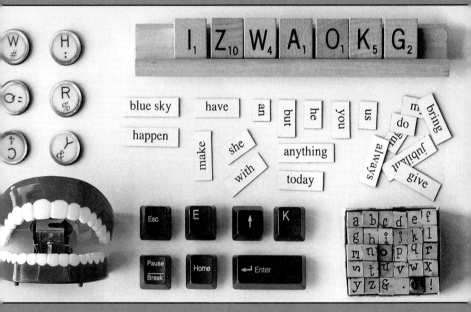

# CHAPTER 27

# Writing to the World

P EOPLE TODAY OFTEN COMMUNICATE instantaneously across vast distances and cultures: students in Ohio take online classes at MIT, and tweets from Tehran find readers in Atlanta. You will almost certainly find yourself writing to (or with) others throughout the country and across the globe, and students in your classes may well come from many countries and cultures. When the whole world can be your potential audience, it's time to step back and think about how to communicate as effectively as possible with a diverse group — how to become a world writer.

> **CONNECT:** How well do you know the audiences for your social media posts? **1a, 2e, 27a**
>
> **CREATE:** Sketch a diagram or write a list of the various communities (defined any way you like) who may view your posts on your favorite social media site.
>
> **REFLECT:** Go to **macmillanhighered.com/smh**, and respond to **27. Writing to the World** > **Video** > **Writing for the real world**.

## 27a Thinking about what seems "normal"

One good place to begin thinking about cross-cultural communication is with a hard look at your own assumptions about others. It's likely that your judgment on what's "normal" is based on assumptions you are not even aware of. But remember: behavior that is considered out of place in one context may appear perfectly normal in another. What's considered "normal" in a Facebook note or text message would be anything but in a request for an internship with a law firm. If you want to communicate with people across cultures, try to learn something about the norms in those cultures and, even more important, be aware of the norms that guide your own behavior.

Remember that most of us tend to see our own way as the "normal" or right way to do things. How do your own values and assumptions guide your thinking and behavior? Keep in mind that if your ways seem inherently right, then — even without thinking about it — you may assume that other ways are somehow less than right.

### Communicating across cultures

- Recognize what you consider "normal." Examine your own customary behaviors and assumptions, and think about how they may affect what you think and say (and write). **(27a)**
- Listen closely to someone from another culture, and ask for clarification if necessary. Carefully define your terms. **(27b)**
- Think about your audience's expectations. **(27c)** How much authority should you have? Should you sound like an expert? a subordinate? something else?
- What kind of evidence will count most with your audience? **(27c)**
- Organize your writing with your audience's expectations in mind. How direct should you be? If in doubt, be formal rather than informal. **(27c)**
- Most ways of communicating are influenced by cultural contexts. Pay close attention to the ways that people from cultures other than your own communicate, and be flexible.
- Don't overgeneralize—respect the differences among individual people within a given culture. Don't assume that all members of a community behave in just the same way or value exactly the same things.
- Remember that your audience may be made up of people from many backgrounds who have very different concepts about what is appropriate. Don't assume that your work will have just one audience!

## 27b  Clarifying meaning

When an instructor called for "originality" in his students' essays, what did he mean? A Filipina student thought *originality* meant going to an original source and explaining it; a student from Massachusetts thought *originality* meant coming up with an idea entirely on her own. The professor, however, expected students to read multiple sources and develop a critical point of their own about those sources. In subsequent classes, this professor defined *originality* as he was using it in his classes, and he gave examples of student work he judged original.

This brief example points to the challenges all writers face in trying to communicate across space, across languages, across cultures. While there are no foolproof rules, here are some tips for communicating with people from cultures other than your own:

- Listen carefully. Don't hesitate to ask people to explain or even repeat a point if you're not absolutely sure you understand.
- Take care to be explicit about the meanings of the words you use.

- Invite response — ask whether you're making yourself clear. This kind of back-and-forth is particularly easy (and necessary) in email.
- Remember that sometimes a picture is worth a thousand words. A visual may help make your meaning absolutely clear.

## 27c Meeting audience expectations

When you do your best to meet an audience's expectations about how a text should work, your writing is more likely to have the desired effect. In practice, figuring out what audiences want, need, or expect can be difficult — especially when you are writing in public spaces online and your audiences can be composed of anyone, anywhere. If you do know something about your readers' expectations, use what you know to present your work effectively. If you know little about your potential audiences, however, err on the side of caution and carefully examine your assumptions about your readers.

### ☐ Meeting expectations about your authority as a writer

In the United States, students are frequently asked to establish authority in their writing — by drawing on certain kinds of personal experience, by reporting on research they or others have conducted, or by taking a position for which they can offer strong evidence and support. But this expectation about writerly authority is by no means universal. Indeed, some cultures view student writers as novices whose job is to reflect what they learn from their teachers — those who hold the most important knowledge, wisdom, and, hence, authority. One Japanese student, for example, said he was taught that it's rude to challenge a teacher: "Are you ever so smart that you should challenge the wisdom of the ages?"

As this student's comment reveals, a writer's tone also depends on his or her relationship with listeners and readers. In this student's case, the valued relationship is one of respect and deference, of what one Indonesian student called "good modesty." As a world writer, you need to remember that those you're addressing may hold a wide range of attitudes about authority.

- Whom are you addressing, and what is your relationship to him or her? (2e)
- What knowledge are you expected to have? Is it appropriate for or expected of you to demonstrate that knowledge — and, if so, how?
- What is your goal — to answer a question? to make a point? to agree? something else? (2b and c)
- What tone is appropriate? If in doubt, show respect: politeness is rarely if ever inappropriate. (4i)
- What level of control do you have over your writing? In a report, you may have the final say. But if you are writing on a wiki, where you share control with others, sensitivity to communal standards is key.

## ☐ Meeting expectations about persuasive evidence

How do you decide what evidence will best support your ideas? The answer depends, in large part, on the audience you want to persuade. American academics generally give great weight to factual evidence.

Differing concepts of what counts as evidence can lead to arguments that go nowhere. Consider, for example, how rare it is for a believer in creationism to be persuaded by what the theory of evolution presents as evidence — or how rare for a supporter of evolutionary theory to be convinced by what creationists present as evidence. A person who regards biblical authority as the supreme evidence in any argument may never see eye to eye with a person who views religion and science as occupying separate spheres, each of which offers its own kind of truth. Think carefully about how you use evidence in writing, and pay attention to what counts as evidence to members of other groups you are trying to persuade.

- Should you rely on facts? concrete examples? firsthand experience? religious or philosophical texts? other sources?

- Should you include the testimony of experts? Which experts are valued most, and why?

- Should you use analogies as support? How much will they count?

- When does evidence from unedited Web sites such as blogs offer credible support, and when should you question or reject it?

- Once you determine what counts as evidence in your own thinking and writing, think about where you learned to use and value this kind of evidence. You can ask these same questions about the use of evidence by members of other cultures.

## ☐ Meeting expectations about organization

As you make choices about how to organize your writing, remember that cultural influences are at work here as well: the patterns that you find pleasing are likely to be ones that are deeply embedded in your own culture. For example, the organizational pattern favored by U.S. engineers, highly explicit and leaving little or nothing unsaid or unexplained, is probably familiar to most U.S. students: introduction and thesis, necessary background, overview of the parts to follow, systematic presentation of evidence, consideration of other viewpoints, and conclusion. If a piece of writing follows this pattern, American readers ordinarily find it "well organized" or "coherent."

In the United States, many audiences (especially those in the academic and business worlds) expect a writer to get to the point as directly as possible and to take on the major responsibility of articulating that point efficiently and unambiguously. But not all audiences have such expectations. For instance, a Chinese student with an excellent command of English found herself struggling in her

American classes. Her writing, U.S. teachers said, was "vague," with too much "beating around the bush." As it turned out, her teachers in China had prized this kind of indirectness, expecting audiences to read between the lines. To be more explicit could send the message that readers aren't capable of such intellectual work.

When writing for audiences who may not share your expectations, then, think about how you can organize material to get your message across effectively. There are no hard and fast rules to help you organize your writing for effectiveness across cultures, but here are a few options to consider:

- Determine when to state your thesis — at the beginning? at the end? somewhere else? not at all?

- Consider whether the addition of tangential topics, what U.S. writers may think of as digressions, is a good idea, a requirement, or best avoided with your intended audience.

- Remember that electronic communication may call for certain ways of organizing. In messages or postings, you need to place the most important information first and be as succinct as possible. Or you may need to follow a template, as in submitting a résumé online.

## ☐ Meeting expectations about style

As with beauty, good style is most definitely in the eye of the beholder — and thus is always affected by language, culture, and rhetorical tradition. In fact, what constitutes effective style varies broadly across cultures and depends on the rhetorical situation — purpose, audience, and so on (see Chapter 2). Even so, there is one important style question to consider when writing across cultures: what level of formality is most appropriate? In most writing to a general audience in the United States, a fairly informal style is often acceptable, even appreciated. Many cultures, however, tend to value a more formal approach. When in doubt, it may be wise to err on the side of formality in writing to people from other cultures, especially to elders or to those in authority.

- Be careful to use proper titles:

  Dr. Faye Spencer Maor          Professor Jaime Mejía

- Be careful in using slang or informal structures such as fragments unless you are doing so for special effect and are certain your audience will understand your purpose.

- Do not use first names of people you do not know in correspondence (even in text messages) unless invited to do so. Note, however, that an invitation to use a first name could come indirectly; if someone signs a message to you with his or her first name, you are implicitly invited to use the first name as a term of address. (See 1f for more on effective digital communication.)

- For formal business correspondence, use complete sentences and words; avoid contractions. Open with the salutation "Dear Mr./Ms." or the person's title, if you know it. Write dates with the day before the month, and spell out the name of the month: *7 June 2014.*

Beyond formality, other stylistic preferences vary widely, and context matters. Long, complex sentences and ornate language may be exactly what some audiences are looking for. On Twitter, on the other hand, writers have to limit their messages to 140 characters — so using abbreviated words, symbols, and fragments is expected, even desirable, there.

World writers, then, should take very little about language for granted. To be an effective world writer, aim to recognize and respect stylistic differences as you move from community to community and to meet expectations whenever you can.

▼ ▼ ▼ ▼ ▼ ▼ ▼ ▼ ▼ ▼ ▼ ▼ ▼ ▼ ▼ ▼ ▼ ▼ ▼ ▼ ▼ ▼ ▼ ▼ ▼ ▼ ▼

## THINKING CRITICALLY ABOUT ASSUMPTIONS IN YOUR WRITING

Choose one or two recent essays or other pieces of writing, and examine them carefully, noting what you assume about what counts as persuasive evidence, good organization, and effective style. How do you represent yourself in relation to your audience? What assumptions do you make about the audience, and are such assumptions warranted? What other unstated assumptions about good writing can you identify?

# CHAPTER 28

# Language That Builds Common Ground

**L**ANGUAGE THAT SHOWS RESPECT for differences and builds common ground can help persuade readers. Few absolute guidelines exist for using such language, but two general rules can help: consider the sensitivities and preferences of others, and watch for words that carry stereotypes and betray your assumptions, even though you have not directly stated them.

---

**CONNECT:** How can you make your work more inclusive for the audiences you want to reach? **28d, p. 267**

**CREATE:** Write or sketch feedback about how well the Web site for an organization you support includes various audiences—and consider submitting your ideas to the site if you see room for improvement.

**REFLECT:** How difficult did you find it to analyze the Web site for inclusiveness? Is thinking this way a habit for you? If not, how can you remain mindful of all kinds of audiences in your own work going forward?

---

## 28a  Avoiding stereotypes and generalizations

Kids like video games; U.S. citizens value individual freedom; people who drop out of high school do not get the best jobs. These broad statements contain stereotypes, standardized or fixed ideas about a group. To some extent, we all think in terms of stereotypes, and sometimes they can be helpful in making a generalization. Stereotyping any individual on the basis of generalizations about a group, however, can lead to inaccurate and even hurtful conclusions.

For example, an instructor who notes a fraternity member's absence from class on the morning after a big frat party and jokes that he must have a hangover is stereotyping the student on the basis of assumptions about fraternity men. But such stereotyping may be far off the mark with this particular student — and with many other fraternity members. By indulging in it, this instructor may well be alienating some of her students and undermining her effectiveness as a teacher.

Because stereotypes are often based on half-truths, misunderstandings, and hand-me-down prejudices, they can lead to intolerance, bias, and bigotry. But even positive stereotypes — for example, *Jewish doctors are the best* — or neutral ones — *college students like pizza* — can hurt, for they inevitably ignore the uniqueness of an individual.

Other kinds of unstated assumptions also destroy common ground by ignoring the differences between others and ourselves. For example, a student in a religion seminar who uses *we* to refer to Christians and *they* to refer to members of other religions had better be sure that everyone in the class is Christian, or some people present may feel left out of the discussion.

Sometimes assumptions even lead writers to call special attention to a group affiliation when it is not relevant to the point, as in a *woman bus driver* or a *white basketball player*. Decisions about whether to generalize about a group or to describe an individual as a member of a group are often difficult for writers. Think about how your language can build — rather than destroy — common ground.

---

**QUICK HELP**

**Editing to build common ground**

- What stereotypes and other assumptions might come between you and your readers? Look, for instance, for language implying approval or disapproval and for the ways you use *we*, *you*, and *they*. (**28a**)
- Avoid potentially sexist language, and omit irrelevant references to gender. Be careful not to assume gender based on occupation, and use gender-neutral nouns when you may be referring to either men or women (*firefighters* instead of *firemen*, for instance). Avoid using a masculine pronoun such as *he* or *him* to refer to a person who may be female. (**28b**)
- Make sure your references to race, religion, gender, sexual orientation, physical ability, age, and so on are relevant or necessary to your discussion. (**28b–d**)
- Are the terms you use to refer to groups accurate and acceptable? Pay attention to the terms that members of the group prefer. (**28c and d**)

---

## 28b Avoiding assumptions about gender

An elementary teacher in Toronto got tired of seeing hands go up every time the children sang the line in Canada's national anthem, "True patriot love in all thy sons command." "When do we get to the part about the daughters?" the children inevitably asked. The children's questions point to the ways in which gender-related words can subtly affect our thinking and behavior. For instance, many young women at one time were discouraged from pursuing careers in medicine at least partially because speakers commonly referred to hypothetical doctors as *he* (and labeled any woman who worked as a doctor a *woman doctor*, as if to say, "She's an exception; doctors are normally men"). Similarly, a label like *male nurse* may offend by reflecting stereotyped assumptions about proper roles for men. Equally problematic is the traditional use of *man* and *mankind* to refer to people of both sexes and the use of *he, him, his,* and *himself* to refer to people of unknown sex. Because such usage ignores half the human race, it hardly helps a writer build common ground.

Sexist language, those words and phrases that stereotype or ignore members of either sex or that unnecessarily call attention to gender, can usually be revised fairly easily. There are several alternatives to using masculine pronouns to refer to persons of unknown sex. (See also 41g.)

One option is to recast the sentence using plural forms.

▶ A ~~lawyer~~ must pass the bar exam before ~~he~~ can begin to practice.
 *Lawyers* *they*

Another option is to substitute *he or she, him or her,* and so on.

▶ A lawyer must pass the bar exam before he *or she* can begin to practice.

Yet another way to revise the sentence is to eliminate the pronouns.

▶ A lawyer must pass the bar exam before ~~he can begin~~ to practice.
 *beginning*

You should also try to eliminate words that make assumptions about gender or emphasize it for no good reason.

| INSTEAD OF | TRY USING |
|---|---|
| anchorman, anchorwoman | anchor |
| businessman | businessperson, business executive |
| chairman, chairwoman | chair, chairperson |
| congressman | member of Congress, representative |
| fireman | firefighter |
| mailman | mail carrier |
| male secretary | secretary |
| man, mankind | humans, human beings, humanity, the human race, humankind |
| manpower | workers, personnel |
| mothering | parenting |
| policeman, policewoman | police officer |
| salesman | salesperson |
| woman engineer | engineer |

◢ **EXERCISE 28.1**

The following excerpt is taken from the 1948 edition of Dr. Benjamin Spock's *Baby and Child Care*. Read it carefully, noting any language we might now consider sexist. Then try bringing it up-to-date by revising the passage, substituting nonsexist language as necessary.

> When you suggest something that doesn't appeal to your baby, he feels he *must* assert himself. His nature tells him to. He just says "no" in words or actions, even about things that he likes to do. The psychologists call it "negativism"; mothers call it "that terrible *no* stage." But stop and think what would happen to him if he never felt like saying "no." He'd become a robot, a mechanical man. You wouldn't be able to resist the temptation to boss him all the time, and he'd stop learning and developing. When he was old enough to go out into the world, to school and later to work, everybody else would take advantage of him, too. He'd never be good for anything.

## 28c Avoiding assumptions about race and ethnicity

Generalizations about racial and ethnic groups can result in especially harmful stereotyping. To build common ground, then, avoid language that ignores differences not only among individual members of a race or ethnic group but also among subgroups. Writers must be aware, for instance, of the diverse places from which Americans of Spanish-speaking ancestry have come.

When writing about an ethnic or racial group, how can you refer to that group in terms that its members actually desire? Doing so is sometimes not an easy task, for terms can change often and vary widely.

The word *colored*, for example, was once widely used in the United States to refer to Americans of African ancestry. By the 1950s, the preferred term had become *Negro*. This changed in the 1960s, however, as *black* came to be preferred by most, though certainly not all, members of that community. Since the late 1980s, both *black* — sometimes capitalized (*Black*) — and *African American* have been widely used.

The word *Oriental*, once used to refer to people of East Asian descent, is now often considered offensive. At the University of California at Berkeley, the Oriental Languages Department is now known as the East Asian Languages Department. One advocate of the change explained that *Oriental* is appropriate for objects — like rugs — but not for people.

Once widely preferred, the term *Native American* is being challenged by those who argue that the most appropriate way to refer to indigenous peoples is by the specific name of the tribe or pueblo, such as *Chippewa* or *Diné*. Many indigenous peoples once referred to as *Eskimos* now prefer *Inuit* or a specific term such as *Tlingit*. It has also become fairly common for tribal groups to refer to themselves as *Indians* or *Indian tribes*.

Among Americans of Spanish-speaking descent, the preferred terms of reference are many: *Chicano/Chicana, Hispanic, Latin American, Latino/Latina, Mexican American, Dominican,* and *Puerto Rican,* to name but a few.

Clearly, then, ethnic terminology changes often enough to challenge the most careful writers — including writers who belong to the groups they are writing about. Consider your words carefully, seek information about ways members of groups refer to themselves (or ask about preferences), but don't expect one person to speak for all members of a group or expect unanimity on such terms. Finally, check any term you are unsure of in a current dictionary. *Random House Webster's College Dictionary* includes particularly helpful usage notes about racial and ethnic designations.

## 28d  Considering other kinds of difference

Gender, race, and ethnicity are among the most frequent challenges to a writer seeking to find common ground with readers, but you will face many others as well.

### Age

Mention age if it is relevant, but be aware that age-related terms can carry derogatory connotations (*matronly, well-preserved,* and so on). Although describing Mr. Fry as *elderly but still active* may sound polite to you, chances are Mr. Fry would prefer being called *an active seventy-eight-year-old* — or just *a seventy-eight-year-old*, which eliminates the unstated assumption of surprise that he is active at his age.

### Class

Take special care to examine your words for assumptions about class. In a *New York Times* column, for example, a young woman wrote about losing her high-paying professional job. Unable to find other "meaningful work," as she put it, she was forced to accept "absurd" jobs like cleaning houses and baby-sitting.

The column provoked a number of angry letters to the *Times,* including this one: "So the young and privileged are learning what we of the working classes have always understood too well: there is no entitlement in life. We have always taken the jobs you label 'absurd.' Our mothers are the women who clean your mothers' houses."

As a writer, then, do not assume that all your readers share your background or values — that your classmates all own or even want to own cars, for instance. And avoid using any words — *redneck, old money,* and the like — that might alienate members of an audience.

## Geography

Geography does not necessarily determine personality, politics, or lifestyle. New Englanders are not all thrifty and tight-lipped; people in "red states" may hold liberal social and political views; midwesterners are not always polite. Check your writing carefully to be sure it doesn't make such simplistic assumptions.

Check also that you use geographic terms accurately:

| | |
|---|---|
| AMERICA, AMERICAN | Although many people use these words to refer to the United States alone, such usage will not necessarily be acceptable to people from Canada, Mexico, and Central or South America. |
| BRITISH, ENGLISH | Use *British* to refer to the island of Great Britain, which includes England, Scotland, and Wales, or to the United Kingdom of Great Britain and Northern Ireland. In general, do not use *English* for these broader senses. |
| ARAB | This term refers only to people of Arabic-speaking descent. Note that Iran is not an Arab nation; its people speak Farsi, not Arabic. Note also that *Arab* is not synonymous with *Muslim* or *Moslem* (a believer in Islam). Most (but not all) Arabs are Muslims, but many Muslims (those in Pakistan, for example) are not Arab. |

## Physical ability or health

When writing about a person with a serious illness or disability, ask yourself whether mentioning the disability is relevant to your discussion and whether the words you use carry negative connotations. You might choose, for example, to say someone *uses* a wheelchair rather than to say he or she is *confined to* one. Similarly, you might note a subtle but meaningful difference between calling someone *a person with AIDS* rather than *an AIDS victim*. Mentioning the person first and the disability second, such as referring to a *child with diabetes* rather than a *diabetic child* or a *diabetic*, is always appropriate. In addition, remember that people with disabilities may well resent the use of euphemisms like "physically challenged" because such terms can minimize the importance of a disability.

## Religion

Religious stereotypes are very often inaccurate and unfair. For example, Roman Catholics hold a wide spectrum of views on abortion, Muslim women do not all wear veils, and many Baptists are not fundamentalists — so beware of making generalizations based on religion. In fact, many people do not believe in or

CONSIDERING DISABILITIES | **KNOWING YOUR READERS**

The American Council on Education reports that nearly 10 percent of all first-year college students — some 155,000 — identify themselves as having one or more disabilities. As this figure suggests, living with a disability is more the norm than many previously thought. And the actual figure may well be higher, since many students with disabilities do not identify themselves as disabled. Effective writers learn as much as possible about their readers so that they can find ways to build common ground.

practice a religion at all, so be careful of such assumptions. As in other cases, do not use religious labels at all unless they are relevant.

### Sexual orientation

If you wish to build common ground, do not assume that readers all share one sexual orientation — that everyone is attracted to the opposite sex, for example. As with any label, reference to sexual orientation should be governed by context. Someone writing about Senator Tammy Baldwin's or Federal Reserve Chair Janet Yellen's economic views would probably have no reason to refer to either person's sexual orientation. On the other hand, someone writing about diversity in U.S. government might find it important to note that Baldwin became the first openly gay person elected to the Senate in 2012.

▼ ▼ ▼ ▼ ▼ ▼ ▼ ▼ ▼ ▼ ▼ ▼ ▼ ▼ ▼ ▼ ▼ ▼ ▼ ▼ ▼ ▼ ▼ ▼ ▼ ▼

## THINKING CRITICALLY ABOUT HOW LANGUAGE CAN BUILD COMMON GROUND

Writer and filmmaker Ruth Ozeki has written widely on issues related to the environment. In this June 2009 posting from her blog, Ozeki appeals to readers to step back and cultivate silence as a necessary prelude to making difficult decisions. Who is the "we" that Ozeki addresses? What views and values do you think she expects her readers to share with her? Note the strategies the writer uses to establish common ground with readers in this paragraph.

> I'm more and more convinced that we need to cultivate mindful silence, and share it with others whenever possible, if we are going to be able to make the careful and difficult choices we will need to make in order to survive in a wired and warming world. This seems to me to be a key piece of activism and eco-pedagogy that we can all learn to cultivate. —RUTH OZEKI, *Ozekiland* (blog)

# CHAPTER 29

# Language Variety

WHEN PULITZER PRIZE–WINNING AUTHOR Junot Díaz spoke to a group of first-year college students in California in 2008, he used colloquial English and Spanish, plus a few four-letter words — and the students loved every minute of it. When he was interviewed a month later on National Public Radio, however, Díaz addressed his nationwide audience in more formal standard English. As a college student, you will be called on to think carefully about how to make appropriate choices. Since standard academic English is still the expected variety of English for most if not all your writing for your classes, you will want to use it effectively. But you may also choose to use another language or another variety of English for rhetorical purpose or special effect. Strong writers recognize these differences and learn to use all their languages and language varieties in the most appropriate and powerful ways.

> **CONNECT:** What varieties of English or other languages should you include in your writing for certain audiences and purposes? **2g, 29a and b**
>
> **CREATE:** Choose something you have written on a social media site, and show how you could include it in a work for an academic course.
>
> **REFLECT:** Go to **macmillanhighered.com/smh**, and respond to **29. Language Variety > Video > Correctness in context**.

## 29a Using varieties of language in academic writing

How do writers decide when to use another language or when to use a particular variety of English — when to insert an eastern Tennessee dialect or African American vernacular patterns into a formal essay, for example? Even writers who are perfectly fluent in several languages must think carefully before switching linguistic gears. The key to shifting effectively among varieties of English and among languages is appropriateness: you need to consider when such shifts will help you connect with your audience, get their attention, make a particular point, or represent the actual words of someone you are writing about.

Sometimes writers' choices are limited by various kinds of pressures. One example is the tendency of many to discriminate against those who fail to use an expected variety of English. Some listeners discriminate against speakers of so-called "nonstandard" varieties of English; in other communities, other audiences distrust speech that they consider "too proper." Used appropriately and wisely, however, all varieties of English are legitimate and effective — and can serve good purposes.

---

**QUICK** | **HELP**

### Using varieties of language effectively

Standard **(29b)** and nonstandard **(29c and d)** varieties of English, as well as other languages **(29e)**, can all be used very effectively for the following purposes in your writing:

- to repeat someone's exact words
- to evoke a particular person, place, or activity
- to establish your credibility
- to build common ground with audiences
- to make a strong point
- to get your audience's attention

---

## 29b Using standard varieties of English

One variety of English, often referred to as "standard" or "standard academic," is taught prescriptively in schools, represented in this and most other textbooks, used in the national media, and written and spoken widely by those wielding the most social and economic power. As the language used in business and most public institutions, standard English is a variety you will want to be completely familiar with — while recognizing that it is only one of many effective and powerful varieties of our language.

Even standard English is hardly a monolith, however; the standard varies according to purpose and audience, from the very formal style used in most academic writing to the informal style characteristic of casual conversation. Thus there is usually more than one "standard" way to say or write something. Nevertheless, recognizable practices and conventions do exist, and they go by the shorthand name of standard English. (For more on academic conventions, see Chapter 1.)

---

## 29c  Using varieties of English to evoke a place or community

"Ever'body says words different," said Ivy. "Arkansas folks says 'em different from Oklahomy folks says 'em different. And we seen a lady from Massachusetts, an' she said 'em differentest of all. Couldn' hardly make out what she was sayin'."
—JOHN STEINBECK, *The Grapes of Wrath*

Using the language of a local community is an effective way to evoke a character or place. Author and radio host Garrison Keillor, for example, peppers his tales of his native Minnesota with the homespun English spoken there: "I once was a tall dark heartbreaker who, when I slouched into a room, women jumped up and asked if they could get me something, and now they only smile and say, 'My mother is a big fan of yours. You sure are a day-brightener for her. You sure make her chuckle.'"

Weaving together regionalisms and standard English can also be effective in creating a sense of place. Here, an anthropologist writing about one Carolina community takes care to let the residents speak their minds — and in their own words:

For Roadville, schooling is something most folks have not gotten enough of, but everybody believes will do something toward helping an individual "get on." In the words of one oldtime resident, "Folks that ain't got no schooling don't get to be nobody nowadays." —SHIRLEY BRICE HEATH, *Ways with Words*

Varieties of language can also help writers evoke other kinds of communities. In this panel from *One! Hundred! Demons!*, Lynda Barry uses playground language to present a vivid image of remembered childhood games. See how kids' use of slang ("Dag") and colloquialisms ("Whose up is it?") helps readers join in the experience.

FROM "TODAY'S DEMON: LOST WORLDS," IN *ONE! HUNDRED! DEMONS!* BY LYNDA BARRY. COPYRIGHT © 2002 BY LYNDA BARRY. PUBLISHED BY SASQUATCH BOOKS AND USED COURTESY OF DARHANSOFF & VERRILL LITERARY AGENTS.

**GLOBAL VARIETIES OF ENGLISH**

Like other world languages, English is used in many countries, so it has many global varieties. For example, British English differs somewhat from U.S. English in certain vocabulary (*bonnet* for *hood of a car*), syntax (*to hospital* rather than *to the hospital*), spelling (*centre* rather than *center*), and pronunciation. If you have learned a non-American variety of English, you will want to recognize, and to appreciate, the ways in which it differs from the variety widely used in U.S. academic settings.

## 29d Using varieties of English to build credibility with a community

Whether you are American Indian or trace your ancestry to Europe, Asia, Latin America, Africa, or elsewhere, your heritage lives on in the diversity of the English language.

See how one Hawaiian writer uses a local variety of English to paint a picture of young teens hearing a "chicken skin" story from their grandmother.

> " — So, rather dan being rid of da shark, da people were stuck with many little ones, for dere mistake."
>
> Then Grandma Wong wen' pause, for dramatic effect, I guess, and she wen' add, "Dis is one of dose times. Dis is da time of da mano." She wen' look at my kid brother 'Analu and said, "Da time of da sharks."
>
> Those words ended another of Grandma's chicken skin stories. The stories she told us had been passed on to her by her grandmother, who had heard them from her grandmother. Always skipping a generation.
>
> —RODNEY MORALES, "When the Shark Bites"

Notice how the narrator of the story uses both standard and nonstandard varieties of English — presenting information necessary to the story line mostly in standard English and using a local, ethnic variety to represent spoken language.

In a similar vein, Zora Neale Hurston's work often effectively mixes African American vernacular with standard English.

> My grandmother worried about my forward ways a great deal. She had known slavery and to her my brazenness was unthinkable.
>
> "Git down offa dat gate-post! You li'l sow, you! Git down! Setting up dere looking dem white folks right in de face! They's gowine to lynch you, yet. And don't stand in dat doorway gazing out at 'em neither. Youse too brazen to live long."
>
> Nevertheless, I kept right on gazing at them, and "going a piece of the way" whenever I could make it.
>
> —ZORA NEALE HURSTON, *Dust Tracks on a Road*

**CHOOSING APPROPRIATE WORDS**

If you are unsure about what words are most appropriate in U.S. English — or if you are unfamiliar with particular regional, occupational, or social varieties — talk with your instructor or ask your classmates for advice.

In each of these examples, one important reason for the shift from standard English is to demonstrate that the writer is a member of the community whose language he or she is representing and thus to build credibility with others in the community.

Take care, however, in using the language of communities other than your own. When used inappropriately, such language can have an opposite effect, perhaps destroying credibility and alienating your audience.

**EXERCISE 29.1**

Identify the purpose and audience for one of this chapter's examples of regional, ethnic, or communal varieties of English. Then rewrite the passage to remove all evidence of any variety of English other than the "standard." Compare your revised version with the original and with those produced by some of your classmates. What differences do you notice in tone (is it more formal? more distant? something else?) and in overall impression? Which version seems most appropriate for the intended audience and purpose? Which do you prefer, and why?

## 29e Using other languages

You might use a language other than English for the same reasons you might use different varieties of English: to represent the actual words of a speaker, to make a point, to connect with your audience, or to get their attention.

See how Gerald Haslam uses Spanish to capture his great-grandmother's words as well as to make a point about his relationship to her.

> "*Expectoran su sangre!*" exclaimed Great-grandma when I showed her the small horned toad I had removed from my breast pocket. I turned toward my mother, who translated: "They spit blood."
>
> "*De los ojos,*" Grandma added. "From their eyes," mother explained, herself uncomfortable in the presence of the small beast.
>
> I grinned, "Awwwwwww."
>
> But my Great-grandmother did not smile. "*Son muy tóxicos,*" she nodded with finality. Mother moved back an involuntary step, her hands suddenly busy at her breast. "Put that thing down," she ordered.
>
> "His name's John," I said. —GERALD HASLAM, *California Childhood*

---

CONSIDERING DISABILITIES | **AMERICAN SIGN LANGUAGE**

One variety of language that is becoming increasingly popular on college campuses is American Sign Language (ASL), a fairly young language that began in this country around 1817. Some colleges now offer ASL courses that satisfy a second language requirement — and also introduce hearing students to Deaf culture.

---

In the following passage, notice how the novelist Michele Herman uses Yiddish to evoke her grandmother's world:

> "Skip *shabes*?" Rivke chuckled. "I don't think this is possible. Once a week comes *shabes*. About this a person doesn't have a choice."
> "What I *mean*" — Myra's impatience was plain — "is skip the preparation. It's too much for you, it tires you out."
> "Ach," Rivke said. "Too much for me it isn't." This wasn't true. For some time she had felt that it really was too much for her. It was only for *shabes* that she cooked; the rest of the week she ate cold cereal, fruit, pot cheese, crackers.
>
> —MICHELE HERMAN, *Missing*

In this passage, Rivke's syntax — the inversion of word order (*Once a week comes* <u>*shabes*</u>, for example, and *Too much for me it isn't*) — reflects Yiddish rhythms. In addition, the use of the Yiddish *shabes* carries a strong association with a religious institution, one that would be lost if it were translated to "sabbath." It is not "sabbath" to Rivke; it is *shabes*.

In the following passage, a linguist uses Spanish, with English translations, in her discussion of literacy in a Mexican community in Chicago:

> *Gracia* (grace, wit) is used to refer to wittiness in talk; people who *tiene gracia* (have grace, are witty) are seen as clever and funny. Not everyone illustrates this quality, but those who do are obvious from the moment they speak. As one middle-aged male said,
> . . . *cuando ellos empiezan a hablar, desde el momento que los oyes hablar, tienen gracia. Entonces, la gente que tiene gracia, se va juntando gente a oírlos. Y hay gente más desabrida, diría yo. No tiene, no le quedan sus chistes. Aunque cuente uno una charrita . . . ya no te vas a reír igual.*
> (. . . when they start to speak, from the moment that you hear them speak, they are witty. So then, the people who are witty begin to have a listening crowd gather about them. And then there are people who are more boring, I would say. They don't have, their jokes just don't make it. Even though they may tell a joke . . . you're not going to laugh in the same manner.)
>
> —MARCIA FARR, "Essayist Literacy and Other Verbal Performances"

Here, Farr provides a translation of the Spanish, for she expects that many of her readers will not know Spanish. She evokes the language of the community she describes, however, by presenting the Spanish first.

In general, you should not assume that all your readers will understand another language. So, in most cases, including a translation (as Marcia Farr does) is appropriate. Occasionally, however, the words from the other language will be clear from the context (as is *shabes* in Michele Herman's passage). At other times, a writer might leave something untranslated to make a point — to let readers know what it's like not to understand, for example.

▼ ▼ ▼ ▼ ▼ ▼ ▼ ▼ ▼ ▼ ▼ ▼ ▼ ▼ ▼ ▼ ▼ ▼ ▼ ▼ ▼ ▼ ▼

## THINKING CRITICALLY ABOUT LANGUAGE VARIETY

The following description of a meal features English that is characteristic of the Florida backwoods in the 1930s. Using this passage as an example, write a description of a memorable event from your daily life. Try to include some informal dialogue. Then look at the language you used—do you use more than one variety of English? What effect does your use of language have on your description?

> Jody heard nothing; saw nothing but his plate. He had never been so hungry in his life, and after a lean winter and a slow spring . . . his mother had cooked a supper good enough for the preacher. There were poke-greens with bits of white bacon buried in them; sandbuggers made of potato and onion and the cooter he had found crawling yesterday; sour orange biscuits and at his mother's elbow the sweet potato pone. He was torn between his desire for more biscuits and another sandbugger and the knowledge, born of painful experience, that if he ate them, he would suddenly have no room for pone. The choice was plain.
> —MARJORIE KINNAN RAWLINGS, *The Yearling*

## CHAPTER 30

# Word Choice

**D**ECIDING WHICH WORD is the right word can be a challenge. English has borrowed and absorbed words from other languages for centuries, so it's not unusual to find many words that have similar but subtly different meanings — and choosing one instead of another can make a very different impression on the audience. For instance, the "pasta with marinara sauce" served in a restaurant may look and taste much like the "macaroni and gravy" served at an Italian American family dinner, but in each case the choice of words says something not only about the food but also about the people serving it — and about the people they expect to serve it to.

---

**CONNECT:** How can you match the words you use with the needs of the rhetorical situation? **2g, 30a**

**CREATE:** Draft a written or video response to Exercise 30.1.

**REFLECT:** Go to **macmillanhighered.com/smh**, and respond to **30. Word Choice > Student Writing > Reflective blog post (Nguyen)**.

---

## 30a Choosing appropriate words for the context

A writer's tone and level of formality vary with context. In an email or letter to a friend or close associate, informal language is often expected and appropriate. But when you are addressing people you do not know well, as in most academic and professional writing, more formal language is likely to have a better effect on your audience. Compare these responses to a request for information about a job candidate:

**EMAIL TO SOMEONE YOU KNOW WELL**
Maisha is great — hire her if you can!

**LETTER OF RECOMMENDATION TO SOMEONE YOU DO NOT KNOW**
I am pleased to recommend Maisha Fisher. She will bring good ideas and extraordinary energy to your organization.

In deciding on the right words to use in a particular piece of writing, a writer needs to be aware of the possibilities and pitfalls of different kinds of language, including slang and colloquial language; technical and occupational language; and pompous language, euphemisms, and doublespeak.

---

**QUICK HELP**

### Editing for appropriate and precise language

- Check to see that your language reflects the appropriate level of formality and courtesy for your audience, purpose, and topic. If you use informal language (such as *yeah*), is it appropriate? **(30a)**
- Unless you are writing for a specialized audience that will understand technical jargon, either define the jargon or replace it with words that will be understood. **(30a)**
- Revise any pompous language, inappropriate euphemisms, or doublespeak. **(30a)**
- Consider the connotations of words carefully. If you say someone is *pushy*, be sure you mean to be critical; otherwise, use a word like *assertive*. **(30b)**
- Be sure to use both general and specific words. If you are writing about the general category of "beds," for example, do you give enough concrete detail (*an antique four-poster bed*)? **(30c)**
- Look for clichés, and replace them with fresher language. **(30d)**

---

### □ Using slang and colloquial language

Slang, or extremely informal language, is often confined to a relatively small group and usually becomes obsolete rather quickly, though some slang gains wide use (*selfie, duh*). Colloquial language, such as *in a bind* or *snooze*, is slightly less informal, more widely used, and longer lasting than most slang.

Writers who use slang and colloquial language in the wrong context run the risk of not being understood or of not being taken seriously. If you are writing for a general audience about gun-control legislation and you use terms like *gat* or *Mac* to refer to weapons, some readers may not know what you mean, and others may be irritated by what they see as a frivolous reference to a serious subject.

**EXERCISE 30.1**

Choose something or someone to describe—a favorite cousin, a stranger on the bus, an automobile, a musical instrument, whatever strikes your fancy. Describe your subject using colloquial language and slang. Then rewrite the description, this time using neither of these. Read the two passages aloud, and note what different effects each version creates.

---

### □ Using technical and occupational language

Those who work—or play—in particular fields sometimes create their own technical language. Businesspeople speak about *vertical integration* and *upside movement,* biologists about *nucleotides* and *immunodestruction,* and baseball fans about *fielder's choices* and *suicide bunts.* If you use any technical or occupation-specific language, make sure that your audience will understand your terms, and replace or define those that they will not. Technical and occupational language can be divided into two overlapping categories: neologisms and jargon.

### Neologisms

Defined as new words that have not yet found their way into dictionaries, neologisms are especially useful in rapidly changing fields, such as business and sciences. Terms like *nanotechnology* (coined in 1974 and popularized in the 1980s) and *vortal* (from "vertical portal"), for example, could not be easily replaced except by much more complex explanations. Some neologisms, however, do not meet a real need and are unlikely to have staying power. Before including a neologism in your writing, then, consider whether your audience will understand and appreciate it.

### Jargon

Jargon is the special vocabulary of a trade or profession, enabling members to speak and write concisely to one another. Reserve jargon for an audience that will understand your terms. The example that follows, from a blog about fonts and typefaces, uses jargon appropriately for an interested and knowledgeable audience.

© FONTSHOP.COM

The Modern typeface classification is usually associated with Didones and display faces that often have too much contrast for text use. The Ingeborg family was designed with the intent of producing a Modern face that was readable at any size. Its roots might well be historic, but its approach is very contemporary. The three text weights (Regular, Bold, and Heavy) are functional and discreet while the Display weights (Fat and Block) catch the reader's eye with a dynamic form and a whole lot of ink on the paper. The family includes a boatload of extras like unicase alternates, swash caps, and a lined fill.

— *FONTSHOP.COM* blog

Depending on the needs of one's audience, jargon can be irritating and incomprehensible — or extremely helpful. Terms that begin as jargon for specialists (such as *asynchronous* or *vertical integration*) can quickly become part of the mainstream if they provide a useful shorthand for an otherwise-lengthy explanation. Before you use technical jargon, remember your readers: if they will not understand the terms, or if you don't know them well enough to judge, then say what you need to say in everyday language.

## ☐ Avoiding pompous language, euphemisms, and doublespeak

Stuffy or pompous language is unnecessarily formal for the purpose, audience, or topic. It gives writing an insincere or unintentionally humorous tone, making a writer's ideas seem insignificant or even unbelievable.

### POMPOUS

Pursuant to the August 9 memorandum regarding petroleum pricing, it is incumbent upon us to endeavor to make maximal utilization of digital and alternate methods of communication in lieu of personal visitation.

### REVISED

As the August 9 memo noted, gas costs are high, so please use email, texting, and phone calls rather than personal visits whenever possible.

As these examples illustrate, some writers use words in an attempt to sound expert or important, and these puffed-up words can easily backfire.

| INSTEAD OF | TRY USING |
|---|---|
| ascertain | find out |
| commence | begin |
| finalize | finish or complete |
| functionality | function |
| impact (as a verb) | affect |
| methodology | method |
| operationalize | start; put into operation |
| optimal | best |
| parameters | boundaries |
| peruse | look at |
| ramp up | increase |
| utilize | use |

Euphemisms are words and phrases that make unpleasant ideas seem less harsh. *Your position is being eliminated* seeks to soften the blow of being fired or laid off. Other euphemisms include *pass on* for *die* and *plus-sized* for *fat*. Although euphemisms can sometimes show that the writer is considerate of people's feelings, such language can also sound insincere or evasive — or can unintentionally insult by implying that the term or idea being avoided is something shameful.

Unlike euphemisms, *doublespeak*, a word coined from the *Newspeak* and *doublethink* of George Orwell's novel *1984*, is language used deliberately to hide or distort the truth. During cutbacks in the business world, companies may speak of layoffs as *employee repositioning* or *proactive downsizing*, and of unpaid time off as a *furlough*. Nevertheless, most people — and particularly those who have lost jobs or taken pay cuts — recognize these terms as doublespeak.

### ◢ EXERCISE 30.2

Revise each of these sentences to use formal language consistently. Example:

> Although   be enthusiastic    as soon as
> **I can ~~get all enthused~~ about writing, ~~but~~ I sit down to write, ~~and~~ my**
>     ^        ^          ^
>              blank.
> **mind goes ~~right to sleep.~~**
>          ^

1. In Shakespeare's *Othello*, Desdemona just lies down like some kind of wimp and accepts her death as inevitable.

2. The budget office doesn't want to cough up the cash to replace the drafty windows, but cranking up the heat in the building all winter doesn't come cheap.

3. Finding all that bling in King Tut's tomb was one of the biggest archeological scores of the twentieth century.

4. In unfamiliar settings or with people he did not know well, Duncan often came off as kind of snooty, but in reality he was scared to death.

5. My family lived in Trinidad for the first ten years of my life, and we went through a lot of bad stuff there, but when we came to the United States, we thought we finally had it made.

---

### ◣ TALKING THE TALK | **TEXTING ABBREVIATIONS**

"Can I use text-message slang when I contact my teacher?" In a chat or text message, abbreviations such as *u* for *you* are conventional usage, but using such shortcuts when communicating with an instructor can be a serious mistake. At least some of your instructors are likely to view these informal shortcuts as disrespectful, unprofessional, or simply sloppy writing. Unless your instructor has invited you to use text-message lingo, keep to the conventions of standard English for your college writing — even in email.

**MULTI-LINGUAL** | **AVOIDING FANCY LANGUAGE**

In writing standard academic English, which is fairly formal, students are often tempted to use many "big words" instead of simple language. Although learning impressive words can be a good way to expand your vocabulary, it is usually best to avoid flowery or fancy language in college writing. Academic writing at U.S. universities tends to value clear, concise prose.

## 30b Using words with appropriate connotations

Thinking of a stone tossed into a pool and ripples spreading out from it can help you understand the distinction between *denotation*, the dictionary meaning of a word (the stone), and *connotation*, the associations that accompany the word (the ripples).

Words with similar denotations may have connotations that vary widely. The words *enthusiasm*, *passion*, and *obsession*, for instance, all have roughly the same dictionary meaning. But the associations called up by each word are quite different: an *enthusiasm* is a pleasurable and absorbing interest; a *passion* has a strong emotional component and may affect someone positively or negatively; an *obsession* is an unhealthy attachment that excludes other interests. *Pushy* and *assertive* also have similar denotations but different connotations — one negative, the other neutral or positive.

Take special care to use words with the appropriate connotations for your intended meaning. Note the differences in connotation among the following three statements:

▶ **The group Students Against Racism erected a temporary barrier on the campus oval. Members say it symbolizes "the many barriers to those discriminated against by university policies."**

▶ **Left-wing agitators planted an eyesore right on the oval to try to stampede the university into giving in to their every demand.**

▶ **Supporters of human rights for all students challenged the university's investment in racism by erecting a protest barrier on campus.**

The first statement is neutral, merely stating facts (and quoting the assertion about university policy to represent it as someone's words rather than as facts); the second, by using words with negative connotations (*agitators*, *eyesore*, *stampede*), is strongly critical; the third, by using words with positive connotations (*supporters of human rights*) and presenting assertions as facts (*the university's investment in racism*), gives a favorable slant to the group's actions. Political parties use words with loaded connotations regularly: during the health care reform debate in 2009–2010, for example, anti-reform groups used the term *death panels* to describe legislation that would reimburse doctors for optional consultations with patients about hospice care, living wills, and similar services.

### ◢ EXERCISE 30.3

From the parentheses, choose the word with the denotation that makes most sense in the context of the sentence. Use a dictionary if necessary.

1. She listened (*apprehensively/attentively*) to the lecture and took notes.
2. The telemarketers were told to (*empathize/emphasize*) more expensive items.
3. The interns were (*conscientious/conscious*) workers who listened carefully and learned fast.
4. Franklin advised his readers to be frugal and (*industrial/industrious*).
5. All (*proceedings/proceeds*) from the bake sale went to the athletics program.

### ◢ EXERCISE 30.4

Study the italicized words in each of the following passages, and decide what each word's connotations contribute to your understanding of the passage. Think of a synonym for each word, and see if you can decide what difference the new word would make on the effect of the passage.

1. If boxing is a sport, it is the most *tragic* of all sports because, more than any human activity, it consumes the very excellence it displays: Its very *drama* is this consumption. —JOYCE CAROL OATES, "On Boxing"
2. Then one evening Miss Glory told me to serve the ladies on the porch. After I set the tray down and turned toward the kitchen, one of the women asked, "What's your name, *girl*?" —MAYA ANGELOU, *I Know Why the Caged Bird Sings*
3. The Kiowas are a summer people; they *abide* the cold and keep to themselves; but when the season *turns* and the land becomes warm and *vital*, they cannot *hold still*. —N. SCOTT MOMADAY, "The Way to Rainy Mountain"

## 30c Balancing general and specific language

Effective writers move their prose along by balancing general words, which name or describe groups or classes of things, with specific words, which refer to individual items. Some general words are abstractions, referring to qualities or ideas, things that the five senses cannot perceive. Specific words are often concrete words, referring to things we can see, hear, touch, taste, or smell. We can seldom draw a clear-cut line between general or abstract words on the one hand

and specific or concrete ones on the other. Instead, most words fall somewhere between these two extremes.

| GENERAL | LESS GENERAL | SPECIFIC | MORE SPECIFIC |
|---|---|---|---|
| book | dictionary | abridged dictionary | *The American Heritage College Dictionary* |

| ABSTRACT | LESS ABSTRACT | CONCRETE | MORE CONCRETE |
|---|---|---|---|
| culture | visual art | painting | van Gogh's *Starry Night* |

Passages that contain too many general terms or abstractions demand that readers supply the specific details with their imaginations, making such writing hard to read. But writing that is full of specifics can also be hard to follow if the main point is lost amid a flood of details. Strong writing usually provides readers both with a general idea or overall picture and with specific examples or concrete details to fill in that picture. In the following passage, the author might have simply made a general statement — *their breakfast was always liberal and good* — or simply described the breakfast. Instead, he is both general and specific.

> There would be a brisk fire crackling in the hearth, the old smoke-gold of morning and the smell of fog, the crisp cheerful voices of the people and their ruddy competent morning look, and the cheerful smells of breakfast, which was always liberal and good, the best meal that they had: kidneys and ham and eggs and sausages and toast and marmalade and tea.
>
> —THOMAS WOLFE, *Of Time and the River*

Here a student writer balances a general statement (*My next-door neighbor is a nuisance*) with specific details:

> My next-door neighbor is a nuisance, poking and prying into my life, constantly watching me as I enter and leave my house, complaining about the noise when I am having a good time, and telling my parents whenever she sees me kissing my date.

### ◢ EXERCISE 30.5

Rewrite each of the following sentences to be more specific and concrete.

1. The entryway of the building was dirty.
2. The sounds at dawn are memorable.
3. Our holiday dinner tasted good.
4. The attendant came toward my car.
5. I woke up.

> **MULTI-LINGUAL** | **MASTERING IDIOMS**
>
> Why do you wear a diamond *on* your finger but *in* your ear? (See 43a.)

# 30d Using figurative language

Figurative language, or figures of speech, can paint pictures in our minds, allowing us to "see" a point readily and clearly. For example, an economist might explain that if you earned one dollar per second, you would need nearly thirty-two years to become a billionaire. When scientists compare certain genetic variants to typographical errors, they too are giving us a picture to help us grasp a difficult concept. Far from being mere decoration, then, figurative language is crucial to understanding.

In important ways, all language is metaphoric, referring to something beyond the word itself for which the word is a symbol. Particularly helpful in building understanding are specific types of figurative language, including similes, metaphors, and analogies.

## ☐ Using similes

Similes use *like, as, as if,* or *as though* to make an explicit comparison between two things.

▶ **Rain slides slowly down the glass, as if the night is crying.**

—PATRICIA CORNWELL

▶ **You can tell the graphic-novels section in a bookstore from afar, by the young bodies sprawled around it like casualties of a localized disaster.**

—PETER SCHJELDAHL

## ☐ Using metaphors

Metaphors are implicit comparisons, omitting the *like, as, as if,* or *as though* of similes.

▶ **The Internet is the new town square.**   —JEB HENSARLING

Often, metaphors are more elaborate.

▶ **Black women are called, in the folklore that so aptly identifies one's status in society, "the mule of the world," because we have been handed the burdens that everyone else — everyone else — refused to carry.**

—ALICE WALKER, *In Search of Our Mothers' Gardens*

## ☐ Using analogies

Analogies compare similar features of two dissimilar things; they explain something unfamiliar by relating it to something familiar. Analogies are often several sentences or paragraphs in length. Here, the writer draws an analogy between corporate pricing strategies and nuclear war:

▶ **One way to establish that peace-preserving threat of mutual assured destruction is to commit yourself beforehand, which helps explain why so many retailers promise to match any competitor's advertised price. Consumers view these guarantees as conducive to lower prices. But in fact offering a price-matching guarantee should make it less likely that competitors will slash prices, since they know that any cuts they make will immediately be matched. It's the retail version of the doomsday machine.**

—JAMES SUROWIECKI

Before you use an analogy, make sure that the two things you are comparing have enough points of similarity to justify the comparison.

## ☐ Avoiding clichés and mixed metaphors

Just as effective figurative language can create the right impression, ineffective figures of speech — such as clichés and mixed metaphors — may wind up boring, irritating, or unintentionally amusing readers.

A cliché is a frequently used expression such as *busy as a bee* or *children are the future*. By definition, we use clichés all the time, especially in speech, and many serve usefully as shorthand for familiar ideas. If you use too many clichés in your writing, however, readers may conclude that what you are saying is not very new or interesting — or true. For example, if you write that a group of schoolgirls looked *pretty as a picture*, this clichéd simile may sound false or insincere. A more original figure of speech, such as *pretty as brand-new red shoes,* might be more effective.

Since people don't always agree on what is a cliché and what is a fresh image, how can you check your writing for clichés? Here is a rule to follow: if you can predict exactly what the upcoming word(s) in a phrase will be, it is probably a cliché.

Mixed metaphors are comparisons that are not consistent. Instead of creating a clear impression, they confuse the reader by pitting one image against another.

▶ **The lectures were brilliant comets streaking through the night sky,** ~~dazzling~~        ~~flashes~~
**~~showering~~ listeners with ~~a torrential rain~~ of insight.**

The images of streaking light and heavy precipitation are inconsistent; in the revised sentence, all of the images relate to light.

## ☐ Using allusions

Allusions are indirect references to cultural works, people, or events. When a sports commentator said, "If the Georgia Tech men have an Achilles heel, it is their inexperience, their youth," he alluded to the Greek myth in which the hero Achilles was fatally wounded in his single vulnerable spot, his heel.

You can draw allusions from history, literature, sacred texts, common wisdom, or current events. Many movies and popular songs are full of allusions. The *Simpsons* episode called "Eternal Moonshine of the Simpson Mind," for example, alludes to the film *Eternal Sunshine of the Spotless Mind*. Remember, however, that allusions work only if your audience recognizes them.

## ☐ Signifying

One distinctive use of figurative language found extensively in African American English is signifying, in which a speaker cleverly needles or insults the listener. In the following passage, two African American men (Grave Digger and Coffin Ed) signify on their white supervisor (Anderson), who ordered them to discover the originators of a riot:

> "I take it you've discovered who started the riot," Anderson said.
> "We knew who he was all along," Grave Digger said.
> "It's just nothing we can do to him," Coffin Ed echoed.
> "Why not, for God's sake?"
> "He's dead," Coffin Ed said.
> "Who?"
> "Lincoln," Grave Digger said.
> "He hadn't ought to have freed us if he didn't want to make provisions to feed us," Coffin Ed said. "Anyone could have told him that."
>
> —CHESTER HIMES, *Hot Day, Hot Night*

Coffin Ed and Grave Digger demonstrate the major characteristics of effective signifying: indirection, ironic humor, fluid rhythm — and a surprising twist, the revelation that Abraham Lincoln caused the riot by ending slavery. This twist leaves the supervisor speechless — and gives Grave Digger and Coffin Ed the last word.

▼ ▼ ▼ ▼ ▼ ▼ ▼ ▼ ▼ ▼ ▼ ▼ ▼ ▼ ▼ ▼ ▼ ▼ ▼ ▼ ▼ ▼ ▼ ▼ ▼

## THINKING CRITICALLY ABOUT WORD CHOICE

### Reflecting on word choice

Read the following brief poem. What dominant feeling or impression does the poem produce in you? Identify the specific words and phrases that help create that impression.

What happens to a dream deferred?

Does it dry up
Like a raisin in the sun?
Or fester like a sore—
And then run?
Does it stink like rotten meat?
Or crust and sugar over—
Like a syrupy sweet?

Maybe it just sags
Like a heavy load.

Or does it explode?

—LANGSTON HUGHES, "Harlem (A Dream Deferred)"

### Thinking about your own word choice

Choose a description you have written. Note any words that carry strong connotations, and identify the concrete and abstract language as well as any use of figurative language. Revise any inappropriate language you find. What do you notice about the words you choose?

# CHAPTER 31

# Dictionaries, Vocabulary, and Spelling

**P**HILOSOPHER **JOHN DEWEY** wrote, "Everyone has experienced how learning an appropriate name for what was dim and vague cleared up and crystallized the whole matter." Such is the power of vocabulary to enrich not only your language but your life as well. Expanding your vocabulary can expand your ability to reach a wide variety of audiences. To communicate effectively, pay careful attention to the meaning, and to the spelling, of the words you use.

> **CONNECT:** How can you choose just the right words when you write? **The Top Twenty, "Wrong Word" (pp. 2–3), 30a and b, 31e**
>
> **CREATE:** Paste some of your informal writing into a new document and spell check the text, accepting all the suggestions it gives you. Share the results with colleagues and classmates. Did the spell check give you any *bad* advice?
>
> **REFLECT:** What advice would you give writers about using spell checkers based on your experience?

## 31a  Finding information in dictionaries

A good dictionary packs a surprising amount of information about words into a relatively small space.

### Dictionary information

Here are the kinds of information dictionaries may give about a word:

- Spelling
- Syllable divisions or *syllabification*, usually indicated by a dot: **let·ter**  ▶

Dictionary information, continued

- Pronunciation, including common alternate pronunciations. Online dictionaries often provide audio links that allow you to hear the pronunciation.
- Parts of speech. Many words can be used as more than one part of speech; for instance, *sign* can be either a noun or a verb.
- Other forms of the word
- Idiomatic uses and phrasal verbs
- Usage notes
- The languages the word comes from, known as *etymology*
- Field labels that indicate how a word is used in a particular discipline or profession
- Synonyms (words with the same or similar meanings)

## ☐ Finding help in usage notes

Usage notes in dictionaries, such as the following note from *Merriam-Webster's Online Dictionary* about the nonstandard word *irregardless*, often provide extensive information about how a particular usage may affect readers:

> *Irregardless* originated in dialectal American speech in the early 20th century. Its fairly widespread use in speech called it to the attention of usage commentators as early as 1927. The most frequently repeated remark about it is that "there is no such word." There is such a word, however. It is still used primarily in speech, although it can be found from time to time in edited prose. Its reputation has not risen over the years, and it is still a long way from general acceptance. Use *regardless* instead.

## ☐ Understanding usage labels

Many dictionaries include usage labels, which let readers know that some or all meanings of a particular word are nonstandard or inappropriate in certain contexts. An explanation of such labels usually occurs at the beginning of the dictionary. Here are some of the labels *Webster's New World Dictionary* uses:

1. **Archaic:** rarely used today except in specialized contexts
2. **Obsolete** or **obs.:** no longer used
3. **Colloquial** or **colloq.:** characteristic of conversation and informal writing
4. **Slang:** extremely informal
5. **Dialect:** used mostly in a particular geographic or linguistic area, often one that is specified, such as Scotland or New England

Many dictionaries also label words that are considered offensive and vulgar.

### EXERCISE 31.1

Look up the spelling, syllable division, and pronunciation of the following words in your dictionary. Note any variants in spelling and pronunciation.

1. heinous
2. exigency
3. schedule
4. greasy
5. macabre
6. mature

### EXERCISE 31.2

Look up the etymology of the following words in your dictionary.

1. rhetoric
2. student
3. tobacco
4. crib
5. cinema
6. okra

## 31b Using different kinds of dictionaries

Abridged, or abbreviated, dictionaries are popular with college writers and are widely available in print and online. Online versions are unbeatable as a quick reference, but print versions may offer more information on usage. Two college dictionaries that offer notably helpful usage notes are *Random House Webster's College Dictionary*, with usage notes and appendices that warn users about offensive or disparaging terms, and *The American Heritage College Dictionary*, which includes extensive notes on usage, including introductory essays in the form of a debate.

Unabridged, or unabbreviated, dictionaries are the most complete and thorough dictionaries of English. Print versions may appear in multiple volumes, and access to online versions often requires a subscription. Libraries offer access to unabridged dictionaries. Two especially important unabridged dictionaries are the *Oxford English Dictionary* and *Webster's Third New International Dictionary of the English Language*. The *OED* offers a full history of each English word: a record of its entry into the language and the development of the word's various meanings, with dated quotations in chronological order. *Webster's Third* aims to describe the way people actually use words today rather than to prescribe standards of correct and incorrect usage.

 **USING THE DICTIONARY TO LEARN IDIOMS**

When you encounter an unfamiliar phrase that seems to involve an idiom, you might find help at the end of a word's dictionary definition, where idioms often are defined. For example, a dictionary entry for the word *point* might define idioms such as *beside the point* and *to the point*. For more help with idioms, see 43a.

**CONSULTING A LEARNER'S DICTIONARY**

In addition to using a good college dictionary, you may want to invest in a dictionary intended especially for learners of English, such as the *Oxford Advanced Learner's Dictionary*. Such dictionaries provide information about count and noncount nouns, idioms and phrasal verbs, grammatical usage, and other topics important to learners of English. Bilingual dictionaries (such as English–Spanish) can be helpful for quick translations of common words but rarely give information about usage or related idioms. Many multilingual writers find it helpful to use multiple dictionaries to get a range of information about a word and its usage.

Sometimes you will need to turn to specialized dictionaries, especially if you are seeking more information on usage, synonyms, or slang. A librarian can help you find an appropriate resource.

## 31c Building your vocabulary

At its largest, your vocabulary includes all the words whose meanings you either recognize or can deduce from context. This group of words, called your *processing vocabulary*, allows you to interpret the meanings of many passages whose words you might not use yourself. Your *producing* or *active vocabulary*, on the other hand, is more limited, made up of words you actually use in writing or speaking.

An important intellectual goal is to consciously strengthen your producing vocabulary — to begin to use in your own speech and writing more of the words that you understand in context. To accomplish this goal, you must become an investigative reporter both of your own language and the language of others.

QUICK HELP

Building your vocabulary

- Keep a list of new words. Each time you come across a new word in a text, try to come up with a definition, and then check the dictionary to see how close you came. Copy the word's definition next to the word on your list.
- Practice naming the opposites of words. If you see *abbreviation*, for example, can you think of *enlargement* or *elaboration*?
- As you read, try to come up with better words than the authors have.
- While reading a work by a writer you admire, identify several words you like but do not yet use. Check the meanings of these words, and then try using them in your speech or writing.

## ☐ Understanding the sources of English

English, like one-third of all languages in the world, descends from Indo-European, a language spoken millennia ago. Scholars began to consider Indo-European a "common source" when they noted striking resemblances among words in a number of languages.

| ENGLISH | LATIN | SPANISH | FRENCH | GREEK | GERMAN | DUTCH | HINDI |
|---------|-------|---------|--------|-------|--------|-------|-------|
| *three* | *tres* | *tres* | *trois* | *treis* | *drei* | *drie* | *teen* |

A version of Indo-European was brought to Britain by the Germanic invasions following 449. This early language, called Anglo-Saxon or Old English, was influenced by Latin and Greek when Christianity was reintroduced into England beginning in 597, shaped by the Viking invasions in the late 700s, and transformed by French after the Norman Conquest (1066).

Although English continued to evolve after the conquest, educated people spoke not English but Latin and French, the languages of the church and court. In the late 1300s, Geoffrey Chaucer, writing *The Canterbury Tales* in the language of the common people, helped establish what is now called Middle English as the legal and literary language of Britain. With the advent of printing in the mid-1400s, that language became more accessible and standardized. By about 1600, it had essentially become the Modern English we use today.

In the past four hundred years, English has continued borrowing from many languages and, as a result, now has one of the world's largest vocabularies. Modern English, then, is a plant growing luxuriously in the soil of multiple language sources.

## ☐ Learning word roots

As its name suggests, a root is a word from which other words grow, usually through the addition of prefixes or suffixes. From the Latin root *-dic-* or *-dict-* ("speak"), for instance, grows a whole range of words in English: *contradict, dictate, dictator, diction, dictionary, predict,* and others. Here are some other Latin (L) and Greek (G) roots and examples of words derived from them.

| ROOT | MEANING | EXAMPLES |
|------|---------|----------|
| -audi- (L) | to hear | audience, audio |
| -bene- (L) | good, well | benevolent, benefit |
| -bio- (G) | life | biography, biosphere |
| -duc(t)- (L) | to lead or to make | ductile, reproduce |
| -gen- (G) | race, kind | genealogy, gene |
| -geo- (G) | earth | geography, geometry |
| -graph- (G) | to write | graphic, photography |

| ROOT | MEANING | EXAMPLES |
|---|---|---|
| -jur-, -jus- (L) | law | justice, jurisdiction |
| -log(o)- (G) | word, thought | biology, logical |
| -luc- (L) | light | lucid, translucent |
| -manu- (L) | hand | manufacture, manual |
| -mit-, -mis- (L) | to send | permit, transmission |
| -path- (G) | feel, suffer | empathy, pathetic |
| -phil- (G) | love | philosopher, bibliophile |
| -photo- (G) | light | photography, telephoto |
| -port- (L) | to carry | transport, portable |
| -psych- (G) | soul | psychology, psychopath |
| -scrib-, -script- (L) | to write | scribble, manuscript |
| -sent-, -sens- (L) | to feel | sensation, resent |
| -tele- (G) | far away | telegraph, telepathy |
| -tend- (L) | to stretch | extend, tendency |
| -terr- (L) | earth | inter, territorial |
| -vac- (L) | empty | vacant, evacuation |
| -vid-, -vis- (L) | to see | video, envision, visit |

## ☐ Recognizing prefixes

Originally individual words, prefixes are groups of letters added to the beginning of words or to roots to create new words. Prefixes modify or extend the meaning of the original word or root. Recognizing common prefixes can help you decipher the meaning of unfamiliar words.

### *Prefixes of negation or opposition*

| PREFIX | MEANING | EXAMPLES |
|---|---|---|
| a-, an- | without, not | amoral, anemia |
| anti- | against | antibody, antiphonal |
| contra- | against | contravene, contradict |
| de- | from, take away from | demerit, declaw |
| dis- | apart, away | disappear, discharge |
| il-, im-, in-, ir- | not | illegal, immature, indistinct, irreverent |
| mal- | wrong | malevolent, malpractice |
| mis- | wrong, bad | misapply, misanthrope |
| non- | not | nonentity, nonsense |
| un- | not | unbreakable, unable |

## Prefixes of quantity

| PREFIX | MEANING | EXAMPLES |
|--------|---------|----------|
| bi- | two | bipolar, bilateral |
| milli- | thousand | millimeter, milligram |
| mono- | one, single | monotone, monologue |
| omni- | all | omniscient, omnipotent |
| semi- | half | semicolon, semiconductor |
| tri- | three | tripod, trimester |
| uni- | one | unitary, univocal |

## Prefixes of time and space

| PREFIX | MEANING | EXAMPLES |
|--------|---------|----------|
| ante- | before | antedate, antebellum |
| circum- | around | circumlocution, circumnavigate |
| co-, col-, com-, con-, cor- | with | coequal, collaborate, commiserate, contact, correspond |
| e-, ex- | out of | emit, extort, expunge |
| hyper- | over, more than | hypersonic, hypersensitive |
| hypo- | under, less than | hypodermic, hypoglycemia |
| inter- | between | intervene, international |
| mega- | enlarge, large | megalomania, megaphone |
| micro- | tiny | micrometer, microscopic |
| neo- | recent | neologism, neophyte |
| post- | after | postwar, postscript |
| pre- | before | previous, prepublication |
| pro- | before, onward | project, propel |
| re- | again, back | review, re-create |
| sub- | under, beneath | subhuman, submarine |
| super- | over, above | supercargo, superimpose |
| syn- | at the same time | synonym, synchronize |
| trans- | across, over | transport, transition |

## □ Recognizing suffixes

Like prefixes, suffixes modify and extend meanings. Suffixes, which are attached to the end of words or roots, often alter the grammatical function or part of speech of the original word — for example, turning the verb *create* into a noun, an adjective, or an adverb.

| VERB | create |
|------|--------|
| NOUNS | creat*or*/creat*ion*/creat*ivity*/creat*ure* |
| ADJECTIVE | creat*ive* |
| ADVERB | creative*ly* |

## Noun suffixes

| SUFFIX | MEANING | EXAMPLES |
|--------|---------|----------|
| -acy | state or quality | democracy, privacy |
| -al | act of | dismissal, refusal |
| -ance, -ence | state or quality of | maintenance, eminence |
| -dom | place or state of being | freedom, kingdom |
| -er, -or | one who | trainer, investor |
| -ism | doctrine or belief characteristic of | liberalism, Taoism |
| -ist | one who | organist, physicist |
| -ity | quality of | veracity, opacity |
| -ment | condition of | payment, argument |
| -ness | state of being | watchfulness, cleanliness |
| -ship | position held | professorship, fellowship |
| -sion, -tion | state of being or action | digression, transition |

## Verb suffixes

| SUFFIX | MEANING | EXAMPLES |
|--------|---------|----------|
| -ate | cause to be | concentrate, regulate |
| -en | cause to be or become | enliven, blacken |
| -ify, -fy | make or cause to be | unify, terrify, amplify |
| -ize | cause to become | magnetize, civilize |

## Adjective suffixes

| SUFFIX | MEANING | EXAMPLES |
|--------|---------|----------|
| -able, -ible | capable of being | readable, edible |
| -al | pertaining to | regional, political |
| -esque | reminiscent of | picturesque, statuesque |
| -ful | having much of a quality | colorful, sorrowful |
| -ic | pertaining to | poetic, mythic |
| -ious, -ous | of or characterized by | famous, nutritious |
| -ish | having the quality of | prudish, clownish |
| -ive | having the nature of | festive, creative, massive |
| -less | without | endless, senseless |

## 31d Understanding vocabulary in context

In addition to using prefixes and suffixes, you can increase your vocabulary by analyzing contexts and reading actively.

If a word is at first unfamiliar to you, look carefully at its context, paying attention to all the clues the context provides; often, you will be able to deduce the meaning. For instance, if the word *accoutrements* is unfamiliar in the sentence *We stopped at a camping-supply store to pick up last-minute accoutrements*, the context — *a camping-supply store* and *last-minute* — suggests strongly that *equipment* or some similar word fits the bill. And that is what *accoutrements* means.

When you are studying a new field, you may encounter words that are completely unfamiliar to you or that have a different meaning in the field than they have in everyday use. You may want to keep a log of new vocabulary in your chosen field. (See also 19d and 30a.)

### EXERCISE 31.3

Identify the contextual clues that help you understand any unfamiliar words in the following sentences. Then write paraphrases of three of the sentences.

1. Before Prohibition, the criminal fringe in the United States had been a self-effacing, scattered class with little popular support.

2. The judge failed to recuse himself from the trial, even though he had a vested interest in the case's outcome.

3. The clownfish lives symbiotically among sea anemones: it is protected from predators by the anemones' poisonous tentacles, and it defends its territory by fighting off anemone-eaters.

4. Some have made the mistake of assuming that the new casinos will be a panacea for the state's financial problems.

5. Health officials warned the population of an extremely virulent strain of flu next season and urged those with compromised immune systems to be vaccinated.

## 31e Checking spelling

Words work best for you, of course, when they are spelled correctly.

### ☐ Using spell checkers

Research conducted for this textbook shows that spelling errors have changed dramatically in the past twenty-five years — and the reason is spell checkers. Although these programs have weeded out many once-common misspellings, spell checkers are not foolproof.

**Common errors with spell checkers**

Spell checkers still allow typical kinds of errors that you should look out for.

- **Homonyms.** Spell checkers cannot differentiate among words such as *affect* and *effect* that sound alike but are spelled differently (see p. 397 for a list of confusing homonyms). Proofread especially carefully for these words.
- **Proper nouns.** You can add names and other proper nouns to your spell checker's dictionary so that the spell checker will not flag these words as incorrect, but first be certain you have spelled the names correctly.
- **Compound words written as two words.** Spell checkers will not identify a problem, for example, when *nowhere* is incorrectly written as *no where*. When in doubt, check a dictionary.
- **Typos.** The spell checker will not flag *heat*, even if you meant to type *heart*. Careful proofreading is still essential.

## ◻ Adapting spell checkers to your needs

To make spell checkers work best for you, you need to learn to adapt them to your own needs.

- Always proofread carefully, even after you have used the spell checker. The more important the message or document, the more careful you should be about its accuracy and clarity.

- Use a dictionary to look up any word the spell checker highlights that you are not absolutely sure of.

- If your spell checker's dictionary allows you to add new words, enter any proper names, non-English words, or specialized language that you use

---

TALKING THE TALK | **SPELL CHECKERS AND WRONG-WORD ERRORS**

"Can I trust spell checkers to give me the correct alternative for a word that I have spelled wrong?" In a word, no. The spell checker may suggest bizarre substitutes for many proper names and specialized terms (even when you spell them correctly) and for certain typographical errors, thus introducing wrong words into your paper if you accept its suggestions automatically. For example, a student who had typed *fantic* instead of *frantic* found that the spell checker's first choice was to substitute *fanatic* — a replacement word that made no sense. Wrong-word errors are the most common surface error in college writing today (see pp. 2–3), and spell checkers are partly to blame. So be careful not to take a spell checker's recommendation without paying careful attention to the replacement word.

regularly and have trouble spelling. Be careful to enter the correct spelling!

- If you know that you mix up certain homonyms, such as *there* and *their*, check for them after running your spell checker.
- Remember that spell checkers are not usually sensitive to capitalization. If you write "the united states," the spell checker won't question it.
- Do *not* automatically accept the spell checker's suggestions: doing so can lead you to choose a word you really don't want.

### EXERCISE 31.4

The following paragraph has been checked with a spell checker. Proofread carefully and correct any errors that the spell checker missed.

I see that you have send me a warning about a computer virus that can destroy my hard drive, mangle my soft ware, and generally reek havoc on my computer. How ever, you may not be aware oft he fact that warnings like this one are almost never real. When a message axes you to foreword it to every one in you're address book, you should know immediately that its a hoax. User who send false warnings about viruses to hundreds of there friends are not doing any one a favor; instead, they are simple slowing down traffic on line and creating problems that maybe worst then any technical difficulties cause by the virus — if the virus even exist. Please insure that warnings contain a grain of true before you past them on. If your worried that my computer might be in danger, set you mind at easy. I will except responsibility if the machine goes hay wire.

### ☐ Learning homonyms

English has many homonyms — words that sound alike but have different spellings and meanings. But a relatively small number of them, just eight groups, cause student writers frequent trouble (see the Quick Help box on p. 397). If you tend to confuse any of these words, create a special memory device to help you remember the differences: "the *weather* will determine *whether* I wear a jacket."

In addition, pay close attention to homonyms that may be spelled as one word or as two, depending on the meaning.

- **Of course, they did not wear *everyday* clothes *every day* of the year.**
- **Though we were *all ready* to dance, our dates had *already* departed.**
- **Sonya *may be* on time for the meeting, or *maybe* she'll be late.**

Other homonyms and frequently confused words can be found in the Glossary of Usage at the back of this book (see p. 751).

## The most troublesome homonyms

accept (to take or receive)

except (to leave out)

affect (an emotion; to have an influence)

effect (a result; to cause to happen)

its (possessive form of *it*)

it's (contraction of *it is* or *it has*)

their (possessive form of *they*)

there (in that place)

they're (contraction of *they are*)

to (in the direction of)

too (in addition; excessive)

two (number between *one* and *three*)

weather (climatic conditions)

whether (if)

who's (contraction of *who is* or *who has*)

whose (possessive form of *who*)

your (possessive form of *you*)

you're (contraction of *you are*)

---

### ◢ EXERCISE 31.5

Choose the appropriate word in parentheses to fill each blank.

If _____ (*your/you're*) looking for summer fun, _____ (*accept/except*) the friendly _____ (*advice/advise*) of thousands of happy adventurers: spend three _____ (*weaks/weeks*) kayaking _____ (*thorough/threw/through*) the inside passage _____ (*to/too/two*) Alaska. For ten years, Outings, Inc., has _____ (*lead/led*) groups of novice kayakers _____ (*passed/past*) some of the most breathtaking scenery in North America. The group's goal is simple: to give participants the time of _____ (*their/there/they're*) lives and show them things they don't see _____ (*every day/everyday*). As one of last year's adventurers said, "_____ (*Its/It's*) a trip that is _____ (*already/all ready*) one of my favorite memories. It _____ (*affected/effected*) me powerfully."

---

## ☐ Considering spelling and pronunciation

Pronunciation often leads spellers astray. Not only do people who live in different regions pronounce words differently, but speakers also tend to blur letters or syllables. To link spelling and pronunciation, try to pronounce words mentally the way they look, including every letter and syllable (so that, for example, you hear the *b* at the end of *crumb*). Doing so will help you "see" words with unpronounced letters or syllables, such as those listed here. The frequently unpronounced letters or syllables are italicized and underlined.

| | | |
|---|---|---|
| can*d*idate | drastica*l*ly | foreig*n* |
| condem*n* | enviro*n*ment | gover*n*ment |
| diff*e*rent | Feb*r*uary | int*e*rest |

| | | |
|---|---|---|
| lib<u>r</u>ary | prob<u>a</u>bly | sep<u>a</u>rate (adjective) |
| mar<u>r</u>iage | quan<u>t</u>ity | su<u>r</u>prise |
| mus<u>c</u>le | rest<u>au</u>rant | We<u>d</u>nesday |

In English words, *a*, *i*, and *e* often sound alike in syllables that are not stressed. Hearing the word *definite*, for instance, gives us few clues as to whether the vowels in the second and third syllables should be *i*'s or *a*'s. In this case, remembering the related word *finite* helps us know that the *i*'s are correct. If you are puzzled about how to spell a word with unstressed vowels, try to think of a related word, and then check your dictionary. You can also use memory cues, or mnemonic devices, to master words that tend to trip you up. Here are two memory cues one student made up:

| WORD | MISSPELLING | CUE |
|---|---|---|
| government | goverment | Government should serve those it *governs*. |
| separate | seperate | *Separate* rates two *a*'s. |

# 31f  Following spelling rules

Some general spelling rules can be of enormous help to writers.

### i *before* e

Here is a slightly expanded version of the "*i* before *e*" rule:

> *i* before *e* except after *c* or when pronounced "ay" as in *neighbor* and *weigh*, or in *weird* exceptions like *either* and *species*

| | |
|---|---|
| *I* BEFORE *E* | ach<u>ie</u>ve, br<u>ie</u>f, f<u>ie</u>ld, fr<u>ie</u>nd |
| EXCEPT AFTER *C* | c<u>ei</u>ling, conc<u>ei</u>vable, dec<u>ei</u>t, rec<u>ei</u>ve |
| OR WHEN PRONOUNCED "AY" | <u>ei</u>ghth, n<u>ei</u>ghbor, r<u>ei</u>gn, w<u>ei</u>gh |
| OR IN WEIRD EXCEPTIONS | anc<u>ie</u>nt, for<u>ei</u>gn, h<u>ei</u>ght, l<u>ei</u>sure, n<u>ei</u>ther, s<u>ei</u>ze |

 **AMERICAN SPELLINGS**

You have likely noticed that different varieties of English often use different spelling conventions. If you have learned a British form of English, for example, you will want to be aware of some of the more common spelling differences in American English. For example, words ending in *-yse* or *-ise* in British English (*analyse*, *criticise*) usually end in *-yze* or *-ize* in American English (*analyze*, *criticize*); words ending in *-our* in British English (*colour*, *labour*) usually end in *-or* in American English (*color*, *labor*); and words ending in *-re* in British English (*theatre*, *centre*) usually end in *-er* in American English (*theater*, *center*).

---

CONSIDERING DISABILITIES | **SPELLING**

---

While some English spellings are hard for anyone to learn, spelling is especially difficult for those who have trouble processing letters and/or sounds in sequence. If spelling seems to be particularly difficult or nearly impossible for you, some technologies can help, including "talking pens" that read words aloud when they're scanned or voice-recognition computer programs that take and transcribe dictated text.

### Prefixes

A prefix, added to the beginning of a word (31c), does not change the spelling of the word it is added to, even when the last letter of the prefix and the first letter of the word are the same (*service, disservice; rate, overrate*). Some prefixes require the use of hyphens (see 63b).

### Suffixes

A suffix, added to the end of a word (31c), may change the spelling of the word it is added to. Pay attention to spell checker recommendations, and consult a dictionary if you are uncertain of the right spelling when you add a suffix.

- **Words ending in a silent -e.** In general, drop the final silent *e* on a word when you add a suffix that starts with a vowel (*exercise, exercising*). Keep the final silent *e* if the suffix starts with a consonant (*force, forceful*).

- **Words ending in -y.** In general, when you add a suffix to words ending in *y*, change the *y* to *i* if the *y* is preceded by a consonant (*try, tried*). Keep the *y* if it is preceded by a vowel (*employ, employed*).

### Plurals

For most words, simply add -*s* to form a plural. For singular nouns ending in *s, ch, sh, x,* or *z,* add -*es* (*church, churches; fox, foxes*).

- **Words ending in o.** In general, add -*es* if the *o* is preceded by a consonant (*potato, potatoes*). Add -*s* if the *o* is preceded by a vowel (*radio, radios*).

- **Words ending in y.** Change *y* to *i* and add -*es* if the *y* is preceded by a consonant (*theory, theories*).

▼ ▼ ▼ ▼ ▼ ▼ ▼ ▼ ▼ ▼ ▼ ▼ ▼ ▼ ▼ ▼ ▼ ▼ ▼ ▼ ▼ ▼ ▼

## THINKING CRITICALLY ABOUT DICTIONARIES, VOCABULARY, AND SPELLING

### Reading with an eye for vocabulary

In his autobiography, Malcolm X says that he taught himself to write by reading and copying the dictionary. You can teach yourself to be a better writer by paying careful attention to the way other writers use words. Choose a writer whose work you admire, and read that author's work for at least thirty minutes, noting six or seven words that you would not ordinarily have thought to use. Do a little dictionary investigative work on these words, and bring your results to class for discussion.

## Thinking about your own vocabulary and spelling

Read over a piece of your recent writing. Underline any words you think could be improved on, and come up with several possible substitutes. Then look for any words whose meanings are not absolutely clear to you, and check them in your dictionary. Have you used any of them incorrectly for your context? Finally, double-check spelling throughout. What do you notice about the words you use?

# PART 7
# Documenting Sources

# CHAPTER 32

# MLA Style

F OR INFORMAL ONLINE WRITING, you might follow conventions for citation simply by linking to source material. But in most formal academic writing, you'll be expected to follow a more rigorous system for citing the information you use. Many writers in the humanities follow Modern Language Association (MLA) style to format manuscripts and document various kinds of sources. For more on MLA style, consult the *MLA Handbook for Writers of Research Papers,* Seventh Edition, 2009.

## 32a  Understanding the basics of MLA style

Why does academic work call for very careful citation practices when writing for the general public may not? The answer is that readers of your academic work expect source citations for several reasons:

- Source citations demonstrate that you've done your homework on your topic and that you are a part of the conversation surrounding it. Careful citation shows your readers what you know, where you stand, and what you think is important.

- Source citations show your readers that you understand the need to give credit when you make use of someone else's intellectual property. Especially in academic writing, when it's better to be safe than sorry, include a citation for any source you think you might need to cite. (See 14b.)

- Source citations give explicit directions to guide readers who want to look for themselves at the works you're using.

The guidelines for MLA style help you with this last purpose, giving you instructions on exactly what information to include in your citation and how to format that information.

### ☐ Types of sources

Look at the Directory to MLA Style on pp. 412–14 for guidelines on citing various types of sources, including print books, articles in print periodicals (journals, magazines, and newspapers), digital written-word sources, and other sources (films, artwork) that consist mainly of material other than written words. A digital version of a source may include updates or corrections that the print version of the same work lacks, so MLA guidelines ask you to indicate the medium and to cite print and digital sources differently. If you can't find a model exactly like the source you've selected, see the Quick Help box on p. 412.

### Web and database sources

MLA asks you to distinguish between Web sources and database sources. Individual researchers almost always gain access to articles in databases through the computer system of a school or public library that pays to subscribe. The easiest way to tell whether a source comes from a database, then, is that its information is *not* generally available to anyone with an Internet connection. Many databases are digital collections of articles that originally appeared in edited print periodicals, ensuring that an authority has vouched for the accuracy of the information. Such sources may have more credibility than free material available on the Web.

### Sources for content beyond the written word

Figuring out which model to follow for media sources online can pose questions. Is a video interview posted on YouTube most like a work from a Web site? an online video? an interview? Talk with your instructor about any complicated sources, and remember that your ultimate goal is to make the source as accessible as possible to your readers.

## ☐ Parts of citations

MLA citations appear in two parts—a brief in-text citation in parentheses in the body of your written text, and a full citation in the list of works cited, to which the in-text citation directs readers. A basic in-text citation includes the author's name and the page number (for a print source), but many variations on this format are discussed in 32c.

In the text of his research project — see 32e and the integrated media at **macmillanhighered.com/smh** — David Craig quotes material from a print book and from an online report. He cites both parenthetically, pointing readers to entries on his list of works cited, as shown in the figure on p. 404.

## ☐ Explanatory notes

MLA citation style asks you to include explanatory notes for information that doesn't readily fit into your text but is needed for clarification or further explanation. In addition, MLA permits bibliographic notes to give information about or evaluate a source, or to list multiple sources that relate to a single point. Use superscript numbers in the text to refer readers to the notes, which may appear

reason. According to David Crystal, an internationally recognized scholar of linguistics at the University of Wales, as young children develop and learn how words string together to express ideas, they go through many phases of language play. The singsong rhymes and nonsensical chants of preschoolers are vital to their learning language, and a healthy appetite for such wordplay leads to a better command of language later in life (182).

Craig 9

*nd in SAT Scores*
*Indicates Increased Emphasis on Math Is Yielding Results: Reading and Writing Are Causes for Concern.* New York: College Board, 2002. Print.

College Board. "2011 SAT Trends." *Collegeboard.org.* College Board, 1 Sept. 2011. Web. 6 Dec. 2014.

Crystal, David. *Language Play.* Chicago: U of Chicago P, 1998. Print.

*The Discouraging Word.* "Re: Messaging and Literacy." Message to the author. 13 Nov. 2014. E-mail.

Ferguson, Niall. "Texting Makes U Stupid." *Newsweek* 158.12 (2011): 11. *Academic Search Premier.* Web. 7 Dec. 2014.

Leibowitz, Wendy R. "Technology Transforms Writing and the Teaching of Writing." *Chronicle of Higher Education* 26 Nov. 1999: A67-68. Print.

Lenhart, Amanda. *Teens, Smartphones, & Texting.* Pew Research Center, 19 Mar. 2012. PDF file.

Lenhart, Amanda, Sousan Arafeh, Aaron Smith, and Alexandra Macgill. *Writing, Technology & Teens.* Pew Research Center, 24 Apr. 2008. Web. 6 Dec. 2014.

Lenhart, Amanda, and Oliver Lewis. *Teenage Life Online: The Rise of the Instant-Message Generation and the Internet's Impact on Friendships and Family Relationships.* Pew Research Center, 21 June 2001. Web. 6 Dec. 2014.

of those aged 12-17 at least occasionally write text messages, instant messages, or comments on social networking sites (Lenhart, Arafeh, Smith, and Macgill). In 2001, the most conservative estimate based on Pew numbers showed that American youths spent, at a minimum, nearly

*essaging Skills Can*
Mar. 2005. Web.

as endnotes (under the heading *Notes* on a separate page immediately before the list of works cited) or as footnotes at the bottom of each page where a super-script number appears.

### EXAMPLE OF SUPERSCRIPT NUMBER IN TEXT

Although messaging relies on the written word, many messagers disregard standard writing conventions. For example, here is a snippet from an IM conversation between two teenage girls:[1]

### EXAMPLE OF EXPLANATORY NOTE

1. This transcript of an IM conversation was collected on 20 Nov. 2012. The teenagers' names are concealed to protect their privacy.

# 32b Formatting MLA manuscripts

The MLA recommends the following format for the manuscript of a research-based print project. If you are creating a nonprint project or have formatting questions, it's always a good idea to check with your instructor before preparing your final draft.

For detailed guidelines on formatting a list of works cited, see 32d. For a sample student essay in MLA style, see 32e.

- **First page and title page.** The MLA does not require a title page. Type each of the following items on a separate line on the first page, beginning one inch from the top and flush with the left margin: your name, the instructor's name, the course name and number, and the date. Double-space between each item; then double-space again and center the title. Double-space between the title and the beginning of the text.

- **Margins and spacing.** Leave one-inch margins at the top and bottom and on both sides of each page. Double-space the entire text, including set-off quotations, notes, and the list of works cited. Indent the first line of a paragraph one-half inch.

- **Page numbers.** Include your last name and the page number on each page, one-half inch below the top and flush with the right margin.

- **Long quotations.** Set off a long quotation (one with more than four typed lines) in block format by starting it on a new line and indenting each line one inch from the left margin. Do not enclose the passage in quotation marks (13b).

- **Headings.** MLA style allows, but does not require, headings. Many students and instructors find them helpful.

- **Visuals.** Place tables, photographs, drawings, charts, graphs, and other figures as near as possible to the relevant text. (See 13e for guidelines on incorporating visuals into your text.) Tables should have a label and number (*Table 1*) and a clear caption. The label and caption should be aligned on the left, on separate lines. Give the source information below the table. All other visuals should be labeled *Figure* (abbreviated *Fig.*), numbered, and captioned. The label and caption should appear on the same line, followed by the source information. Remember to refer to each visual in your text, indicating how it contributes to the point you are making.

# 32c Creating MLA in-text citations

MLA style requires a citation in the text of an essay for every quotation, paraphrase, summary, or other material requiring documentation (see 14b). In-text citations document material from other sources with both signal phrases and parenthetical references. Parenthetical references should include the information your readers need to locate the full reference in the list of works cited at the end of the text (32d). An in-text citation in MLA style aims to give the reader two kinds of information: (1) it indicates *which source* on the works-cited page the writer is referring to, and (2) it explains *where in the source* the material quoted, paraphrased, or summarized can be found, if the source has page numbers or other numbered sections.

The basic MLA in-text citation includes the author's last name either in a signal phrase introducing the source material (13b) or in parentheses at the end of the sentence. For sources with stable page numbers, it also includes the page number in parentheses at the end of the sentence.

**SAMPLE CITATION USING A SIGNAL PHRASE**

In his discussion of Monty Python routines, Crystal notes that the group relished "breaking the normal rules" of language (107).

**SAMPLE PARENTHETICAL CITATION**

A noted linguist explains that Monty Python humor often relied on "bizarre linguistic interactions" (Crystal 108).

(For digital sources without print page numbers, see model 3.)

---

## DIRECTORY TO MLA STYLE  IN-TEXT CITATIONS

Note in the following examples where punctuation is placed in relation to the parentheses.

**1. Author named in a signal phrase**   The MLA recommends using the author's name in a signal phrase to introduce the material and citing the page number(s), if any, in parentheses.

> Lee claims that his comic-book creation, Thor, was "the first regularly published superhero to speak in a consistently archaic manner" (199).

**2. Author named in a parenthetical reference**   When you do not mention the author in a signal phrase, include the author's last name before the page number(s), if any, in parentheses. Use no punctuation between the author's name and the page number(s).

> The word *Bollywood* is sometimes considered an insult because it implies that Indian movies are merely "a derivative of the American film industry" (Chopra 9).

**3. Digital or nonprint source**   Give enough information in a signal phrase or in parentheses for readers to locate the source in your list of works cited. Many works found online or in electronic databases lack stable page numbers; you can omit the page number in such cases. However, if you are citing a work with stable pagination, such as an article in PDF format, include the page number in parentheses.

> DIGITAL SOURCE WITHOUT STABLE PAGE NUMBERS
>
> As a *Slate* analysis has noted, "Prominent sports psychologists get praised for their successes and don't get grief for their failures" (Engber).
>
> DIGITAL SOURCE WITH STABLE PAGE NUMBERS
>
> According to Whitmarsh, the British military had experimented with using balloons for observation as far back as 1879 (328).

If the source includes numbered sections, paragraphs, or screens, include the abbreviation (*sec.*), paragraph (*par.*), or screen (*scr.*) and the number in parentheses.

> Sherman notes that the "immediate, interactive, and on-the-spot" nature of Internet information can make nondigital media seem outdated (sec. 32).

**4. Two or three authors**   Use all the authors' last names in a signal phrase or in parentheses.

> Gortner, Hebrun, and Nicolson maintain that "opinion leaders" influence other people in an organization because they are respected, not because they hold high positions (175).

**5. Four or more authors** Use the first author's name and *et al.* ("and others"), or to give credit to all authors, name all the authors in a signal phrase or in parentheses.

> Similarly, as Belenky et al. assert, examining the lives of women expands our understanding of human development (7).

> Similarly, as Belenky, Clinchy, Tarule, and Goldberger assert, examining the lives of women expands our understanding of human development (7).

**6. Organization as author** Give the group's full name or a shortened form of it in a signal phrase or in parentheses.

> Any study of social welfare involves a close analysis of "the impacts, the benefits, and the costs" of its policies (Social Research Corporation iii).

**7. Unknown author** Use the full title, if it is brief, in your text — or a shortened version of the title in parentheses.

> One analysis defines *hype* as "an artificially engendered atmosphere of hysteria" (*Today's Marketplace* 51).

**8. Author of two or more works cited in the same project** If your list of works cited has more than one work by the same author, include a shortened version of the title of the work you are citing in a signal phrase or in parentheses to prevent reader confusion.

> Gardner shows readers their own silliness in his description of a "pointless, ridiculous monster, crouched in the shadows, stinking of dead men, murdered children, and martyred cows" (*Grendel* 2).

**9. Two or more authors with the same last name** Include the author's first *and* last names in a signal phrase or first initial and last name in a parenthetical reference.

> Children will learn to write if they are allowed to choose their own subjects, James Britton asserts, citing the Schools Council study of the 1960s (37-42).

**10. Indirect source (author quoting someone else)** Use the abbreviation *qtd. in* to indicate that you are quoting from someone else's report of a source.

> As Arthur Miller says, "When somebody is destroyed everybody finally contributes to it, but in Willy's case, the end product would be virtually the same" (qtd. in Martin and Meyer 375).

**11. Multivolume work**   In a parenthetical reference, note the volume number first and then the page number(s), with a colon and one space between them.

> Modernist writers prized experimentation and gradually even sought to blur the line between poetry and prose, according to Forster (3: 150).

If you name only one volume of the work in your list of works cited, include only the page number in the parentheses.

**12. Work in an anthology or collection**   For an essay, short story, or other piece of prose reprinted in an anthology, use the name of the author of the work, not the editor of the anthology, but use the page number(s) from the anthology.

> Narratives of captivity play a major role in early writing by women in the United States, as demonstrated by Silko (219).

**13. Government source**   Because entries for sources authored by government agencies will appear on your list of works cited under the name of the country (see 32d, item 79), your in-text citation for such a source should include the name of the country as well as the name of the agency responsible for the source.

> To reduce the agricultural runoff into the Chesapeake Bay, the United States Environmental Protection Agency has argued that "[h]igh nutrient loading crops, such as corn and soybean, should be replaced with alternatives in environmentally sensitive areas" (26).

**14. Entire work**   Include the reference in the text, without any page numbers.

> In *Into the Wild*, Krakauer both criticizes and admires the solitary impulses of its young hero, which end up killing him.

**15. Two or more sources in one citation**   Separate the information with semicolons.

> Economists recommend that *employment* be redefined to include unpaid domestic labor (Clark 148; Nevins 39).

**16. Personal communication or social media source**   Provide information that will allow readers to locate the source in your list of works cited, such as a name (if you know it) or username.

> George Hahn posted a self-portrait with a Citibike on Instagram with the caption, "Citibike is fabulous. Don't let anyone tell you differently."

**17. Literary work** Because literary works are often available in many different editions, cite the page number(s) from the edition you used followed by a semicolon; then give other identifying information that will lead readers to the passage in any edition. Indicate the act and / or scene in a play (*37; sc. 1*). For a novel, indicate the part or chapter (*175; ch. 4*).

> In utter despair, Dostoyevsky's character Mitya wonders aloud about the "terrible tragedies realism inflicts on people" (376; bk. 8, ch. 2).

For a poem, cite the part (if there is one) and line(s), separated by a period.

> Whitman speculates, "All goes onward and outward, nothing collapses, / And to die is different from what anyone supposed, and luckier" (6.129-30).

If you are citing only line numbers, use the word *line(s)* in the first reference (*lines 21–22*) and the line numbers alone in subsequent references.

> The duke criticizes his late wife for having a "heart . . . too soon made glad" (line 22).

For a verse play, give only the act, scene, and line numbers, separated by periods.

> The witches greet Banquo as "Lesser than Macbeth, and greater" (1.3.65).

**18. Sacred text** To cite a sacred text such as the Qur'an or the Bible, give the title of the edition you used, and the book, chapter, and verse (or their equivalent), separated by a period. In your text, spell out the names of books. In parenthetical references, use abbreviations for books with names of five or more letters (*Gen.* for *Genesis*).

> He ignored the admonition "Pride goes before destruction, and a haughty spirit before a fall" (*New Oxford Annotated Bible,* Prov. 16.18).

**19. Encyclopedia or dictionary entry** An entry for a reference work that does not list an author's name — for example, an encyclopedia or dictionary— will appear on the works-cited list under the entry's title. Enclose the title in quotation marks and place it in parentheses. Omit the page number if the reference work arranges entries alphabetically.

> The term *prion* was coined by Stanley B. Prusiner from the words *proteinaceous* and *infectious* and a suffix meaning *particle* ("Prion").

**20. Visual** When you include an image in your text, number it and include a parenthetical reference that precedes the image in your text (*see Fig. 2*). Number figures (photos, drawings, cartoons, maps, graphs, and charts) and tables separately. Each visual should include a caption with the figure or table number and information about the source (see the Quick Help box on p. 439).

This trend is illustrated in a chart distributed by the College Board as part of its 2011 analysis of aggregate SAT data (see Fig. 1).

Soon after the preceding sentence, readers find the following figure and caption (see 32e):

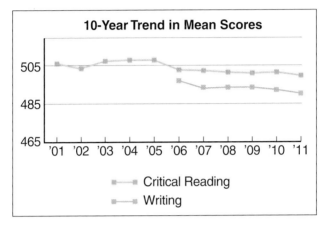

Fig. 1. Ten-year trend in mean SAT reading and writing scores (2001-2011). Data source: College Board, "2011 SAT Trends."

An image that you create might appear with a caption like this:

Fig. 4. Young woman reading a magazine. Personal photograph by author.

## 32d  Preparing an MLA list of works cited

A list of works cited is an alphabetical list of the sources you have referred to in your essay. (If your instructor asks you to list everything you have read as background, call the list *Works Consulted.*) You begin the works-cited list on a separate page or slide after the text of your project and any notes, under the centered heading *Works Cited* (not italicized or in quotation marks).

- Do not indent the first line of each entry, but indent subsequent lines for the entry one-half inch. (This makes the author names easy to scan.) Double-space the entire list.
- List sources alphabetically by the author's last names or by title for works without authors. For titles beginning with the article *A, An,* or *The,* don't count the article when alphabetizing.

- List the author's last name first, followed by a comma and the first name. If a source has more than one author, subsequent authors' names appear first name first (see model 2).

- Italicize titles of books and long works. Put titles of articles and other short works in quotation marks.

- Give a medium, such as *Print* or *Web*, for each entry.

---

### Citing sources that don't match any model exactly

What should you do if your source doesn't match the model exactly? Suppose, for instance, that your source is a translated essay that appears in the fifth edition of an anthology.

- Identify a basic model to follow. If you decide that your source looks most like an essay in an anthology, you would start with a citation that looks like **model 10**.

- Look for models that show the additional elements in your source. For this example, you would need to add elements of **model 13** (for the translation) and **model 19** (for an edition other than the first).

- Add new elements from other models to your basic model in the order indicated.

- If you aren't sure how to arrange the pieces to create a combination model, ask your instructor.

   To cite a source for which you cannot find a model, collect as much information as you can find—about the creator, title, sponsor, date of posting or latest update, your access date, and the site's location—with the goal of helping your readers find the source for themselves, if possible. Then look at the models in this section to see which one most closely matches the type of source you are using. If possible, seek your instructor's advice to find the best model.

---

## DIRECTORY TO MLA STYLE  WORKS-CITED ENTRIES

### Guidelines for author listings

### Print books

## ☐ Guidelines for author listings

The list of works cited is arranged alphabetically. The in-text citations in your writing point readers toward particular sources on the list (32c).

**NAME CITED IN SIGNAL PHRASE IN TEXT**

Crystal explains . . .

**NAME IN PARENTHETICAL CITATION IN TEXT**

. . . (Crystal 107).

**BEGINNING OF ENTRY ON LIST OF WORKS CITED**

Crystal, David.

Models 1–6 explain how to arrange author names. The information that follows the name depends on the type of work you are citing — a print book (models 7–28); a print periodical (models 29–36); a written text from a digital source, such as an article from a Web site or database (models 37–54); sources from art, film, comics, or other media, including live performances (models 55–77); and academic, government, and legal sources (models 78–85). Consult the model that most closely resembles the source you are using.

**1. One author** Put the last name first, followed by a comma, the first name (and initial, if any), and a period.

Crystal, David.

**2. Multiple authors** List the first author's last name first (see model 1). Then, give the names of any other authors with the first name first. Separate authors' names with commas, and include the word *and* before the last person's name.

Martineau, Jane, Desmond Shawe-Taylor, and Jonathan Bate.

For four or more authors, either list all the names, or list the first author followed by a comma and *et al.* ("and others").

Lupton, Ellen, Jennifer Tobias, Alicia Imperiale, Grace Jeffers, and Randi Mates.

Lupton, Ellen, et al.

**3. Organization or group author** Give the name of the group, government agency, corporation, or other organization listed as the author.

Getty Trust.

United States. Government Accountability Office.

**4. Unknown author** When the author is not identified, begin the entry with the title, and alphabetize by the first important word. Italicize titles of books and long works, but put titles of articles and other short works in quotation marks.

"California Sues EPA over Emissions."

*New Concise World Atlas.*

**5. Author using a pseudonym (pen name) or screen name** Give the author's name as it appears in the source, followed by the real name in brackets. If you don't know the author's real name, use only the pseudonym or screen name.

Grammar Girl [Mignon Fogarty].

JennOfArk.

**6. Two or more works by the same author** Arrange the entries alphabetically by title. Include the author's name in the first entry, but in subsequent entries, use three hyphens followed by a period. (For the basic format for citing a book, see model 7. For the basic format for citing an article from an online newspaper, see model 40.)

> Chopra, Anupama. "Bollywood Princess, Hollywood Hopeful." *New York Times.* New York Times, 10 Feb. 2008. Web. 13 Feb. 2008.

> ---. *King of Bollywood: Shah Rukh Khan and the Seductive World of Indian Cinema.* New York: Warner, 2007. Print.

*Note:* Use three hyphens only when the work is by *exactly* the same author(s) as the previous entry.

## □ Print books

**7. Basic format for a book** Begin with the author name(s). (See models 1–6.) Then include the title and subtitle, the city of publication and the publisher, the publication year, and the medium (*Print*). The source map on pp. 418–19 shows where to find this information in a typical book.

> Crystal, David. *Language Play.* Chicago: U of Chicago P, 1998. Print.

*Note:* Place a period and a space after the name, title, and date. Place a colon after the city and a comma after the publisher, and shorten the publisher's name — omit *Co.* or *Inc.*, and abbreviate *University Press* to *UP*.

### 8. Author and editor both named

> Bangs, Lester. *Psychotic Reactions and Carburetor Dung.* Ed. Greil Marcus. New York: Knopf, 1988. Print.

To cite the editor's contribution instead, begin the entry with the editor's name.

> Marcus, Greil, ed. *Psychotic Reactions and Carburetor Dung.* By Lester Bangs. New York: Knopf, 1988. Print.

### 9. Editor, no author named

> Wall, Cheryl A., ed. *Changing Our Own Words: Essays on Criticism, Theory, and Writing by Black Women.* New Brunswick: Rutgers UP, 1989. Print.

**10. Anthology** Cite an entire anthology the same way you would cite a book with an editor and no named author (see model 9).

> Walker, Dale L., ed. *Westward: A Fictional History of the American West.* New York: Forge, 2003. Print.

**11. Work in an anthology or chapter in a book with an editor**  List the author(s) of the selection; the selection title, in quotation marks; the title of the book, italicized; the abbreviation *Ed.* and the name(s) of the editor(s); publication information; the selection's page numbers; and the medium (*Print*).

> Komunyakaa, Yusef. "Facing It." *The Seagull Reader.* Ed. Joseph Kelly. New
> York: Norton, 2000. 126-27. Print.

*Note:* Use the following format to provide original publication information for a reprinted selection:

> Byatt, A. S. "The Thing in the Forest." *New Yorker* 3 June 2002: 80-89. Rpt.
> in *The O. Henry Prize Stories 2003.* Ed. Laura Furman. New York: Anchor,
> 2003. 3-22. Print.

**12. Two or more items from the same anthology**  List the anthology as one entry (see model 10). Also list each of the selections separately with a cross-reference to the anthology.

> Estleman, Loren D. "Big Tim Magoon and the Wild West." Walker 391-404.

> Salzer, Susan K. "Miss Libbie Tells All." Walker 199-212.

**13. Translation**

> Bolaño, Roberto. *2666.* Trans. Natasha Wimmer. New York: Farrar, 2008. Print.

**14. Book with both translator and editor**  List the editor's and translator's names after the title, in the order they appear on the title page.

> Kant, Immanuel. *"Toward Perpetual Peace" and Other Writings on Politics,*
> *Peace, and History.* Ed. Pauline Kleingeld. Trans. David L. Colclasure. New
> Haven: Yale UP, 2006. Print.

**15. Translation of a section of a book**  If different translators have worked on various parts of the book, identify the translator of the part you are citing.

> García Lorca, Federico. *"The Little Mad Boy."* Trans. W. S. Merwin. *The Selected*
> *Poems of Federico García Lorca.* Ed. Francisco García Lorca and Donald M.
> Allen. London: Penguin, 1969. Print.

**16. Translation of a book by an unknown author**  Place the title first unless you wish to emphasize the translator's work.

> *Grettir's Saga.* Trans. Denton Fox and Hermann Palsson. Toronto: U of Toronto
> P, 1974. Print.

# Books

Take information from the book's title page and copyright page (on the reverse side of the title page), not from the book's cover or a library catalog.

1. **Author.** List the last name first. End with a period. For variations, see models 2–6.

2. **Title.** Italicize the title and any subtitle; capitalize all major words. End with a period.

3. **City of publication and publisher.** If more than one city is given, use the first one listed. For foreign cities, add an abbreviation of the country or province (*Cork, Ire.*). Follow it with a colon and a shortened version of the publisher's name (*Oxford UP* for *Oxford University Press*). Follow it with a comma.

4. **Year of publication.** If more than one copyright date is given, use the most recent one. End with a period.

5. **Medium of publication.** End with the medium (*Print*) followed by a period.

**A citation for the book on p. 419 would look like this:**

Patel, Raj. *The Value of Nothing: How to Reshape Market Society and Redefine Democracy.* New York: Picador, 2009. Print.

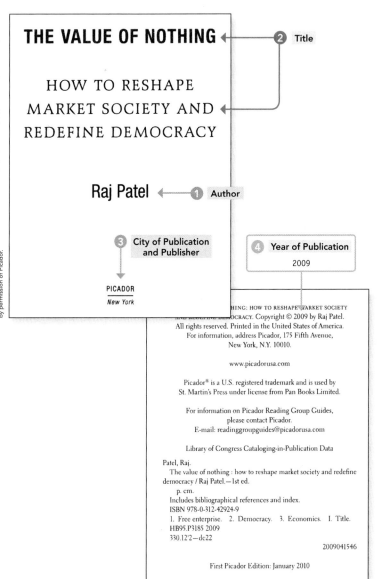

# THE VALUE OF NOTHING ◄

**2** Title

## HOW TO RESHAPE
## MARKET SOCIETY AND ◄
## REDEFINE DEMOCRACY

## Raj Patel ◄

**1** Author

**3** City of Publication and Publisher

PICADOR
*New York*

**4** Year of Publication

2009

HING: HOW TO RESHAPE MARKET SOCIETY AND REDEFINE DEMOCRACY. Copyright © 2009 by Raj Patel. All rights reserved. Printed in the United States of America. For information, address Picador, 175 Fifth Avenue, New York, N.Y. 10010.

www.picadorusa.com

Picador® is a U.S. registered trademark and is used by St. Martin's Press under license from Pan Books Limited.

For information on Picador Reading Group Guides, please contact Picador. E-mail: readinggroupguides@picadorusa.com

Library of Congress Cataloging-in-Publication Data

Patel, Raj.
  The value of nothing : how to reshape market society and redefine democracy / Raj Patel.—1st ed.
    p. cm.
  Includes bibliographical references and index.
  ISBN 978-0-312-42924-9
  1. Free enterprise.   2. Democracy.   3. Economics.   I. Title.
  HB95.P3185 2009
  330.12'2—dc22

2009041546

First Picador Edition: January 2010

**17. Book in a language other than English**  Include a translation of the title in brackets, if necessary.

> Benedetti, Mario. *La borra del café* [*The Coffee Grind*]. Buenos Aires:
>     Sudamericana, 2000. Print.

**18. Graphic narrative**  If the words and images are created by the same person, cite a graphic narrative just as you would with a book (model 7).

> Bechdel, Alison. *Are You My Mother? A Comic Drama*. New York: Houghton,
>     2012. Print.

If the work is a collaboration, indicate the author or illustrator who is most important to your research before the title of the work. List other contributors after the title, in the order of their appearance on the title page. Label each person's contribution to the work.

> Stavans, Ilan, writer. *Latino USA: A Cartoon History*. Illus. Lalo Arcaraz. New
>     York: Basic, 2000. Print.

**19. Edition other than the first**

> Walker, John A. *Art in the Age of Mass Media*. 3rd ed. London: Pluto, 2001.
>     Print.

**20. One volume of a multivolume work**  Give the number of the volume cited after the title. Including the total number of volumes after the publication date is optional.

> Ch'oe, Yong-Ho, Peter Lee, and William Theodore De Barry, eds. *Sources of
>     Korean Tradition*. Vol. 2. New York: Columbia UP, 2000. Print. 2 vols.

**21. More than one volume of a multivolume work**

> Ch'oe, Yong-Ho, Peter Lee, and William Theodore De Barry, eds. *Sources of
>     Korean Tradition*. 2 vols. New York: Columbia UP, 2000. Print.

**22. Preface, foreword, introduction, or afterword**  Following the writer's name, describe the contribution. After the title, indicate the book's author (with *By*) or editor (with *Ed.*).

> Atwan, Robert. Foreword. *The Best American Essays 2002*. Ed. Stephen Jay
>     Gould. Boston: Houghton, 2002. viii-xii. Print.

> Moore, Thurston. Introduction. *Confusion Is Next: The Sonic Youth Story*. By
>     Alec Foege. New York: St. Martin's, 1994. xi. Print.

**23. Entry in a reference book** For a well-known encyclopedia, note the edition (if identified) and year of publication. If the entries are alphabetized, omit publication information and page number.

> Kettering, Alison McNeil. "Art Nouveau." *World Book Encyclopedia*. 2002 ed.
> Print.

**24. Book that is part of a series** After the medium (*Print*), cite the series name (and number, if any) from the title page.

> Nichanian, Marc, and Vartan Matiossian, eds. *Yeghishe Charents: Poet of the Revolution*. Costa Mesa: Mazda, 2003. Print. Armenian Studies Ser. 5.

**25. Republication (modern edition of an older book)** Indicate the original publication date after the title.

> Austen, Jane. *Sense and Sensibility*. 1813. New York: Dover, 1996. Print.

**26. Publisher's imprint** If the title page gives a publisher's imprint, hyphenate the imprint and the publisher's name.

> Hornby, Nick. *About a Boy*. New York: Riverhead-Penguin Putnam, 1998.
> Print.

**27. Book with a title within the title** Do not italicize a book title within a title. For an article title within a title, italicize as usual and place the article title in quotation marks.

> Mullaney, Julie. *Arundhati Roy's* The God of Small Things: *A Reader's Guide*.
> New York: Continuum, 2002. Print.

> Rhynes, Martha. *"I, Too, Sing America": The Story of Langston Hughes*.
> Greensboro: Morgan, 2002. Print.

**28. Sacred text** To cite any individual published editions of sacred books, begin the entry with the title.

> *Qur'an: The Final Testament (Authorized English Version) with Arabic Text*.
> Trans. Rashad Khalifa. Fremont: Universal Unity, 2000. Print.

□ **Articles and short works in print periodicals**

Begin with the author name(s). (See models 1–6.) Then include the article title, the title of the periodical, the date or volume information, the page numbers,

## Articles in Print Periodicals

1 **Author.** List the last name first. End with a period. For variations, see models 2–6.

2 **Article title.** Put the title and any subtitle in quotation marks; capitalize all major words. Place a period inside the closing quotation mark.

3 **Periodical title.** Italicize the title; capitalize all major words. Omit any initial *A*, *An*, or *The*.

4 **Volume and issue / Date of publication.** For journals, give the volume number and issue number (if any), separated by a period; then list the year in parentheses and follow it with a colon.

   For magazines, list the day (if given), month, and year.

5 **Page numbers.** List inclusive page numbers. If the article skips pages, put the first page number and a plus sign. End with a period.

6 **Medium.** Give the medium (*Print*). End with a period.

**A citation for the article on p. 423 would look like this:**

Quart, Alissa. "Lost Media, Found Media: Snapshots from the Future of

   Writing." *Columbia Journalism Review* May/June 2008: 30-34. Print.

**3** Periodical Title

**COLUMBIA**
**JOURNALISM**
**REVIEW**

May / June 2008 • cjr.org

**4** Date of Publication
May/June 2008

*The Future of*
**Writing**

Nonfiction's di...
**ALISSA QUART**

Kindle isn't it,
**EZRA KLEIN**

**UNDER THE**
A reporter rec...
that got him t...
**CAMERON MCW**

**LOVE THY N**
The religion b...
**TIM TOWNSEND**

**2** Article Title

## Lost Media, Found Media

*Snapshots from the future of writing*

BY ALISSA QUART

**1** Author
ALISSA QUART

If there were an ashram for people who worship contemplative long-form journalism, it would be the Nieman Conference on Narrative Journalism. This March, at the Sheraton Boston Hotel, hundreds of journalists, authors, students, and aspirants came for the weekend event. Seated on metal chairs in large conference rooms, we learned about muscular storytelling (the Q-shaped narrative structure—who knew?). We sipped cups of coffee and ate bagels and heard about reporting history through letters and public documents and how to evoke empathy for our subjects, particularly our most marginal ones. As we listened to reporters discussing great feats—exposing Walter Reed's fetid living quarters for wounded soldiers, for instance—we also renewed our pride in our profession. In short, the conference exemplified the best of the older media models, the ones that have so recently fallen into economic turmoil.

Yet even at the weekend's strongest lectures on interview techniques or the long-form profile, we couldn't ignore the digital elephant in the room. We all knew as writers that the kinds of pieces we were discussing require months of work to be both deep and refined, and that we were all hard-pressed for the time and the money to do that. It was always hard for nonfiction writers, but something seems to have changed. For those of us who believed in the value of the journalism and literary nonfiction of the past, we had

become like the people at the ashram after the guru has died.

Right now, journalism is more or less divided into two camps, which I will call Lost Media and Found Media. I went to the Nieman conference partially because I wanted to see how the forces creating this new division are affecting and afflicting the Lost Media world that I love best, not on the institutional level, but for reporters and writers themselves. This world includes people who write for all the newspapers and magazines that are currently struggling with layoffs, speedups, hiring freezes, buyouts, the death or shrinkage of film- and book-review sections, limits on expensive investigative work, the erasure of foreign bureaus, and the general narrowing of institutional ambition. It includes freelance writers competing with hordes of ever-younger competitors willing to write and publish online for free, the fade-out of established journalistic career paths, and, perhaps most crucially, a muddled sense of the meritorious, as blogs level and scramble the value and status of print publications, and of professional writers. The glamour and influence once associated with a magazine elite seem to have faded, becoming a sort of pastiche of winsome articles about yearning and boxers and dinners at Elaine's.

Found Media-ites, meanwhile, are the bloggers, the contributors to Huffington Post-type sites that aggregate blogs, as well as other work that somebody else paid for, and the new nonprofits and pay-per-article schemes that aim to save journalism from 20 percent profit-margin demands. Although these elements are often disparate, together they compose the new media landscape. In economic terms, I mean all the outlets for nonfiction writing that seem to be thriving in the new era or striving to fill niches that Lost Media is giving up in a new order. Stylistically, Found Media tends to feel spontaneous, almost accidental. It's a domain dominated by the young, where writers get points not for following traditions or burnishing them but for amateur and hybrid vigor, for creating their own venues and their own genres. It is about public expression and community—not quite John Dewey's Great Community, which the critic Eric Alterman alluded to in a recent *New Yorker* article on newspapers, but rather a fractured form of Dewey's ideal: call it Great Communities.

To be a Found Media journalist or pundit, one need not be elite, expert, or trained; one must simply produce punchy intellectual property that is in conversation with groups of

*Illustration by Tomer Hanuka*

**5** Page Numbers
30-34

423

and the medium (*Print*). The source map on pp. 422–23 shows where to find this information in a sample periodical.

### Formatting print periodical entries

- Place the **title of the article** from a periodical (journal, magazine, or newspaper) in quotation marks. Put the period inside the closing quotation mark.
- Give the **title of the periodical** as it appears on the magazine's or journal's cover or the newspaper's front page; omit any initial *A*, *An*, or *The*. Italicize the title.
- For **journals**, include the volume number, a period, the issue number, if given, and the year in parentheses.
- For **magazines and newspapers**, give the date in this order: day (if given), month, year. Abbreviate months except for May, June, and July.
- List inclusive **page numbers** if the article appears on consecutive pages. If it skips pages, give only the first page number and a plus sign (*34+*).
- End with the **medium** (*Print*).

**29. Article in a print journal**    Follow the journal title with the volume number, a period, the issue number (if given), and the year (in parentheses).

> Gigante, Denise. "The Monster in the Rainbow: Keats and the Science of Life."
> *PMLA* 117.3 (2002): 433-48. Print.

**30. Article in a print magazine**    Provide the date from the magazine cover, and do not include volume or issue numbers.

> Sanneh, Kelefa. "Skin in the Game." *New Yorker* 24 Mar. 2014: 48-55.
> Print.

> Taubin, Amy. "All Talk?" *Film Comment* Nov.-Dec. 2007: 45-47. Print.

**31. Article in a print newspaper**    Include the edition (if listed) and the section number or letter (if listed).

> Fackler, Martin. "Japan's Foreign Minister Says Apologies to Wartime
> Victims Will Be Upheld." *New York Times* 9 Apr. 2014, late ed.: A6.
> Print.

*Note:* For locally published newspapers, add the city in brackets after the name if it is not part of the name: *Globe and Mail [Toronto].*

**32. Editorial in a print periodical**   Include the writer's name, if given, and the title, if any, followed by the label *Editorial.*

"California Dreaming." Editorial. *Nation* 25 Feb. 2008: 4. Print.

**33. Letter to the editor of a print periodical**   Include the writer's name, if given, and the title, if any, followed by the label *Letter.* Provide relevant information for the type of source (journal, magazine, newspaper).

MacEwan, Valerie. Letter. *Believer* Jan. 2014: 4. Print.

**34. Review in a print periodical**   Include the writer's name and the title of the review, if given, then *Rev. of* and the title of the work under review.

Nussbaum, Emily. "Change Agents." Rev. of *Silicon Valley,* by Mike Judge. *New Yorker* 31 Mar. 2014: 68. Print.

Schwarz, Benjamin. Rev. of *The Second World War: A Short History,* by R. A. C. Parker. *Atlantic Monthly* May 2002: 110-11. Print.

**35. Interview in a print periodical**   List the person interviewed and either the title of the interview (if any) or the label *Interview,* along with the interviewer's name, if relevant.

Blume, Judy. Interview by Lena Dunham. *Believer* Jan. 2014: 39+. Print.

**36. Unsigned article in a print periodical**

"Performance of the Week." *Time* 6 Oct. 2003: 18. Print.

□ **Digital written-word sources**

Digital sources such as Web sites differ from print sources in the ease with which they can be changed, updated, or eliminated. In addition, the various digital media do not organize their works the same way. The most commonly cited digital sources are documents from Web sites and databases. For help determining which is which, see 32a.

## Citing digital sources

When citing sources accessed online or from a digital database, give as many of the following elements as you can find:

1. **Author.** Give the author's name, if available.

2. **Title.** Put titles of articles or short works in quotation marks. Italicize book titles.

**FOR WORKS FROM DATABASES:**

3. **Title of periodical,** italicized.

4. **Publication information.** After the volume/issue/year or date, include page numbers (or *n. pag.* if no page numbers are listed).

5. **Name of database,** italicized, if you used a subscription service such as Academic Search Premier.

**FOR WORKS FROM THE WEB:**

3. **Title of the site,** italicized.

4. **Name of the site's publisher or sponsor.** This information usually appears at the bottom of the page.

5. **Date of online publication or most recent update.** This information often appears at the bottom of the page. If no date is given, use *n.d.*

6. **Medium of publication.** Use *Web* for works from both databases and the Web.

7. **Date of access.** Give the most recent date you accessed the source.

If you think your readers will have difficulty finding the source without a URL, put it after the period following the date of access, inside angle brackets, with a period after the closing bracket.

---

**37. Work from an online database**   The basic format for citing a work from a database appears in the source map on pp. 428–29.

For a periodical article that is available in print but that you access in an online database through a library subscription service such as Academic Search Premier, begin with the author's name (if given); the title of the work, in quotation marks; the title of the periodical, italicized; and the volume/issue and date of the print version of the work (see models 29–36). Include the page numbers from the print version; if no page numbers are available, use *n. pag.* Then give the name of the online database, italicized; the medium (*Web*); and your most recent date of access.

> Collins, Ross F. "Cattle Barons and Ink Slingers: How Cow Country Journalists Created a Great American Myth." *American Journalism* 24.3 (2007): 7-29. *Communication and Mass Media Complete.* Web. 7 Feb. 2013.

**38. Article from a journal on the Web**   Begin an entry for an online journal article as you would one for a print journal article (see model 29). If an article does not have page numbers, use *n. pag.* End with the medium consulted (*Web*) and the date of access.

> Gallagher, Brian. "Greta Garbo Is Sad: Some Historical Reflections on the Paradoxes of Stardom in the American Film Industry, 1910-1960." *Images: A Journal of Film and Popular Culture* 3 (1997): n. pag. Web. 7 Aug. 2013.

**39. Article from a magazine on the Web**   List the author, article title, and name of the magazine. Then identify the sponsor of the Web site and the date of publication, the medium (*Web*), and your date of access.

> Sullivan, Barbara Apple. "Big Data: Where Does Intuition Fit In?" *Below the Fold.* Sullivan, Apr. 2014. Web. 11 Apr. 2014.

**40. Article from a newspaper on the Web**   After the name of the newspaper, give the publisher, publication date, medium (*Web*), and access date.

> Shyong, Frank. "Sriracha Showdown Intensifies as Irwindale Declares Public Nuisance." *Los Angeles Times.* Los Angeles Times, 10 Apr. 2014. Web. 16 May 2014.

**41. Digital book (online or e-reader)**   Provide information as for a print book (see models 7–28); then give the digital publication information, the medium, and the date of access.

> Euripides. *The Trojan Women.* Trans. Gilbert Murray. New York: Oxford UP, 1915. *Internet Sacred Text Archive.* Web. 12 Oct. 2014.

If you read the book on an e-reader such as a Kindle or Nook, the medium should specify the type of reader file you used. No access date is required.

> Schaap, Rosie. *Drinking with Men: A Memoir.* New York: Riverhead-Penguin, 2013. Kindle file.

**42. Part of a digital book**   Cite as you would a part of a print book (see models 11 and 22). Give the print (if any) and digital publication information, the medium (*Web*), and the date of access.

> Riis, Jacob. "The Genesis of the Gang." *The Battle with the Slum.* New York: Macmillan, 1902. N. pag. *Bartleby.com: Great Books Online.* Web. 31 Mar. 2014.

**43. Online poem**   Include the poet's name, the title of the poem, and the print publication information (if any). End with the electronic publication information, the medium (*Web*), and the date of access.

> Geisel, Theodor. "Too Many Daves." *The Sneetches and Other Stories.* New York: Random House, 1961. N. pag. *Poetry Foundation.* Web. 2 Feb. 2014.

## Articles from Databases

Library subscriptions—such as EBSCOhost and Academic Search Premier—provide access to huge databases of articles.

**1** **Author.** List the last name first. End with a period. For variations, see models 2–6.

**2** **Article title.** Enclose the title and any subtitle in quotation marks.

**3** **Periodical title.** Italicize it. Exclude any initial *A*, *An*, or *The*.

**4** **Volume and issue / Date of publication.** List the volume and issue number, if any. Then, add the date of publication, including the day (if given), month, and year, in that order. Last, add a colon.

**5** **Page numbers.** Give the inclusive page numbers. If an article has no page numbers, write *n. pag.*

**6** **Database name.** Italicize the name of the database.

**7** **Medium.** For an online database, use *Web*.

**8** **Date of access.** Give the day, month, and year, then a period.

**A citation for the article on p. 429 would look like this:**

Arnett, Robert P. "*Casino Royale* and Franchise Remix: James Bond as Superhero." *Film Criticism* 33.3 (2009): 1-16. *Academic Search Premier*. Web. 16 May 2014.

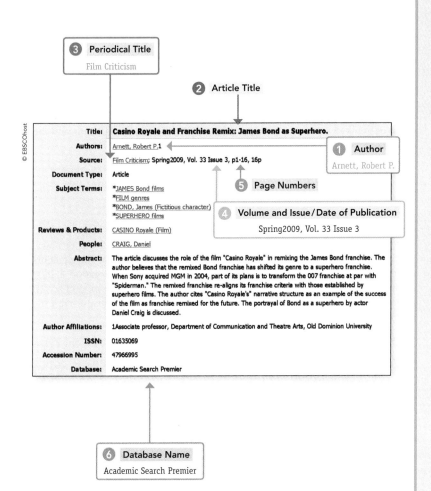

**3** Periodical Title

Film Criticism

**2** Article Title

**1** Author

Arnett, Robert P.

| | |
|---|---|
| **Title:** | **Casino Royale and Franchise Remix: James Bond as Superhero.** |
| **Authors:** | Arnett, Robert P.1 |
| **Source:** | Film Criticism; Spring2009, Vol. 33 Issue 3, p1-16, 16p |
| **Document Type:** | Article |
| **Subject Terms:** | *JAMES Bond films |
| | *FILM genres |
| | *BOND, James (Fictitious character) |
| | *SUPERHERO films |
| **Reviews & Products:** | CASINO Royale (Film) |
| **People:** | CRAIG, Daniel |
| **Abstract:** | The article discusses the role of the film "Casino Royale" in remixing the James Bond franchise. The author believes that the remixed Bond franchise has shifted its genre to a superhero franchise. When Sony acquired MGM in 2004, part of its plans is to transform the 007 franchise at par with "Spiderman." The remixed franchise re-aligns its franchise criteria with those established by superhero films. The author cites "Casino Royale's" narrative structure as an example of the success of the film as franchise remixed for the future. The portrayal of Bond as a superhero by actor Daniel Craig is discussed. |
| **Author Affiliations:** | 1Associate professor, Department of Communication and Theatre Arts, Old Dominion University |
| **ISSN:** | 01635069 |
| **Accession Number:** | 47966995 |
| **Database:** | Academic Search Premier |

**5** Page Numbers

**4** Volume and Issue / Date of Publication

Spring2009, Vol. 33 Issue 3

**6** Database Name

Academic Search Premier

© EBSCOhost

429

**44. Online editorial or letter to the editor** Include the author's name (if given) and the title (if any). Then give the label *Editorial* or *Letter*. Follow the appropriate model for the type of source you are using. (Check the directory on pp. 412–14.)

> "Shorter Drug Sentences." Editorial. *New York Times*. New York Times, 10 Apr. 2014. Web. 5 May 2014.

> Starr, Evva. "Local Reporting Thrives in High Schools." Letter. *Washington Post*. Washington Post, 4 Apr. 2014. Web. 16 Apr. 2014.

**45. Online review** Cite an online review as you would a print review (see model 34), and include information about the work under review. End with the name of the Web site, the sponsor, the date of publication, the medium, and the date of access.

> O'Hehir, Andrew. "Aronofsky's Deranged Biblical Action Flick." Rev. of *Noah*, dir. Darren Aronofsky. *Salon*. Salon Media Group, 27 May 2014. Web. 24 Apr. 2014.

**46. Short work from a Web site** For basic information for citing a work on a Web site that is not part of a regularly published journal, magazine, or newspaper, see the source map on pp. 432–33. Include all of the following elements that are available: the author; the title of the document, in quotation marks; the name of the Web site, italicized; the name of the publisher or sponsor (if none is available, use *N.p.*); the date of publication (if not available, use *n.d.*); the medium consulted (*Web*); and the date of access.

> Bali, Karan. "Kishore Kumar." *Upperstall.com*. Upperstall, n.d. Web. 7 May 2014.

> "Our Mission." *Trees for Life International*. Trees for Life International, 2011. Web. 31 May 2014.

**47. Entire Web site** Follow the guidelines for a specific work from the Web, beginning with the name of the author or editor (if any), followed by the title of the Web site, italicized; the name of the sponsor or publisher (if none, use *N.p.*); the date of publication or last update; the medium of publication (*Web*); and the date of access.

> Glazier, Loss Pequeño, dir. *Electronic Poetry Center*. SUNY Buffalo, 2014. Web. 26 Sept. 2014.

> *Weather.com*. Weather Channel Interactive, 2014. Web. 13 Mar. 2014.

For a personal Web site, include the name of the person who created the site; the title, in quotation marks if it is part of a larger work or italicized if it is not, or (if there is no title) a description such as *Home page*, not italicized; the name of the larger site, if different from the personal site's title; the publisher or sponsor of the site (if none, use *N.p.*); the date of the last update (if there is no date, use *n.d.*); the medium of publication (*Web*); and the date of access.

Enright, Mike. Home page. *Menright.com.* N.p., n.d. Web. 17 May 2014.

**48. Entry in an online reference work or wiki**  Begin with the title unless the author is named. (A wiki, which is collectively edited, will not include an author.) Treat an online reference entry as you would a work from a Web site (see model 46). Include the title of the entry; the name of the work, italicized; the sponsor or publisher (use *N.p.* if none is named); the date of the latest update; the medium (*Web*); and the date of access. Before using a wiki as a source, check with your instructor.

"Gunpowder Plot." *Wikipedia.* Wikimedia Foundation, 28 Mar. 2014. Web.
    10 Apr. 2014.

**49. Academic course or department Web site**  For a course site, include the name of the instructor, the title of the course in quotation marks, the title of the site in italics, the department (if relevant) and institution sponsoring the site, the date (or *n.d.* if none is given), the medium consulted (*Web*), and the access information.

Creekmur, Corey K., and Philip Lutgendorf. "Topics in Asian Cinema: Popular
    Hindi Cinema." *University of Iowa.* Depts. of English, Cinema, and
    Comparative Literature, U of Iowa, 2007. Web. 13 Mar. 2014.

For a department Web site, give the department name, the description *Dept. home page*, the institution (in italics), the site sponsor, the date (or *n.d.*), the medium (*Web*), and the access information.

English Dept. home page. *Amherst College.* Amherst Coll., n.d. Web. 5 Apr. 2014.

**50. Blog**  For an entire blog, give the author's name, if any; the title of the blog, italicized; the sponsor or publisher of the blog (if there is none, use *N.p.*); the date of the most recent update; the medium (*Web*); and the date of access.

Levy, Carla Miriam. *Filmi Geek.* N.p., 2 Apr. 2014. Web. 14 Apr. 2014.

*Little Green Footballs.* Little Green Footballs, 14 Apr. 2014. Web. 14 Apr. 2014.

*Note:* To cite a blogger who writes under a pseudonym, begin with the pseudonym and then put the writer's real name (if you know it) in square brackets. (See model 5, p. 415.)

Atrios [Duncan Black]. *Eschaton.* N.p., 27 Apr. 2014. Web. 27 Apr. 2014.

# Works from Web Sites

You may need to browse other parts of a site to find some of the following elements, and some sites may omit elements. Uncover as much information as you can.

**1** **Author.** List the last name first. End with a period. If no author is given, begin with the title. For variations, see models 2–6.

**2** **Title of work.** Enclose the title and any subtitle of the work in quotation marks.

**3** **Title of Web site.** Give the title of the entire Web site, italicized.

**4** **Publisher or sponsor.** Look for the sponsor's name at the bottom of the home page. If no information is available, write *N.p.* Follow it with a comma.

**5** **Date of publication or latest update.** Give the most recent date, followed by a period. If no date is available, use *n.d.*

**6** **Medium.** Use *Web* and follow it with a period.

**7** **Date of access.** Give the date you accessed the work. End with a period.

**A citation for the work on p. 433 would look like this:**

Tønnesson, Øyvind. "Mahatma Gandhi, the Missing Laureate."

> *Nobelprize.org.* Nobel Foundation, 1 Dec. 1999. Web. 4 May 2013.

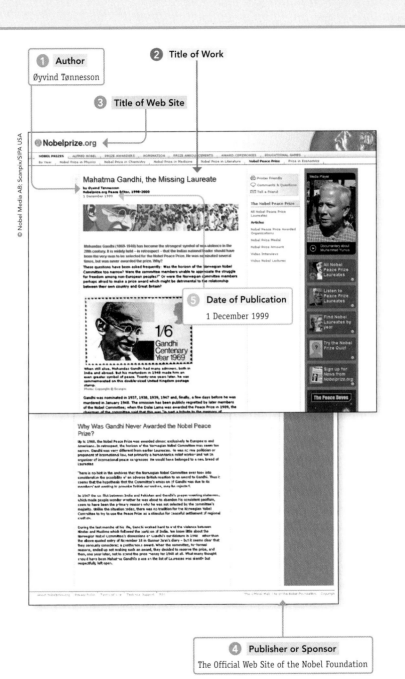

**1** Author

Øyvind Tønnesson

**2** Title of Work

**3** Title of Web Site

Nobelprize.org

**Mahatma Gandhi, the Missing Laureate**

by Øyvind Tønnesson
Nobel.org Peace Editor, 1998-2000
1 December 1999

**5** Date of Publication

1 December 1999

Why Was Gandhi Never Awarded the Nobel Peace Prize?

**4** Publisher or Sponsor

The Official Web Site of the Nobel Foundation

433

**51. Post or comment on a blog or discussion group**   Give the author's name; the title of the post, in quotation marks (if there is no title, use the description *Online posting*, not italicized); the title of the site, italicized; the sponsor (if there is none, use *N.p.*); the date of the most recent update; the medium (*Web*); and the date of access.

> Edroso, Roy. "Friends in High Places." *Alicublog.* N.p., 16 Apr. 2014. Web.
> 18 Apr. 2014.

For a comment on an online post, give the writer's name or screen name (see model 5); the title of the comment or a label such as *Online comment*, not italicized; the title of the article commented on, in quotation marks; the label *by* and the article author's name. End with the citation information for the type of article.

> JennOfArk. Online comment. "Friends in High Places," by Roy Edroso.
> *Alicublog.* N.p., 16 Apr. 2014. Web. 18 Apr. 2014.

**52. Tweet**   Include the writer's real name, if known, with the user name (if different) in parentheses. If you don't know the real name, give just the user name. Include the entire tweet, in quotation marks. End with date and time of message and the medium *Tweet*.

> Patterson, Amy (amycep). "So many cool student projects at the @BedfordPub
> Celebration of Multimodal Composition! #4c14 pic.twitter.com/
> pZpxYgmpbj." 21 Mar. 2014, 4:46 p.m. Tweet.

**53. Posting on a social networking site**   To cite a posting on Facebook, Instagram, or another social networking site, include the writer's name; up to 140 characters of the posting, in quotation marks (or a description such as *Photograph*, not italicized and not in quotation marks, if no text appears); the date of the post; and the medium of delivery (such as *Facebook post*). (The MLA does not provide guidelines for citing postings or messages on such sites; this model is based on the MLA's guidelines for citing a tweet.)

> Cannon, Kevin. "Portrait of Norris Hall in #Savannah, GA — home (for a few
> more months, anyway) of #SCAD's sequential art department." Mar. 2014.
> Instagram post.

**54. Email or message on a social networking site**   Include the writer's name; the subject line, in quotation marks, if one is provided; *Message to* (not italicized or in quotation marks) followed by the recipient's name; the date of the message; and the medium of delivery (such as *E-mail* or *Facebook message*—note that MLA style hyphenates *e-mail*).

> Carbone, Nick. "Screen vs. Print Reading." Message to the author. 17 Apr.
> 2013. E-mail.

> Natiello, Michael. Message to the author. 31 Mar. 2014. Facebook message.

□ **Visual, audio, multimedia, and live sources**

**55. Film (theatrical, DVD, or other format)**   If you cite a particular person's work, start with that name. If not, start with the title of the film; then name the director, distributor, and year of release. Other contributors, such as writers or performers, may follow the director. If you cite a DVD or Blu-ray disc instead of a theatrical release, include the original film release date and the label *DVD* or *BD*. Treat a film that you viewed streaming online as a theatrical release.

> *Spirited Away.* Dir. Hayao Miyazaki. 2001. Walt Disney Video, 2003.
> DVD.

> *Twelve Years a Slave.* Dir. Steve McQueen. Perf. Chiwetel Ejiofor. Fox
> Searchlight, 2013. Film.

**56. Online video clip**   Cite an online video as you would a work from a Web site (see model 46).

> Weber, Jan. "As We Sow, Part 1: Where Are the Farmers?" *YouTube.* YouTube,
> 15 Mar. 2008. Web. 27 Sept. 2014.

**57. Television broadcast**   Begin with the title of the program, italicized (for an entire series) or the title of the episode, in quotation marks. Then list important contributors (narrator, writer, director, actors); the network; the local station and city, if the show appeared on a local channel; the broadcast date(s); and the medium. To cite a particular person's work, begin with that name. When citing an entire series, give inclusive dates.

> *Breaking Bad.* Creator Vince Gilligan. Perf. Bryan Cranston, Aaron Paul, Anna
> Gunn. AMC, 2008-2013. Television.

> "Time Zones." *Mad Men.* Writ. Matthew Weiner. Dir. Scott Hornbacher. AMC,
> 13 Apr. 2014. Television.

**58. Television on the Web**   For a show accessed on a network Web site, begin as for a television broadcast (model 57). After the network, include the date of posting, the Web site title, the medium (*Web*), and the access date.

> "Time Zones." *Mad Men.* Writ. Matthew Weiner. Dir. Scott Hornbacher. AMC,
> 13 Apr. 2014. *AMCTV.com.* Web. 15 Apr. 2014.

**59. Radio broadcast**   If you are citing a particular episode or segment, begin with the title, in quotation marks. Then give the program title in italics. List important contributors (narrator, writer, director, actors); the network; the local station and city, if the show appeared locally; the broadcast date(s);

and the medium (*Radio*). To cite a particular person's work, begin with that name.

> "Tarred and Feathered." *This American Life.* Narr. Ira Glass. WNYC, New York, 11 Apr. 2013. Radio.

**60. Radio on the Web** For a show or segment accessed on the Web, begin as for a radio broadcast (model 59). After the network, include the date of posting, the Web site title, the medium (*Web*), and the access date. (For downloaded versions, see model 73.)

> "Obama's Failures Have Made Millennials Give Up Hope." *The Rush Limbaugh Show.* Narr. Rush Limbaugh. Premiere Radio Networks, 14 Apr. 2014. *RushLimbaugh.com.* Web. 15 Apr. 2014.

**61. Television or radio interview** List the person interviewed and then the title, if any. If the interview has no title, use the label *Interview* and name the interviewer, if relevant. Then identify the source. End with information about the program, the date(s) the interview took place, and the medium.

> Russell, David O. Interview by Terry Gross. *Fresh Air.* WNYC, New York, 20 Feb. 2014. Radio.

*Note:* If you found an archived version of a television or radio interview online, provide the site's sponsor (if known), the date of the interview, the name of the Web site, the medium (*Web*), and the access date. For a podcast interview, see model 72.

> Revkin, Andrew. Interview by Terry Gross. *Fresh Air.* NPR, 14 June 2006. *NPR.org.* Web. 12 Jan. 2014.

**62. Online interview** Start with the name of the person interviewed. Give the title or the label *Interview* and the interviewer (if named), then the title of the site, the sponsor or publisher (or *N.p.* if none is identified), the date of publication, the medium (*Web*), and the access date.

> Ladd, Andrew. "What Ends: An Interview with Andrew Ladd." *Looks & Books.* N.p., 25 Feb. 2014. Web. 10 Apr. 2014.

**63. Personal interview** List the person interviewed; the label *Telephone interview*, *Personal interview*, or *E-mail interview*; and the date the interview took place.

> Freedman, Sasha. Personal interview. 10 Nov. 2014.

**64. Sound recording** List the name of the person or group you wish to emphasize (such as the composer, conductor, or band); the title of the recording or composition; the artist, if appropriate; the manufacturer; and the year of issue. Give the medium (such as *CD*, *MP3 file*, or *LP*). If you are citing a particular song or selection, include its title, in quotation marks, before the title of the recording.

> Bach, Johann Sebastian. *Bach: Violin Concertos.* Perf. Itzhak Perlman and
> Pinchas Zukerman. English Chamber Orch. EMI, 2002. CD.

> Sonic Youth. "Incinerate." *Rather Ripped.* Geffen, 2006. MP3 file.

*Note:* If you are citing instrumental music that is identified only by form, number, and key, do not underline, italicize, or enclose it in quotation marks.

> Grieg, Edvard. Concerto in A minor, op. 16. Cond. Eugene Ormandy.
> Philadelphia Orch. RCA, 1989. LP.

**65. Musical composition**   When you are not citing a specific published version, first give the composer's name, followed by the title.

> Mozart, Wolfgang Amadeus. *Don Giovanni,* K527.

> Mozart, Wolfgang Amadeus. Symphony no. 41 in C major, K551.

**66. Published score**   Cite a published score as you would a book. If you include the date the composition was written, do so immediately after the title.

> Schoenberg, Arnold. *Chamber Symphony No. 1 for 15 Solo Instruments, Op. 9.*
> 1906. New York: Dover, 2002. Print.

**67. Video game**   Start with the developer or author (if any). After the title, give the version (*Vers.*), if given, then the distributor, the date of publication, and the medium.

> Harmonix. *Rock Band Blitz.* MTV Games, 2012. Xbox 360.

*Note:* If you play the game on the Web, give the name of the site, the medium *Web,* and the date after the game publication information.

**68. Computer software or app**   Cite as a video game (see model 67), giving the available information about the version, distributor, date, and platform.

> *Angry Birds.* Vers. 4.1.0. Rovio, 2014. Android 4.0.4.

**69. Lecture or speech (live)**   List the speaker; the title, in quotation marks; the sponsoring institution or group; the place; and the date. If the speech is untitled, use a label such as *Lecture.*

> Eugenides, Jeffrey. Portland Arts and Lectures. Arlene Schnitzer Concert Hall,
> Portland, OR. 30 Sept. 2003. Lecture.

**70. Lecture or speech on the Web**    Cite as you would a short work from a Web site (model 46).

> Burden, Amanda. "How Public Spaces Make Cities Work." *TED.com*. TED
> Conferences, Mar. 2014. Web. 15 Apr. 2014.

**71. Live performance**    List the title, the appropriate names (such as the writer or performer), the place, and the date. To cite a particular person's work, begin the entry with that name.

> *Anything Goes*. By Cole Porter. Perf. Klea Blackhurst. Shubert Theater, New
> Haven. 7 Oct. 2003. Performance.

**72. Podcast (streaming)**    Cite a podcast that you view or listen to online as a short work from a Web site (model 46). For a downloaded podcast, see model 73.

> Fogarty, Mignon. "Begs the Question: Update." *QuickandDirtyTips.com*.
> Macmillan, 6 Mar. 2014. Web. 27 June 2014.

**73. Downloaded digital file**    A citation for a file that you can download — one that exists independently, not only on a Web site — begins with citation information required for the type of source (a photograph or sound recording, for example). For the medium, indicate the type of file (*MP3 file, JPEG file*).

> *Officers' Winter Quarters, Army of Potomac, Brandy Station*. Mar. 1864. Prints
> and Photographs Div., Lib. of Cong. TIFF file.

> "Return to the Giant Pool of Money." *This American Life*. Narr. Ira Glass. NPR,
> 25 Sept. 2009. MP3 file.

**74. Work of art or photograph**    List the artist's or photographer's name; the work's title, italicized; the date of composition (if unknown, use *n.d.*); and the medium of composition (*Oil on canvas, Bronze*). Then cite the name of the museum or other location and the city. To cite a reproduction in a book, add the publication information (see the second model below). To cite artwork found online, omit the medium of composition, and after the location, add the title of the database or Web site, italicized; the medium consulted (*Web*); and the date of access.

> Bronzino, Agnolo. *Lodovico Capponi*. 1550-55. Oil on poplar panel. Frick
> Collection, New York.

> *General William Palmer in Old Age*. 1810. National Army Museum, London.
> *White Mughals: Love and Betrayal in Eighteenth-Century India*. By William
> Dalrymple. New York: Penguin, 2002. 270. Print.

Theotolopoulos, Domenikos. *Christ Driving the Money Changers from the Temple.* c. 1570. Minneapolis Inst. of Arts. *artsmia.org.* Web. 6 Oct. 2014.

**75. Map or chart**   Cite a map or chart as you would a book or a short work within a longer work, and include the word *Map* or *Chart* after the title. Then, add the medium of publication. For an online source, end with the date of access.

"Australia." Map. *Perry-Castañeda Library Map Collection.* U of Texas, 1999. Web. 4 Nov. 2014.

*California.* Map. Chicago: Rand, 2002. Print.

**76. Cartoon or comic strip**   List the artist's name; the title (if any) of the cartoon or comic strip, in quotation marks; the label *Cartoon* or *Comic strip*; and the usual publication information for a print periodical (see models 29–36) or a work from a Web site (model 46).

Lewis, Eric. "The Unpublished Freud." Cartoon. *New Yorker* 11 Mar. 2002: 80. Print.

Munroe, Randall. "Heartbleed Explanation." Comic strip. *xkcd.com.* N.p., n.d. Web. 15 Apr. 2014.

**77. Advertisement**   Include the label *Advertisement* after the name of the item or organization being advertised.

Ameritrade. Advertisement. *Wired* Jan. 2014: 47. Print.

Lufthansa. Advertisement. *New York Times.* New York Times, 16 Apr. 2014. Web. 16 Apr. 2014.

---

**QUICK HELP**

## Citing visuals that appear in your text

If you choose to include images in your text, you need to cite and caption them correctly (see pp. 410–11).

- For a work that you have created, the works-cited entry should begin with a descriptive phrase from the image's caption ("L.A. Bus Stop"), a label ("Photograph by author"), and the date. (For an example, see **model 20** on pp. 410–11.)
- For a visual reproduced from another source, you can include the complete citation information in the caption, or you can indicate the source to allow readers to find it on the list of works cited. If you give the complete citation in the caption and do not cite the visual elsewhere in your text, you can omit the visual from your works-cited page.

## ☐ Other sources (including online versions)

If an online version is not shown in this section, use the appropriate model for the source and then end with the medium and date of access.

**78. Report or pamphlet** Follow the guidelines for a print book (models 7–28) or a digital book (model 41).

> Allen, Katherine, and Lee Rainie. *Parents Online.* Washington: Pew Internet and Amer. Life Project, 2002. Print.

> Environmental Working Group. *Dead in the Water.* Washington: Environmental Working Group, 2006. Web. 24 Apr. 2014.

**79. Government publication** Begin with the author, if identified. Otherwise, start with the name of the government, followed by the agency. For congressional documents, cite the number, session, and house of Congress (*S* for Senate, *H* for House of Representatives); the type (*Report, Resolution, Document*) in abbreviated form; and the number. End with the publication information. The print publisher is often the Government Printing Office (GPO). For online versions, follow the models for a work from a Web site (model 46), an entire Web site (model 47), or a downloadable file (model 73).

> Gregg, Judd. *Report to Accompany the Genetic Information Act of 2003.* US 108th Cong., 1st sess. S. Rept. 108-22. Washington: GPO, 2003. Print.

> Kinsella, Kevin, and Victoria Velkoff. *An Aging World: 2001.* US Bureau of the Census. Washington: GPO, 2001. Print.

> United States. Dept. of Health and Human Services. *Keep the Beat Recipes: Deliciously Healthy Dinners.* National Institutes of Health, Oct. 2009. PDF file.

**80. Published proceedings of a conference** Cite the proceedings as you would a book.

> Cleary, John, and Gary Gurtler, eds. *Proceedings of the Boston Area Colloquium in Ancient Philosophy 2002.* Boston: Brill Academic, 2003. Print.

**81. Dissertation** Enclose the title in quotation marks. Add the label *Diss.*, the school, and the year the work was accepted.

> Paris, Django. "Our Culture: Difference, Division, and Unity in Multicultural Youth Space." Diss. Stanford U, 2008. Print.

*Note*: Cite a published dissertation as a book, adding the identification *Diss.* and the university after the title.

**82. Dissertation abstract** Cite the abstract as you would an unpublished dissertation (see model 81). For the abstract of a dissertation using *Disserta-*

*tion Abstracts International* (*DAI*), include the *DAI* volume, year, and page number.

> Huang-Tiller, Gillian C. "The Power of the Meta-Genre: Cultural, Sexual, and Racial Politics of the American Modernist Sonnet." Diss. U of Notre Dame, 2000. *DAI* 61 (2000): 1401. Print.

**83. Unpublished letter**   Cite a published letter as a work in an anthology (see model 11). If the letter is unpublished, follow this form:

> Anzaldúa, Gloria. Letter to the author. 10 Sept. 2002. MS.

**84. Manuscript or other unpublished work**   List the author's name; the title (if any) or a description of the material; the form of the material (such as *MS* for manuscript or *TS* for typescript) and any identifying numbers; and the name and location of the library or research institution housing the material, if applicable.

> Woolf, Virginia. "The Searchlight." N.d. TS. Ser. III, Box 4, Item 184. Papers of Virginia Woolf, 1902-1956. Smith Coll., Northampton.

**85. Legal source**   To cite a court case, give the names of the first plaintiff and defendant, the case number, the name of the court, and the date of the decision. To cite an act, give the name of the act followed by its Public Law (*Pub. L.*) number, the date the act was enacted, and its Statutes at Large (*Stat.*) cataloging number.

> Eldred v. Ashcroft. No. 01-618. Supreme Ct. of the US. 15 Jan. 2003. Print.

> Museum and Library Services Act of 2003. Pub. L. 108-81. 25 Sept. 2003. Stat. 117.991. Print.

*Note:* You do not need an entry in the list of works cited when you cite articles of the U.S. Constitution and laws in the U.S. Code.

## 32e  A student research essay, MLA style

STUDENT WRITER
David Craig

David Craig's research project appears on the following pages. In preparing this essay, he followed the MLA guidelines described in this chapter. His complete project appears with an activity in the integrated media at **macmillanhighered.com/smh**. (Photo © David Craig)

Craig 1

1″   ½″

David Craig

Professor Turkman

English 219

18 December 2014

Messaging: The Language of Youth Literacy

The English language is under attack. At least, that is what many people seem to believe. From concerned parents to local librarians, everyone seems to have a negative comment on the state of youth literacy today. They fear that the current generation of grade school students will graduate with an extremely low level of literacy, and they point out that although language education hasn't changed, kids are having more trouble reading and writing than in the past. When asked about the cause of this situation, many adults pin the blame on technologies such as texting and instant messaging, arguing that electronic shortcuts create and compound undesirable reading and writing habits and discourage students from learning conventionally correct ways to use language. But although the arguments against messaging are passionate, evidence suggests that they may not hold up.

The disagreements about messaging shortcuts are profound, even among academics. John Briggs, an English professor at the University of California, Riverside, says, "Americans have always been informal, but now the informality of precollege culture is so ubiquitous that many students have no practice in using language in any formal setting at all" (qtd. in McCarroll). Such objections are not new; Sven Birkerts of Mount Holyoke College argued in 1999 that "[students] read more casually. They strip-mine what they read" online and consequently produce "quickly generated, casual prose" (qtd. in Leibowitz A67). However, academics are also among the defenders of texting and instant messaging (IM), with some suggesting that messaging may be a beneficial force in the development of youth literacy because it promotes regular contact with words and the use of a written medium for communication.

Texting and instant messaging allows two individuals who are separated by any distance to engage in real-time, written communication. Although

*Marginal annotations (left column):*

Name, instructor, course, date aligned at left

Title centered

Opens with attention-getting statement

Background on the problem of youth literacy

Explicit thesis statement concludes introductory paragraph

Indirect quotation uses "qtd. in" and name of Web source on list of works cited

Definition and example of messaging

---

Marginal annotations indicate effective choices or MLA-style formatting.

Craig 2  Writer's last name and page number at upper right corner of every page

such communication relies on the written word, many messagers disregard standard writing conventions. For example, here is a snippet from an IM conversation between two teenage girls:[1]

> Teen One: sorry im talkinto like 10 ppl at a time
>
> Teen Two: u izzyful person
>
> Teen Two: kwel
>
> Teen One: hey i g2g

As this brief conversation shows, participants must use words to communicate via texting and messaging, but their words do not have to be in standard English.

The issue of youth literacy does demand attention because standardized test scores for language assessments, such as the verbal and writing sections of the College Board's SAT, have declined in recent years. This trend is illustrated in a chart distributed by the College Board as part of its 2011 analysis of aggregate SAT data (see Fig. 1).

Writer considers argument that youth literacy is in decline

Figure explained in text and cited in parenthetical reference

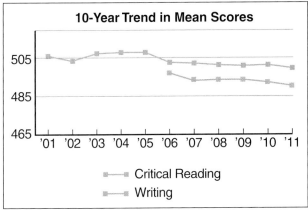

Fig. 1. Ten-year trend in mean SAT reading and writing scores (2001-2011). Data source: College Board, "2011 SAT Trends."

Figure labeled, titled, and credited to source; inserted at appropriate point in text

---

[1] This transcript of an IM conversation was collected on 20 Nov. 2014. The teenagers' names are concealed to protect privacy.

Explanatory note adds information about field research not found on list of works cited

Craig 3

Discussion of
Figure 1

The trend lines illustrate a significant pattern that may lead to
the conclusion that youth literacy is on the decline. These lines display
the ten-year paths (from 2001 to 2011) of reading and writing scores,
respectively. Within this period, the average verbal score dropped a few
points—and appears to be headed toward a further decline in the future.

Writer accepts
part of critic's
argument;
transition to next
point

Based on the preceding statistics, parents and educators appear to
be right about the decline in youth literacy. And this trend coincides
with another phenomenon: digital communication is rising among the
young. According to the Pew Internet & American Life Project, 85 percent

For Web source
with no page
numbers, only
author names
appear in
parentheses

of those aged 12-17 at least occasionally write text messages, instant
messages, or comments on social networking sites (Lenhart, Arafeh,
Smith, and Macgill). In 2001, the most conservative estimate based on

Statistical
evidence cited

Pew numbers showed that American youths spent, at a minimum, nearly
three million hours per day on instant messaging services (Lenhart and
Lewis 20). These numbers are now exploding thanks to texting, which
was "the dominant daily mode of communication" for teens in 2012
(Lenhart), and messaging on popular social networking sites such as
Facebook and Tumblr.

In the interest of establishing the existence of a messaging

Writer's field
research
described

language, I analyzed 11,341 lines of text from IM conversations
between youths in my target demographic: U.S. residents aged twelve to
seventeen. Young messengers voluntarily sent me chat logs, but they were
unaware of the exact nature of my research. Once all of the logs had been
gathered, I went through them, recording the number of times messaging
language was used in place of conventional words and phrases. Then I
generated graphs to display how often these replacements were used.

During the course of my study, I identified four types of messaging
language: phonetic replacements, acronyms, abbreviations, and inanities. An
example of phonetic replacement is using *ur* for *you are*. Another popular
type of messaging language is the acronym; for a majority of the people in
my study, the most common acronym was *lol*, a construction that means

Findings of
field research
presented

*laughing out loud*. Abbreviations are also common in messaging, but I
discovered that typical IM abbreviations, such as *etc.*, are not new to the

Craig 4

English language. Finally, I found a class of words that I call "inanities." These words include completely new words or expressions, combinations of several slang categories, or simply nonsensical variations of other words. My favorite from this category is *lolz*, an inanity that translates directly to *lol* yet includes a terminating *z* for no obvious reason.

In the chat transcripts that I analyzed, the best display of typical messaging lingo came from the conversations between two thirteen-year-old Texan girls, who are avid IM users. Figure 2 is a graph showing how often they used certain phonetic replacements and abbreviations. On the *y*-axis, frequency of replacement is plotted, a calculation that compares the number of times a word or phrase is used in messaging language with the total number of times that it is communicated in any form. On the *x*-axis, specific messaging words and phrases are listed.

My research shows that the Texan girls use the first ten phonetic replacements or abbreviations at least 50 percent of the time in their normal messaging writing. For example, every time one of them writes *see*, there is a parallel time when *c* is used in its place. In light of this finding, it appears that the popular messaging culture contains at least some elements of its own language. It also seems that much of this language is new: no formal dictionary yet identifies the most common messaging words and phrases. Only in the heyday of the telegraph or on

*Figure introduced and explained*

*Discussion of findings presented in Figure 2*

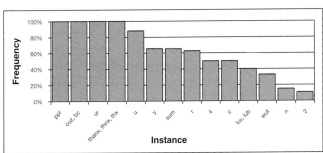

Fig. 2. Usage of phonetic replacements and abbreviations in messaging.

*Figure labeled and titled*

Craig 5

the rolls of a stenographer would you find a similar situation, but these "languages" were never a popular medium of youth communication. Texting and instant messaging, however, are very popular among young people and continue to generate attention and debate in academic circles.

My research shows that messaging is certainly widespread, and it does seem to have its own particular vocabulary, yet these two factors alone do not mean it has a damaging influence on youth literacy. As noted earlier, however, some people claim that the new technology is a threat to the English language. In an article provocatively titled "Texting Makes U Stupid," historian Niall Ferguson argues, "The good news is that today's teenagers are avid readers and prolific writers. The bad news is that what they are reading and writing are text messages." He goes on to accuse texting of causing the United States to "[fall] behind more literate societies."

The critics of messaging are numerous. But if we look to the field of linguistics, a central concept — metalinguistics — challenges these criticisms and leads to a more reasonable conclusion — that messaging has no negative impact on a student's development of or proficiency with traditional literacy.

Scholars of metalinguistics offer support for the claim that messaging is not damaging to those who use it. As noted earlier, one of the most prominent components of messaging language is phonetic replacement, in which a word such as *everyone* becomes *every1*. This type of wordplay has a special importance in the development of an advanced literacy, and for good reason. According to David Crystal, an internationally recognized scholar of linguistics at the University of Wales, as young children develop and learn how words string together to express ideas, they go through many phases of language play. The singsong rhymes and nonsensical chants of preschoolers are vital to their learning language, and a healthy appetite for such wordplay leads to a better command of language later in life (182).

As justification for his view of the connection between language play and advanced literacy, Crystal presents an argument for

---

**Writer returns to opposition argument**

For author of Web source named in signal phrase, no parenthetical citation needed

**Transition to support of thesis and refutation of critics**

**Linguistic authority cited in support of thesis**

Author of print source named in signal phrase, so parenthetical citation includes only page number

metalinguistic awareness. According to Crystal, *metalinguistics* refers to the ability to "step back" and use words to analyze how language works:

> If we are good at stepping back, at thinking in a more abstract way about what we hear and what we say, then we are more likely to be good at acquiring those skills which depend on just such a stepping back in order to be successful — and this means, chiefly, reading and writing. . . . [T]he greater our ability to play with language, . . . the more advanced will be our command of language as a whole. (Crystal 181)

If we accept the findings of linguists such as Crystal that metalinguistic awareness leads to increased literacy, then it seems reasonable to argue that the phonetic language of messaging can also lead to increased metalinguistic awareness and, therefore, increases in overall literacy. As messagers develop proficiency with a variety of phonetic replacements and other types of texting and messaging words, they should increase their subconscious knowledge of metalinguistics.

Metalinguistics also involves our ability to write in a variety of distinct styles and tones. Yet in the debate over messaging and literacy, many critics assume that either messaging or academic literacy will eventually win out in a person and that the two modes cannot exist side by side. This assumption is, however, false. Human beings ordinarily develop a large range of language abilities, from the formal to the relaxed and from the mainstream to the subcultural. Mark Twain, for example, had an understanding of local speech that he employed when writing dialogue for *Huckleberry Finn*. Yet few people would argue that Twain's knowledge of this form of English had a negative impact on his ability to write in standard English.

However, just as Mark Twain used dialects carefully in dialogue, writers must pay careful attention to the kind of language they use in any setting. The owner of the language Web site *The Discouraging Word*, who is an anonymous English literature graduate student at the University of Chicago, backs up this idea in an e-mail to me:

**Block format for a quotation of more than four lines**

**Ellipses and brackets indicate omissions and changes in quotation**

**Writer links Crystal's views to thesis**

**Another refutation of critics' assumptions**

**Example from well-known work of literature used as support**

Craig 7

Email correspondence cited in support of claim

What is necessary, we feel, is that students learn how to shift between different styles of writing—that, in other words, the abbreviations and shortcuts of messaging should be used online . . . but that they should not be used in an essay submitted to a teacher. . . . Messaging might even be considered . . . a different way of reading and writing, one that requires specific and unique skills shared by certain communities.

The analytical ability that is necessary for writers to choose an appropriate tone and style in their writing is, of course, metalinguistic in nature because it involves the comparison of two or more language systems. Thus, youths who grasp multiple languages will have a greater

Writer synthesizes evidence for claim

natural understanding of metalinguistics. More specifically, young people who possess both messaging and traditional skills stand to be better off than their peers who have been trained only in traditional or conventional systems. Far from being hurt by their online pastime, instant messagers can be aided in standard writing by their experience with messaging language.

Transition to final point

The fact remains, however, that youth literacy seems to be declining. What, if not messaging, is the main cause of this phenomenon? According to the College Board, which collects data on several questions

Alternate explanation for decline in literacy

from its test takers, course work in English composition and grammar classes has decreased by 14 percent between 1992 and 2002 (Carnahan and Coletti 11). The possibility of messaging causing a decline in literacy seems inadequate when statistics on English education for US youths provide other evidence of the possible causes. Simply put, schools in the United States are not teaching English as much as they used to. Rather than blaming texting and messaging language alone for the decline in literacy and test scores, we must also look toward our schools' lack of focus on the teaching of standard English skills.

Transition to conclusion

My findings indicate that the use of messaging poses virtually no threat to the development or maintenance of formal language skills among American youths aged twelve to seventeen. Diverse language skills

Craig 8

tend to increase a person's metalinguistic awareness and, thereby, his or her ability to use language effectively to achieve a desired purpose in a particular situation. The current decline in youth literacy is not due to the rise of texting and messaging. Rather, fewer young students seem to be receiving an adequate education in the use of conventional English. Unfortunately, it may always be fashionable to blame new tools for old problems, but in the case of messaging, that blame is not warranted. Although messaging may expose literacy problems, it does not create them.

Concluding paragraph sums up argument and reiterates thesis

Craig 9

Works Cited

Carnahan, Kristin, and Chiara Coletti. *Ten-Year Trend in SAT Scores Indicates Increased Emphasis on Math Is Yielding Results: Reading and Writing Are Causes for Concern*. New York: College Board, 2002. Print.

College Board. "2011 SAT Trends." *Collegeboard.org*. College Board, 14 Sept. 2011. Web. 6 Dec. 2014.

Crystal, David. *Language Play*. Chicago: U of Chicago P, 1998. Print.

*The Discouraging Word*. "Re: Messaging and Literacy." Message to the author. 13 Nov. 2014. E-mail.

Ferguson, Niall. "Texting Makes U Stupid." *Newsweek* 158.12 (2011): 11. *Academic Search Premier*. Web. 7 Dec. 2014.

Leibowitz, Wendy R. "Technology Transforms Writing and the Teaching of Writing." *Chronicle of Higher Education* 26 Nov. 1999: A67-68. Print.

Lenhart, Amanda. *Teens, Smartphones, & Texting*. Pew Research Center, 19 Mar. 2012. PDF file.

Lenhart, Amanda, Sousan Arafeh, Aaron Smith, and Alexandra Macgill. *Writing, Technology & Teens*. Pew Research Center, 24 Apr. 2008. Web. 6 Dec. 2014.

Lenhart, Amanda, and Oliver Lewis. *Teenage Life Online: The Rise of the Instant-Message Generation and the Internet's Impact on Friendships and Family Relationships*. Pew Research Center, 21 June 2001. Web. 6 Dec. 2014.

McCarroll, Christina. "Teens Ready to Prove Text-Messaging Skills Can Score SAT Points." *Christian Science Monitor* 11 Mar. 2005. Web. 10 Dec. 2014.

Heading centered

Report

Graph

Book

Email

Article from database

Print newspaper article

Downloaded file

Online report

Subsequent lines of each entry indented

Online newspaper article

# CHAPTER 33

# APA Style

**C**HAPTER 33 DISCUSSES THE BASIC FORMATS prescribed by the American Psychological Association (APA), guidelines that are widely used for research in the social sciences. For further reference, consult the *Publication Manual of the American Psychological Association,* Sixth Edition (2010).

## 33a  Understanding the basics of APA style

Why does academic work call for very careful citation practices when writing for the general public may not? The answer is that readers of academic work expect source citations for several reasons:

- Source citations demonstrate that you've done your homework on your topic and that you are a part of the conversation surrounding it.
- Source citations show that you understand the need to give credit when you make use of someone else's intellectual property. (See Chapter 14.)
- Source citations give explicit directions to guide readers who want to look for themselves at the works you're using.

The guidelines for APA style tell you exactly what information to include in your citation and how to format that information.

### ☐  Types of sources

Look at the Directory to APA Style on pp. 459–61 for guidelines on citing various types of sources—print books (or parts of print books), articles in print periodicals (journals, magazines, and newspapers), and digital written-word sources (an online article or a book on an e-reader). A digital version of a source may include updates or corrections that the print version lacks, so it's important to provide the correct citation information for readers. For sources that consist mainly of material other than written words—such as a film, song, or artwork—consult the other sections of the directory. And if you can't find a model exactly like the source you've selected, see the Quick Help box on p. 459.

*Articles from Web and database sources*

You need a subscription to look through most databases, so individual researchers almost always gain access to articles in databases through the computer system of a school or public library that pays to subscribe. The easiest way to tell whether a source comes from a database, then, is that its information is *not* generally available for free. Many databases are digital collections of articles that originally appeared in edited print periodicals, ensuring that an authority has vouched for the accuracy of the information. Such sources often have more credibility than free material available on the Web.

## ☐ Parts of citations

APA citations appear in two parts of your text — a brief in-text citation in the body of your written text and a full citation in the list of references, to which the in-text citation directs readers. The most straightforward in-text citations include the author's name, the publication year, and the page number, but many variations on this basic format are discussed in 33c.

In the text of her research essay — see 21c as well as the integrated media at **macmillanhighered.com/smh** — Tawnya Redding includes a paraphrase of material from an online journal that she had accessed through the publisher's Web site. She cites the authors' names and the year of publication in a parenthetical reference, pointing readers to the entry for "Baker, F., & Bor, W. (2008)" in her references list, as shown in the figure on p. 453.

## ☐ Content notes

APA style allows you to use content notes, either at the bottom of the page or on a separate page at the end of the text, to expand or supplement your text. Indicate such notes in the text by superscript numerals ([1]). Double-space all entries. Indent the first line of each note five spaces, but begin subsequent lines at the left margin.

**SUPERSCRIPT NUMBER IN TEXT**

The age of the children involved in the study was an important factor in the selection of items for the questionnaire.[1]

**FOOTNOTE**

[1]Marjorie Youngston Forman and William Cole of the Child Study Team provided great assistance in identifying appropriate items for the questionnaire.

# 33b Formatting APA manuscripts

The following formatting guidelines are adapted from the APA recommendations for preparing manuscripts for publication in journals. However, check with your instructor before preparing the final draft of a print text.

MOOD MUSIC                                                          9

References

Baker, F., & Bor, W. (2008). Can music preference indicate mental
    health status in young people? *Australasian Psychiatry, 16*(4),
    284 – 288. Retrieved from http://www3.interscience.wiley.com
    /journal/118565538/home

George, D., Stickle, K., Rachid, F., & Wopnford, A. (2007). The association
    ... and personality

alter the mood of at-risk youth in a negative way. This view of the
correlation between music and suicide risk is supported by a meta-
analysis done by Baker and Bor (2008), in which the authors assert
that most studies reject the notion that music is a causal factor
and suggest that music preference is more indicative of emotional
vulnerability. However, it is still unknown whether these genres can

... music and ... . 30(3),

Taiwan. *Issues in Mental Health Nursing, 20,* 229 – 246. doi:
    10.1080/016128499248637

- **Title page.** If your instructor wants you to include a running head, place
  it flush left on the first line. Write the words *Running head*, a colon, and a
  short version of the title (fifty characters or fewer, including spaces) using
  all capital letters. On the same line, flush with the right margin, type the
  number *1*.

    Center the title and include your name and school affiliation. An
  author's note at the bottom of the page can give the course name and contact
  information, if desired.

- **Margins and spacing.** Leave margins of one inch at the top and bottom and
  on both sides of the page. Do not justify the right margin. Double-space the
  entire text, including any headings, set-off quotations (13b), content notes,
  and the list of references. Indent one-half inch for the first line of a paragraph
  and all lines of a quotation over forty words long.

- **Short title and page numbers.** Place the short title in the upper left corner
  of each page. Place the page number in the upper right corner of each page,
  in the same position as on the title page.

- **Long quotations.** To set off a long quotation (more than forty words),
  indent it one-half inch from the left margin. Do not use quotation marks.
  Place the page reference in parentheses one space after the final punctuation.

- **Abstract.** If your instructor asks for an abstract, the abstract should go immediately after the title page, with the word *Abstract* centered an inch from the
  top of the page. Double-space the text of the abstract. In most cases, a one-
  paragraph abstract of about one hundred words will be sufficient to introduce

readers to your topic and provide a brief summary of your major thesis and supporting points.

- **Headings.**   Headings are used within the text of many APA-style projects. In a text with only one or two levels of headings, use boldface type; center the main headings, and position the subheadings flush with the left margin. Capitalize all major words; however, do not capitalize articles, short prepositions, and coordinating conjunctions unless they are the first word or follow a colon.

- **Visuals.**   Tables should be labeled *Table*, numbered, and captioned. All other visuals (such as charts, graphs, photographs, and drawings) should be labeled *Figure*, numbered, and captioned with a description and the source information. Remember to refer to each visual in your text, stating how it contributes to the point(s) you are making. Tables and figures should generally appear near the relevant text; check with your instructor for guidelines on the placement of visuals.

## 33c   Creating APA in-text citations

An in-text citation in APA style always indicates which source on the references page the writer is referring to, and it explains in what year the material was published; for quoted material, the in-text citation also indicates where in the source the quotation can be found.

Note that APA style generally calls for using the past tense or present perfect tense for signal verbs: *Baker (2003) showed* or *Baker (2003) has shown*. Use the present tense only to discuss results (*the experiment demonstrates*) or widely accepted information (*researchers agree*).

*1. Basic format for a quotation*    Generally, use the author's name in a signal phrase to introduce the cited material, and place the date, in parentheses, immediately after the author's name. The page number, preceded by *p.,* appears in parentheses after the quotation.

> Gitlin (2001) pointed out that "political critics, convinced that the media are rigged against them, are often blind to other substantial reasons why their causes are unpersuasive" (p. 141).

If the author is not named in a signal phrase, place the author's name, the year, and the page number in parentheses after the quotation: (Gitlin, 2001, p. 141). For a long, set-off quotation (more than forty words), place the page reference in parentheses one space after the final quotation.

For quotations from works without page numbers, you may use paragraph numbers, if the source includes them, preceded by the abbreviation *para.*

> Driver (2007) has noticed "an increasing focus on the role of land" in policy debates over the past decade (para. 1).

*2. Basic format for a paraphrase or summary*    Include the author's last name and the year as in model 1, but omit the page or paragraph number unless the reader will need it to find the material in a long work.

> Gitlin (2001) has argued that critics sometimes overestimate the influence of the media on modern life.

*3. Two authors*    Use both names in all citations. Use *and* in a signal phrase, but use an ampersand (&) in parentheses.

> Babcock and Laschever (2003) have suggested that many women do not negotiate their salaries and pay raises as vigorously as their male counterparts do.

> A recent study has suggested that many women do not negotiate their salaries and pay raises as vigorously as their male counterparts do (Babcock & Laschever, 2003).

*4. Three to five authors*    List all the authors' names for the first reference.

> Safer, Voccola, Hurd, and Goodwin (2003) reached somewhat different conclusions by designing a study that was less dependent on subjective judgment than were previous studies.

In subsequent references, use just the first author's name followed by *et al.*

> Based on the results, Safer et al. (2003) determined that the apes took significant steps toward self-expression.

**5. Six or more authors** Use only the first author's name and *et al.* in every citation.

> As Soleim et al. (2002) demonstrated, advertising holds the potential for manipulating "free-willed" consumers.

**6. Corporate or group author** If the name of the organization or corporation is long, spell it out the first time you use it, followed by an abbreviation in brackets. In later references, use the abbreviation only.

> FIRST CITATION    (Centers for Disease Control and Prevention [CDC], 2006)

> LATER CITATIONS   (CDC, 2006)

**7. Unknown author** Use the title or its first few words in a signal phrase or in parentheses. A book's title is italicized, as in the following example; an article's title is placed in quotation marks.

> The employment profiles for this time period substantiated this trend (*Federal Employment,* 2001).

**8. Two or more authors with the same last name** Include the authors' initials in each citation.

> S. Bartolomeo (2000) conducted the groundbreaking study on teenage childbearing.

**9. Two or more works by an author in a single year** Assign lowercase letters (*a, b,* and so on) alphabetically by title, and include the letters after the year.

> Gordon (2004b) examined this trend in more detail.

**10. Two or more sources in one parenthetical reference** List any sources by different authors in alphabetical order by the authors' last names, separated by semicolons: (Cardone, 1998; Lai, 2002). List works by the same author in chronological order, separated by commas: (Lai, 2000, 2002).

**11. Source reported in another source** Use the phrase *as cited in* to indicate that you are reporting information from a secondary source. Name the original source in a signal phrase, but list the secondary source in your list of references.

> Amartya Sen developed the influential concept that land reform was necessary for "promoting opportunity" among the poor (as cited in Driver, 2007, para. 2).

**12. Personal communication** Cite personal letters, email messages, electronic postings, telephone conversations, or interviews as shown. Do not include personal communications in the reference list.

> R. Tobin (personal communication, November 4, 2006) supported his claims about music therapy with new evidence.

**13. Digital source** Cite a Web or electronic document as you would a print source, using the author's name and date.

> Link and Phelan (2005) argued for broader interventions in public health that would be accessible to anyone, regardless of individual wealth.

The APA recommends the following for electronic sources without names, dates, or page numbers:

AUTHOR UNKNOWN

Use a shortened form of the title in a signal phrase or in parentheses (see model 7). If an organization is the author, see model 6.

DATE UNKNOWN

Use the abbreviation *n.d.* (for "no date") in place of the year: (*Hopkins, n.d.*).

NO PAGE NUMBERS

Many works found online or in electronic databases lack stable page numbers. (Use the page numbers for an electronic work in a format, such as PDF, that has stable pagination.) If paragraph numbers are included in such a source, use the abbreviation *para.*: (*Giambetti, 2014, para.* 7). If no paragraph numbers are included but the source includes headings, give the heading and identify the paragraph in the section:

> Jacobs and Johnson (2007) have argued that "the South African media is still highly concentrated and not very diverse in terms of race and class" (South African Media after Apartheid, para. 3).

**14. Entire Web site** If you are citing an entire Web site, not simply a page or document from a site, list the URL in parentheses in the text of your writing project. Do not include it in the list of references.

**15. Table or figure reproduced in the text** Number figures (illustrations, graphs, charts, and photographs) and tables separately.

For a table, place the label (*Table 1*) and an informative heading (*Hartman's Key Personality Traits*) above the table; below, provide information about its source.

Table 1

*Hartman's Key Personality Traits*

| Trait category | Color | | | |
|---|---|---|---|---|
| | Red | Blue | White | Yellow |
| Motive | Power | Intimacy | Peace | Fun |
| Strengths | Loyal to tasks | Loyal to people | Tolerant | Positive |
| Limitations | Arrogant | Self-righteous | Timid | Uncommitted |

*Note:* Adapted from *The Hartman Personality Profile,* by N. Hayden. Retrieved February 24, 2013, from http://students.cs.byu.edu/~nhayden/Code/index .php

For a figure, place the label (*Figure 3*) and a caption indicating the source below the image. If you do not cite the source of the table or figure elsewhere in your text, you do not need to include the source on your list of references.

## 33d Preparing the APA list of references

A list of references is an alphabetical list of the sources you have referred to in your essay. (If your instructor asks you to list everything you have read, not just the sources you cite, call the list *Bibliography.*) Begin the references list on a separate page or slide after the text of your project and any notes, under the centered heading *References* (not italicized or in quotation marks).

- Do not indent the first line of each entry, but indent subsequent lines for the entry one-half inch. (This makes the author names easy to scan.) Double-space the entire list.

- List sources alphabetically by authors' last names, or by the title for a work without an author. For titles beginning with the articles *A, An,* or *The,* don't count the article when alphabetizing.

- List the author's last name first, followed by a comma and initials. For more than one author, use an ampersand (&) before the name of the last author, and separate the names with commas.

- Italicize the titles of books and long works. Do not italicize titles of articles and other short works, and do not enclose them in quotation marks.

- For titles of books and articles, capitalize only the first word of the title and subtitle and any proper nouns or proper adjectives. For titles of periodicals, capitalize all major words.

## Citing sources that don't match any model exactly

What should you do if your source doesn't match the model exactly? Suppose, for instance, that your source is a translation of a republished book with an editor.

- Identify a basic model to follow. If you decide that your source looks most like a republished book, start with a citation that looks like **model 18**.
- Look for models that show the additional elements in your source. For this example, you would need to add elements of **model 13** (for the translation) and **model 8** (for the editor).
- Add new elements from other models to your basic model in the order indicated.
- If you aren't sure how to arrange the pieces to create a combination model, ask your instructor.

To cite a source for which you cannot find a model, collect as much information as you can find about the creator, title, sponsor, date, and so on, with the goal of helping your readers find the source for themselves. Then look at the models in this section to see which one most closely matches the type of source you are using. If possible, seek your instructor's advice to find the best model.

## DIRECTORY TO APA STYLE   REFERENCES

### Guidelines for author listings

### Print books

☐ **Guidelines for author listings**

The list of references is arranged alphabetically. The in-text citations in your writing point readers toward particular sources on the list (33c).

**NAME CITED IN SIGNAL PHRASE IN TEXT**

Driver (2007) has noted . . .

**NAME IN PARENTHETICAL CITATION IN TEXT**

. . . (Driver, 2007).

**BEGINNING OF ENTRY IN LIST OF REFERENCES**

Driver, T. (2007).

Models 1–9 below explain how to arrange author and editor names. The information that follows the name of the author depends on the type of work you are citing—a book (models 10–22), a print periodical (models 23–29), a digital written-word source (models 30–47), a media or live source (models 48–64), an academic source (models 65–68), or a personal communication (models 69–71).

**1. One author**   Give the last name, a comma, the initial(s), and the date in parentheses.

Zimbardo, P. G. (2007). *The Lucifer effect: Understanding how good people turn evil.* New York, NY: Random House.

**2. Multiple authors**    List up to seven authors, last name first, with commas separating authors' names and an ampersand (&) before the last author's name.

> Miller, S. J., O'Hea, E. L., Lerner, J. B., Moon, S., & Foran-Tuller, K. A.
>     (2011).

For a work with more than seven authors, list the first six, then an ellipsis (. . .), and then the final author's name.

> Lahmann, C., Henrich, G., Henningsen, P., Baessler, A., Fischer, M., Loew, T., . . .
>     Pieh, C. (2011).

**3. Organization or group author**

> Resources for Rehabilitation. (2003).

**4. Unknown author**    Begin with the work's title. Italicize book titles, but do not italicize article titles or enclose them in quotation marks. Capitalize only the first word of the title and subtitle (if any) and proper nouns and proper adjectives.

> *Safe youth, safe schools.* (2009).

**5. Author using a pseudonym (pen name) or screen name**    Give the author's real name, if known, and give the pen or screen name in brackets. If the real name is unknown, use only the screen name.

> Psych Babbler. (2013, August 4). Blogging under a pseudonym
>     [Blog post]. Retrieved from http://www.overacuppacoffee.com
>     /blogging-under-a-pseudonym/

**6. Two or more works by the same author**    List works by the same author in chronological order. Repeat the author's name in each entry.

> Goodall, J. (1999).
>
> Goodall, J. (2002).

**7. Two or more works by the same author in the same year**    If the works appeared in the same year, list them alphabetically by title, and assign lowercase letters (*a, b,* etc.) after the dates.

> Shermer, M. (2002a). On estimating the lifetime of civilizations. *Scientific*
>     *American, 287*(2), 33.
>
> Shermer, M. (2002b). Readers who question evolution. *Scientific American,*
>     *287*(1), 37.

**8. Editor**   If the source has an editor but no author, alphabetize the entry under the editor's last name.

> Mishra, P. (Ed.). (2005). *India in mind*. New York, NY: Random House-Vintage.

**9. Author and editor**   To cite a work with an author and an editor, place the editor's name, with a comma and the abbreviation *Ed.*, in parentheses after the title.

> Austin, J. (1995). *The province of jurisprudence determined*. (W. E. Rumble, Ed.). Cambridge, England: Cambridge University Press.

## ☐ Print books

**10. Basic format for a book**   Begin with the author name(s). (See models 1–9.) Then include the publication year, title and subtitle, city of publication, country or state abbreviation, and publisher. The source map on pp. 464–65 shows where to find this information in a typical book.

> Levick, S. E. (2003). *Clone being: Exploring the psychological and social dimensions*. Lanham, MD: Rowman & Littlefield.

**11. Entire anthology or collection**   Begin with the editor's name, and use the label *Ed.* or *Eds.*

> Rudd, E., & Descartes, L. (Eds.). (2008). *The changing landscape of work and family in the American middle class: Reports from the field*. Lanham, MD: Lexington.

**12. Work in an anthology or collection**   Give the name of the work's author first. List editors after the work's title, and include page numbers after the collection's title.

> Pash, D. M. (2008). Gay family values: Gay co-father families in straight communities. In E. Rudd & L. Descartes (Eds.), *The changing landscape of work and family in the American middle class: Reports from the field* (pp. 159–187). Lanham, MD: Lexington.

**13. Translator**   After the title, give the translator's name and the abbreviation *Trans.* in parentheses.

> Al-Farabi, A. N. (1998). *On the perfect state* (R. Walzer, Trans.). Chicago, IL: Kazi.

# Books

Take information from the book's title page and copyright page (on the reverse side of the title page), not from the book's cover or a library catalog.

1 **Author.** List all authors' last names first, and use only initials for first and middle names. For more about citing authors, see models 1–9.

2 **Publication year.** Enclose the year of publication in parentheses.

3 **Title.** Italicize the title and any subtitle. Capitalize only the first word of the title and the subtitle and any proper nouns or proper adjectives.

4 **City and state of publication, and publisher.** List the city of publication and the country or state abbreviation, a colon, and the publisher's name, dropping any *Inc.*, *Co.*, or *Publishers*.

**A citation for the book on p. 465 would look like this:**

Tsutsui, W. (2004). *Godzilla on my mind: Fifty years of the king of monsters.*
New York, NY: Palgrave Macmillan.

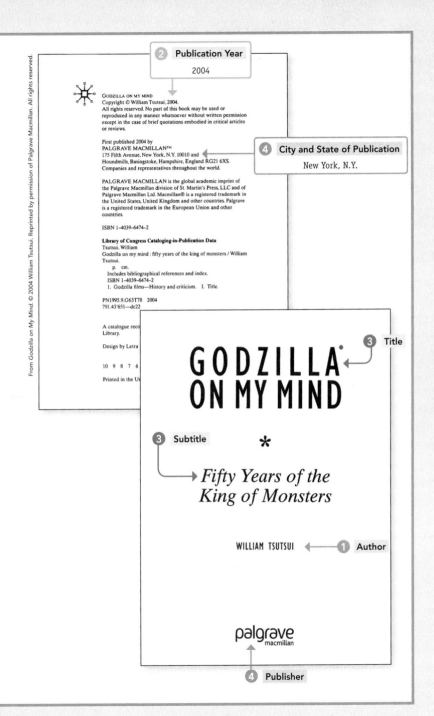

**2 Publication Year**

2004

GODZILLA ON MY MIND.
Copyright © William Tsutsui, 2004.
All rights reserved. No part of this book may be used or reproduced in any manner whatsoever without written permission except in the case of brief quotations embodied in critical articles or reviews.

First published 2004 by
PALGRAVE MACMILLAN™
175 Fifth Avenue, New York, N.Y. 10010 and
Houndmills, Basingstoke, Hampshire, England RG21 6XS.
Companies and representatives throughout the world.

PALGRAVE MACMILLAN is the global academic imprint of the Palgrave Macmillan division of St. Martin's Press, LLC and of Palgrave Macmillan Ltd. Macmillan® is a registered trademark in the United States, United Kingdom and other countries. Palgrave is a registered trademark in the European Union and other countries.

ISBN 1-4039-6474-2

**Library of Congress Cataloging-in-Publication Data**
Tsutsui, William
Godzilla on my mind : fifty years of the king of monsters / William Tsutsui.
     p.   cm.
   Includes bibliographical references and index.
   ISBN 1-4039-6474-2
   1. Godzilla films—History and criticism.   I. Title.

PN1995.9.G63T78   2004
791.43'651—dc22

A catalogue reco
Library.

Design by Letra

10  9  8  7  6

Printed in the U

**4 City and State of Publication**

New York, N.Y.

**3 Title**

# GODZILLA®
# ON MY MIND

**3 Subtitle**

✳

*Fifty Years of the King of Monsters*

WILLIAM TSUTSUI ← **1 Author**

palgrave
macmillan

**4 Publisher**

**14. Book in a language other than English** Include the English translation (in brackets) after the title.

Andre, C. (2004). *Psychologie de la peur* [The psychology of fear]. Paris, France: Odile Jacob.

**15. Edition other than the first**

Moore, G. S. (2002). *Living with the earth: Concepts in environmental health science* (2nd ed.). New York, NY: Lewis.

**16. One volume of a multivolume work** List the volume in parentheses after the title.

Barnes, J. (Ed.). (1995). *Complete works of Aristotle* (Vol. 2). Princeton, NJ: Princeton University Press.

**17. More than one volume of a multivolume work** List the complete span of volumes in parentheses after the title.

Barnes, J. (Ed.). (1995). *Complete works of Aristotle* (Vols. 1–2). Princeton, NJ: Princeton University Press.

**18. Republished book (more recent version of an older book)**

Piaget, J. (1952). *The language and thought of the child.* London, England: Routledge & Kegan Paul. (Original work published 1932)

**19. Introduction, preface, foreword, or afterword**

Klosterman, C. (2007). Introduction. In P. Shirley, *Can I keep my jersey?: 11 teams, 5 countries, and 4 years in my life as a basketball vagabond* (pp. v–vii). New York, NY: Villard-Random House.

**20. Government publication**

Office of the Federal Register. (2003). *The United States government manual 2003/2004.* Washington, DC: U.S. Government Printing Office.

**21. Book with a title within the title** Do not italicize or enclose in quotation marks a title within a book title.

Klarman, M. J. (2007). Brown v. Board of Education *and the civil rights movement.* New York, NY: Oxford University Press.

### 22. Article in a reference book

Dean, C. (1994). Jaws and teeth. In *The Cambridge encyclopedia of human evolution* (pp. 56–59). Cambridge, England: Cambridge University Press.

If no author is listed, begin with the title.

## □ Articles and short works in print periodicals

Begin with the author name(s). (See models 1–9.) Then include the publication date (year only for journals, and year, month, and day for all other periodicals); the article title; the periodical title; the volume number and issue number, if any; and the page numbers. The source map on pp. 468–69 shows where to find this information in a sample periodical.

**23. Article in a print journal**    Include the issue number (in parentheses and not italicized) after the volume number (italicized).

Hall, R. E. (2000). Marriage as vehicle of racism among women of color. *Psychology: A Journal of Human Behavior, 37*(2), 29–40.

**24. Article in a print magazine**    Include the month (as well as the day, if given).

Solomon, A. (2014, March 17). The reckoning. *The New Yorker, 90*(4), 36–45.

**25. Article in a print newspaper**    Use *p.* or *pp.* with the page numbers.

Fackler, M. (2014, April 9). Japan's foreign minister says apologies to wartime victims will be upheld. *The New York Times,* p. A6.

**26. Editorial or unsigned article in a print publication**    Add an identifying label such as *[Editorial]*.

The tyranny of the glass boxes [Editorial]. (2014, April 22). *The New York Times,* p. A24.

**27. Letter to the editor in a print publication**    Add an identifying label.

MacEwan, V. (2014, January). [Letter to the editor]. *The Believer, 12*(1), 4.

# Articles from Print Periodicals

1 **Author.** List all authors' last names first, and use only initials for first and middle names. For more about citing authors, see models 1–9.

2 **Publication date.** Enclose the date in parentheses. For journals, use only the year. For magazines and newspapers, use the year, a comma, the month (spelled out), and the day, if given.

3 **Article title.** Do not italicize or enclose article titles in quotation marks. Capitalize only the first word of the article title and subtitle and any proper nouns or proper adjectives.

4 **Periodical title.** Italicize the periodical title (and subtitle, if any), and capitalize all major words. Follow the periodical title with a comma.

5 **Volume and issue numbers.** Give the volume number (italicized) and, without a space in between, the issue number (if given) in parentheses. Follow with a comma.

6 **Page numbers.** Give the inclusive page numbers of the article. For newspapers only, include the abbreviation *p.* ("page") or *pp.* ("pages") before the page numbers. End the citation with a period.

**A citation for the periodical article on p. 469 would look like this:**

Etzioni, A. (2006). Leaving race behind: Our growing Hispanic population creates a golden opportunity. *The American Scholar, 75*(2), 20–30.

*The* **AMERICAN**
# SCHOLAR

← **4** Periodical Title

Spring 2006 | Vol. 75, No. 2 ← **5** **Volume and Issue Numbers**

**2** **Publication Date**

ROBERT WILSON
*Editor*

JEAN STIPICEVIC
*Managing Editor*

SANDRA COSTICH
*Associate Editor*

*The* **AMERICAN**
## SCHOLAR

**3** Article Title

# Leaving Race Behind

*Our growing Hispanic population creates a golden opportunity*

**AMITAI ETZIONI** ← **1** Author

Some years ago the United States government asked me what my race was. I was reluctant to respond because my 50 years of practicing sociology—and some powerful personal experiences—have underscored for me what we all know to one degree or another, that racial divisions bedevil America, just as they do many other societies across the world. Not wanting to encourage these divisions, I refused to check off one of the specific racial options on the U.S. Census form and instead marked a box labeled "Other." I later found out that the federal government did not accept such an attempt to de-emphasize race, by me or by some 6.75 million other Americans who tried it. Instead the government assigned me to a racial category, one I chose for me. Learning this made me conjure up what I admit is a far-fetched association. I was in this place once before. When I was a Jewish child in Nazi Germany in the early 1930s, many Jews who saw themselves as good Germans wanted to "pass" as Aryans. But the Nazi regime would have none of it. Never mind, they told these Jews, *we determine* who is Jewish and who is not. A similar practice prevailed in the Old South, where if you had one drop of African blood you were a Negro, disregarding all other facts and considerations, including how you saw yourself.

You might suppose that in the years since my little Census-form protest

～ Amitai Etzioni is University Professor at George Washington University and the author of *The Monochrome Society*.

20 ← **6** Page Numbers

**28. Review in a print publication**    Include the author and title of the review, if given. In brackets, give the type of work, the title, and the author (for a book) or year (for a motion picture).

> Lane, A. (2014, March 17). Double trouble [Review of the motion picture *Enemy*, 2014]. *The New Yorker, 90*(4), 78–79.

**29. Interview in a print publication**

> Blume, J. (2014, January). Judy Blume in conversation with Lena Dunham [Interview by Dunham]. *The Believer, 12*(1), 39–48.

□ **Digital written-word sources**

Updated guidelines for citing digital resources are maintained at the APA's Web site (www.apa.org).

---

**QUICK HELP**

**Citing digital sources**

When citing sources accessed online or from an electronic database, include as many of the following elements as you can find:

- **Author.** Give the author's name, if available.

- **Publication date.** Include the date of electronic publication or of the latest update, if available. When no publication date is available, use *n.d.* ("no date").

- **Title.** If the source is not from a larger work, italicize the title.

- **Print publication information.** For articles from online journals, magazines, or reference databases, give the publication title and other publishing information as you would for a print periodical (see **models 23–29**).

- **Retrieval information.** For a work from a database, do the following: if the article has a DOI (digital object identifier), include that number after the publication information; do not include the name of the database. If there is no DOI, write *Retrieved from* followed by the URL for the journal's home page (not the database URL). For a work found on a Web site, write *Retrieved from* and include the URL. If the work seems likely to be updated, include the retrieval date. If the URL is longer than one line, break it only before a punctuation mark; do not break *http://*.

---

**30. Work from an online database**    Give the author, date, title, and publication information as you would for a print document. Include both the volume and issue numbers for all journal articles. If the article has a digital object identifier (DOI), include it. If there is no DOI, write *Retrieved from* and the URL of the journal's home page (not the URL of the database). The source map on pp. 472–73 shows where to find this information for a typical article from a database.

> Hazleden, R. (2003, December). Love yourself: The relationship of the self with itself in popular self-help texts. *Journal of Sociology, 39*(4), 413–428. Retrieved from http://jos.sagepub.com

> Morley, N. J., Ball, L. J., & Ormerod, T. C. (2006). How the detection of insurance fraud succeeds and fails. *Psychology, Crime, & Law, 12*(2), 163–180. doi:10.1080/10683160512331316325

**31. Article from a journal on the Web**   Give information as for an article in a print journal (see model 23). If the article has a DOI (digital object identifier), include it. If there is no DOI, include the URL for the journal's home page or for the article, if it is difficult to find from the home page.

> Cleary, J. M., & Crafti, N. (2007). Basic need satisfaction, emotional eating, and dietary restraint as risk factors for recurrent overeating in a community sample. *E-Journal of Applied Psychology, 2*(3), 27–39. Retrieved from http://ojs.lib.swin.edu.au/index.php/ejap/article /view/90/116

**32. Article from a magazine on the Web**   Give information as for an article from a print magazine (see model 24). If the article has a DOI (digital object identifier), include it. If there is no DOI, include the URL for the magazine's home page.

> Kinsley, M. (2014, April 28). Have you lost your mind? *The New Yorker, (10)*12, 24–31. Retrieved from http://www.newyorker.com/

**33. Article from a newspaper on the Web**   Include information as for a print newspaper article (see model 25). Add the URL of the searchable Web site.

> Barringer, F. (2008, February 7). In many communities, it's not easy going green. *The New York Times.* Retrieved from http://www.nytimes.com/

**34. Abstract for a journal article online**   Include a label.

> Gudjonsson, G. H., & Young, S. (2010). Does confabulation in memory predict suggestibility beyond IQ and memory? [Abstract]. *Personality & Individual Differences, 49*(1), 65–67. doi:10.1016/j.paid.2010.03.014

## Articles from Databases

1. **Author.** Include the author's name as you would for a print source. List all authors' last names first, and use initials for first and middle names. For more about citing authors, see models 1–9.

2. **Publication date.** Enclose the date in parentheses. For journals, use only the year. For magazines and newspapers, use the year, a comma, the month, and the day if given.

3. **Article title.** Capitalize only the first word of the article title and the subtitle and any proper nouns or proper adjectives.

4. **Periodical title.** Italicize the periodical title.

5. **Volume and issue numbers.** For journals and magazines, give the volume number (italicized) and the issue number (in parentheses).

6. **Page numbers.** For journals only, give inclusive page numbers.

7. **Retrieval information.** If the article has a DOI (digital object identifier), include that number after the publication information; do not include the name of the database. If there is no DOI, write *Retrieved from* followed by the URL of the journal's home page (not the database URL).

**A citation for the article on p. 473 would look like this:**

Knobloch-Westerwick, S., & Crane, J. (2012). A losing battle: Effects

of prolonged exposure to thin-ideal images on dieting and

body satisfaction. *Communication Research, 39*(1), 79–102.

doi:10.1177/0093650211400596

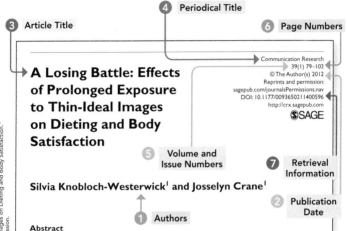

**Periodical Title**

**Article Title**

**Page Numbers**

Communication Research
39(1) 79–102
© The Author(s) 2012
Reprints and permission:
sagepub.com/journalsPermissions.nav
DOI: 10.1177/0093650211400596
http://crx.sagepub.com
**$SAGE**

# A Losing Battle: Effects of Prolonged Exposure to Thin-Ideal Images on Dieting and Body Satisfaction

**Volume and Issue Numbers**

**Retrieval Information**

**Publication Date**

**Silvia Knobloch-Westerwick[1] and Josselyn Crane[1]**

**Authors**

## Abstract

The present study examined prolonged exposure effects of thin-ideal media messages. College-aged females participated in seven online sessions over 10 days including a baseline measures session, five daily measures, and a posttest. Two experimental groups viewed magazine pages with thin-ideal imagery. One of those groups was induced to engage in social comparisons with the thin-ideal models. The control group viewed messages with body-neutral images of women. Prolonged exposure to thin-ideal messages led to greater body satisfaction. This finding was attributed to the fact that the experimental groups reported more dieting behaviors. A mediation analysis showed that the impact of thin-ideal message exposure on body satisfaction was mediated by dieting.

## Keywords

body dissatisfaction, body image, dieting, prolonged exposure, social comparison

Idealized body images in the media have been linked to unrealistic body shape aspirations and body dissatisfaction (see meta-analysis by Grabe, Ward, & Hyde, 2008), which, in turn, have been linked to numerous pathological problems, including depression, obesity, dieting, and eating disorders (e.g., Johnson & Wardle, 2005; Neumark-Sztainer, Paxton, Hannan, Haines, & Story, 2006; Ricciardelli & McCabe, 2001). However, another meta-analysis by Holmstrom (2004) found that the longer the media exposure, the *better* the individuals felt about their body. This inconsistency indicates that the factors and processes at work have not yet been fully understood and captured by the research at hand and deserve further investigation. Social comparison theory is the theoretical framework that has guided much

[1]The Ohio State University

**Corresponding Author:**
Silvia Knobloch-Westerwick, The Ohio State University, 154 N Oval Mall, Columbus, OH 43210
Email: knobloch-westerwick.1@osu.edu

**35. Comment on an online article**   Give the writer's real name (if known) or screen name. If both are given, follow the real name with the screen name in brackets. Use *Re:* before the title of the article, and add the label *Comment* in brackets.

The Lone Ranger. (2014, April 22). Re: The American middle class is no
longer the world's richest [Comment]. *The New York Times.* Retrieved from
http://www.nytimes.com/

**36. Digital book (online or e-reader)**   For a book you read online, give the URL for the home page of the site after the book title.

Stossel, S. (2013). *My age of anxiety: Fear, hope, dread, and the search for*
*peace of mind.* Retrieved from http://books.google.com/

If you downloaded the book to an e-reader such as a Kindle or Nook, give the version after the title. Include the DOI, if given, or the URL of the home page for the site from which you downloaded the file.

Schaap, R. (2013). *Drinking with men: A memoir* [Nook version]. Retrieved
from http://www.barnesandnoble.com/

**37. Online editorial or letter to the editor**   Include the author's name (if given) and the title (if any). For an editorial, give the label *[Editorial]*. For a letter, give the label *[Letter to the editor]*.

Shorter drug sentences [Editorial]. (2014, April 10). *The New York Times.*
Retrieved from http://www.nytimes.com/

Starr, E. (2014, April 4). Local reporting thrives in high schools [Letter to the
editor]. *The Washington Post.* Retrieved from http://www.washingtonpost
.com/

**38. Online review**   Cite an online review as you would a print review (see model 28), and end with a retrieval statement.

Miller, L. (2014, April 20). How the American office worker wound up in a box
[Rev. of the book *Cubed,* by N. Saval]. *Salon.* Retrieved from http://www
.salon.com/

**39. Interview published online**

Ladd, A. (2014, February 25). What ends: An interview with Andrew Ladd
[Interview by J. Gallagher]. Retrieved from http://www.looksandbooks
.com/

**40. Entry in an online reference work or wiki**   Begin with the title unless the author is named. (A wiki, which is collectively edited, will not include an author.)

Gunpowder plot. (2014). In *Wikipedia*. Retrieved April 10, 2014, from http://
www.wikipedia.org/

**41. Report or document from a Web site**  List all of the following that are
available: the author's name; the publication date (or *n.d.* if no date is given);
the title of the document, italicized; and URL. If the publisher is identified and
is not the same as the author, list the publisher in the retrieval statement. The
source map on pp. 476–77 shows where to find this information for a report
from a Web site.

Institute of Medicine of the National Academies. (2011, August 25). *Adverse
effects of vaccines: Evidence and causality.* Retrieved from http://
www.iom.edu/Reports/2011/Adverse-Effects-of-Vaccines-Evidence-and
-Causality.aspx

**42. Section of a Web document**  Cite as you would a chapter in a book (see
model 12).

Fox, S., & Rainie, L. (2014, February 27). Part 1: How the Internet has woven
itself into American life. In *The web at 25 in the U.S.* Retrieved from Pew
Research Center website: http://www.pewinternet.org/2014/02/27
/part-1-how-the-internet-has-woven-itself-into-american-life/

**43. Entire Web site**  Do not cite an entire Web site in your list of references.
Give the URL in parentheses when you mention the site in the body of your
writing project.

**44. Government source online**  If the document is numbered, give the number in parentheses.

U.S. Census Bureau. (2013, September). *Income, poverty, and health insurance
coverage in the United States: 2012* (Report No. P60-245). Retrieved from
http://www.census.gov/prod/2013pubs/p60-245.pdf

**45. Online report from a private organization**  If the publisher and author
are the same, start with the publisher. If they are different, identify the publisher
in the retrieval statement.

Southern Poverty Law Center. (2013, February). *Easy money, impossible debt:
How predatory lending traps Alabama's poor.* Retrieved from http://
www.splcenter.org/sites/default/files/downloads/publication/Payday
_Lending_Report_web.pdf

# Reports and Long Works from Web Sites

1. **Author.** If one is given, include the author's name (see models 1–9). List last names first, and use only initials for first names. The site's sponsor may be the author. If no author is identified, begin the citation with the title of the document.

2. **Publication date.** Enclose the date of publication or latest update in parentheses. Use *n.d.* ("no date") when no publication date is available.

3. **Title of work.** Italicize the title. Capitalize only the first word of the title and subtitle and any proper nouns or proper adjectives.

4. **Retrieval information.** Write *Retrieved from* and include the URL. For a report from an organization's Web site, identify the organization in the retrieval statement. (The APA uses *website*, one word, not capitalized.) If the work seems likely to be updated, include the retrieval date. If you need to break a long URL in the retrieval statement, do so before a punctuation mark.

**A citation for the Web document on p. 477 would look like this:**

Parker, K., & Wang, W. (2013, March 14). *Modern parenthood: Roles of moms and dads converge as they balance work and family.* Retrieved from the Pew Research Center website: http://www.pewsocialtrends .org/2013/03/14/modern-parenthood-roles-of-moms-and-dads -converge-as-they-balance-work-and-family/

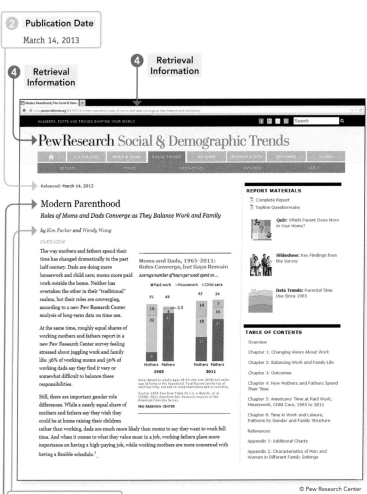

© Pew Research Center

**46. Blog post** Give the author's real name (if known) or screen name; the date of the post (or *n.d.* if no date is given); the title, followed by the label *Web log post* in brackets; and the URL.

> Black, D. (2014, April 22). Wealthy white people from good backgrounds are never involved in crime [Web log post]. Retrieved from http://www .eschatonblog.com/2014/04/wealthy-white-people-from-good.html

**47. Blog comment** Follow model 46 for a blog post, but put *Re:* before the title of the article commented on, and use the label *Web log comment* in brackets.

> JennOfArk. (2014, April 16). Re: Friends in high places [Web log comment]. Retrieved from http://alicublog.blogspot.com/2014/04/friends-in-high -places.html

□ **Visual, audio, multimedia, and live sources**

**48. Film (theatrical, DVD, or other format)** Begin with the director, the producer, and other relevant contributors.

> Bigelow, K. (Director, Producer), Boal, M. (Producer), & Ellison, M. (Producer). (2012). *Zero dark thirty* [Motion picture]. United States: Annapurna.

If you watched the film in another medium, such as on a DVD or Blu-ray disc, indicate the medium in brackets. If the DVD or Blu-ray and the film were not released in the same year, put *Original release* and the year in parentheses at the end of the entry.

> Hitchcock, A. (Director, Producer). (2010). *Psycho* [Blu-ray disc]. United States: Universal. (Original release 1960.)

**49. Video or audio on the Web** Use the label *Audio file* or *Video file* in brackets after the title. If the video or audio is a segment or episode of a show rather than a standalone file, identify the show, as in the first model below.

> Buckner, T. (2013, May 7). *Last laugh* [Audio file]. In *The moth*. Retrieved from http://www.themoth.org/

> Klusman, P. (2008, February 13). *An engineer's guide to cats* [Video file]. Retrieved from http://www.youtube.com/watch?v5=mHXBL6bzAR4

**50. Transcript of video or audio file**

> Glass, I. (2014, March 28). *Bad baby* [Transcript of audio file no. 521]. In *This American life*. Retrieved from http://www.thisamericanlife.org

### 51. Television episode broadcast

Weiner, M. (Writer), & Hornbacher, S. (Director). (2014, April 13). Time zones [Television series episode]. In M. Weiner (Executive producer), *Mad men.* New York, NY: AMC.

### 52. Television series

Gilligan, V. (Executive producer). (2008–2013). *Breaking bad* [Television series]. New York, NY: AMC.

### 53. Television episode on the Web

Weiner, M. (Writer), & Hornbacher, S. (Director). (2014, April 13). Time zones [Television series episode]. In M. Weiner (Executive producer), *Mad men.* Retrieved from http://www.amctv.com/

**54. Podcast (downloaded file)**   For an episode of a podcast series, follow model 53. For a standalone podcast, follow model 41 for a document from the Web. Include an identifying label in brackets.

Britt, M. A. (Writer & Producer). (2013, December 13). Ep. 211: Is a little deception okay? Paid crowds and native advertising [Audio podcast]. In M. A. Britt (Producer), *The psych files.* Retrieved from http://www .thepsychfiles.com/

Spack, N. (2014, April 16). *How I help transgender teens become who they want to be* [Video podcast]. Retrieved from http://www.ted.com/

### 55. Sound recording

The Avalanches. (2001). Frontier psychiatrist. On *Since I left you* [CD]. Los Angeles, CA: Elektra/Asylum Records.

**56. Video game**   Begin with the game's creator, if possible. Follow with the label *[Video game].* If you accessed the game on the Web, give the URL; if you played on a game console, identify the type.

Harmonix. (2012). *Rock band blitz* [Video game]. New York, NY: MTV Games. Xbox 360.

King. (2014). *Candy crush saga* [Video game]. Retrieved from http://www .candycrushsaga.com/

**57. Computer software or app**   If an individual can be identified as the developer, use that person's name. Otherwise, start with the name of the product and give the version. Use the label *Computer software* or *Mobile application software* in brackets.

> MediaWiki (Version 1.22.0) [Mobile application software]. Retrieved from
> http://www.microsoft.com/web/gallery

### 58. Lecture or speech (live)

> Khan, S. (2014, April 16). *Education reimagined.* Address at the Stanford
> University Ventures Program, Stanford University, Stanford, CA.

### 59. Lecture or speech viewed on the Web    Cite as you would a work from a Web site (model 41).

> Burden, A. (2014, March). *How public spaces make cities work* [Video file].
> Retrieved from http://www.ted.com/

### 60. Data set or graphic representation of data    If the graphic appears as part of a larger document, do not italicize the title. Give information about the type of source in brackets.

> U.S. Census Bureau. (2012, December 20). *State-to-state migration for states
> of 8 million or more* [Graph]. Retrieved from http://www.census.gov
> /dataviz/visualizations/028/

### 61. Presentation slides

> Mader, S. L. (2007, March 27). *The Zen aesthetic* [Presentation slides].
> Retrieved from http://www.slideshare.net/slmader/the-zen-aesthetic

### 62. Work of art or photograph

> Bronzino, A. (1550–1555). *Lodovico Capponi* [Painting]. Frick Collection, New
> York, NY.

> Theotolopoulos, D. (ca. 1570). *Christ driving the money changers from the
> temple* [Painting]. Retrieved from http://www.artsmia.org/

### 63. Map

> Australia [Map]. (1999). Retrieved from the University of Texas at Austin
> Perry-Castañeda Library Map Collection website: http://www.lib.utexas
> .edu/maps/australia/australia_pol99.jpg

### 64. Advertisement

> Ameritrade [Advertisement]. (2014, January). *Wired, 22*(1), 47.

☐ **Academic sources (including online versions)**

### 65. Published proceedings of a conference

Robertson, S. P., Vatrapu, R. K., & Medina, R. (2009). YouTube and Facebook: Online video "friends" social networking. In *Conference proceedings: YouTube and the 2008 election cycle* (pp. 159–176). Amherst, MA: University of Massachusetts. Retrieved from http://scholarworks.umass.edu/jitpc2009

### 66. Paper presented at a meeting or symposium, unpublished   Cite the month of the meeting if it is available.

Jones, J. G. (1999, February). *Mental health intervention in mass casualty disasters.* Paper presented at the Rocky Mountain Region Disaster Mental Health Conference, Laramie, WY.

### 67. Poster session

Barnes Young, L. L. (2003, August). *Cognition, aging, and dementia.* Poster session presented at the 2003 Division 40 APA Convention, Toronto, Ontario, Canada.

### 68. Dissertation   If you retrieved the dissertation from a database, give the database name and the accession number, if one is assigned.

Lengel, L. L. (1968). *The righteous cause: Some religious aspects of Kansas populism.* Retrieved from ProQuest Digital Dissertations. (AAT 6900033)

If you retrieve a dissertation from a Web site, give the type of dissertation and the institution after the title, and provide a retrieval statement. If you retrieve the dissertation from an institution's own site, omit the institution after the title.

Meeks, M. G. (2006). *Between abolition and reform: First-year writing programs, e-literacies, and institutional change* (Doctoral dissertation). Retrieved from http://dc.lib.unc.edu/etd/

☐ **Personal communications and social media**

### 69. Tweet   Include the writer's real name, if known, with the user name (if different) in brackets. If you don't know the real name, give just the user name. Include the entire tweet as the title, followed by the label *Tweet* in brackets.

Waldman, K. [xwaldie]. (2014, April 24). The psychology of unfriending someone on Facebook: slate.com/blogs/future_t . . . [Tweet]. Retrieved from https://twitter.com/xwaldie/status/459336732232912896

**70. Posting on a public Facebook page**   When citing a posting on a public Facebook page or another social networking site that is visible to anyone, include the writer's name as it appears in the post. Give a few words from the post, and add an identifying label. Include the date you retrieved the post and the URL for the public page. Do not include a page on the list of references if your readers will not be able to access the source; instead, cite it as a personal communication in the text (see model 12 on p. 457).

> American Psychological Association. (2014, April 24). Why do many people do their best thinking while walking? [Facebook post]. Retrieved April 24, 2014, from https://www.facebook.com/AmericanPsychologicalAssociation

**71. Email, private message, or post on a social networking site**   Email messages, letters, and any personal messages or privacy-protected postings on Facebook and other social media sites are not included in the list of references because the APA stresses that all sources in your list of references should be retrievable by your readers. (See model 12 on p. 457 for information on citing personal communication in your text.)

## 33e   A student research essay, APA style

STUDENT WRITER
Martha Bell

On the following pages is a paper by Martha Bell that conforms to the APA guidelines described in this chapter. Her project also appears with an activity in the integrated media at **macmillanhighered.com/smh**. (Photo © Martha Bell)

Running head: POST-LYME MYSTERY                                    1

Running head
(fifty characters
or fewer) appears
flush left on first
line of title page

Page number
appears flush
right on first line
of every page

The Mystery of Post-Lyme Disease Syndrome

Martha Bell

Eastern Mennonite University

Title, name,
and affiliation
centered and
double-spaced

Author Note: This paper was prepared for College Writing 130C, taught by Professor Eads.

Author's note
lists specific
information
about course
(and can
include contact
information)

Annotations indicate effective choices or APA-style formatting.

Running head
appears in all
capital letters
flush left on each
page

Heading
centered

No indentation
for abstract

Double-spaced
text

## Abstract

Lyme disease, prevalent in parts of the United States, is a preventable
illness spread by tick bites. Lyme disease is considered treatable with
a course of antibiotics in the early stages of infection. In some cases,
however, symptoms of Lyme disease persist in individuals who have
completed antibiotic treatment. The causes of post-Lyme disease
syndrome, sometimes called "chronic Lyme disease," are unknown, and
treatment of those suffering post-Lyme disease syndrome is controversial,
with some physicians arguing for long-term antibiotic treatment and
others convinced that such treatments are harmful to patients. There
is a need for more research with a focus on developing the technology
to perform replicable studies and eventually an effective treatment
algorithm for post-Lyme disease syndrome.

The Mystery of Post-Lyme Disease Syndrome

The Centers for Disease Control and Prevention (CDC) estimates a total of 300,000 cases of Lyme disease annually. Many medical professionals believe Lyme disease can be cured in a matter of weeks with a simple antibiotic treatment. In some cases, however, patients develop post-Lyme disease syndrome, sometimes called "chronic Lyme disease," exhibiting persistent symptoms of Lyme after initial treatment is completed. The scientific community, divided over the causes of post-Lyme disease syndrome, cannot agree on the best treatment for the syndrome. Although Lyme disease is preventable, people are still vulnerable to infection; consequently, there is a need for more research and collaboration with a focus on developing the technology to perform replicable studies, which may subsequently lead to an effective treatment algorithm for post-Lyme disease syndrome.

## Prevention

Ixodes ticks, also known as blacklegged and deer ticks, are infected with the bacterium *Borrelia burgdorferi*, responsible for Lyme disease (Hawker et al., 2012). Since being bitten by an infected tick is the only known way of contracting Lyme disease, evading Ixodes ticks is an effective measure. According to M'ikanatha et al. (2013), "Lyme disease is acquired peridomestically and the risk is highest in residential settings abutting areas with forests, meadows, and high prevalence of deer" (p. 168). While adult ticks are more active in the cooler months, developing Ixodes ticks, called nymphs, feed the most during the spring and summer months (Centers for Disease Control and Prevention [CDC], 2011b). Therefore, avoiding areas such as meadows and grasslands in the spring and summer seasons aids in preventing Lyme disease.

Using permethrin repellent on clothes and 20 to 30 percent DEET insect repellent on the skin also keeps ticks away (U.S. Department of Health and Human Services [HHS], 2012). Other measures include wearing light-colored clothing to make ticks more visible, wearing long sleeves and long pants, tucking shirts into pants and pants into socks, and taping closed open areas of clothing when spending time outdoors

---

*Full title centered*

*Paragraphs indented*

*Background information supplied*

*Boldface headings help organize review*

*Reference to work with six or more authors uses et al.*

*First reference to organization gives abbreviation for later references*

in areas where ticks are prevalent (Hawker et al., 2012; HHS, 2012).
Additionally, individuals should keep yards and houses clean to avert
mammals, such as deer and rodents, that carry Ixodes ticks, and should
check pets for ticks (HHS, 2012).

Though all of these measures greatly reduce the chance of receiving
a tick bite, they are not foolproof. The bacterium *B. burgdorferi* takes
approximately 36 to 48 hours to become infectious after the tick has bitten
an individual (Hawker et al., 2012). A bull's-eye rash called erythema
migrans is the only unique symptom of Lyme disease (HHS, 2012). It
appears 3 to 32 days after infection (Hawker et al., 2012). According to
one study, only 70 to 80 percent of Lyme disease victims develop erythema
migrans; therefore, other symptoms must be assessed (Steere & Sikand,
2003). Other characteristics of Lyme disease include fevers, headaches, stiff
neck, swollen lymph nodes, body aches, fatigue, facial palsy, polyarthritis,
aseptic meningitis, peripheral root lesions, radiculopathy, and myocarditis
(CDC, 2011a; Hawker, 2012; HHS, 2012).

On average, it takes a few weeks for infected individuals to
produce antibodies against *B. burgdorferi* (HHS, 2012). Consequently,
most cases of Lyme disease have better outcomes and recovery rates
when antibiotics are administered quickly (Steere & Sikand, 2003).
Administered in the beginning stages of Lyme disease, antibiotics help
speed recovery and prevent more serious symptoms, such as heart and
nervous system problems, from developing (HHS, 2012).

Erythema migrans is not always present, and other symptoms of
Lyme disease are similar to other illnesses. Therefore, Lyme disease may
be misdiagnosed and untreated. Raphael B. Stricker (2007), a doctor
at the University of California at San Francisco, explained that "in the
absence of typical features of Lyme disease, patients may go on to
develop a syndrome with multiple nonspecific symptoms that affect
various organ systems, including the joints, muscles, nerves, brain, and
heart" (p. 149). Conversely, even when patients receive proper antibiotic
treatment of two to four weeks they can continue to experience
symptoms.

*More than one reference included in citation*

*Parenthetical citation for quotation from print source includes page number*

### Post-Lyme Disease Syndrome

The majority of Lyme disease patients are cured after multiple weeks of antibiotics; however, 10 to 15 percent of patients acquire relapsing nonspecific symptoms such as fatigue, arthritis, and short-term memory problems that can persist for months or even years (Brody, 2013). When there is no other possible origin of the nonspecific symptoms, and the individual has had proper treatment for Lyme disease, the patient is classified as having post-Lyme disease syndrome (Lantos, 2011). Adriana Marques (2008) of the Laboratory of Clinical Infectious Diseases explains, "The appearance of post-Lyme disease symptoms seems to correlate with disseminated diseases, a greater severity of illness at presentation, and delayed antibiotic therapy; but not with the duration of the initial antibiotic therapy." The medical community is unsure of how to treat the nonspecific symptoms or what causes them (Lantos, 2011).

### Possible Sources of Post-Lyme Disease Syndrome

Scientists are unable to identify the exact source of post-Lyme disease syndrome for several reasons. Identifying patients is difficult because of the general nature of the symptoms. Several surveys demonstrate that a relatively high percentage of the overall population reports nonspecific symptoms, such as fatigue, chronic pain, or cognitive dysfunction after a tick bite (Lantos, 2011). In addition, researchers struggle to find participants for their studies (Marques, 2008). Study participants must have previous documentation of contracting Lyme disease, which significantly diminishes the testing population (Lantos, 2011).

Scientists and physicians suspect the source of post-Lyme disease syndrome to be multifactorial (Marques, 2008). Plausible causes of reoccurring nonspecific symptoms include persistent infection of *B. burgdorferi*, other tick-borne infections, a natural healing process after infection, post-infective fatigue syndrome, autoimmune mechanisms, and intercurrent conditions (Marques, 2008). Nevertheless, only a few ideas have been thoroughly explored thus far by the scientific community. The majority of scientists believe remaining damage to tissue and the immune system from the infection causes post-Lyme disease syndrome; however, some believe persistent infection of the bacteria is the source (CDC, 2014).

Despite complications, a majority of the medical community considers persistent symptoms as a result from residual damage to the tissues and the immune system that occurred during the infection. These "auto-immune" reactions, which the body uses against foreign elements, occur in infections similar to Lyme disease such as Campylobacter, Chlamydia, and Strep throat (CDC, 2014). Patients report their nonspecific symptoms improving over time after the typical antibiotic treatment (Marques, 2008). Physicians who followed their patients with post-Lyme disease syndrome for extended times also see nonspecific symptoms resolve without further antibiotic treatment (Marques, 2008). Consequently, post-Lyme disease syndrome may be a natural evolution of the body healing after an intense infection.

A smaller portion of the medical community considers persistent infection of the microorganism *B. burgdorferi* as the cause of post-Lyme disease syndrome. Recently published studies performed on animals show signs of ongoing infection of the bacterium. One scientific study infected mice with *B. burgdorferi* and gave them intense treatment of antibiotics that should wipe out the bacterium (Bockenstedt, Gonzalez, Haberman, & Belperron, 2012). Bockenstedt et al. observed the mice over a period of time and found "that infectious spirochetes are rapidly eliminated after institution of antibiotics, but inflammatory *B. burgdorferi* antigens persist adjacent to cartilage and in the enthuses" (2012). This is one of the first studies to show continuous effects of the harmful microorganism in post-Lyme disease syndrome. Another recent scientific study was conducted on nonhuman primates, Rhesus macaques. Once again the scientists infected the animals with *B. burgdorferi* and then four to six months later administered an antibiotic treatment to half of the monkeys (Embers et al., 2012). Their results also confirmed that *B. burgdorferi* could withstand antibiotic treatment in Rhesus macaques and proceed to cause post-Lyme disease syndrome (Embers et al., 2012). Nonetheless, these results showing perpetual infection as the cause of post-Lyme disease syndrome have yet to be replicated in humans.

In contrast, many studies over the years contradict the theory of ongoing infection, though these studies have not been confirmed true in humans. Lantos (2011), an MD Medical Instructor in the Department of Medicine at Duke University School of Medicine, clarifies that "[n]o adequately controlled, hypothesis-driven study using a repeatable method has demonstrated that viable *B. burgdorferi* is found in patients with persistent post-Lyme symptoms any more frequently than in those with favorable outcomes" (p. 790). Most scientific studies trying to prove persistent infection of *B. burgdorferi* have not been replicated because their procedures and techniques are at fault (Marques, 2008). The problem derives from the technology that detects the microorganism (Lantos, 2011). PCR and *B. burgdorferi* culture are commonly used to find evidence of the bacteria in the body; however, both have "low sensitivity in most body fluids from patients with Lyme disease" (Marques, 2008). Even though other methods, such as finding antibodies in immune complexes, changes in C6 antibody levels, and PCR in urine samples, have been tried, none prove helpful (Marques, 2008). Therefore, the persistent infection of *B. burgdorferi* has not yet successfully been proven as the cause of post-Lyme disease syndrome.

### Post-Lyme Disease Syndrome Treatment

Since the cause of post-Lyme disease syndrome is controversial, treatment for the infection varies from patient to patient and physician to physician. Treatment is still in the experimental stages, meaning no set treatment algorithm currently exists. Numerous patients rely on long-term antibiotic medication, despite the overwhelming defying scientific evidence against this treatment (CDC, 2014). The research studies that focus on prolonged antibiotic treatment observe no dramatic difference in benefits or recoveries of those who had the treatment and those who did not (Marques, 2008). On the contrary, many long-term antibiotic research studies found that post-Lyme disease syndrome patients develop harmful side effects (Lantos, 2011). These adverse health effects include

POST-LYME MYSTERY                                                    8

"catheter-associated venous thromboembolism, catheter-associated septicemia, allergic reactions and ceftriaxone-induced gallbladder toxicity" (Lantos, 2011, p. 792). Therefore, most of the scientific community considers long-term antibiotic treatment for chronic Lyme disease a harmful, risky, and unbeneficial plan.

Most of the scientific community advises against the use of long-term antibiotics because of potential adverse effects. Nevertheless, a small minority of physicians have observed improvements with long-term antibiotics. Because numerous studies show a lack of benefit to long-term antibiotics, these hopeful patients may be experiencing a placebo effect, which occurs when patients improve because they believe they are receiving an effective treatment (Marques, 2008).

### Solving the Mystery

Individuals can take various simple preventive measures to avoid contracting Lyme disease. If the infection is contracted, those who seek prompt treatment increase the chance of full recovery and decrease the chance of developing post-Lyme disease syndrome. However, these steps do not guarantee complete avoidance of post-Lyme disease syndrome. Finding the source of post-Lyme disease syndrome will lead to a specific treatment plan that effectively heals patients. Many scientists deem the source of post-Lyme disease syndrome to be a natural autoimmune reaction; conversely, a few other scientists consider persistent infection as the cause. Both theories, however, need better technology to prove their accuracy. Since scientists disagree about the source of post-Lyme disease syndrome, a variety of experimental treatments have arisen. Replicable studies are needed so that an effective treatment for post-Lyme disease syndrome can be found.

Conclusion indicates need for further research

### References

Bockenstedt, L., Gonzalez, D., Haberman, A., & Belperron, A. (2012). Spirochete antigens persist near cartilage after murine Lyme borreliosis therapy. *The Journal of Clinical Investigation, 122*(7), 2652–2660. doi:10.1172/JCI58813

Brody, J. (2013, July 8). When Lyme disease lasts and lasts. *The New York Times*. Retrieved from http://nytimes.com/

Centers for Disease Control and Prevention. (2014, February 24). *Post-treatment Lyme disease syndrome*. Retrieved from http://www.cdc.gov/lyme/

Centers for Disease Control and Prevention. (2011a, April 12). *Signs and symptoms*. Retrieved from http://www.cdc.gov/lyme/

Centers for Disease Control and Prevention. (2011b, April 12). *Transmission*. Retrieved from http://www.cdc.gov/lyme/

Embers, M. E., Barthold, S. W., Borda, J. T., Bowers, L., Doyle, L., Hodzic, E., . . . & Philipp, M. T. (2012). *Persistence of* Borrelia burgdorferi *in rhesus macaques following antibiotic treatment of disseminated infection. PLoS ONE, 7*(1). doi:10.1371/journal.pone.0029914

Hawker, J., Begg, N., Blair, L., Reintjes, R., Weinberg, J., & Ekdahl, K. (2012). *Communicable disease control and health protection handbook* (3rd ed.) [Electronic book]. Retrieved from http://reader.eblib.com.hartzler.emu.edu

Lantos, P. (2011). Chronic Lyme disease: The controversies and the science. *Expert Review of Anti-Infective Therapy, 9*(7), 787–797. doi:10.1586/eri.11.63

Marques, A. (2008). Chronic Lyme disease: An appraisal. *Infectious Disease Clinics of North America, 22*(2), 341–360. doi:10.1016/j.idc.2007.12.011

M'ikanatha, N. M., Lynfield, R., Van Beneden, C. A., & de Valk, H. (2013). *Infectious disease surveillance* (2nd ed.) [Electronic book]. Retrieved from http://reader.eblib.com.hartzler.emu.edu

References begin on a new page

Article from an online newspaper

Two works by the same author in the same year

Work with more than seven authors

Journal article with DOI

Electronic book

Steere, A., & Sikand, V. (2003). The presenting manifestations of Lyme
    disease and the outcomes of treatment. *The New England Journal of
    Medicine, 348*(24), 2472–2474. doi:10.1056/NEJM200306123482423

Stricker, R. (2007). Counterpoint: Long-term antibiotic therapy improves
    persistent symptoms associated with Lyme disease. *Clinical Infectious
    Diseases, 45*(2), 147–157. doi:10.1086/518853

U.S. Department of Health and Human Services, National Institutes
    of Health, National Institute of Allergy and Infectious Diseases.
    (2012, October 9). *A history of Lyme disease, symptoms, diagnosis,
    treatment, and prevention.* Retrieved from http://www.niaid.nih
    .gov/topics/lymedisease/understanding/pages/intro.aspx

# CHAPTER 34

# *Chicago* Style

T HE STYLE GUIDE of the University of Chicago Press has long been used in history as well as in other areas of the arts and humanities. The Sixteenth Edition of *The Chicago Manual of Style* (2010) provides a complete guide to *Chicago* style, including two systems for citing sources. This chapter presents the notes and bibliography system.

## 34a  Understanding the basics of *Chicago* style

Why does academic work call for very careful citation practices when writing for the general public may not? The answer is that readers of academic work expect source citations for several reasons:

- Source citations demonstrate that you've done your homework on your topic and that you are a part of the conversation surrounding it.
- Source citations show that you understand the need to give credit when you make use of someone else's intellectual property. (See Chapter 14.)
- Source citations give explicit directions to guide readers who want to look for themselves at the works you're using.

Guidelines from *The Chicago Manual of Style* will tell you exactly what information to include in your citation and how to format that information.

### ☐  Types of sources

Look at the Directory to *Chicago* Style on p. 497. You will need to be careful to tell your readers whether you read a print version or a digital version of a source that consists mainly of written words. Digital magazine and newspaper articles may include updates or corrections that the print version lacks; digital books may not number pages or screens the same way the print book does. If you are citing a source with media elements—such as a film, song, or artwork—consult the other sections of the directory. And if you can't find a model exactly like the source you've selected, see the Quick Help box on p. 498.

### Articles from Web and database sources

You need a subscription to look through most databases, so individual researchers almost always gain access to articles in databases through the computer system of a school or public library that pays to subscribe. The easiest way to tell whether a source comes from a database, then, is that its information is *not* generally available free to anyone with an Internet connection. Many databases are digital collections of articles that originally appeared in edited print periodicals, ensuring that an authority has vouched for the accuracy of the information. Such sources may have more credibility than free material available on the Web.

## ☐ Parts of citations

Citations in *Chicago* style will appear in three places in your text—a note number in the text marks the material from the source, a footnote or an endnote includes information to identify the source (or information about supplemental material), and the bibliography provides the full citation. In her research essay (see 34c), Amanda Rinder uses a footnote to link a source in her text to a numbered note and then to a bibliography entry, as shown in the figure below.

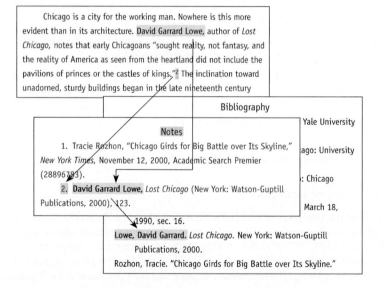

Chicago is a city for the working man. Nowhere is this more evident than in its architecture. David Garrard Lowe, author of *Lost Chicago*, notes that early Chicagoans "sought reality, not fantasy, and the reality of America as seen from the heartland did not include the pavilions of princes or the castles of kings."² The inclination toward unadorned, sturdy buildings began in the late nineteenth century

**Bibliography**

**Notes**

1. Tracie Rozhon, "Chicago Girds for Big Battle over Its Skyline," *New York Times*, November 12, 2000, Academic Search Premier (2889683).

2. David Garrard Lowe, *Lost Chicago* (New York: Watson-Guptill Publications, 2000), 123.

1990, sec. 16.

Lowe, David Garrard. *Lost Chicago*. New York: Watson-Guptill Publications, 2000.

Rozhon, Tracie. "Chicago Girds for Big Battle over Its Skyline."

Yale University

ago: University

: Chicago

March 18,

## 34b Formatting *Chicago* manuscripts

- **Title page.** About halfway down the title page, center the full title of your project and your name. Unless otherwise instructed, at the bottom of the page also list the course name, the instructor's name, and the date submitted.

Do not type a number on this page. Check to see if your instructor has a preference on whether to count the title page as part of the text (if so, the first text page will be page 2) or as part of the frontmatter (if so, the first text page will be page 1).

- **Margins and spacing.** Leave one-inch margins on all sides. Double-space the entire text, including block quotations. Single-space notes and bibliographic entries, but double-space between entries.
- **Page numbers.** Number all pages (except the title page) in the upper right-hand corner. Also use a short title or your name before page numbers.
- **Long quotations.** For a long quotation, indent one-half inch (or five spaces) from the left margin and do not use quotation marks. *Chicago* defines a long quotation as one hundred words or eight lines, though you may set off shorter quotes for emphasis.
- **Headings.** *Chicago* style allows, but does not require, headings.
- **Visuals.** Visuals (photographs, drawings, charts, graphs, and tables) should be placed as near as possible to the relevant text. (See 13e for guidelines on incorporating visuals into your text.) Tables should be labeled *Table*, numbered, and captioned. All other visuals should be labeled *Figure* (abbreviated *Fig.*), numbered, and captioned. Remember to refer to each visual in your text, pointing out how it contributes to the point(s) you are making.

## ☐ Notes

Notes can be footnotes (each one appearing at the bottom of the page on which its citation appears) or endnotes (in a list on a separate page at the end of the text). (Check your instructor's preference.) Indent the first line of each note one-half inch and begin with a number, a period, and one space before the first word. All remaining lines of the entry are flush with the left margin. Single-space footnotes and endnotes, with a double space between entries.

Use superscript numbers ([1]) to mark citations in the text. Place the superscript number for each note just after the relevant quotation, sentence, clause, or phrase. Type the number after any punctuation mark except the dash, and do not leave a space before the superscript. Number citations sequentially throughout the text. When you use signal phrases to introduce source material, note that *Chicago* style requires you to use the present tense (*citing Bebout's studies, Meier points out . . .*).

**IN THE TEXT**

Sweig argues that Castro and Che Guevara were not the only key players in the Cuban Revolution of the late 1950s.[19]

**IN THE FIRST NOTE REFERRING TO THE SOURCE**

19. Julia Sweig, *Inside the Cuban Revolution* (Cambridge, MA: Harvard University Press, 2002), 9.

After giving complete information the first time you cite a work, shorten additional references to that work: list only the author's last name, a comma, a short version of the title, a comma, and the page number. If you refer to the same source cited in the previous note, you can use the Latin abbreviation *Ibid.* ("in the same place") instead of the name and title.

**IN FIRST AND SUBSEQUENT NOTES**

19. Julia Sweig, *Inside the Cuban Revolution* (Cambridge, MA: Harvard University Press, 2002), 9.

20. Ibid., 13.

21. Ferguson, "Comfort of Being Sad," 63.

22. Sweig, *Cuban Revolution*, 21.

## □ Bibliography

Begin the list of sources on a separate page after the main text and any endnotes. Continue numbering pages consecutively. Center the title *Bibliography* (without underlining, italics, or quotation marks) one inch below the top of the page. Begin each entry at the left margin. Indent the second and subsequent lines of each entry one-half inch, or five spaces.

List sources alphabetically by authors' last names or by the first major word in the title if the author is unknown. Italicize titles of books and periodicals, and enclose titles of short works in quotation marks. See p. 517 for an example of a *Chicago*-style bibliography.

In the bibliographic entry, include the same information as in the first note for that source, but omit the page reference. Give the *first* author's last name first, followed by a comma and the first name; separate the main elements of the entry with periods rather than commas; and do not enclose the publication information for books in parentheses.

**IN THE BIBLIOGRAPHY**

Sweig, Julia. *Inside the Cuban Revolution*. Cambridge, MA: Harvard University Press, 2002.

## 34c Preparing *Chicago* notes and bibliographic entries

The following examples demonstrate how to format both notes and bibliographic entries according to *Chicago* style. The note, which is numbered, appears first; the bibliographic entry, which is not numbered, appears below the note.

# DIRECTORY TO *CHICAGO* STYLE
# NOTES AND BIBLIOGRAPHIC ENTRIES

## Citing sources that don't match any model exactly

What should you do if your source doesn't match the model exactly? Suppose, for instance, that your source is a translation of a republished book with an editor.

- Identify a basic model to follow. If you decide that your source looks most like a republished book, start with a citation that looks like **model 12**.

- Look for models that show the additional elements in your source. For this example, you would need to add elements of **model 11** (for the translation) and either **model 7** or **model 8** (for the editor).

- Add new elements from other models to your basic model in the order indicated.

- If you aren't sure how to arrange the pieces to create a combination model, ask your instructor.

To cite a source for which you cannot find a model, collect as much information as you can about the creator, title, sponsor, date, and so on, with the goal of helping your readers find the source for themselves. Then look at the models in this section to see which one most closely matches the type of source you are using. If possible, seek your instructor's advice to find the best model.

## ▢ Print and digital books

For the basic format for citing a print book, see the source map on pp. 500–501. The note for a book typically includes five elements: author's name, title and subtitle, city of publication and publisher, year, and page number(s) or electronic locator information for the information in the note. The bibliographic entry usually includes all these elements but the page number (and does include a URL or other locator if the book is digitally published), but it is styled differently: commas separate major elements of a note, but a bibliographic entry uses periods.

### 1. One author

1. Nell Irvin Painter, *The History of White People* (New York: W. W. Norton, 2010), 119.

Painter, Nell Irvin. *The History of White People.* New York: W. W. Norton, 2010.

### 2. Multiple authors

2. Margaret Macmillan and Richard Holbrooke, *Paris 1919: Six Months That Changed the World* (New York: Random House, 2003), 384.

Macmillan, Margaret, and Richard Holbrooke. *Paris 1919: Six Months That Changed the World.* New York: Random House, 2003.

With more than three authors, you may give the first-listed author followed by *et al.* in the note. In the bibliography, list all the authors' names.

2. Stephen J. Blank et al., *Conflict, Culture, and History: Regional Dimensions* (Miami: University Press of the Pacific, 2002), 276.

Blank, Stephen J., Lawrence E. Grinter, Karl P. Magyar, Lewis B. Ware, and Bynum E. Weathers. *Conflict, Culture, and History: Regional Dimensions.* Miami: University Press of the Pacific, 2002.

### 3. Organization as author

3. World Intellectual Property Organization, *Intellectual Property Profile of the Least Developed Countries* (Geneva: World Intellectual Property Organization, 2002), 43.

World Intellectual Property Organization. *Intellectual Property Profile of the Least Developed Countries.* Geneva: World Intellectual Property Organization, 2002.

### 4. Unknown author

4. *Broad Stripes and Bright Stars* (Kansas City, MO: Andrews McMeel, 2002), 10.

*Broad Stripes and Bright Stars.* Kansas City, MO: Andrews McMeel, 2002.

### 5. Online book

5. Dorothy Richardson, *Long Day: The Story of a New York Working Girl, as Told by Herself* (1906; UMDL Texts, 2010), 159, http://quod.lib.umich.edu /cgi/t/text/text-idx?c=moa;idno=AFS7156.0001.001.

Richardson, Dorothy. *Long Day: The Story of a New York Working Girl, as Told by Herself.* 1906. UMDL Texts, 2010. http://quod.lib.umich.edu/cgi/t/text /text-idx?c=moa;idno=AFS7156.0001.001.

### 6. Electronic book (e-book)

6. Manal M. Omar, *Barefoot in Baghdad* (Naperville, IL: Sourcebooks, 2010), Kindle edition, ch. 4.

Omar, Manal M. *Barefoot in Baghdad.* Naperville, IL: Sourcebooks, 2010. Kindle edition.

### 7. Edited book with no author

7. James H. Fetzer, ed., *The Great Zapruder Film Hoax: Deceit and Deception in the Death of JFK* (Chicago: Open Court, 2003), 56.

Fetzer, James H., ed. *The Great Zapruder Film Hoax: Deceit and Deception in the Death of JFK.* Chicago: Open Court, 2003.

# Books

Take information from the book's title page and copyright page (on the reverse side of the title page), not from the book's cover or a library catalog. Look carefully at the differences in punctuation between the note and the bibliographic entry.

**1** **Author.** In a note, list the author(s) first name first. In a bibliographic entry, list the first author last name first. List other authors first name first.

**2** **Title.** Italicize the title and subtitle and capitalize all major words.

**3** **City of publication and publisher.** List the city (and country or state abbreviation for an unfamiliar city) followed by a colon. In a note only, city, publisher, and year appear in parentheses. Drop *Inc., Co., Publishing,* or *Publishers.* Follow with a comma.

**4** **Publication year.** In a bibliographic entry only, end with a period.

**5** **Page number.** In a note only, end with the page number and a period.

**Citations for the book on p. 501 would look like this:**

ENDNOTE

1. Alex von Tunzelmann, *Red Heat: Conspiracy, Murder, and the Cold War in the Caribbean* (New York: Picador, 2011), 178.

BIBLIOGRAPHIC ENTRY

von Tunzelmann, Alex. *Red Heat: Conspiracy, Murder, and the Cold War in the Caribbean.* New York: Picador, 2011.

**4  Publication Year**

2011

# RED HEAT

**2  Title**

## CONSPIRACY, MURDER, AND THE COLD WAR IN THE CARIBBEAN

## ALEX VON TUNZELMANN

**1  Author**

PICADOR
HENRY HOLT AND COMPANY
NEW YORK

**3  Publisher and City of Publication**

### 8. Edited book with author

8. Leopold von Ranke, *The Theory and Practice of History,* ed. Georg G. Iggers (New York: Routledge, 2010), 135.

von Ranke, Leopold. *The Theory and Practice of History.* Edited by Georg G. Iggers. New York: Routledge, 2010.

### 9. Selection in an anthology or chapter in a book with an editor

9. Denise Little, "Born in Blood," in *Alternate Gettysburgs,* ed. Brian Thomsen and Martin H. Greenberg (New York: Berkley Publishing Group, 2002), 245.

Give the inclusive page numbers of the selection or chapter in the bibliographic entry.

Little, Denise. "Born in Blood." In *Alternate Gettysburgs.* Edited by Brian Thomsen and Martin H. Greenberg, 242–55. New York: Berkley Publishing Group, 2002.

### 10. Introduction, preface, foreword, or afterword

10. Robert B. Reich, introduction to *Making Work Pay: America after Welfare,* ed. Robert Kuttner (New York: New Press, 2002), xvi.

Reich, Robert B. Introduction to *Making Work Pay: America after Welfare,* vii–xvii. Edited by Robert Kuttner. New York: New Press, 2002.

### 11. Translation

11. Suetonius, *The Twelve Caesars,* trans. Robert Graves (London: Penguin Classics, 1989), 202.

Suetonius. *The Twelve Caesars.* Translated by Robert Graves. London: Penguin Classics, 1989.

### 12. Edition other than the first

12. Dee Brown, *Bury My Heart at Wounded Knee: An Indian History of the American West,* 4th ed. (New York: Owl Books, 2007), 12.

Brown, Dee. *Bury My Heart at Wounded Knee: An Indian History of the American West,* 4th ed. New York: Owl Books, 2007.

### 13. Multivolume work

13. John Watson, *Annals of Philadelphia and Pennsylvania in the Olden Time,* vol. 2 (Washington, DC: Ross & Perry, 2003), 514.

Watson, John. *Annals of Philadelphia and Pennsylvania in the Olden Time.* Vol. 2. Washington, DC: Ross & Perry, 2003.

**14. Reference work**    In a note, use *s.v.,* the abbreviation for the Latin *sub verbo* ("under the word") to help your reader find the entry. Do not list reference works such as encyclopedias or dictionaries in your bibliography.

> 14. *Encyclopaedia Britannica,* s.v. "carpetbagger."

**15. Work with a title within the title**    Use quotation marks around any title within a book title.

> 15. John A. Alford, *A Companion to "Piers Plowman"* (Berkeley: University of California Press, 1988), 195.

> Alford, John A. *A Companion to "Piers Plowman."* Berkeley: University of California Press, 1988.

**16. Sacred text**    Do not include sacred texts in the bibliography.

> 16. Luke 18:24–25 (New International Version)
> 16. Qur'an 7:40–41

**17. Source quoted in another source**    Identify both the original and the secondary source.

> 17. Frank D. Millet, "The Filipino Leaders," *Harper's Weekly,* March 11, 1899, quoted in Richard Slotkin, *Gunfighter Nation: The Myth of the Frontier in Twentieth-Century America* (New York: HarperCollins, 1992), 110.

> Millet, Frank D. "The Filipino Leaders." *Harper's Weekly,* March 11, 1899. Quoted in Richard Slotkin, *Gunfighter Nation: The Myth of the Frontier in Twentieth-Century America* (New York: HarperCollins, 1992), 110.

□ **Print and digital periodicals**

The note for an article in a periodical typically includes the author's name, the article title, and the periodical title. The format for other information, including the volume and issue numbers (if any) and the date of publication, as well as the page number(s) to which the note refers, varies according to the type of periodical and whether you consulted it in print, on the Web, or in a database. In a bibliographic entry for a journal or magazine article from a database or a print periodical, also give the inclusive page numbers.

**18. Article in a print journal**

> 18. Karin Lützen, "The Female World: Viewed from Denmark," *Journal of Women's History* 12, no. 3 (2000): 36.

> Lützen, Karin. "The Female World: Viewed from Denmark." *Journal of Women's History* 12, no. 3 (2000): 34–38.

**19. Article in an online journal**    Give the DOI if there is one. If not, include the article URL. If page numbers are provided, include them as well.

> 19. Jeffrey J. Schott, "America, Europe, and the New Trade Order," *Business and Politics* 11, no. 3 (2009), doi:10.2202/1469-3569.1263.

> Schott, Jeffrey J. "America, Europe, and the New Trade Order." *Business and Politics* 11, no. 3 (2009). doi:10.2202/1469-3569.1263.

**20. Journal article from a database**    For basic information on citing a periodical article from a database in *Chicago* style, see the source map on pp. 506–7.

> 20. W. Trent Foley and Nicholas J. Higham, "Bede on the Britons," *Early Medieval Europe* 17, no. 2 (2009), 157, doi:10.1111/j.1468-0254.2009.00258.x.

> Foley, W. Trent, and Nicholas J. Higham. "Bede on the Britons." *Early Medieval Europe* 17, no. 2 (2009). 154–85. doi:10.1111/j.1468-0254.2009.00258.x.

**21. Article in a print magazine**

> 21. Terry McDermott, "The Mastermind: Khalid Sheikh Mohammed and the Making of 9/11," *New Yorker,* September 13, 2010, 42.

> McDermott, Terry. "The Mastermind: Khalid Sheikh Mohammed and the Making of 9/11." *New Yorker,* September 13, 2010, 38–51.

**22. Article in an online magazine**

> 22. Tracy Clark-Flory, "Educating Women Saves Kids' Lives," *Salon,* September 17, 2010, http://www.salon.com/life/broadsheet/2010/09/17/education_women/index.html.

> Clark-Flory, Tracy. "Educating Women Saves Kids' Lives." *Salon,* September 17, 2010. http://www.salon.com/life/broadsheet/2010/09/17/education_women/index.html.

**23. Magazine article from a database**

> 23. Sami Yousafzai and Ron Moreau, "Twisting Arms in Afghanistan," *Newsweek,* November 9, 2009, 8, Academic Search Premier (44962900).

> Yousafzai, Sami, and Ron Moreau. "Twisting Arms in Afghanistan." *Newsweek,* November 9, 2009. 8. Academic Search Premier (44962900).

**24. Article in a newspaper**    Do not include page numbers for a newspaper article, but you may include the section, if any.

> 24. Katherine Q. Seelye, "A Heinous Crime, Secret Histories, and a Sinn Fein Leader's Arrest," *New York Times,* May 2, 2014, sec. A.

> Seelye, Katherine Q. "A Heinous Crime, Secret Histories, and a Sinn Fein Leader's Arrest." *New York Times,* May 2, 2014, sec. A.

If you provide complete documentation of a newspaper article in a note, you may not need to include it in the bibliography. Check your instructor's preference.

**25. Article in an online newspaper**   If the URL for the article is very long, use the URL for the newspaper's home page.

> 25. Katherine Q. Seelye, "A Heinous Crime, Secret Histories, and a Sinn Fein Leader's Arrest," *New York Times,* May 2, 2014, http://www.nytimes.com.

> Seelye, Katherine Q. "A Heinous Crime, Secret Histories, and a Sinn Fein Leader's Arrest." *New York Times,* May 2, 2014. http://www.nytimes.com.

**26. Newspaper article from a database**

> 26. Demetria Irwin, "A Hatchet, Not a Scalpel, for NYC Budget Cuts," *New York Amsterdam News,* November 13, 2008, Academic Search Premier (35778153).

> Irwin, Demetria. "A Hatchet, Not a Scalpel, for NYC Budget Cuts." *New York Amsterdam News,* November 13, 2008. Academic Search Premier (35778153).

**27. Book review**   After the information about the book under review, give publication information for the appropriate kind of source (see models 18–26).

> 27. Arnold Relman, "Health Care: The Disquieting Truth," review of *Tracking Medicine: A Researcher's Quest to Understand Health Care,* by John E. Wennberg, *New York Review of Books* 57, no. 14 (2010), 45.

> Relman, Arnold. "Health Care: The Disquieting Truth." Review of *Tracking Medicine: A Researcher's Quest to Understand Health Care,* by John E. Wennberg. *New York Review of Books* 57, no. 14 (2010), 45–48.

□ **Other online sources**

In general, include the author (if given); the title of a work from a Web site (in quotation marks); the name of the site (in italics, if the site is an online publication, but otherwise neither italicized nor in quotation marks); the sponsor of the site, if different from the name of the site or name of the author; the date of publication or most recent update; and a URL. If the online source does not indicate when it was published or last modified, or if your instructor requests an access date, place it before the URL.

For basic information on citing works from Web sites in *Chicago* style, see the source map on pp. 510–11.

**28. Web site**   If the site does not list the date of publication or date last modified, identify your access date ("accessed March 12, 2014").

> 28. Rutgers School of Arts and Sciences, The Rutgers Oral History Archives, accessed May 6, 2014, http://oralhistory.rutgers.edu/.

> Rutgers School of Arts and Sciences. The Rutgers Oral History Archives. Accessed May 6, 2014. http://oralhistory.rutgers.edu/.

# Articles from Databases

1. **Author.** In a note, list the author(s) first name first. In the bibliographic entry, list the first author last name first, comma, first name; list other authors first name first.

2. **Article title.** Enclose the title and subtitle (if any) in quotation marks, and capitalize major words. In the notes section, put a comma before and after the title. In the bibliography, put a period before and after.

3. **Periodical title.** Italicize the title and subtitle, and capitalize all major words. For a magazine or newspaper, follow with a comma.

4. **Volume and issue numbers (for journals) and date.** For journals, follow the title with the volume number, a comma, the abbreviation *no.*, and the issue number; enclose the publication year in parentheses and follow with a comma (in a note) or with a period (in a bibliography). For other periodicals, give the month and year or month, day, and year, not in parentheses, followed by a comma.

5. **Page numbers.** In a note, give the page where the information is found. In the bibliographic entry, give the page range.

6. **Retrieval information.** Provide the article's DOI, if one is given, the name of the database and an accession number, or a "stable or persistent" URL for the article in the database. Because you provide stable retrieval information, you do not need to identify the electronic format of the work (i.e., PDF, as in the example shown here). End with a period.

**Citations for the journal article on p. 507 would look like this:**

ENDNOTE

    1. Elizabeth Tucker, "Changing Concepts of Childhood: Children's Folklore Scholarship since the Late Nineteenth Century," *Journal of American Folklore* 125, no. 498 (2012), 399, http://www.jstor.org/stable/10.5406/jamerfolk.125.498.0389.

BIBLIOGRAPHIC ENTRY

Tucker, Elizabeth. "Changing Concepts of Childhood: Children's Folklore Scholarship since the Late Nineteenth Century." *Journal of American Folklore* 125, no. 498 (2012). 389–410. http://www.jstor.org/stable/10.5406/jamerfolk.125.498.0389.

**④ Volume and Issue Numbers and Date**

**③ Periodical Title**

Changing Concepts of Childhood: Children's Folklore Scholarship since the Late Nineteenth Century
Author(s): Elizabeth Tucker
Source: *The Journal of American Folklore*, Vol. 125, No. 498 (Fall 2012), pp. 389–410
Published by: University of Illinois Press on behalf of American Folklore Society
Stable URL: http://www.jstor.org/stable/10.5406/jamerfolk.125.498.0389

**⑥ Retrieval Information**          **⑤ Page Numbers**

ELIZABETH TUCKER

**① Author**

**② Article Title and Subtitle** ➔

# Changing Concepts of Childhood: Children's Folklore Scholarship since the Late Nineteenth Century

*This essay examines children's folklore scholarship from the late nineteenth century to the present, tracing key concepts from the Gilded Age to the contemporary era. These concepts reflect significant social, cultural, political, and scientific changes. From the "savage child" to the "secret-keeping child," the "magic-making child," the "cerebral child," the "taboo-breaking child," the "monstrous child," and others, scholarly representations of young people have close connections to the eras in which they developed. Nineteenth-century children's folklore scholarship relied on evolutionism; now evolutionary biology provides a basis for children's folklore research, so we have re-entered familiar territory.*

SINCE 1977, WHEN THE American Folklore Society decided to form a new section for scholars interested in young people's traditions, I have belonged to the Children's Folklore Section. It has been a joy to contribute to this dynamic organization, which has significantly influenced children's folklore scholarship and children's book authors' focus on folk tradition. This essay examines children's folklore scholarship from the late nineteenth century to the present, tracing key concepts from the Gilded Age to the contemporary era in the English language. These concepts reflect significant social, cultural, political, and scientific changes that have occurred since William Wells Newell, the first secretary of the American Folklore Society and the first editor of the *Journal of American Folklore*, published *Games and Songs of American Children* in 1883. They also reveal some very interesting commonalities. Those of us who pursue children's folklore scholarship today may consider ourselves to be light years away from nineteenth-century scholars' research but may find, when reading nineteenth-century works, that we have stayed fairly close to our scholarly "home base."

Before examining concepts of childhood that folklorists have developed, I will offer a working definition of this life stage and briefly explain the beginning of childhood studies. I will also summarize the Children's Folklore Section's work during the past thirty-four years. According to the *Oxford English Dictionary*, childhood consists of "the state or stage of life of a child; the time during which one is a child; the time from birth to puberty" (2011). Scholars of childhood tend to draw a line between childhood and adolescence, which begins at puberty and follows pre-adolescence. The folklore

ELIZABETH TUCKER is Professor of English at Binghamton University

*Journal of American Folklore* 125(498):389–410
Copyright © 2012 by the Board of Trustees of the University of Illinois

**29. Work from a Web site** If the site does not list the date of publication or date last modified, identify your access date ("accessed March 12, 2014").

> 29. Kheel Center, "Timeline of Events," Remembering the 1911 Triangle Factory Fire, Cornell University, accessed May 5, 2014, http://www.ilr.cornell .edu/trianglefire/supplemental/timeline.html.

> Kheel Center. "Timeline of Events." Remembering the 1911 Triangle Factory Fire. Cornell University. Accessed May 5, 2014. http://www.ilr.cornell .edu/trianglefire/supplemental/timeline.html.

**30. Blog post** Treat a blog post as a short work from a Web site (see model 29), but italicize the name of the blog.

> 30. Kate Beaton, "Ida B. Wells," *Hark! A Vagrant* (blog), accessed May 2, 2014, http://harkavagrant.com/.

*Chicago* recommends that blog posts appear in the notes section only, not in the bibliography, unless the blog is cited frequently. Check your instructor's preference. A bibliography reference to an entire blog would look like this:

> Beaton, Kate. *Hark! A Vagrant* (blog). http://harkavagrant.com/.

**31. Email, Facebook, Twitter, and personal communications** *Chicago* style recommends that email and communications that are not archived and accessible to all readers, such as Facebook and Twitter posts and telephone calls, be cited in notes only, not in the bibliography. If you cite a public Facebook page, give both the access date and the URL; for an individual's account, omit the URL. (Note that *Chicago* style recommends hyphenating *e-mail*.)

> 31. Kareem Adas, e-mail message to author, February 11, 2014.

> 31. Supraja Iyer, Facebook post, accessed March 1, 2014.

> 31. U.S. Department of Education, Twitter feed, accessed April 24, 2014, https://twitter.com/usedgov.

**32. Podcast** Treat a podcast as a short work from a Web site (see model 29) and give as much of the following information as you can find: the author or speaker, the title or a description of the podcast, the title of the site, the site sponsor (if different from the author or site name), the type of podcast or file format, the date of posting or access, and the URL.

> 32. Rob Attar, "Victorian Burials and the History of Psychology," History Extra, podcast audio, May 1, 2014, http://www.historyextra.com/podcast /victorian-burials-and-history-psychology.

> Attar, Rob. "Victorial Burials and the History of Psychology." History Extra. Podcast audio. May 1, 2014. http://www.historyextra.com/podcast /victorian-burials-and-history-psychology.

**33. Online audio or video**   Treat an online audio or video source as a short work from a Web site (see model 29). If the source is downloadable, give the medium or file format before the URL (see model 32).

>      33. Alyssa Katz, "Did the Mortgage Crisis Kill the American Dream?" NYCRadio, June 24, 2009, http://www.youtube.com/watch?v =uivtwjwd_Qw.

>   Katz, Alyssa. "Did the Mortgage Crisis Kill the American Dream?" NYCRadio. June 24, 2009. http://www.youtube.com/watch?v=uivtwjwd_Qw.

□ **Other sources**

**34. Published or broadcast interview**

>      34. Nina Totenberg, interview by Charlie Rose, *The Charlie Rose Show,* PBS, June 29, 2010.

>   Totenberg, Nina. Interview by Charlie Rose. *The Charlie Rose Show.* PBS, June 29, 2010.

Any interviews you conduct are considered personal communications (see model 31).

**35. Video, DVD, or Blu-ray disc**

>      35. Edward Norton and Edward Furlong, *American History X,* directed by Tony Kaye (1998; Los Angeles: New Line Studios, 2002), DVD.

>   Norton, Edward, and Edward Furlong. *American History X.* Directed by Tony Kaye, 1998. Los Angeles: New Line Studios, 2002. DVD.

**36. Sound recording**

>      36. Paul Robeson, *The Collector's Paul Robeson,* recorded 1959, Monitor MCD-61580, 1989, compact disc.

>   Robeson, Paul. *The Collector's Paul Robeson*. Recorded 1959. Monitor MCD-61580, 1989, compact disc.

**37. Work of art**   Begin with the artist's name and the title of the work. If you viewed the work in person, give the medium, the date the work was created, and the name of the place where you saw it.

>      37. Mary Cassatt, *The Child's Bath,* oil on canvas, 1893, The Art Institute of Chicago, Chicago, IL.

>   Cassatt, Mary. *The Child's Bath*. Oil on canvas, 1893. The Art Institute of Chicago, Chicago, IL.

## Works from Web Sites

1. **Author.** In a note, list the author(s) first name first. In a bibliographic entry, list the first author last name first, comma, first name; list additional authors first name first. Note that the host may serve as the author.

2. **Document title.** Enclose the title in quotation marks, and capitalize all major words. In a note, put a comma before and after the title. In the bibliography, put a period before and after.

3. **Title of Web site.** Capitalize all major words. If the site's title is analogous to a book or periodical title, italicize it. In the notes section, put a comma after the title. In the bibliography, put a period after the title.

4. **Sponsor of site.** If the sponsor is the same as the author or site title, you may omit it. End with a comma (in the note) or a period (in the bibliographic entry).

5. **Date of publication or last modification.** If no date is available, or if your instructor requests it, include your date of access (with the word *accessed*).

6. **Retrieval information.** Give the URL for the Web site. If you are required to include a date of access, put the word *accessed* and the date in parentheses after the URL. End with a period.

### Citations for the Web site on p. 511 would look like this:

**ENDNOTE**

1. Rebecca Edwards, "The Populist Party," 1896: The Presidential Campaign: Cartoons & Commentary, Vassar College, 2000, http://projects .vassar.edu/1896/populists.html.

**BIBLIOGRAPHIC ENTRY**

Edwards, Rebecca. "The Populist Party." 1896: The Presidential Campaign: Cartoons & Commentary. Vassar College. 2000. http://projects.vassar .edu/1896/populists.html.

**6** Retrieval Information
projects.vassar.edu/1896/populists.html

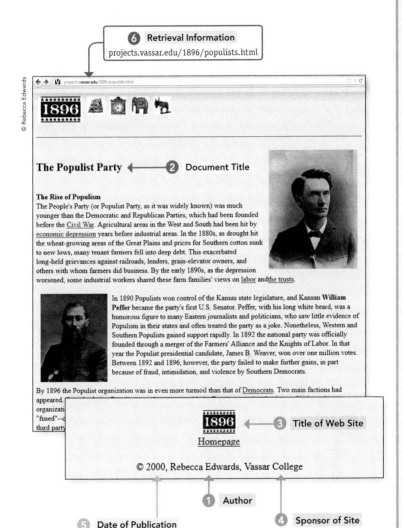

projects.**vassar.edu**/1896/populists.html

## The Populist Party ← **2** Document Title

**The Rise of Populism**
The People's Party (or Populist Party, as it was widely known) was much
younger than the Democratic and Republican Parties, which had been founded
before the Civil War. Agricultural areas in the West and South had been hit by
economic depression years before industrial areas. In the 1880s, as drought hit
the wheat-growing areas of the Great Plains and prices for Southern cotton sunk
to new lows, many tenant farmers fell into deep debt. This exacerbated
long-held grievances against railroads, lenders, grain-elevator owners, and
others with whom farmers did business. By the early 1890s, as the depression
worsened, some industrial workers shared these farm families' views on labor and the trusts.

In 1890 Populists won control of the Kansas state legislature, and Kansan **William
Peffer** became the party's first U.S. Senator. Peffer, with his long white beard, was a
humorous figure to many Eastern journalists and politicians, who saw little evidence of
Populism in their states and often treated the party as a joke. Nonetheless, Western and
Southern Populists gained support rapidly. In 1892 the national party was officially
founded through a merger of the Farmers' Alliance and the Knights of Labor. In that
year the Populist presidential candidate, James B. Weaver, won over one million votes.
Between 1892 and 1896, however, the party failed to make further gains, in part
because of fraud, intimidation, and violence by Southern Democrats.

By 1896 the Populist organization was in even more turmoil than that of Democrats. Two main factions had
appeared.
organizati
"fused"--d
third party

**1896**
Homepage ← **3** Title of Web Site

© 2000, Rebecca Edwards, Vassar College

**1** Author

**5** Date of Publication

**4** Sponsor of Site

511

If you refer to a reproduction, give the publication information.

> 37. Mary Cassatt, *The Child's Bath,* oil on canvas, 1893, on *Art Access,* The Art Institute of Chicago, August 2004, http://www.artic.edu/artaccess/AA_Impressionist/pages/IMP_6.shtml#.

> Cassatt, Mary. *The Child's Bath.* Oil on canvas, 1893. On *Art Access,* The Art Institute of Chicago. August 2004. http://www.artic.edu/artaccess/AA_Impressionist/pages/IMP_6.shtml#.

**38. Pamphlet, report, or brochure**  Information about the author or publisher may not be readily available, but give enough information to identify your source.

> 38. Jamie McCarthy, *Who Is David Irving?* (San Antonio, TX: Holocaust History Project, 1998).

> McCarthy, Jamie. *Who Is David Irving?* San Antonio, TX: Holocaust History Project, 1998.

**39. Government document**

> 39. U.S. House Committee on Ways and Means, *Report on Trade Mission to Sub-Saharan Africa,* 108th Cong., 1st sess. (Washington, DC: Government Printing Office, 2003), 28.

> U.S. House Committee on Ways and Means. *Report on Trade Mission to Sub-Saharan Africa.* 108th Cong., 1st sess. Washington, DC: Government Printing Office, 2003.

## 34d  A student research essay, *Chicago* style

**STUDENT WRITER**
**Amanda Rinder**

On the following pages are excerpts from an essay by Amanda Rinder that conforms to the *Chicago* guidelines described in this chapter. To read her complete project, go to the integrated media page at **macmillanhighered.com/smh**. (Photo © Amanda Rinder)

Sweet Home Chicago: Preserving the Past,
Protecting the Future of the Windy City

Title announces
topic clearly and
succinctly

Amanda Rinder

Title and writer's
name centered

Twentieth-Century U.S. History

Professor Goldberg

November 27, 2014

Course title,
instructor's
name, and date
centered at
bottom of title
page

Marginal annotations indicate effective choices or *Chicago*-style formatting.

Rinder 2

Only one city has the "Big Shoulders" described by Carl Sandburg: Chicago (fig. 1). So renowned are its skyscrapers and celebrated building style that an entire school of architecture is named for Chicago. Presently, however, the place that Frank Sinatra called "my kind of town" is beginning to lose sight of exactly what kind of town it is. Many of the buildings that give Chicago its distinctive character are being torn down in order to make room for new growth. Both preserving the classics and encouraging new creation are important; the combination of these elements gives Chicago architecture its unique flavor. Witold Rybczynski, a professor of urbanism at the University of Pennsylvania, told the *New York Times,* "Of all the cities we can think of . . . we associate Chicago with new things, with building new. Combining that with preservation is a difficult task, a tricky thing. It's hard to find the middle ground in Chicago."[1] Yet finding a middle ground is essential if the city is to retain the original character that sets it apart from the rest. In order to maintain Chicago's distinctive identity and its delicate balance between the old and the new, the city government must provide a comprehensive urban plan that not only directs growth, but calls for the preservation of landmarks and historic districts as well.

Chicago is a city for the working man. Nowhere is this more evident than in its architecture. David Garrard Lowe, author of *Lost Chicago,*

Fig. 1. Chicago skyline, circa 1940s. (Postcard courtesy of Minnie Dangberg.)

Rinder 3

notes that early Chicagoans "sought reality, not fantasy, and the reality
of America as seen from the heartland did not include the pavilions
of princes or the castles of kings."[2] The inclination toward unadorned,
sturdy buildings began in the late nineteenth century with the aptly
named Chicago School, a movement led by Louis Sullivan, John Wellborn
Root, and Daniel Burnham and based on Sullivan's adage, "Form follows
function."[3] The early skyscraper, the very symbol of the Chicago style,
represents the triumph of function and utility over sentiment, America
over Europe, and perhaps even the frontier over the civilization of the
East Coast.[4] These ideals of the original Chicago School were expanded
upon by architects of the Second Chicago School. Frank Lloyd Wright's
legendary organic style and the famed glass and steel constructions of
Mies van der Rohe are often the first images that spring to mind when
one thinks of Chicago.

Second paragraph provides background

  Yet the architecture that is the city's defining attribute is being
threatened by the increasing tendency toward development. The root
of Chicago's preservation problem lies in the enormous drive toward
economic expansion and the potential in Chicago for such growth. The
highly competitive market for land in the city means that properties sell
for the highest price if the buildings on them can be obliterated to make
room for newer, larger developments. Because of this preference on the
part of potential buyers, the label "landmark" has become a stigma for
property owners. "In other cities, landmark status is sought after—in
Chicago, it's avoided at all costs," notes Alan J. Shannon of the *Chicago
Tribune*.[5] Even if owners wish to keep their property's original structure,
designation as a landmark is still undesirable as it limits the renovations
that can be made to a building and thus decreases its value. Essentially,
no building that has even been recommended for landmark status may
be touched without the approval of the Commission on Chicago Historical
and Architectural Landmarks, a restriction that considerably diminishes
the appeal of the real estate. "We live in a world where the owners say,
'If you judge my property a landmark you are taking money away from
me.' And in Chicago the process is stacked in favor of the economics,"

Clear transition from previous paragraph

Signal verb "notes" introduces quotation

Notes

Newspaper article in database

1. Tracie Rozhon, "Chicago Girds for Big Battle over Its Skyline," *New York Times,* November 12, 2000, Academic Search Premier (28896783).

On Notes page, sources indented, numbered, and listed in order of appearance in body text

2. David Garrard Lowe, *Lost Chicago* (New York: Watson-Guptill Publications, 2000), 123.

3. *Columbia Encyclopedia,* 6th ed., s.v. "Louis Sullivan."

4. Daniel Bluestone, *Constructing Chicago* (New Haven: Yale University Press, 1991), 105.

Indirect source

5. Alan J. Shannon, "When Will It End?" *Chicago Tribune,* September 11, 1987, quoted in Karen J. Dilibert, *From Landmark to Landfill* (Chicago: Chicago Architectural Foundation, 2000), 11.

6. Steve Kerch, "Landmark Decisions," *Chicago Tribune,* March 18, 1990, sec. 16.

7. John W. Stamper, *Chicago's North Michigan Avenue* (Chicago: University of Chicago Press, 1991), 215.

Newspaper article online

8. Alf Siewers, "Success Spoiling the Magnificent Mile?" *Chicago Sun-Times,* April 9, 1995, http://www.sun-times.com/.

9. Paul Gapp, "McCarthy Building Puts Landmark Law on a Collision Course with Developers," *Chicago Tribune,* April 20, 1986, quoted in Karen J. Dilibert, *From Landmark to Landfill* (Chicago: Chicago Architectural Foundation, 2000), 4.

"Ibid." refers to previous source

10. Ibid.

11. Rozhon, "Chicago Girds for Big Battle."

Second reference to source identified by last name and title

12. Kerch, "Landmark Decisions."

13. Robert Bruegmann, *The Architects and the City* (Chicago: University of Chicago Press, 1997), 443.

Bibliography

Bluestone, Daniel. *Constructing Chicago.* New Haven: Yale University Press, 1991.

Bruegmann, Robert. *The Architects and the City.* Chicago: University of Chicago Press, 1997.

Dilibert, Karen J. *From Landmark to Landfill.* Chicago: Chicago Architectural Foundation, 2000.

Kerch, Steve. "Landmark Decisions." *Chicago Tribune,* March 18, 1990, sec. 16.

Lowe, David Garrard. *Lost Chicago.* New York: Watson-Guptill Publications, 2000.

Rozhon, Tracie. "Chicago Girds for Big Battle over Its Skyline." *New York Times,* November 12, 2000. Academic Search Premier (28896783).

Siewers, Alf. "Success Spoiling the Magnificent Mile?" *Chicago Sun-Times,* April 9, 1995. http://www.sun-times.com/.

Stamper, John W. *Chicago's North Michigan Avenue.* Chicago: University of Chicago Press, 1991.

Bibliography starts on new page. Sources in bibliography arranged alphabetically.

Book

Pamphlet

Newspaper article

Article from database

Bibliography entries use hanging indent and are not numbered

# CHAPTER 35

# CSE Style

W RITERS IN THE PHYSICAL SCIENCES, the life sciences, and mathematics often use the documentation style set forth by the Council of Science Editors (CSE). Guidelines for citing print sources can be found in *Scientific Style and Format: The CSE Manual for Authors, Editors, and Publishers,* Eighth Edition (2014).

## 35a Formatting CSE manuscripts

- **Title page.** Center the title of your paper. Beneath it, center your name. Include other relevant information, such as the course name and number, the instructor's name, and the date submitted.

- **Margins and spacing.** Leave standard margins at the top and bottom and on both sides of each page. Double-space the text and the references list.

- **Page numbers.** Type a short version of the paper's title and the page number in the upper right-hand corner of each page.

- **Abstract.** CSE style frequently calls for a one-paragraph abstract (about one hundred words). The abstract should be on a separate page, right after the title page, with the title *Abstract* centered one inch from the top of the page.

- **Headings.** CSE style does not require headings, but it notes that they can help readers quickly find the contents of a section of the paper.

- **Tables and figures.** Tables and figures must be labeled *Table* or *Figure* and numbered separately, one sequence for tables and one for figures. Give each table and figure a short, informative title. Be sure to introduce each table and figure in your text, and comment on its significance.

- **List of references.** Start the list of references on a new page at the end of the essay, and continue to number the pages consecutively. Center the title *References* one inch from the top of the page, and double-space before beginning the first entry.

# 35b Creating CSE in-text citations

In CSE style, citations within an essay follow one of three formats.

- The **citation-sequence format** calls for a superscript number or a number in parentheses after any mention of a source. The sources are numbered in the order they appear. Each number refers to the same source every time it is used. The first source mentioned in the paper is numbered *1*, the second source is numbered *2*, and so on.

- The **citation-name format** also calls for a superscript number or a number in parentheses after any mention of a source. The numbers are added after the list of references is completed and alphabetized, so that the source numbered *1* is alphabetically first in the list of references, *2* is alphabetically second, and so on.

- The **name-year format** calls for the last name of the author and the year of publication in parentheses after any mention of a source. If the last name appears in a signal phrase, the name-year format allows for giving only the year of publication in parentheses.

Before deciding which system to use, ask your instructor's preference.

### 1. In-text citation using citation-sequence or citation-name format

VonBergen[12] provides the most complete discussion of this phenomenon.

For the citation-sequence and citation-name formats, you would use the same superscript ([12]) for each subsequent citation of this work by VonBergen.

### 2. In-text citation using name-year format

VonBergen (2003) provides the most complete discussion of this phenomenon.

Hussar's two earlier studies of juvenile obesity (1995, 1999) examined only children with diabetes.

The classic examples of such investigations (Morrow 1968; Bridger et al. 1971; Franklin and Wayson 1972) still shape the assumptions of current studies.

# 35c Preparing a CSE list of references

The citations in the text of an essay correspond to items on a list titled *References*, which starts on a new page at the end of the essay. Continue to number the pages consecutively, center the title *References* one inch from the top of the page, and double-space before beginning the first entry.

The order of the entries depends on which format you follow:

- **Citation-sequence format:** number and list the references in the order the references are first cited in the text.
- **Citation-name format:** list and number the references in alphabetical order.
- **Name-year format:** list the references, unnumbered, in alphabetical order.

In the following examples, you will see that both the citation-sequence and citation-name formats call for listing the date after the publisher's name in references for books and after the periodical name in references for articles. The name-year format calls for listing the date immediately after the author's name in any kind of reference.

CSE style also specifies the treatment and placement of the following basic elements in the list of references:

- **Author.** List all authors last name first, and use only initials for first and middle names. Do not place a comma after the author's last name, and do not place periods after or spaces between the initials. Use a period after the last initial of the last author listed.
- **Title.** Do not italicize titles and subtitles of books and titles of periodicals. Do not enclose titles of articles in quotation marks. For books and articles, capitalize only the first word of the title and any proper nouns or proper adjectives. Abbreviate and capitalize all major words in a periodical title.

As you refer to these examples, pay attention to how publication information (publishers for books, details about periodicals for articles) and other specific elements are styled and punctuated.

## ☐ Books

For the basic format for citing a print book in your project, consult the source map on pp. 522–23.

### 1. One author

CITATION-SEQUENCE AND CITATION-NAME

1. Buchanan M. Nexus: small worlds and the groundbreaking theory of networks. New York: Norton; 2003.

NAME-YEAR

Buchanan M. 2003. Nexus: small worlds and the groundbreaking theory of networks. New York: Norton.

## DIRECTORY TO CSE STYLE  REFERENCES

### Books

### Periodicals

### Digital sources

### 2. Two or more authors

CITATION-SEQUENCE AND CITATION-NAME

2. Wojciechowski BW, Rice NM. Experimental methods in kinetic studies. 2nd ed. St. Louis (MO): Elsevier Science; 2003.

NAME-YEAR

Wojciechowski BW, Rice NM. 2003. Experimental methods in kinetic studies. 2nd ed. St. Louis (MO): Elsevier Science.

### 3. Organization as author

CITATION-SEQUENCE AND CITATION-NAME

3. World Health Organization. The world health report 2002: reducing risks, promoting healthy life. Geneva (Switzerland): The Organization; 2002.

# Books

Note that, depending on whether you are using the citation-sequence or citation-name format or the name-year format, the date placement will vary.

1 **Author.** List author(s) last name first, and use initials for first and middle names, with no periods or spaces. Use a period only after the last initial of the last author.

2, 5 **Publication year.** In name-year format, put the year of publication immediately after the author name(s). In citation-sequence or citation-name format, put the year of publication after the publisher's name.

3 **Title.** Do not italicize or put quotation marks around titles and subtitles of books. Capitalize only the first word of the title and any proper nouns or proper adjectives. If an edition number is given, list it after the title.

4 **City of publication and publisher.** List the city of publication (and the country or state abbreviation for unfamiliar cities) followed by a colon. Give the publisher's name. In citation-sequence or citation-name format, follow with a semicolon. In name-year format, follow with a period.

**A citation for the book on p. 523 would look like this:**

CITATION-SEQUENCE OR CITATION-NAME FORMAT

1. Creighton TE. Proteins: structures and molecular properties. 2nd ed. New York: WH Freeman; 1993.

NAME-YEAR FORMAT

Creighton TE. 1993. Proteins: structures and molecular properties. 2nd ed. New York: WH Freeman.

# PROTEINS

*Structures and Molecular Properties*

*Second Edition*

③ Title and Subtitle

① Author

Thomas E. Creighton

*European Molecular Biology Laboratory*
*Heidelberg, Germany*

Cover image provided by

**Library of Congress Ca**
Creighton, Thomas E., 19
    Proteins : structures
Creighton.—2nd ed.
        p.   cm.
    Includes bibliograph
    ISBN-13: 978-0-716
    ISBN-10: 0-7167-70
    1. Proteins—Structu
QP551.C737   1993
574.19'245—dc20

92-6664
CIP

④ **Publisher and City of Publication**

W. H. Freeman and Company • New York

②, ⑤ **Publication Year**

Printed in the United States of America

Eighth printing

W. H. Freeman and Company
41 Madison Avenue
New York, NY 10010

www.whfreeman.com

Place the organization's abbreviation at the beginning of the name-year entry, and use the abbreviation in the corresponding in-text citation. Alphabetize the entry by the first word of the full name, not by the abbreviation.

NAME-YEAR

[WHO] World Health Organization. 2002. The world health report 2002: reducing risks, promoting healthy life. Geneva (Switzerland): The Organization.

### 4. Book prepared by editor(s)

CITATION-SEQUENCE AND CITATION-NAME

4. Torrence ME, Isaacson RE, editors. Microbial food safety in animal agriculture: current topics. Ames: Iowa State University Press; 2003.

NAME-YEAR

Torrence ME, Isaacson RE, editors. 2003. Microbial safety in animal agriculture: current topics. Ames: Iowa State University Press.

### 5. Section of a book with an editor

CITATION-SEQUENCE AND CITATION-NAME

5. Kawamura A. Plankton. In: Perrin MF, Wursig B, Thewissen JGM, editors. Encyclopedia of marine mammals. San Diego: Academic Press; 2002. p. 939–942.

NAME-YEAR

Kawamura A. 2002. Plankton. In: Perrin MF, Wursig B, Thewissen JGM, editors. Encyclopedia of marine mammals. San Diego: Academic Press. p. 939–942.

### 6. Chapter of a book

CITATION-SEQUENCE AND CITATION-NAME

6. Honigsbaum M. The fever trail: in search of the cure for malaria. New York: Picador; 2003. Chapter 2, The cure; p. 19–38.

NAME-YEAR

Honigsbaum M. 2003. The fever trail: in search of the cure for malaria. New York: Picador. Chapter 2, The cure; p. 19–38.

### 7. Paper or abstract in conference proceedings

CITATION-SEQUENCE AND CITATION-NAME

7. Gutierrez AP. Integrating biological and environmental factors in crop system models [abstract]. In: Integrated Biological Systems Conference; 2003 Apr 14–16; San Antonio, TX. Beaumont (TX): Agroeconomics Research Group; 2003. p. 14–15.

NAME-YEAR

Gutierrez AP. 2003. Integrating biological and environmental factors in crop system models [abstract]. In: Integrated Biological Systems Conference; 2003 Apr 14–16; San Antonio, TX. Beaumont (TX): Agroeconomics Research Group. p. 14–15.

## □ Periodicals

Provide volume and issue numbers for journals. For newspaper and magazine articles, include the section designation and column number, if any, and the date. For all periodicals, give inclusive page numbers. For rules on abbreviating journal titles, consult the CSE manual or ask an instructor.

### 8. Article in a journal

CITATION-SEQUENCE AND CITATION-NAME

8. Mahmud K, Vance ML. Human growth hormone and aging. New Engl J Med. 2003;348(2):2256–2257.

NAME-YEAR

Mahmud K, Vance ML. 2003. Human growth hormone and aging. New Engl J Med. 348(2):2256–2257.

### 9. Article in a weekly journal

CITATION-SEQUENCE AND CITATION-NAME

9. Holden C. Future brightening for depression treatments. Science. 2003 Oct 31:810–813.

NAME-YEAR

Holden C. 2003. Future brightening for depression treatments. Science. Oct 31:810–813.

### 10. Article in a magazine

CITATION-SEQUENCE AND CITATION-NAME

10. Livio M. Moving right along: the accelerating universe holds secrets to dark energy, the Big Bang, and the ultimate beauty of nature. Astronomy. 2002 Jul:34–39.

NAME-YEAR

Livio M. 2002 Jul. Moving right along: the accelerating universe holds secrets to dark energy, the Big Bang, and the ultimate beauty of nature. Astronomy. 34–39.

### 11. Article in a newspaper

**CITATION-SEQUENCE AND CITATION-NAME**

11. Kolata G. Bone diagnosis gives new data but no answers. New York Times (National Ed.). 2003 Sep 28;Sect. 1:1 (col. 1).

**NAME-YEAR**

Kolata G. 2003 Sep 28. Bone diagnosis gives new data but no answers. New York Times (National Ed.). Sect. 1:1 (col. 1).

## □ Digital sources

These examples use the citation-sequence or citation-name system. To adapt them to the name-year system, delete the note number and place the update date immediately after the author's name.

The basic entry for most sources accessed through the Internet should include the following elements:

- **Author.** Give the author's name, if available, last name first, followed by the initial(s) and a period.
- **Title.** For book, journal, and article titles, follow the style for print materials. For all other types of electronic material, reproduce the title that appears on the screen.
- **Medium.** Indicate, in brackets, that the source is not in print format by using a designation such as *[Internet]*.
- **Place of publication.** The city usually should be followed by the two-letter abbreviation for the state. No state abbreviation is necessary for well-known cities such as New York, Chicago, Boston, and London or for a publisher whose location is part of its name (for example, University of Oklahoma Press). If the city is implied, put the city and state in brackets. If the city cannot be inferred, use the words *place unknown* in brackets.
- **Publisher.** For material other than journal articles from Web sites and online databases, include the individual or organization that produces or sponsors the site. If no publisher can be determined, use the words *publisher unknown* in brackets.
- **Dates.** Cite three important dates, if possible: either the date that the publication was placed on the Internet or the copyright date; the most recent date of any update or revision; and the date that the publication was accessed by you.
- **Page, document, volume, and issue numbers.** When citing a portion of a larger work or site, list the inclusive page numbers or document numbers of

the specific item being cited. For journals or journal articles, include volume and issue numbers. If exact page numbers are not available, include in brackets the approximate length in computer screens, paragraphs, or bytes: [2 screens], [10 paragraphs], [332K bytes].

- **Address.** Include the URL or other electronic address; use the phrase *Available from:* to introduce the address. Only URLs that end with a slash are followed by a period.

### 12. Material from an online database

For the basic format for citing an article from a database, see the source map on pp. 528–29. (Because CSE does not provide guidelines for citing an article from an online database, this model has been adapted from CSE guidelines for citing an online journal article.)

> 12. Shilts E. Water wanderers. Can Geographic [Internet]. 2002 [accessed 2014 Jan 27];122(3):72–77. Academic Search Premier. Ipswich (MA): EBSCO. Available from: http://www.ebscohost.com/ Document No.: 6626534.

### 13. Article in an online journal

> 13. Perez P, Calonge TM. Yeast protein kinase C. J Biochem [Internet]. 2002 Oct [accessed 2014 Nov 3];132(4):513–517. Available from: http://edpex104.bcasj.or.jp/jb-pdf/132-4/jb132-4-513.pdf

### 14. Article in an online newspaper

> 14. Brody JE. Reasons, and remedies, for morning sickness. New York Times [Internet]. 2004 Apr 27 [accessed 2014 Apr 30]. Available from: http://www.nytimes.com/2009/04/27/health/27BROD.html

### 15. Online book

> 15. Patrick TS, Allison JR, Krakow GA. Protected plants of Georgia [Internet]. Social Circle (GA): Georgia Department of Natural Resources; c1995 [accessed 2014 Dec 3]. Available from: http://www.georgiawildlife.com/content/displaycontent.asp?txtDocument=89&txtPage=9

To cite a portion of an online book, give the name of the part after the publication information: *Chapter 6, Encouraging germination.* See model 6.

### 16. Web site

> 16. Geology and public policy [Internet]. Boulder (CO): Geological Society of America; c2010 [updated 2010 Jun 3; accessed 2014 Sep 19]. Available from: http://www.geosociety.org/geopolicy.htm

# Articles from Databases

Note that date placement will vary depending on whether you are using the citation-sequence or citation-name format or the name-year format.

**①** **Author.** List author(s) last name first, and use only initials for first and middle names.

**②, ⑤** **Publication date.** For name-year format, put publication date after author name(s). In citation-sequence or citation-name format, put it after periodical title. Use year only (for journals) or year month day (for other periodicals).

**③** **Article title.** Capitalize first word and proper nouns/adjectives.

**④** **Periodical title.** Capitalize major words. Abbreviate journal titles. Follow with *[Internet]* and a period.

**⑥** **Date of access.** In brackets, write *cited* and the year, month, and day. End with a semicolon.

**⑦** **Publication information for article.** Give volume number, issue number (in parentheses), and a colon.

**⑧** **Page numbers.** Give page range. End with a period.

**⑨** **Name of database.** End with a period.

**⑩** **Publication information for database.** Include the city, the state abbreviation in parentheses, a colon, the publisher's name, and a period.

**⑪** **Web address and document number.** Write *Available from* and the brief URL, then *Document no.* and the identifying number.

## A citation for the article on p. 529 would look like this:

**CITATION-SEQUENCE OR CITATION-NAME FORMAT**

1. Miller AL. Epidemiology, etiology, and natural treatment of seasonal affective disorder. Altern Med Rev [Internet]. 2005 [accessed 2014 25 May]; 10(1):5–13. Academic Search Premier. Ipswich (MA): EBSCO. Available from http://www.ebscohost.com Document No.: 16514813.

**NAME-YEAR FORMAT**

Miller AL. 2005. Epidemiology, etiology, and natural treatment of seasonal affective disorder. Altern Med Rev [Internet]. [accessed 2014 25 May]; 10(1):5–13. Academic Search Premier. Ipswich (MA): EBSCO. Available from http://www.ebscohost.com Document No.: 16514813.

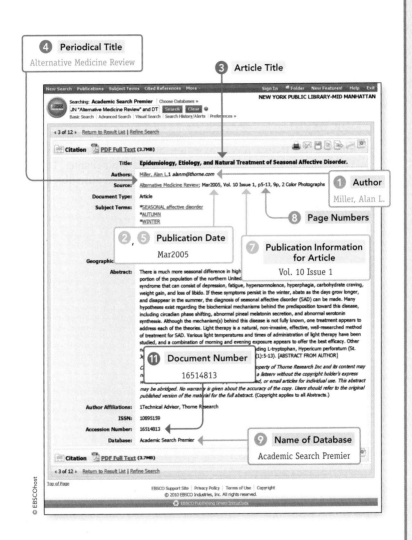

**Periodical Title**
Alternative Medicine Review

**Article Title**

NEW YORK PUBLIC LIBRARY-MID MANHATTAN

Searching: **Academic Search Premier** | Choose Databases »
JN "Alternative Medicine Review" and DT | Search | Clear
Basic Search | Advanced Search | Visual Search | Search History/Alerts | Preferences »

‹ 3 of 12 › | Return to Result List | Refine Search

Citation | PDF Full Text (3.7MB)

Title: **Epidemiology, Etiology, and Natural Treatment of Seasonal Affective Disorder.**

Authors: Miller, Alan L,1 alanm@thorne.com

Source: Alternative Medicine Review; Mar2005, Vol. 10 Issue 1, p5-13, 9p, 2 Color Photographs

Document Type: Article

Subject Terms: *SEASONAL affective disorder
*AUTUMN
*WINTER

**Author**
Miller, Alan L.

**Page Numbers**

**Publication Date**
Mar2005

**Publication Information for Article**
Vol. 10 Issue 1

Geographic

Abstract: There is much more seasonal difference in high
portion of the population of the northern United
syndrome that can consist of depression, fatigue, hypersomnolence, hyperphagia, carbohydrate craving,
weight gain, and loss of libido. If these symptoms persist in the winter, abate as the days grow longer,
and disappear in the summer, the diagnosis of seasonal affective disorder (SAD) can be made. Many
hypotheses exist regarding the biochemical mechanisms behind the predisposition toward this disease,
including circadian phase shifting, abnormal pineal melatonin secretion, and abnormal serotonin
synthesis. Although the mechanism(s) behind this disease is not fully known, one treatment appears to
address each of the theories. Light therapy is a natural, non-invasive, effective, well-researched method
of treatment for SAD. Various light temperatures and times of administration of light therapy have been
studied, and a combination of morning and evening exposure appears to offer the best efficacy. Other
n                                        ding L-tryptophan, Hypericum perforatum (St.

**Document Number**
16514813

C                                          operty of Thorne Research Inc and its content may
n                                          a listserv without the copyright holder's express
                                          d, or email articles for individual use. This abstract
may be abridged. No warranty is given about the accuracy of the copy. Users should refer to the original
published version of the material for the full abstract. (Copyright applies to all Abstracts.)

Author Affiliations: 1Technical Advisor, Thorne Research

ISSN: 10895159

Accession Number: 16514813

Database: Academic Search Premier

**Name of Database**
Academic Search Premier

Citation | PDF Full Text (3.7MB)

‹ 3 of 12 › | Return to Result List | Refine Search

Top of Page

529

### 17. Government Web site

17. Health disparities: reducing health disparities in cancer [Internet].
Atlanta (GA): Centers for Disease Control and Prevention (US); 2010
[updated 2010 Apr 5; accessed 2014 May 1]. Available from: http://www
.cdc.gov/cancer/healthdisparities/basic_info/disparities.htm

## 35d  A student research project, CSE style

The following excerpt from a literature review by Joanna Hays conforms to
the name-year format in the CSE guidelines described in this chapter. To read
her complete project, go to the integrated media page at **macmillanhighered
.com/smh**.

Running head has
short title, page
number

### Overview

Niemann-Pick disease (NP) occurs in patients with deficient
acid sphingomyelinase (ASM) activity as well as with the lysosomal
accumulation of sphingomyelin. It is an autosomal recessive disorder
(Levran et al. 1991). As recently as 1991, researchers had classified
two major phenotypes: type A and type B (Levran et al. 1991). In more
recent studies several more phenotypes have been identified, including
types C and D. Each type of NP has distinct characteristics and effects on
the patient. NP is distributed worldwide, but is closely associated with
Ashkenazi Jewish descendants. Niemann-Pick disease is relevant to the
molecular world today because of advances being made in the ability
to identify mutations, to trace ancestry where the mutation may have
originated, and to counsel patients with a high potential of carrying
the disease. Genetic counseling primarily consists of confirmation of the
particular disease and calculation of the possible future reappearance in
the same gene line (Brock 1974). The following discussion will summarize
the identification of mutations causing the various forms of NP, the
distribution of NP, as well as new genotypes and phenotypes that are
correlated with NP.

### Mutations Causing NP

Headings
organize project

Levran et al. (1991) inform readers of the frequent identification
of missense mutations in the gene associated with Ashkenazi Jewish
persons afflicted by type A and type B NP. This paper identifies the
mutations associated with NP and the beginning of many molecular
techniques to develop diagnoses. Greer et al. (1998) identify a new
mutation that is specifically identified to be the cause of type D. NP
in various forms is closely associated with the founder effect caused
by a couple married in the early 1700s in what is now Nova Scotia.
Simonaro et al. (2002) discuss the distribution of type B NP as well as
new phenotypes and genotypes. All three of these papers identify

Annotations indicate CSE-style formatting.

Niemann-Pick Disease 9

## References

Brock DJH. 1974. Prenatal diagnosis and genetic counseling. J Clin Pathol Suppl. (R Coll Path.) 8:150–155.

Greer WL, Ridell DC, Gillan TL, Girouard GS, Sparrow SM, Byers DM, Dobson MJ, Neumann PE. 1998. The Nova Scotia (type D) form of Niemann-Pick disease is caused by a $G_{3097} \rightarrow T$ transversion in NPC1. Am J Hum Genet 63:52–54.

Levran O, Desnick RJ, Schuchman EH. 1991. Niemann-Pick disease: a frequent missense mutation in the acid sphingomyelinase gene of Ashkenazi Jewish type A and B patients. P Natl Acad Sci USA 88:3748–3752.

Simonaro CM, Desnick RJ, McGovern MM, Wasserstein MP, Schuchman EH. 2002. The demographics and distribution of type B Niemann-Pick disease: novel mutations lead to new genotype/phenotype correlations. Am J Hum Genet 71:1413–1419.

Alphabetical by name

# PART 8
# Grammar

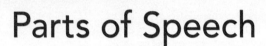

# CHAPTER 36

# Parts of Speech

G RAMMATICAL CORRECTNESS ALONE is not enough to ensure that a
sentence is effective and artful — or that it serves an appropriate purpose
in your writing. Understanding grammatical structures can, however, help you
produce sentences that are appropriate and effective as well as grammatically
correct. The English language includes eight different categories of words called
the *parts of speech* — verbs, nouns, pronouns, adjectives, adverbs, prepositions,
conjunctions, and interjections. Many English words can function as more than
one part of speech. When you *book an airplane flight*, the word *book* is a verb;
when you *take a good book to the beach*, it is a noun; and when you have *book
knowledge*, it is an adjective.

## 36a Verbs

Verbs move the meaning of sentences along by showing action (*glance, speculate*), occurrence (*become, happen*), or being (*be, seem*). Verbs change form to
show *time, person, number, voice*, and *mood* (Chapter 39).

| | |
|---|---|
| TIME | we *work*, we *worked* |
| PERSON | I *work*, she *works* |
| NUMBER | one person *works*, two people *work* |
| VOICE | she *asks*, she *is asked* |
| MOOD | we *see*, if I *were to see* |

Helping verbs (also called *auxiliary verbs*) combine with main verbs to create
verb phrases. Auxiliaries include the forms of *be, do*, and *have*, which are also
used as main verbs, and *can, could, may, might, must, shall, should, will*, and
*would* (39b).

▶ **I could have danced all night.**

▶ **She would prefer to learn Italian rather than Spanish.**

▶ **When do you need the spreadsheet?**

◢ **EXERCISE 36.1**

Identify each verb or verb phrase in the following sentences. Example:

**Drivers should expect weather-related delays.**

**Verb phrase:** should expect

1. The story was released to the press late on Friday evening.
2. Most athletes will be arriving well before the games.
3. Housing prices have fallen considerably in the past year.
4. No one spoke in the room where the students were taking the exam.
5. The suspect has been fingerprinted and is waiting for his lawyer.

# 36b Nouns

Nouns name persons (*aviator, child*), places (*lake, library*), things (*truck, suitcase*), or concepts (*happiness, balance*). Proper nouns, which are capitalized, name specific persons, places, things, or concepts: *Bill, Iowa, Supreme Court, Buddhism*. Collective nouns (40d) name groups: *flock, jury*.

Most nouns change from singular (one) to plural (more than one) when you add *-s* or *-es*: *horse, horses; kiss, kisses*. Some nouns, however, have irregular plural forms: *woman, women; mouse, mice; deer, deer*. Noncount nouns (38a) cannot be made plural because they name things that cannot easily be counted: *dust, peace, prosperity*.

The possessive form of a noun shows ownership. Possessive forms add an apostrophe plus *-s* to most singular nouns or just an apostrophe to most plural nouns: *the horse's owner, the boys' department*.

Nouns are often preceded by the article (or determiner) *a, an,* or *the*: *a rocket, an astronaut, the launch* (38c).

◢ **EXERCISE 36.2**

Identify the nouns and the articles in each of the following sentences. Example:

**The Puritans hoped for a different king, but Charles II regained the throne.**

**Nouns:** Puritans, king, Charles II, throne
**Articles:** the, a, the

1. After Halloween, the children got sick from eating too much candy.
2. Although June is technically the driest month, severe flooding has occurred in the late spring.
3. Baking is no longer a common activity in most households around the country.
4. A sudden frost turned the ground into a field of ice.
5. The cyclist swerved to avoid an oncoming car that had run a red light.

# Parts of Speech

**1** **Verbs show action, occurrence, or being.**

Anita is running for mayor, and maybe she will win. Hey, who knows? This could finally be her big chance. She is honest—unlike the former mayor, who was caught in a financial scandal that made the newspapers shortly before he resigned.

> Verbs and verb phrases: *is running*—present progressive form; *will win*—future tense; *knows*—present tense; *could be*—present tense (*could* is a modal); *is*—present tense; *was caught*—past tense of irregular verb *catch* (passive voice); *made*—past tense; *resigned*—past tense.

**2** **Nouns name persons, places, things, or concepts.**

Anita is running for mayor, and maybe she will win. Hey, who knows? This could finally be her big chance. She is honest—unlike the former mayor, who was caught in a financial scandal that made the newspapers shortly before he resigned.

> Proper noun: *Anita*—subject. Common nouns: *mayor* (first use)—object of preposition *for*; *chance*—subject complement; *mayor* (second use)—object of preposition *unlike*; *scandal*—object of preposition *in*; *newspapers*—direct object of verb.

**3** **Pronouns substitute for nouns.**

Anita is running for mayor, and maybe she will win. Hey, who knows? This could finally be her big chance. She is honest—unlike the former mayor, who was caught in a financial scandal that made the newspapers shortly before he resigned.

> Personal pronouns: *she* (two uses) and *he*—subject. Interrogative pronoun: *who* (first use). Demonstrative pronoun: *this* (refers to the fact that Anita is running for mayor). Possessive pronoun: *her*. Relative pronouns: *who* (second use—refers to *the former mayor*) and *that* (refers to *a financial scandal*).

**4** **Adjectives modify nouns or pronouns.**

Anita is running for mayor, and maybe she will win. Hey, who knows? This could finally be her big chance. She is honest—unlike the former mayor, who was caught in a financial scandal that made the newspapers shortly before he resigned.

> Articles: *the*; *a*. Subject complement: *honest*. Other adjectives: *big*—modifies *chance*; *former*—modifies *mayor*; *financial*—modifies *scandals*.

**⑤** **Adverbs** modify **verbs**, **adjectives**, other **adverbs**, or entire clauses.

Anita is running for mayor, and maybe she will win. Hey, who knows? This could finally be her big chance. She is honest—unlike the former mayor, who was caught in a financial scandal that made the newspapers shortly before he resigned.

> *Maybe*—modifies the clause *he will win*; *finally*—modifies the verb phrase *could be*; *shortly*—modifies the clause *before he resigned*.

**⑥** **Prepositions** express relationships between **nouns or pronouns** and other words.

Anita is running for mayor, and maybe she will win. Hey, who knows? This could finally be her big chance. She is honest—unlike the former mayor, who was caught in a financial scandal that made the newspapers shortly before he resigned.

> *For*—object is the noun *mayor*; *unlike*—object is the noun phrase *the former mayor*; *in*—object is the noun phrase *a financial scandal*.

**⑦** **Conjunctions** join words or groups of words.

Anita is running for mayor, and maybe she will win. Hey, who knows? This could finally be her big chance. She is honest—unlike the former mayor, who was caught in a financial scandal that made the newspapers shortly before he resigned.

> Coordinating conjunction: *and*. Subordinating conjunction: *before*.

**⑧** **Interjections** express surprise or emotion and do not relate grammatically to other parts of speech.

Anita is running for mayor, and maybe she will win. Hey, who knows? This could finally be her big chance. She is honest—unlike the former mayor, who was caught in a financial scandal that made the newspapers shortly before he resigned.

Here is the paragraph again, with each of the eight parts of speech identified as above.

Anita is running for mayor, and maybe she will win. Hey, who knows? This could finally be her big chance. She is honest—unlike the former mayor, who was caught in a financial scandal that made the newspapers shortly before he resigned.

---

| MULTI-LINGUAL | **COUNT AND NONCOUNT NOUNS** |

Do people conduct *research* or *researches*? See 38a for a discussion of count and non-count nouns.

## 36c Pronouns

Pronouns often take the place of nouns or other words functioning as nouns so that you do not have to repeat words that have already been mentioned. A word or word group that a pronoun replaces or refers to is called the antecedent of the pronoun (41f).

ANTECEDENT                                          PRONOUN
▶ **Caitlin refused the invitation even though she wanted to go.**

Pronouns fall into several categories.

### Personal pronouns

Personal pronouns refer to specific persons or things. Each can take several forms (*I, me, my, mine*) depending on its function in the sentence (41a).

*I, me, you, he, she, him, her, it, we, they, them*

▶ **When Keisha saw the dogs again, she called them, and they ran to her.**

### Possessive pronouns

Possessive pronouns are personal pronouns that indicate ownership (41a and 57b).

*my, mine, your, yours, her, hers, his, its, our, ours, their, theirs*

▶ **My roommate lost her keys.**

### Reflexive pronouns

Reflexive pronouns refer to the subject of the sentence or clause in which they appear. They end in *-self* or *-selves*.

*myself, yourself, himself, herself, itself, oneself, ourselves, yourselves, themselves*

▶ **The seals sunned themselves on the warm rocks.**

### Intensive pronouns

Intensive pronouns have the same form as reflexive pronouns. They emphasize a noun or another pronoun.

▶ **He decided to paint the apartment himself.**

## Indefinite pronouns

Indefinite pronouns do not refer to specific nouns, although they may refer to identifiable persons or things (40e and 41k). The following is a partial list:

*all, another, anybody, both, each, either, everything, few, many, most, neither, none, no one, nothing, one, some, something*

▶ **Everybody screamed, and someone fainted, when the lights went out.**

## Demonstrative pronouns

Demonstrative pronouns identify or point to specific nouns.

*this, that, these, those*

▶ **These are Peter's books.**

## Interrogative pronouns

Interrogative pronouns are used to ask questions.

*who, which, what*

▶ **Who can help set up the chairs for the meeting?**

## Relative pronouns

Relative pronouns introduce dependent clauses and relate the dependent clause to the rest of the sentence (37e). The interrogative pronoun *who* and the relative pronouns *who* and *whoever* have different forms depending on how they are used in a sentence (41b).

*who, which, that, what, whoever, whichever, whatever*

▶ **Maya, who hires interns, is the manager whom you should contact.**

## Reciprocal pronouns

Reciprocal pronouns refer to individual parts of a plural antecedent.

*each other, one another*

▶ **The business failed because the partners distrusted each other.**

### ◢ EXERCISE 36.3

Identify the pronouns and any antecedents in each of the following sentences. Example:

**As identical twins, they really do understand each other.**

**Pronoun:** they      **Antecedent:** twins
**Pronoun:** each other      **Antecedent:** they

1. He told the volunteers to help themselves to the leftovers.
2. There are two kinds of people: those who divide people into two kinds and those who don't.
3. Who is going to buy the jeans and wear them if the designer himself finds them uncomfortable?
4. Before an annual performance review, employees are asked to take a hard look at themselves and their work habits.
5. Forwarding an email warning about a computer virus to everyone in your address book is never a good idea.

## 36d Adjectives

Adjectives modify (limit the meaning of) nouns and pronouns, usually by describing, identifying, or quantifying those words (see Chapter 42). Adjectives that identify or quantify are sometimes called *determiners* (38b).

▶ **The red Corvette ran off the road.** [describes]
▶ **That Corvette needs to be repaired.** [identifies]
▶ **We saw several other Corvettes race by.** [quantifies]

In addition to their basic forms, most descriptive adjectives have other forms that allow you to make comparisons: *small, smaller, smallest; foolish, more foolish, most foolish, less foolish, least foolish.*

▶ **This year's attendance was smaller than last year's.**

Adjectives usually precede the words they modify, though they may follow linking verbs: *The car was defective.* Many pronouns (36c) can function as identifying adjectives when they are followed by a noun.

▶ **That is a dangerous intersection.** [pronoun]
▶ **That intersection is dangerous.** [identifying adjective]

Other kinds of adjectives that identify or quantify are the articles *a, an,* and *the* (38c) and numbers (*three, sixty-fifth, five hundred*).

Proper adjectives, which are capitalized (60b), form from or relate to proper nouns (*Egyptian, Emersonian*).

## 36e Adverbs

Adverbs modify verbs, adjectives, other adverbs, or entire clauses (see Chapter 42). Many adverbs end in *-ly*, though some do not (*always, never, very, well*), and some words that end in *-ly* are not adverbs but adjectives (*friendly, lovely*). One of the most common adverbs is *not*.

- **Business writers frequently communicate with strangers.** [modifies the verb *communicate*]
- **How can they attract customers in an increasingly difficult economy?** [modifies the adjective *difficult*]
- **They must work especially hard to avoid offending readers.** [modifies the adverb *hard*]
- **Obviously, they need to weigh their words with care.** [modifies the independent clause that makes up the rest of the sentence]

Adverbs often answer the questions *when? where? why? how? to what extent?*

Many adverbs, like many adjectives, take different forms when making comparisons: *forcefully, more forcefully, most forcefully, less forcefully, least forcefully.*

- **Of all the candidates, she speaks the most forcefully.**

Conjunctive adverbs modify an entire clause, and they express the connection in meaning between that clause and the preceding clause (or sentence). More common conjunctive adverbs include *however, furthermore, therefore,* and *likewise.* (See 36g.)

### EXERCISE 36.4

Identify the adjectives and adverbs in each of the following sentences. Remember that articles and some pronouns are used as adjectives. Example:

> **Inadvertently, the two agents misquoted their major client.**
>
> **Adjectives:** the, two, their, major
> **Adverb:** inadvertently

1. The small, frightened child firmly squeezed my hand and refused to take another step forward.
2. Meanwhile, she learned that the financial records had been completely false.
3. Koalas are generally quiet creatures that make loud grunting noises during mating season.
4. The huge red tomatoes looked lovely, but they tasted disappointingly like cardboard.
5. The youngest dancer in the troupe performed a brilliant solo.

# 36f Prepositions

Prepositions express relationships — in space, time, or other senses — between nouns or pronouns and other words in a sentence.

▶ We did not want to leave **during** the game.

▶ The contestants waited nervously **for** the announcement.

A prepositional phrase (see Chapter 43) begins with a preposition and ends with the noun or pronoun it connects to the rest of the sentence.

▶ Drive **across** the bridge and go **down** the avenue **past** three stoplights.

**SOME COMMON PREPOSITIONS**

| | | | | |
|---|---|---|---|---|
| about | at | down | near | since |
| above | before | during | of | through |
| across | behind | except | off | toward |
| after | below | for | on | under |
| against | beneath | from | onto | until |
| along | beside | in | out | up |
| among | between | inside | over | upon |
| around | beyond | into | past | with |
| as | by | like | regarding | without |

**SOME COMPOUND PREPOSITIONS**

| | | |
|---|---|---|
| according to | except for | instead of |
| as well as | in addition to | next to |
| because of | in front of | out of |
| by way of | in place of | with regard to |
| due to | in spite of | |

Research for this book shows that many writers — including native speakers of English — have trouble choosing appropriate prepositions. If you are not sure which preposition to use, consult your dictionary.

 **EXERCISE 36.5**

Identify the prepositions in the following sentences. Example:

**In the dim interior of the hut crouched an old man.**

**Prepositions:** in, of

1. The supervisor of the night shift requested that all available personnel work extra hours from October through December.
2. The hatchlings emerged from their shells, crawled across the sand, and swam into the sea.
3. Instead of creating a peaceful new beginning, the tribunal factions are constantly fighting among themselves.
4. After some hard thinking on a weeklong camping trip, I decided I would quit my job and join the Peace Corps for two years.
5. The nuclear power plant about ten miles from the city has the worst safety record of any plant in the country.

# 36g Conjunctions

Conjunctions connect words or groups of words to each other and tell something about the relationship between these words.

## Coordinating conjunctions

Coordinating conjunctions (51a) join equivalent structures, such as two or more nouns, pronouns, verbs, adjectives, adverbs, prepositions, conjunctions, phrases, or clauses.

▶ **A strong but warm breeze blew across the desert.**
▶ **Please print or type the information on the application form.**
▶ **Taiwo worked two shifts today, so she is tired tonight.**

COORDINATING CONJUNCTIONS

| and | but | for | nor | or | so | yet |
|-----|-----|-----|-----|-----|-----|-----|

## Correlative conjunctions

Correlative conjunctions join equal elements, and they come in pairs.

▶ **Both Bechtel and Kaiser submitted bids on the project.**
▶ **Maisha not only sent a card but also visited me in the hospital.**

CORRELATIVE CONJUNCTIONS

| both . . . and | just as . . . so | not only . . . but also |
|----------------|------------------|-------------------------|
| either . . . or | neither . . . nor | whether . . . or |

## Subordinating conjunctions

Subordinating conjunctions (51b) introduce adverb clauses and signal the relationship between the adverb clause and another clause, usually an independent clause. For instance, in the following sentence, the subordinating conjunction *while* signals a time relationship, letting us know that the two events in the sentence happened simultaneously:

▶ **Sweat ran down my face while I frantically searched for my child.**

SOME COMMON SUBORDINATING CONJUNCTIONS

| | | |
|---|---|---|
| after | if | unless |
| although | in order that | until |
| as | once | when |
| as if | since | where |
| because | so that | whether |
| before | than | while |
| even though | that | who |
| how | though | why |

### Conjunctive adverbs

Conjunctive adverbs connect independent clauses and often act as transitional expressions (54f) that show how the second clause relates to the first clause. As their name suggests, conjunctive adverbs can act as both adverbs and conjunctions because they modify the second clause in addition to connecting it to the preceding clause. Like many other adverbs yet unlike other conjunctions, they can move to different positions in a clause.

▶ **The cider tasted bitter; however, each of us drank a tall glass of it.**
▶ **The cider tasted bitter; each of us, however, drank a tall glass of it.**

SOME CONJUNCTIVE ADVERBS

| | | |
|---|---|---|
| also | indeed | now |
| anyway | instead | otherwise |
| besides | likewise | similarly |
| certainly | meanwhile | still |
| finally | moreover | then |
| furthermore | namely | therefore |
| however | nevertheless | thus |
| incidentally | next | undoubtedly |

Independent clauses connected by a conjunctive adverb must be separated by a semicolon or a period, not just a comma (46d).

▶ **Some of these problems could occur at any company; still, many could happen only here.**

**EXERCISE 36.6**

Identify the coordinating, correlative, and subordinating conjunctions as well as the conjunctive adverbs in each of the following sentences. Example:

> **We used sleeping bags, even though the cabin had sheets and blankets.**
>
> **Subordinating conjunction:** even though
> **Coordinating conjunction:** and

1. After waiting for an hour and a half, both Jenny and I were disgruntled, so we went home.
2. The facilities were not only uncomfortable but also dangerous.
3. I usually get a bonus each January; however, sales were down this year, so the company did not give us any extra money.
4. Although I had completed a six-week training regimen of running, swimming, and cycling, I did not feel ready, so I withdrew from the competition.
5. Enrique was not qualified for the job because he knew one of the programming languages but not the other; still, the interview encouraged him.

# 36h Interjections

Interjections express surprise or emotion: *oh, ouch, hey.* Interjections often stand alone. Even when they are included in a sentence, they do not relate grammatically to the rest of the sentence.

▶ **Hey, no one suggested that we would find an easy solution.**

▼ ▼ ▼ ▼ ▼ ▼ ▼ ▼ ▼ ▼ ▼ ▼ ▼ ▼ ▼ ▼ ▼ ▼ ▼ ▼ ▼ ▼ ▼ ▼ ▼ ▼

## THINKING CRITICALLY ABOUT PARTS OF SPEECH

Some students in U.S. schools study parts of speech and other grammatical terms before college, and others don't. Jot down notes describing what you know about basic structures of English grammar and how you acquired this knowledge (from explicit instruction? from your own reading and intuition? somewhere else?). How confident are you that you understand English grammar? Do you think having such knowledge is (or would be) useful? Why or why not?

# CHAPTER 37

# Parts of Sentences

THE GRAMMAR OF YOUR FIRST LANGUAGE comes to you almost automatically. Listen in on a conversation between two four-year-olds:

AUDREY: My new bike that Aunt Andrea got me has a red basket and a loud horn, and I love it.

LILA: Can I ride it?

AUDREY: Yes, as soon as I take a turn.

This simple conversation features sophisticated grammar — the subordination of one clause to another, a compound object, and a number of adjectives — used effortlessly. If you are like many English speakers, you may never really have reflected on the details of how the language works. Paying close attention to how you put sentences together can help you understand the choices available to you whenever you write.

## 37a  The basic grammar of sentences

A sentence is a grammatically complete group of words that expresses a thought. Words in a sentence can be identified by parts of speech (see Chapter 36), but you should also understand how words and phrases function in sentences.

### □  Recognizing subjects and predicates

To be grammatically complete, a sentence must contain both a subject, which identifies what the sentence is about, and a predicate, which says or asks something about the subject or tells the subject to do something.

| SUBJECT | PREDICATE |
|---|---|
| I | have a dream. |
| The rain in Spain | stays mainly in the plain. |
| Her skill as an archer | makes her a formidable opponent. |

---

**TALKING THE TALK | UNDERSTANDING GRAMMATICAL TERMS**

"I never learned any grammar." You may lack *conscious* knowledge of grammar and grammatical terms (and if so, you are not alone — American students today rarely study English grammar). But you probably understand the ideas that grammatical terms such as *auxiliary verb* and *direct object* represent, even if the terms themselves are unfamiliar. Brushing up on the terms commonly used to talk about grammar will make it easier for you and your instructor — as well as other readers and reviewers — to share a common language when you discuss the best ways to get your ideas across clearly and with few distractions.

---

Some sentences contain only a one-word predicate with an implied subject; for example, *Stop!* is a complete sentence, with the unspoken subject *you*. Most sentences, however, contain some words that expand upon the basic subject and predicate.

The central elements of subjects and predicates are nouns (36b) and verbs (36a).

```
┌──── SUBJECT ────┬──── PREDICATE ────┐
          NOUN    VERB
```
▶ **A solitary figure waited on the platform.**

```
┌──── SUBJECT ────┬──── PREDICATE ────┐
     NOUN              VERB
```
▶ **Her skill as an archer makes her a formidable opponent.**

## ☐ Using conventional English word order

In general, subjects, verbs, and objects must all be placed in specific positions within a sentence.

SUBJECT VERB OBJECT ADVERB
▶ **Mario left Venice reluctantly.**

The only word in this sentence that you can move to different locations is the adverb *reluctantly* (*Mario reluctantly left Venice* or *Reluctantly, Mario left Venice*). The three key elements of subject, verb, and object rarely move out of their normal order.

## ☐ Recognizing sentence patterns

Knowing a word's part of speech (see Chapter 36) helps you understand how to use it, but you also have to look at the part it plays in a particular sentence. In the following sentences, the noun *description* plays different roles:

SUBJECT

 This **description** conveys the ecology of the Everglades.

DIRECT OBJECT

 I read a **description** of the ecology of the Everglades.

In the first sentence, *description* serves as the subject of the verb *conveys*, while in the second it serves as the direct object of the verb *read*.

---

**QUICK HELP**

**Basic sentence patterns**

1. Subject / verb

   ┌─ S ─┐ ┌─V─┐
   Babies drool.

2. Subject / verb / subject complement

   ┌─ S ─┐ ┌─V─┐┌─SC─┐
   Babies smell sweet.

3. Subject / verb / direct object

   ┌─ S ─┐ ┌─V─┐┌DO┐
   Babies drink milk.

4. Subject / verb / indirect object / direct object

   ┌─ S ─┐┌─V─┐┌───── IO ─────┐┌─DO─┐
   Babies give grandparents pleasure.

5. Subject / verb / direct object / object complement

   ┌─ S ─┐┌─V─┐┌─DO─┐┌─OC─┐
   Babies keep parents awake.

---

## 37b Subjects

The subject of a sentence identifies what the sentence is about. The simple subject consists of one or more nouns (36b) or pronouns (36c); the complete subject consists of the simple subject with all its modifiers.

 **Baseball** is a summer game.

┌────── COMPLETE SUBJECT ──────┐

 Sailing over the fence, the **ball** crashed through Mr. Wilson's window.

┌────── COMPLETE SUBJECT ──────┐

 **Those** who sit in the bleachers have the most fun.

A compound subject contains two or more simple subjects joined with a coordinating conjunction (*and, but, or*) or a correlative conjunction (*both ... and, either ... or, neither ... nor, not only ... but also*). (See 36g.)

 **Baseball** *and* **softball** developed from cricket.

 *Both* **baseball** *and* **softball** developed from cricket.

sentence

## ☐ Positioning subjects

The subject usually comes before the predicate (37a), but sometimes writers reverse this order to achieve a particular effect.

▶ **Up to the plate stepped Casey.**

In questions, the subject appears between the helping verb and the main verb.

▶ **Can statistics lie?**
▶ **How did the manager turn these players into a winning team?**

In sentences beginning with *there* or *here* followed by a form of the verb *be*, the subject always follows the verb. *There* and *here* are never the subject.

▶ **There was no joy in Mudville.**

## ☐ Using explicit subjects

While many languages can omit a sentence subject, English very rarely allows this. You might write *Responsible for analyzing data* on a résumé, but in most varieties of spoken and written English, you must state the subject explicitly. In fact, with only a few exceptions, all clauses in English must have an explicit subject.

▶ **They took the Acela Express to Boston because** it **was fast.**

English even requires a kind of "dummy" subject to fill the subject position in certain kinds of sentences.

▶ *It* **is raining.**
▶ *There* **is a strong wind.**

Imperative sentences (37f), which express requests or commands, are an exception to the rule of explicit subjects; the subject *you* is usually implied rather than stated.

▶ **(You) Keep your eye on the ball.**

### ◢ EXERCISE 37.1

Identify the complete subject and the simple subject in each sentence. Example:

**The tall, powerful woman defiantly blocked the doorway.**

**Complete subject:** The tall, powerful woman
**Simple subject:** woman

1. That container of fried rice has spent six weeks in the back of the refrigerator.
2. Did the new tour guide remember to stop in the Ancient Greek gallery?
3. There was one student still taking the exam when the bell rang.

4. Japanese animation, with its cutting-edge graphics and futuristic plots, has earned many American admirers.

5. Sniffer dogs trained to detect drugs, blood, and explosives can help solve crimes and save lives.

## 37c Predicates

In addition to a subject, every sentence has a predicate, which asserts or asks something about the subject or tells the subject to do something. The key word of most predicates is a verb. The simple predicate of a sentence consists of the main verb and any auxiliaries; the complete predicate includes the simple predicate and any modifiers of the verb and any objects or complements (37a) and their modifiers.

COMPLETE PREDICATE

▶ Both of us **are planning to major in history.**

A compound predicate contains two or more verbs that have the same subject, usually joined by a coordinating or a correlative conjunction (36g).

▶ Omar **shut the book, put** it back on the shelf, *and* **sighed.**

On the basis of how they function in predicates, verbs can be divided into three categories: linking, transitive, and intransitive.

### □ Identifying linking verbs

A linking verb connects a subject with a subject complement (SC), a word or word group that identifies or describes the subject.

    S  V   SC
▶ Christine **is** an excellent teacher.

    S V  SC
▶ She **is** patient.

A subject complement can be either a noun or pronoun (*teacher*) or an adjective (*patient*).

The forms of *be*, when used as main verbs, are common linking verbs. Other verbs, such as *appear, become, feel, grow, look, make, seem, smell,* and *sound,* can also function as linking verbs, depending on the sense of the sentence.

    S   V  SC
▶ The neighborhood **looked** prosperous.

### □ Identifying transitive verbs

MULTI-LINGUAL

A transitive verb expresses action that is directed toward a noun or pronoun called the *direct object* (DO).

    S V   DO
▶ He **peeled** all the rutabagas.

Here, the subject and verb do not express a complete thought. The direct object completes the thought by saying *what* he peeled.

A direct object may be followed by an object complement (OC), a word or word group that describes or identifies the direct object. Object complements may be adjectives, as in the first example below, or nouns, as in the second example.

▸ I **find** cell-phone conversations in restaurants very annoying.

▸ Alana **considers** Keyshawn her best friend.

Some transitive verbs may also be followed by an indirect object (IO), which is the recipient of the direct object. The indirect object tells to whom or what, or for whom or what, the verb does its action.

▸ The sound of the traffic **gave** me a splitting headache.

Transitive verbs typically require you to state the object explicitly. For example, you can't just say *Give!* even if it is clear that you mean *Give me the phone.*

## ☐ Identifying intransitive verbs

An intransitive verb does not have a direct object.

▸ The Red Sox **persevered.**

▸ Their fans **watched** anxiously.

The verb *persevered* has no object (it makes no sense to ask, *persevered what?*), and the verb *watched* is directed toward an object that is implied but not expressed.

Some verbs that express action can be only transitive or only intransitive, but most can be used either way, with or without a direct object.

▸ The butler **opened** the door. [transitive]

▸ The door **opened** silently. [intransitive]

### ◢ EXERCISE 37.2

Identify the predicate in each of the following sentences. Label each verb as linking, transitive, or intransitive. Finally, label any subject complements, object complements, direct objects, and indirect objects. Example:

We considered city life unbearable.

**Predicate:** considered city life unbearable
**Transitive verb:** considered
**Direct object:** city life
**Object complement:** unbearable

1. He is proud of his heritage.
2. The horrifying news story made me angry.
3. The old house looks deserted.
4. Rock and roll will never die.
5. Chloe's boss offered her a promotion.

## 37d Phrases

A phrase is a group of words that lacks a subject or a predicate or both.

### □ Identifying noun phrases

Made up of a noun and all its modifiers, a noun phrase can function in a sentence as a subject, object, or complement.

SUBJECT
▶ **Delicious, gooey peanut butter is surprisingly healthful.**

OBJECT
▶ **I craved a green salad with plenty of fresh vegetables.**

COMPLEMENT
▶ **Soup is a popular lunch.**

### □ Identifying verb phrases

A main verb and its auxiliary verbs make up a verb phrase, which can function in a sentence only as a verb.

▶ **Frank can swim for a long time.**
▶ **His headaches might have been caused by tension.**

### □ Identifying prepositional phrases

A prepositional phrase begins with a preposition and includes a noun or pronoun (the object of the preposition) and any modifiers of the object. Prepositional phrases usually function as adjectives or adverbs.

ADJECTIVE
▶ **Our house in Maine was a cabin.**

ADVERB
▶ **From Cadillac Mountain, you can see the northern lights.**

### □ Identifying verbal phrases

Verbals look like verbs, but they function as nouns, adjectives, or adverbs. There are three kinds of verbals: participles, gerunds, and infinitives.

## Participles and participial phrases

The present participle is the *-ing* form of a verb (*spinning*). The past participle of most verbs ends in *-ed* (*accepted*), but some verbs have an irregular past participle (*worn, frozen*). Participles function as adjectives (42a).

▶ A kiss awakened the dreaming princess.

▶ The cryptographers deciphered the hidden meaning in the message.

Participial phrases, which also act as adjectives, consist of a present or past participle and any modifiers, objects, or complements.

▶ Irritated by the delay, Luisa complained.

▶ A dog howling at the moon kept me awake.

## Gerunds and gerund phrases

The gerund has the same *-ing* form as the present participle but functions as a noun.

SUBJECT
▶ Writing takes practice.

DIRECT OBJECT
▶ The organization promotes recycling.

Gerund phrases, which function as nouns, consist of a gerund and any modifiers, objects, or complements.

SUBJECT
▶ Opening their eyes to the problem was not easy.

DIRECT OBJECT
▶ They suddenly heard a loud wailing from the sandbox.

## Infinitives and infinitive phrases

The infinitive is the *to* form of a verb (*to dream, to be*). An infinitive can function as a noun, an adjective, or an adverb.

NOUN
▶ She wanted to write.

ADJECTIVE
▶ They had no more time to waste.

ADVERB
▶ The corporation was ready to expand.

Infinitive phrases consist of an infinitive and any modifiers, objects, or complements. Like infinitives, they function as nouns, adjectives, or adverbs.

▷ My goal is **to be a biology teacher.** ⟵ NOUN

▷ **A party to end the semester** would be a good idea. ⟵ ADJECTIVE

▷ **To perfect a draft,** always proofread carefully. ⟵ ADVERB

---

**QUICK HELP**

### Choosing between infinitives and gerunds

In general, infinitives tend to indicate intentions, desires, or expectations, and gerunds tend to indicate facts. Knowing whether to use an infinitive or a gerund in a sentence can be a challenge for many students.

**INFINITIVES TO STATE INTENTIONS**

▷ Kumar **expected to get** a good job after graduation.

▷ Last year, Fatima **decided to change** her major.

▷ The strikers have **refused to go** back to work.

Verbs such as *expect*, *decide*, and *refuse*, which indicate intentions, must always be followed by an infinitive.

**GERUNDS TO STATE FACTS**

▷ Jerzy **enjoys going** to the theater.

▷ We **resumed working** after our coffee break.

▷ Kim **appreciated getting** a card from Sean.

Verbs like *enjoy*, *resume*, and *appreciate*, which indicate that something has actually happened, can be followed only by gerunds, not by infinitives.

**OTHER RULES AND GUIDELINES**

A few verbs can be followed by either an infinitive or a gerund. With some, such as *begin* and *continue*, the choice doesn't affect the meaning. With others, however, the difference is important.

▷ Carlos was working as a medical technician, but he **stopped to study** English.

The infinitive shows that Carlos quit because he intended to study English.

▷ When Carlos left the United States, he **stopped studying** English.

The gerund indicates that Carlos gave up his English studies when he left. ▶

---

### Choosing between infinitives and gerunds, continued

You can use only a gerund—never an infinitive—right after a preposition.

> *eating.*
> This fruit is safe for ~~to eat~~.
> ^

> This fruit is safe ~~for~~ to eat.

> us
> This fruit is safe for to eat.
> ^

Consult a learner's dictionary for more information on whether to follow a verb with an infinitive or a gerund.

## ☐ Identifying absolute phrases

An absolute phrase usually includes a noun or pronoun and a participle. It modifies an entire sentence rather than a particular word and is usually set off from the rest of the sentence with commas (54d).

> I stood on the deck, **the wind whipping my hair.**
> **My fears laid to rest,** I set off on my first solo flight.

When the participle is *being*, it is often omitted.

> The ambassador, **her head [being] high,** walked out of the room.

## ☐ Identifying appositive phrases

An appositive phrase is a noun phrase that renames the noun or pronoun that immediately precedes it (54d).

> The report, **a hefty three-volume work,** included more than ninety recommendations.
> We had a single desire, **to change the administration's policies.**

### ◢ EXERCISE 37.3

Read the following sentences, and identify all of the prepositional, verbal, absolute, and appositive phrases. Notice that one kind of phrase may appear within another kind. Example:

His voice breaking with emotion, Ed thanked us for the award.

**Prepositional phrases:** with emotion, for the award
**Absolute phrase:** His voice breaking with emotion

1. Chantelle, the motel clerk, hopes to be certified as a river guide.
2. Carpets made by hand are usually the most valuable.
3. My stomach doing flips, I answered the door.

4. Floating on my back, I ignored my practice requirements.
5. Driving across town during rush hour can take thirty minutes or more.

## 37e Clauses

A clause is a group of words containing a subject and a predicate. There are two kinds of clauses: independent and dependent. Independent clauses (also known as main clauses) can stand alone as complete sentences.

▶ **The window is open.**

Pairs of independent clauses may be joined with a coordinating conjunction and a comma (36g and 54c).

▶ **The window is open, so the room feels cool.**

Like independent clauses, dependent clauses (also referred to as subordinate clauses) contain a subject and a predicate. They cannot stand alone as complete sentences, however, for they begin with a subordinating word — a subordinating conjunction (36g) or a relative pronoun (36c) — that connects them to an independent clause.

▶ **Because the window is open, the room feels cool.**

The subordinating conjunction *because* transforms the independent clause *the window is open* into a dependent clause. In doing so, it indicates a causal relationship between the two clauses.

Dependent clauses function as nouns, adjectives, or adverbs.

☐ **Identifying noun clauses**

Noun clauses are always contained within another clause. They usually begin with a relative pronoun (*that, which, what, who, whom, whose, whatever, whoever, whomever, whichever*) or with *when, where, whether, why,* or *how.*

SUBJECT
▶ **What the archeologists found was startling.**

DIRECT OBJECT
▶ **She explained that the research was necessary.**

SUBJECT COMPLEMENT
▶ **The mystery was why the ancient city had been abandoned.**

OBJECT OF PREPOSITION
▶ **They were looking for whatever information was available.**

Like a noun, a noun clause is an integral part of the sentence; for example, in the second sentence the independent clause is not just *She explained* but *She explained that the research was necessary.* This complex sentence is built out of two sentences; one of them (*The research was necessary*) is embedded in the other (*She explained [something]*). The relative pronoun *that* introduces the noun clause that is the object of *explained.*

A *that* clause can serve as the subject of a sentence, but the effect is very formal:

> ┌─────── SUBJECT ───────┐
> **That the city had been abandoned was surprising.**

In less formal contexts, and in spoken English, a long noun clause is usually moved to the end of the sentence and replaced with the "dummy subject" *it.*

> *It* **was surprising that the city had been abandoned.**

□ **Identifying adjective clauses**

Adjective clauses modify nouns and pronouns in another clause. Usually, they immediately follow the words they modify.

> **The surgery, which took three hours, was a complete success.**

> **It was performed by the surgeon who had developed the procedure.**

> **The hospital was the one where I was born.**

Sometimes the relative pronoun introducing an adjective clause may be omitted, as in the following examples:

> **That is one book [that] I intend to read.**

> **The company [that] the family had invested in grew rapidly.**

To see how the adjective clause fits into this sentence, rewrite it as two sentences: *The company grew rapidly. The family had invested in it.* To make *The family had invested in it* a relative clause, change it to a relative pronoun and move it to the beginning of the clause: *The family had invested in it* becomes *that the family had invested in.* Then position the new clause after the word it describes (in this case, *company*): *The company that the family had invested in grew rapidly.*

In very formal writing, when the pronoun you are changing is the object of a preposition, select *which* (or *whom* for people, 41b) and move the whole prepositional phrase to the beginning of the clause: *The company in which the family had invested grew rapidly.* In many American English contexts, however, such constructions may sound too formal, so consider your audience carefully.

## □ Identifying adverb clauses

Adverb clauses modify verbs, adjectives, or other adverbs. They begin with a subordinating conjunction (36g). Like adverbs, they usually tell when, where, why, how, or to what extent.

▶ We hiked **where few other hikers went.**

▶ My backpack felt heavier **than it ever had.**

▶ Climbers ascend Mount Everest **because it is there.**

### ◢ EXERCISE 37.4

Identify the independent and dependent clauses and any subordinating conjunctions and relative pronouns in each of the following sentences. Example:

> **If I were going on a really long hike, I would carry a lightweight stove.**
>
> **Independent clause:** I would carry a lightweight stove
> **Dependent clause:** If I were going on a really long hike
> **Subordinating conjunction:** if

1. The hockey game was postponed because one of the players collapsed on the bench.
2. She eventually discovered the secret admirer who had been leaving notes in her locker.
3. After completing three advanced drawing classes, Jason was admitted into the fine arts program, and he immediately rented a small studio space.
4. The test was easier than I had expected.
5. I could tell that it was going to rain, so I tried to get home quickly.

### ◢ EXERCISE 37.5

Expand each of the following sentences by adding at least one dependent clause to it. Be prepared to explain how your addition improves the sentence. Example:

> As the earth continued to shake, the
> ~~The~~ books tumbled from the shelves.
> ^

1. The economy gradually began to recover.
2. Simone waited nervously by the phone.
3. New school safety rules were instituted this fall.

4. Rob always borrowed money from friends.
5. The crowd grew louder and more disorderly.

# 37f  Types of sentences

Noticing how many and what types of clauses sentences contain and identifying whether they make a statement, ask a question, issue a command, or express an exclamation can help you analyze sentences as you write and revise.

## ☐ Identifying sentences by grammatical structure

Grammatically, sentences may be simple, compound, complex, or compound-complex.

### Simple sentences

A simple sentence consists of one independent clause and no dependent clause. The subject or the verb, or both, may be compound.

⏵    ┌──────── INDEPENDENT CLAUSE ────────┐
**The trailer is surrounded by a wooden deck.**

⏵    ┌──────── INDEPENDENT CLAUSE ────────┐
**Pompeii and Herculaneum disappeared under tons of lava and ash.**

### Compound sentences

A compound sentence consists of two or more independent clauses and no dependent clause. The clauses may be joined by a comma and a coordinating conjunction (36g) or by a semicolon.

⏵    ┌──── INDEPENDENT CLAUSE ────┐   ┌ INDEPENDENT CLAUSE ┐
**Occasionally a car goes up the dirt trail, and dust flies everywhere.**

⏵    ┌──── INDEPENDENT CLAUSE ────┐ ┌──── INDEPENDENT CLAUSE ────┐
**Alberto is obsessed with soccer; he eats, breathes, and lives the game.**

### Complex sentences

A complex sentence consists of one independent clause and at least one dependent clause.

⏵    INDEPENDENT CLAUSE ┌──── DEPENDENT CLAUSE ────┐
**Many people believe that anyone can earn a living.**

⏵    ┌──── DEPENDENT CLAUSE ────┐ ┌──── INDEPENDENT CLAUSE ────┐
**As I awaited my interview, I sat with another candidate**

   ┌── DEPENDENT CLAUSE ──┐
**who smiled nervously.**

### Compound-complex sentences

A compound-complex sentence consists of two or more independent clauses and at least one dependent clause.

> INDEPENDENT CLAUSE ┌── DEPENDENT CLAUSE ──┐ INDEPENDENT CLAUSE
> **I complimented Luis when he finished the job, and he seemed pleased.**

> ┌── INDEPENDENT CLAUSE ──┐ ┌── INDEPENDENT CLAUSE ──┐
> **The actors performed well, but the audience hated the play,**
>
> ┌──────── DEPENDENT CLAUSE ────────┐
> **which was confusing and far too long.**

## □ Identifying sentences by function

In terms of function, sentences can be declarative (making a statement), interrogative (asking a question), imperative (giving a command), or exclamatory (expressing strong feeling).

| | |
|---|---|
| DECLARATIVE | He sings with the Grace Church Boys' Choir. |
| INTERROGATIVE | How long has he sung with them? |
| IMPERATIVE | Comb his hair before the performance starts. |
| EXCLAMATORY | What voices those boys have! |

### ◢ EXERCISE 37.6

Classify the following sentences as simple, compound, complex, or compound-complex. In addition, note any sentence that may be classified as interrogative, imperative, or exclamatory.

1. The boat rocked and lurched over the rough surf as the passengers groaned in agony.
2. Is this the coldest winter on record, or was last year even worse?
3. After waiting for over an hour, I was examined by the doctor for only three minutes!
4. Keeping in mind the terrain, the weather, and the length of the hike, decide what you need to take.
5. The former prisoner, who was cleared by DNA evidence, has lost six years of his life, and he needs a job right away.

▼ ▼ ▼ ▼ ▼ ▼ ▼ ▼ ▼ ▼ ▼ ▼ ▼ ▼ ▼ ▼ ▼ ▼ ▼ ▼ ▼ ▼ ▼ ▼

## THINKING CRITICALLY ABOUT SENTENCES

The following sentences come from the openings of well-known works. Identify the independent and dependent clauses in each sentence. Then choose one sentence, and write a sentence of your own imitating its structure, clause for clause and phrase for phrase. Example:

> When I wake up, the other side of the bed is cold.
>
> —SUZANNE COLLINS, *The Hunger Games*

Before the detectives arrived, our friend Nastassia found a passageway behind the wall.

1. We observe today not a victory of party but a celebration of freedom, symbolizing an end as well as a beginning, signifying renewal as well as change.

   —JOHN F. KENNEDY, *Inaugural Address*

2. Once in a long while, four times so far for me, my mother brings out the metal tube that holds her medical diploma.

   —MAXINE HONG KINGSTON, "Photographs of My Parents"

# CHAPTER 38

# Nouns and Noun Phrases

**A**LTHOUGH ALL LANGUAGES HAVE NOUNS, English nouns differ from those in some other languages in various ways, such as their division into count and noncount nouns and the use of plural forms, articles, and other modifiers.

## 38a Using count and noncount nouns

Nouns in English can be either count nouns or noncount nouns. Count nouns refer to distinct individuals or things that can be directly counted: *a doctor, an egg, a child; doctors, eggs, children.* Noncount nouns refer to masses, collections, or ideas without distinct parts: *milk, rice, courage.* You cannot count noncount nouns except with a preceding phrase: *a glass of milk, three grains of rice, a little courage.*

Count nouns usually have singular and plural forms: *tree, trees.* Noncount nouns usually have only a singular form: *grass.*

| COUNT | NONCOUNT |
|---|---|
| people (plural of person) | humanity |
| tables, chairs, beds | furniture |
| letters | mail |
| pebbles | gravel |
| suggestions | advice |

Some nouns can be either count or noncount, depending on their meaning.

| | |
|---|---|
| COUNT | Before video games, children played with marbles. |
| NONCOUNT | The palace floor was made of marble. |

When you learn a noun in English, you need to learn whether it is count, non-count, or both. Many dictionaries provide this information.

# 38b Using determiners

Determiners are words that identify or quantify a noun, such as *this study*, *all people*, *his suggestions*.

**COMMON DETERMINERS**

- the articles *a, an, the*
- *this, these, that, those*
- *my, our, your, his, her, its, their*
- possessive nouns and noun phrases (*Sheila's paper, my friend's book*)
- *whose, which, what*

| These determiners . . . | . . . can precede these noun types | Examples |
|---|---|---|
| *a, an, each, every* | singular count nouns | *a* book<br>*an* American<br>*each* word<br>*every* Buddhist |
| *this, that* | singular count nouns<br>noncount nouns | *this* book<br>*that* milk |
| *(a) little, much* | noncount nouns | *a little* milk<br>*much* affection |
| *some, any, enough* | noncount nouns<br><br>plural count nouns | *some* milk<br>*any* fruit<br>*enough* trouble<br>*some* books<br>*any* questions<br>*enough* problems |
| *the* | singular count nouns<br>plural count nouns<br>noncount nouns | *the* doctor<br>*the* doctors<br>*the* information |
| *these, those,<br>(a) few, many,<br>both, several* | plural count nouns | *these* books<br>*those* plans<br>*a few* ideas<br>*many* students<br>*both* hands<br>*several* trees |

- *all, both, each, every, some, any, either, no, neither, many, much, (a) few, (a) little, several, enough*
- the numerals *one, two,* etc.

### ☐ Using determiners with singular count nouns

Every singular count noun must be preceded by a determiner. Place any adjectives between the determiner and the noun.

▷ my
   **sister**
   ^

▷ the
   **growing population**
   ^

▷ that
   **old neighborhood**
   ^

### ☐ Using determiners with plural nouns or noncount nouns

Noncount and plural nouns sometimes have determiners and sometimes do not. For example, *This research is important* and *Research is important* are both acceptable but have different meanings.

## 38c Using articles

Articles (*a, an,* and *the*) are a type of determiner. In English, choosing which article to use—or whether to use an article at all—can be challenging. Although there are exceptions, the following general guidelines can help.

### ☐ Using *a* or *an*

Use the indefinite articles *a* and *an* with singular count nouns. Use *a* before a consonant sound (*a car*) and *an* before a vowel sound (*an uncle*). Consider sound rather than spelling: *a house, an hour.*

   *A* or *an* tells readers they do not have enough information to identify specifically what the noun refers to. Compare these sentences:

▷ **I need a new coat for the winter.**

▷ **I saw a coat that I liked at Dayton's, but it wasn't heavy enough.**

The coat in the first sentence is hypothetical rather than actual. Since it is indefinite to the writer and the reader, it is used with *a,* not *the.* The second sentence refers to an actual coat, but since the writer cannot expect the reader to know which one, it is used with *a* rather than *the.*

If you want to speak of an indefinite quantity rather than just one indefinite thing, use *some* or *any* with a noncount noun or a plural count noun. Use *any* in negative sentences and questions.

▷ This stew needs **some** more salt.

▷ I saw **some** plates that I liked at Gump's.

▷ This stew doesn't need **any** more salt.

## ☐ Using *the*

Use the definite article *the* with both count and noncount nouns whose identity is known or is about to be made known to readers. The necessary information for identification can come from the noun phrase itself, from elsewhere in the text, from context, from general knowledge, or from a superlative.

▷ Let's meet at ^the fountain in front of Dwinelle Hall.

The phrase *in front of Dwinelle Hall* identifies the specific fountain.

▷ Last Saturday, a fire that started in a restaurant spread to a nearby clothing store. The ^Store was saved, although it suffered water damage.

The word *store* is preceded by *the*, which directs our attention to the information in the previous sentence, where the store is first identified.

▷ She asked him to shut ^the door when he left her office.

The context shows that she is referring to her office door.

▷ The ^Pope is expected to visit Africa in October.

There is only one living pope.

▷ Bill is now ^the best singer in the choir.

The superlative *best* identifies the noun *singer*.

## ☐ Using no article

Noncount and plural count nouns can be used without an article when making generalizations:

▷ In this world nothing is certain but death and taxes.

—BENJAMIN FRANKLIN

Franklin refers not to a particular death or specific taxes but to death and taxes in general, so no article is used with *death* or with *taxes*.

English differs from many other languages that use the definite article to make generalizations. In English, a sentence like *The ants live in colonies* can refer only to particular, identifiable ants, not to ants in general.

It is sometimes possible to make general statements with *the* or *a/an* and singular count nouns.

▶ *First-year college students* **are confronted with many new experiences.**

▶ *A first-year student* **is confronted with many new experiences.**

▶ *The first-year student* **is confronted with many new experiences.**

These sentences all make the same general statement, but the emphasis of each sentence is different. The first sentence refers to first-year college students as a group, the second focuses on a hypothetical student taken at random, and the third sentence, which is characteristic of formal written style, projects the image of a typical student as representative of the whole class.

### ◢ EXERCISE 38.1

Each of the following sentences contains an error. Rewrite each sentence correctly.

1. Before a middle of the nineteenth century, surgery was usually a terrifying, painful ordeal.
2. Because anesthesia did not exist yet, only painkiller available for surgical patients was whiskey.
3. The pain of surgical procedures could be so severe that much people were willing to die rather than have surgery.
4. In 1846, one of the hospital in Boston gave ether to a patient before he had surgery.
5. The patient, who had a large on his neck tumor, slept peacefully as doctors removed it.

### ◢ EXERCISE 38.2

Rewrite the following passage from *The Silent Language*, by Edward T. Hall, inserting articles as necessary. Some blanks may not need an article.

Hollywood is famous for hiring _____ various experts to teach _____ people technically what most of us learn informally. _____ case in point is _____ story about _____ children of one movie couple who noticed _____ new child in _____ neighborhood climbing _____ tree. _____ children immediately wanted to be given _____ name of his instructor in _____ tree climbing.

# CHAPTER 39

# Verbs

USED SKILLFULLY, verbs can be the heartbeat of prose, moving it along, enlivening it, carrying its action: *As the little girl skipped in, she bounced a red rubber ball and smiled from ear to ear.*

> **CONNECT:** How can you use verbs effectively to say what you really mean? **39e, 53b**
>
> **CREATE:** Write a response to "Thinking about Your Own Use of Verbs" on p. 589.
>
> **REFLECT:** Think about a text you have read, seen, or heard that uses verbs especially effectively. Write or record a reflection on what made the verbs work well in the context of that text.

## 39a  Using appropriate verb forms

Except for *be*, all English verbs have five possible forms.

| BASE FORM | PAST TENSE | PAST PARTICIPLE | PRESENT PARTICIPLE | -S FORM |
|-----------|------------|-----------------|--------------------|---------| 
| talk | talked | talked | talking | talks |
| adore | adored | adored | adoring | adores |

### ☐  Using the base form

The base form is the one listed in the dictionary. For all verbs except *be*, use the base form to indicate an action or condition in the present when the subject is plural or when the subject is *I* or *you*.

> ◉  **During the ritual, the women go into trances.**

### ☐  Using the past-tense form

Use the past tense to indicate an action or condition that occurred entirely in the past. For most verbs, the past tense is formed by adding *-ed* or *-d* to the base form. Some verbs, however, have irregular past-tense forms. *Be* has two past-tense forms, *was* and *were*.

▶ **The Globe was the stage for many of Shakespeare's most famous works.**

▶ **In 1613, it caught fire and burned to the ground.**

### ☐ Using the past participle form

Use the past participle to form perfect tenses and the passive voice (39g). A past participle usually has the same form as the past tense, though some verbs have irregular past participles (39c).

▶ **She had accomplished the impossible.** [past perfect]

▶ **No one was injured in the explosion.** [passive voice]

### ☐ Using the present participle form

The present participle is constructed by adding *-ing* to the base form. Use it with auxiliary verbs to indicate a continuing action or condition.

▶ **Many students are competing in the race.** [continuing action]

Present participles sometimes function as adjectives or nouns (gerunds), and past participles can also serve as adjectives; in such cases they are not verbs but verbals (see 37d).

### ☐ Using the -s form

Except for *be* and *have*, the *-s* form consists of the base form plus *-s* or *-es*. This form indicates an action in the present for third-person singular subjects. All singular nouns; *he, she,* and *it*; and many other pronouns (such as *this* and *someone*) are third-person singular.

|  | SINGULAR | PLURAL |
|---|---|---|
| FIRST PERSON | I wish | we wish |
| SECOND PERSON | you wish | you wish |
| THIRD PERSON | he/she/it wishes | they wish |
|  | Joe wishes | children wish |
|  | someone wishes | many wish |

The third-person singular form of *have* is *has*.

**Editing for -s and -es endings**

If you tend to leave off or misuse the -s and -es verb endings in academic writing, check for them systematically.

1. Underline every verb, and then circle all of the verbs in the present tense.

2. Find the subject of every verb you circled.

3. If the subject is a singular noun; *he, she,* or *it*; or a singular indefinite pronoun, be sure the verb ends in -s or -es. If the subject is not third-person singular, the verb should not have an -s or -es ending.

4. Be careful with auxiliary verbs such as *can* or *may*. These auxiliaries are used with the base form, never with the -s or -es form (**39b**).

□ **Using forms of *be***

*Be* has three forms in the present tense (*am, is, are*) and two in the past tense (*was, were*).

*Present tense*

|  | SINGULAR | PLURAL |
|---|---|---|
| FIRST PERSON | I am | we are |
| SECOND PERSON | you are | you are |
| THIRD PERSON | he/she/it is | they are |
|  | Juan is | children are |
|  | somebody is | many are |

*Past tense*

|  | SINGULAR | PLURAL |
|---|---|---|
| FIRST PERSON | I was | we were |
| SECOND PERSON | you were | you were |
| THIRD PERSON | he/she/it was | they were |
|  | Juan was | children were |
|  | somebody was | many were |

# 39b Forming verb phrases

English sentences must have at least one verb or verb phrase that is not simply an infinitive (*to write*), a gerund (*writing*), or a participle (*written*) without any helping verbs. Use helping (also called *auxiliary*) verbs with a main verb — in its base form or in a present participle or past participle form — to create verb phrases.

The most common auxiliaries are forms of *be, have,* and *do. Have* is used to form perfect tenses that indicate completed action (39e); *be* is used with progressive forms that show continuing action (39e) and to form the passive voice (39g).

▶ **The engineers have considered possible problems.** [completed action]

▶ **The college is building a new dormitory.** [continuing action]

▶ **The activists were warned to stay away.** [passive voice]

As an auxiliary, *do* is used to show emphasis, to form questions, and to make negative statements.

▶ **I do respect my opponent's viewpoint.** [emphasis]

▶ **Do you know the answer?** [question]

▶ **He does not like wearing a tie.** [negative statement]

## ☐ Arranging helping (auxiliary) verbs

MULTI-LINGUAL

Verb phrases can be built up out of a main verb and one or more auxiliaries.

▶ **Immigration figures rise every year.**

▶ **Immigration figures are rising every year.**

▶ **Immigration figures have risen every year.**

▶ **Immigration figures have been rising every year.**

Verb phrases have strict rules of order. The only permissible change to word order is to form a question, moving the first auxiliary to the beginning of the sentence: *Have immigration figures been rising every year?*

When two or more auxiliaries appear in a verb phrase, they must follow a particular order based on the type of auxiliary:

1. A modal (*can, could, may, might, must, shall, should, will, would,* or *ought to*)

2. A form of *have* used to indicate a perfect tense (39e)

3. A form of *be* used to indicate a progressive tense (39e)

4. A form of *be* used to indicate the passive voice, followed by a past participle (39g)

Very few sentences include all four kinds of auxiliaries.

| | Modal | Perfect *Have* | Progressive *Be* | Passive *Be* | Main Verb | |
|---|---|---|---|---|---|---|
| Sonia | — | has | — | been | invited | to visit her relatives in Prague. |
| Her travel arrange-ments | will | — | — | be | made | by the relatives. |
| The invitation | must | have | — | been | sent | in the spring. |
| She | — | has | been | — | studying | Czech. |
| She | may | — | be | — | feeling | nervous. |
| She | might | have | been | — | expect-ing | to travel else-where. |
| The trip | will | have | been | — | planned | for months by the time she leaves. |

## ☐ Using modals

The modal auxiliaries — *can, could, may, might, shall, should, will, would, must,* and *ought to* — indicate future action, possibility, necessity, or obligation.

- ▶ They **will explain** the procedure. [future action]
- ▶ You **can see** three states from the top of the mountain. [possibility]
- ▶ Students **must manage** their time wisely. [necessity]
- ▶ They **should examine** the results of the study. [obligation]

No verb phrase can include more than one modal.

     *be able to*
- ▶ She will ~~can~~ speak Czech much better soon.
      ∧

*Shall* was once used instead of *will* with the first person (*I* or *we*), but in U.S. English today, *shall* rarely appears except in legal documents and other very formal contexts. In earlier English, *could, would, should,* and *might* were used as past-tense forms. Today, *could* still functions to some extent as the past tense of *can.*

▶ **Ingrid can ski.**

▶ **Ingrid could ski when she was five years old.**

### Modals for requests or instructions

Modals are often used in requests and instructions. If you use a modal such as *could* or *would,* you are politely acknowledging that the person you are talking to may be unable or unwilling to do what you ask.

▶ ***Could* you bring me a pillow?**

Modals appearing in instructions usually indicate whether an action is suggested or required:

1. You *can* / You *may* post your work online. [Posting online is allowed.]
2. You *should* submit your report electronically. [Posting online is recommended or required.]
3. You *must* / You *will* submit your report electronically. [Posting online is required.]

### Modals to show doubt or certainty

Modals can also indicate how confident the writer is about his or her claims. Using *may* or *might* results in a tentative suggestion, while *will* indicates complete confidence:

▶ **The study might help explain the findings of previous research.**

▶ **The study will help explain the findings of previous research.**

☐ **Forming phrases with modals**

Use the base form of a verb after a modal.

▶ **Alice can read Latin.**

▶ **Sanjay should have studied for the test.**

▶ **They must be going to a fine school.**

In many other languages, modals such as *can* and *must* are followed by an infinitive (*to* + base form). In English, only the base form follows a modal.

⬤ **Alice can ~~to~~ read Latin.**

Notice that a modal auxiliary never changes form to agree with the subject.

For the most part, modals refer to present or future time. When you want to use a modal to refer to the past, you follow the modal with a perfect form of the main verb (see 39e).

⬤ **If you have a fever, you should see a doctor.**

⬤ **If you had a fever, you should have seen a doctor.**

The modal *must* is a special case. The past tense of *must* is *had to* or *needed to*.

⬤ **You must renew your visa by the end of this week.**

⬤ **You had to renew / You needed to renew your visa by last Friday.**

Note, too, the different meanings of the negative forms *must not* and *don't have to*.

⬤ **You must not go to the party.** [You are forbidden to go.]

⬤ **You don't have to go to the party.** [You are not required to go, but you may.]

## 39c Understanding regular and irregular verbs

A verb is regular when its past tense and past participle are formed by adding *-ed* or *-d* to the base form.

| BASE FORM | PAST TENSE | PAST PARTICIPLE |
|-----------|-----------|-----------------|
| love | loved | loved |
| honor | honored | honored |
| obey | obeyed | obeyed |

---

**QUICK HELP**

### Editing for *-ed* or *-d* endings

Speakers who delete the *-ed* or *-d* endings in conversation may forget to include them in academic writing. If you tend to drop these endings, make a point of checking for them when proofreading. Underline all the verbs, and then underline a second time any that are past tense or past participles. Check each of these for an *-ed* or *-d* ending. Unless the verb is irregular (see the following list), it should end in *-ed* or *-d*.

vf

A verb is irregular when it does not follow the *-ed* or *-d* pattern. If you are unsure about whether a verb is regular or irregular, or what the correct form is, consult the following list or a dictionary. Dictionaries list any irregular forms under the entry for the base form.

## Common irregular verbs

| BASE FORM | PAST TENSE | PAST PARTICIPLE |
| --- | --- | --- |
| arise | arose | arisen |
| be | was/were | been |
| bear | bore | borne, born |
| beat | beat | beaten |
| become | became | become |
| begin | began | begun |
| bite | bit | bitten, bit |
| blow | blew | blown |
| break | broke | broken |
| bring | brought | brought |
| broadcast | broadcast | broadcast |
| build | built | built |
| burn | burned, burnt | burned, burnt |
| burst | burst | burst |
| buy | bought | bought |
| catch | caught | caught |
| choose | chose | chosen |
| come | came | come |
| cost | cost | cost |
| cut | cut | cut |
| dig | dug | dug |
| dive | dived, dove | dived |
| do | did | done |
| draw | drew | drawn |
| dream | dreamed, dreamt | dreamed, dreamt |
| drink | drank | drunk |
| drive | drove | driven |
| eat | ate | eaten |
| fall | fell | fallen |
| feel | felt | felt |
| fight | fought | fought |
| find | found | found |

| BASE FORM | PAST TENSE | PAST PARTICIPLE |
|---|---|---|
| fly | flew | flown |
| forget | forgot | forgotten, forgot |
| freeze | froze | frozen |
| get | got | gotten, got |
| give | gave | given |
| go | went | gone |
| grow | grew | grown |
| hang (suspend)[1] | hung | hung |
| have | had | had |
| hear | heard | heard |
| hide | hid | hidden |
| hit | hit | hit |
| keep | kept | kept |
| know | knew | known |
| lay | laid | laid |
| lead | led | led |
| leave | left | left |
| lend | lent | lent |
| let | let | let |
| lie (recline)[2] | lay | lain |
| lose | lost | lost |
| make | made | made |
| mean | meant | meant |
| meet | met | met |
| pay | paid | paid |
| prove | proved | proved, proven |
| put | put | put |
| read | read | read |
| ride | rode | ridden |
| ring | rang | rung |
| rise | rose | risen |
| run | ran | run |
| say | said | said |
| see | saw | seen |
| send | sent | sent |

[1]*Hang* meaning "execute by hanging" is regular: *hang, hanged, hanged.*
[2]*Lie* meaning "tell a falsehood" is regular: *lie, lied, lied.*

| BASE FORM | PAST TENSE | PAST PARTICIPLE |
|---|---|---|
| set | set | set |
| shake | shook | shaken |
| shoot | shot | shot |
| show | showed | showed, shown |
| shrink | shrank | shrunk |
| sing | sang | sung |
| sink | sank | sunk |
| sit | sat | sat |
| sleep | slept | slept |
| speak | spoke | spoken |
| spend | spent | spent |
| spread | spread | spread |
| spring | sprang, sprung | sprung |
| stand | stood | stood |
| steal | stole | stolen |
| strike | struck | struck, stricken |
| swim | swam | swum |
| swing | swung | swung |
| take | took | taken |
| teach | taught | taught |
| tear | tore | torn |
| tell | told | told |
| think | thought | thought |
| throw | threw | thrown |
| wake | waked, woke | waked, woken |
| wear | wore | worn |
| win | won | won |
| wind | wound | wound |
| write | wrote | written |

## EXERCISE 39.1

Complete each of the following sentences by writing the past tense or past participle of the verb listed in parentheses. Example:

> **They had already _____ (eat) the entrée; later they _____ (eat) the dessert.**

> **Answers:** eaten, ate

1. The babysitter _____ (let) the children play with my schoolbooks, and before I _____ (come) home, they had _____ (tear) out several pages.

2. After they had _____ (review) the evidence, the jury _____ (find) the defendant not guilty.

3. Hypnosis _____ (work) only on willing participants.

4. My parents _____ (plant) a tree for me in the town where I was born, but I have never _____ (go) back to see it.

5. Some residents _____ (know) that the levee was leaking long before the storms, but authorities _____ (ignore) the complaints.

6. I _____ (paint) a picture from a photograph my sister had _____ (take) at the beach.

7. When the buzzer sounded, the racers _____ (spring) into the water and _____ (swim) toward the far end of the pool.

8. We had _____ (assume) for some time that surgery was a possibility, and we had _____ (find) an excellent facility.

9. Once the storm had _____ (pass), we could see that the old oak tree had _____ (fall).

10. Some high-level employees _____ (decide) to speak publicly about the cover-up before the company's official story had _____ (be) released to the media.

## 39d Using *lay* and *lie*, *sit* and *set*, *raise* and *rise*

*Lay* and *lie*, *sit* and *set*, and *raise* and *rise* cause problems for many writers because both verbs in each pair have similar-sounding forms and related meanings. In each pair, one of the verbs is transitive, meaning that it takes a direct object; the other is intransitive, meaning that it does not take an object. The best way to avoid confusing the two is to memorize their forms and meanings. All these verbs except *raise* are irregular.

| BASE FORM | PAST TENSE | PAST PARTICIPLE | PRESENT PARTICIPLE | -S FORM |
|---|---|---|---|---|
| lie (recline) | lay | lain | lying | lies |
| lay (put) | laid | laid | laying | lays |
| sit (be seated) | sat | sat | sitting | sits |
| set (put) | set | set | setting | sets |
| rise (get up) | rose | risen | rising | rises |
| raise (lift) | raised | raised | raising | raises |

*Lie* is intransitive and means "recline" or "be situated." *Lay* is transitive and means "put" or "place." This pair is especially confusing because *lay* is also the past-tense form of *lie*.

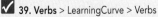

**macmillanhighered.com/smh**

**39. Verbs** > LearningCurve > Verbs
**39. Verbs** > LearningCurve > Verbs for multilingual writers

| INTRANSITIVE | He lay on the floor when his back ached. |
| TRANSITIVE | I laid the cloth on the table. |

*Sit* is intransitive and means "be seated." *Set* usually is transitive and means "put" or "place."

| INTRANSITIVE | She sat in the rocking chair. |
| TRANSITIVE | We set the bookshelf in the hallway. |

*Rise* is intransitive and means "get up" or "go up." *Raise* is transitive and means "lift" or "cause to go up."

| INTRANSITIVE | He rose up in bed and glared at me. |
| TRANSITIVE | He raised his hand eagerly. |

### EXERCISE 39.2

Identify the appropriate verb form in each of the following sentences. Example:

**The guests (*raised*/*rose*) their glasses to the happy couple.**

**Answer:** raised

1. That cat (*lies*/*lays*) on the sofa all morning.
2. The chef (*lay*/*laid*) his knives carefully on the counter.
3. The two-year-old walked carefully across the room and (*set*/*sat*) the glass vase on the table.
4. Grandpa used to love (*sitting*/*setting*) on the front porch and telling stories of his childhood.
5. Immediately, the dough (*sitting*/*setting*) by the oven began to (*raise*/*rise*).

## 39e Indicating verb tenses

In English, you must clearly indicate the time of the action in every verb or verb phrase by using the correct tense form. Tenses show when the action or condition expressed by a verb occurs. The three simple tenses are present tense, past tense, and future tense.

| PRESENT TENSE | I ask, I write |
| PAST TENSE | I asked, I wrote |
| FUTURE TENSE | I will ask, I will write |

More complex aspects of time are expressed through progressive, perfect, and perfect progressive forms of the simple tenses. (Although this terminology may sound complicated, native English speakers regularly use all these tense forms.)

| PRESENT PROGRESSIVE | she is asking, she is writing |
|---|---|
| PAST PROGRESSIVE | she was asking, she was writing |
| FUTURE PROGRESSIVE | she will be asking, she will be writing |
| PRESENT PERFECT | she has asked, she has written |
| PAST PERFECT | she had asked, she had written |
| FUTURE PERFECT | she will have asked, she will have written |
| PRESENT PERFECT PROGRESSIVE | she has been asking, she has been writing |
| PAST PERFECT PROGRESSIVE | she had been asking, she had been writing |
| FUTURE PERFECT PROGRESSIVE | she will have been asking, she will have been writing |

The simple tenses locate an action only within the three basic time frames of present, past, and future. Progressive forms express continuing actions; perfect forms express actions completed before another action or time in the present, past, or future; perfect progressive forms express actions that continue up to some point in the present, past, or future.

## ☐ Using present-tense forms

The present tense includes simple, progressive, perfect, and perfect progressive forms.

### Simple present

The simple present tense indicates actions or conditions occurring now and those occurring habitually.

▶ **They are very angry about the decision.**

▶ **I eat breakfast every day at 8:00 AM.**

▶ **Love conquers all.**

The simple present can also indicate a scheduled future event if the sentence explains when the event will take place.

▶ **Classes begin next week.**

Write about general truths or scientific facts in the simple present, even when the predicate of the sentence is in the past tense.

makes
▶ **Pasteur demonstrated that his boiling process made milk safe.**
^

Use the simple present, not the past tense, when writing about action in literary works.

▶ Ishmael slowly ~~realized~~ all that ~~was~~ at stake in the search for the white
                <sub>realizes</sub>       <sub>is</sub>

   whale.

In general, use the simple present when you are quoting, summarizing, or paraphrasing someone else's writing.

▶ Keith Walters ~~wrote~~ that the "reputed consequences and promised
            <sub>writes</sub>

   blessings of literacy are legion."

But in an essay using APA (American Psychological Association) style (see Chapter 33), report your experiments or another researcher's work in the past tense (*wrote, noted*) or the present perfect (*has reported*).

▶ Comer (1995) ~~notes~~ that protesters who deprive themselves of food are
            <sub>has noted</sub>

   seen as "caring, sacrificing, even heroic" (p. 5).

### Present progressive

Use the present progressive form when an action is in progress now. The present progressive uses a present form of *be* (*am, is, are*) and the *-ing* form of the main verb.

▶ He is directing a new film.

In contrast, use the simple present tense for actions that frequently occur during a period that might include the present, but that is not necessarily happening now.

        SIMPLE PRESENT    PRESENT PROGRESSIVE

▶ My sister drives a bus. She is taking a vacation now.

With an appropriate expression of time, you can use the present progressive to indicate a scheduled event in the future.

▶ We are having friends over for dinner tomorrow night.

Some verbs are rarely used in progressive forms in formal writing. These verbs are said to express unchanging conditions or mental states: *believe, belong, hate, know, like, love, need, own, resemble, understand.* However, in spoken and informal written English, progressive forms like *I'm loving this* and *You're not understanding me correctly* are becoming increasingly common.

*Present perfect*

The present perfect tense indicates actions begun in the past and either completed at some unspecified time in the past or continuing into the present. To form the present perfect, use a present form of *have* (*has, have*) and a perfect participle such as *talked*.

- Uncontrolled logging **has destroyed** many tropical forests.

*Present perfect progressive*

Use the present perfect progressive form to indicate continuous actions begun in the past and continuing into the present. To form the present perfect progressive, use the present perfect form of *be* (*have been, has been*) and the *-ing* form of the main verb.

- The two sides **have been trying** to settle the case out of court.
- Since September, he **has been writing** a novel in his spare time.

## ☐ Using past-tense forms

In the past tense, you can use simple past, past progressive, past perfect, and past perfect progressive forms.

*Simple past*

Use the simple past to indicate actions or conditions that occurred at a specific time and do not extend into the present.

- Germany **invaded** Poland on September 1, 1939.

*Past progressive*

Use the past progressive when an action was in progress in the past. It is used relatively infrequently in English, and it focuses on duration or calls attention to a past action that went on at the same time as something else. The present progressive uses a past form of *be* (*was, were*) and the *-ing* form of the main verb.

- Lenin **was living** in exile in Zurich when the tsar was overthrown.

*Past perfect*

Use the past perfect to indicate actions or conditions completed by a specific time in the past or before some other past action occurred. To form the past perfect, use *had* and a perfect participle such as *talked*.

- By the fourth century, Christianity **had become** the state religion.

### Past perfect progressive

Use the past perfect progressive form to indicate a continuing action or condition in the past that had already been happening when some other past action happened. (You will probably need the simple past tense for the other past action.) To form the past perfect progressive, use the past perfect form of *be* (*had been*) and the *-ing* form of the main verb.

▶ Carter **had been planning** a naval career until his father died.

## ☐ Using future-tense forms

The future tense includes simple, progressive, perfect, and perfect progressive forms.

### Simple future

Use the simple future (*will* plus the base form of the verb) to indicate actions or conditions that have not yet begun.

▶ The exhibition **will come** to Washington in September.

### Future progressive

Use the future progressive to indicate continuing actions or conditions in the future. The future progressive uses the future form of *be* (*will be*) and the *-ing* form of the main verb.

▶ The loans **will be coming** due over the next two years.

### Future perfect

Use the future perfect to indicate actions or conditions that will be completed by or before some specified time in the future. To form the future perfect, use *will have* and a perfect participle such as *talked*.

▶ By next summer, she **will have published** the results of the research study.

### Future perfect progressive

Use the future perfect progressive to indicate continuing actions or conditions that will be completed by some specified time in the future. To form the future perfect progressive, use the future perfect form of *be* (*will have been*) and the *-ing* form of the main verb.

▶ As of May 1, I **will have been living** in Tucson for five years.

### ◢ EXERCISE 39.3

Complete each of the following sentences by writing an appropriate form of the verb listed in parentheses. Since more than one form will sometimes be possible, be prepared to explain the reasons for your choices. Example:

**The supply of a product _____ (rise) when the demand is great.**

**Answer:** rises

1. History _____ (show) that crime usually decreases as the economy improves.
2. Ever since the first nuclear power plants were built, opponents _____ (fear) disaster.
3. Thousands of Irish peasants _____ (emigrate) to America after the potato famine of the 1840s.
4. The soap opera *General Hospital* _____ (be) on the air since 1963.
5. Olivia _____ (direct) the play next year.
6. While they _____ (eat) in a local restaurant, they saw a minor accident.
7. By this time next week, each of your clients _____ (receive) an invitation to the opening.
8. By the time a child born today enters first grade, he or she _____ (watch) thousands of television commercials.
9. In one of the novel's most famous scenes, Huck _____ (express) his willing-ness to go to hell rather than report Jim as an escaped slave.
10. A cold typically _____ (last) for about a week and a half.

# 39f Sequencing verb tenses

Careful and accurate use of tenses is important to clear writing. Even the simplest narrative describes actions that take place at different times; when you use the appropriate tense for each action, readers can follow such time changes easily.

▶ **By the time he offered her the money, she had declared bankruptcy.**

---

**QUICK HELP**

### Editing verb tenses

Errors in verb tenses take several forms. If you have trouble with verb tenses, check for common errors as you proofread.

- Errors of verb form: for example, writing *seen* for *saw*, which confuses the past-participle and past-tense forms (**39c**)
- Omitted auxiliary verbs: for example, using the simple past (*Uncle Charlie arrived*) when meaning requires the present perfect (*Uncle Charlie has arrived*) (**39b and e**)  ▶

Editing verb tenses, continued

- Nonstandard varieties of English in situations calling for academic English: for example, writing *they eat it all up* when the situation requires *they ate it all up* **(29b)**

  The sequence of tenses shows the relationship between the tense of the verb in the independent clause of a sentence and the tense of a verb in a dependent clause or a verbal **(Chapter 37)**.

## ☐ Using infinitives in sequences

Use the infinitive of a verb — *to* plus the base form (*to go, to be*) — to indicate actions occurring at the same time as or later than the action of the main verb in the clause.

▶ **The child waved to greet the passing trains.**

The waving and the greeting occurred at the same time in the past.

▶ **Each couple hopes to win the dance contest.**

The hoping is present; the winning is in the future.

Use *to have* plus the past participle (*to have asked*) to indicate that an action occurred before the action of the main verb.

▶ **He appeared to have left his wallet at home.**

The leaving of the wallet took place before the appearing.

## ☐ Using participles in sequences

Use the present participle (the base form plus *-ing*) to indicate actions occurring at the same time as the action of the main verb.

▶ **Seeking to relieve unemployment, Roosevelt established several public-works programs.**

Use *having* plus the past participle to indicate action occurring before that of the main verb.

▶ **Having changed his mind, he voted against the proposal.**

## ☐ Using habitual actions in sequences

In conversation, people often use *will* or *would* to describe habitual actions. In writing, however, stick to the present and past tenses for this purpose.

▶ **When I have a deadline, I ~~will~~ work all night.**

▶ **While we sat on the porch, the children ~~would play~~.**  played.

## EXERCISE 39.4

Rewrite each of the following sentences to create the appropriate sequence of tenses. Example:

*have sent*
**He needs to ~~send~~ in his application before today.**

1. When she saw *Chicago*, it had made her want to become an actress even more.
2. Leaving England in December, the settlers arrived in Virginia in May.
3. I hoped to make the football team, but injuries prevented me from trying out.
4. Working with great dedication as a summer intern at the magazine, Mohan called his former supervisor in the fall to ask about a permanent position.
5. As we waited for the bus, we would watch the taxis pass by.

# 39g Using active and passive voice

Voice tells whether the subject is acting (*he questions us*) or being acted upon (*he is questioned*). When the subject is acting, the verb is in the active voice; when the subject is being acted upon, the verb is in the passive voice.

| | |
|---|---|
| ACTIVE VOICE | The storm uprooted huge pine trees. |
| PASSIVE VOICE | Huge pine trees were uprooted by the storm. |

The passive voice uses the appropriate form of the auxiliary verb *be* followed by the past participle of the main verb: *he is being questioned, he was questioned, he will be questioned, he has been questioned.*

Most contemporary writers use the active voice as much as possible because it livens up their prose. Passive-voice verbs often make a passage hard to understand and remember. In addition, writers sometimes use the passive voice to avoid taking responsibility for what they have written. A government official who admits that "mistakes were made" skirts the question: who made them?

To shift a sentence from the passive to the active voice (44c), make the performer of the action the subject of the sentence, and make the recipient of the action an object.

*My sister took the*
▷ **The prizewinning photograph. ~~was taken by my sister.~~**

The passive voice can work to good advantage in some situations. Journalists often use the passive voice when the performer of an action is unknown or less important than the recipient.

▷ **Colonel Muammar el-Qaddafi was killed during an uprising in his hometown of Surt.**

Much technical and scientific writing uses the passive voice to highlight what is being studied.

▷ **The volunteers' food intake was closely monitored.**

### ◢ EXERCISE 39.5

Convert each sentence from active to passive voice or from passive to active, and note the differences in emphasis these changes make. Example:

> The ~~Machiavelli advises the~~ prince to gain the friendship of the people. *is advised by Machiavelli*
> ^                                                    ^

1. The surfers were informed by the lifeguard of a shark sighting.
2. The cartoonist sketched a picture of Sam with huge ears and a pointy chin.
3. The baby kangaroo is protected, fed, and taught how to survive by its mother.
4. The gifts were given out to the children by volunteers dressed as elves.
5. A new advertising company was chosen by the board members.

## 39h Using mood and forming conditional sentences

The mood of a verb indicates the attitude of the writer. The indicative mood states facts and opinions or asks questions. The imperative mood gives commands and instructions. The subjunctive mood (used mainly in clauses beginning with *that* or *if*) expresses wishes or conditions that are contrary to fact.

| | |
|---|---|
| INDICATIVE | I did the right thing. |
| IMPERATIVE | Do the right thing. |
| SUBJUNCTIVE | If I had done the right thing, I would not be in trouble now. |

### ◻ Forming subjunctives

The present subjunctive uses the base form, no matter what the subject of the verb is.

▷ **It is important that children be psychologically ready for a new sibling.**

The past subjunctive is the same as the simple past except for the verb *be*, which uses *were* for all subjects.

▷ **He spent money as if he had infinite credit.**

▷ **If the store were better located, it would attract more customers.**

## ☐ Using the subjunctive mood

Because the subjunctive can create a rather formal tone, many people today tend to substitute the indicative mood in informal conversation.

▶ **If I *was* a better swimmer, I would try out for the team.** [informal]

Nevertheless, formal writing still requires the use of the subjunctive in the following kinds of dependent clauses:

*Clauses expressing a wish*

▶ **He wished that his mother were still living nearby.**

As if *and* as though *clauses*

▶ **He started down the trail as if he were walking on ice.**

That *clauses expressing a request or demand*

▶ **The job requires that the employee be in good physical condition.**

If *clauses expressing a condition that does not exist*

▶ **If the sale of tobacco were banned, tobacco companies would suffer a great loss.**

One common error is to use *would* in both clauses. Use the subjunctive in the *if* clause and *would* in the main clause.

▶ **If I ~~would~~ <sub>had</sub> have played harder, I would have won.**

## ☐ Forming conditional sentences

Sentences that use an *if* clause don't always require subjunctive forms. Each of the following conditional sentences makes different assumptions about whether or not the *if* clause is true.

▶ **If you practice writing frequently, you know what your chief problems are.**

This sentence assumes that what is stated in the *if* clause is probably true. Any tense that is appropriate may be used in both the *if* clause and the main clause.

▶ **If you practice writing for the rest of this term, you will understand the process better.**

This sentence makes a prediction. The main clause uses the future tense (*will understand*) or some other modal that can indicate future time (*may understand*). The *if* clause uses the present tense.

⦿ **If you practiced writing every single day, it would eventually seem** much
easier to you.

This sentence indicates doubt. In the *if* clause, the verb is past subjunctive, even
though it refers to future time. The main clause contains *would* + the base form
of the main verb.

⦿ **If you practiced writing on Mars, you would find** no one to read your
work.

This sentence imagines an impossible situation. The past subjunctive is used in
the *if* clause, although past time is not being referred to, and *would* + the base
form is used in the main clause.

⦿ **If you had practiced writing in ancient Egypt, you would have used**
hieroglyphics.

This sentence shifts the impossibility to the past; obviously, you aren't going to
find yourself in ancient Egypt. But a past impossibility demands a form that is
"more past": the past perfect in the *if* clause and *would* + the perfect form of the
verb in the main clause.

### ⬛ EXERCISE 39.6

Revise any of the following sentences that do not use the appropriate subjunctive
verb forms required in formal writing. Example:

> *were*
> I saw how carefully he moved, as if he was holding an infant.
>                                            ^

1. Josh kept spending money as if he was still earning high commissions.
2. Marvina wished that she was able to take her daughter along on the business
   trip.
3. Protesters demanded that the senator resign from her post.
4. If the vaccine was more readily available, the county health department would
   recommend that everyone receive the shot.
5. It is critical that the liquid remains at room temperature for at least seven
   hours.

▼ ▼ ▼ ▼ ▼ ▼ ▼ ▼ ▼ ▼ ▼ ▼ ▼ ▼ ▼ ▼ ▼ ▼ ▼ ▼ ▼ ▼ ▼ ▼

## THINKING CRITICALLY ABOUT VERBS

### Reading with an eye for verbs

Some years ago a newspaper in San Francisco ran the headline "Giants Crush
Cardinals, 3–1," provoking the following friendly advice from John Updike about the
art of sports-headline verbs:

The correct verb, San Francisco, is *whip*. Notice the vigor, force, and scorn obtained. . . . [These examples] may prove helpful: 3–1 — *whip*; 3–2 — *shade*; 2–1 — *edge*. 4–1 gets the coveted verb *vanquish*. Rule: Any three-run margin, *provided the winning total does not exceed ten*, may be described as a vanquishing.

Take the time to study a newspaper with an eye for its verbs. Copy down several examples of strong verbs as well as a few examples of weak or overused verbs. For the weak ones, try to come up with better choices.

### Thinking about your own use of verbs

Writing that relies too heavily on the verbs *be*, *do*, and *have* almost always bores readers. Look at something you've written recently to see whether you rely too heavily on these verbs, and revise accordingly.

# CHAPTER 40

# Subject-Verb Agreement

I N EVERYDAY TERMS, the word *agreement* refers to an accord of some sort: friends agree to go to a movie; the United States and Russia negotiate an agreement about reducing nuclear arms. In most sentences, making subjects and verbs agree is fairly simple; only a few subject-verb constructions cause confusion.

> **CONNECT:** How can you determine which verb forms to use with which subjects? **39a, 40a**
>
> **CREATE:** Start a log to record any subject-verb agreement issues that you have found (or that others have identified) in your writing.
>
> **REFLECT:** Write or record a reflection about the subject-verb agreement questions you find most puzzling. When do you think subject-verb agreement is most and least important?

## 40a  Understanding subject-verb agreement

In academic varieties of English, verbs must agree with their subjects in number (singular or plural) and in person (first, second, or third).

To make a verb in the present tense agree with a third-person singular subject, add *-s* or *-es* to the base form.

▶ **A vegetarian diet lowers the risk of heart disease.**

To make a verb in the present tense agree with any other subject, use the base form of the verb.

▶ **I miss my family.**
▶ **They live in another state.**

The verbs *have* and *be* do not follow the *-s* or *-es* pattern with third-person singular subjects. *Have* changes to *has*; *be* has irregular forms in both the present and past tenses and in the first person as well as the third person. (See Chapter 39.)

🔵 **War is hell.**

🔵 **The soldier was brave beyond the call of duty.**

In some varieties of African American or regional English, third-person singular verb forms do not end with *-s* or *-es*: *She go to work every day.* In most academic writing, however, your audience will expect third-person singular verb forms to end in *-s* or *-es* (39a).

---

**QUICK HELP**

### Editing for subject-verb agreement

- Identify the subject that goes with each verb. Cover up any words between the subject and the verb to identify agreement problems more easily. **(40b)**
- Check compound subjects. Those joined by *and* usually take a plural verb form. With those subjects joined by *or* or *nor*, however, the verb agrees with the part of the subject closest to the verb. **(40c)**
- Check collective-noun subjects. These nouns take a singular verb form when they refer to a group as a single unit but a plural form when they refer to the multiple members of a group. **(40d)**
- Check indefinite-pronoun subjects. Most take a singular verb form. *Both, few, many, others,* and *several* take a plural form; and *all, any, enough, more, most, none,* and *some* can be either singular or plural, depending on the noun they refer to. **(40e)**

---

## 40b  Making separated subjects and verbs agree

Make sure the verb agrees with the subject and not with another noun that falls in between.

🔵 **A vase of flowers makes a room attractive.**

🔵 **Many books on the best-seller list has little literary value.**
> *have*

The simple subject is *books,* not *list.*

Be careful when you use phrases beginning with *as well as, along with, in addition to, together with,* or similar prepositions. They do not make a singular subject plural.

🔵 **The president, along with many senators, opposes the bill.**

🔵 **A passenger, as well as the driver, were injured in the accident.**
> *was*

Though this sentence has a grammatically singular subject, it suggests the idea of a plural subject. The sentence makes better sense with a compound subject: *The driver and a passenger were injured in the accident.*

---

▰ **EXERCISE 40.1**

Identify the appropriate verb form in each of the following sentences. Example:

> **The benefits of family planning (*is/are*) not apparent to many peasants.**
>
> **Answer:** are

1. Soldiers who are injured while fighting for their country (*deserves/deserve*) complete medical coverage.

2. The dog, followed by his owner, (*races/race*) wildly down the street every afternoon.

3. Just when I think I can go home, another pile of invoices (*appears/appear*) on my desk.

4. The pattern of secrecy and lies (*needs/need*) to stop in order for counseling to be successful.

5. A substance abuser often (*hides/hide*) the truth to cover up his or her addiction.

6. The police chief, in addition to several soldiers and two civilians, (*was/were*) injured in the explosion.

7. Garlic's therapeutic value as well as its flavor (*comes/come*) from sulfur compounds.

8. The fiber content of cereal (*contributes/contribute*) to its nutritional value.

9. The graphics on this computer game often (*causes/cause*) my system to crash.

10. Current research on AIDS, in spite of the best efforts of hundreds of scientists, (*leaves/leave*) serious questions unanswered.

---

# 40c  Making verbs agree with compound subjects

Two or more subjects joined by *and* generally require a plural verb form.

▶ Tony and his friend commute from Louisville.

▶ A backpack, a canteen, and a rifle ~~was~~ *were* issued to each recruit.

When subjects joined by *and* are considered a single unit or refer to the same person or thing, they take a singular verb form.

▶ George W. Bush's older brother and political ally was the governor of Florida.

▶ Drinking and driving ~~remain~~ *remains* a major cause of highway fatalities.

> In this sentence, *drinking and driving* is considered a single activity, and a singular verb is used.

If the word *each* or *every* precedes subjects joined by *and*, the verb form is singular.

▷ **Each boy and girl chooses one gift to take home.**

With subjects joined by *or* or *nor*, the verb agrees with the part closest to the verb.

▷ **Neither my roommate nor my neighbors *like* my loud music.**

▷ **Either the witnesses or the defendant** is **are lying.**

If you find this sentence awkward, put the plural noun closest to the verb: *Either the defendant or the witnesses are lying.*

## 40d Making verbs agree with collective nouns

Collective nouns — such as *family, team, audience, group, jury, crowd, band, class,* and *committee* — refer to a group. Collective nouns can take either singular or plural verb forms, depending on whether they refer to the group as a single unit or to the multiple members of the group. The meaning of a sentence as a whole is your guide to whether a collective noun refers to a unit or to the multiple parts of a unit.

▷ **After deliberating, the jury *reports* its verdict.**

The jury acts as a single unit.

▷ **The jury still *disagree* on a number of counts.**

The members of the jury act as multiple individuals.

▷ **The duck family** scatter **scatters when the cat approaches.**

*Family* here refers to the many ducks; they cannot scatter as one.

Treat fractions that refer to singular nouns as singular and those that refer to plural nouns as plural.

SINGULAR    Two-thirds of the park *has* burned.
PLURAL      Two-thirds of the students *were* commuters.

Treat phrases starting with *the number of* as singular and with *a number of* as plural.

SINGULAR    The number of applicants for the internship *was* unbelievable.
PLURAL      A number of applicants *were* put on the waiting list.

## 40e  Making verbs agree with indefinite pronouns

Indefinite pronouns do not refer to specific persons or things. Most take singular verb forms.

SOME COMMON INDEFINITE PRONOUNS

| | | | |
|---|---|---|---|
| another | each | much | one |
| any | either | neither | other |
| anybody | everybody | nobody | somebody |
| anyone | everyone | no one | someone |
| anything | everything | nothing | something |

▶ Of the two jobs, **neither holds** much appeal.

▶ Each of the plays <del>depict</del> *depicts* a hero undone by a tragic flaw.

*Both, few, many, others,* and *several* are plural.

▶ Though **many apply**, **few are** chosen.

*All, any, enough, more, most, none,* and *some* can be singular or plural, depending on the noun they refer to.

▶ **All of the cake** *was* eaten.

▶ **All of the candidates** *promise* to improve the schools.

## 40f  Making verbs agree with *who, which,* and *that*

When the relative pronouns *who, which,* and *that* are used as a subject, the verb agrees with the antecedent of the pronoun.

▶ Fear is an **ingredient that** *goes* into creating stereotypes.

▶ Guilt and fear are **ingredients that** *go* into creating stereotypes.

Problems often occur with the words *one of the.* In general, *one of the* takes a plural verb, while *only one of the* takes a singular verb.

▶ Carla is one of the employees who always <del>works</del> *work* overtime.

Some employees always work overtime. Carla is among them. Thus *who* refers to *employees*, and the verb is plural.

▶ **Ming is the only one of the employees who always ~~work~~ overtime.**
   *works*

Only one employee always works overtime, and that employee is Ming. Thus *one*, and not *employees*, is the antecedent of *who*, and the verb form is singular.

## 40g Making linking verbs agree with subjects

A linking verb should agree with its subject, which usually precedes the verb, not with the subject complement, which follows it (37a).

▶ **Three key treaties ~~is~~ the topic of my talk.**
   *are*

The subject is *treaties*, not *topic*.

▶ **Nero Wolfe's passion ~~were~~ orchids.**
   *was*

The subject is *passion*, not *orchids*.

## 40h Making verbs agree with subjects ending in -s

Some words that end in *-s* appear plural but are singular and thus take singular verb forms.

▶ **Measles still ~~strike~~ many Americans.**
   *strikes*

Some nouns of this kind (such as *statistics* and *politics*) may be either singular or plural, depending on context.

SINGULAR    Statistics *is* a course I really dread.
PLURAL      The statistics in that study *are* highly questionable.

## 40i Making verbs agree with following subjects

In English, verbs usually follow subjects. When this order is reversed, make the verb agree with the subject, not with a noun that happens to precede it.

▶ **Beside the barn ~~stands~~ silos filled with grain.**
   *stand*

The subject is *silos*; it is plural, so the verb must be *stand*.

In sentences beginning with *there is, there are, there was,* or *there were,* the word *there* serves only as a placeholder; the subject follows the verb.

▶ **There are five basic positions in classical ballet.**

The subject, *positions,* is plural, so the verb must also be plural.

## 40j Making verbs agree with titles and with words used as words

When the subject is the title of a book, film, or other work of art, the verb form is singular even if the title is plural in form.

▶ *One Writer's Beginnings* **describes** Eudora Welty's childhood.

Similarly, a word referred to as a word requires a singular verb form even if the word itself is plural.

▶ *Steroids* **is a little word that packs a big punch in the world of sports.**

### EXERCISE 40.2

Revise any of the following sentences as necessary to establish subject-verb agreement. (Some of the sentences do not require any change.) Example:

> *darts*
> Into the shadows d̶a̶r̶t̶ the frightened raccoon.
>                    ^

1. Room and board are the most expensive part of my college education.
2. *Goodfellas* tell the story of a boy growing up to be a mobster.
3. Hanging near the *Mona Lisa* is many more Renaissance paintings.
4. Most of the students oppose the shortened dining hall hours.
5. Each of the security workers are considered trained after viewing a twenty-minute videotape.
6. Neither his expensive clothes nor his charm were enough to get him the job.
7. The committee were expected to produce its annual report two weeks early.
8. My grandmother is the only one of my relatives who still goes to church.
9. Sweden was one of the few European countries that was neutral in 1943.
10. Economics involve the study of the distribution of goods and services.

▼ ▼ ▼ ▼ ▼ ▼ ▼ ▼ ▼ ▼ ▼ ▼ ▼ ▼ ▼ ▼ ▼ ▼ ▼ ▼ ▼ ▼ ▼ ▼ ▼ ▼

## THINKING CRITICALLY ABOUT SUBJECT-VERB AGREEMENT

### Reading with an eye for subject-verb agreement

The following passage, from a 1990 essay questioning a "traditional" view of marriage, includes several instances of complicated subject-verb agreement. Note the rules governing subject-verb agreement in each case.

> Marriage seems to me more conflict-ridden than ever, and the divorce rate—with or without new babies in the house—remains constant. The fabric of men-and-women-as-they-once-were is so thin in places no amount of patching can weave that cloth together again. The longing for connection may be strong, but even stronger is the growing perception that only people who are real to themselves can connect. Two shall be as one is over, no matter how lonely we get.
>
> —VIVIAN GORNICK, "Who Says We Haven't Made a Revolution?"

### Thinking about your own use of subject-verb agreement

*Visiting relatives is/are treacherous.* Either verb makes a grammatically acceptable sentence, yet the verbs result in two very different statements. Write a brief explanation of the two possible meanings. Then write a paragraph or two about visiting relatives. Using the information in this chapter, examine each subject and its verb. Do you maintain subject-verb agreement throughout? Revise to correct any errors you find. If you find any patterns, make a note to yourself of things to look for routinely as you revise your writing.

# CHAPTER 41

# Pronouns

**T**HESE DIRECTIONS SHOW ONE REASON why it's important to use pronouns clearly:

> When you see a dirt road turning left off Winston Lane, follow it for two more miles.

The word *it* could mean either the dirt road or Winston Lane. Pronouns can improve understanding, but only when they're used carefully and accurately.

---

**CONNECT:** How can you avoid sexist pronouns? **28b, 41g**

**CREATE:** Keep a record of any pronoun questions from your own writing.

**REFLECT:** Write or record a reflection about the pronoun questions you find most puzzling.

---

## 41a  Understanding pronoun case

Most speakers of English know intuitively when to use *I*, *me*, or *my*. The choice reflects differences in case, the form a pronoun takes to indicate its function in a sentence. Pronouns functioning as subjects are in the subjective case; those functioning as objects are in the objective case; and those functioning as possessives are in the possessive case.

**SUBJECTIVE PRONOUNS**

| | | | | |
|---|---|---|---|---|
| I/we | you | he/she/it | they | who/whoever |

**OBJECTIVE PRONOUNS**

| | | | | |
|---|---|---|---|---|
| me/us | you | him/her/it | them | whom/whomever |

**POSSESSIVE PRONOUNS**

| | | | | |
|---|---|---|---|---|
| my/our | your | his/hers/its | their | whose |
| mine/ours | yours | his/hers/its | theirs | |

### Editing for case

- Are all pronouns after forms of the verb *be* in the subjective case in formal writing? **(41a)**
- To check for correct use of *who* and *whom* (and *whoever* and *whomever*), try answering the question or rewriting the clause using *he* or *him*. If *he* is correct, use *who* or *whoever*; if *him*, use *whom* or *whomever*. **(41b)**
- In compound structures, make sure pronouns are in the same case they would be in if used alone (*Jake and she were living in Spain*). **(41c)**
- When a pronoun follows *than* or *as*, complete the sentence mentally to see whether the pronoun should be subjective or objective. **(41d)**
- Circle all the pronouns to see if you rely too heavily on any one pronoun or case, especially *I*. If you find that you do, try rewriting some sentences to change *I* to *me*, *she* to *her*, and so on.

## ☐ Using pronouns as subjects

Use a subjective pronoun as a subject of a clause, a subject complement, or an appositive renaming a subject or subject complement (37a).

**SUBJECT OF A CLAUSE**

They could either fight or face certain death with the lions.

Who is your closest friend?

Pedro told the story to Lizzie, who told all her friends.

**SUBJECT COMPLEMENT**

The person in charge was she.

**APPOSITIVE RENAMING A SUBJECT OR SUBJECT COMPLEMENT**

Three colleagues — Peter, John, and she — worked on the program.

Americans often use the objective case for subject complements, especially in conversation: *Who's there? It's me.* However, expect to use the subjective case in formal writing. If you find the subjective case stilted or awkward, try rewriting the sentence using the pronoun as the subject.

> She was the
> ⊙ The first person to see Kishore after the awards was she.

## ☐ Using pronouns as objects

Use an objective pronoun as a direct or indirect object (of a verb or verbal), an object of a preposition, an appositive renaming an object, or when the pronoun is followed by an infinitive (37a and c).

OBJECT OF A VERB OR VERBAL

The professor surprised us with a quiz. [direct object of *surprised*]

The grateful owner gave him a reward. [indirect object of *gave*]

The Parisians were always wonderful about helping me. [direct object of gerund]

OBJECT OF A PREPOSITION

Several friends went with him.

APPOSITIVE RENAMING AN OBJECT

The committee elected two representatives, Sach and me.

PRONOUN FOLLOWED BY AN INFINITIVE

The students convinced him to vote for the school bond.

## ☐ Using pronouns as possessives

Use a possessive pronoun to show possession or ownership. Notice that there are two forms of possessive pronouns: those that function as adjectives (*my, your, his, her, its, our, their, whose*) and those that take the place of a noun (*mine, yours, his, hers, its, ours, theirs, whose*).

ADJECTIVE FORMS

People were buying their tickets weeks in advance of the show.

Whose fault was the accident?

NOUN FORMS

The responsibility is hers.

Whose is this blue backpack?

---

TALKING THE TALK | **CORRECTNESS OR STUFFINESS?**

"I think *Everyone has their opinion* sounds better than *Everyone has his or her opinion.* And nobody says *whom.* Why should I write that way?" Over time, the conventions governing certain usages have become much more relaxed. To many Americans, *Whom did you talk to?* — which is technically "correct" — sounds unpleasantly fussy. However, other people object to less formal constructions such as *Who did you talk to?* Unfortunately, you can't please everyone. Use whatever constructions you are most comfortable with in speaking, but be more careful in your formal writing. If you don't know whether your audience will prefer more or less formality, try recasting your sentence.

When a pronoun appears before a verbal (37d) that ends in *-ing*, using a possessive pronoun leads to a different meaning than using an objective pronoun.

▶ **I remember *his* singing.**

   The possessive pronoun *his* makes *singing* the object of *remember.*

▶ **I remember *him* singing.**

   The pronoun *him* is the object of *remember,* and *singing* modifies *him.*

Choose the pronoun that makes sense for the meaning you want to convey.


# 41b  Using *who, whoever, whom,* and *whomever*

A common problem with pronoun case is deciding whether to use *who* or *whom.* Even when traditional grammar requires *whom,* many Americans use *who* instead, especially in speech. Nevertheless, you should understand the difference between *who* and *whom* so that you can make informed choices in situations such as formal college writing that may call for the use of *whom* (or *whomever*) in the objective case.

   Two particular situations lead to confusion with *who* and *whom*: when they begin a question and when they introduce a dependent clause.


## ☐ Choosing *who* or *whom* in questions

You can determine whether to use *who* or *whom* at the beginning of a question by answering the question using a personal pronoun. If the answer is a subject pronoun, use *who*; if it is an object pronoun, use *whom.*

   *Who*
▶ **Whom do you think wrote the story?**
   ^
   I think *she* wrote the story. *She* is subjective, so *who* is correct.

   *Whom*
▶ **Who did you visit?**
   ^
   I visited *them. Them* is objective, so *whom* is correct.


## ☐ Using *who, whoever, whom,* and *whomever* in dependent clauses

The function a pronoun serves in a dependent clause determines whether you should choose *who* or *whom, whoever* or *whomever* — no matter how that clause functions in the sentence. If the pronoun acts as a subject or subject complement in the clause, use *who* or *whoever.* If the pronoun acts as an object, use *whom* or *whomever.*

> whoever
> **The center is open to ~~whomever~~ wants to use it.**
>   ^

*Whoever* is the subject of the clause *whoever wants to use it.* (The clause is the object of the preposition *to*, but the clause's function in the sentence does not affect the case of the pronoun.)

> whom
> **The new president was not ~~who~~ she had expected.**
>   ^

Here, *whom* is the object of the verb *had expected* in the clause *whom she had expected.*

If you are not sure which case to use, try separating the dependent clause from the rest of the sentence. Rewrite the clause as a new sentence, and substitute a personal pronoun for *who*(*ever*) or *whom*(*ever*). If the pronoun is in the subjective case, use *who* or *whoever*; if it is in the objective case, use *whom* or *whomever*.

> **The minister glared at (*whoever/whomever*) made any noise.**

Isolate the clause *whoever/whomever made any noise.* Substituting a personal pronoun gives you *they made any noise. They* is in the subjective case; therefore, *The minister grimaced at <u>whoever</u> made any noise.*

> **The minister smiled at (*whoever/whomever*) she greeted.**

Isolate and transpose the clause to get *she greeted whoever/whomever.* Substituting a personal pronoun gives you *she greeted them. Them* is in the objective case; therefore, *The minister smiled at <u>whomever</u> she greeted.*

> **The minister glared at whoever ~~she thought~~ made any noise.**

Ignore such expressions as *he thinks* and *she says* when you isolate the clause.

---

### EXERCISE 41.1

Choose *who, whoever, whom,* or *whomever* to complete the blank in each of the following sentences. Example:

> **She is someone _____ will go far.**
>
> **Answer:** who

1. _____ did you say was our most likely suspect?
2. _____ the audience chooses will move up to the next level.
3. The awards banquet will recognize _____ made the honor roll.
4. Professor Quiñones asked _____ we wanted to collaborate with.
5. _____ received the highest score?

## 41c   Considering case in compound structures

When a pronoun is part of a compound structure, put it in the same case you would use if the pronoun were alone.

- Come to the park with José and ~~I.~~ <sup>me.</sup>

  Eliminating the other part of the compound, *José and,* leaves *Come to the park with me.*

- When ~~him~~ <sup>he</sup> and Zelda were first married, they lived in New York.

- The next two speakers will be Philip and ~~her.~~ <sup>she.</sup>

- The boss invited ~~she~~ <sup>her</sup> and her family to dinner.

- This morning saw yet another conflict between my sister and ~~I.~~ <sup>me.</sup>

Pronoun case in a compound appositive (54d) is determined by the word the appositive renames. If the word functions as a subject or subject complement, the pronoun should be subjective; if it functions as an object, the pronoun should be objective.

- Both panelists — Tony and ~~me~~ <sup>I</sup> — were stumped.

  *Panelists* is the subject of the sentence, so the pronoun in the appositive *Tony and I* should be in the subjective case.

## 41d   Considering case in elliptical constructions

In elliptical constructions, some words are left out but understood. A pronoun in an elliptical construction should be in the case it would be in if the construction were complete.

- His brother has always been more athletic than *he* [is].

Sometimes the case depends on the meaning intended.

- Willie likes Lily more than *she* [likes Lily].

  *She* is the subject of the implied clause *she likes Lily.*

- Willie likes Lily more than [he likes] *her.*

  *Her* is the object of the verb *likes* in the implied clause *he likes her.*

## 41e Using *we* or *us* before a noun

If you aren't sure whether to use *we* or *us* before a noun, recast the sentence without the noun. Use the pronoun that would be correct without the noun.

> We
> **◉ ~~Us~~ fans never give up hope.**
> ^
>
> *Fans* is the subject, so the pronoun should be subjective.

> us
> **◉ The Rangers depend on ~~we~~ fans.**
> ^
>
> *Fans* is the object of a preposition, so the pronoun should be objective.

---

### ◢ EXERCISE 41.2

Identify the appropriate pronoun from the pair in parentheses in each of the following sentences. Example:

> **The possibility of (*their*/*them*) succeeding never occurred to me.**
>
> **Answer:** their

1. Max has had more car accidents than Gabriella, but he still insists he is a better driver than (*she*/*her*).
2. Swimming with Hank and (*they*/*them*) reminded me of summers at the lake.
3. The coach gave honorable-mention ribbons to the two who didn't win any races—Aiden and (*I*/*me*).
4. There seemed to be no reason for (*them*/*their*) voluntarily studying on a Saturday night.
5. Tomorrow (*we*/*us*) recruits will have our first on-the-job test.

---

## 41f Making pronouns agree with antecedents

The antecedent of the pronoun is the word the pronoun refers to. The antecedent usually appears before the pronoun — earlier in the sentence or in a previous sentence. Pronouns and antecedents are said to agree when they match up in person, number, and gender.

> **◉ The conductor raised her baton, and the boys picked up their music.**

### ☐ Using compound antecedents

Compound antecedents joined by *and* require plural pronouns.

> **◉ My parents and I tried to resolve our disagreement.**

A compound antecedent preceded by *each* or *every*, however, takes a singular pronoun.

◯ **Every plant and animal has its own ecological niche.**

With a compound antecedent joined by *or* or *nor*, the pronoun agrees with the nearest antecedent. If the parts of the antecedent are of different genders or persons, however, this kind of sentence can be awkward.

AWKWARD      Neither Annie nor Barry got *his* work done.

REVISED      Annie didn't get *her* work done, and neither did Barry.

When a compound antecedent contains both singular and plural parts, the sentence may sound awkward unless the plural part comes last.

newspaper          radio stations          their
◯ **Neither the radio stations nor the newspaper would reveal its sources.**

## ▢ Using collective-noun antecedents

A collective-noun antecedent (*herd*, *team*, *audience*) that refers to a single unit requires a singular pronoun.

◯ **The audience fixed *its* attention on center stage.**

When such an antecedent refers to the multiple parts of the unit, however, it requires a plural pronoun.

◯ **The director chose this cast because *they* had experience in their roles.**

## ▢ Using indefinite-pronoun antecedents

Indefinite pronouns (40e) do not refer to specific persons or things. A pronoun whose antecedent is an indefinite pronoun should agree with it in number. Many indefinite pronouns are always singular (as with *one*); a few are always plural (as with *many*). Some can be singular or plural depending on the context.

◯ **One of the ballerinas lost *her* balance.**
◯ **Many in the audience jumped to *their* feet.**
◯ **Some of the antique furniture was showing *its* age.** [singular meaning for *some*]
◯ **Some of the local farmers abandoned *their* land.** [plural meaning for *some*]

**Editing for pronoun-antecedent agreement**

- Check all subjects joined by *and*, *or*, or *nor* to be sure they are treated as singular or plural, as appropriate. Recast any sentence in which agreement creates awkwardness.
- Check all uses of *anyone*, *each*, *everybody*, *many*, and other indefinite pronouns (see list in **40e**) to be sure they are treated as singular or plural, as appropriate.
- If you find *he*, *his*, or *him* used to refer to persons of either sex, revise the pronouns, or recast the sentences altogether. **(41g)**

## 41g Avoiding sexist pronouns

Indefinite pronouns (40e) often refer to antecedents that may be either male or female. Writers used to use a masculine pronoun, known as the generic *he*, in such cases. However, many people have pointed out that wording that ignores or excludes females should be avoided.

When an antecedent is a singular indefinite pronoun, some people avoid the generic *he* by using a plural pronoun.

▶ **Everybody had *their* own theories about Jennifer's sudden resignation.** [informal]

Although this usage is gaining acceptance, many readers still consider it incorrect. In formal writing, do not use a plural pronoun to refer to a grammatically singular indefinite pronoun.

▶ **Everybody had a theory about Jennifer's sudden resignation.**

**Editing out the generic use of *he*, *his*, or *him***

▶ **Every citizen should know *his* legal rights under the law.**

Here are three ways to express the same idea without *his*:

1. Revise to make the antecedent plural.
   *All citizens should know* their *legal rights.*

2. Revise the sentence altogether.
   *Every citizen should have some knowledge of basic legal rights.*

3. Use both masculine and feminine pronouns.
   *Every citizen should know* his or her *legal rights.*

The last option can be awkward when repeated several times in a passage.

⬛ **EXERCISE 41.3**

Revise the following sentences as needed to create pronoun-antecedent agreement and to eliminate the generic *he* and any awkward pronoun references. Some can be revised in more than one way. Examples:

*or her*
**Every graduate submitted his diploma card.**
^

*All graduates          their          cards.*
~~Every graduate submitted his diploma card.~~
^                    ^          ^

1. While shopping for a new computer for school, I noticed that a laptop costs much less than they used to.

2. Congress usually resists a president's attempt to encroach on what they consider their authority.

3. Marco and Ellen were each given a chance to voice their opinion.

4. An ER doctor needs to be swift; he also needs to be calm and careful.

5. Every dog and cat has their own personality.

# 41h Revising ambiguous pronoun references

If a pronoun can refer to more than one antecedent, revise the sentence to make the meaning clear.

*the bridge*
◉ **The car went over the bridge just before it fell into the water.**
^

What fell into the water — the car or the bridge? The revision makes the meaning clear by replacing the pronoun *it* with *the bridge.*

"I                                       "
◉ **Kerry told Ellen, she should be ready soon.**
^                    ^

Reporting Kerry's words directly, in quotation marks, eliminates the ambiguity.

If a pronoun and its antecedent are too far apart, you may need to replace the pronoun with the appropriate noun.

◉ **The right-to-life coalition believes that a *zygote*, an egg at the moment**

**of fertilization, is as deserving of protection as is the born human being**

**and thus that abortion is as much murder as is the killing of a child. The**

*the zygote*
**coalition's focus is on what it will become as much as on what it is now.**
^

In the original, the pronoun *it* is too far away from the antecedent *zygote* in the first sentence, thus making the second sentence unclear to readers.

**Editing for clear pronoun reference**

1.  Identify a specific antecedent that each pronoun refers to. If you cannot find a specific antecedent, supply one. **(41h, i, and k)**

2.  If the pronoun refers to more than one antecedent, revise the sentence. If the pronoun and its antecedent are so far apart that the reader cannot connect the two, replace the pronoun with the appropriate noun. **(41h)**

3.  Be sure that any use of *you* refers to your specific reader or readers. **(41k)**

## 41i  Revising vague use of *it*, *this*, *that*, and *which*

Writers often use *it*, *this*, *that*, or *which* as a shortcut for referring to something mentioned earlier. But such shortcuts can cause confusion. Make sure that these pronouns refer clearly to a specific antecedent.

▶ When the senators realized the bill would be defeated, they tried to

                               The entire effort

   postpone the vote but failed. ~~It~~ was a fiasco.

                                       and her sudden wealth

▶ Nancy just found out that she won the lottery, ~~which~~ explains her

   resignation.

If a *that* or *which* clause refers to a specific noun, put the clause directly after the noun, if possible.

▶ We worked all night on the float ~~for the Rose Parade~~ that our club was

                       for the Rose Parade.

   going to sponsor.

Does *that* refer to the float or the parade? The editing here makes the meaning clear.

## 41j  Using *who*, *which*, or *that* to refer to people

Use *who* to refer primarily to people or to animals with names. *Which* and *that* generally refer to animals or to things.

              who

▶ The veterinarian ~~that~~ operated saved my dog's life.

       which

▶ Cats, ~~who~~ are my favorite animals, often seem aloof.

# 41k  Revising indefinite use of *you*, *it*, and *they*

In conversation, we frequently use *you*, *it*, and *they* in an indefinite sense in such expressions as *you never know*; *it said in the paper*; and *on television, they said*. In college writing, however, use *you* only to mean "you, the reader," and *they* only to refer to a clear antecedent.

▷ Commercials try to make ~~you~~ ^people^ buy without thinking.

▷ ^The^ ~~On the~~ Weather Channel/ it reported that the earthquake devastated parts of Pakistan.

▷ ~~In France, they~~ ^Most restaurants in France^ allow dogs. ~~in most restaurants.~~

# 41l  Revising implied antecedents

Though an adjective or possessive may imply a noun antecedent, it does not serve as a clear antecedent.

▷ In Alexa's ^her^ formal complaint, ~~she~~ ^Alexa^ showed why the test question was wrong.

## ◢ EXERCISE 41.4

Revise each of the following items to clarify pronoun reference. Most of the items can be revised in more than one way. If a pronoun refers ambiguously to more than one possible antecedent, revise the sentence to reflect each possible meaning. Examples:

^Miranda found Jane's keys after^
After Jane left/. ~~Miranda found her keys.~~

^Miranda found her own keys after^
After Jane left/. ~~Miranda found her keys.~~

1. All scholarship applicants must fill out a financial aid form, meet with the dean, and write a letter to the committee members. The deadline is October 24, so they should start the process as soon as possible.

2. Patients on medication may relate better to their therapists, be less vulnerable to what disturbs them, and be more responsive to them.

3. Ms. Dunbar wanted to speak to my mother before she spoke to me.

4. In Texas, you often hear about the influence of big oil corporations.

5. A small band of protestors picketed the new shopping center, which outraged many residents.

### EXERCISE 41.5

Revise the following paragraph to establish a clear antecedent for every pronoun that needs one.

In the summer of 2005, the NCAA banned the use of mascots that could be considered offensive to American Indians at any of their championship games. In order to understand this, it is important to consider that movies and television programs for years portrayed them as savage warriors that were feared and misunderstood. That is why some schools have chosen to use Indians as their mascot, a role typically played by wild animals or fictional beasts. You would not tolerate derogatory terms for other ethnic groups being used for school mascots. In the NCAA's new ruling, they ask schools to eliminate mascots that may be hurtful or offensive to America's Indian population.

▼ ▼ ▼ ▼ ▼ ▼ ▼ ▼ ▼ ▼ ▼ ▼ ▼ ▼ ▼ ▼ ▼ ▼ ▼ ▼ ▼ ▼ ▼ ▼ ▼ ▼ ▼ ▼

## THINKING CRITICALLY ABOUT PRONOUNS

Turn to a recent piece of your writing (something at least four pages long), and analyze your use of pronouns. Look carefully at the pronoun case you tend to use most; if it is first person, ask whether *I* is used too much. And if you find that you rely heavily on any one case (*you*, for example), decide whether your writing seems monotonous as a result. Take a look as well at whether you tend to use masculine pronouns exclusively to refer to people generally; if so, ask whether you would be more inclusive if you used both masculine and feminine pronouns or if you should revise to use plural pronouns that are not marked as either masculine or feminine (such as *we* or *they*). Finally, check to make sure that your pronouns and their antecedents agree and that the pronouns refer clearly and directly to antecedents.

# CHAPTER 42

# Adjectives and Adverbs

**A**S WORDS THAT DESCRIBE OTHER WORDS, adjectives and adverbs add liveliness and color to writing, helping writers show rather than just tell. In addition, adjectives and adverbs often provide indispensable meanings to the words they modify. In basketball, for example, there is an important difference between a *flagrant* foul and a *technical* foul, or an *angry* coach and an *abusively angry* coach. In each instance, the modifiers are crucial to accurate communication.

> **CONNECT:** Why are adjectives sometimes used in place of adverbs in informal language? **29c and d, 42c**
>
> **CREATE:** Keep a log of situations in which you hear adjectives used in place of adverbs in speech (for example, in phrases like *They played great*).
>
> **REFLECT:** Write or record a reflection about spoken use of adjectives and adverbs.

## 42a  Understanding adjectives and adverbs

Adjectives modify nouns and pronouns, answering the question *which? how many?* or *what kind?* Adverbs modify verbs, adjectives, other adverbs, or entire clauses; they answer the question *how? when? where?* or *to what extent?* Many adverbs are formed by adding *-ly* to adjectives (*slight, slightly*), but many are not (*outdoors, very*). And some words that end in *-ly* are adjectives (*lovely, homely*). To tell adjectives and adverbs apart, identify the word's function in the sentence.

 **HELP**

Editing adjectives and adverbs

- Scrutinize each adjective and adverb. Consider synonyms for each one to see whether you have chosen the best word possible.
- See if a more specific noun would eliminate the need for an adjective (*mansion* rather than *enormous house*, for instance); do the same with verbs and adverbs. ▶

**611**

Editing adjectives and adverbs, continued

- Consider adding an adjective or adverb that might make your writing more vivid or specific.
- Make sure all adjectives modify nouns or pronouns and all adverbs modify verbs, adjectives, or other adverbs. Check especially for proper use of *good* and *well*, *bad* and *badly*, *real* and *really*. **(42c)**
- Make sure all comparisons are complete. **(42d)**
- If English is not your first language, check that adjectives are in the right order. **(42g)**

## 42b Using adjectives after linking verbs

When adjectives come after linking verbs, they usually describe the subject: *I am patient*. Note that in specific sentences, some verbs may or may not act as linking verbs — *look, appear, sound, feel, smell, taste, grow,* and *prove,* for instance. When a word following one of these verbs modifies the subject, use an adjective; when the word modifies the verb, use an adverb.

ADJECTIVE         **Fluffy looked angry.**

ADVERB            **Fluffy looked angrily at the poodle.**

Linking verbs suggest a state of being, not an action. In the preceding examples, *looked angry* suggests the state of being angry; *looked angrily* suggests an angry action.

## 42c Using adverbs

In everyday conversation, you will often hear (and perhaps use) adjectives in place of adverbs. When you write in standard academic English, however, use adverbs to modify verbs, adjectives, and other adverbs.

○ You can feel the song's meter if you listen ~~careful.~~ *carefully.*

○ The audience was ~~real~~ *really* disappointed by the show.

### □ Using *good* and *well*, *bad* and *badly*

The modifiers *good, well, bad,* and *badly* cause problems for many writers because the distinctions between *good* and *well* and between *bad* and *badly* are often not observed in conversation. Problems also arise because *well* can function as either an adjective or an adverb. *Good* and *bad* are always adjectives, and both can be used after a linking verb. In formal writing, do not use them to modify a verb, an adjective, or an adverb; use *well* or *badly* instead.

○ The weather looks **good** today.

○ We had a **bad** night with the new baby.

          *well*                                *badly.*

○ He plays the trumpet ~~good~~ and the trombone ~~bad~~.
                      ^                         ^

*Badly* is an adverb and can modify a verb, an adjective, or another adverb. Do not use it after a linking verb in formal writing; use *bad* instead.

○ In her first recital, the soprano sang **badly**.

   *bad*

○ I feel ~~badly~~ for the Cubs' fans.
   ^

As an adjective, *well* means "in good health"; as an adverb, it means "in a good manner" or "thoroughly."

| | |
|---|---|
| ADJECTIVE | After a week of rest, Julio felt well again. |
| ADVERB | She plays well enough to make the team. |

□ **Using regional modifiers (*right* smart, *wicked* fun)**

Most regions have certain characteristic adjectives and adverbs. Some of the most colorful are intensifiers, adverbs meaning *very* or *absolutely*. In parts of the South, for example, and particularly in Appalachia, you are likely to hear the following: *He paid a right smart price for that car* or *She was plumb tuckered out*. In New England, you might hear *That party was wicked fun*. In each case, the adverb (*right*, *plumb*, *wicked*) acts to intensify the meaning of the adjective (*smart, tuckered out, fun*).

    As with all language, use regional adjectives and adverbs only when they are appropriate (29d). In writing about a family member in Minnesota, for example, you might well quote her, bringing midwestern expressions into your writing. For most academic writing, however, you should use academic English.

◢ **EXERCISE 42.1**

Revise the following sentences to correct adverb and adjective use. Then identify each adjective or adverb you have revised and the word each modifies. Example:

               *superbly*

**The attorney delivered a ~~superb~~ conceived summation.**
                           ^

    **Adverb:** superbly
    **Modifies:** conceived

1. Getting tickets at this late date is near impossible.
2. Derek apologized for behaving so immature on the football field.
3. Nora felt badly that the package would arrive one week later than promised.

**MULTI-LINGUAL** | **ADJECTIVES WITH PLURAL NOUNS**

In Spanish, Russian, and many other languages, adjectives agree in number with the nouns they modify. In English, however, adjectives do not change number this way: *her kittens are cute* (not *cutes*).

4. It is real dangerous to hike those mountains in the winter.
5. He spoke confident about winning the race, but we doubted his abilities.
6. Paramedics rushed to help the victim, who was bleeding bad from the head.
7. The car ran good until the last two miles of the trip.
8. Arjun felt terrifically about his discussion with Professor Greene.
9. After we added cinnamon, the stew tasted really well.
10. Scientists measured the crater as accurate as possible.

## 42d Comparatives and superlatives

Most adjectives and adverbs have three forms: positive, comparative, and superlative.

| POSITIVE | COMPARATIVE | SUPERLATIVE |
|----------|-------------|-------------|
| large | larger | largest |
| early | earlier | earliest |
| careful | more careful | most careful |
| delicious | more delicious | most delicious |

▶ **Canada is larger than the United States.**
▶ **My son needs to be more careful with his money.**
▶ **This is the most delicious coffee we have tried.**

The comparative and superlative of most short (one-syllable and some two-syllable) adjectives are formed by adding *-er* and *-est*. With some two-syllable adjectives, longer adjectives, and most adverbs, use *more* and *most*: *scientific, more scientific, most scientific; elegantly, more elegantly, most elegantly*. If you are not sure whether a word has *-er* and *-est* forms, consult the dictionary entry for the simple form.

### ▢ Using irregular forms

A number of adjectives and adverbs have irregular comparative and superlative forms.

| POSITIVE | COMPARATIVE | SUPERLATIVE |
|---|---|---|
| good, well | better | best |
| bad, badly, ill | worse | worst |
| little (quantity) | less | least |
| many, some, much | more | most |

## ▢ Choosing comparatives or superlatives

In academic writing, use the comparative to compare two things; use the superlative to compare three or more.

▶ Rome is a much **older** city than New York.

▶ Damascus is one of the ~~older~~ *oldest* cities in the world.

▶ Which of the two candidates is the ~~strongest~~ *stronger* for the job?

## ▢ Considering double comparatives and superlatives

Double comparatives and superlatives, used in some informal contexts, use both *more* or *most* and the *-er* or *-est* ending. Occasionally they can act to build a special emphasis, as in the title of Spike Lee's movie *Mo' Better Blues*. In college writing, however, double comparatives and superlatives may count against you. Make sure not to use *more* or *most* before adjectives or adverbs ending in *-er* or *-est* in formal situations.

▶ Paris is the ~~most~~ loveliest city in the world.

## ▢ Considering incomplete comparisons

Even if you think your audience will understand an implied comparison, you will be safer if you make sure that comparisons in formal writing are complete and clear (49e).

▶ The patients taking the drug appeared healthier. *than those receiving a placebo.*

## ▢ Considering absolute concepts

Some readers consider modifiers such as *perfect* and *unique* to be absolute concepts; according to this view, a construction such as *more unique* is illogical because a thing is either unique or it isn't, so modified forms of the concept don't make sense. However, many seemingly absolute words have multiple meanings, all of which are widely accepted as correct. For example, *unique* may mean *one of a kind* or *unequaled*, but it can also simply mean *distinctive* or *unusual*.

If you think your readers will object to a construction such as *more perfect* (which appears in the U.S. Constitution) or *somewhat unique*, then avoid such uses.

## □ Considering multiple negatives

One common type of repetition is to use more than one negative term in a negative statement. In *I can't hardly see you,* for example, both *can't* and *hardly* carry negative meanings. Emphatic double negatives — and triple, quadruple, and more — are especially common in the South and among speakers of some African American varieties of English, who may say, for example, *Don't none of my people come from up North.*

Multiple negatives have a long history in English (and in other languages) and can be found in the works of Chaucer and Shakespeare. In the eighteenth century, however, in an effort to make English more logical, double negatives came to be labeled as incorrect. In college writing, you may well have reason to quote passages that include them (whether from Shakespeare, Toni Morrison, or your grandmother), but it is safer to avoid other uses of double negatives in academic writing.

## 42e Using nouns as modifiers

Sometimes a noun can function as an adjective by modifying another noun, as in *chicken soup* or *money supply.* If noun modifiers pile up, however, they can make your writing harder to understand.

| | |
|---|---|
| AWKWARD | The cold war–era Rosenberg espionage trial and execution continues to arouse controversy. |
| REVISED | The Rosenbergs' trial and execution for espionage during the cold war continues to arouse controversy. |

### ◢ EXERCISE 42.2

Revise each of the following sentences to use modifiers correctly, clearly, and effectively. Many of the sentences can be revised in more than one way. Example:

He is sponsoring a housing project. ~~financial plan approval bill.~~ bill to approve a financial plan for the

1. Alicia speaks both Russian and German, but she speaks Russian best.
2. The summers are more rainier in New York than they are in Seattle.
3. He glanced at the menu and ordered the expensivest wine on the list.
4. Most of the elderly are women because women tend to live longer.

5. Minneapolis is the largest of the Twin Cities.

6. She came up with the most silliest plan for revenge.

7. Our theater company has produced several of the famousest classical Greek plays.

8. The student cafeteria is operated by a college food service system chain.

9. It is safer to jog in daylight.

10. Evan argued that subtitled films are boringer to watch than films dubbed in English.

## 42f   Using adjectives ending in *-ed* and *-ing*

Many verbs refer to feelings — for example, *bore, confuse, excite, frighten, interest.* The present participles of such verbs, which end in *-ing*, and the past participles, which end in *-ed*, can be used as adjectives (36d).

Use the *-ed* (past participle) form to describe a person having the feeling.

○   The *frightened* boy started to cry.

Use the *-ing* (present participle) form to describe the thing or person causing the feeling.

○   The *frightening* movie gave him nightmares.

Be careful not to confuse the two types of adjectives.

○   I am **interesting** in African literature.
        interested

○   African literature seems **interested.**
        interesting.

## 42g   Putting adjectives in order

Modifiers are words that give more information about a noun; that is, they *modify* the meaning of the noun in some way. Some modifiers precede the noun, and others follow it, as indicated in the chart on p. 618.

If there are two or more adjectives, their order is variable, but English has strong preferences, described below.

- Subjective adjectives (those that show the writer's opinion) go before objective adjectives (those that merely describe): *these old-fashioned kitchen tiles.*
- Adjectives of size generally come early: *these large old-fashioned kitchen tiles.*

| Modifier Type | Arrangement | Examples |
|---|---|---|
| determiners | at the beginning of the noun phrase | _these_ old-fashioned tiles |
| _all_ or _both_ | before any other determiners | _all_ these tiles |
| numbers | after any other determiners | these _six_ tiles |
| noun modifiers | directly before the noun | these _kitchen_ tiles |
| adjectives | between determiners and noun modifiers | these _old-fashioned_ kitchen tiles |
| phrases or clauses | after the noun | the tiles _on the wall_ <br> the tiles _that we bought_ |

- Adjectives of color generally come late: _these beautiful blue kitchen tiles._
- Adjectives derived from proper nouns or from nouns that refer to materials generally come after color terms and right before noun modifiers: _these beautiful blue Portuguese ceramic kitchen tiles._
- All other objective adjectives go in the middle, separated by commas (see 54e): _these decorative, heat-resistant, old-fashioned blue Portuguese ceramic kitchen tiles._

Of course, very long noun phrases are usually out of place in most kinds of writing. Academic and professional types of writing tend to avoid long strings of adjectives.

▼ ▼ ▼ ▼ ▼ ▼ ▼ ▼ ▼ ▼ ▼ ▼ ▼ ▼ ▼ ▼ ▼ ▼ ▼ ▼ ▼ ▼ ▼ ▼ ▼

## THINKING CRITICALLY ABOUT ADJECTIVES AND ADVERBS

### Reading with an eye for adjectives and adverbs

[Gwendolyn Brooks] describes the "graceful life" as one where people glide over floors in softly glowing rooms, smile correctly over trays of silver, cinnamon, and cream, and retire in quiet elegance.

—MARY HELEN WASHINGTON, "Taming All That Anger Down"

Identify the adjectives and adverbs in the preceding passage, and comment on what they add to the writing. What would be lost if they were removed?

## Thinking about your own use of adjectives and adverbs

Take a few minutes to study something you can observe or examine closely. In a paragraph or two, describe your subject for someone who has never seen it. Using the guidelines in this chapter, check your use of adjectives and adverbs, and revise your paragraphs. How would you characterize your use of adjectives and adverbs?

# CHAPTER 43

# Prepositions and Prepositional Phrases

WORDS SUCH AS *to, from, over,* and *under* show the relations between other words; these words are prepositions, and they are one of the more challenging elements of English writing. If you speak languages other than English, knowing which preposition your home language uses in an expression will not necessarily help you figure out which preposition to use in English. And if English is your home language, you may still choose the wrong prepositions from time to time in formal communication. Thus, you will almost certainly want to pay very careful attention to these little words.

> **CONNECT:** Why are prepositions tricky to use correctly?
> **The Top Twenty, "Wrong Word" (pp. 2–3); 43a**
>
> **CREATE:** Keep a log of the questionable preposition usage you find in your own writing or in texts you encounter, and note the context.
>
> **REFLECT:** Write or record a reflection about the prepositions that cause you the most trouble and what you plan to do to teach yourself to use them more effectively.

## 43a Using prepositions idiomatically

Each of the most common prepositions has a wide range of applications, and this range never coincides exactly from one language to another. See, for example, how *in* and *on* are used in English.

- The peaches are **in** the refrigerator.
- The peaches are **on** the table.
- Is that a diamond ring **on** your finger?

In some other languages (Spanish, for instance), these sentences might all use the same preposition. Be careful not to assume that what you know about prepositions in another language will help in English.

Is that a ruby ring ~~in~~ *on* your finger?

There is no easy solution to the challenge of using English prepositions idiomatically. However, the following strategies can make learning idiomatic uses of prepositions less troublesome.

> **QUICK HELP**
>
> ### Strategies for learning prepositions idiomatically
>
> 1. **Keep in mind typical examples of each preposition.**
>
>    IN    The peaches are *in* the refrigerator.
>    There are still some pickles *in* the jar.
>    The book you are looking for is *in* the bookcase.
>
>    Here the object of the preposition *in* is a container that encloses something.
>
>    ON    The peaches are *on* the table.
>    There are still some pickles *on* the plate.
>    The book you are looking for is *on* the top shelf.
>
>    Here the object of the preposition *on* is a horizontal surface that supports something with which it is in direct contact.
>
> 2. **Learn other examples that show some similarities and some differences in meaning.**
>
>    IN    You shouldn't drive *in* a snowstorm.
>
>    Here there is no container, but like a container, the falling snow surrounds the driver. The preposition *in* is used for other weather-related expressions as well: *in a tornado, in the sun, in the rain.*
>
>    ON    Is that a diamond ring *on* your finger?
>
>    The preposition *on* is used to describe things we wear: *the hat on his head, the shoes on her feet, the tattoo on his back.*
>
> 3. **Use your imagination to create mental images that can help you remember figurative uses of prepositions.**
>
>    IN    Michael is *in* love.
>
>    The preposition *in* is often used to describe a state of being: *in love, in pain, in a panic.* As a way to remember this, you might imagine the person immersed *in* this state of being. ▶

Strategies for learning prepositions idiomatically, continued

4. **Try to learn prepositions not in isolation but as part of a system.** For example, in identifying the location of a place or an event, you can use the three prepositions *at*, *in*, and *on*.

*At* specifies the exact point in space or time.

AT     There will be a meeting tomorrow *at* 9:30 AM *at* 160 Main Street.

Expanses of space or time within which a place is located or an event takes place might be seen as containers and so require *in*.

IN     I arrived *in* the United States *in* January.

*On* must be used in two cases: with the names of streets (but not the exact address) and with days of the week or month.

ON     The airline's office is *on* Fifth Avenue.
       I'll be moving to my new apartment *on* September 30.

---

**EXERCISE 43.1**

Revise the following paragraph to include any needed prepositions.

The children's soccer game happened _____ 10:00 _____ Saturday morning. The families sat _____ blankets to watch the game. Everyone was _____ a good mood. When the game ended, both teams stood _____ a circle to cheer.

---

# 43b Using two-word verbs idiomatically [MULTI-LINGUAL]

Some words that look like prepositions do not always function as prepositions. Consider the following two sentences:

▶ **The balloon rose *off* the ground.**

▶ **The plane took *off* without difficulty.**

In the first sentence, *off* is a preposition that introduces the prepositional phrase *off the ground*. In the second, *off* does not function as a preposition. Instead, it combines with *took* to form a two-word verb with its own meaning. Such a verb is called a phrasal verb, and the word *off*, when used this way, is called an adverbial particle. Many prepositions can function as particles to form phrasal verbs.

## ▢ Using phrasal verbs

The verb + particle combination that makes up a phrasal verb is a single entity that often cannot be torn apart.

⊙ The plane took *off* without difficulty. ~~off.~~

However, when a phrasal verb takes a direct object (37a), the particle may sometimes be separated from the verb by the object.

⊙ I *picked up* my baggage at the terminal.

⊙ I *picked* my baggage *up* at the terminal.

If a personal pronoun (such as *it*, *her*, or *him*) is used as the direct object, that pronoun must separate the verb from its particle.

⊙ I *picked it up* at the terminal.

□ **Using prepositional verbs**

Some idiomatic two-word verbs are not phrasal verbs.

⊙ We *ran into* our neighbor on the train.

Here, *into* is a preposition, and *our neighbor* is its object. You can't separate the verb from the preposition (*We ran our neighbor into on the train* does not make sense in English). Verbs like *run into* are called prepositional verbs.

Notice that *run into our neighbor* is different from a normal verb and prepositional phrase, such as *run into a room*. The combination *run + into* has a special meaning, "meet by chance," that you could not guess from the meanings of *run* and *into*.

English has many idiomatic prepositional verbs. Here is a small sample.

| PREPOSITIONAL VERB | MEANING |
|---|---|
| take after | resemble (usually a parent or older relative) |
| get over | recover from |
| count on | trust |

Other prepositional verbs have predictable meanings but require you to use a particular preposition that you should learn along with the verb: *depend on, look at, listen to, approve of.*

Finally, look out for phrasal-prepositional verbs such as these, which include a verb, a particle, and a preposition in a set order.

| PHRASAL-PREPOSITIONAL VERB | MEANING |
|---|---|
| put up with | tolerate |
| look forward to | anticipate with pleasure |
| get away with | avoid punishment for |

### EXERCISE 43.2

Each of the following sentences contains a two-word verb. In some sentences, the verb is used correctly; in others, it is used incorrectly. Identify each two-word verb, indicate whether it is a phrasal or prepositional verb, and rewrite any incorrect sentences correctly.

1. Soon after I was hired for my last job, I learned that the company might lay off me.

2. I was counting on the job to pay my way through school, so I was upset.

3. I decided to pick up a newspaper and see what other jobs were available.

4. As I looked the newspaper at, I was surprised to see that I was qualified for a job that paid much better than mine.

5. I gave my old job up and took the new one, which made attending school much easier.

# PART 9
# Clarity

# CHAPTER 44

# Confusing Shifts

A SHIFT IS AN ABRUPT CHANGE of some sort that results in inconsistency. Sometimes writers and speakers create deliberate shifts, as linguist Geneva Smitherman does in this passage from *Word from the Mother*: "In the larger realm of Hip Hop culture, there is cause for optimism as we witness Hip Hop younguns tryna git they political activist game togetha."

Unintentional shifts, however, can be jolting and confusing to readers.

> **CONNECT:** Why are verb tense shifts confusing to readers? **The Top Twenty, "Unnecessary shift in verb tense" (p. 7); 44a**
>
> **CREATE:** Keep a log of the confusing verb tense shifts you find in your own writing or in texts you encounter, and note the context.
>
> **REFLECT:** Write or record a reflection about the situations that cause you the most trouble with verb tenses and what you can do to make yourself more aware of avoiding confusing shifts.

## 44a Revising shifts in tense

If verbs in a passage refer to actions occurring at different times, they may require different tenses. Be careful, however, not to change tenses for no clear reason.

> **A few countries produce almost all of the world's illegal drugs, but**
>    affects
> **addiction ~~affected~~ many countries.**

## 44b Revising shifts in mood

Be careful not to shift from one mood to another without good reason. The mood of a verb can be indicative (*he closes the door*), imperative (*close the door*), or subjunctive (*if the door were closed*). (See 39h.)

⊙ **Keep your eye on the ball, and ~~you should~~ bend your knees.**

The writer's purpose is to give orders, but the original version shifts unnecessarily from the imperative to the indicative; the editing makes both verbs imperative.

## 44c  Revising shifts in voice

Do not shift without reason between the active voice (*she sold it*) and the passive voice (*it was sold*). (See 39g.) Sometimes a shift in voice is justified, but often it only confuses readers.

⊙ **Two youths approached ~~me,~~ and ~~I was~~ asked for my wallet.**
                              *me*

The original sentence shifts from the active (*youths approached*) to the passive (*I was asked*), so it is unclear who asked for the wallet. Making both verbs active clears up the confusion.

## 44d  Revising shifts in person and number

Unnecessary shifts in point of view between first person (*I, we*), second person (*you*), and third person (*he, she, it, one,* or *they*) or between singular and plural can be very confusing to readers.

     *You*
⊙ **~~One~~ can do well on this job if you budget your time.**

Is the writer making a general statement or giving advice to someone? Eliminating the shift eliminates this confusion.

Many shifts in number are actually problems with pronoun-antecedent agreement (41f).

| | |
|---|---|
| INCONSISTENT | A patient should be able to talk to their doctor. |
| REVISED | Patients should be able to talk to their doctors. |
| REVISED | A patient should be able to talk to his or her doctor. |

## 44e  Revising shifts between direct and indirect discourse

 MULTI-LINGUAL

When you quote someone's exact words, you are using direct discourse: *She said, "I'm an editor."* When you report what someone says without repeating the exact words, you are using indirect discourse: *She said she was an editor.*

| | |
|---|---|
| DIRECT | She said, "My work *is* now complete." |
| INDIRECT | She *told* me that her work *was* now complete. |
| INDIRECT | She *tells* me that her work *is* now complete. |

In general, the verb introducing the indirect quotation (sometimes called the reporting verb) agrees in tense with the verb in the indirect quotation; there are, however, some exceptions. For example, if the reporting verb is in the past tense but the information that follows holds true in the present, shifting to a present-tense verb is acceptable.

▶ She *told* me that her work *is* as exciting as ever.

Shifting between direct and indirect discourse within the same sentence can cause problems, especially when the sentence is a question.

▶ Viet asked what could ^he^ do to help?̠

The editing eliminates an awkward shift by reporting Viet's question indirectly. The sentence could also be edited to quote Viet directly: *Viet asked, "What can I do to help?"*

---

**EXERCISE 44.1**

Revise the following sentences to eliminate unnecessary shifts in tense, mood, voice, or person and number and between direct and indirect discourse. Most of the items can be revised in more than one way. Examples:

> When a person goes to college, you face many new situations.
> When a person goes to college, he or she faces many new situations.
> When people go to college, they face many new situations.

1. The greed of the 1980s gave way to the occupational insecurity of the 1990s, which in turn gives way to reinforced family ties in the early 2000s.
2. The building inspector suggested that we apply for a construction permit and that we should check with his office again when the plans are complete.
3. The instructor grabbed her coat, wondered why was the substitute late, and ran out of the room.
4. Suddenly, we heard an explosion of wings off to our right, and you could see a hundred or more ducks lifting off from the water.
5. In my previous job, I sold the most advertising spots and was given a sales excellence award.
6. A cloud of snow powder rose as skis and poles fly in every direction.
7. The flight attendant said, "Please turn off all electronic devices," but that we could use them again after takeoff.
8. The real estate market was softer than it had been for a decade, and a buyer could practically name their price.
9. When in Florence, be sure to see the city's famed cathedral, and many tourists also visit Michelangelo's statue *David*.
10. The freezing weather is threatening crops such as citrus fruits, which were sensitive to cold.

## 44f   Revising shifts in tone and diction

Tone, a writer's attitude toward a topic or audience, is related to diction or word choice and to overall formality or informality. Watch out for tone or diction shifts that could confuse readers and leave them wondering what your real attitude is. (See 4i.)

### INCONSISTENT TONE

The question of child care forces a society to make profound decisions about its economic values. Can most families with children actually live adequately on only one salary? If some conservatives had their way, June Cleaver would still be stuck in the kitchen baking cookies for Wally and the Beaver and waiting for Ward to bring home the bacon, except that with only one income, the Cleavers would be lucky to afford hot dogs.

In the preceding version, the first two sentences set a serious, formal tone as they discuss child care in fairly general, abstract terms. But in the third sentence, the writer shifts suddenly to sarcasm, to references to television characters of an earlier era, and to informal language like *stuck* and *bring home the bacon*. Readers cannot tell whether the writer is presenting a serious analysis or preparing for a humorous satire. The revision makes the tone consistently formal.

### REVISED

The question of child care forces a society to make profound decisions about its economic values. Can most families with young children actually live adequately on only one salary? Some conservatives believe that women with young children should not work outside the home, but many mothers are forced to do so for financial reasons.

▼ ▼ ▼ ▼ ▼ ▼ ▼ ▼ ▼ ▼ ▼ ▼ ▼ ▼ ▼ ▼ ▼ ▼ ▼ ▼ ▼ ▼ ▼ ▼ ▼

## THINKING CRITICALLY ABOUT SHIFTS

### Reading with an eye for shifts

The following paragraph includes several necessary shifts in person and number. Read the paragraph carefully, marking all such shifts. Notice how careful the author must be as he shifts back and forth among pronouns.

It has been one of the great errors of our time to think that by thinking about thinking, and then talking about it, we could possibly straighten out and tidy up our minds. There is no delusion more damaging than to get the idea in your head that you understand the functioning of your own brain. Once you acquire such a notion, you run the danger of moving in to take charge, guiding your thoughts, shepherding your mind from place to place, controlling it, making lists of regulations. The human mind is not meant to be governed, certainly not by any book of rules yet written; it is supposed to run itself, and we are obliged to follow it along, trying to keep up with it as best we can. It is all very well to be aware of your awareness, even proud of it, but never try to operate it. You are not up to the job.                                    —LEWIS THOMAS, "The Attic of the Brain"

## Thinking about any shifts in your own writing

Find an article about a well-known person you admire. Then write a paragraph or two about him or her, making a point of using both direct and indirect discourse. Using the information in 44e, check your writing for any inappropriate shifts between direct and indirect discourse, and revise as necessary.

# CHAPTER 45

# Parallelism

**S**EE HOW JONATHAN FRANZEN uses parallelism in talking about a job:

> _Since_ I was paid better than the minimum wage, and _since_ I enjoyed topological packing puzzles, and _since_ the Geyers liked me and gave me lots of cake, it was remarkable _how_ fiercely I hated the job — _how_ I envied even those friends of mine who _manned_ the deep-fry station at Long John Silver's or _cleaned_ the oil traps at Kentucky Fried Chicken.

The parallelism indicated by the underscores brings a sense of orderliness to a long yet cohesive sentence. Making similar structures parallel will help clarify your writing.

## 45a  Making items in a series parallel

All items in a series should be in parallel form — all nouns, all prepositional phrases, all adverb clauses, and so on. Such parallelism makes a series graceful and easy to follow.

- The quarter horse skipped, pranced, and ~~was sashaying.~~ sashayed.

- The children ran down the hill, raced over the lawn, and ^jumped into the swimming pool.

- The duties of the job include baby-sitting, house-cleaning, and ^preparing ~~preparation of~~ meals.

Items in a list should be parallel.

- Kitchen rules: (1) Coffee to be made only by library staff. (2) Coffee service to be closed at 4:00 PM. (3) Doughnuts to be kept in cabinet. (4) ~~No faculty members should handle coffee materials.~~ ^Coffee materials not to be handled by faculty.

**631**

Items on a formal outline and headings in a paper should be parallel. The headings in this chapter, for example, use parallel phrases.

---

**QUICK HELP**

### Editing for parallelism

* Look for any series of three or more items, and make all of the items parallel in structure. If you want to emphasize one particular item, try putting it at the end of the series. **(45a and d)**
* Be sure items in lists and headings are parallel in form. **(45a)**
* Check for sentences that compare, contrast, or otherwise pair two ideas. Often these ideas will appear on either side of *and, but, or, nor, for, so,* or *yet* or after each part of *either . . . or, both . . . and, neither . . . nor, not only . . . but also, just as . . . so,* or *whether . . . or.* Edit to make the two ideas parallel in structure. **(45b)**
* Check all parallel structures to be sure you have included all necessary words—articles, prepositions, the *to* of the infinitive, and so on. **(45c)**

---

## 45b Using parallel structures to pair ideas

Parallel structures can help you pair two ideas effectively. The more nearly parallel the two structures are, the stronger the connection between the ideas will be. Parallel structures are especially appropriate when two ideas are compared or contrasted.

▶ **History became popular, and historians became alarmed.**    —WILL DURANT

▶ **I type in one place, but I write all over the house.**    —TONI MORRISON

To create an especially forceful impression, writers may construct a balanced sentence, one with two clauses that mirror each other.

▶ **Mankind must put an end to war, or war will put an end to mankind.**

—JOHN F. KENNEDY

### Using coordinating conjunctions

When you link ideas with a coordinating conjunction — *and, but, or, nor, for, so, yet* — try to make the ideas parallel in structure.

▶ **We performed whenever folks would listen and wherever they would pay.**

▶ **Consult a friend in your class** ~~or~~ who is **good at math.**
           who is
              ^

### Using correlative conjunctions

Always use the same structure after both parts of any correlative conjunction **(36g)** — *either . . . or, both . . . and, neither . . . nor, not . . . but, not only . . . but also, just as . . . so, whether . . . or.*

> The organization provided both **scholarships for young artists** and **grants for established ones.**

> I wanted not only to go away to school but also ~~to~~ New England.

<small>live in</small>

The edited sentence is more balanced. Both parts of the correlative conjunction (*not only . . . but also*) precede a verb.

### EXERCISE 45.1

Complete the following sentences, using parallel words or phrases in each case. Example:

**The wise politician *promises the possible, faces the unavoidable,* and *accepts the inevitable.***

1. Before buying a used car, you should ____, ____, and ____.
2. Three activities I'd like to try are ____, ____, and ____.
3. Working in a restaurant taught me not only ____ but also ____.
4. We must either ____ or ____.
5. To pass the time in the waiting room, I ____, ____, and ____.

### EXERCISE 45.2

Revise the following sentences as necessary to eliminate any errors in parallel structure.

walking

**I enjoy skiing, playing the guitar, and ~~I walk~~ on the beach in warm weather.**

1. I remember watching it for the first time, realizing I'd never seen anything like it, and immediately vowed never to miss even one episode of *The Daily Show*.
2. A crowd stood outside the school and were watching as the graduates paraded by.
3. An effective Web site is well designed, provides useful information, and links are given to other relevant sites.
4. It is impossible to watch *The Office* and not seeing a little of yourself in one of the characters.
5. Lila was the winner not only of the pie-eating contest but also won the yodeling competition.

## 45c  Including all necessary words

In addition to making any parallel elements grammatically similar, be careful to include all words — prepositions, articles, verb forms, and so on — that are necessary for clarity or grammar. (See also 39e.)

▶ We'll move to a city in the Southwest or *in* Mexico.

   To a city in Mexico or to Mexico in general? The editing makes the meaning clear.

▶ I had never before *seen* and would never again see such a sight.

   In the unedited version, *had . . . see* is not grammatically correct.

## 45d  Using parallel structures for emphasis and effect

Parallel structures can help a writer emphasize a point, as Joan Didion does in this passage about people living in California's San Bernardino Valley in the late 1960s:

> Here is where the hot wind blows and the old ways do not seem relevant, where the divorce rate is double the national average and where one person in every thirty-eight lives in a trailer. Here is the last stop for all those who come from somewhere else, for all those who drifted away from the cold and the past and the old ways. Here is where they are trying to find a new life style, trying to find it in the only places they know to look: the movies and the newspapers.    —JOAN DIDION, "Some Dreamers of the Golden Dream"

The parallel phrases — *Here is, Here is* — introduce parallel details (*the hot wind* versus *the cold*; *the old ways* versus *a new life style*) that emphasize the emotional distance between *here* and the *somewhere else* that was once home for these new Californians.

▼ ▼ ▼ ▼ ▼ ▼ ▼ ▼ ▼ ▼ ▼ ▼ ▼ ▼ ▼ ▼ ▼ ▼ ▼ ▼ ▼ ▼ ▼ ▼ ▼ ▼

### THINKING CRITICALLY ABOUT PARALLELISM

#### Reading with an eye for parallelism

Read the following paragraph about a bareback rider practicing her circus act, and identify all the parallel structures. Consider what effect they create on you as a reader, and try to decide why the author chose to put his ideas in such overtly parallel form. Try imitating the next-to-last sentence, the one beginning *In a week or two.*

> The richness of the scene was in its plainness, its natural condition — of horse, of ring, of girl, even to the girl's bare feet that gripped the bare back of her proud

and ridiculous mount. The enchantment grew not out of anything that happened or was performed but out of something that seemed to go round and around and around with the girl, attending her, a steady gleam in the shape of a circle — a ring of ambition, of happiness, of youth. (And the positive pleasures of equilibrium under difficulties.) In a week or two, all would be changed, all (or almost all) lost: the girl would wear makeup, the horse would wear gold, the ring would be painted, the bark would be clean for the feet of the horse, the girl's feet would be clean for the slippers that she'd wear. All, all would be lost.

—E. B. WHITE, "The Ring of Time"

### Thinking about your own use of parallelism

Read carefully several paragraphs from a draft you have recently written, noting any series of words, phrases, or clauses. Using the guidelines in this chapter, determine whether the series are parallel, and if not, revise them for parallelism. Then reread the paragraphs, looking for places where parallel structures would add emphasis or clarity, and revise accordingly. Can you draw any conclusions about your use of parallelism?

# CHAPTER 46

# Comma Splices and Fused Sentences

W RITERS SOMETIMES USE comma splices for special effect in fiction or essays and especially in advertising or on bumper stickers, where they can give slogans a catchy rhythm: *Dogs have owners, cats have staff.*

> **CONNECT:** When might you choose to use a comma splice for a particular effect? **2a, 46a**
>
> **CREATE:** Keep a log of the comma splices you see in a day on social networking platforms that you use regularly, and note the context of each one.
>
> **REFLECT:** Write or record a reflection about when comma splices seem appropriate and when they are distracting.

## 46a Identifying comma splices and fused sentences

A comma splice results from placing only a comma between two independent clauses, as in this tweet:

○ **One thing is certain, girls everywhere need education.**

A related construction is a fused, or run-on, sentence, which results from joining two independent clauses with no punctuation or connecting word between them. As a fused sentence, the tweet above would read *One thing is certain girls everywhere need education.*

Using comma splices is increasingly common in writing that aims for a casual, informal feel, but comma splices and fused sentences in academic writing are likely to draw an instructor's criticism. If you use comma splices and fused sentences in formal writing, be sure your audience can tell that you are doing so for a special effect.

## Editing for comma splices and fused sentences

If you find no punctuation between two of your independent clauses—groups of words that can stand alone as sentences—you have identified a fused sentence. If you find two such clauses joined only by a comma, you have identified a comma splice. Revise comma splices and fused sentences with one of these methods.

1.  Separate the clauses into two sentences. **(46b)**

    ▶ Education is an elusive idea/. *It* it means different things to different people.

2.  Link the clauses with a comma and a coordinating conjunction (*and*, *but*, *or*, *nor*, *for*, *so*, or *yet*). **(46c)**

    ▶ Education is an elusive idea, *for* it means different things to different people.

3.  Link the clauses with a semicolon. **(46d)**

    ▶ Education is an elusive idea/; it means different things to different people.

    If the clauses are linked with only a comma and a conjunctive adverb—a word like *however*, *then*, *therefore*—add a semicolon.

    ▶ Education is an elusive idea/; *indeed,* it means different things to different people.

4.  Recast the two clauses as one independent clause. **(46e)**

    ▶ *An elusive idea, education* ~~Education is an elusive idea, it~~ means different things to different people.

5.  Recast one independent clause as a dependent clause. **(46f)**

    ▶ Education is an elusive idea/ *because* it means different things to different people.

6.  In informal writing, link the clauses with a dash. **(46g)**

    ▶ Education is an elusive idea/ —it means different things to different people.

## 46b Separating the clauses into two sentences

The simplest way to revise comma splices or fused sentences is to separate them into two sentences.

COMMA
SPLICE

My mother spends long hours every spring tilling the soil
                                                          This
and moving manure/. this part of gardening is nauseating.
                           ^

FUSED
SENTENCE

My mother spends long hours every spring tilling the soil
                                                     This
and moving manure. this part of gardening is nauseating.
                         ^

If the two clauses are very short, making them two sentences may sound abrupt and terse, so some other method of revision is probably preferable.

## 46c Linking the clauses with a comma and a coordinating conjunction

If the ideas in the two clauses are closely related and equally important, you can join them with a comma and a coordinating conjunction: *and, but, or, nor, for, so,* or *yet.* (See Chapter 54.) The conjunction helps indicate what kind of link exists between the two clauses. For instance, *but* and *yet* signal opposition or contrast; *for* and *so* signal cause-effect relationships.

COMMA
SPLICE

                            so
I got up feeling bad, I took some aspirin.
                     ^

FUSED
SENTENCE

                              but
I should pay my tuition, I need a new car.
                       ^

## 46d Linking the clauses with a semicolon

If the ideas in the two clauses are closely related and you want to give them equal emphasis, you can link them with a semicolon.

COMMA
SPLICE

This photograph is not at all realistic/; it uses dreamlike
                                     ^
images to convey its message.

FUSED
SENTENCE

The practice of journalism is changing dramatically;
                                                   ^
advances in technology have sped up news cycles.

Be careful when you link clauses with either a conjunctive adverb or a transitional phrase. Precede such words and phrases with a semicolon (see Chapter 55), with a period, or with a comma combined with a coordinating conjunction (36g).

| | |
|---|---|
| COMMA SPLICE | **Many developing countries have very high birthrates;**<br><br>**therefore, most of their citizens are young.** |
| FUSED SENTENCE | **Many developing countries have very high birthrates.**<br><br>**therefore, most of their citizens are young.** |
| FUSED SENTENCE | **Many developing countries have very high birthrates,**<br>and<br>**therefore, most of their citizens are young.** |

SOME CONJUNCTIVE ADVERBS AND TRANSITIONAL PHRASES

| | | |
|---|---|---|
| also | in contrast | next |
| anyway | indeed | now |
| besides | in fact | otherwise |
| certainly | instead | similarly |
| finally | likewise | still |
| furthermore | meanwhile | then |
| however | moreover | therefore |
| in addition | namely | thus |
| incidentally | nevertheless | undoubtedly |

**MULTI-LINGUAL** | **SENTENCE LENGTH**

In U.S. academic contexts, readers sometimes find a series of short sentences "choppy" and undesirable. If you want to connect two independent clauses into one sentence, be sure to join them with a comma followed by a coordinating conjunction (*and, but, for, so, nor, or,* or *yet*) or with a semicolon. Doing so will help you avoid a comma splice, which is often considered an error in formal writing. Another useful tip for writing in American English is to avoid writing several very long sentences in a row. If you find this pattern in your writing, try breaking it up by including a shorter sentence occasionally. See the tips in Chapter 52 for altering the sentence lengths and patterns in your writing.

## 46e Recasting two clauses as one independent clause

Sometimes you can reduce two spliced or fused clauses to a single independent clause that is more direct and concise.

> COMMA SPLICE
>
> and
> A large part of my mail is advertisements,/ ~~most of the~~
> ~~rest is bills.~~

## 46f Recasting one independent clause as a dependent clause

When one independent clause is more important than the other, try converting the less important one to a dependent clause.

> COMMA SPLICE
>
> which reacted against mass production,
> The arts and crafts movement, called for handmade
> objects,/. ~~it reacted against mass production.~~

In the revision, the writer chooses to emphasize the first clause, the one describing what the movement advocated, and to make the second clause, the one describing what it reacted against, into a dependent clause.

> FUSED SENTENCE
>
> Although
> Zora Neale Hurston is regarded as one of America's major
> novelists, she died in obscurity.

In the revision, the writer chooses to emphasize the second clause and to make the first one into a dependent clause by adding the subordinating conjunction *although* (36g).

## 46g Linking two independent clauses with a dash

In informal writing, you can use a dash to join two independent clauses, especially when the second clause elaborates on the first.

> COMMA SPLICE
>
> Exercise has become too much like work,/— it's a bad
> trend.

▰ **EXERCISE 46.1**

Using two of the methods in this chapter, revise each item to correct its comma splice or fused sentence. Use each of the methods at least once. Example:

> so
> I had misgivings about the marriage, I did not attend the ceremony.
> ^
>
> *Because*
> I had misgivings about the marriage, I did not attend the ceremony.
> ^

1. Many motorists are unaware of the dangers of texting while driving, lawmakers have taken the matter into their own hands.

2. The tallest human on record was Robert Wadlow he reached an amazing height of eight feet, eleven inches.

3. Some employers provide on-site care for the children of their employees, others reimburse workers for day-care costs.

4. The number of vaccine manufacturers has plummeted the industry has been hit with a flood of lawsuits.

5. Most crustaceans live in the ocean, some also live on land or in freshwater habitats.

6. She inherited some tribal customs from her grandmother, she knows the sewing technique called Seminole patchwork.

7. Don't throw your soda cans in the trash recycle them.

8. My West Indian neighbor has lived in New England for years, nevertheless, she always feels betrayed by winter.

9. The Hope diamond in the Smithsonian Institution is impressive in fact, it looks even larger in person than online.

10. You signed up for the course now you'll have to do the work.

▰ **EXERCISE 46.2**

Revise the following paragraph, eliminating all comma splices by using a period or a semicolon. Then revise the paragraph again, this time using any of the other methods in this chapter. Comment on the two revisions. What differences in rhythm do you detect? Which version do you prefer, and why?

> We may disagree on the causes of global warming, however, we cannot ignore that it is happening. Of course we still experience cold winters, on the other hand, average global temperatures have risen drastically for the last three decades. Polar ice caps are melting, as a result, sea levels are rising. Scientists predict more extreme weather in the coming decades, droughts will probably be more common, in addition, flooding and tropical storm activity may increase. Some experts fear that rising temperatures may cause large amounts of methane

gases to be released, this could be disastrous for our atmosphere. Climate change may have human causes, it might be a natural occurrence, nevertheless, we must find ways to save our planet.

▼ ▼ ▼ ▼ ▼ ▼ ▼ ▼ ▼ ▼ ▼ ▼ ▼ ▼ ▼ ▼ ▼ ▼ ▼ ▼ ▼ ▼ ▼ ▼ ▼ ▼ ▼ ▼

## THINKING CRITICALLY ABOUT COMMA SPLICES AND FUSED SENTENCES

### Reading with an eye for special effects

Roger Angell is known as a careful and correct stylist, yet he often deviates from the "correct" to create special effects, as in this passage about pitcher David Cone:

> And then he won. Next time out, on August 10th, handed a seven-run lead against the A's, he gave up two runs over six innings, with eight strike-outs. He had tempo, he had poise. —ROGER ANGELL, "Before the Fall"

Angell uses a comma splice in the last sentence to emphasize parallel ideas; any conjunction, even *and*, would change the causal relationship he wishes to show. Because the splice is unexpected, it attracts just the attention that Angell wants for his statement.

Look through some stories or essays to find comma splices and fused sentences. Copy down one or two and enough of the surrounding text to show context, and comment in writing on the effects they create.

### Thinking about any comma splices and fused sentences in your own writing

Go through some essays you have written, checking for comma splices and fused sentences. Revise any you find, using one of the methods in this chapter. Comment on your chosen methods.

# CHAPTER 47

# Fragments

S ENTENCE FRAGMENTS are often used to make writing sound conversational, as in this Facebook status update:

> Realizing that there are no edible bagels in this part of Oregon. Sigh.

Fragments — groups of words that are punctuated as sentences but are not sentences — are often seen in intentionally informal writing and in public writing, such as advertising, that aims to attract attention or give a phrase special emphasis. Think carefully before using fragments in academic or professional writing, where some readers might regard them as errors.

---

**CONNECT:** When might you choose to use a fragment for a particular effect? **2a, 47a**

**CREATE:** Keep a log of the fragments you see in professional writing (such as advertising) in a single day. Note the context of each one.

**REFLECT:** Write or record a reflection about the effect of fragments in professional writing.

---

## 47a Identifying fragments

A group of words must meet the following three criteria to form a complete sentence. If it does not meet all three, it is considered a fragment.

1. A sentence must have a subject. (37b)

2. A sentence must have a verb, not just a verbal. A verbal (such as the participle *singing*) needs a helping verb in order to function as a sentence's verb.

   | | |
   |---|---|
   | VERBAL | She *singing*. |
   | VERB | She *is singing*. |

3. Unless it is a question, a sentence must have at least one clause that does not begin with a subordinating conjunction such as *because, if, that,* or *when*. See 36g for a list of common subordinating conjunctions.

## 47b Revising phrase fragments

Phrases are groups of words that lack a subject, a verb, or both (37d). When phrases are punctuated like sentences, they become fragments. To revise such a fragment, either attach it to an independent clause or make it a separate sentence.

▶ NBC is broadcasting the debates./, *with* ~~With~~ discussions afterward.

> The word group *with discussions afterward* is a prepositional phrase, not a sentence. The editing combines the phrase with an independent clause.

▶ The town's growth is controlled by zoning laws./, *a* ~~A~~ strict set of regulations for builders and corporations.

> *A strict set of regulations for builders and corporations* is an appositive phrase renaming the noun *zoning laws*. The editing attaches the fragment to the sentence containing that noun.

▶ Kamika stayed out of school for three months after Linda was born.
  *She wanted to*
  ~~To~~ recuperate and to take care of the baby.

> *To recuperate and to take care of the baby* includes verbals, not verbs. The revision — adding a subject (*she*) and a verb (*wanted*) — turns the fragment into a separate sentence.

☐ Avoiding fragments beginning with transitions

If you introduce an example or explanation with a transition, such as one of the following, be certain you write a sentence, not a fragment.

| | | |
|---|---|---|
| again | but | instead |
| also | finally | like |
| and | for example | or |
| as a result | for instance | such as |
| besides | however | that is |

▶ Barbara Ehrenreich has written on many subjects./, *such* ~~Such~~ as underemployment and positive psychology.

> In the original, the second word group is a phrase, not a sentence. The editing combines it with an independent clause.

# 47c Revising compound-predicate fragments

A compound predicate consists of two or more verbs, along with their modifiers and objects, that share the same subject. Fragments occur when one part of a compound predicate lacks a subject but is punctuated as a separate sentence. These fragments usually begin with *and*, *but*, or *or*. You can revise them by attaching them to the independent clause that contains the rest of the predicate.

> **They sold their house. And moved into an apartment.** *(and)*

## EXERCISE 47.1

Revise each of the following items to eliminate any sentence fragments, either by combining fragments with independent clauses or by rewriting them as separate sentences. Example:

> **Zoe looked close to tears. Standing with her head bowed.** *Zoe looked close to tears.*

> **Zoe looked close to tears. Standing with her head bowed.** *She was standing*

1. Long stretches of white beaches and shady palm trees. Give tourists the impression of an island paradise.
2. Forgetting to study for an exam. That is what many college students are afraid of.
3. Much of New Orleans is below sea level. Making the city susceptible to flooding.
4. Uncle Ron forgot to bring his clarinet to the party. Fortunately for us.
5. Oscar night is an occasion for celebrating the film industry. And criticizing the fashion industry.
6. Diners in Creole restaurants might try shrimp gumbo. Or order turtle soup.
7. In the late 1940s, women began hosting Tupperware parties. Casual gatherings in which the hosts act as salespersons.
8. Attempting to lose ten pounds in less than a week. I ate only cottage cheese and grapefruit.
9. Our parents did not realize that we were hoarding our candy. Under our beds.
10. Thomas Edison was famous for his inventions. For example, the phonograph and the first practical lightbulb.

## 47d Revising dependent-clause fragments

Dependent clauses contain both a subject and a verb, but they cannot stand alone as sentences because they depend on an independent clause to complete their meaning. Dependent clauses usually begin with words such as *after, because, before, if, since, though, unless, until, when, where, while, who, which,* and *that* (36g and 37e). You can usually combine dependent-clause fragments with a nearby independent clause.

▶ The team had a dismal record~~.~~, ~~Which~~ which spurred the owner to fire the

manager.

If you cannot smoothly attach a dependent clause to a nearby independent clause, try deleting the opening subordinating word and turning the dependent clause into a sentence.

▶ The majority of injuries in automobile accidents occur in two ways.
~~When an~~ An occupant either is hurt by something inside the car or is

thrown from the car.

### ◢ EXERCISE 47.2

Identify all the sentence fragments in the following items, and explain why each is grammatically incomplete. Then revise each one in at least two ways. Example:

Controlling my temper~~.~~/ ~~That~~ has been one of my goals this year.

One of my goals this year has been controlling
~~Controlling~~ my temper. ~~That has been one of my goals this year.~~

1. As soon as the seventy-five-year-old cellist walked onstage. The audience burst into applause.

2. The patient has only one intention. To smoke behind the doctor's back.

3. Some reality shows feature people working in dangerous situations. Such as fishing for Alaskan king crab or logging in swamps.

4. After writing and rewriting for almost three years. She finally felt that her novel was complete.

5. In the wake of the earthquake. Relief workers tried to provide food and shelter to victims.

6. Forster stopped writing novels after *A Passage to India*. Which is one of the greatest novels of the twentieth century.

7. Because only two students signed up. The class was canceled this semester.

8. I started running in April. And ran my first marathon in September.

9. We sat stunned as she delivered her monologue. A ten-minute speech about everything we had done to annoy her.

10. All primates have opposable thumbs. Which sets them apart from other mammals.

▼ ▼ ▼ ▼ ▼ ▼ ▼ ▼ ▼ ▼ ▼ ▼ ▼ ▼ ▼ ▼ ▼ ▼ ▼ ▼ ▼ ▼ ▼ ▼ ▼ ▼ ▼ ▼

## THINKING CRITICALLY ABOUT FRAGMENTS

### Reading with an eye for fragments

Identify the fragments in the following passage. What effect does the writer achieve by using fragments rather than complete sentences?

> On Sundays, for religion, we went up on the hill. Skipping along the hexagon-shaped tile in Colonial Park. Darting up the steps to Edgecomb Avenue. Stopping in the candy store on St. Nicholas to load up. Leaning forward for leverage to finish the climb up to the church. I was always impressed by this particular house of the Lord. —KEITH GILYARD, *Voices of the Self*

### Thinking about any fragments in your own writing

Read through some essays you have written. Using the guidelines in 47a, see whether you find any sentence fragments. If so, do you recognize any patterns? Do you write fragments when you're attempting to add emphasis? Are they all dependent clauses? phrases? Note any patterns you discover, and make a point of routinely checking your writing for fragments. Finally, revise any fragments to form complete sentences.

# Modifier Placement

C **ONSIDER THE FOLLOWING** notice in a guidebook:

> Visit the old Dutch cemetery where early settlers are buried from noon to five daily.

Does the old cemetery really bury early settlers for five hours every day? Repositioning the modifier *from noon to five daily* eliminates the confusion and makes it clear when the cemetery is open: *From noon to five daily, visit the old Dutch cemetery where early settlers are buried.* To be effective, modifiers should refer clearly to the words they modify and be placed close to those words.

## 48a Revising misplaced modifiers

Misplaced modifiers cause confusion because they are not close enough to the words they modify or because they seem to modify more than one thing.

▶ ~~Clearly~~ I could hear the instructor lecturing ^*clearly.*^

The editing repositions the modifier *clearly* next to the word *lecturing*, which the writer wants to describe.

Phrases should usually be placed right before or after the words they modify.

▶ She teaches a seminar this term ^*on voodoo*^ ~~on voodoo~~ at Skyline College.

The voodoo is not at the college; the seminar is.

▶ ~~Billowing from every window,~~ ^*We*^ we saw clouds of smoke ^*billowing from every window.*^

People cannot billow from windows.

Although you have some flexibility in the placement of dependent clauses, try to position them close to what they modify.

> After he lost the 1962 race,
> **Nixon said he would get out of politics. ~~after he lost the 1962 race.~~**

The unedited sentence implies that Nixon planned to lose the race.

---

**QUICK HELP**

### Editing for misplaced or dangling modifiers

1. Identify all the modifiers in each sentence, and draw an arrow from each modifier to the word it modifies.

2. If a modifier is far from the word it modifies, try to move the two closer together. **(48a)**

3. Does any modifier seem to refer to a word other than the one it is intended to modify? If so, move the modifier so that it refers clearly to only the intended word. **(48a and b)**

4. If you cannot find the word to which a modifier refers, revise the sentence: supply such a word, or revise the modifier itself so that it clearly refers to a word already in the sentence. **(48c)**

---

 **EXERCISE 48.1**

Revise each of the following sentences by moving any misplaced modifiers so that they clearly modify the words they should. Example:

> When they propose sensible plans, politicians
> **Politicians earn support from the people. ~~when they propose sensible plans.~~**

1. The comedian had the audience doubled over with laughter relating her stories in a deadpan voice.

2. News reports can increase a listener's irrational fears that emphasize random crime or rare diseases.

3. Studying legal documents and court records from hundreds of years ago, ordinary people in the Middle Ages teach us about everyday life at that time.

4. Risking their lives in war zones, civilians learn about the conflict from the first-hand accounts of journalists abroad.

5. Melena saw lions in the wild on a safari in Africa last spring.

6. Doctors recommend a new test for cancer, which is painless.

7. Every afternoon I find flyers for free pizza left on my windshield.

8. Screeching strings told the audience that the killer was coming after the opening credits.

9. The coach awarded a medal to the most valuable player made of solid brass.

10. Hanging on by a thread, the five-year-old finally lost her tooth.

## ☐ Using limiting modifiers

Be especially careful with the placement of limiting modifiers such as *almost, even, hardly, just, merely, nearly, only, scarcely,* and *simply.* In general, these modifiers should be placed right before or after the words they modify. Putting them in other positions may produce not just ambiguity but a completely different meaning.

| | |
|---|---|
| AMBIGUOUS | **The court *only* hears civil cases on Tuesdays.** |
| CLEAR | **The court hears only civil cases on Tuesdays.** |
| CLEAR | **The court hears civil cases on Tuesdays only.** |

In the first sentence, placing *only* before *hears* makes the meaning ambiguous. The revised versions clarify the meaning.

▶ **The city** ~~almost~~ *almost* **spent $20 million on the new stadium.**

The original sentence suggests the money was almost spent; moving *almost* makes clear that the amount spent was almost $20 million.

## ☐ Avoiding squinting modifiers

If a modifier can refer to *either* the word before it *or* the word after it, it is a squinting modifier. Put the modifier where it clearly relates to only a single word in the sentence.

| | |
|---|---|
| SQUINTING | **Students who practice writing *often* will benefit.** |

Does the writer mean that students often benefit from practice or that they benefit from practicing often?

| | |
|---|---|
| REVISED | **Students who often practice writing will benefit.** |
| REVISED | **Students who practice writing will often benefit.** |

◢ **EXERCISE 48.2**

Revise each of the following sentences in at least two ways. Move the limiting or squinting modifier so that it unambiguously modifies one word or phrase in the sentence. Example:

*completely*

**The course we hoped would engross us** ~~completely~~ **bored us.**

*completely.*

**The course we hoped would engross us** ~~completely~~ **bored us.**

1. The division that profited most deserves the prize.
2. The soldier was apparently injured by friendly fire.
3. The collector who owned the painting originally planned to leave it to a museum.
4. Alcoholics who try to quit drinking on their own frequently tend to relapse.
5. Ever since I was a child, I have only liked green peas with ham.

## 48b Revising disruptive modifiers

Disruptive modifiers interrupt the connections between parts of a sentence, making it hard for readers to follow the progress of the thought. Most disruptive modifiers are adverbial clauses or phrases that appear between the parts of a verb phrase, between a subject and a verb, or between a verb and an object.

> ~~Vegetables will, if they are cooked too long,~~ lose most of their nutritional value.
>
> *If they are cooked too long, vegetables will*

Separating the parts of the verb phrase, *will* and *lose*, disrupts the flow of the sentence.

> The books~~,~~ ~~because they were no longer useful,~~ ~~were discarded.~~
>
> *were discarded*

Separating the subject *books* from the verb *were discarded* is awkward.

> He bought ~~with his first paycheck~~ ~~a secondhand car.~~
>
> *a secondhand car*

Separating the verb *bought* from the object *a secondhand car* makes it hard to follow the thought.

### □ Splitting infinitives

A modifier placed between the *to* and verb of an infinitive (*to boldly go*) is known as a split infinitive. Once considered a serious writing error, split infinitives are no longer taboo. Few readers will object to a split infinitive in a clear and understandable sentence.

> Students need to *really* know the material to pass the exam.

Sometimes, however, split infinitives can be distracting to readers — especially when more than one word comes between the parts of the infinitive. In such cases, move the modifier before or after the infinitive, or reword the sentence, to remove the distracting interruption.

> Hitler expected the British to fairly quickly ~~surrender.~~
>
> *surrender*

▰ **EXERCISE 48.3**

Revise each of the following sentences by moving the disruptive modifier so that the sentence reads smoothly. Example:

*During the recent economic depression, many*
**Many unemployed college graduates** ~~during the recent economic~~
^
~~depression~~ **attended graduate school.**

1. Strong economic times have, statistics tell us, led to increases in the college dropout rate.

2. During finals an otherwise honest student, facing high levels of stress, may consider cheating to achieve a higher grade.

3. The director encouraged us to loudly and enthusiastically applaud after each scene.

4. Michael Jordan earned, at the pinnacle of his career, roughly $40 million a year in endorsements.

5. The stock exchange became, because of the sudden trading, a chaotic circus.

## 48c Revising dangling modifiers

Dangling modifiers *seem* to modify something that is implied but not actually present in the sentence and can be distracting for readers. Dangling modifiers frequently appear at the beginnings or ends of sentences.

| | |
|---|---|
| DANGLING | Driving nonstop, Salishan Lodge is two hours from Portland. |
| REVISED | Driving nonstop from Portland, you can reach Salishan Lodge in two hours. |
| REVISED | If you drive nonstop, Salishan Lodge is two hours from Portland. |

The preceding revised sentences illustrate two ways to fix a dangling modifier. Often you need to add a subject that the modifier clearly refers to. Sometimes, however, you have to turn the dangling modifier itself into a phrase or clause.

*our family gave*
▸ **Reluctantly, the hound** ~~was given~~ **away to a neighbor.**
^

In the original sentence, was the dog reluctant, or was someone else who is not mentioned reluctant?

*When he was*
▸ **As a young boy, his aunt told stories of her years as a country doctor.**
^

His aunt was never a young boy.

> ~~Thumbing through the magazine, my~~ eyes automatically noticed the  
>   My  
> perfume ads. as I was thumbing through the magazine.
>
> Eyes cannot thumb through a magazine.

> he was  
> Although a reserved and private man, everyone enjoyed his company.
>
> The original clause does not refer to *everyone* or *his company*. It needs its own subject and verb.

### EXERCISE 48.4

Revise each of the following sentences to correct the dangling phrase. Example:

a viewer gets  
**Watching television news, an impression ~~is given~~ of constant disaster.**

1. No longer obsessed with being the first to report a story, information is now presented as entertainment.
2. Trying to attract younger viewers, news is blended with comedy on late-night talk shows.
3. Highlighting local events, important international news stories may get overlooked.
4. Chosen for their looks, the journalistic credentials of newscasters may be weak.
5. As an interactive medium, people can find information online that reinforces views they already hold.

▼ ▼ ▼ ▼ ▼ ▼ ▼ ▼ ▼ ▼ ▼ ▼ ▼ ▼ ▼ ▼ ▼ ▼ ▼ ▼ ▼ ▼ ▼ ▼ ▼

## THINKING CRITICALLY ABOUT MODIFIERS

### Reading with an eye for modifiers

Look at the limiting modifier italicized in the following passage. Identify which word or words it modifies. Then try moving the modifier to some other spot in the sentence, and consider how the meaning of the sentence changes as a result.

> It was, among other things, the sort of railroad you would occasionally ride *just* for the hell of it, a higher existence into which you would escape unconsciously and without hesitation. —E. B. WHITE, "Progress and Change"

### Thinking about your own use of modifiers

As you examine two pages of a draft, check for clear and effective modifiers. Can you identify any misplaced, disruptive, or dangling modifiers? Using the guidelines in this chapter, revise as need be. Then look for patterns—in the kinds of modifiers you use and in any problems you have placing them. Make a note of what you find.

# CHAPTER 49

# Consistent and Complete Structures

YOU HEAR INCONSISTENT and incomplete structures all the time in conversation. For instance, during an interview with journalist Bill Moyers, Jon Stewart discussed the supposed objectivity of news reporting:

> But news has never been objective. It's always ... what does every newscast start with? "Our top stories tonight." That's a list. That's a subjective ... some editor made a decision: "Here's our top stories. Number one: there's a fire in the Bronx."

Stewart is talking casually, so some of his sentences begin one way but then move in another direction. The mixed structures pose no problem for the listener, but sentences such as these can be confusing in writing.

## 49a Revising faulty sentence structure

Faulty sentence structure poses problems for both writers and readers. A mixed structure results from beginning a sentence with one grammatical pattern and then switching to another one:

MIXED       The fact that I get up at 5:00 AM, a wake-up time that explains why I'm always tired in the evening.

The sentence starts out with a subject (*The fact*) followed by a dependent clause (*that I get up at 5:00 AM*). The sentence needs a predicate to complete the independent clause (37a), but instead it moves to another phrase (*a wake-up time*) followed by a dependent clause (*that explains why I'm always tired in the evening*), and what results is a fragment (Chapter 47).

REVISED       The fact that I get up at 5:00 AM explains why I'm always tired in the evening.

Deleting *a wake-up time that* changes the rest of the sentence into a predicate.

REVISED    I get up at 5:00 AM, a wake-up time that explains why
            I'm always tired in the evening.

Deleting *The fact that* turns the beginning of the sentence into an independent clause.
Here is another example of a mixed structure:

▷ **Because hope was the only thing left when Pandora finally closed up the**

**mythical box, explains why even today we never lose hope.**
                    ^

The dependent clause beginning with *Because* is followed by a predicate (beginning with *explains*) without a subject. Deleting *explains why* changes the predicate into an independent clause.

### Editing for consistency and completeness

* Check every confusing sentence to see whether it has a subject and a predicate. If not, revise as necessary. (**49a**) If you find both a subject and a predicate and you are still confused, see whether the subject and verb make sense together. If not, revise so that they do. (**49b**)
* Revise any *is when, is where,* and *the reason . . . is because* constructions. (**49b**)

              the practice of sending
    ▷ Spamming is ~~where companies send~~ electronic junk mail.
                    ^

* Check all comparisons for completeness. (**49e**)

              we like
    ▷ We like Marian better than Margaret.
                              ^

## 49b  Matching subjects and predicates

Another kind of faulty sentence structure, called faulty predication, occurs when a subject and predicate do not fit together grammatically or simply do not make sense together. Many cases of faulty predication result from using forms of *be* when another verb would be stronger.

▷ A characteristic ~~that I admire is~~ a generous person.

A person is not a characteristic.

                          require
▷ The rules of the corporation ~~expect~~ employees to be on time.
                                 ^

Rules cannot expect anything.

Constructions using *is when, is where,* and *the reason ... is because* are used frequently in informal contexts, but they may be inappropriate in formal academic writing because they use an adverb clause rather than a noun as their subject complement (37a).

- A stereotype is ~~when someone characterizes~~ a group *an unfair characterization of*~~. unfairly.~~

- A confluence is ~~where~~ *a place* two rivers join to form one.

- ~~The reason~~ I like to play soccer ~~is because~~ it provides aerobic exercise.

<hr>

### ⊿ EXERCISE 49.1

Revise each of the following sentences in two ways to make its structure consistent in grammar and meaning. Example:

*Because*
~~The fact that~~ our room was cold, we put a heater between our beds.

*led us to*
The fact that our room was cold/ we put a heater between our beds.

1. To enroll in film school being my primary goal, so I am always saving my money and watching for scholarship opportunities.
2. The reason air-pollution standards should not be relaxed is because many people would suffer.
3. By turning off the water when you brush your teeth, saving up to eight gallons of water per day.
4. Irony is when you expect one thing and get something else.
5. The best meal I've ever eaten was sitting by a river eating bread and cheese from a farmers' market.

<hr>

## 49c Completing elliptical constructions

Sometimes writers omit a word in a compound structure. They succeed with such an elliptical construction when the word omitted later in the compound is exactly the same as the word earlier in the compound.

- That bell belonged to the figure of Miss Duling as though it grew directly out of her right arm, as wings grew out of an angel or a tail [grew] out of the devil.　　　　　—EUDORA WELTY, *One Writer's Beginnings*

The omitted word, *grew*, is exactly the same verb that follows *it* and *wings* in the earlier parts of the compound. You should not omit a word that does not exactly match the word used in the other part(s) of the compound.

> His skills are weak, and his performance only ~~is~~ average.

The verb *is* does not match the verb in the other part of the compound (*are*), so the writer needs to include it.

## 49d Checking for missing words

The best way to catch inadvertent omissions is to proofread carefully, reading each sentence slowly — and aloud.

> The new Web site makes it easier to look ~~at~~ and choose from the company's inventory.

## 49e Making complete comparisons

When you compare two or more things, the comparison must be complete, logically consistent, and clear.

> I was embarrassed because my parents were so different. ~~from my friends' parents.~~

Different from what? Adding *from my friends' parents* completes the comparison.

UNCLEAR     Aneil likes his brother more than his sister.

Does Aneil like his brother more than his sister does — or does he like his brother more than he likes his sister?

CLEAR     Aneil likes his brother more *than his sister does.*

CLEAR     Aneil likes his brother more *than he likes his sister.*

 MULTI-
LINGUAL **DECIDING WHICH ARTICLES TO USE**

Do you say "I'm working on *a* paper" or "I'm working on *the* paper"? Deciding when to use the articles *a*, *an*, and *the* can be challenging for multilingual writers since many languages have nothing directly comparable to them. See 38c for help using articles.

**EXERCISE 49.2**

Revise each of the following sentences to eliminate any inappropriate elliptical constructions; to make comparisons complete, logically consistent, and clear; and to supply any other omitted words that are necessary for meaning. Example:

> is
> **Most of the candidates are bright, and one brilliant.**
> ^

1. Convection ovens cook more quickly and with less power.
2. Argentina and Peru were colonized by Spain, and Brazil by Portugal.
3. She argued that children are even more important for men than women.
4. Do you think the barbecue sauce in Memphis is better than North Carolina?
5. The equipment in our new warehouse is guaranteed to last longer than our current facility.

▼ ▼ ▼ ▼ ▼ ▼ ▼ ▼ ▼ ▼ ▼ ▼ ▼ ▼ ▼ ▼ ▼ ▼ ▼ ▼ ▼ ▼ ▼ ▼ ▼ ▼

## THINKING CRITICALLY ABOUT CONSISTENCY AND COMPLETENESS

Read over three or four paragraphs from a draft or completed essay you have written recently. Check for mixed sentences and incomplete or missing structures. Revise the paragraphs to correct any problems you find. If you find any, do you recognize any patterns? If so, make a note of them for future reference.

# PART 10
# Style

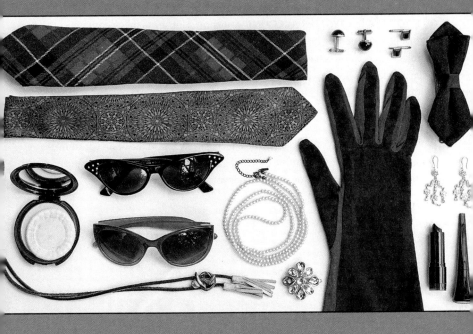

# CHAPTER 50

# Concise Writing

**I**F YOU HAVE A TWITTER ACCOUNT, you know a lot about being concise — that is, about getting messages across without wasting words — since Twitter limits writers to 140 characters. Recently, *New York Times* editor Bill Keller started a discussion by tweeting, "Twitter makes you stupid. Discuss." That little comment drew a large number of responses, including one from his wife that read, "I don't know if Twitter makes you stupid, but it's making you late for dinner. Come home."

No matter how you feel about the effects of Twitter on the brain (or stomach!), you can make any writing more effective by using clear structures and choosing words that convey exactly what you mean to say.

---

**CONNECT:** How can you identify the essentials of a piece of writing? **7d, 50a**

**CREATE:** Choose a text (such as a blog post, a film, or a scholarly article) on a topic of interest to you. Summarize the contents in a tweet of no more than 140 characters.

**REFLECT:** Write or record a reflection about how you decided what information to keep.

---

## 50a Eliminating unnecessary words

Sometimes writers say that something is large *in size* or red *in color* or that two ingredients should be combined *together*. The italicized words are unnecessarily repetitive; delete such redundant words.

▶ ~~Compulsory~~ attendance at assemblies is required.

Attendance ^

▶ Many different forms of hazing occur, such as physical abuse and

mental abuse.

## ☐ Deleting meaningless modifiers

Many modifiers are so overused that they have little meaning.

**MEANINGLESS MODIFIERS**

absolutely, awfully, definitely, fine, great, interesting, quite, really, very

## ☐ Replacing wordy phrases

Wordy phrases can be reduced to a word or two with no loss in meaning.

| WORDY | CONCISE |
|---|---|
| at all times | always |
| at that point in time | then |
| at the present time | now, today |
| due to the fact that | because |
| for the purpose of | for |
| in order to | to |
| in spite of the fact that | although |
| in the event that | if |

---

**QUICK HELP**

### Editing for conciseness

- Look for redundant words. If you are unsure about a word, read the sentence without it; if the meaning is not affected, leave the word out. **(50a)**
- Replace wordy phrases with a single word. Instead of *because of the fact that*, try *because*. **(50a)**
- Simplify grammatical structures whenever possible. For example, you might rewrite a sentence to make it more specific or combine two sentences that have the same subject or predicate. **(50b)**
- Identify all uses of *it is*, *there is*, and *there are*, and delete any that do not give your writing necessary emphasis. **(50b)**
- Note noun phrases whose meaning could be expressed by a verb, and try revising using the verb. **(50b)**
- Look for sentences that use the passive voice without a good reason. If the active voice would make the sentence livelier, clearer, or more concise, rewrite the sentence. **(50c)**

---

# 50b Simplifying sentence structure

Using simple grammatical structures will often strengthen your sentences considerably.

▶ Hurricane Katrina, ~~which was certainly~~ one of the most powerful storms
ever to hit the Gulf Coast, caused damage . *widespread* ~~to a very wide area.~~

Deleting unnecessary words and replacing five words with one tightens the sentence
and makes it easier to read.

▶ When ~~she was~~ questioned about her previous job, she seemed
nervous, *and* ~~She also~~ tried to change the subject.

Combining two sentences produces one concise sentence.

☐ Avoiding unnecessary *there is, there are, it is, it seems* constructions

In general, do not use *there is, there are, it is, it seems,* or similar phrases unless you
are introducing an idea to give it extra emphasis:

▶ It is for us, the living, to ensure that We the People shall become the
powerful.                    —JUNE JORDAN, "Inside America"

Here, *it is* slows down the opening of the sentence and sets up a formal rhythm
that emphasizes what follows. Often, however, writers merely overuse expletives.
Note how the following sentences are strengthened by deleting the expletives:

▶ *Many* ~~There are many people who~~ fear success because they do not believe
they deserve it.

▶ *Presidential* ~~It is necessary for presidential~~ candidates ~~to~~ *must* perform well on television.

☐ Avoiding wordy noun forms

Forming nouns from verbs, a process sometimes called *nominalization,* can help
make prose more concise — for example, using *abolition* instead of *the process of
abolishing* — but it can also make a sentence wordy and hard to read. Using noun
phrases when verbs will do can bury the action of a sentence and force the writer
to use weak verbs and too many prepositional phrases. Too often, writers change
verbs to nouns not to simplify a complex explanation but to make an idea sound
more complex than it is.

▶ The firm is now *assessing* ~~engaged in an assessment of~~ its procedures for
*developing* ~~the development of~~ new products.

The original sentence sounds pretentious, and the noun phrases cloud the message. In contrast, the edited version is clear and forceful.

## 50c   Using active and passive voice appropriately

In addition to choosing strong, precise verbs, you can help make your prose concise by using those verbs appropriately in active or passive voice (39g). Look at the passive voice in the following passage:

▷   [John F. Kennedy] died of a wound in the brain **caused** by a rifle bullet that **was fired** at him as he was riding through downtown Dallas in a motorcade.
   Vice President Lyndon Baines Johnson, who was riding in the third car behind Mr. Kennedy's, **was sworn in** as the 36th President of the United States 99 minutes after Mr. Kennedy's death.          —TOM WICKER, *New York Times*

As this passage indicates, the passive voice works effectively in certain situations: when the performer is unknown, unwilling to be identified, or less important than the recipient of the action. In general, however, try to use the active voice whenever possible. Because the passive voice diverts attention from the performer of an action and because it is usually wordier than the active voice, using it excessively makes for dull and difficult reading.

   Edit an unnecessary passive construction to make it active.

▷   In ~~Gower's~~ research, ~~it was~~ found that pythons often dwell in trees.
   his ^           Gower ^

### ▰ EXERCISE 50.1

Look at the following sentences, which use the passive voice. Then rewrite each sentence in the active voice, and decide which version you prefer and why. Example:

   I                                you
   ~~You are~~ hereby relieved of your duties. ~~by me.~~
   ^                                ^           ^

1. Mistakes were made.
2. The chair's address was interrupted by hecklers.
3. Numerous reports of loud music from bars and shouting neighbors were taken by the city's new noise complaint hotline.
4. The violin solo was performed by an eight-year-old.
5. In a patient with celiac disease, intestinal damage can be caused by the body's immunological response to gluten.

◢ **EXERCISE 50.2**

Revise the following paragraph to eliminate unnecessary words, nominalizations, expletives, and inappropriate use of the passive voice.

As dogs became tamed and domesticated by humans over many thousands of years, the canine species underwent an evolution into hundreds of breeds designed to perform particular, specific tasks, such as pulling sleds and guarding sheep. Over time, there was a decreased need for many breeds. For example, as humans evolved from hunter-gatherers into farmers, it was no longer at all necessary for them to own hunting dogs. Later, as farming societies became industrialized, there was a disappearance of herd animals, and fewer shepherds watching sheep meant that there were fewer sheepdogs. But by this time humans had grown accustomed to dogs' companionship, and breeding continued. Today, most dogs are kept by their owners simply as companions, but some dogs still do the work they were intentionally bred for, such as following a scent, guarding a home, or leading the blind.

▼ ▼ ▼ ▼ ▼ ▼ ▼ ▼ ▼ ▼ ▼ ▼ ▼ ▼ ▼ ▼ ▼ ▼ ▼ ▼ ▼ ▼ ▼ ▼ ▼ ▼ ▼

## THINKING CRITICALLY ABOUT CONCISE WRITING

### Reading with an eye for conciseness

Bring two pieces of writing to class: one that is not just short, but concise—wasting no words but conveying its meaning clearly—and one that uses too many words to say too little. Bring both pieces to class to compare with those chosen by your classmates.

### Thinking about your own writing

Find two or three paragraphs you have written recently, and study them with an eye for empty words. Using 50a for guidance, eliminate meaningless words such as *quite* and *very*. Compare notes with one or two classmates to see what empty words, if any, you tend to use. Finally, make a note of the empty words you use, and try to avoid them in the future.

# CHAPTER 51

# Coordination and Subordination

**I**N SPEECH, people tend to use *and* and *so* as all-purpose connectors.

> He enjoys psychology, and the course requires a lot of work.

The meaning of this sentence may be perfectly clear in speech, which provides clues through voice, facial expressions, and gestures. But in writing, the sentence could have multiple meanings, including these:

> Although he enjoys psychology, the course requires a lot of work.

> He enjoys psychology even though the course requires a lot of work.

Coordinating conjunctions like *and* give ideas equal weight, whereas subordinating conjunctions like *although* emphasize one idea over another.

---

**CONNECT:** What can you do to use subordination for special emphasis in your sentences? **36g, 37e, 51b**

**CREATE:** Rewrite a post from a blog you enjoy, adding subordination to at least three sentences.

**REFLECT:** Write or record a reflection explaining how you decided what material to subordinate and how the effect of your revision is different from the effect of the original.

---

## 51a   Relating equal ideas

When you want to give equal emphasis to different ideas in a sentence, link them with a coordinating conjunction (*and, but, for, nor, or, so, yet*) or a semicolon.

▶ **They acquired horses, and their ancient nomadic spirit was suddenly free of the ground.** —N. SCOTT MOMADAY, *The Way to Rainy Mountain*

---

▶ **There is perfect freedom in the mountains, but it belongs to the eagle and the elk, the badger and the bear.**

—N. SCOTT MOMADAY, *The Way to Rainy Mountain*

---

**QUICK HELP**

### Editing for coordination and subordination

How do your ideas flow from one sentence to another? Do they connect smoothly and clearly? Are the more important ideas given more emphasis than the less important ones? These guidelines will help you edit with such questions in mind.

- Look for strings of short sentences that might be combined to join related ideas. **(51a)**

  but                    it
  ▶ The report was short, ~~It was persuasive~~, ~~It~~ changed my mind.

- If you often link ideas with the conjunctions *and*, *but*, and *so*, are the linked ideas equally important? If not, edit to subordinate the less important ones. **(51b)**

- Are the most important ideas in independent clauses? If not, edit so that they are. **(51b)**

  Even though the
  ▶ ~~The~~ report was short, ~~even though~~ it changed my mind.

---

Coordination can help to make explicit the relationship between two separate ideas.

forced
▶ **My son watches *The Simpsons* religiously, ~~Forced~~ to choose, he would**

**probably take Lisa Simpson over his sister.**

Connecting these two sentences with a semicolon strengthens the connection between two closely related ideas.

When you connect ideas in a sentence, make sure that the relationship between the ideas is clear.

but
▶ **Surfing the Internet is a common way to spend leisure time, ~~and~~ it**

**should not replace human contact.**

What does being a common form of leisure have to do with replacing human contact? Changing *and* to *but* better relates the two ideas.

---

◻ **Using coordination for special effect**

Coordination can create special effects, as in a passage by Carl Sandburg describing the American reaction to Abraham Lincoln's assassination.

Men tried to talk about it and the words failed and they came back to silence.

To say nothing was best.

Lincoln was dead.

Was there anything more to say?

Yes, they would go through the motions of grief and they would take part in a national funeral and a ceremony of humiliation and abasement and tears.

But words were no help.

Lincoln was dead. —CARL SANDBURG, *Abraham Lincoln: The War Years*

Everything in the passage is grammatically equal, flattened out by the pain and shock of the death. In this way, the sentence structure and grammar mirror the dazed state of the populace. The short sentences and independent clauses are almost like sobs that illustrate the thought of the first sentence, that "the words failed."

### EXERCISE 51.1

Using coordination to signal equal importance or to create special effects, combine and revise the following twelve short sentences into several longer and more effective ones. Add or delete words as necessary.

The auditorium was filled with people. The sea of faces did not intimidate me. I had decided to appear in a musical with my local community theater group. There was no going back now. I reminded myself of how I had gotten here. It took hard work. I refused to doubt my abilities. Besides, the director and her staff had held auditions. I had read the heroine's part. I had sung a song. They had chosen me for the role. I was untrained. My skills as an actor would now be judged publicly. I felt ready to rise to the challenge.

## 51b  Distinguishing main ideas

Subordination allows you to distinguish major points from minor points or to bring supporting details into a sentence. If, for instance, you put your main idea in an independent clause, you might then put any less significant ideas in dependent clauses, phrases, or even single words. The following sentence highlights the subordinated point:

> **Mrs. Viola Cullinan was a plump woman who lived in a three-bedroom house somewhere behind the post office.**
>
> —MAYA ANGELOU, "My Name Is Margaret"

The dependent clause adds important information about Mrs. Cullinan, but it is subordinate to the independent clause.

Notice that the choice of what to subordinate rests with the writer and depends on the intended meaning. Angelou might have given the same basic information differently:

▶ **Mrs. Viola Cullinan, a plump woman, lived in a three-bedroom house somewhere behind the post office.**

Subordinating the information about Mrs. Cullinan's size to that about her house would suggest a slightly different meaning, of course. As a writer, you must think carefully about what you want to emphasize and must subordinate information accordingly.

Subordination also establishes logical relationships among different ideas. These relationships are often specified by subordinating conjunctions.

SOME COMMON SUBORDINATING CONJUNCTIONS

| | | |
|---|---|---|
| after | if | though |
| although | in order that | unless |
| as | once | until |
| as if | since | when |
| because | so that | where |
| before | than | while |
| even though | that | |

The following sentence highlights the subordinate clause and italicizes the subordinating word:

▶ **She usually rested her smile until late afternoon *when* her women friends dropped in and Miss Glory, the cook, served them cold drinks on the closed-in porch.** —MAYA ANGELOU, "My Name Is Margaret"

Using too many coordinate structures can be monotonous and can make it hard for readers to recognize the most important ideas. Subordinating lesser ideas can help highlight the main ideas.

▶ **Many people check email in the evening, and so they turn on the**
   Though they
   **computer. ~~They~~ may intend to respond only to urgent messages, a friend**
                                                    which
   **sends a link to a blog post, ~~and~~ they decide to read ~~it~~ for just a short**
            Eventually,
   **while~~,~~. ~~and~~ they get engrossed in Facebook or Twitter, and they end up**

   **spending the whole evening in front of the screen.**

## ☐ Determining what to subordinate

> *Although our*
> ~~Our~~ new boss can be difficult, ~~although~~ she has revived and maybe even
>   ^
> saved the division.

The editing puts the more important information—that the new boss has saved part of the company—in an independent clause and subordinates the rest.

## ☐ Avoiding excessive subordination

When too many subordinate clauses are strung together, readers may have trouble keeping track of the main idea expressed in the independent clause.

**TOO MUCH SUBORDINATION**

> Philip II sent the Spanish Armada to conquer England, which was ruled by Elizabeth, who had executed Mary because she was plotting to overthrow Elizabeth, who was a Protestant, whereas Mary and Philip were Roman Catholics.

**REVISED**

> Philip II sent the Spanish Armada to conquer England, which was ruled by Elizabeth, a Protestant. She had executed Mary, a Roman Catholic like Philip, because Mary was plotting to overthrow her.

Putting the facts about Elizabeth executing Mary into an independent clause makes key information easier to recognize.

You can employ a variety of grammatical structures — not merely dependent clauses — to subordinate a less important element within a sentence:

> The parks report was persuasively written. It contained five typed pages. [no subordination]
> The parks report, *which contained five typed pages*, was persuasively written. [dependent clause]
> The parks report, *containing five typed pages*, was persuasively written. [participial phrase]
> The *five-page* parks report was persuasively written. [adjective]
> The parks report, *five typed pages*, was persuasively written. [appositive]
> The parks report, *its five pages neatly typed*, was persuasively written. [absolute]

### ▲ EXERCISE 51.2

Combine each of the following sets of sentences into one sentence that uses subordination to signal the relationships among ideas. Example:

> **I was looking through the cupboard.**
> **I noticed the cookies were gone.**
> **This snack is a favorite of my roommate.**
>
> *While I was looking through the cupboard, I noticed that the cookies, one of my roommate's favorite snacks, were gone.*

1. The original *Star Trek* television show ran from 1966 to 1969.
   It was critically acclaimed.
   It had low ratings and was canceled by the network.
2. Athena was the goddess of wisdom.
   Ancient Greeks relied on Athena to protect the city of Athens.
   Athens was named in Athena's honor.
3. Harry Potter is a fictional wizard.
   He turns eleven years old.
   He is taken to Hogwarts School of Witchcraft and Wizardry.
4. Flappers seemed rebellious to their parents' generation.
   They broke with 1920s social conventions.
   They cut their hair short and smoked in public.
5. Skateboarding originated in Venice, California.
   The time was the mid-seventies.
   There was a drought.
   The swimming pools were empty.

□ **Using subordination for special effect**

Some particularly fine examples of subordination come from Martin Luther King Jr. In the following passage, he piles up dependent clauses beginning with *when* to build up suspense for his main statement, given in the independent clause at the end:

> Perhaps it is easy for those who have never felt the stinging darts of segregation to say, "Wait." But *when* you have seen vicious mobs lynch your mothers and fathers at will and drown your sisters and brothers at whim; *when* you have seen hate-filled policemen curse, kick, and even kill your black brothers and sisters; . . . *when* you have to concoct an answer for a five-year-old son who is asking: "Daddy, why do white people treat colored people so mean?"; *when* you take a cross-country drive and find it necessary to sleep night after night

in the uncomfortable corners of your automobile because no motel will accept you; . . . *when* your first name becomes "nigger," your middle name becomes "boy" (however old you are) and your last name becomes "John," and your wife and mother are never given the respected title "Mrs."; . . . *when* you are forever fighting a degenerating sense of "nobodiness" — then you will understand why we find it difficult to wait.

—MARTIN LUTHER KING JR., "Letter from Birmingham Jail"

A dependent clause can also create an ironic effect if it somehow undercuts the independent clause. A master of this technique, Mark Twain once opened a paragraph with this sentence:

▶ **Always obey your parents,** *when they are present.*

—MARK TWAIN, "Advice to Youth"

▼ ▼ ▼ ▼ ▼ ▼ ▼ ▼ ▼ ▼ ▼ ▼ ▼ ▼ ▼ ▼ ▼ ▼ ▼ ▼ ▼ ▼ ▼ ▼ ▼

## THINKING CRITICALLY ABOUT COORDINATION AND SUBORDINATION

### Reading with an eye for coordination and subordination

Read over the first draft of "All-Powerful Coke" (see p. 59), paying special attention to the coordination and subordination. Do you notice any patterns—is there some of each? more of one than the other? Identify the coordination and subordination in one paragraph. Are they used appropriately? If not, revise the paragraph by following the guidelines in this chapter.

### Thinking about your own use of coordination and subordination

Analyze two paragraphs from one of your drafts. Do the independent clauses contain the main ideas? How many dependent clauses do you find? Should the ideas in the dependent clauses be subordinate to those in the independent clauses? Revise the paragraphs to use coordination and subordination effectively. What conclusions can you draw about your use of coordination and subordination?

# Sentence Variety

I N ONE COLLEGE CLASSROOM, a peer-response group worked on an essay for almost an hour, but its overall effect still seemed boring. Finally, one student exclaimed, "These sentences all look the same!"

And they were: every sentence in the essay was about the same length, and every sentence started with the subject. The group went to work again, shortening some sentences and revising others to create new rhythms. With the resulting sentence variety, the essay took on new life; it flowed.

> **CONNECT:** What about your sentences would you most like to improve? **Chapter 52, 53a**
>
> **CREATE:** Write or record a brief memo to yourself in which you describe the improvements you would like to see in your sentences.
>
> **REFLECT:** Do the "Thinking Critically about Sentence Variety" exercise at the end of this chapter.

## 52a  Varying sentence length

Deciding how and when to vary sentence length is not always easy. Is there a "just right" length for a particular sentence or idea? The answer depends on, among other things, the writer's purpose, intended audience, and topic. A children's story, for instance, may call for mostly short sentences, whereas an article on nuclear disarmament may call for considerably longer ones.

Although a series of short or long sentences can sometimes be effective, alternating sentence length is usually the best approach in formal writing. For example, after one or more long sentences with complex ideas or images, the punch of a short sentence can be dramatic:

▶ **The fire of, I think, five machine-guns was pouring upon us, and there was a series of heavy crashes caused by the Fascists flinging bombs over their own parapet in the most idiotic manner. It was intensely dark.**

—GEORGE ORWELL, *Homage to Catalonia*

Similarly, try using a long sentence after several short ones.

 *Sith.* **What kind of a word is that? It sounds to me like the noise that emerges when you block one nostril and blow through the other, but to George Lucas it is a name that trumpets evil.** —ANTHONY LANE

---

**QUICK HELP**

### Editing for sentence variety

- Check sentence *length* by counting the words in each sentence. If the difference between the longest and the shortest sentences is fairly small—say, five words or fewer—try revising some sentences to create greater variety. Should two or more short sentences be combined because they deal with closely related ideas? Should a long sentence be split up because it contains too many important ideas? **(52a)**
- Look at sentence *openings*. If most sentences start with a subject, try recasting some to begin with a transition, a phrase, or a dependent clause. **(52b)**
- Vary *types* of sentences to make your writing more interesting. Do you use simple, compound, complex, and compound-complex sentences—or does one type predominate? Would a particular declarative sentence be more effective as a command or question or exclamation? Could you use a periodic or cumulative sentence for special effect? **(52c)**

---

### ◢ EXERCISE 52.1

The following paragraph can be improved by varying sentence length. Read it aloud to get a sense of how it sounds. Then revise it, creating some short, emphatic sentences and combining other sentences to create more effective long sentences. Add words or change punctuation as you need to.

> Before planting a tree, a gardener needs to choose a good location and dig a deep enough hole. The location should have the right kind of soil, sufficient drainage, and enough light for the type of tree chosen. The hole should be slightly deeper than the root-ball and about twice as wide. The gardener must unwrap the root-ball, for even burlap, which is biodegradable, may be treated with chemicals that will eventually damage the roots. The roots may have grown into a compact ball if the tree has been in a pot for some time, and they should be separated or cut apart in this case. The gardener should set the root-ball into the hole and then begin to fill the hole with loose dirt. After filling the hole completely, he or she should make sure to water the tree thoroughly. New plantings require extra water and extra care for about three years before they are well rooted.

## 52b Varying sentence openings

If sentence after sentence begins with a subject, a passage may become monotonous or even hard to read.

> The way football and basketball are played is as interesting as the
> players. ~~Football~~ is a game of precision/ ~~Each~~ play is diagrammed
> to accomplish a certain goal. Basketball, is a game of endurance.
> ~~A~~ basketball game looks like a track meet/; ~~The~~ team that drops of
> exhaustion first loses.

*Handwritten annotations: "Because football" above struck-through "Football"; "each" above struck-through "Each"; "however," above "Basketball,"; "In fact, a" above struck-through "A"; "the" above struck-through "The"*

The editing adds variety by using a subordinating word (*Because*) and transitions (*however* and *In fact*) and by linking sentences. Varying sentence openings prevents the passage from seeming to jerk or lurch along.

You can add variety to your sentence openings by using transitions, various kinds of phrases, and introductory dependent clauses.

☐ Using transitional expressions for variety

See how transitions bring variety and clarity to this passage.

> In order to be alert Friday morning in New York, I planned to take the shuttle from Washington Thursday night. *On Thursday morning* it began to snow in Washington and to snow even harder in New York. *By mid-afternoon* I decided not to risk the shuttle and caught a train to New York. *Seven hours later* the train completed its three-hour trip. I arrived at Penn Station to find a city shut down by the worst blizzard since 1947.
> —LINDA ELLERBEE, "And So It Goes"

Here the transitional words establish chronology as well as help carry readers smoothly through the paragraph. (For more on transitions, see 5f.)

☐ Using phrases for variety

Prepositional, verbal, and absolute phrases can also provide variety in sentence openings.

PREPOSITIONAL PHRASES

> **Before dawn,** tired commuters drink their first cups of coffee.

> **From a few scraps of wood in the Middle Ages to a precisely carved, electrified instrument in our times,** the guitar has gone through uncounted changes.

VERBAL PHRASES

> **Frustrated by the delays,** the driver shouted at his car radio.

> **To qualify for the finals,** a speller must win a regional championship.

ABSOLUTE PHRASES

▶ **Our hopes for victory shattered,** we started home.

In general, use a comma after such phrases whenever they open a sentence (54b).

## ☐ Using dependent clauses for variety

Dependent clauses are another way to open a sentence.

▶ **While the boss sat on his tractor,** I was down in a ditch, pounding in stakes.

▶ **What they want** is a place to call home.

In general, use a comma after adverb clauses whenever they open a sentence (54b).

# 52c Varying sentence types

In addition to using different lengths and openings, you can use different types of sentences. Sentences can be classified grammatically and functionally (as discussed in Chapter 37) as well as rhetorically.

## ☐ Varying grammatical types

Grammatically, sentences fall into four categories — simple, compound, complex, and compound-complex — based on the number of independent and dependent clauses they contain (37f). Varying your sentences among these grammatical types can help you create readable, effective prose.

## ☐ Varying functional types

In terms of function, sentences are declarative (making a statement), interrogative (asking a question), imperative (giving a command), or exclamatory (expressing strong feeling). Most sentences are declarative, but occasionally a command, a question, or an exclamation may be appropriate.

COMMAND

▶ Coal-burning plants undoubtedly harm the environment in various ways; for example, they contribute to acid rain. **But consider the alternatives.**

QUESTION

▶ **Why would sixteen middle-aged people try to backpack thirty-seven miles?** At this point, I was not at all sure.

EXCLAMATION

▷ **Divorcés! They were everywhere! Sometimes he felt like a new member of an enormous club, the Divorcés of America, that he had never before even heard of.**

## ☐ Varying rhetorical types

By highlighting sentence endings and beginnings, periodic and cumulative sentences can create strong effects.

### Periodic sentences

Periodic sentences postpone the main idea (usually in an independent clause) until the very end of the sentence. They are especially useful for creating tension or building toward a climactic, surprise, or inspirational ending.

▷ **Even though large tracts of Europe and many old and famous states have fallen or may fall into the grasp of the Gestapo and all the odious apparatus of Nazi rule, we shall not flag or fail.**  —WINSTON CHURCHILL

Look at the following sentence and its revision to see how periodic order can provide emphasis:

ORIGINAL SENTENCE

The nations of the world have no alternative but coexistence because another world war would be unwinnable and because total destruction would certainly occur.

REVISED AS A PERIODIC SENTENCE

Because another world war would be unwinnable and because total destruction would certainly occur, the nations of the world have no alternative but coexistence.

Nothing is wrong with the first sentence. But to emphasize the idea in the independent clause — *no alternative but coexistence* — the writer chose to revise it using the periodic pattern.

### Cumulative sentences

Cumulative sentences, which begin with an independent clause and then add details in phrases and in dependent clauses (as does the preceding sentence labeled *original*), are far more common than periodic sentences. They are useful when you want to provide both immediate understanding of the main idea and a great deal of supporting detail.

▷ **I can still see her, a tiny nun with a sharp pink nose, confidently drawing a dead-straight horizontal line like a highway across the blackboard,**

**flourishing her chalk at the end of it, her veil flapping out behind her as she turned back to class.** —KITTY BURNS FLOREY

### EXERCISE 52.2

Revise each of the following sentences twice, once as a periodic sentence and once as a cumulative sentence.

1. Obviously not understanding reporters, the politician did not know their names, did not answer their questions, and did not read their stories.

2. Able to think only of my mother's surgery the next morning, I could not even eat my dinner, much less get any sleep, nor could I do my homework.

## THINKING CRITICALLY ABOUT SENTENCE VARIETY

### Reading with an eye for sentence variety

Read something by an author you admire. Analyze two paragraphs for sentence length, opening, and type. Compare the sentence variety in these paragraphs with that in one of your paragraphs. What similarities or differences do you recognize, and what conclusions can you draw about sentence variety?

### Thinking about your own sentence variety

Choose a piece of writing you have recently completed, and analyze two or three pages for sentence variety. Note sentence length, opening, and type (grammatical, functional, and rhetorical). Choose a passage you think can be improved for variety, and make those revisions.

# CHAPTER 53

# Memorable Prose

GREAT WRITERS MAY HAVE A GENIUS for choosing the perfect words, but with practice, anyone can learn to write more memorable prose. When you notice a piece of writing that you admire — whether it's an advertisement, a magazine article, dialogue from a film, or a friend's Facebook status update — reflect on what the writing does well and try to understand how it achieves its goals.

---

**CONNECT:** How can you use strong verbs to make a presentation memorable? **17b, 53b**

**CREATE:** Choose a paragraph from a piece of your writing that you want to present to a listening audience, and revise it to replace every use of *be, do,* or *have* with a more vivid word. Ask a friend or classmate to listen to both paragraphs and provide feedback.

**REFLECT:** Record the revised paragraph along with your comments on how the changes affected the response to your writing.

---

## 53a Writing emphatic sentences

When you speak, you achieve emphasis by raising your voice or stressing an important word or phrase. And much of the writing you see — in advertisements, on Web sites, in magazines — gains emphasis in similar fashion, with color or bold type, for instance. Even though academic writing can't always rely on such graphic devices, writers use other techniques to emphasize parts of their sentences.

---

QUICK HELP

### Editing for memorable prose

- Identify the words you want to emphasize. If you've buried those words in the middle of a sentence, edit the sentence to change their position. The end and the beginning are generally the most emphatic. **(53a)** ▶

Editing for memorable prose, continued

- Note any sentences that include a series of words, phrases, or clauses. Arrange the items in the series in climactic order, with the most important item last. **(53a)**
- Underline all verbs, and look to see whether you rely too much on *be*, *do*, and *have*. If so, try to substitute more specific verbs. **(53b)**

☐ **Using closing and opening positions for emphasis**

When you read a sentence, you usually remember the ending. This part of the sentence moves the writing forward by providing new information, as in the following example:

▷ **Employers today expect college graduates to have excellent writing skills.**

A less emphatic but still important position in a sentence is the opening, which often connects the new sentence with what has come before.

▷ **Today's employers want a college-educated workforce that can communicate well. Excellent writing skills are high on the list of qualifications.**

If you place relatively unimportant information in the memorable closing position of a sentence, you may undercut what you want to emphasize or give more emphasis to the closing words than you intend.

Last month, she                                                    $500,000.
▷ **She gave $500,000 to the school capital campaign last month.**
   ^                                                   ^
Moving *$500,000* to the end of the sentence emphasizes the amount.

☐ **Using climactic order**

Presenting ideas in climactic order means arranging them in order of increasing importance or drama so that your writing builds to a climax. By saving its most dramatic item for last, a sentence can make its point more forcefully.

▷ **After they've finished with the pantry, the medicine cabinet, and the attic, [neat people] will throw out the red geranium (too many leaves), sell the dog (too many fleas), and send the children off to boarding school (too many scuffmarks on the hardwood floors).**
                        —SUSANNE BRITT, "Neat People vs. Sloppy People"

                              "appetizer ribs" and "entrée ribs," with
▷ **The barbecue stand's menu offered "more ribs" for dessert.**
                        ^                                    ^
**after "appetizer ribs" and "entrée ribs."**

The original version of the preceding sentence fails to achieve strong emphasis; the editing provides climactic order.

### EXERCISE 53.1

Revise each of the following sentences to highlight what you take to be the main or most important ideas. Example:

His video soon went viral, bringing in increased advertising revenue, ~~and~~ ^accolades from everyone he knew on Facebook,^ an offer to edit a feature film/. ~~and accolades from everyone he knew on Facebook.~~

1. The president persuaded the American people, his staff, and Congress.
2. We can expect a decade of record-breaking tropical storms and hurricanes, if meteorologists are correct in their predictions.
3. From the sightseeing boat, we saw a whale dive toward us and then, before crashing its tail on the waves, lift itself out of the water.
4. I did not realize that living in the city would mean eating canned soup every night, selling my car, and losing half my closet space.
5. Jake experienced several side effects from the medication, including dizziness, severe abdominal pain, and dry mouth.

## 53b Choosing strong verbs

Verbs serve as the real workhorses of our language. Look, for instance, at the strong, precise verbs in the following passage:

> A fire engine, out for a trial spin, **roared** past Emerson's house, hot with readiness for public duty. Over the barn roofs the martens **dipped** and **chittered**. A swarthy daughter of an asparagus grower, in culottes, shirt, and bandanna, **pedalled** past on her bicycle.      —E. B. WHITE, "Walden"

If White had used more general verbs — such as *drove, flew, called,* and *rode* — the passage would be much less effective. With White's verbs, however, readers can hear the roar of the fire engine, see the martens swooping downward and hear them chirping shrilly, and feel the young woman pushing on the pedals of her bicycle.

Some of the most commonly used verbs in English — especially *be, do,* and *have* — carry little or no sense of specific action. Try not to overuse them in situations where precise verbs would be more effective. Look at how much stronger the following sentences become when precise verbs are used:

○ Malnutrition ~~is harmful to~~ children's development.
*stunts and distorts*

○ Sidewalk artists offered to do my portrait in ten minutes.
*sketch*

○ The young marines had basic training at Parris Island.
*sweated through*

# 53c  Using special effects

Contemporary movies often succeed on the basis of their special effects. Similarly, special effects like repetition, antithesis, and inverted word order can animate your prose and help make it memorable.

## ☐ Using repetition for emphasis

Carefully used, repetition of sounds, words, phrases, or other grammatical constructions serves as a powerful stylistic device. Orators have long known its power. Here is a famous use of repetition from one of British prime minister Winston Churchill's addresses to the British people during World War II:

○ We shall not flag or fail, we shall go on to the end. We shall fight in France, we shall fight on the seas and oceans, we shall fight with growing confidence and growing strength in the air, we shall defend our island, whatever the cost may be; we shall fight on the beaches, . . . we shall fight in the fields and in the streets, . . . we shall never surrender.

—WINSTON CHURCHILL

In this passage, Churchill uses the constant hammering of *we shall* accompanied by the repetition of *f* sounds ( *flag, fail, fight, France, confidence, defend, fields*) to strengthen his listeners' resolve.

Though you may not be a prime minister, you can use repetition to equally good effect. Here is another example:

○ So my dream date turned into a nightmare. Where was the quiet, considerate, caring guy I thought I had met? In his place appeared this jerk. He postured, he preened, he bragged, he bellowed. He practically brayed — just like the donkey he so much reminded me of.

Be careful, however, to use repetition only for a deliberate purpose.

## ☐ Using antithesis to emphasize contrast

Antithesis is the use of parallel structures to highlight contrast or opposition (see Chapter 45). Like other uses of parallelism, antithesis provides a pleasing rhythm that calls readers' attention to the contrast, often in a startling or amusing way.

▶ Love is an ideal thing, marriage a real thing.

▶ The congregation didn't think much of the new preacher, and what the new preacher thought of the congregation she didn't wish to say.

▶ It is a sin to believe evil of others — but it is not a mistake.

—H. L. MENCKEN

### EXERCISE 53.2

Using one of the preceding examples as a guide, create a sentence of your own that uses antithesis. You might begin by thinking of opposites you could build on: hope/despair, good/evil, fire/ice. Or you might begin with a topic you want to write about: success, greed, generosity, and so on.

## ☐ Using inverted word order

Writers may invert the usual word order, such as putting the verb before the subject or the object before the subject and verb, to create surprise or to emphasize a particular word or phrase.

> *Out of the tree          two dead birds.*
> ▶ ~~Two dead birds~~ plummeted ~~out of the tree.~~
>       ^                        ^
>
> The inverted word order creates a more dramatic sentence by putting the emphasis at the end, on *two dead birds.*

As with any unusual sentence pattern, use inverted word order sparingly, only to create occasional special effects.

▶ Into this grey lake plopped the thought, I know this man, don't I?

—DORIS LESSING

▶ In a hole in the ground there lived a hobbit.          —J. R. R. TOLKIEN

### EXERCISE 53.3

Look at something you have written, and find a sentence that might be more effective with inverted word order. Experiment with the word order. Read the results aloud, and compare the effects.

▼ ▼ ▼ ▼ ▼ ▼ ▼ ▼ ▼ ▼ ▼ ▼ ▼ ▼ ▼ ▼ ▼ ▼ ▼ ▼ ▼ ▼ ▼ ▼ ▼ ▼

## THINKING CRITICALLY ABOUT PROSE STYLE

### Reading with an eye for prose style

One entertaining way to practice the elements of effective prose is to imitate them. Choose a writer you admire. Reread (or listen to) this writer's work, getting a feel for the rhythms, the structures, the special effects. Make a list of the elements that contribute to the distinctive style. Then choose a well-known story, and retell it in that writer's style. Following is the opening of "The Three Little Pigs" as one student imagined Edgar Allan Poe might have told it.

> It began as a mere infatuation. I admired them from afar, with a longing that only a wolf may know. Soon, these feelings turned to torment. Were I even to set eyes upon their porcine forms, the bowels of my soul raged, as if goaded by some festering poison. As the chilling winds of November howled, my gullet yearned for them. I soon feasted only upon an earnest and consuming desire for the moment of their decease.

## Thinking about your own prose style

Read over something you have written, looking for memorable sentences. If few sentences catch your eye, choose some that show promise — ones with strong verbs or a pleasing rhythm, perhaps. Using this chapter for guidance, try revising one or two sentences to make them more effective and memorable. Finally, note some ways in which your writing is effective and some strategies for making it more effective.

# PART 11
# Punctuation

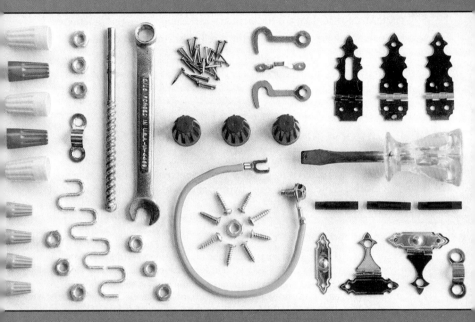

CHAPTER 54

# Commas

C OMMAS OFTEN PLAY A CRUCIAL ROLE in meaning. Even the directions for making hot cereal depend on the careful placement of a comma: *Add Cream of Wheat slowly, stirring constantly.* Here the comma tells the cook to *add the cereal slowly.* If the comma came before the word *slowly,* however, the cook might add the cereal all at once and *stir slowly.*

## 54a Understanding comma use

Because the comma can play many roles in a sentence, comma use often doesn't follow hard and fast rules. Using commas effectively requires you to make decisions that involve audience, purpose, rhythm, and style — not just grammar.

---

 **HELP**

### Editing for commas

Research for this book shows that five of the most common errors in college writing involve commas. Check your writing for these errors:

- Check every sentence that doesn't begin with the subject to see whether it opens with an introductory element (a word, phrase, or clause that tells when, where, how, or why the main action of the sentence occurs). Use a comma to separate the introductory material from the main part of the sentence. **(54b)**
- Look at every sentence that contains one of the conjunctions *and, but, for, nor, or, so,* or *yet.* If the groups of words before and after the conjunction both function as complete sentences, you have a compound sentence. Use a comma before the conjunction. **(54c)**
- Look at each adjective clause beginning with *which, who, whom, whose, when,* or *where,* and at each phrase and appositive. Decide whether the element is essential to the meaning of the sentence. If the rest of the sentence would be unclear without it, you should not set off the element with commas. **(54d)**
- Identify all adjective clauses beginning with *that,* and make sure they are not set off with commas. **(54d and 54k)**
- Do not use commas to set off restrictive elements; between subjects and verbs, verbs and objects or complements, or prepositions and objects; to separate parts of compound constructions other than compound sentences; or before the first or after the last item in a series. **(54k)**

# 54b  Using commas after introductory elements

A comma usually follows an introductory word, expression, phrase, or clause.

- **However, health care costs keep rising.**

- **In the end, only you can decide.**

- **Wearing new running shoes, Logan prepared for the race.**

- **To win the contest, Connor needed skill and luck.**

- **Pencil poised in anticipation, Audrey waited for the drawing contest to begin.**

- **While her friends watched, Lila practiced her gymnastics routine.**

Some writers omit the comma if the introductory element is short and does not seem to require a pause after it.

- *At the racetrack* **Henry lost nearly his entire paycheck.**

However, you will seldom be wrong if you use a comma after an introductory element. If the introductory element is followed by inverted word order, with the verb preceding the subject, do not use a comma unless misreading might occur.

- **From directly behind my seat/ came huge clouds of cigar smoke.**

- **Before he went, on came the rains.**

---

◢ **EXERCISE 54.1**

Rewrite the following sentences to add any commas that are needed. Example:

**To find a good day-care provider, parents usually need both time and money.**

1. After the concession speech the senator's supporters drifted out of the room.
2. To our surprise the charity auction raised enough money to build a new technology center.
3. Unaware that the microphone was on the candidate made an offensive comment.

4. Whenever someone rings the doorbell her dog goes berserk.
5. Therefore Sasha must take a summer course to receive her diploma.
6. With the fifth century came the fall of the Roman Empire.
7. A tray of shrimp in one hand and a pile of napkins in the other the waiter avoided me.
8. Toward the rapids floated an empty rubber raft.
9. When they woke up the exhausted campers no longer wanted to hike.
10. Tears in his eyes Keflezighi won the marathon.

## 54c Using commas in compound sentences

A comma usually precedes a coordinating conjunction (*and, but, for, nor, or, so,* or *yet*) that joins two independent clauses in a compound sentence.

▷ **The title sounds impressive‸ but *administrative clerk* is just another word for *photocopier.***

▷ **The show started at last‸ and the crowd grew quiet.**

With very short clauses, writers sometimes omit the comma before *and* or *or.* You will never be wrong to include it, however.

▷ **She saw her chance and she took it.**
▷ **She saw her chance, and she took it.**

Always use the comma if there is any chance of misreading the sentence without it.

▷ **The game ended in victory‸ and pandemonium erupted.**

You may want to use a semicolon rather than a comma when the clauses are long and complex or contain their own commas.

▷ **When these early migrations took place, the ice was still confined to the lands in the far north; but eight hundred thousand years ago, when man was already established in the temperate latitudes, the ice moved southward until it covered large parts of Europe and Asia.**

—ROBERT JASTROW, *Until the Sun Dies*

Be careful not to use *only* a comma between independent clauses in formal writing. Doing so creates a comma splice (see Chapter 46). Either use a coordinating conjunction after the comma, or use a semicolon.

| COMMA SPLICE | Luck isn't the only thing responsible for your new job, give yourself the credit you deserve. |
| REVISED | Luck isn't the only thing responsible for your new job, so give yourself the credit you deserve. |
| REVISED | Luck isn't the only thing responsible for your new job; give yourself the credit you deserve. |

### EXERCISE 54.2

Use a comma and a coordinating conjunction (*and, but, for, nor, or, so,* or *yet*) to combine each of the following pairs of sentences into one sentence. Delete or rearrange words if necessary. Example:

*so*
I had finished studying for the test, I went to bed.

1. The chef did not want to serve a heavy dessert. She was planning to have a rich stew for the main course.
2. My mother rarely allowed us to eat sweets. Halloween was a special exception.
3. Scientists have mapped the human genome. They learn more every day about how genes affect an individual's health.
4. Perhaps I will change my name when I get married. Maybe I will keep my maiden name.
5. Penguins cannot fly. They cannot walk the way other birds do.

## 54d  Using commas with nonrestrictive elements

Nonrestrictive elements are word groups that do not limit, or restrict, the meaning of the noun or pronoun they modify. Setting nonrestrictive elements off with commas shows your readers that the information is not essential to the meaning of the sentence. Restrictive elements, on the other hand, *are* essential to meaning and should *not* be set off with commas. The same sentence may mean different things with and without the commas:

- **The bus drivers rejecting the management offer remained on strike.**
- **The bus drivers, rejecting the management offer, remained on strike.**

The first sentence says that only *some* bus drivers, the ones rejecting the offer, remained on strike. The second says that *all* the drivers did.

Since the decision to include or omit commas influences how readers will interpret your sentence, you should think especially carefully about what you mean and use commas (or omit them) accordingly.

RESTRICTIVE

Drivers *who have been convicted of drunken driving* should lose their licenses.

In the preceding sentence, the clause *who have been convicted of drunken driving* is essential because it explains that only drivers who have been convicted of drunken driving should lose their licenses. Therefore, it is *not* set off with commas.

NONRESTRICTIVE

The two drivers involved in the accident, *who have been convicted of drunken driving*, should lose their licenses.

In this sentence, however, *who have been convicted of drunken driving* is nonrestrictive because it merely provides additional information about the particular drivers who were involved in the accident. Therefore, the clause *is* set off with commas.

To decide whether an element is restrictive or nonrestrictive, mentally delete the element, and see if the deletion changes the meaning of the rest of the sentence. If the deletion *does* change the meaning, you should probably not set the element off with commas. If it *does not* change the meaning, the element probably requires commas.

## ☐ Using commas with adjective and adverb clauses

An adjective clause that begins with *that* is always restrictive; do not set it off with commas. An adjective clause beginning with *which* may be either restrictive or nonrestrictive; however, some writers prefer to use *which* only for nonrestrictive clauses, which they set off with commas. (See 37e.)

### RESTRICTIVE CLAUSES

▶ The claim that men like seriously to battle one another to some sort of finish is a myth.                —JOHN McMURTRY, "Kill 'Em! Crush 'Em! Eat 'Em Raw!"

The adjective clause is necessary to the meaning because it explains which claim is a myth; therefore, the clause is not set off with commas.

▶ The man⁄ who rescued Jana's puppy⁄ won her eternal gratitude.

The adjective clause is necessary to the meaning because it identifies the man, so it takes no commas.

### NONRESTRICTIVE CLAUSES

▶ I borrowed books from the rental library of Shakespeare and Company, which was the library and bookstore of Sylvia Beach at 12 rue de l'Odeon.                —ERNEST HEMINGWAY, *A Moveable Feast*

The adjective clause is not necessary to the meaning of the independent clause and therefore is set off with a comma.

An adverb clause that follows a main clause does *not* usually require a comma to set it off unless the adverb clause expresses contrast.

▶ **The park became a popular gathering place, although nearby residents complemented about the noise.**

The adverb clause expresses contrast; therefore, it is set off with a comma.

## □ Using commas with phrases

Participial phrases may be restrictive or nonrestrictive. Prepositional phrases are usually restrictive, but sometimes they are not essential to the meaning of a sentence and thus are set off with commas.

**NONRESTRICTIVE PHRASES**

▶ **The singer's children, refusing to be ignored, interrupted the recital.**

Using commas around the participial phrase makes it nonrestrictive, telling us that all of the singer's children interrupted.

**RESTRICTIVE PHRASES**

▶ **Wood cut from living trees does not burn as well as dead wood.**

The participial phrase *cut from living trees* is essential to the meaning.

▶ **The bodyguards were the men in dark suits and matching ties.**

The prepositional phrase *in dark suits and matching ties* is essential to the meaning.

## □ Using commas with appositives

An appositive is a noun or noun phrase that renames a nearby noun in a sentence. When an appositive is not essential to identify what it renames, it is set off with commas.

**NONRESTRICTIVE APPOSITIVES**

▶ **Savion Glover, the award-winning dancer, taps like poetry in motion.**

Savion Glover's name identifies him; the appositive *the award-winning dancer* provides extra information.

**RESTRICTIVE APPOSITIVES**

▶ **Mozart's opera/ The Marriage of Figaro/ was considered revolutionary.**

The phrase is restrictive because Mozart wrote more than one opera. Therefore, it is *not* set off with commas.

◢ **EXERCISE 54.3**

Use commas to set off nonrestrictive clauses, phrases, and appositives in any of the following sentences that contain such elements.

1. What can you buy for the person who has everything?
2. Embalming is a technique that preserves a cadaver.
3. The enormous new house which was the largest in the neighborhood had replaced a much smaller old home.
4. The rescue workers exhausted and discouraged stared ahead without speaking.
5. The new mall has the same stores and restaurants as all the other malls in town.
6. Viruses unlike bacteria can reproduce only by infecting live cells.
7. Napoléon was imprisoned after his defeat at the battle of Waterloo.
8. Hammurabi an ancient Babylonian king created laws that were carved on a stone for public display.
9. Birds' hearts have four chambers whereas reptiles' have three.
10. A female cheetah hisses and swats if another animal gets too close to her young.

# 54e Using commas to separate items in a series

Use a comma to separate items in a series of three or more words, phrases, or clauses.

◯ **I bumped into professors, horizontal bars, agricultural students, and swinging iron rings.** —JAMES THURBER, "University Days"

◯ **He has plundered our seas, ravaged our coasts, burnt our towns, and destroyed the lives of our people.**
—THOMAS JEFFERSON, Declaration of Independence

You may see a series with no comma after the next-to-last item, particularly in newspaper writing. Occasionally, however, omitting the comma can cause confusion.

◯ **All the vegetables in the cafeteria — broccoli, green beans, peas, and carrots — were cooked to an unrecognizable mush.**

Without the comma after *peas*, you wouldn't know if the cafeteria offered three vegetables (the third being a *mixture* of peas and carrots) or four.

When the items in a series contain commas of their own or other punctuation, separate them with semicolons rather than commas (55b).

Coordinate adjectives, those that relate equally to the noun they modify, should be separated by commas.

◯ **The *long, twisting, muddy* road led to a shack in the woods.**

In a sentence like *The cracked bathroom mirror reflected his face,* however, *cracked* and *bathroom* are not coordinate because *bathroom mirror* is the equivalent of a single word, which is modified by *cracked*. Hence, they are *not* separated by commas.

You can usually determine whether adjectives are coordinate by inserting the word *and* between them. If the sentence still makes sense with the *and*, the adjectives are coordinate and should be separated by commas.

▶ **They are sincere *and* talented *and* inquisitive researchers.**

The sentence makes sense with the *and*s, so the adjectives should be separated by commas: *They are sincere, talented, inquisitive researchers.*

▶ **Byron carried an elegant ~~and~~ gold ~~and~~ pocket watch.**

The sentence does not make sense with the *and*s, so the adjectives should not be separated by commas: *Byron carried an elegant gold pocket watch.*

### ◢ EXERCISE 54.4

Revise any of the following sentences that require commas to set off words, phrases, or clauses in a series.

1. The students donated clothing school supplies and nonperishable food.
2. The hot humid weather did not stop the fans from flocking to the free outdoor concert.
3. The ball sailed over the fence across the yard and through the Wilsons' window
4. Several art historians inspected the Chinese terra-cotta figures.
5. The young athletes' parents insist on calling every play judging every move and telling everyone within earshot exactly what is wrong with the team.

## 54f Using commas with parenthetical and transitional expressions

Parenthetical and transitional expressions often interrupt the flow of a sentence or digress, so they are usually set off with commas. Parenthetical expressions (*in fact, by the way*) add comments. Transitional expressions (5e and f), including conjunctive adverbs (36g) such as *however* and *furthermore*, clarify how parts of sentences relate to what has come before them.

▶ **Roald Dahl's stories, it turns out, were often inspired by his own childhood.**

▶ **Ceiling fans are, moreover, less expensive than air conditioners.**

## 54g Using commas with contrasting elements, interjections, direct address, and tag questions

**CONTRASTING ELEMENTS**

▶ **On official business it was she, not my father, one would usually hear on the phone or in stores.**

> —RICHARD RODRIGUEZ, "Aria: A Memoir of a Bilingual Childhood"

**INTERJECTIONS**

▶ **My God, who wouldn't want a wife?**  —JUDY BRADY, "I Want a Wife"

**DIRECT ADDRESS**

▶ **Remember, sir, that you are under oath.**

**TAG QUESTIONS**

▶ **The governor did not veto the unemployment bill, did she?**

### ◢ EXERCISE 54.5

Revise each of the following sentences, using commas to set off parenthetical and transitional expressions, contrasting elements, interjections, words used in direct address, and tag questions.

1. One must consider the society as a whole not just its parts.
2. Drinking caffeinated beverages can in fact be good for your health.
3. You don't expect me to read this speech do you?
4. Coming in ahead of schedule and under budget it appears is the only way to keep this client happy.
5. Believe me Jenna I had no idea things would turn out this way.

## 54h Using commas with dates, addresses, titles, and numbers

*Dates*

Use a comma between the day of the week and the month, between the day of the month and the year, and between the year and the rest of the sentence, if any.

▶ **On Wednesday, November 26, 2008, gunmen arrived in Mumbai by boat.**

Do not use commas with dates in inverted order or with dates consisting of only the month and the year.

- She dated the letter **18 October 2014.**
- Thousands of Germans swarmed over the Berlin Wall in **November 1989.**

### Addresses and place-names

Use a comma after each part of an address or place-name, including the state if no zip code is given. Do not precede a zip code with a comma.

- Forward my mail to the Department of English, The Ohio State University, Columbus, Ohio 43210.

- Portland, Oregon, is much larger than Portland, Maine.

### Titles

Use commas to set off a title such as *MD* or *PhD* from the name preceding it and from the rest of the sentence. The titles *Jr.* and *Sr.*, however, often appear without commas.

- Jaime Mejía, PhD, will speak about his ethnographic research.

- Martin Luther King Jr. was one of the twentieth century's greatest orators.

### Numbers

In numerals of five digits or more, use a comma between each group of three digits, starting from the right.

- The city's population rose to **158,000** in the 2000 census.

The comma is optional in four-digit numerals but is never used in years.

- The college had an enrollment of **1,789 [or 1789]** in the fall of 2006.

Do not use a comma in building numbers, zip codes, or page numbers.

- My parents live at **11311** Wimberly Drive, Richmond, Virginia **23233.**
- Turn to page **1566.**

### ◢ EXERCISE 54.6

Revise each of the following sentences, using commas appropriately with dates, addresses, place-names, titles, and numbers.

1. The city of Dublin Ireland has a population of over 500000.
2. I rode a total of almost 1200 miles on my bike in 2009.

3. New Delhi India and Islamabad Pakistan became the capitals of two independent nations at midnight on August 15 1947.

4. MLA headquarters are still located at 26 Broadway New York New York 10004.

5. I was convinced that the nameplate I. M. Well MD was one of my sister's pranks.

## 54i   Commas with quotations

Commas set off a quotation from words used to introduce or identify the source of the quotation. A comma following a quotation goes inside the closing quotation mark.

▶ A German proverb warns, "Go to law for a sheep, and lose your cow."

▶ "All I know about grammar," said Joan Didion, "is its infinite power."

Do not use a comma after a question mark or exclamation point.

▶ "What's a thousand dollars?," asks Groucho Marx in *The Cocoanuts.* "Mere chicken feed. A poultry matter."

▶ "Out, damned spot!," cries Lady Macbeth.

Do not use a comma to introduce a quotation with *that.*

▶ The writer of Ecclesiastes concludes that, "all is vanity."

Do not use a comma with a quotation when the rest of the sentence does more than introduce or identify the source of the quotation.

▶ People who say, "Have a nice day" irritate me.

▶ He put off military service because he had, "other priorities."

Do not use a comma before an indirect quotation — one that does not use the speaker's exact words.

▶ Patrick Henry declared, that he wanted either liberty or death.

▲ **EXERCISE 54.7**

Insert a comma in any of the following sentences that require one.

1. "The public be damned!" William Henry Vanderbilt was reported to have said. "I'm working for my stockholders."
2. My mother was fond of telling me "You'd make coffee nervous!"
3. I refuse to believe the old saying that "nice guys finish last."
4. "Learning without thought is labor lost; thought without learning is perilous" Confucius argued.
5. "Do you have any idea who I am?" the well-dressed young man asked belligerently.

# 54j Using commas for clarity

Use a comma if it will make a sentence easier to read or understand.

⊙ **The members of the dance troupe strutted in, in matching tuxedos and top hats.**

⊙ **Before, I had planned to major in biology.**

# 54k Avoiding unnecessary commas

Excessive use of commas can spoil an otherwise fine sentence.

## ▢ Avoiding commas with restrictive elements

Do not use commas to set off restrictive elements — elements that limit, or define, the meaning of the words they modify or refer to (54d).

⊙ **My mother dislikes films, that include foul language.**

⊙ **A law, reforming campaign financing, was passed in 2002.**

⊙ **My only defense, against my allergies, is to stay indoors.**

⊙ **The actress, Cate Blanchett, won an Oscar in 2014.**

☐ **Avoiding commas between subjects and verbs, verbs and objects or complements, and prepositions and objects**

Do not use a comma between a subject and its verb, a verb and its object or complement, or a preposition and its object — not even if the subject, object, or complement is a long phrase or clause.

▶ Watching old movies late at night⁄ is a way for me to relax.

▶ Parents must decide⁄ how much television their children should watch.

▶ The winner of⁄ the community-service award stepped forward.

☐ **Using commas in compound constructions**

In compound constructions (other than compound sentences — see 54c), do not use a comma before or after a coordinating conjunction that joins the two parts.

▶ Donald Trump was born rich⁄ and has used his money to make even

more money.

The *and* here joins parts of the compound predicate *was born* and *has used*, which should not be separated by a comma.

▶ Ellen Johnson Sirleaf⁄ and George Weah both claimed to have won

the election.

The *and* here joins parts of a compound subject, which should not be separated by a comma.

☐ **Using commas in a series**

Do not use a comma before the first or after the last item in a series (54e).

▶ The auction included⁄ furniture, paintings, and china.

▶ The swimmer took slow, powerful⁄ strokes.

## THINKING CRITICALLY ABOUT COMMAS

### Reading with an eye for commas

The following poem uses commas to create rhythm and guide readers. Read the poem aloud, listening especially to the effect of the commas at the end of the first and fifth lines. Then read it again as if those commas were omitted, noting the difference. What is the effect of the poet's decision not to use a comma at the end of the third line?

> Some say the world will end in fire,
> Some say in ice.
> From what I've tasted of desire
> I hold with those who favor fire.
> But if it had to perish twice,
> I think I know enough of hate
> To say that for destruction ice
> Is also great
> And would suffice.
> —ROBERT FROST, "Fire and Ice"

### Thinking about your own use of commas

Choose a paragraph that you have written. Remove all of the commas, and read it aloud. What is the effect of leaving out the commas? Now, punctuate the passage with commas, consulting this chapter. Did you replace all of your original commas? Did you add any new ones? Explain why you added the commas you did.

# CHAPTER 55

# Semicolons

THE FOLLOWING PUBLIC SERVICE ANNOUNCEMENT, posted in New York City subway cars, reminds commuters what to do with a used newspaper at the end of the ride:

> Please put it in a trash can; that's good news for everyone.

A *New York Times* article praised the writer of the announcement for choosing to use a semicolon, "that distinct division between statements that are closely related but require a separation more prolonged than a conjunction and more emphatic than a comma."

## 55a  Using semicolons with independent clauses

You can join independent clauses in several ways: with a comma and a coordinating conjunction (54c), with a colon (59d), with a dash (59c), or with a semicolon. Semicolons provide writers with subtle ways of signaling closely related clauses. The clause following a semicolon often restates an idea expressed in the first clause; it can also expand on or present a contrast to the first.

▶ **Immigration acts were passed; newcomers had to prove, besides moral correctness and financial solvency, their ability to read.**
 —MARY GORDON, "More Than Just a Shrine"

In this example, Gordon uses a semicolon to lead to a clause that expands on the first one. The semicolon also gives the sentence an abrupt rhythm that suits the topic: laws that imposed strict requirements.

A semicolon should link independent clauses joined by conjunctive adverbs such as *therefore, however,* and *indeed* or transitional expressions such as *in a way, in fact, in addition,* and *for example* (46d).

▶ **The circus comes as close to being the world in microcosm as anything I know; in a way, it puts all the rest of show business in the shade.**
 —E. B. WHITE, "The Ring of Time"

If two independent clauses joined by a coordinating conjunction contain commas, you may use a semicolon instead of a comma before the conjunction to make the sentence easier to read.

 **Every year, whether the Republican or the Democratic Party is in office, more and more power drains away from the individual to feed vast reservoirs in far-off places; and we have less and less say about the shape of events which shape our future.**

> —WILLIAM F. BUCKLEY JR., "Why Don't We Complain?"

---

 **QUICK HELP**

## Editing for semicolons

- Use semicolons only between independent clauses—groups of words that can stand alone as sentences **(55a)**—or between items in a series. **(55b)**
- If you find few or no semicolons in your writing, ask yourself whether closely related ideas in two sentences might be better expressed in one sentence with a semicolon.
- If you find too many semicolons in your writing, try deleting some of them. Would making some clauses into separate sentences make your writing smoother or less monotonous? **(55d)**

---

### EXERCISE 55.1

Combine each of the following pairs of sentences into one sentence by using a semicolon. Example:

>      *meet*
> Take the bus to Henderson Street,/; Meet me under the clock at half past
>
> three.

1. Abalone fishing in California is strictly regulated. A person is allowed to harvest only twenty-four of these large mollusks per year.
2. City life offers many advantages. In many ways, however, life in a small town is much more pleasant.
3. The door contains an inflatable slide to be used in an emergency. In addition, each seat can become a flotation device.
4. Most car accidents occur within twenty-five miles of the home. Therefore, you should wear a seat belt on every trip.
5. Involvement in team sports provides more than just health benefits for young girls. It also increases their self-confidence.

## 55b Using semicolons to separate items in a series

Ordinarily, commas separate items in a series (54e). But when the items themselves contain commas or other punctuation, using semicolons to separate the items will make the sentence clearer and easier to read.

▶ **Anthropology encompasses archaeology, the study of ancient civilizations through artifacts; linguistics, the study of the structure and development of language; and cultural anthropology, the study of customs, language, and behavior.**

## 55c Using semicolons with quotation marks

A semicolon goes *outside* closing quotation marks (58e).

▶ **Shirley Jackson's most famous story is "The Lottery"; its horrifying ending depicts a result of relying too heavily on tradition.**

## 55d Avoiding misused or overused semicolons

A comma, not a semicolon, should separate an independent clause from a dependent clause or a phrase.

▶ **The police found a set of fingerprints; which they used to identify the thief.**

A colon, not a semicolon, should introduce a series.

▶ **The reunion tour includes the following bands; Urban Waste, Murphy's Law, Rapid Deployment, and Ism.**

Be careful not to use semicolons too often. Sentence upon sentence punctuated with semicolons may sound monotonous and jerky.

▶ **Like many people in public life, he spoke with confidence; perhaps
    ^ that
he even spoke with arrogance; yet I noted a certain anxiety; it touched
       He
and puzzled me; he seemed too eager to demonstrate his control of a
situation.**

### EXERCISE 55.2

Revise the following passage, eliminating any misused or overused semicolons and, if necessary, replacing them with other punctuation.

Hosting your first dinner party can be very stressful; but careful planning and preparation can make it a success. The guest list must contain the right mix of people; everyone should feel comfortable; good talkers and good listeners are both important; while they don't need to agree on everything, you don't want them to have fistfights, either. Then you need to plan the menu; which should steer clear of problem areas; for vegans; no pork chops; for guests with shellfish allergies, no lobster; for teetotallers; no tequila. In addition; make sure your home is clean and neat, and check that you have enough chairs; dishes; glasses; napkins; and silverware. Leave enough time to socialize with your guests; and save a little energy to clean up when it's over!

▼ ▼ ▼ ▼ ▼ ▼ ▼ ▼ ▼ ▼ ▼ ▼ ▼ ▼ ▼ ▼ ▼ ▼ ▼ ▼ ▼ ▼ ▼ ▼ ▼

## THINKING CRITICALLY ABOUT SEMICOLONS

### Reading with an eye for semicolons

Read the following paragraph, which describes a solar eclipse, with attention to the use of semicolons. What different effect would the paragraph have if the author had used periods instead of semicolons? What if she had used commas and coordinating conjunctions? What is the effect of all the semicolons?

You see the wide world swaddled in darkness; you see a vast breadth of hilly land, and an enormous, distant, blackened valley; you see towns' lights, a river's path, and blurred portions of your hat and scarf; you see your husband's face looking like an early black-and-white film; and you see a sprawl of black sky and blue sky together, with unfamiliar stars in it, some barely visible bands of cloud, and over there, a small white ring. The ring is as small as one goose in a flock of migrating geese—if you happen to notice a flock of migrating geese. It is one 360th part of the visible sky. The sun we see is less than half the diameter of a dime held at arms' length.                    —ANNIE DILLARD, "Solar Eclipse"

### Thinking about your own use of semicolons

Think of something you might take five or ten minutes to observe—a football game, a brewing storm, an argument between friends—and write a paragraph describing your observations point by point and using semicolons to separate each point, as Annie Dillard does in the preceding paragraph. Then, look at the way you used semicolons. Are there places where a period or a comma and a coordinating conjunction would better serve your meaning? Revise appropriately. What can you conclude about effective ways of using semicolons?

# CHAPTER 56

# End Punctuation

MAKING APPROPRIATE CHOICES with end punctuation allows your readers to understand exactly what you mean.

> **CONNECT:** Do you use exclamation points differently in different writing contexts? **1a, 56c**
>
> **CREATE:** Compare samples of your informal writing and your formal college writing, and briefly describe how you use exclamation points in each one.
>
> **REFLECT:** Ask one or two classmates or friends to look at these pieces of writing and tell you what effect the exclamation points have in each piece. What do their responses suggest to you about when and where it's appropriate to use exclamation points?

## 56a  Using periods

Use a period to close sentences that make statements or give mild commands.

- **All books are either dreams or swords.** —AMY LOWELL
- **Don't use a fancy word if a simpler word will do.**
  —GEORGE ORWELL, "Politics and the English Language"

A period also closes indirect questions, which report rather than ask questions.

- **I asked how old the child was.**
- **We all wonder who will win the election.**

Until recently, periods have been used with most abbreviations (see Chapter 61) in American English. However, more and more abbreviations are appearing without periods.

| | | |
|---|---|---|
| Mr. | MD | BC *or* B.C. |
| Ms. | PhD | BCE *or* B.C.E. |
| Mrs. | MBA | AD *or* A.D. |
| Dr. | RN | AM *or* a.m. |
| Jr. | Sen. | PM *or* p.m. |

Some abbreviations rarely if ever appear with periods. These include the postal abbreviations of state names, such as *FL* and *TN* (though the traditional abbreviations, such as *Fla.* and *Tenn.*, do call for periods), and most groups of initials (*MLA, CIA, AIDS, UNICEF*). If you are not sure whether a particular abbreviation should include periods, check a dictionary or follow the style guidelines (such as those of the Modern Language Association) you are using in a research project.

## 56b Using question marks

Use a question mark to close sentences that ask direct questions.

- **Have you finished the essay, or do you need more time?**

Question marks do not close *indirect* questions, which report rather than ask questions.

- **She asked whether I opposed his nomination?.**

Do not use a comma or a period immediately after a question mark that ends a direct quotation (58e).

- **"Am I my brother's keeper?/" Cain asked.**
- **Cain asked, "Am I my brother's keeper?"/**

Questions in a series may have question marks even when they are not separate sentences.

- **I often confront a difficult choice: should I go to practice? finish my homework? spend time with my friends?**

A question mark in parentheses can be used to indicate that a writer is unsure of a date, a figure, or a word.

- **Quintilian died in 96 CE (?).**

## 56c Using exclamation points

Use an exclamation point to show surprise or strong emotion.

- **In those few moments of geologic time will be the story of all that has happened since we became a nation. And what a story it will be!** —JAMES RETTIE, "But a Watch in the Night"
- **Look out!**

Today, we live in a world of excess exclamations, such as *Best Sale Ever!!!!!* But college writers will do well to use exclamation points sparingly in academic work because they can distract your readers or suggest that you are exaggerating. In general, try to create emphasis through diction and sentence structure rather than with exclamation points.

▶ **This university is so large, so varied, that attempting to tell someone**

**everything about it would take three years!.**

Do not use a comma or a period after an exclamation point that ends a direct quotation.

▶ **On my last visit, I looked out the sliding glass doors and ran breathlessly**

**to Connor in the kitchen: "There's a *huge* black pig in the backyard!".**

—ELLEN ASHDOWN, "Living by the Dead"

△ **EXERCISE 56.1**

Revise each of the following sentences, adding appropriate punctuation and deleting any unnecessary punctuation you find. Example:

**She asked the travel agent, "What is the air fare to Greece?".**

1. Social scientists face difficult questions: should they use their knowledge to shape society, merely describe human behavior, or try to do both.
2. The court denied a New Jersey woman's petition to continue raising tigers in her backyard!
3. I screamed at Jamie, "You rat. You tricked me."
4. The reporter wondered whether anything more could have been done to save lives?
5. Zane called every store within fifty miles and asked if they had the Wii game he wanted
6. "Have you seen the new George Clooney film?," Mia asked.

# 56d Using end punctuation in informal writing

In informal writing, especially texts and tweets with character limits, writers today are increasingly likely to omit end punctuation entirely. In informal writing that does use end punctuation, research shows that ellipses (. . .), or "dots," are on the rise; they can be used to signal a trailing off of a thought, to raise questions about what is being left out, to leave open the possibility of further communication, or simply to indicate that the writer doesn't want or need to finish the sentence (59f). Exclamation marks can convey an excited or a chatty tone, so they are used more frequently in social media and other informal writing situations than in academic writing (where they tend to be rare). And some writers have argued that using a period at the end of a text or tweet rather than no punctuation at all can suggest that the writer is irritated or angry. The meaning of end punctuation is changing in informal contexts, so pay attention to how others communicate, and use what you learn in your own social writing.

▼ ▼ ▼ ▼ ▼ ▼ ▼ ▼ ▼ ▼ ▼ ▼ ▼ ▼ ▼ ▼ ▼ ▼ ▼ ▼ ▼ ▼ ▼ ▼ ▼

## THINKING CRITICALLY ABOUT END PUNCTUATION

### Reading with an eye for end punctuation

Consider the use of end punctuation in the following paragraph. Then experiment with the end punctuation. What would be the effect of deleting the exclamation point from the quotation by Cicero or of changing it to a question mark? What would be the effect of changing Cicero's question to a statement?

> To be admired and praised, especially by the young, is an autumnal pleasure enjoyed by the lucky ones (who are not always the most deserving). "What is more charming," Cicero observes in his famous essay *De Senectute*, "than an old age surrounded by the enthusiasm of youth! . . . Attentions which seem trivial and conventional are marks of honor—the morning call, being sought after, precedence, having people rise for you, being escorted to and from the forum. . . . What pleasures of the body can be compared to the prerogatives of influence?" But there are also pleasures of the body, or the mind, that are enjoyed by a greater number of older persons.
>
> —MALCOLM COWLEY, *The View from 80*

### Thinking about your own use of end punctuation

Look through something you have written recently, noting its end punctuation. Using the guidelines in this chapter, see if your use of end punctuation follows any patterns. Try revising the end punctuation in a paragraph or two to emphasize (or de-emphasize) some point. What conclusions can you draw about ways of using end punctuation to draw attention to (or away from) a sentence?

# CHAPTER 57

# Apostrophes

**T**HE LITTLE APOSTROPHE can make a big difference in meaning. The following sign at a neighborhood swimming pool, for instance, probably doesn't say quite what the writer intended:

> Please deposit your garbage (and your guests) in the trash receptacles before leaving the pool area.

Adding a single apostrophe would offer a more neighborly statement: *Please deposit your garbage (and your guests') in the trash receptacles before leaving the pool area* asks residents to remove the guests' garbage, not the guests themselves.

---

**CONNECT:** What makes apostrophe use tricky for you?
**The Top Twenty, "Unnecessary or missing apostrophe"
(pp. 7–8); 57a–d**

**CREATE:** Write a brief paragraph beginning, "I've always wondered about my best friend's . . . ," noting every word you use that includes an apostrophe. Then type the same paragraph on your smartphone or other device, and note every time the device inserts the apostrophe for you.

**REFLECT:** Write or record a reflection on what you learned about depending on a device to insert appropriate apostrophes. Do you think you need the device's help? Did you find any instances where the device was wrong?

---

## 57a Understanding apostrophes

Apostrophes are used for two main purposes: to show the possessive case and to show where a letter has been omitted from a contraction. Apostrophe placement can be confusing, especially today when smart devices sometimes put them in for you, and they are sometimes left out in informal writing. But they are still important in writing, so it's best to learn how to use them accurately.

### Editing for apostrophes

- Check each noun that ends in -s and shows ownership or possession. Verify that the apostrophe is in the right place, either before or after the -s. **(57b)**
- Check the possessive form of each indefinite pronoun, such as *someone's*. Be sure an apostrophe comes before the -s. **(57b)**
- Check each possessive personal pronoun ending in -s (*yours*, *hers*, *his*, *its*, *ours*, *theirs*), and make sure that it does not include an apostrophe. **(57b)**
- Check each *its*. Does it show possession? If not, add an apostrophe before the -s. **(57c)**
- Check each *it's*. Does it mean "it is" or "it has"? If not, remove the apostrophe. **(57c)**

## 57b Using apostrophes to signal possessive case

The possessive case denotes ownership or possession of one thing by another (41a).

### ☐ Forming possessives of singular nouns and indefinite pronouns

Add an apostrophe and -*s* to form the possessive of most singular nouns, including those that end in -*s*, and of indefinite pronouns (40e).

- **The bus's fumes overpowered her.**
- ***Star Wars* made George Lucas's fortune.**
- **Anyone's guess is as good as mine.**

Apostrophes are never used with the possessive forms of personal pronouns: *yours, his, hers, its, ours, theirs.*

- **His favorite movies have nothing in common with her̶'̶s.**

### ☐ Forming possessives of plural nouns

For plural nouns that do not end in -*s*, add an apostrophe and -*s*.

men's
- **Most suits in the mens̶'̶ department are appropriate business attire.**
                        ^

For plural nouns ending in -*s*, add only the apostrophe.

clowns'
- **The three c̶l̶o̶w̶n̶s̶'̶s̶ costumes were bright green and orange.**
                ^

## ☐ Forming possessives of compound words

For compound words, make the last word in the group possessive.

▶ The secretary of state's speech was televised.

▶ My in-laws' disapproval dampened our enthusiasm.

## ☐ Showing possession by more than one owner

To signal individual possession by two or more owners, make each noun possessive.

▶ The differences between Ridley Scott's and Jerry Bruckheimer's films are enormous.

> Scott and Bruckheimer make different films.

To signal joint possession, make only the last noun possessive.

▶ Wallace and Gromit's creator is Nick Park.

> Wallace and Gromit have the same creator.

### ▲ EXERCISE 57.1

Revise each of the following sentences to form the possessive case of the italicized words. Example:

> A. J.'s older brother's name is Griffin.

1. Grammar is not *everybody* favorite subject.
2. An *ibis* wingspan is about half as long as a *flamingo*.
3. *Charles and Camilla* first visit to the United States as a married couple included a stop at the White House.
4. The long debate over *states* rights culminated in the Civil War.
5. *Kobe Bryant and Tiger Woods* personal crises have threatened to overshadow their athletic careers.
6. She insists that her personal life is *nobody* business.
7. Parents often question their *children* choice of friends.
8. This dog has a *beagle* ears and a *St. Bernard* face.
9. The sidewalk smokers disregarded the *surgeon generals* warnings.
10. *Anna and Tobias* income dropped dramatically after Anna lost her job.

# 57c  Using apostrophes to signal contractions

Contractions are two-word combinations formed by leaving out certain letters, which are indicated by an apostrophe.

| | | |
|---|---|---|
| it is, it has/it's | I would, I had/I'd | will not/won't |
| was not/wasn't | he would, he had/he'd | let us/let's |
| I am/I'm | would not/wouldn't | who is, who has/who's |
| he is, he has/he's | do not/don't | cannot/can't |
| you will/you'll | does not/doesn't | |

Contractions are common in both conversation and informal writing. Some academic and professional work, however, calls for greater formality.

## □ Distinguishing *its* and *it's*

*Its* is the possessive form of *it*. *It's* is a contraction for *it is* or *it has*.

▶ **This disease is unusual; it's symptoms vary from person to person.**

▶ **It's a difficult disease to diagnose.**

## □ Signaling omissions

An apostrophe signals omissions in some common phrases:

| | | |
|---|---|---|
| ten of the clock | rock and roll | class of 2003 |
| ten o'clock | rock 'n' roll | class of '03 |

In addition, writers can use an apostrophe to signal omitted letters in approximating the sound of speech or a specific dialect.

▶ **You should'a seen 'em playin' together.**

# 57d  Using guidelines for apostrophes with plurals

Many style guides advise against apostrophes for any plurals.

▶ **The gymnasts need marks of 8s and 9s to qualify for the finals.**

Others use an apostrophe and *-s* to form the plural of numbers, letters, symbols, and words referred to as terms.

▶ **The five *Shakespeare*'s in the essay were spelled five different ways.**

Check your instructor's preference. In any case, italicize numbers, letters, symbols, and terms but not the plural ending.

### EXERCISE 57.2

The following sentences, from which all apostrophes have been deleted, appear in Langston Hughes's "Salvation." Insert apostrophes where appropriate. Example:

> **"Sister Reed, what is this child's name?"**

1. There was a big revival at my Auntie Reeds church.
2. I heard the songs and the minister saying: "Why dont you come?"
3. Finally Westley said to me in a whisper: . . . "Im tired of sitting here. Lets get up and be saved."
4. So I decided that maybe to save further trouble, Id better lie. . . .
5. That night . . . I cried, in bed alone, and couldnt stop.

▼ ▼ ▼ ▼ ▼ ▼ ▼ ▼ ▼ ▼ ▼ ▼ ▼ ▼ ▼ ▼ ▼ ▼ ▼ ▼ ▼ ▼ ▼ ▼ ▼ ▼

## THINKING CRITICALLY ABOUT APOSTROPHES

Write a brief paragraph, beginning "I've always been amused by my neighbor's (or roommate's) _____." Then note every use of an apostrophe. Use the guidelines in this chapter to check that you have used apostrophes correctly.

# CHAPTER 58

# Quotation Marks

A S A WAY OF BRINGING other people's words into our own, quotation can be a powerful writing tool.

> Mrs. Macken urges parents to get books for their children, to read to them when they are "li'l," and when they start school to make certain they attend regularly. She holds herself up as an example of a "millhand's daughter who wanted to be a schoolteacher and did it through sheer hard work."
>
> —SHIRLEY BRICE HEATH, *Ways with Words*

The writer could have paraphrased, but by quoting, she lets her subject speak for herself — and lets readers hear that person's voice.

## 58a  Using quotation marks to signal direct quotations

Use double quotation marks to signal a direct quotation.

- ▶ **The president asked Congress to "try common sense."**
- ▶ **She smiled and said, "Son, this is one incident I will never forget."**

Single quotation marks enclose a quotation within a quotation. Open and close the quoted passage with double quotation marks, and change any quotation marks that appear *within* the quotation to single quotation marks.

- ▶ **James Baldwin says, "The title 'The Uses of the Blues' does not refer to music; I don't know anything about music."**

---

**Editing for quotation marks**

- Use quotation marks around direct quotations and titles of short works. **(58a and b)**
- Do not use quotation marks around set-off quotations of more than four lines of prose or three lines of poetry or around titles of long works. **(58a and b)** ▶

**713**

**Editing for quotation marks, continued**

- Use quotation marks to signal irony and invented words, but do so sparingly. **(58c)**
- Never use quotation marks around indirect quotations. **(58d)**
- Do not use quotation marks to add emphasis to words. **(58d)**
- Check other punctuation used with closing quotation marks. **(58e)**
  Periods and commas should be *inside* the quotation marks.
  Colons, semicolons, and footnote numbers should be *outside*.
  Question marks, exclamation points, and dashes should be *inside* if they are part of the quoted material, *outside* if they are not.

## ☐ Quoting longer passages

If the prose passage you wish to quote exceeds four typed lines, set it off from the rest of the text by starting it on a new line and indenting it one inch from the left margin. This format, known as block quotation, does not require quotation marks.

> In *Winged Words: American Indian Writers Speak*, Leslie Marmon Silko describes her early education:
>> I learned to love reading, and love books, and the printed page, and therefore was motivated to learn to write. The best thing . . . you can have in life is to have someone tell you a story . . . but in lieu of that . . . I learned at an early age to find comfort in a book, that a book would talk to me when no one else would. (145)

This block quotation, including the ellipses and the page number in parentheses at the end, follows the style of the Modern Language Association (MLA). Other organizations, such as the American Psychological Association (APA) and the University of Chicago Press, have different guidelines for ellipses and block quotations. (See Chapters 32–35.)

## ☐ Quoting poetry

If the quotation is fewer than four lines, include it within your text, enclosed in double quotation marks. Separate the lines of the poem with slashes, each preceded and followed by a space, to tell the reader where one line of the poem ends and the next begins.

> In one of his best-known poems, Robert Frost remarks, "Two roads diverged in a wood, and I — / I took the one less traveled by, / And that has made all the difference" (lines 18-20).

To quote four or more lines of poetry, indent the block one inch from the left margin, and do not use quotation marks.

**QUOTING IN AMERICAN ENGLISH**

American English and British English use opposite conventions for double and single quotation marks. Writers of British English use single quotation marks first and, if necessary, double quotation marks for quotations within quotations. If you have studied British English, be careful to follow the U.S. conventions for quotation marks: double quotation marks first and, if necessary, single quotation marks within double.

The duke in Robert Browning's "My Last Duchess" is clearly a jealous, vain person, whose own words illustrate his arrogance:

> She thanked men — good! but thanked
> Somehow — I know not how — as if she ranked
> My gift of a nine-hundred-years-old name
> With anybody's gift. (lines 31–34)

When you quote poetry, take care to follow the indention, spacing, capitalization, punctuation, and other features of the original poem.

### □ Quoting dialogue

When you write dialogue or quote a conversation, enclose the words of each speaker in quotation marks, and mark each shift in speaker by beginning a new paragraph.

**"I want no proof of their affection," said Elinor, "but of their engagement I do."**

**"I am perfectly satisfied of both."**

**"Yet not a syllable has been said to you on the subject, by either of them."** —JANE AUSTEN, *Sense and Sensibility*

Because of the paragraph breaks in this example, we know when Elinor is speaking and when her mother is speaking without the author's having to repeat *said Elinor, her mother said,* and so on.

## 58b Using quotation marks to signal titles and definitions

Quotation marks are used to enclose the titles of short poems, short stories, articles, essays, songs, sections of books, and episodes of television and radio programs.

---

**MULTI-LINGUAL** | **QUOTATION MARKS**

Remember that the way you mark quotations in English (" ") may not be the same as in other languages. In French, for example, quotations are marked with *guillemets* (« »), while in German, quotations take split-level marks („ ").

---

- ▶ "Dover Beach" moves from calm to sadness. [poem]
- ▶ Walker's "Everyday Use" is not just about quilts. [short story]
- ▶ The White Stripes released ten different versions of "The Denial Twist." [song]
- ▶ The *Atlantic* published an article titled "Illiberal Education." [article]
- ▶ In the chapter called "Complexion," Richard Rodriguez describes his sensitivity about his skin color. [section of book]
- ▶ The *Nature* episode "Echo of the Elephants" denounces ivory hunters. [television series episode]

Use italics rather than quotation marks for the titles of television series, books, magazines, and other longer works (62a).

Definitions are sometimes set off with quotation marks.

- ▶ The French phrase *idée fixe* means literally "fixed idea."

## 58c Using quotation marks to signal irony and invented words

To show readers that you are using a word or phrase ironically, or that you invented it, enclose it in quotation marks.

- ▶ The "banquet" consisted mainly of dried-out chicken and canned vegetables.

The quotation marks suggest that the meal was anything but a banquet.

- ▶ Your whole first paragraph or first page may have to be guillotined in any case after your piece is finished: it is a kind of "forebirth."

—JACQUES BARZUN, "A Writer's Discipline"

The writer made up the term *forebirth*.

⊿ **EXERCISE 58.1**

Revise each of the following sentences, using quotation marks appropriately to signal titles, definitions, irony, or invented terms.

1. Stephen Colbert introduced Americans to the concept he calls truthiness on the first episode of *The Colbert Report*.

2. Margaret Talbot's article A Risky Proposal examines the constitutionality of state laws that ban gay marriage.

3. "The little that is known about gorillas certainly makes you want to know more," writes Alan Moorehead in his essay A Most Forgiving Ape.

4. My father's way of helping usually meant doing the whole project for me.

5. Should America the Beautiful replace The Star-Spangled Banner as the national anthem?

6. In the chapter called The Last to See Them Alive, Truman Capote shows the utterly ordinary life of the Kansas family.

7. The *30 Rock* episode Reunion won an Emmy for outstanding comedy writing.

8. Several popular films, including *Mamma Mia!* and *Muriel's Wedding*, have used Abba hits such as Dancing Queen and Take a Chance on Me.

9. My dictionary defines *isolation* as the quality or state of being alone.

10. In his poem The Shield of Achilles, W. H. Auden depicts the horror of modern warfare.

## 58d Avoiding misused quotation marks

Do not use quotation marks for *indirect* quotations — those that do not relay someone's exact words. (See 44e.)

▶ The teacher warned us that ⸢we could be expelled.⸣

Do not use quotation marks just to emphasize particular words or phrases.

▶ Julia said that her views might not be ⸢politically correct⸣ but that she wasn't going to change them for anything.

▶ Much time was spent speculating about their ⸢relationship.⸣

Do not use quotation marks around slang or colloquial language; they create the impression that you are apologizing for using those words. Instead, try to express the idea in formal language. If you have a good reason to use a slang or colloquial term, use it without quotation marks (30a).

▶ After our twenty-mile hike, we were ready to ⸢turn in.⸣

# 58e Using quotation marks with other punctuation

Periods and commas go *inside* closing quotation marks.

▶ **"Don't compromise yourself," said Janis Joplin. "You are all you've got."**

## Exception

When you use parenthetical documentation with a short quotation, place the period after the parentheses with source information (32c, 33c).

▶ **In places, de Beauvoir "sees Marxists as believing in subjectivity" (Whitmarsh 63).**

Colons, semicolons, and footnote numbers go *outside* closing quotation marks.

▶ **I felt only one emotion after reading "Eveline": sorrow.**

▶ **Everything is dark, and "a visionary light settles in her eyes"; this light is her salvation.**

▶ ***Tragedy* is defined by Aristotle as "an imitation of an action that is serious and of a certain magnitude."[1]**

Question marks, exclamation points, and dashes all go *inside* closing quotation marks if they are part of the quotation, *outside* if they are not.

PART OF THE QUOTATION

▶ **The cashier asked, "Would you like to super-size that?"**

▶ **"Jump!" one of the firefighters shouted.**

NOT PART OF THE QUOTATION

▶ **What is the theme of "A Good Man Is Hard to Find"?**

▶ **"Break a leg" — that phrase is supposed to bring good luck to a performer.**

For help using quotation marks in various documentation styles, see Chapters 32–35.

▼ ▼ ▼ ▼ ▼ ▼ ▼ ▼ ▼ ▼ ▼ ▼ ▼ ▼ ▼ ▼ ▼ ▼ ▼ ▼ ▼ ▼ ▼ ▼ ▼ ▼

## THINKING CRITICALLY ABOUT QUOTATION MARKS

### Reading with an eye for quotation marks

Read the following passage about the painter Georgia O'Keeffe, and pay particular attention to the use of quotation marks. What effect is created by the author's use of quotation marks with *hardness, crustiness,* and *crusty*? How do the quotations by O'Keeffe help support the author's description of her?

"Hardness" has not been in our century a quality much admired in women, nor in the past twenty years has it even been in official favor for men. When hardness surfaces in the very old we tend to transform it into "crustiness" or eccentricity, some tonic pepperiness to be indulged at a distance. On the evidence of her work and what she has said about it, Georgia O'Keeffe is neither "crusty" nor eccentric. She is simply hard, a straight shooter, a woman clean of received wisdom and open to what she sees. This is a woman who could early on dismiss most of her contemporaries as "dreamy," and would later single out one she liked as "a very poor painter." (And then add, apparently by way of softening the judgment: "I guess he wasn't a painter at all. He had no courage and I believe that to create one's own world in any of the arts takes courage.") This is a woman who in 1939 could advise her admirers that they were missing her point, that their appreciation of her famous flowers was merely sentimental. "When I paint a red hill," she observed coolly in the catalogue for an exhibition that year, "you say it is too bad that I don't always paint flowers. A flower touches almost everyone's heart. A red hill doesn't touch everyone's heart."

—JOAN DIDION, "Georgia O'Keeffe"

## Thinking about your own use of quotation marks

Choose a topic that is of interest on your campus, and interview one of your friends about it. On the basis of your notes from the interview, write two or three paragraphs about your friend's views, using several direct quotations that support the points you are making. Then see how closely you followed the conventions for quotation marks explained in this chapter. Note any usages that caused you problems.

# CHAPTER 59

# Other Punctuation Marks

P ARENTHESES, BRACKETS, DASHES, colons, slashes, and ellipses are everywhere. Every URL includes colons and slashes, and dashes and ellipses are increasingly common in writing that expresses conversational informality.

You can also use these punctuation marks for more formal purposes: to signal relationships among parts of sentences, to create particular rhythms, and to help readers follow your thoughts.

---

**CONNECT:** How and when do you tend to use ellipses? **13b, 56d, 59f**

**CREATE:** Sketch a brief comparison of the way you use ellipses in social media and the way you use them in your college writing assignments.

**REFLECT:** Write or record a reflection on your different purposes for using ellipses. What do you tend to omit? Do you think the meaning of your ellipses is clear to your readers?

---

## 59a  Using parentheses

Parentheses enclose material of minor or secondary importance in a sentence — material that supplements, clarifies, comments on, or illustrates what precedes or follows it. Parentheses also enclose numbers or letters that precede items in a list, and sometimes they enclose source citations or publication information.

☐ **Enclosing less important material**

▶ **Inventors and men of genius have almost always been regarded as fools at the beginning (and very often at the end) of their careers.**

—FYODOR DOSTOYEVSKY

▶ **During my research, I found problems with the flat-rate income tax (a single-rate tax with no deductions).**

A period may be placed either inside or outside a closing parenthesis. If the parenthetical material is part of a larger sentence, put the period after the parentheses; if the entire sentence is in parentheses, put the period inside the parentheses. A comma, if needed, is always placed *outside* a closing parenthesis (and never before an opening one).

○ **Gene Tunney's single defeat in an eleven-year career was to a flamboyant and dangerous fighter named Harry Greb ("The Human Windmill"), who seems to have been, judging from boxing literature, the dirtiest fighter in history.** —JOYCE CAROL OATES, "On Boxing"

If the material in parentheses is a question or an exclamation, use a question mark or exclamation point inside the closing parenthesis.

○ **Our laughing (so deep was the pleasure!) became screaming.**
—RICHARD RODRIGUEZ, "Aria: A Memoir of a Bilingual Childhood"

In general, parentheses create more of an interruption than commas (Chapter 54) but less of an interruption than dashes (59c).

□ **Enclosing numbers or letters in a list**

○ **Five distinct styles can be distinguished: (1) Old New England, (2) Deep South, (3) Middle American, (4) Wild West, and (5) Far West or Californian.** —ALISON LURIE, *The Language of Clothes*

□ **Enclosing textual citations**

The first of the following in-text citations shows the style of the American Psychological Association (see Chapter 33); the second shows the style of the Modern Language Association (see Chapter 32).

A later study resulted in somewhat different conclusions (Murphy & Orkow, 1985).

Zamora notes that Kahlo referred to her first self-portrait, given to a close friend, as "your Botticelli" (110).

# 59b Using brackets

Use brackets to enclose parenthetical elements in material that is itself within parentheses and to enclose explanatory words or comments that you are inserting into a quotation.

☐ **Setting off material within parentheses**

▷ The investigation examined the major agencies (including the National Security Agency [NSA]) that were conducting covert operations.

☐ **Inserting material within quotations**

▷ Massing notes that "on average, it [Fox News] attracts more than eight million people daily — more than double the number who watch CNN."

The bracketed words clarify *it* in the original quotation.

In the quotation in the following sentence, the artist Gauguin's name is misspelled. The bracketed Latin word *sic*, which means "so," tells readers that the person being quoted — not the writer using the quotation — made the mistake.

▷ One admirer wrote, "She was the most striking woman I'd ever seen — a sort of wonderful combination of Mia Farrow and one of Gaugin's [*sic*] Polynesian nymphs."

---

🔺 **EXERCISE 59.1**

Revise the following sentences, using parentheses and brackets correctly. Example:

**She was in fourth grade (or was it third?) when she became blind.**
$\wedge$ $\qquad\qquad$ $\wedge$

1. The committee was presented with three options to pay for the new park: 1 increase vehicle registration fees, 2 install parking meters downtown, or 3 borrow money from the reserve fund.

2. The FISA statute authorizes government wiretapping only under certain circumstances for instance, the government has to obtain a warrant.

3. The health care expert informed readers that "as we progress through middle age, we experience intimations of our own morality *sic*."

4. Some hospitals train nurses in a pseudoscientific technique called therapeutic touch TT that has been discredited by many rigorous studies.

5. Because I was carrying an umbrella, which, as it turned out, wasn't even necessary, I was required to enter the stadium through the high-security gate.

---

# 59c Using dashes

In contrast to parentheses, dashes give more rather than less emphasis to the material they enclose. A typed dash is made with two hyphens (--) with *no* spaces before, between, or after. Many word-processing programs will automatically convert two typed hyphens into a solid dash (—).

□ **Inserting a comment**

▷ Leeches — yuck — turn out to have valuable medical uses.

□ **Emphasizing explanatory material**

▷ Indeed, several of modern India's greatest scholars — such as the Mughal historian Muzaffar Alam of the University of Chicago — are madrasa graduates. —WILLIAM DALRYMPLE

A single dash toward the *end* of a sentence may serve to emphasize the material at the end, to mark a shift in tone or a hesitation in speech, or to summarize or explain what has come before.

□ **Emphasizing material at the end of a sentence**

▷ In the twentieth century it has become almost impossible to moralize about epidemics — except those which are transmitted sexually.
—SUSAN SONTAG, "AIDS and Its Metaphors"

□ **Marking a sudden change in tone**

▷ New York is a catastrophe — but a magnificent catastrophe.
—LE CORBUSIER

□ **Indicating hesitation in speech**

▷ As the officer approached his car, the driver stammered, "What — what have I done?"

□ **Introducing a summary or explanation**

▷ In walking, the average adult person employs a motor mechanism that weighs about eighty pounds — sixty pounds of muscle and twenty pounds of bone. —EDWIN WAY TEALE

◢ **EXERCISE 59.2**

Revise the following sentences to add dashes where appropriate. Example:

He is quick, violent, and mean—they don't call him Dirty Harry for
 ^
nothing—but appealing nonetheless.
 ^

1. Most people would say that Labradors are easy dogs to train but they never met our Millie.

2. Even if marijuana is dangerous an assertion disputed by many studies it is certainly no more harmful to human health than alcohol and cigarettes, which remain legal.

3. If too much exposure to negative news stories makes you feel depressed or anxious and why wouldn't it? try going on a media fast.

4. Union Carbide's plant in Bhopal, India, sprang a leak that killed more than 2,000 people and injured an additional 200,000.

5. Refrigerators especially side-by-side models use up more energy than most people realize.

## 59d Using colons

Use a colon to introduce explanations, examples, lists, and sometimes quotations. In addition, follow conventions for using colons to separate some elements (such as titles and subtitles) from one another.

### ☐ Introducing an explanation or example

▶ **The men may also wear the getup known as Sun Belt Cool: a pale beige suit, open-collared shirt (often in a darker shade than the suit), cream-colored loafers and aviator sunglasses.**

—ALISON LURIE, *The Language of Clothes*

### ☐ Introducing a series, list, or quotation

▶ **At the baby's one-month birthday party, Ah Po gave him the Four Valuable Things: ink, inkslab, paper, and brush.**

—MAXINE HONG KINGSTON, *China Men*

▶ **The teachers wondered: "Do boys and girls really learn differently? Do behavioral differences reflect socialization or biology?"**

The preceding example could have used a comma instead of a colon before the quotation (54i). You can use a colon rather than a comma to introduce a quotation when the lead-in is a complete sentence on its own.

▶ **The State of the Union address contained one surprising statement: "America is addicted to oil."**

## ☐ Separating elements

SALUTATIONS IN FORMAL LETTERS

▶ **Dear Dr. Mahiri:**

HOURS, MINUTES, AND SECONDS

▶ **4:59 PM**

▶ **2:15:06**

RATIOS

▶ **a ratio of 5:1**

BIBLICAL CHAPTERS AND VERSES

▶ **I Corinthians 3:3–5**

TITLES AND SUBTITLES

▶ *Better: A Surgeon's Notes on Performance*

CITIES AND PUBLISHERS IN BIBLIOGRAPHIC ENTRIES

▶ **New York: Farrar, Straus & Giroux, 2010**

## ☐ Eliminating misused colons

Do not put a colon between a verb and its object or complement, unless the object is a quotation.

▶ **Some natural fibers are⫶ cotton, wool, silk, and linen.**

Do not put a colon between a preposition and its object or after such expressions as *such as, especially,* or *including.*

▶ **In poetry, additional power may come from devices such as⫶ simile, metaphor, and alliteration.**

◢ **EXERCISE 59.3**

In the following items, insert a colon in any sentence that needs one and delete any unnecessary colons. Some sentences may be correct as written. Example:

> *Images: My Life in Film* includes revealing material written by Ingmar
> ^
> Bergman.

1. After discussing the case study, the class reached one main conclusion in any business, the most important asset is the customer.
2. Another example is taken from Psalm 139 16.
3. Roberto tried to make healthier choices, such as: eating organic food, walking to work, and getting plenty of rest.

4. A number of quotable movie lines come from *Casablanca*, including "Round up the usual suspects."

5. Sofi rushed to catch the 5 45 express but missed it and had to wait for the 6 19.

## 59e Using slashes

Use slashes to mark line divisions in poetry quoted within running text (58a) and to separate alternative terms. Whenever a slash separates lines of poetry, it should be preceded and followed by a space.

### ▢ Marking line divisions in poetry

◉ In "Digging," Seamus Heaney observes, "Between my finger and my thumb / The squat pen rests; snug as a gun."

### ▢ Separating alternatives

◉ Then there was Daryl, the cabdriver/bartender.

—JOHN L'HEUREUX, *The Handmaid of Desire*

Slashes also separate parts of fractions and Internet addresses.

## 59f Using ellipses

Ellipses are three equally spaced dots. Ellipses usually indicate that something has been omitted from a quoted passage, but they can also signal a pause or hesitation in speech in the same way that a dash can.

### ▢ Indicating omissions

Just as you should carefully use quotation marks around any material that you quote directly from a source, so you should carefully use ellipses to indicate that you have left out part of a quotation that otherwise appears to be a complete sentence.

The ellipses in the following example indicate two omissions — one in the middle of the sentence and one at the end. When you omit the last part of a quoted sentence, add a period before the ellipses, for a total of four dots. Be sure a complete sentence comes before and after the four points. If you are adding your own ellipses to a quotation that already has other ellipses, enclose yours in brackets.

ORIGINAL TEXT

◉ The quasi-official division of the population into three economic classes called high-, middle-, and low-income groups rather misses the point,

because as a class indicator the amount of money is not as important as
the source. —PAUL FUSSELL, "Notes on Class"

**WITH ELLIPSES**

▷ As Paul Fussell argues, "The quasi-official division of the population
into three economic classes . . . rather misses the point. . . ."

If your shortened quotation ends with a source (such as a page number, a
name, or a title), follow these steps:

1. Use three ellipsis points but no period after the quotation.

2. Add the closing quotation mark, closed up following the third ellipsis
point.

3. Add the source documentation in parentheses.

4. Use a period to indicate the end of the sentence.

▷ Packer then argues, "The Administration is right to reconsider its
strategy . . ." (34).

## ▢ Indicating a pause or hesitation

Ellipses are becoming more common in informal communication, where many
writers prefer them to a period at the end of a sentence.

▷ Let me know where you want to meet tonight. . . .

### ◢ EXERCISE 59.4

The following sentences use the punctuation marks presented in this chapter very
effectively. Read the sentences carefully; then choose one, and use it as a model for
writing a sentence of your own, making sure to use the punctuation marks in the
same way in your sentence.

1. The dad was—how can you put this gracefully?—a real blimp, a wide load,
   and the white polyester stretch-pants only emphasized the cargo.
   —GARRISON KEILLOR, "Happy to Be Here"

2. Not only are the distinctions we draw between male nature and female nature
   largely arbitrary and often pure superstition: they are completely beside the
   point. —BRIGID BROPHY, "Women"

3. If no one, including you, liked the soup the first time round (and that's why
   you've got so much left over), there is no point in freezing it for some hopeful
   future date when, miraculously, it will taste delicious. But bagging leftovers—say, stews—in single portions can be useful for those evenings when
   you're eating alone. —NIGELLA LAWSON, How to Eat

▼ ▼ ▼ ▼ ▼ ▼ ▼ ▼ ▼ ▼ ▼ ▼ ▼ ▼ ▼ ▼ ▼ ▼ ▼ ▼ ▼ ▼ ▼ ▼ ▼ ▼ ▼ ▼

## THINKING CRITICALLY ABOUT PUNCTUATION

### Reading with an eye for punctuation

In the following passage, Tom Wolfe uses dashes, parentheses, ellipses, and a colon to create rhythm and build momentum in a very long (178-word) sentence. The editorial comment inserted in brackets calls attention to the fact that the "right stuff" was, in the world Wolfe describes here, always male. Look carefully at how Wolfe and the editors use these punctuation marks, and then try writing a description of something that effectively uses as many of them as possible. Your description should be about the same length as Wolfe's passage, but it need not be all one sentence.

> Likewise, "hassling"—mock dogfighting—was strictly forbidden, and so naturally young fighter jocks could hardly wait to go up in, say, a pair of F-100s and start the duel by making a pass at each other at 800 miles an hour, the winner being the pilot who could slip in behind the other one and get locked in on his [never *her* or *his or her*!] tail ("wax his tail"), and it was not uncommon for some eager jock to try too tight an outside turn and have his engine flame out, whereupon, unable to restart it, he has to eject . . . and he shakes his fist at the victor as he floats down by parachute and his million-dollar aircraft goes *kaboom!* on the palmetto grass or the desert floor, and he starts thinking about how he can get together with the other guy back at the base in time for the two of them to get their stories straight before the investigation: "I don't know what happened, sir. I was pulling up after a target run, and it just flamed out on me."
>
> —TOM WOLFE, *The Right Stuff*

### Thinking about your own use of punctuation

Look through a draft you have recently written or are working on, and check your use of parentheses, brackets, dashes, colons, slashes, and ellipses. Do you follow the conventions presented in this chapter? If not, revise accordingly. Check the material in parentheses to see if it could use more emphasis and thus be set off instead with dashes. Then check any material in dashes to see if it could do with less emphasis and thus be punctuated with commas or parentheses.

# PART 12
# Mechanics

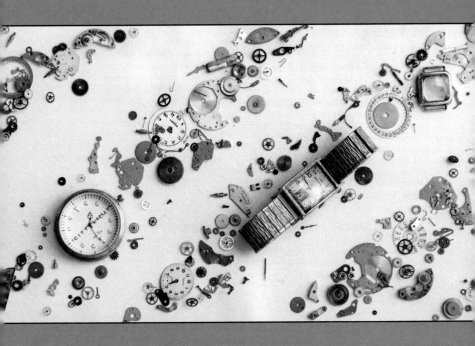

# CHAPTER 60

# Capital Letters

MANY WRITERS STRUGGLE to determine which words should be capitalized and which should not — so many, in fact, that capitalization errors have become one of the most common problems facing student writers. As with other "mechanical" aspects of writing, following established conventions for capitalizing words can help you meet your readers' expectations.

## 60a Capitalizing the first word of a sentence or line of poetry

Capitalize the first word of a sentence.

▶ **Posing relatives for photographs is a challenge.**

If you are quoting a full sentence, capitalize its first word.

▶ **Kennedy said, "Let us never negotiate out of fear."**

Capitalizing a sentence following a colon is optional.

▶ **Gould cites the work of Darwin: The [or the] theory of natural selection incorporates the principle of evolutionary ties between all animals.**

Capitalize a sentence within parentheses unless the parenthetical sentence is inserted into another sentence.

▶ **Gould cites the work of Darwin. (Other researchers cite more recent evolutionary theorists.)**

▶ **Gould cites the work of Darwin (see page 150).**

When citing poetry, follow the capitalization of the original poem. Though most poets capitalize the first word of each line in a poem, some poets do not.

▶ **Morning sun heats up the young beech tree**
   **leaves and almost lights them into fireflies**

                             —JUNE JORDAN, "Aftermath"

### Editing for capitalization

- Capitalize the first word of each sentence. If you quote a poem, follow its original capitalization. **(60a)**
- Check to make sure you have appropriately capitalized proper nouns and proper adjectives. **(60b)**
- Review titles of people or of works to be sure you have capitalized them correctly. **(60b and c)**
- Double-check the capitalization of geographic directions (*north* or *North*?), family relationships (*dad* or *Dad*?), and seasons of the year (*winter*, not *Winter*). **(60d)**

## 60b Capitalizing proper nouns and proper adjectives

Capitalize proper nouns (those naming specific persons, places, and things) and most proper adjectives (those formed from proper nouns). All other nouns are common nouns and are not capitalized unless they begin a sentence or are used as part of a proper noun: *the street where you live*, but *Elm Street*. Here, proper nouns and adjectives appear on the left and related common nouns and adjectives on the right.

**PEOPLE**

| | |
|---|---|
| Ang Lee | the film's director |
| Nixonian | political |

**NATIONS, NATIONALITIES, ETHNIC GROUPS, AND LANGUAGES**

| | |
|---|---|
| Brazil, Brazilian | their native country, his citizenship |
| Italian American | an ethnic group |
| Cantonese | one of the nation's languages |

**PLACES**

| | |
|---|---|
| Pacific Ocean | an ocean |
| Hawaiian Islands | tropical islands |

**STRUCTURES AND MONUMENTS**

| | |
|---|---|
| the Lincoln Memorial | a monument |
| the Eiffel Tower | a landmark |

**SHIPS, TRAINS, AIRCRAFT, AND SPACECRAFT**

| the *Queen Mary* | a cruise ship |
| the *City of New Orleans* | the 6:00 train |

**ORGANIZATIONS, BUSINESSES, AND GOVERNMENT INSTITUTIONS**

| United Auto Workers | a trade union |
| Library of Congress | a federal agency |
| Desmond-Fish Library | the local library |

**ACADEMIC INSTITUTIONS AND COURSES**

| University of Maryland | a state university |
| Political Science 102 | my political science course |

**HISTORICAL EVENTS AND ERAS**

| the Whiskey Rebellion | a revolt |
| the Renaissance | the fifteenth century |

**RELIGIONS AND RELIGIOUS TERMS**

| God | a deity |
| the Qur'an | a holy book |
| Catholicism, Catholic | a religion, their religious affiliation |

**TRADE NAMES**

| Nike | running shoes |
| Cheerios | cereal |

☐ **Capitalizing product names**

Some companies use capitals in the middle of their own or their product's names. Follow the style you see in company advertising or on the product itself — *eBay, FedEx, iPad*.

☐ **Capitalizing titles before names**

Capitalize titles used before a proper name. When used alone or following a proper name, most titles are not capitalized. One common exception is the word *president*, which many writers capitalize whenever it refers to the President of the United States.

| Chief Justice Roberts | John Roberts, the chief justice |
| Professor Lisa Ede | my English professor |
| Dr. Edward A. Davies | Edward A. Davies, our doctor |

**ENGLISH CAPITALIZATION**

Capitalization systems vary considerably among languages, and some languages do not use capital letters at all. English may be the only language to capitalize the first-person singular pronoun (*I*), but Dutch and German capitalize some forms of the second-person pronoun (*you*). German capitalizes all nouns; English used to capitalize more nouns than it does now (see, for instance, the Declaration of Independence).

## 60c  Capitalizing titles of works

Capitalize most words in titles (of books, articles, plays, poems, songs, films, paintings, and so on). Do not capitalize an article (*a, an, the*), a preposition, a conjunction, or the *to* in an infinitive unless it is the first or last word in a title or subtitle.

| | |
|---|---|
| *Walt Whitman: A Life* | "The Gift of the Magi" |
| "As Time Goes By" | Declaration of Independence |
| "Shooting an Elephant" | *Charlie and the Chocolate Factory* |
| *The Producers* | *Rebel without a Cause* |

### EXERCISE 60.1

Capitalize words as needed in the following sentences. Example:

T. S. Eliot,　　　　*The Waste Land,*　　　　Faber　　Faber.
t. s. eliot, who wrote *the waste land,* was an editor at faber and faber.

1. the town in the south where i was raised had a statue of a civil war soldier in the center of main street.

2. sarah palin, the former governor, frequently complained that the press had treated her harshly before she accepted a position as an analyst for fox news.

3. the corporation for public broadcasting relies on donations as well as on grants from the national endowment for the arts.

4. during the economic recession, companies such as starbucks had to close some of their stores; others, such as circuit city, went completely out of business.

5. most americans remember where they were when they heard about the 9/11 disaster.

6. accepting an award for his score for the john wayne film *the high and the mighty,* dimitri tiomkin thanked beethoven, brahms, wagner, and strauss.

# 60d Avoiding unnecessary capitalization

Do not capitalize a compass direction unless the word designates a specific geographic region.

▶ **Voters in the South and much of the West tend to favor socially conservative candidates.**

▶ **John Muir headed ~~West,~~ motivated by the need to explore.**
*west,*

Do not capitalize a word indicating a family relationship unless the word is used as part of the name or as a substitute for the name.

▶ **I could always tell when Mother was annoyed with Aunt Rose.**

▶ **When she was a child, my ~~Mother~~ shared a room with my ~~Aunt.~~**
*mother* *aunt.*

Do not capitalize seasons of the year and parts of the academic or financial year.

| | |
|---|---|
| spring | fall semester |
| winter | winter term |
| autumn | third-quarter earnings |

Capitalizing whole words or phrases for emphasis may come across to readers as SHOUTING. Use italics, underlining, or asterisks to add emphasis.

▶ **Sorry for the abrupt response, but I am \*very\* busy.**

### EXERCISE 60.2

Correct any unnecessary or missing capitalization in the following sentences. Some sentences may be correct as written. Example:

*southern governors* *Washington,*
**A group of ~~Southern Governors~~ meets annually in ~~washington,~~ DC.**

1. The Sandy Hook School Shootings in 2012 prompted yet another debate about Gun Control Laws in the United States.
2. Every Professor in the department of english has a degree in literature.
3. The Cast included several children, but only two of them had Speaking Roles.
4. Airport checkpoints are the responsibility of the Transportation Security Administration.
5. The price of oil has fluctuated this Winter.

▼ ▼ ▼ ▼ ▼ ▼ ▼ ▼ ▼ ▼ ▼ ▼ ▼ ▼ ▼ ▼ ▼ ▼ ▼ ▼ ▼ ▼ ▼ ▼ ▼ ▼ ▼

## THINKING CRITICALLY ABOUT CAPITALIZATION

The following poem uses unconventional capitalization. Read it over a few times, at least once aloud. What effect does the capitalization have? Why do you think the poet chose to use capitals as she did?

> A little Madness in the Spring
> Is wholesome even for the King,
> But God be with the Clown—
> Who ponders this tremendous scene—
> This whole Experiment of Green—
> As if it were his own!
> —EMILY DICKINSON

# CHAPTER 61

# Abbreviations and Numbers

A NY TIME YOU LOOK UP AN ADDRESS, you see an abundance of abbreviations and numbers, as in the following movie theater listing from a Google map of Berkeley, California:

Oaks Theater, 1875 Solano Ave, Berkeley, CA

Abbreviations and numbers allow writers to present detailed information in a small amount of space. In academic writing, abbreviations and numbers follow conventions that vary from field to field.

---

**QUICK HELP**

### Editing abbreviations and numbers

- Use abbreviations and numbers according to the conventions of a specific field (see p. 740): for example, *57%* might be acceptable in a math paper, but *57 percent* may be more appropriate in a sociology essay. **(61g)**
- If you use an abbreviation readers might not understand, spell out the term the first time you use it, and give the abbreviation in parentheses. **(61c)**
- If you use an abbreviation more than once, use it consistently.
- Consider your context. In informal writing, abbreviated terms and symbols are much more conventional than in formal writing. **(30a)**

---

## 61a Abbreviating titles and academic degrees

When used before or after a name, some personal and professional titles and academic degrees are abbreviated, even in academic writing.

| | |
|---|---|
| Ms. Susanna Moller | Henry Louis Gates Jr. |
| Mr. Aaron Oforlea | Gina Tartaglia, MD |
| Dr. Edward Davies | Jamie Barlow Kayes, PhD |

Most other titles — including any religious, military, academic, and governmental titles — should be spelled out in academic writing. In other writing, they may be abbreviated when they appear before a full name but should be spelled out when used with only a last name.

| | |
|---|---|
| Rev. Franklin Graham | Reverend Graham |
| Prof. Beverly Moss | Professor Moss |
| Gen. Colin Powell | General Powell |

Academic degrees may be abbreviated when used alone, but other titles used alone are never abbreviated.

▶ She received her **PhD** this year.

▶ He was a demanding ~~prof.~~, and we worked hard.
  *professor,*

Use either a title or an academic degree, but not both, with a person's name. Instead of *Dr. James Dillon, PhD*, write *Dr. James Dillon* or *James Dillon, PhD*. (Note that academic degrees such as *PhD* and *RN* often appear without periods; see 56a.)

# 61b Abbreviating years and hours

You can use the following abbreviations with numerals in formal academic writing. Notice that AD precedes the numeral; all other abbreviations follow the numeral. Today, BCE and CE are generally preferred over BC and AD, and periods in all four of these abbreviations are optional.

399 BCE ("before the common era") or 399 BC ("before Christ")

49 CE ("common era") or AD 49 (*anno Domini*, Latin for "year of our Lord")

11:15 AM (*or* a.m.)

9:00 PM (*or* p.m.)

For abbreviations, you may use full-size capital letters or small caps, a typographical option in word-processing programs.

# 61c Using acronyms and initial abbreviations

Acronyms are abbreviations that can be pronounced as words: OPEC, for example, is the acronym for the Organization of Petroleum Exporting Countries. Initial abbreviations, on the other hand, are pronounced as separate initials: NRA for National Rifle Association, for instance. Many of these abbreviations come from business, government, and science: NASA, PBS, DNA, GE, UNICEF, AIDS, SAT.

As long as you are sure your readers will understand them, use such abbreviations in your formal college writing. If the abbreviation may be unfamiliar to your readers, however, spell out the term the first time you use it, and give the abbreviation in parentheses. After that, you can use the abbreviation by itself.

▶ **The International Atomic Energy Agency (IAEA) is the central intergovernmental forum for cooperation in the nuclear arena.**

## 61d Abbreviating company names

Use such abbreviations as *Co.*, *Inc.*, *Corp.*, and *&* if they are part of a company's official name. Do not, however, use these abbreviations in most other contexts.

▶ **Sears, Roebuck & Co. was the only large** ~~corp.~~ **in town.** *corporation*

## 61e Using Latin abbreviations

In general, avoid these Latin abbreviations except when citing sources:

| | | | |
|---|---|---|---|
| cf. | compare (*confer*) | etc. | and so forth (*et cetera*) |
| e.g. | for example (*exempli gratia*) | i.e. | that is (*id est*) |
| et al. | and others (*et alia*) | N.B. | note well (*nota bene*) |

▶ **Many firms have policies to help working parents — e.g., flexible hours,** *for example,*

**parental leave, and day care.**

▶ **Before the conference began, Haivan unpacked the name tags,**

**programs, pens,** ~~etc.~~ *and so forth.*

## 61f Abbreviating reference information, geographic terms, and months

Though abbreviations for such words as *chapter* (ch.), *edition* (ed.), *page* (p.), or *pages* (pp.) are common in source citations, they are not appropriate in the body of a formal academic text.

▶ **The 1851** ~~ed.~~ **of** *Twice-Told Tales* **is now a valuable collectible.** *edition*

Place-names and months of the year are often abbreviated in source citations, but they should almost always be written out within sentences.

▶ **In** ~~Aug.,~~ **I moved from Lodi,** ~~Calif.,~~ **to** ~~L.A.~~ *August,* *California,* *Los Angeles.*

Common exceptions are *Washington, DC,* and *U.S.* The latter is acceptable as an adjective but not as a noun.

▶ **The *U.S. delegation* negotiated the treaty.**

▶ **The exchange student enjoyed the ~~U.S.~~** United States.

# 61g Using symbols and units of measurement

In academic writing for English and the other humanities, symbols such as %, +, $, and = are acceptable in charts and graphs. Dollar signs are acceptable with figures: *$11* (but not with words: *eleven dollars*). Units of measurement can be abbreviated in charts and graphs (*4 in.*) but not in the body of a formal text (*four inches*). Check with your instructor about using a word or a figure with the word *percent*: some documentation styles, such as MLA, require a word (*ten percent*), while others, such as *Chicago*, require a figure whether the word (*10 percent*) or the symbol (*10%*) is used.

▶ **The ball sailed 425 ~~ft.~~ over the fence.** feet

Informal writing also has strong conventions for using certain symbols, such as the hashtag (#) for categorizing social-media posts (see 18c) and the symbol @ for tagging Twitter users. Consider what symbols may be conventional in your context.

---

◢ **EXERCISE 61.1**

Revise each of the following sentences to eliminate any abbreviations that would be inappropriate in most academic writing. Example:

The population of the ~~U.S.~~ grew considerably in the 1980s. United States

1. Every Fri., my grandmother would walk a mi. to the P.O. and send a care package to her brother in Tenn.

2. The blue whale can grow to be 180 ft. long and can weigh up to 380,000 lbs.

3. Many a Mich.-based auto co., incl. GM, requested financial aid from the govt.

---

◆ **MULTI-LINGUAL** **THE TERM *HUNDRED***

The term *hundred* is used idiomatically in English. When it is linked with numbers like two, eight, and so on, the word *hundred* remains singular: *Eight <u>hundred</u> years have passed, and still old animosities run deep.* Add the plural *-s* to *hundred* only when no number precedes the term: <u>*Hundreds*</u> *of priceless books were lost in the fire.*

---

TALKING THE TALK | **ABBREVIATIONS AND NUMBERS IN DISCIPLINES**

Use of abbreviations and numbers varies in different fields. See a typical example from a biochemistry textbook:

> The energy of a green photon . . . is 57 kilocalories per mole (kcal/mol). An alternative unit of energy is the joule ( J), which is equal to 0.239 calorie; 1 kcal/mol is equal to 4.184 kJ/mol.   —LUBERT STRYER, *Biochemistry*

These two sentences demonstrate how useful figures and abbreviations can be; reading the same sentences would be very difficult if the numbers and units of measurement had to be written out.

Be sure to use the appropriate system of measurement for the field you are discussing and for the audience you are addressing. Scientific fields generally use metric measurements, which are the standard in most nations other than the United States.

Become familiar with the conventions governing abbreviations and numbers in your field. The following reference books provide guidelines:

*MLA Handbook for Writers of Research Papers* for literature and the humanities

*Publication Manual of the American Psychological Association* for the social sciences

*Scientific Style and Format: The CSE Manual for Authors, Editors, and Publishers* for the natural sciences

*The Chicago Manual of Style* for the humanities

*AIP Style Manual* for physics and the applied sciences

---

4. A large corp. like AT&T may help finance an employee's M.B.A.

5. Rosie began by saying, "If you want my two ¢," but she did not wait to see if listeners wanted it or not.

---

# 61h  Using numbers within sentences

In formal writing, if you can write out the number in one or two words, you should generally do so, and use figures for longer numbers.

⊙ Her screams were heard by ~~38~~ <sup>thirty-eight</sup> people, but not one person called the police.

⊙ A baseball is held together by ~~two hundred sixteen~~ <sup>216</sup> red stitches.

If one of several numbers *of the same kind* in the same sentence requires a figure, use figures for all the numbers in that sentence.

$100

▶ Our audio systems range in cost from ~~one hundred dollars~~ to $2,599.
                                        ^

## 61i Using numbers to begin sentences

When a sentence begins with a number, either spell out the number or rewrite the sentence.

One hundred nineteen
▶ ~~119~~ years of CIA labor cost taxpayers sixteen million dollars.
   ^

Most readers find it easier to read figures than three-word numbers; thus the best solution may be to rewrite this sentence: *Taxpayers spent sixteen million dollars for 119 years of CIA labor.*

## 61j Following conventions for figures

| | |
|---|---|
| ADDRESSES | 23 Main Street; 175 Fifth Avenue |
| DATES | September 17, 1951; 6 June 1983; 4 BCE; the 1860s |
| DECIMALS AND FRACTIONS | 65.34; 8½ |
| PERCENTAGES | 77 percent (*or* 77%) |
| EXACT AMOUNTS OF MONEY | $7,348; $1.46 trillion; $2.50; thirty-five (*or* 35) cents |
| SCORES AND STATISTICS | an 8–3 Red Sox victory; a verbal score of 600; an average age of 22; a mean of 53 |
| TIME OF DAY | 6:00 AM (*or* a.m.) |

### EXERCISE 61.2

Revise the numbers in the following sentences as necessary for correctness and consistency. Some sentences may be correct as written. Example:

twenty-first
Did the ~~21st~~ century begin in 2000 or 2001?
       ^

1. In 2000, Al Gore won the popular presidential vote with 50,996,116 votes, but he was still short by 5 electoral votes.

2. 200,000 people may have perished in the 2010 Haitian earthquake.

3. The senator who voted against the measure received 6817 angry emails and only twelve in support of her decision.

4. Walker signed a three-year, $4.5-million contract.

5. In that age group, the risk is estimated to be about one in 2,500.

▼ ▼ ▼ ▼ ▼ ▼ ▼ ▼ ▼ ▼ ▼ ▼ ▼ ▼ ▼ ▼ ▼ ▼ ▼ ▼ ▼ ▼ ▼ ▼ ▼ ▼ ▼

## THINKING CRITICALLY ABOUT ABBREVIATIONS AND NUMBERS

### Reading with an eye for abbreviations and numbers

The paragraph by Roger Angell at the end of Chapter 63 follows the style of the *New Yorker* magazine, which often spells out numbers in situations where this chapter recommends using figures. Read the paragraph carefully, and then consider whether it would have been easier to read if figures had been used for some of the numbers. If so, which ones? Then consider how the paragraph would have been different if Angell had used *semi-professional* instead of *semi-pro*. What effect does the abbreviated form create?

### Thinking about your own use of abbreviations and numbers

Compare the way you have used abbreviations and numbers in a piece of formal writing for a class and in a sample of your informal writing. How are they different? Have you followed conventions for correctness, consistency, and appropriateness in both pieces of writing? If you discover a problem with abbreviations or numbers, make a note of it so that you can follow conventions appropriately in the future.

# CHAPTER 62

# Italics

THE SLANTED TYPE known as *italics* is more than just a pretty typeface. In the sentence "Many people read *People* on the subway every day," the italics (and the capital letter) tell us that *People* is a publication. Italics give words special meaning or emphasis. But remember not to overuse italics to emphasize important words: doing so will get *very boring* to readers *very quickly*.

## 62a  Using italics for titles

In general, use italics for titles of long works; use quotation marks for shorter works (58b and 60c).

| | |
|---|---|
| BOOKS | *Fun Home: A Family Tragicomic* |
| CHOREOGRAPHIC WORKS | Agnes de Mille's *Rodeo* |
| FILMS AND VIDEOS | *12 Years a Slave* |
| LONG MUSICAL WORKS | *Brandenburg Concertos* |
| LONG POEMS | *Bhagavad Gita* |
| MAGAZINES | *Ebony* |
| JOURNALS | the *New England Journal of Medicine* |
| NEWSPAPERS | the *Cleveland Plain Dealer* |
| PAINTINGS AND SCULPTURE | Georgia O'Keeffe's *Black Iris* |
| PAMPHLETS | Thomas Paine's *Common Sense* |
| PLAYS | *The Book of Mormon* |
| RADIO SERIES | *All Things Considered* |
| RECORDINGS | *Slade Alive!* |
| SOFTWARE | *Final Cut Pro* |
| TELEVISION SERIES | *Orange Is the New Black* |

Do not use italics for sacred books, such as the Bible and the Qur'an; for public documents, such as the Constitution and the Magna Carta; or for the titles of your own papers. With magazines and newspapers, do not italicize or capitalize an initial *the*, even if part of the official name.

### Editing for italics

- Check that all titles of long works are italicized. **(62a)**
- If you use any words, letters, or numbers as terms, make sure they are in italics. **(62b)**
- Italicize any non-English words or phrases that are not in an English dictionary. **(62c)**
- If you use italics to emphasize words, be sure you use the italics sparingly. **(62e)**

## 62b Using italics for words, letters, and numbers referred to as terms

Italicize words, letters, and numbers referred to as terms.

▷ One characteristic of some New York speech is the absence of postvocalic *r*, with some New Yorkers pronouncing *four* as "fouh."

▷ The first four orbitals are represented by the letters *s*, *p*, *d*, and *f*.

▷ On the back of his jersey was the famous *24*.

## 62c Using italics for non-English words and phrases

Italicize words and phrases from other languages unless they have become part of English, such as the French word "bourgeois" and the Italian "pasta." If a word is in an English dictionary, it does not need italics.

▷ At last one of the phantom sleighs gliding along the street would come to a stop, and with gawky haste Mr. Burness in his fox-furred *shapka* would make for our door. —VLADIMIR NABOKOV, *Speak, Memory*

Always italicize Latin genus and species names.

▷ The caterpillars of *Hapalia*, when attacked by the wasp *Apanteles machaeralis*, drop suddenly from their leaves and suspend themselves in air by a silken thread. —STEPHEN JAY GOULD, "Nonmoral Nature"

## 62d Using italics for names of vehicles

Italicize names of specific aircraft, spacecraft, ships, and trains. Do not italicize types and classes, such as Learjet and space shuttle.

| AIRCRAFT AND SPACECRAFT | the *Spirit of St. Louis*, the *Discovery* |
| SHIPS | the *Santa Maria*, the *USS Iowa* |
| TRAINS | the *Orient Express*, Amtrak's *Lakeshore Limited* |

# 62e  Using italics for emphasis

Italics can help create emphasis in writing, but use them sparingly for this purpose. It is usually better to create emphasis with sentence structure and word choice.

▶ **Great literature and a class of literate readers are nothing new in India. What is new is the emergence of a gifted generation of Indian writers *working in English*.** ——SALMAN RUSHDIE

### ◣ EXERCISE 62.1

In each of the following sentences, identify any words that should be italicized and any italicized words that should not be. Example:

**The film Good Night, and Good Luck tells the story of a CBS newsman who helped to end the career of Senator Joseph McCarthy.**

**Italicize:** *Good Night, and Good Luck*

1. One critic claimed that few people listened to *The Velvet Underground* and *Nico* when the record was issued but that everyone who did formed a band.
2. Homemade *sushi* can be dangerous, but so can deviled eggs kept too long in a picnic basket.
3. The Web site Poisonous Plants and Animals lists tobacco (Nicotiana tabacum) as one of the most popular poisons in the world.
4. The monster in the Old English epic Beowulf got to tell his own side of the story in John Gardner's novel Grendel.
5. The 2009 film Star Trek imagines the youthful life of James T. Kirk and the crew of the Enterprise.

▼ ▼ ▼ ▼ ▼ ▼ ▼ ▼ ▼ ▼ ▼ ▼ ▼ ▼ ▼ ▼ ▼ ▼ ▼ ▼ ▼ ▼ ▼ ▼ ▼

## THINKING CRITICALLY ABOUT ITALICS

### Reading with an eye for italics

Read the following passage about a graduate English seminar carefully, particularly noting the effects created by the italics. How would it differ without any italic emphasis? What other words or phrases might the author have italicized?

There were four big tables arranged in a square, with everyone's feet sticking out into the open middle of the square. You could tell who was nervous, and how much, by watching the pairs of feet twist around each other. The Great Man presided awesomely from the high bar of the square. His head was a majestic granite-gray, like a centurion in command; he *looked* famous. His clean shoes twitched only slightly, and only when he was angry.

It turned out he was angry at me a lot of the time. He was angry because he thought me a disrupter, a rioter, a provocateur, and a fool; also crazy. And this was twenty years ago, before these things were *de rigueur* in the universities. Everything was very quiet in those days: there were only the Cold War and Korea and Joe McCarthy and the Old Old Nixon, and the only revolutionaries around were in Henry James's *The Princess Casamassima.*

—CYNTHIA OZICK, "We Are the Crazy Lady"

### Thinking about your own use of italics

Write a paragraph or two describing the most eccentric person you know, italicizing some words for special emphasis. Read your passage aloud to hear the effect of the italics. Now explain each use of italics. If you find yourself unable to give a reason, ask yourself whether the word should be italicized at all.

Then revise the passage to eliminate *all but one* use of italics. Try revising sentences and choosing more precise words to convey emphasis. Decide which version is more effective. Can you reach any conclusions about using italics for emphasis?

# CHAPTER 63

# Hyphens

**H**YPHEN PROBLEMS are now one of the twenty most common surface errors in student writing. The confusion is understandable. Over time, the conventions for hyphen use in a given word can change (*tomorrow* was once spelled *to-morrow*). New words, even compounds such as *firewall*, generally don't use hyphens, but style manuals still differ over whether to hyphenate *email* (or is it *e-mail*?). And some words are hyphenated when they serve one kind of purpose in a sentence and not when they serve another.

## 63a  Using hyphens with compound words

Some compounds are one word (*rowboat*), some are separate words (*hard drive*), and some require hyphens (*sister-in-law*). You should consult a dictionary to be sure. However, the following conventions can help you decide when to use hyphens with compound words.

### ☐ Hyphenating compound adjectives

Hyphenate most compound adjectives that precede a noun but not those that follow a noun.

| | |
|---|---|
| a *well-liked* boss | My boss is *well liked*. |
| a *six-foot* plank | The plank is *six feet long*. |

In general, the reason for hyphenating most compound adjectives is to facilitate reading.

▶ **Designers often use potted plants as living‑room dividers.**

Without the hyphen, *living* may seem to modify *room dividers*.

Commonly used compound adjectives, however, do not usually need to be hyphenated for clarity — *income tax reform* or *first class mail* would seldom if ever be misunderstood.

Never hyphenate an *-ly* adverb and an adjective.

▶ **They used a widely‑distributed mailing list.**

Compound adjectives formed from compound proper nouns are hyphenated if the noun is hyphenated: *Austro-Hungarian history* but *Latin American literature*.

## ▢ Hyphenating coined compounds

You may need hyphens to link coined compounds, combinations of words that you are using in an unexpected way, especially as an adjective.

▶ **She gave me her I-told-you-so look before leaving the party.**

## ▢ Hyphenating fractions and compound numbers

Use a hyphen to write out fractions and to spell out compound numbers from twenty-one to ninety-nine, both when they stand alone and when they are part of larger numbers. (Usually such larger numbers should be written as numerals. See Chapter 61.)

| | |
|---|---|
| one-seventh | thirty-seven |
| two and seven-sixteenths | three hundred fifty-four thousand |

## ▢ Using suspended hyphens

A series of compound words that share the same base word can be shortened by the use of suspended hyphens.

▶ **Each student should do the work him- or herself.**

# 63b Using hyphens with prefixes and suffixes

Most words containing prefixes or suffixes are written without hyphens: *anti-war, Romanesque.* Here are some exceptions:

BEFORE CAPITALIZED BASE WORDS   un-American, non-Catholic

| | |
|---|---|
| **WITH FIGURES** | pre-1960, post-1945 |
| **WITH CERTAIN PREFIXES AND SUFFIXES** | all-state, ex-partner, self-possessed, quasi-legislative, mayor-elect, fifty-odd |
| **WITH COMPOUND BASE WORDS** | pre-high school, post-cold war |
| **FOR CLARITY OR EASE OF READING** | re-cover, anti-inflation, un-ionized |

*Re-cover* means "cover again"; the hyphen distinguishes it from *recover*, meaning "get well." In *anti-inflation* and *un-ionized*, the hyphens separate confusing clusters of vowels and consonants.

# 63c Avoiding unnecessary hyphens

Unnecessary hyphens are at least as common a problem as omitted ones. Do not hyphenate the parts of a two-word verb such as *depend on, turn off,* or *tune out* (43b).

▶ **Players must pick⁄up a medical form before football tryouts.**

> The words *pick up* act as a verb and should not be hyphenated.

However, be careful to check that the two words do indeed function as a verb in the sentence; if they function as an adjective, a hyphen may be needed (36a and d).

▶ **Let's sign up for the early class.**

> The verb *sign up* should not have a hyphen.

▶ **Where is the sign-up sheet?**

> The compound adjective *sign-up*, which modifies the noun *sheet*, needs a hyphen.

Do not hyphenate a subject complement — a word group that follows a linking verb (such as a form of *be* or *seem*) and describes the subject (37b).

▶ **Audrey is almost three⁄years⁄old.**

## ◢ EXERCISE 63.1

Insert or delete hyphens as necessary in the following sentences. Use your dictionary if you are not sure whether or where to hyphenate a word. Example:

> **The governor⁻elect joked about the polls.**
> ^

1. The group seeks volunteers to set-up chairs in the meeting room before the event.

2. Despite concerns about reliability, police line-ups are still frequently used to identify suspects.

3. I was ill-prepared for my first calculus exam, but I managed to pass anyway.

4. Some passengers were bumped from the over-sold flight.

5. Having an ignore the customer attitude may actually make a service-industry job less pleasant.

6. Both pro and antiState Department groups registered complaints.

7. At a yard sale, I found a 1964 pre CBS Fender Stratocaster in mint condition.

8. Applicants who are over fifty-years-old may face age discrimination.

9. Neil Armstrong, a selfproclaimed "nerdy engineer," was the first person to set foot on the moon.

10. Carefully-marketed children's safety products suggest to new parents that the more they spend, the safer their kids will be.

▼ ▼ ▼ ▼ ▼ ▼ ▼ ▼ ▼ ▼ ▼ ▼ ▼ ▼ ▼ ▼ ▼ ▼ ▼ ▼ ▼ ▼ ▼ ▼ ▼

## THINKING CRITICALLY ABOUT HYPHENATION

The following paragraph uses many hyphens. Read it carefully, and note how the hyphens make the paragraph easier to read. Why do you think *semi-pro* is hyphenated? Why is *junior-college* hyphenated in the last sentence?

All semi-pro leagues, it should be understood, are self-sustaining, and have no farm affiliation or other connection with the twenty-six major-league clubs, or with the seventeen leagues and hundred and fifty-two teams . . . that make up the National Association—the minors, that is. There is no central body of semi-pro teams, and semi-pro players are not included among the six hundred and fifty major-leaguers, the twenty-five-hundred-odd minor-leaguers, plus all the managers, coaches, presidents, commissioners, front-office people, and scouts, who, taken together, constitute the great tent called organized ball. (A much diminished tent, at that; back in 1949, the minors included fifty-nine leagues, about four hundred and forty-eight teams, and perhaps ten thousand players.) Also outside the tent, but perhaps within its shade, are five college leagues, ranging across the country from Cape Cod to Alaska, where the most promising freshman, sophomore, and junior-college ballplayers . . . compete against each other. —ROGER ANGELL, "In the Country"

# GLOSSARY OF USAGE

Conventions of usage might be called the "good manners" of discourse. And just as manners vary from culture to culture and time to time, so do conventions of usage. Matters of usage, like other language choices you must make, depend on what your purpose is and on what is appropriate for a particular audience at a particular time.

**a, an** Use *a* with a word that begins with a consonant (*a book*), a consonant sound such as "y" or "w" (*a euphoric moment*, *a one-sided match*), or a sounded *h* (*a hemisphere*). Use *an* with a word that begins with a vowel (*an umbrella*), a vowel sound (*an X-ray*), or a silent *h* (*an honor*).

**accept, except** The verb *accept* means "receive" or "agree to." *Except* is usually a preposition that means "aside from" or "excluding." *All the plaintiffs except Mr. Kim decided to accept the settlement.*

**advice, advise** The noun *advice* means "opinion" or "suggestion"; the verb *advise* means "offer advice." *Doctors advise everyone not to smoke, but many people ignore the advice.*

**affect, effect** As a verb, *affect* means "influence" or "move the emotions of"; as a noun, it means "emotions" or "feelings." *Effect* is a noun meaning "result"; less commonly, it is a verb meaning "bring about." *The storm affected a large area. Its effects included widespread power failures. The drug effected a major change in the patient's affect.*

**aggravate** The formal meaning is "make worse." *Having another mouth to feed aggravated their poverty.* In academic and professional writing, avoid using *aggravate* to mean "irritate" or "annoy."

**all ready, already** *All ready* means "fully prepared." *Already* means "previously." *We were all ready for Lucy's party when we learned that she had already left.*

**all right, alright** Avoid the spelling *alright*.

**all together, altogether** *All together* means "all in a group" or "gathered in one place." *Altogether* means "completely" or "everything considered." *When the board members were all together, their mutual distrust was altogether obvious.*

**allude, elude** *Allude* means "refer indirectly." *Elude* means "avoid" or "escape from." *The candidate did not even allude to her opponent. The suspect eluded the police for several days.*

**allusion, illusion** An *allusion* is an indirect reference. An *illusion* is a false or misleading appearance. *The speaker's allusion to the Bible created an illusion of piety.*

**a lot** Avoid the spelling *alot*.

**already** See *all ready, already*.

**alright** See *all right, alright*.

**altogether** See *all together, altogether*.

**among, between** In referring to two things or people, use *between*. In referring to three or more, use *among*. *The* *relationship <u>between</u> the twins is different from that <u>among</u> the other three children.*

**amount, number** Use *amount* with quantities you cannot count; use *number* for quantities you can count. *A small <u>number</u> of volunteers cleared a large <u>amount</u> of brush.*

**an** See *a, an.*

**and/or** Avoid this term except in business or legal writing. Instead of *fat and/ or protein,* write *fat, protein, or both.*

**any body, anybody, any one, anyone** *Anybody* and *anyone* are pronouns meaning "any person." *<u>Anyone</u> [or <u>anybody</u>] would enjoy this film. Any body is an adjective modifying a noun. <u>Any body</u> of water has its own ecology. Any one is two adjectives or a pronoun modified by an adjective. Customers could buy only two sale items at <u>any one</u> time. The winner could choose <u>any one</u> of the prizes.*

**anyplace** In academic and professional discourse, use *anywhere* instead.

**anyway, anyways** In writing, use *anyway,* not *anyways.*

**apt, liable, likely** *Likely to* means "probably will," and *apt to* means "inclines or tends to." In many instances, they are interchangeable. *Liable* often carries a more negative sense and is also a legal term meaning "obligated" or "responsible."

**as** Avoid sentences in which it is not clear if *as* means "when" or "because." For example, does *Carl left town <u>as</u> his father was arriving* mean "at the same time as his father was arriving" or "because his father was arriving"?

**as, as if, like** In academic and professional writing, use *as* or *as if* instead of *like* to introduce a clause. *The dog howled <u>as if</u> [not *like*] it were in pain. She did <u>as</u> [not *like*] I suggested.*

**assure, ensure, insure** *Assure* means "convince" or "promise"; its direct object is usually a person or persons. *She <u>assured</u> voters she would not raise taxes. Ensure and insure both mean "make certain," but insure usually refers specifically to protection against financial loss. When the city rationed water to <u>ensure</u> that the supply would last, the Browns could no longer afford to <u>insure</u> their car-wash business.*

**as to** Do not use *as to* as a substitute for *about. Karen was unsure <u>about</u> [not *as to*] Bruce's intentions.*

**at, where** See *where.*

**awhile, a while** Always use *a while* after a preposition such as *for, in,* or *after. We drove <u>awhile</u> and then stopped for <u>a while</u>.*

**bad, badly** Use *bad* after a linking verb such as *be, feel,* or *seem.* Use *badly* to modify an action verb, an adjective, or another verb. *The hostess felt <u>bad</u> because the dinner was <u>badly</u> prepared.*

**bare, bear** Use *bare* to mean "uncovered" and *bear* to refer to the animal or to mean "carry" or "endure": *The walls were <u>bare</u>. The emptiness was hard to <u>bear</u>.*

**because of, due to** Use *due to* when the effect, stated as a noun, appears before the verb *be. His illness was <u>due to</u> malnutrition.* (*Illness,* a noun, is the effect.) Use *because of* when the effect is stated as a clause. *He was sick <u>because of</u> malnutrition.* (*He was sick,* a clause, is the effect.)

**being as, being that** In academic or professional writing, use *because* or *since* instead of these expressions. *<u>Because</u> [not *being as*] Romeo killed Tybalt, he was banished to Padua.*

**beside, besides** *Beside* is a preposition meaning "next to." *Besides* can be a preposition meaning "other than" or an adverb meaning "in addition." *No one <u>besides</u> Francesca would sit <u>beside</u> him.*

**between** See *among, between.*

**brake, break** *Brake* means "to stop" and also refers to a stopping mechanism: *Check the brakes. Break* means "fracture" or an interruption: *The coffee break was too short.*

**breath, breathe** *Breath* is a noun; *breathe,* a verb. "*Breathe,*" *said the nurse, so June took a deep breath.*

**bring, take** Use *bring* when an object is moved from a farther to a nearer place; use *take* when the opposite is true. *Take the box to the post office; bring back my mail.*

**but that, but what** Avoid using these as substitutes for *that* in expressions of doubt. *Hercule Poirot never doubted that* [not *but that*] *he would solve the case.*

**but yet** Do not use these words together. *He is strong but* [not *but yet*] *gentle.*

**can, may** *Can* refers to ability and *may* to possibility or permission. *Since I can ski the slalom well, I may win the race.*

**can't hardly** *Hardly* has a negative meaning; therefore, *can't hardly* is a double negative. This expression is commonly used in some varieties of English but is not used in academic English. *Tim can* [not *can't*] *hardly wait.*

**can't help but** This expression is not used in academic English. Use *I can't help going* rather than *I can't help but go.*

**censor, censure** *Censor* means "remove that which is considered offensive." *Censure* means "formally reprimand." *The newspaper censored stories that offended advertisers. The legislature censured the official for misconduct.*

**compare to, compare with** *Compare to* means "regard as similar." *Jamie compared the loss to a kick in the head. Compare with* means "examine to find

differences or similarities." *Compare Tim Burton's films with David Lynch's.*

**complement, compliment** *Complement* means "go well with." *Compliment* means "praise." *Guests complimented her on how her earrings complemented her gown.*

**comprise, compose** *Comprise* means "contain." *Compose* means "make up." *The class comprises twenty students. Twenty students compose the class.*

**conscience, conscious** *Conscience* means "a sense of right and wrong." *Conscious* means "awake" or "aware." *Lisa was conscious of a guilty conscience.*

**consensus of opinion** Use *consensus* instead of this redundant phrase. *The family consensus was to sell the old house.*

**consequently, subsequently** *Consequently* means "as a result"; *subsequently* means "then." *He quit, and subsequently his wife lost her job; consequently, they had to sell their house.*

**continual, continuous** *Continual* means "repeated at regular or frequent intervals." *Continuous* means "continuing or connected without a break." *The damage done by continuous erosion was increased by the continual storms.*

**could of** *Have,* not *of,* should follow *could, would, should,* or *might. We could have* [not *of* ] *invited them.*

**criteria, criterion** *Criterion* means "standard of judgment" or "necessary qualification." *Criteria* is the plural form. *Image is the wrong criterion for choosing a president.*

**data** *Data* is the plural form of the Latin word *datum,* meaning "fact." Although *data* is used informally as either singular or plural, in academic or professional writing, treat *data* as plural. *These data indicate that fewer people are smoking.*

**different from, different than**
*Different from* is generally preferred in academic and professional writing, although both of these phrases are widely used. *Her lab results were no different from* [not *than*] *his*.

**discreet, discrete** *Discreet* means "tactful" or "prudent." *Discrete* means "separate" or "distinct." *The leader's discreet efforts kept all the discrete factions unified.*

**disinterested, uninterested** *Disinterested* means "unbiased." *Uninterested* means "indifferent." *Finding disinterested jurors was difficult. She was uninterested in the verdict.*

**distinct, distinctive** *Distinct* means "separate" or "well defined." *Distinctive* means "characteristic." *Germany includes many distinct regions, each with a distinctive accent.*

**doesn't, don't** *Doesn't* is the contraction for *does not*. Use it with *he, she, it,* and singular nouns. *Don't* stands for *do not*; use it with *I, you, we, they,* and plural nouns.

**due to** See *because of, due to*.

**each other, one another** Use *each other* in sentences involving two subjects and *one another* in sentences involving more than two.

**effect** See *affect, effect*.

**elicit, illicit** The verb *elicit* means "draw out." The adjective *illicit* means "illegal." *The police elicited from the criminal the names of others involved in illicit activities.*

**elude** See *allude, elude*.

**emigrate from, immigrate to** *Emigrate from* means "move away from one's country." *Immigrate to* means "move to another country." *We emigrated from Norway in 1999. We immigrated to the United States.*

**ensure** See *assure, ensure, insure*.

**enthused, enthusiastic** Use *enthusiastic* rather than *enthused* in academic and professional writing.

**equally as good** Replace this redundant phrase with *equally good* or *as good*.

**every day, everyday** *Everyday* is an adjective meaning "ordinary." *Every day* is an adjective and a noun, meaning "each day." *I wore everyday clothes almost every day.*

**every one, everyone** *Everyone* is a pronoun. *Every one* is an adjective and a pronoun, referring to each member of a group. *Because he began after everyone else, David could not finish every one of the problems.*

**except** See *accept, except*.

**explicit, implicit** *Explicit* means "directly or openly expressed." *Implicit* means "indirectly expressed or implied." *The explicit message of the ad urged consumers to buy the product, while the implicit message promised popularity if they did so.*

**farther, further** *Farther* refers to physical distance. *How much farther is it to Munich? Further* refers to time or degree. *I want to avoid further delays.*

**fewer, less** Use *fewer* with nouns that can be counted. Use *less* with general amounts that you cannot count. *The world needs fewer bombs and less hostility.*

**finalize** *Finalize* is a pretentious way of saying "end" or "make final." *We closed* [not *finalized*] *the deal.*

**firstly, secondly, etc.** *First, second,* etc., are more common in U.S. English.

**flaunt, flout** *Flaunt* means to "show off." *Flout* means to "mock" or "scorn." *The drug dealers flouted authority by flaunting their wealth.*

**former, latter** *Former* refers to the first and *latter* to the second of two things previously mentioned. *Kathy and Anna are athletes; the former plays tennis, and the latter runs.*

**further** See *farther, further.*

**good, well** *Good* is an adjective and should not be used as a substitute for the adverb *well. Gabriel is a good host who cooks well.*

**good and** *Good and* is colloquial for "very"; avoid it in academic and professional writing.

**hanged, hung** *Hanged* refers to executions; *hung* is used for all other meanings.

**hardly** See *can't hardly.*

**herself, himself, myself, yourself** Do not use these reflexive pronouns as subjects or as objects unless they are necessary. *Jane and I* [not *myself*] *agree. They invited John and me* [not *myself*].

**he/she, his/her** Better solutions for avoiding sexist language are to write out *he or she,* to eliminate pronouns entirely, or to make the subject plural. Instead of writing *Everyone should carry his/her driver's license,* try *Drivers should carry their licenses* or *People should carry their driver's licenses.*

**himself** See *herself, himself, myself, yourself.*

**hisself** Use *himself* instead in academic or professional writing.

**hopefully** *Hopefully* is often used informally to mean "it is hoped," but its formal meaning is "with hope." *Sam watched the roulette wheel hopefully* [not *Hopefully, Sam will win*].

**hung** See *hanged, hung.*

**illicit** See *elicit, illicit.*

**illusion** See *allusion, illusion.*

**immigrate to** See *emigrate from, immigrate to.*

**impact** Some readers object to the colloquial use of *impact* or *impact on* as a verb meaning "affect." *Population control may reduce* [not *impact*] *world hunger.*

**implicit** See *explicit, implicit.*

**imply, infer** To *imply* is to suggest indirectly. To *infer* is to guess or conclude on the basis of an indirect suggestion. *The note implied they were planning a small wedding; we inferred we would not be invited.*

**inside of, outside of** Use *inside* and *outside* instead. *The class regularly met outside* [not *outside of* ] *the building.*

**insure** See *assure, ensure, insure.*

**interact, interface** *Interact* is a vague word meaning "do something that somehow involves another person." *Interface* is computer jargon; when used as a verb, it means "discuss" or "communicate." Avoid both verbs in academic and professional writing.

**irregardless, regardless** *Irregardless* is a double negative. Use *regardless.*

**is when, is where** These vague expressions are often incorrectly used in definitions. *Schizophrenia is a psychotic condition in which* [not *is when* or *is where*] *a person withdraws from reality.*

**its, it's** *Its* is the possessive form of *it. It's* is a contraction for *it is* or *it has. It's important to observe the rat before it eats its meal.*

**kind, sort, type** These singular nouns should be modified with *this* or *that,* not *these* or *those,* and followed by other singular nouns, not plural nouns. *Wear this kind of dress* [not *those kind of dresses*].

**kind of, sort of** In formal writing, avoid these colloquialisms. *Amy was somewhat* [not *kind of* ] *tired.*

**know, no** Use *know* to mean "understand." *No* is the opposite of *yes.*

**later, latter** *Later* means "after some time." *Latter* refers to the second of two items named. *Juan and Chad won all their early matches, but the latter was injured later in the season.*

**latter**   See *former, latter* and *later, latter.*

**lay, lie**   *Lay* means "place" or "put." Its main forms are *lay, laid, laid.* It generally has a direct object, specifying what has been placed. *She laid her books on the desk. Lie* means "recline" or "be positioned" and does not take a direct object. Its main forms are *lie, lay, lain. She lay awake until two.*

**leave, let**   *Leave* means "go away." *Let* means "allow." *Leave alone* and *let alone* are interchangeable. *Let me leave now, and leave* [or *let*] *me alone from now on!*

**lend, loan**   In academic and professional writing, do not use *loan* as a verb; use *lend* instead. *Please lend me your pen so that I may fill out this application for a loan.*

**less**   See *fewer, less.*

**let**   See *leave, let.*

**liable**   See *apt, liable, likely.*

**lie**   See *lay, lie.*

**like**   See *as, as if, like.*

**likely**   See *apt, liable, likely.*

**literally**   *Literally* means "actually" or "exactly as stated." Use it to stress the truth of a statement that might otherwise be understood as figurative. Do not use *literally* as an intensifier in a figurative statement. *Mirna was literally at the edge of her seat* may be accurate, but *Mirna is so hungry that she could literally eat a horse* is not.

**loan**   See *lend, loan.*

**loose, lose**   *Lose* is a verb meaning "misplace." *Loose* is an adjective that means "not securely attached." *Sew on that loose button before you lose it.*

**lots, lots of**   Avoid these informal expressions meaning "much" or "many" in academic or professional discourse.

**man, mankind**   Replace these terms with *people, humans, humankind, men and women,* or similar wording.

**may**   See *can, may.*

**may be, maybe**   *May be* is a verb phrase. *Maybe* is an adverb that means "perhaps." *He may be the head of the organization, but maybe someone else would handle a crisis better.*

**media**   *Media* is the plural form of the noun *medium* and takes a plural verb. *The media are* [not *is*] *obsessed with scandals.*

**might of**   See *could of.*

**moral, morale**   A *moral* is a succinct lesson. *The moral of the story is that generosity is rewarded. Morale* means "spirit" or "mood." *Office morale was low.*

**myself**   See *herself, himself, myself, yourself.*

**no**   See *know, no.*

**nor, or**   Use *either* with *or* and *neither* with *nor.*

**number**   See *amount, number.*

**off, of**   Use *off* without *of. The spaghetti slipped off* [not *off of*] *the plate.*

**OK, O.K., okay**   All are acceptable spellings, but avoid the term in academic and professional discourse.

**on account of**   Use this substitute for *because of* sparingly or not at all.

**one another**   See *each other, one another.*

**or**   See *nor, or.*

**outside of**   See *inside of, outside of.*

**owing to the fact that**   Avoid this and other wordy expressions for *because.*

**passed, past** Use *passed* to mean "went by" or "received a passing grade": *The marching band passed the reviewing stand.* Use *past* to refer to a time before the present: *Historians study the past.*

**per** Use the Latin *per* only in standard technical phrases such as *miles per hour.* Otherwise, find English equivalents. *As mentioned in* [not *As per*] *the latest report, the country's average food consumption each day* [not *per day*] *is only 2,000 calories.*

**percent, percentage** Use *percent* with a specific number; use *percentage* with an adjective such as *large* or *small. Last year, 80 percent of the members were female. A large percentage of the members are women.*

**plenty** *Plenty* means "enough" or "a great abundance." *They told us America was a land of plenty.* Colloquially, it is used to mean "very," a usage you should avoid in academic and professional writing. *He was very* [not *plenty*] *tired.*

**plus** *Plus* means "in addition to." *Your salary plus mine will cover our expenses.* In academic writing, do not use *plus* to mean "besides" or "moreover." *That dress does not fit me. Besides* [not *Plus*], *it is the wrong color.*

**precede, proceed** *Precede* means "come before"; *proceed* means "go forward." *Despite the storm that preceded the ceremony, the wedding proceeded on schedule.*

**pretty** Except in informal situations, avoid using *pretty* as a substitute for "rather," "somewhat," or "quite." *Bill was quite* [not *pretty*] *disagreeable.*

**principal, principle** When used as a noun, *principal* refers to a head official or an amount of money; when used as an adjective, it means "most significant."

*Principle* means "fundamental law or belief." *Albert went to the principal and defended himself with the principle of free speech.*

**proceed** See *precede, proceed.*

**quotation, quote** *Quote* is a verb, and *quotation* is a noun. *He quoted the president, and the quotation* [not *quote*] *was preserved in history books.*

**raise, rise** *Raise* means "lift" or "move upward." (Referring to children, it means "bring up.") It takes a direct object; someone raises something. *The guests raised their glasses to toast. Rise* means "go upward." It does not take a direct object; something rises by itself. *She saw the steam rise from the pan.*

**rarely ever** Use *rarely* by itself, or use *hardly ever. When we were poor, we rarely went to the movies.*

**real, really** *Real* is an adjective, and *really* is an adverb. Do not substitute *real* for *really.* In academic and professional writing, do not use *real* or *really* to mean "very." *The old man walked very* [not *real* or *really*] *slowly.*

**reason is because** Use either *the reason is that* or *because*—not both. *The reason the copier stopped is that* [not *is because*] *the paper jammed.*

**reason why** Avoid this expression in formal writing. *The reason* [not *reason why*] *this book is short is market demand.*

**regardless** See *irregardless, regardless.*

**respectfully, respectively** *Respectfully* means "with respect." *Respectively* means "in the order given." *Karen and David are, respectively, a juggler and an acrobat. The children treated their grandparents respectfully.*

**rise** See *raise, rise.*

**set, sit** *Set* usually means "put" or "place" and takes a direct object. *Sit* refers to taking a seat and does not take an object. <u>*Set*</u> *your cup on the table, and* <u>*sit*</u> *down.*

**should of** See *could of.*

**since** Be careful not to use *since* ambiguously. In <u>*Since*</u> *I broke my leg, I've stayed home,* the word *since* might be understood to mean either "because" or "ever since."

**sit** See *set, sit.*

**so** In academic and professional writing, avoid using *so* alone to mean "very." Instead, follow *so* with *that* to show how the intensified condition leads to a result. *Aaron was* <u>*so*</u> *tired* <u>*that*</u> *he fell asleep at the wheel.*

**someplace** Use *somewhere* instead in academic and professional writing.

**some time, sometime, sometimes** *Some time* refers to a length of time. *Please leave me* <u>*some time*</u> *to dress. Sometime* means "at some indefinite later time." <u>*Sometime*</u> *I will take you to London. Sometimes* means "occasionally." <u>*Sometimes*</u> *I eat sushi.*

**sort** See *kind, sort, type.*

**sort of** See *kind of, sort of.*

**stationary, stationery** *Stationary* means "standing still"; *stationery* means "writing paper." *When the bus was* <u>*stationary*</u>, *Pat took out* <u>*stationery*</u> *and wrote a note.*

**subsequently** See *consequently, subsequently.*

**supposed to, used to** Be careful to include the final *-d* in these expressions. *He is* <u>*supposed to*</u> *attend.*

**sure, surely** Avoid using *sure* as an intensifier. Instead, use *certainly. I was* <u>*certainly*</u> *glad to see you.*

**take** See *bring, take.*

**than, then** Use *than* in comparative statements. *The cat was bigger* <u>*than*</u> *the dog.* Use *then* when referring to a sequence of events. *I won, and* <u>*then*</u> *I cried.*

**that, which** A clause beginning with *that* singles out the item being described. *The book* <u>*that*</u> *is on the table is a good one* specifies the book on the table as opposed to some other book. A clause beginning with *which* may or may not single out the item, although some writers use *which* clauses only to add more information about an item being described. *The book,* <u>*which*</u> *is on the table, is a good one* contains a *which* clause between the commas. The clause simply adds extra, nonessential information about the book; it does not specify which book.

**theirselves** Use *themselves* instead in academic and professional writing.

**then** See *than, then.*

**thorough, threw, through** *Thorough* means "complete": *After a* <u>*thorough*</u> *inspection, the restaurant reopened. Threw* is the past tense of *throw,* and *through* means "in one side and out the other": *He* <u>*threw*</u> *the ball* <u>*through*</u> *a window.*

**to, too, two** *To* generally shows direction. *Too* means "also." *Two* is the number. *We,* <u>*too*</u>, *are going* <u>*to*</u> *the meeting in* <u>*two*</u> *hours.* Avoid using *to* after *where. Where are you flying* [not *flying to*]*?*

**two** See *to, too, two.*

**type** See *kind, sort, type.*

**uninterested** See *disinterested, uninterested.*

**unique** Some people argue that *unique* means "one and only" and object to usage that suggests it means merely "unusual." In formal writing, avoid constructions such as *quite unique.*

**used to** See *supposed to, used to.*

**very** Avoid using *very* to intensify a weak adjective or adverb; instead, replace the adjective or adverb with a stronger, more precise, or more colorful word. Instead of *very nice,* for example, use *kind, warm, sensitive, endearing,* or *friendly.*

**way, ways** When referring to distance, use *way. Graduation was a long <u>way</u>* [not *ways*] *off.*

**well** See *good, well.*

**where** Use *where* alone, not with words such as *at* and *to*. *<u>Where</u> are you going* [not *going to*]?

**which** See *that, which.*

**who, whom** Use *who* if the word is the subject of the clause and *whom* if the word is the object of the clause. *Monica, <u>who</u> smokes incessantly, is my godmother.* (*Who* is the subject of the clause; the verb is *smokes.*) *Monica, <u>whom</u> I saw last winter, lives in Tucson.* (*Whom* is the object of the verb *saw.*)

**who's, whose** *Who's* is a contraction for *who is* or *who has*. *<u>Who's</u> on the patio? Whose* is a possessive form. *<u>Whose</u> sculpture is in the garden? <u>Whose</u> is on the patio?*

**would of** See *could of.*

**yet** See *but yet.*

**your, you're** *Your* shows possession. *Bring <u>your</u> sleeping bag along. You're* is the contraction for *you are. <u>You're</u> in the wrong sleeping bag.*

**yourself** See *herself, himself, myself, yourself.*

# Acknowledgments

**Derek Bok.** "Protecting Freedom of Expression at Harvard." Reprinted by permission of the author.

**Emily Dickinson.** "A little Madness in the Spring." Reprinted by permission of the publishers and the Trustees of Amherst College from *The Poems of Emily Dickinson*, edited by Thomas H. Johnson, Cambridge, Mass.: The Belknap Press of Harvard University Press. Copyright © 1951, 1955, 1979, 1983 by the President and Fellows of Harvard College.

**Robert Frost.** Excerpt from "The Road Not Taken." From *The Poetry of Robert Frost*, edited by Edward Connery Lathem. Copyright © 1916, 1969 by Henry Holt and Company, LLC. Copyright © 1944 by Robert Frost. Used by permission of Henry Holt and Company, LLC. All rights reserved.

**Langston Hughes.** "Harlem [2]." From *The Collected Poems of Langston Hughes*, by Langston Hughes, edited by Arnold Rampersad with David Roessel, Associate Editor. Copyright © 1994 by The Estate of Langston Hughes. Used by permission of Harold Ober Associates, Inc., and Alfred A. Knopf, an imprint of the Knopf Doubleday Publishing Group, a division of Random House, LLC. All rights reserved. Any third-party use of this material, outside of this publication, is prohibited. Interested parties must apply directly to Random House, LLC, for permission.

**James Hunter.** "Outlaw Classics." From *Rolling Stone*, March 9, 2006. Copyright © 2006 Rolling Stone, LLC. All rights reserved. Reprinted by permission.

**Andrea A. Lunsford and Karen J. Lunsford.** "'Mistakes Are a Fact of Life': A National Comparative Study." From *College Composition and Communication*, Vol. 59, No. 4, June 2008. Copyright © 2008 by the National Council of Teachers of English. Reprinted with permission.

**Joshua Oppenheimer.** Excerpt from "Director's Statement." From *The Act of Killing*. Reprinted by permission of Final Cut for Real.

## PART-OPENING ART

**Openers for Parts 1–12:** Photos by Mike Enright/www.menright.com; photo styling by Barbara Lipp.

## LAUNCHPAD MEDIA

*Chicago*-style project, **Amanda Rinder**
   **p. 5,** Courtesy College of Architecture and the Arts, University of Illinois at Chicago

**Critical analysis, Shuqiao Song**
   **p. 2,** René Magritte, *The Treason of Images*. Digital Image © 2013 Museum Associates/ LACMA. Licensed by Art Resource, NY. © 2014 C. Herscovici/Artists Rights Society (ARS), New York.
   **pp. 3, 5, 6,** From *Fun Home: A Family Tragicomic* by Alison Bechdel. Copyright © 2006 by Alison Bechdel. Reprinted by permission of Houghton Mifflin Harcourt Publishing Company. All rights reserved.

# INDEX
## with Glossary of Terms

Words in **blue** are followed by a definition. **Boldface** terms in definitions are themselves defined elsewhere in this index.

looping, 41–42
*loose, lose,* 756
*lots, lots of,* 756
*-ly* adverbs, 540–41, 748

# M

magazines. *See* periodical articles
main clauses. *See* independent clause
main idea. *See* thesis
main verbs, 534, 550, 569–73
major premises, 173–74
*man, mankind,* 362, 756
manuscript format. *See* formatting
*many, few,* 563–64
maps, 270. *See also* visuals and media
margins, 266, 267–68. *See also* design;
    formatting
marking up drafts, 68–69, 71–75. *See*
    *also* annotating
*may,* as helping verb, 534, 570–72
*may, can,* 753
*maybe, may be,* 397, 756
*me, I,* 598, 603
meaning
    clarifying, 355–56
    reading for, 64, 128
measurement, units of, 739, 740
mechanical errors. *See* capital letters;
    italics; punctuation; quotations
*media,* 756
media. *See* multimodal text; visuals and
    media
medium of publication. *See also* visuals
    and media
    adapting material for, 37, 66
    for arguments, 182–83
    in CSE references, 526
    genre and, 34–36, 37
    in MLA works cited, 412
    online texts, 14–16, 20–22, 285–90
    previewing, 126
    print or digital, 124–25, 263
    for public writing, 345, 346

reading critically, 124–25
reflecting on, 66
for research projects, 191–92
rhetorical situation and, 20–23,
    34–37, 262–63
memorable prose, 678–83
    antithesis, 681–82
    emphatic sentences, 678–80
    inverted word order, 682
    for presentations, 274–76
    Quick Help, 678–79
    repetition, 681
    strong verbs, 680–81
memos, 323–24, 339–40
metacognitive learning, 125
metaphors, 43–44, 176, 382–83
metric measurements, 739, 740
microblogs. *See* Twitter and microblogs
*might,* as helping verb, 534, 570–72
*might of, could of,* 753
minor premises, 173–74
misplaced modifiers, 648–49
missing words, 6, 634, 656–57
mixed metaphors, 383
mixed structures, 6, 654–55

**MLA style,** 402–50  The citation style
guidelines issued by the Modern
Language Association.
    basics of, 402–4
    citing sources without models, 412
    explanatory notes, 403–4
    integrating quotations, 233–34
    in-text citations
        directory, 406
        models for, 405–12
    long quotations in, 234, 405, 714
    manuscript format, 405
    sample student research project,
        441–50
    signal phrases in, 405–6
    source maps
        articles from databases, 428–29
        articles in print periodicals,
            422–23

**modal**, 570, 571–73 A kind of **helping verb** that has only one form and shows possibility, necessity, or obligation: *can, could, may, might, must, shall, should, will, would, ought to.*

**modifier** A word, phrase, or **clause** that acts as an **adjective** or an **adverb**, qualifying the meaning of another word, phrase, or clause.

**mood**, 586, 626–27 The form of a **verb** that indicates the writer's attitude toward the idea expressed. The indicative mood states fact or opinion (*I am happy*); the imperative gives commands (*Keep calm*); and the subjunctive refers to a condition that does not exist (*If I were rich . . .* ).

## O

A **noun** or **pronoun** receiving the
action of a **verb** (*We mixed paints*) or
following a **preposition** (*on the road*).

participle, 553, 568, 573–76  A word formed from the **base form** of a **verb**. The present participle always ends in -*ing* (*going*). The past participle ends in -*ed* (*ruined*) unless the verb is **irregular**. A participle can function as an **adjective** (*the singing frog, a ruined shirt*) or form part of a **verb phrase** (*You have ruined my shirt*).

**possessive form** The form of a **noun** or **pronoun** that shows possession. Personal pronouns in the possessive case don't use apostrophes (*ours, hers*), but possessive nouns and indefinite pronouns do (*Harold's, everyone's*).

surveys
as field research, 210–11, 242
Quick Help, 211
in the social sciences, 307
suspended hyphens, 748
*s.v.* ("under the word"), 503
syllables, in dictionary, 386
syllogisms, 173–74
symbols, 739
synonyms, in dictionary, 387

**syntax**, 78, 276 The arrangement of words in a sentence.

**synthesis**, 222–23 Grouping ideas and information together in such a way that the relationship among them is clear.
critical reading and, 125
of field research, 211
student sample, 223–24

## T

table of contents, for portfolio, 340
tables, 269. *See also* visuals and media
tag questions, 694
*take, bring,* 753
take-home exams, 335
Talking the Talk. *See also the directory of boxed tips on p. 815*
abbreviations
in the disciplines, 740
texting, 378
arguments, 162
assignments, 26
audience, reaching, 194
collaboration or cheating, 119
conventions, 17
correctness or stuffiness, 600
critical thinking, 126
disciplines, academic, 740
first person, 296
genre names, 35
grammatical terms, 547
numbers, 740
originality, 239

paragraph length, 96
research with an open mind, 215
revision, 65
saying something new, 239
spell checkers, 395
texting abbreviations, 378
visual texts, 137
wikis as sources, 208
wrong-word errors, 395
team projects. *See* collaboration
technical language, 294–95, 375–78
television. *See* visuals and media
templates, design
for portfolios, 338
for print and digital texts, 265
for Web sites and Web pages, 288, 338, 347

**tense**, 578–83 The form of a **verb** that indicates the time when an action takes place—past, present, or future. Each tense has **simple** (*I enjoy*), **perfect** (*I have enjoyed*), **progressive** (*I am enjoying*), and **perfect progressive** (*I have been enjoying*) forms.
APA style, 308, 454, 580
*Chicago* style, 495
of irregular verbs, 573–76
literary present, 580
MLA style, 580
for multilingual writers, 578–83
Quick Help, 583–84
of regular verbs, 573
in science writing, 318, 579
sequence of, 583–84
shifts in, 7, 626
subject-verb agreement and, 590–91
testimony, in argument, 171–72
tests, 331–36

**text** Traditionally, words on paper, but now anything that conveys a message. *See also* visuals and media
analyzing, 133–39
designing, 262–71
multimodal, 56–57, 285–90

regular, 573
signal, 234–35
strong, 680–81
transitive, 550–51, 623
two-word, 10, 622–23, 749

**verbal** A **verb** form that functions as a **noun**, an **adjective**, or an **adverb**.
gerunds, 553, 554–55
infinitives, 553–56, 584, 651
participles, 573–76
verbal phrases, 552, 674–75

**verb phrase**, 534, 552, 569–73 A main verb and one or more **helping verbs**, acting as a single verb.

*very,* 759
video prompts. *See the directory of online activities on p. 817*
videos. *See* multimodal text; visuals and media
videotaping presentations, 121–22
virtual libraries, 207
visual rhetoric, 262
visuals and media
accessibility of, 270, 275, 287
acknowledgment required for, 243, 270
altering, 152–53, 270–71
analyzing
as argumentative appeals, 145–46, 149
for fallacies, 152–53, 270–71
student example of, 135–36, 137–39
as texts, 135–39, 149
for arguments
analyzing, 145–46, 149
emotional appeals (*pathos*) with, 177–78
ethical appeals (*ethos*) with, 167–68
integrating, 182–83
logical appeals (*logos*) with, 174–75
choosing, 238, 268–71

citing, 270–71
APA style, 451, 478–81
*Chicago* style, 508–9
MLA style, 403, 435–40
Considering Disabilities, 267, 275, 287
creating, 285–90
in design, 262–63, 268–71
details in, 99–100
to explore a topic, 43–44
for global communication, 356
integrating, 182–83, 237–39
italics for titles, 743
labeling, 238–39, 270–71
APA style, 454, 457–58
*Chicago* style, 495
CSE style, 318, 518
MLA style, 405, 410–11, 439
misleading, 152–53, 270–71
for multimodal texts, 289–90
note-taking, 230
for online texts, 268–71, 289–90
organizing, 50–54, 56–57
permission for, 238, 270
positioning, 270
for presentations, 122, 275, 279–81
Quick Help, 53, 268–69
quotation marks for titles, 715–16
reflecting on, 66
for research projects, 192
in résumés, 327, 329
revising, 86
rhetorical situation, 29, 37
sample student writing, 135–36, 137–39
in scientific writing, 316, 318
slides, media, 279–80
sources of, 206, 270
Talking the Talk, 137
as texts, 262
tone and, 37
types of
audio, 289–90
bar graphs, 269

## W

# ADVICE FOR MULTILINGUAL WRITERS

 **MULTI- LINGUAL** *Look for the multilingual writers icon to find advice of special interest to international students and others whose home language is not English.*

## For Multilingual Writers boxes

# TALKING THE TALK BOXES

*These boxes offer advice about conventions of U.S. academic writing.*

# ADVICE FOR CONSIDERING DISABILITIES

# STUDENT WRITING MODELS

 Go to **macmillanhighered.com/smh** *for complete versions of all these student models with assignable activities. Click on the Resources tab in LaunchPad for the full list.*

## Drafts

Early draft: Lesk, 59

Final draft: Lesk, 88

## Reflective writing

Blog post: Nguyen, 92

Cover letter: Kung, 340

## Critical reading and argument

Annotations of scholarly article: Sanchez and Lum, 129

Critical reading: Song, 137

Researched argument project: Mercer-Golden, 183

Rhetorical analysis: Ateyea, 155

## Researched writing

Annotated bibliography: Chan, 214

Annotated bibliography (reflective): Sriram, 214

APA research project: Bell, 482

*Chicago* research project: Rinder, 512

CSE research project: Hays, 530

MLA research project: Craig, 441

Researched argument: Mercer-Golden, 183

Synthesis project: Warner, 223

## Writing for the public

Pitch package: Jane and Burke, 349

Presentation: Song, 273–82

Résumés: Lange, 327–29

Web site: Dart, 347

## Writing in other disciplines

Close reading (literature): Sillay, 303

Lab report (chemistry): Goldberg, 318

Review of literature (biology): Hays, 530

Review of literature (psychology): Redding, 309

Review of literature (public health): Bell, 482

## Multimodal writing

Blog post: Nguyen, 92

Pitch package: Jane and Burke, 349

Presentation: Song, 273–82

Résumés: Lange, 327–29

Web site: Dart, 347

# ONLINE ACTIVITIES

## ▶ Videos and tutorials

*Go to* **macmillanhighered.com/smh**, *and click on the Resources tab for access to tutorials and to short video prompts featuring student writers.*

### Videos

Lessons from informal writing

Something to learn from each other

Developing a sense of audience

Pay attention to what you're interested in

Looking for the essential points [on genres and media]

Writing processes

Brain mapping [on clustering]

Getting ideas from social media

This will take longer than I thought [on planning]

Filling in the gaps [on drafting]

It's hard to delete things

You just have to start

Lessons from peer review

Lessons from being a peer reviewer

Revision happens

Working with other people

Facing a challenging argument

Researching something exciting

When to stop researching

If I were in the audience [on presenting]

You want them to hear you [on slide design]

Presentation is performance

Improving with practice

Writing for the real world

Correctness in context

### Tutorials

Word processing

Active reading

Reading visuals for audience

Reading visuals for purpose

Online research tools

Do I need to cite that?

Presentations

Photo editing with GIMP

Audio editing with Audacity

Job search and personal branding

How to cite a book in MLA style

How to cite an article in MLA style

How to cite a database in MLA style

How to cite a Web site in MLA style

How to cite a book in APA style

How to cite an article in APA style

How to cite a database in APA style

How to cite a Web site in APA style

# ONLINE ACTIVITIES, CONTINUED

### e Quizzes and visual exercises

Go to **macmillanhighered.com/smh**, and click on the Resources tab for these quizzes and activities.

**Top Twenty editing quizzes**

Editing quiz 1

Editing quiz 2

**Storyboard visual exercises**

Rhetorical situations

Working thesis

Being a peer reviewer

Getting help from peer reviewers

Revising and editing

Reading critically

Synthesis

### ✓ LearningCurve adaptive quizzing

Go to **macmillanhighered.com/smh** to test yourself on these topics.

Active and passive voice

Apostrophes

Argument

Articles and nouns for multilingual writers

Capital letters

Commas

Comma splices and fused sentences

Coordination and subordination

Critical reading

Evaluating, integrating, and acknowledging sources [APA]

Evaluating, integrating, and acknowledging sources [MLA]

Fragments

Modifiers

Nouns and pronouns

Parallelism

Prepositions and conjunctions

Prepositions for multilingual writers

Pronouns

Semicolons and colons

Sentence structure for multilingual writers

Shifts

Subject-verb agreement

Topics and main ideas

Topic sentences and supporting details

Verbs

Verbs, adjectives, and adverbs

Verbs for multilingual writers

Vocabulary

Word choice

# REVISION SYMBOLS

*Some instructors use these symbols as a kind of shorthand to guide you in revision. The numbers refer to a chapter number or a section of a chapter.*

| | | | | |
|---|---|---|---|---|
| abb | abbreviation 61 | paraph | paraphrase 13a and c |
| ad | adjective/adverb 42 | pass | inappropriate passive 39g, 50c |
| agr | agreement 40, 41 | | |
| awk | awkward | ref | unclear pronoun reference 41h |
| cap | capitalization 60 | | |
| case | case 41 | run-on | run-on (fused) sentence 46 |
| cliché | cliché 30d | sexist | sexist language 28b, 41g |
| cohere | coherence 5e | shift | shift 44 |
| com | incomplete comparison 49e | slang | slang 30a |
| concl | weak conclusion 4h, 5g, 15c | sp | spelling 31e and f |
| coord | coordination 51a | subord | subordination 51b |
| cs | comma splice 46 | sum | summarize 13a and d |
| d | diction 30 | t | tone 4i, 30a and d, 44f |
| def | define 5d | trans | transition 5e–g, 52b |
| dev | development needed 5d | u | unity 5b |
| dm | dangling modifier 48c | verb | verb form 39a–d |
| doc | documentation 32–35 | vs | verb sequence 39f |
| emph | emphasis unclear 53a | vt | verb tense 39e, f, and h |
| ex | example needed 5c and d | wrdy | wordy 50 |
| frag | sentence fragment 47 | wv | weak verb 53b |
| fs | fused sentence 46 | ww | wrong word 30a and b |
| hyph | hyphen 63 | , | comma 54 |
| inc | incomplete construction 49 | ; | semicolon 55 |
| intro | weak introduction 4h, 5g | . ? ! | period, question mark, exclamation point 56 |
| ital | italics (or underlining) 62 | | |
| jarg | jargon 30a | ' | apostrophe 57 |
| lc | lowercase letter 60d | " " | quotation marks 58 |
| log | logic 8f, 9g | ( ) [ ] — | parentheses, brackets, dash 59 |
| lv | language variety 29 | | |
| mix | mixed construction 49a | : / ... | colon, slash, ellipses 59 |
| mm | misplaced modifier 48a | ^ | insert |
| ms | manuscript form 16 | ~ | transpose |
| no , | no comma 54k | ⌒ | close up |
| num | number 61 | x | obvious error |
| org | organization 3e, 9j | | |
| ¶ | paragraph 5 | | |
| // | faulty parallelism 45 | | |

# CONTENTS